ORACLE®

Oracle Press™

Oracle Developer Advanced Forms & Reports

D1303557

Peter Koletzke
Dr. Paul Dorsey

Osborne/**McGraw-Hill**

Berkeley New York St. Louis San Francisco
Auckland Bogotá Hamburg London Madrid
Mexico City Milan Montreal New Delhi Panama City.
Paris São Paulo Singapore Sydney Tokyo Toronto

Osborne/**McGraw-Hill**
2600 Tenth Street
Berkeley, California 94710
U.S.A.

For information on translations or book distributors outside the U.S.A., or to arrange bulk purchase discounts for sales promotions, premiums, or fund-raisers, please contact Osborne/**McGraw-Hill** at the above address.

Oracle Developer Advanced Forms & Reports

1234567890 AGM AGM 019876543210

ISBN 0-07-212048-7

Publisher
   Brandon A. Nordin

**Associate Publisher and
Editor-in-Chief**
   Scott Rogers

Acquisitions Editor
   Jeremy Judson

Project Editor
   Mark Karmendy

Editorial Assistant
   Monika Faltiss

Technical Editors
   Claire Dessaux
   Michael Olin

Copy Editors
   Jan Jue
   Claire Splan

Proofreader
   Pat Mannion

Indexer
   Caryl Lee Fisher

Computer Designers
   Roberta Steele
   Mickey Galicia
   Gary Corrigan

Illustrators
   Beth Young
   Robert Hansen
   Brian Wells

Series Design
   Jani Beckwith

This book was composed with Corel VENTURA™ Publisher.

About the Authors...

Peter Koletzke is a consulting manager who specializes in Designer and Developer work for Millennia Vision Corporation. He is also a Principal Instructor for the company and a member of the Board of Directors of the International Oracle Users Group – Americas. Peter is a frequent contributor to national and international Oracle newsletters and user group conferences; his paper on Developer and Designer help systems won the ODTUG 1999 Editor's Choice Award. http://ourworld.compuserve.com/homepages/Peter_Koletzke

Millennia Vision Corporation (MVC) is a new breed of business consulting firm, dedicated to improving its clients' business performance and position in the expanding e-business economy. MVC's unique, integrated approach enables companies to align their people, processes, and technologies in support of their business strategy. Global leaders in a wide variety of industries rely on MVC's proven methodologies, knowledge of products, professional expertise, and technical depth to extend their existing business models and seize new opportunities. MVC is based in Redwood Shores, California. http://www.mvsn.com

Dr. Paul Dorsey is the founder and President of Dulcian, Inc. Dulcian specializes in Oracle Client-Server and Web custom application development and data migration. Paul is co-author with Peter Koletzke of *The Oracle Designer Handbook* (now in its second edition) and with Joseph R. Hudicka of *Oracle8 Design Using UML Object Modeling*, both from Oracle Press, 1999. Paul is an Associate Editor of *SELECT* Magazine. He is the President of the New York Oracle Users' Group. Paul and Peter shared the Pinnacle Publishing Technical Achievement Award at ECO '95 for their work on a Forms template that became the basis for this book. Paul has won best presentation awards at both ECO and IOUW conferences.

Dulcian, Inc. offers a wide variety of consulting services, customized training, and products for the Oracle development environment. Dulcian provides products and services to large government and private sector companies worldwide. Services include developing new projects, auditing existing efforts, and rescuing failed projects. Dulcian's vision is to deliver top-quality systems in record time. To this end, Dulcian has automated or streamlined every possible portion of the development life cycle to create a flexible strategy that is adapted for each project. http://www.dulcian.com

Contents

PART I
Overview

PART II
Basic Developer Standards

PART III
Forms Templates

PART IV
Advanced Forms Topics

PART V
Reports Topics

PART VI
Developer Tips and Techniques

Foreword

he Internet changes everything. It changes the way we work, the way we live, and even the way we think. Companies are rethinking and redirecting their core business. They are examining their business models and competitors in light of this new way of thinking. In short, they are redefining how they operate. By leveraging the Internet, a company can transform itself into an e-business.

In an e-business, timely and accurate information is critical. E-business is powered by database applications developed and deployed using Internet standards, and demands that companies redefine their relationship with their suppliers, partners, and customers. Using the Internet, database applications that were traditionally accessible only within an enterprise are now accessible beyond the enterprise. These virtual enterprises, integrating suppliers, partners, and customers, are now being realized by the new generation of Internet-enabled database applications. This significantly increases the number of users that require access to the business-critical information stored in the database. As a result, the applications to access these databases must be high performance, easy to use, and available all the time. The increased opportunity and competition, enabled by the Internet, is dramatically shortening the product lifecycles. To remain competitive, these applications must be developed and adapted in record time.

Oracle is the world's largest supplier of e-business software. Sixty-five percent of the Fortune 100 companies use Oracle for e-business. This is because Oracle offers a complete Internet platform including the Oracle8i database, application servers, and tools.

Oracle tools include an integrated suite of Business Intelligence tools to easily answer any question about your business. Oracle also offers development tools to productively develop transaction-processing applications. Oracle Business Intelligence tools include the award-winning Oracle Discoverer for ad hoc query and analysis, Oracle Reports for high-fidelity database publishing, and Express tools for developing analytical applications. Oracle Development Tools include the productive, model-based development tools, Designer and Developer, and the flexible component-based Java development tool, JDeveloper. Oracle tools automate application development and reduce both the labor as well as the time required to deliver database applications. Better yet, by reducing the error-prone manual coding process, Oracle tools dramatically improve the overall quality of the applications.

Oracle delivers general-purpose and optimized application servers for deploying these applications on the Internet. JDeveloper enables flexible deployment of multi-tier Java business logic using the Oracle Application Server and Oracle8i JServer. Developer Server is tuned for deploying transaction processing and enterprise reporting applications. Discoverer Server is optimized for high-performance query and analysis. As a result, database applications can run efficiently on centrally-managed servers. Users can access these applications simply by using a standard web browser.

Often, users spend an inordinate amount of time looking for the applications and information that they need. Oracle has developed a *portal framework*, Oracle WebDB, that provides a unified desktop for users to easily access the essential database applications and information. The portal framework is open and extensible to enable access to all applications and information. Now, users can easily access all their database applications as well as any web site from a single corporate portal. Users can also personalize the content and layout of the portal based on their role or personal preference. Current, up-to-date information is immediately accessible through the portal.

Oracle Developer is the leading development tool on the market for building database applications. It provides the productivity tools and facilities to build world-class database applications that automate business functions and processes within and beyond the enterprise. Today, Oracle Developer is the tool of choice for companies worldwide to develop custom enterprise-class applications. In addition, application vendors, like Oracle Applications, use Oracle Developer to deliver global, packaged applications for Enterprise Resource Planning (ERP) and Customer Relationship Management (CRM). In fact, powered by Developer Server, these applications are even available as a subscription service from Oracle Business Online, the number one application service provider (ASP) on the Internet. Simply put, Oracle Developer is the only tool available on the market that has been used to deliver an entire suite of e-business applications.

The authors of this book have tackled a large subject—how to use Oracle Developer Release 6.0 to quickly produce database applications that you can fit into the Oracle portal framework. Peter and Paul offer the Oracle user community valuable resources: a reference for best practices using the object-oriented features of Oracle Developer, an exploration of standards for Oracle Developer to help ensure your project's success, and an explanation of key techniques that will save you time and effort when developing applications. With Oracle Developer and the guidance of this book, you can quickly build easy-to-use, powerful database applications that will serve as the foundation for your e-business.

Sohaib Abbasi
Senior Vice President
Tools Product Division
Oracle Corporation

Acknowledgments

here's nothing in life that is quite like writing a book. If I had to make an analogy for this book project, I'd pick the Spinning Plates Trick. You've probably seen this although the last time I remember watching it was on the Ed Sullivan Show. As the music begins, the performer runs onstage carrying a stack of china plates and stands in front of a long set of head-high metal rods. One at a time, the performer places a plate on a rod and sets it spinning—shaking the rod to establish momentum—and then moves on to the next rod. At some point in this process, the plate that was first in line starts to tip and looks as if it will fall. The performer leaps over to the rod under it and shakes it again to continue the plate's progress. As more and more plates start to spin, the complexity of keeping all of the plates on the rods increases but the plates never fall. The performer finally completes the line of plates after many near-disasters and the camera cuts to a wide-shot of the entire assembly happily spinning. Wild applause ensues.

Writing a book consists of sending chapters through various reviews. At any point in time, a chapter can be in one of five or six stages. The trick with maintaining the momentum in the book process is to keep the chapters spinning. If one chapter starts to falter, it is quickly given attention and equilibrium is reestablished. There are many near disasters, but, in the end, all chapters are happily spinning together. While the plate trick only uses one performer, this book project required a team of people to maintain the momentum. It is due to the credit and skills of this team that we reached the end without any broken china. Thanks are therefore due.

A huge amount of credit goes to Caryl Lee Fisher who, through flood, illness, pressures of work, and hard-disk crashes, kept the lines of communication between the two authors open despite a continental separation. She was the main reason that the collaboration succeeded. I'd like to give my sincere appreciation to Paul for hiring Caryl Lee and for somehow managing to squeeze book work into the rare "leisure" moments that are available to someone who is running a company.

Thanks go to my company, Millennia Vision Corporation, and Guy Wilnai, Director, Custom Solutions, for a generous donation of my time towards the completion of the project. Thanks, Guy, too, for helping with that quote.

Our technical editors helped add much to the quality of the material. Unlike some authors, I have to state that any inaccuracies that have sneaked into the text are probably due to my misinterpretation of the technical editors' comments.

I appreciate the challenging and sometimes brutally truthful comments that Michael Olin (Systematic Solutions, Inc.) gave us from his expert user's viewpoint on our code, technical details, and general strategies. Claire Dessaux, Senior Product Marketing Manager of Oracle Developer, also provided valuable information on the directions of the product and features that we might otherwise have missed. She also frequently challenged our technical statements. Claire, you'll be happy to know we finally realize that Oracle Developer is the premier web application development tool.

The Osborne staff provided many contributions above and beyond their normal duties that added to the quality of the book and we thank them for their professional work. Jeremy Judson, Acquisitions Editor, stuck with us through the long first draft period. Monika Faltiss managed our schedule and many versions of the document. Mark Karmendy, our project editor, kept all of our author quirks under control with the patience of a saint. Our copy editors, Jan Jue and Claire Splan, and proofreader, Pat Mannion, expertly helped us fine-tune the prose. The unseen production folks helped us stay on a schedule that was quite ambitious.

All of the "plate spinners" just mentioned contributed to the entire book. There were many others who helped us directly with individual chapters and credit goes to them, too, for their contributions. Tim Eicher (Senior Director of Oracle Developer), Juliana Lerc (Senior Manager of Product Management Enterprise Tools), and Mark Doran (formerly Senior Product Manager)—all from Oracle—reviewed and contributed to the material on web-deploying Forms that became Chapter 13. Joe Strano (Premier Design Systems) provided technical comments on a number of our chapters and gave us inspiration for some of the material in Chapter 4. Thanks to David Anstey (Aris Corporation), Editor-in-Chief of the *ODTUG Technical Journal*, for allowing us to print some code from that journal. Howard Fujimoto, of MVC and a Master of Generic Coding (and many other things), supplied some code for Chapter 25.

There are also many people whose indirect contributions supported the work of the book. Nancy Taslitz, Director of User Group Programs at Oracle, provided us with advice on Oracle resources. Ofer Herzog gave us a seed for the material on how to sort blocks using buttons. The staff of the Menlo Park Public Library assisted us on attributing some of our quotations, as did Rabbi Yitzchok Feldman, of Emek Beracha.

We have taken great inspiration from the Oracle User Groups we belong to and have to thank the IOUG-A and ODTUG for sharing information that has become integral to the way we work with the Oracle products.

I have to say a big "Thanks" to my parents and brother who stuck with me through yet another round of book writing. I appreciate their interest and support. Thanks, too, to my wife, Anne, who was without my companionship on the many weekends that were dedicated to "booking."

Finally, we are honored to have Sohaib Abassi's views on the vision for Oracle Developer in the foreword to this book. Thanks to Sohaib for this contribution.

Peter Koletzke
Menlo Park, CA
October 1999

Well, it's finally here. This is the book Peter and I originally started to write four years ago when Osborne/McGraw-Hill convinced us to write a book about Designer instead. Perhaps we are now more sympathetic to what we recognize are inevitable delays in product releases.

It is difficult to acknowledge all of the contributions to this project since they have come from so many different sources. The developers with whom I've had the privilege to work and whose ideas and development practices I've freely stolen without any acknowledgments whatsoever include I. Michael Snyder, Joseph P. Strano, and Edward Van Orden. These skilled individuals have probably had a greater impact on this project than any of us remember.

Also thanks to the members of ODTUG who attended my presentations and provided valuable feedback. I also appreciate all of the contributors to the ODTUG Internet list whose questions and answers helped provide source material for and guide the direction of this book. Clearly, every Oracle developer should be a member of ODTUG for the valuable resources it provides.

As always, Peter Koletzke has done his usual, thorough, and often thankless job of making the book clear and consistent, but not always concise (we were only supposed to write 400 pages). Peter's seemingly endless font of knowledge about the ins and outs of the Developer product is a major reason for the quality, thoroughness, and usefulness of this book.

I would like to thank Michael Olin for doing a tremendous job as technical editor for this book. He caught enough mistakes, faux pas, omissions, and other inaccuracies that any errors remaining are clearly his fault, so please direct all criticisms about this book to him.

Merci beaucoup to Claire Dessaux of Oracle Corporation who was willing to read all of this material and provide feedback and guidance.

I appreciate all of the efforts of the OMH team to produce the quality end result that you see on the bookshelves, namely Jeremy Judson, Monika Faltiss, Mark Karmendy, Jan Jue, Claire Splan, and Pat Mannion.

Thanks to Ken Burkholder, Walter Burkholder and Wayne Ebersole of Good's Store for allowing us to use screenshots of their system in this book.

Thank you to Charlie Fisher (age 7) for loaning us your mother, Caryl Lee, to perform the tireless edits, myriad screenshots, research of cool quotes and endless rewrites that go into each book project we undertake. We promise to wait at least two months before we start another book and you don't get to play with your mom again for a while.

Much love and appreciation to my wife, Katherine Duliba, who has given up on spending weekends with me without book writing work.

Last but not least, thanks to my dog, Popper, who is now old enough not to miss all of the time I spend not playing with him but still greets me with as much love and enthusiasm whenever I get home.

Paul Dorsey
Colonia, NJ
October 1999

PART
I

Overview

CHAPTER

1

Introduction

And, as imagination bodies forth
The forms of things unknown, the poet's pen
Turns them into shapes, and gives to airy nothing
A local habitation and a name.
        —William Shakespeare (1564–1616), *A Midsummer Night's Dream* (V, i, 7)

racle Developer is a great product. When a skilled development team builds an application system using Oracle Developer Forms and Reports to access an Oracle database, they can quickly create a sophisticated, user-friendly system that can satisfy even the most complex user requirements. Within Developer, the capability exists to support most of the commonly needed user interface requirements. In addition, Developer also provides sufficient flexibility so that you can tune your applications to provide superior performance. With the current release, the Oracle Developer Server has come of age and provides a solid environment for deploying applications that exploit the other strengths of Oracle Developer on the Web.

Despite all of these reasons to build applications using the Oracle Developer tools, the following questions come to mind:

- Why do many developers still complain about how hard Developer is to use?

- Why do organizations purchase Developer, have developers attend training classes and, six months later, end up with a failed project?

- Why are there no generally recognized Oracle Developer standards in the user community?

- Why are developers not aware of the strengths of template systems and the object- and code-sharing features provided by Oracle Developer?

- Why do some systems professionals give up on Oracle Developer and go back to writing applications in Visual Basic or C++?

Why Don't They Use Oracle Developer?

Most of these questions do not make sense. On one side of the development community, there exists a set of satisfied and productive developers who extol the benefits of Oracle Developer, and on the other side there are many users of

Forms and Reports who are frustrated with trying to use the tool productively. A number of factors have contributed to this paradox:

- **Evolution of the Products** Both the Forms and Reports components of Oracle Developer have evolved significantly as products. Each evolution was built to satisfy the demands of the existing developer community at the time. If you started working with SQL*Forms Release 2.3 or 3.0, the basic concepts of the current products will make sense to you. However, if the first version of Oracle Developer you have worked with is Release 6.0, there is a very high learning curve to overcome. Most of the development resources over the life of the Developer tool suite have concentrated on making the product richer functionally. While additional attention has been given to making the product developer-friendly, as the feature-set becomes richer, the ability to provide ease of use to all levels also becomes more difficult and, in a sense, will never catch up.

- **The Need for Experience** With the current release, first-time developers will be able to be productive in Oracle Developer with minimal effort. However, until you understand the way that the components of the Developer tool suite work and interact together and you have achieved some level of mastery, using Developer will be challenging. When one of the authors first worked with Developer, figuring out how to do something new sometimes took four hours. Even after that time, he wondered if the method he came up with was the best method. With more experience building real forms and reports, this process decreased to an hour or less. If you try to use Developer without any training or mentoring, you will have a hard time figuring out how to build any useful form or report. Experience is everything. If you don't have it, you have to learn from the experience of others.

- **The Need for a Template System and Standards** The Forms component of Oracle Developer is a good product on its own. It provides an adequate development environment for building an application. However, to build efficiently and effectively with Forms requires a carefully thought-out template and set of GUI and coding standards. This is true for any development product. Building a production system with any product used "out of the box" without some basic set of reusable components will be a laborious process. However, the productivity improvements possible in Forms with a solid template and set of standards are enormous. This is true, to a large extent, with the Reports component of Developer as well.

■ **The Abundance of Techniques** There are "right" ways to accomplish specific tasks using Oracle Forms and Reports. The authors estimate that there are at least a thousand techniques you need to know to be a good Forms developer and an additional few hundred to be an effective Reports developer. This is a very large body of knowledge. Only a few, experienced members of the development community are aware of the majority of these features, properties, tips, tricks, and techniques. Without this knowledge or access to it, you will spend much more time building less user-friendly applications with poorer performance.

■ **Inadequate Availability of Documentation and Training** While the situation is getting better with each new release, in many cases, the available documentation and training are inadequate. Development products evolve very quickly and it is often difficult for the documentation and training to keep up. The main documentation that ships with Developer is supplied online (with hard copy available for purchase) and covers the area of reference (for the language and properties aspects), web deployment, getting started building applications, and an overview. There are no books on best practices and standards. Many training organizations, including Oracle, teach developers how to perform various tasks in the tools but don't provide sufficient knowledge on building a production form or report from template systems and reusable code and object libraries.

The Solution

What can be done to improve this situation? One solution for us was to write this book. Our objectives for this book were the following:

■ Document and explain many of the necessary techniques needed to use Oracle Developer Forms and Reports effectively.

■ Discuss the template architecture in Forms and Reports and the concepts behind creating reusable components.

■ Present the framework for building standards that you can use when creating applications using Oracle Developer.

We do not claim that this book fills all of the gaps in Oracle Developer knowledge that exist in the user community. However, we feel that this book accurately presents the essence of our current thinking. It explains our philosophy, our core techniques, our approach to standards, and the best architecture for building an application using Oracle Developer.

The Scope of the Book

To support our objectives in writing the book and to fit the material within the allotted number of pages, we have had to declare a scope that may not have universal appeal. This book will not serve the purpose of those who just want to read about techniques because we feel that only discussing those kinds of topics will not serve the purpose of those requiring advanced knowledge. For example, you will not find in this book an explanation of how to use the Forms API, Oracle Terminal, or the PL/SQL debugger because these topics are sufficiently explained in the beginner books and in the Oracle Developer help system.

The title of the book, if read precisely with its subtitle, reflects its contents. We discuss techniques that are in the advanced category (which means that a large percentage of Oracle Developer users do not know about or understand them) and standards (which we feel are missing from most Oracle Developer projects) for the Forms and Reports components of the product.

While an advanced book on all components of Oracle Developer would discuss techniques for Graphics Builder, Procedure Builder, Project Builder, Query Builder, Schema Builder, and Translation Builder, we decided to concentrate on only two of these: the component that developers use most frequently—Forms, and the component that is sorely misunderstood and underused—Reports. Since our intended audience already uses Oracle Developer, we assume knowledge of the basics of the Forms component. The Reports component of Oracle Developer (also sold as Oracle Reports) offers a huge gain in productivity if you use it in an object-based way. However, many developers do not understand even the basics of Reports. Therefore, we explain the basics of this component in a little more detail than we do for the Forms component. We also discuss the same kind of standards and techniques for Reports that we do for Forms.

Web Coverage

This is not a book about deploying applications on the Web. The book does not explain the full realm of the Oracle Developer Server that allows you to deploy Oracle Developer applications to the Web. That subject deserves an entire book covering details about installing, configuring, and optimizing the Oracle Developer Server. The audience for that book will be database administrators and network administrators who are the ones currently held responsible for web server installations. We do not attempt to explore these subjects in this book since our primary audience is developers who need to know about techniques and managers who need to know about standards.

On the other hand, this book does explain some basics and details about deploying Forms to the Web in Chapter 13. Also, the book is about techniques and best practices for building applications with Oracle Developer; all of these are applicable to any work performed using Oracle Developer regardless of the deployment platform.

What Does this Book Cover?

As long-time users of the Oracle tools, we have developed methods that have evolved over time as the tool has evolved. As we have worked more and more with the product, we have been able to examine the best ways to approach development work with these tools. We have frequently retuned our thoughts on object-orientation with Oracle Developer as our sense of how to produce applications has grown and (hopefully) matured. The book does not present everything we know about Forms and Reports. However, it does accomplish the following:

- **Explain our philosophy of Forms and Reports development** and what we believe are the most important techniques for creating applications using Oracle Developer.

- **Give direction for discovering more information** about specific topics.

- **Discuss the heretofore unpublished area of Oracle Developer standards**. Oracle has sold standards solutions for years in products such as the Custom Development Environment (CDM) and the ERP (Enterprise Resource Planning) and CRM (Customer Relationship Management) suites (called Oracle Applications). Third-party vendors have also sold these solutions for many years but standards for Oracle Developer are not yet universally known or accepted.

Why Discuss Standards?

Why do standards fit in the same book with development techniques? Since standards are the most important consideration for reusability and maintainability, the book provides an exploration of the standards you would use to create Oracle Developer applications. Standards are also important from a development point of view and are also important for providing the user with a consistent and intuitive interface. We feel that development techniques and standards are really one and the same. As we discuss various techniques, we will usually present just one way to accomplish a task. By presenting one particular way, we are saying that we have found this way to be the best. For example, we feel that hard-coding values into poplists in Forms is the wrong way to work because it requires ongoing development work to modify the available values. A better way is to load the poplist from a database table. That way, if the list needs modification, the only change required is to update the table that the list is based on. There is a certain technique for accomplishing this (see Chapter 25) that is a standard for our applications. Therefore, our standards document would contain a section on how to accomplish the development work with a note that this is the standard way to do this.

Thus, there is a blurry line between techniques and standards. Why would you want to use a certain technique if it was not a standard? Similarly, why would you develop a standard if you had no preconceived idea for the best way to implement it? Of course, you can elaborate techniques and standards separately, but a development strategy is not complete without both because they support each other. Therefore, this book discusses standards. Although this is not the most glamorous subject for developers, it is important for managers and people in the technical lead role on projects who are tasked with the duty of creating an application that has the maximum level of maintainability.

The book provides advice in some areas of standards and gives some options for various ways you can go in other areas. While you cannot use the book as an integrated development standards document, there are sections that you can use "out of the box" as standards. There are also sections that will provide you with options from which you can select a final standard.

The Version Number Game

Writing about changing technology is akin to hitting a moving target. As soon as you have the target in your scope, it moves. An advanced book should reflect some experience with the most recent version. Once you have the experience and start to write about it, the next version of the tool is released and you have to start over. We have experienced this to some degree in working with this book and realize that it is the reason for the rarity of advanced books. With the current release of Oracle Developer (Release 6.0), we felt that there was a window of opportunity. The differences between this and the previous release are evolutionary and did not change the way we develop and build applications using Oracle Developer. Since the features for this architecture did not change, we are finally able to write up the best practices we have established and proven. We also discuss the differences between the current Oracle Developer release and previous versions so you can get a sense of the improvements.

Some of the techniques described in this book are specific to Oracle Developer Release 6.0 working with Windows (95, 98, or NT) as a development platform. However, the standards chapters, template architecture discussions, and many of the techniques are viable for release 2 of Oracle Developer as well as for other development operating systems such as Sun Solaris. Some techniques will even work with Oracle Developer Release 1, but the object-based features changed enough between releases 1 and 2 that the template architecture discussions will not be usable in release 1.

Release 6.0 (also called R.6 in this book) is the first time in our experience that the various components of Oracle Developer use the same release numbers. Therefore, Forms, Reports, Graphics, Procedure Builder, Project Builder, and the other components of Oracle Developer now all use the same number—6.0. (Oracle calls a major version number such as this a *release*.) In the past, these components have been thought of as different products. In fact, earlier versions of the product were available for sale separately. Even though the Reports product is still available as a separate purchase, Oracle Developer is an integrated product. Therefore, our current thought is that this is one product—Oracle Developer—with many components—Forms (the Form Builder), Reports (the Report Builder), and others. This book often refers to the Form Builder component of Oracle Developer separately (sometimes just using the term Forms); it also refers to the Report Builder component of Oracle Developer separately (sometimes just using the term Reports); however, these are really *components* of one product—Oracle Developer.

You may also see a reference to *Oracle Forms*, the old name of the product, but the term that Oracle currently uses for this is *the Forms component of Oracle Developer* (or Form Builder). As you read through this book, keep in mind that all of these terms refer to the same parts of Oracle Developer, whether the term is the official Oracle term or the short-hand term used by the development community.

Who Should Read this Book?

This is an advanced book. The word "advanced" means different things to different people. To the authors, "advanced" means that the reader has a thorough knowledge of Forms concepts, has done some hands-on development work, and has access to and knowledge of how to use basic Oracle Developer documentation. The reader may not know much about the Reports component or about the nuances of the object-based features of the Forms and Reports products; the reader also may not have extensive experience with the template approach to development. These are all ideas that this book explores and promotes. Developers will gain an understanding of these subjects as well as of specific techniques for working in the tools.

In addition, the book targets managers and technical leaders who need to establish and maintain standards for their applications and enterprise. The standards chapters in this book explore the major areas required for application standards as well as standards for database SQL and PL/SQL code that are accessed from the Oracle Developer tools.

How this Book Is Organized

There are a number of different areas that are within the scope of this book and the book is divided into sections that correspond to these areas:

I. **Overview**   This part discusses the contents of this book (this chapter). Chapter 2 of this part gives an explanation of the new features of the Forms and Reports components of Oracle Developer Release 6.0 for those who have worked with previous releases. It also mentions some of the features that were new with release 2 of Oracle Developer in case you know the release 1 features and want to move to Release 6.

II. Basic Developer Standards   This part explores the heart of development work—the standards that you will need to develop applications using Oracle Developer. SQL and PL/SQL standards are important to the scripting requirements for Forms and Reports code as well as database code. These are discussed in Chapters 3 and 7. Chapter 4 contains a discussion on the topic that will work into your standards for what to base a block on. Other standards that affect the development environment and user experience of an Oracle Developer application are the subject of Chapters 5 and 6. Standards for creating Reports are explained in Chapters 8 and 9.

III. Forms Templates   One of the most powerful techniques you can use to reduce development time of Forms applications is a template system. Chapters 10 through 12 in this section explain the features you can design into a template system, how to build the template system, and how to build a form based on the template system.

IV. Advanced Forms Topics   Part IV provides an in-depth view of several Forms application concepts. Chapter 13 (built from a presentation that was voted the best in overall quality for the Oracle OpenWorld 1998 conference) discusses the special considerations you need to take into account when deploying Oracle Developer Forms on the Web. Chapter 14 (seed material for a presentation that won the Editor's Choice award at the ODTUG 1999 conference) explains the options for creating help systems. Chapter 15 contains techniques for creating forms that allow users to find records without having to know about Query Mode or Query-By-Example. Specific techniques and concepts for checkboxes, radio groups, and other selection items are the subject of Chapter 16. Chapter 17 explains how to integrate the Oracle Developer components and provides some examples.

V. Reports Topics   This part of the book explores the Reports component of Oracle Developer. Since many developers do not have a good basic knowledge of this component, Chapters 18 through 20 explain the basics of Reports and its modeling areas—the Data Model and the Layout Model. Chapter 21 discusses how to use and build templates in Reports. Chapter 22 goes through the process of creating a sample report using the report template and techniques discussed in the earlier chapters.

VI. Developer Tips and Techniques   The last part of the book delves into some of our favorite techniques. Chapter 23 discusses a number of Forms and Reports techniques in the form of a question-and-answer session that is suitable for interviewing candidates who claim to know Oracle Developer. You can use this to quiz yourself on your level of knowledge of the Forms and Reports components of Oracle Developer. The remaining chapters in the book explain other intermediate and advanced techniques grouped by category of the topics: items, blocks, forms, menus, and system techniques. There are techniques and tips for old and new features as well as "recipes" for creating specific objects in Forms and Reports.

The appendices contain supporting material to the main chapters with descriptions of the template form library packages, a listing of interview questions from Chapter 23, information on the WinHelp help engine, a tutorial on the Reports Wizard, a description on how to audit reports and specify reports requirements, and a list of Oracle white papers about deploying forms on the Web.

Where Do You Go from Here?

Throughout this book, we point you to other sources for information because the information in this book lies somewhere in the middle of the life cycle of how to learn the best ways to use Oracle Developer. The first phases of this life cycle include running the online manual available from **Help→Quick Tour** in the Form Builder or Report Builder menu. There are also *cue cards* available from the Help menu. These help screens explain fundamental techniques that are required for all work in the tools. The subjects covered in the cue cards are required skills for all Oracle Developer users.

TIP
An often-overlooked resource for learning Oracle Developer techniques are the demonstration files. These are installed as a separate component by the Oracle Installer and contain examples of specific techniques. Many of these techniques also include a help system topic on how to use the demonstrated feature. Also, the ORACLE_HOME/tools/ devdem60 directory contains sample files with their source code that you can browse. In addition to the learning potential, many of the demonstration files contain ideas and code that you can use for your production applications.

The alternative to working through the Quick Tour and cue cards is to take a basic class on the tools from Oracle or a third-party vendor. A class will get you up to speed quickly (usually within a week) so you can progress to the intermediate topics with a firm foundation. In addition, there are books (such as the Oracle Press book, *Oracle Developer Starter Kit*, by Robert Muller) that provide views from an expert Oracle user on how best to start learning and using the tools.

Strategies for Getting More Information

Part of the knowledge of how to use Oracle Developer is in knowing where to turn for more information. When you run into a problem that cannot be solved with information in the help system, online documentation, or third-party books, it is good to know that there are many other sources for help. Given that the ultimate goal is to be able to build production forms and reports, you may still be missing some key concepts. What else can you do? There are two alternatives:

- **Build your first system without help from anyone and throw it away.** Over time, after building some number of complex forms and reports, you will eventually figure out most of the things you will need to know about the product.

- **Learn from the experts.** All Oracle professionals should belong to their local, regional, and national Oracle user groups. This will put you in touch with experienced Oracle professionals in your area who can often provide invaluable help in getting started using the products effectively. You should also try to work with an experienced developer for your first project. If you work in a large organization, try to pair up with an experienced developer who can act as a mentor. If your organization is using Developer for the first time, you may need to hire some outside consulting and training resources in order to get assistance with your first Developer project.

Oracle User Information

There is no substitute for real-world user information. Great places to interactively ask and answer questions on how people use the tools in real life are independent user group mailing lists such as those sponsored by the Oracle Development Tools User Group (http://www.odtug.com) and online discussion forums such as the ones run by the International Oracle Users Group - Americas (http://www.ioug.org). The Internet-accessibility of these groups makes finding an answer to a question or a solution to a problem an almost instantaneous process.

Both of these Oracle user groups hold annual conferences in the United States as well. These are events that offer access to networking with other users, the ability to talk to the Oracle development teams and see the new products directly, and rich technical presentations by users and Oracle employees. Oracle also sponsors an annual event in numerous locations around the world called Oracle OpenWorld where you can get a preview of the trends and products that will be Oracle's future. While marketing is the main focus of this conference, there are also numerous user technical presentations that provide the real-world spin on the products.

There are other local and regional user group conferences held by groups such as ECO (East Coast Oracle, www.oracle-users.com), RMOUG (Rocky Mountain Oracle Users Group, www.rmoug.org), and SEOUG (Southeast Oracle Users Group, metalab.unc.edu/ncoug/seoug/seoug.htm). Attendance at user conferences is so important that it needs be written into the training budgets for all IT shops that use Oracle products.

In addition, there are many third-party Oracle-related web sites that provide tips and techniques as well as white papers on Oracle Developer topics. The authors' web sites (mentioned in the author biography section in the beginning of this book) and the user group web sites are a starting place for finding this information. Follow the links from sites such as these to gain a portal to the world of Oracle user information available through the Internet.

Oracle also maintains technical information on their web site. The Oracle Technology Network (OTN) is available at technet.oracle.com. This is a free service that Oracle offers for users to interact through discussion forums. The site also offers downloads of trial versions of Oracle products (such as Developer and the database) as well as online documentation. Oracle MetaLink (http://www.oracle.com/support/), a site available to Oracle Support Services customers, contains technical forums that you can search for issues you may be dealing with. You can also browse the problem and bug databases to see workarounds for feature restrictions and limitations of the tools. Oracle Support Services customers can also log a *Technical Assistance Request* (TAR) through this online service just as they can by telephone.

The best advice is to become familiar with all information venues that relate to the Oracle products because each has its own strengths, as mentioned. As an Oracle Developer user, you will need to turn to the one that best serves your needs for a particular problem.

A Review of the Developer Forms Data Architecture

Although this book assumes that the reader has had hands-on contact with Oracle Developer and understands the basic architecture, it is useful to review the data architecture used in Forms. Chapter 18 contains a similar discussion for the Reports component of Oracle Developer.

A *form* is a Form Builder module that stores a set of objects in a single file. A form acts as a user interface that allows the user to display or manipulate data in the database. The strength of Oracle Developer Forms is its close ties to the Oracle database. The main link to the database is through a *block* that is associated with a database object such as a table or procedure (Chapter 4 describes how to make the decision about whether a block should be based on a procedure, table, or view. It also contains techniques for implementing blocks based on those data sources.)

Each form can contain one or more blocks. Data can be queried, inserted, updated, and deleted into *items* that correspond to the columns in a table or elements of a record in a PL/SQL table or cursor variable. Items are usually displayed on the screen so that the user can interact with them. Each block can contain one or more items. Standard GUI controls such as text items, display items, check boxes, and radio groups are used as the interface representations of data elements. Figure 1-1 shows the major form objects, the ties to a table, and how the objects relate on a mandatory one-to-many level.

The Forms and Reports components of Oracle Developer have different data architectures. There is an object in Reports, called the *column*, which represents a piece of data (usually a column value in the row of a table) in a data model query. Reports uses a separate object in the Layout Model, the *field*, to display the column's data. There may be columns without fields and there may be columns with more than one field. The data model and layout model contain separate representations. In the Forms component (at least up to and including release 6), there is only one object, the item, that references the column value in the database and displays the data.

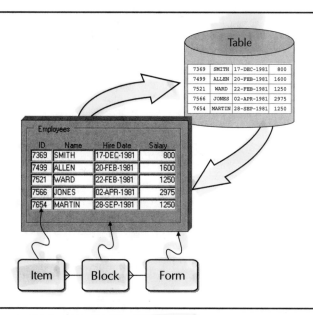

FIGURE 1-1.   *Major form object relationships*

Forms automatically creates DML and query SQL statements (INSERT, UPDATE, DELETE, and SELECT) from the block and item objects contained in the form. No SQL coding is required for these SQL statements because of the embedded functionality of the block. Another facility of Forms is the Query-By-Example (QBE) feature. The user can place the form into Enter Query mode, enter matching values in the items in the block, and execute the query. The form will construct a WHERE clause to add to the SELECT statement it generates to retrieve data. Another feature (and strength) of the tool is its ability to automatically manage row locking and handle concurrency without any extra coding. These principles are used throughout your work with the Form Builder and are required knowledge for even the beginning developer.

Sample Files

Files that were used to develop examples for this book are available from the publisher's and authors' web sites. This medium provides universal availability and allows the authors to update the files and make new files easily available to the book's readers. The authors' web site addresses are listed in the biography pages in the beginning of the book.

NOTE
Throughout the book you will find references to a directory called ORACLE_HOME. This is the directory into which you have installed the Oracle Developer software from the installation CD. If you are in a Windows environment, this will be written into the registry's Oracle node (under HKEY_LOCAL_MACHINE\SOFTWARE). For example, ORACLE_HOME might be defined as "C:\ORANT" or "C:\ORAWIN95." On UNIX operating systems, ORACLE_HOME is an environment (shell) variable. Directory listings in this book refer to the ORACLE_HOME directory because the actual location is installation-specific.

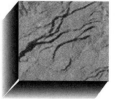

CHAPTER
2

New Features in Oracle Developer Release 6

If we do not find anything pleasant,
at least we shall find something new.

—Voltaire (1694–1778), *Candide*

racle has always offered strong development tools. Oracle Developer Release 6 (R.6) continues this tradition. It is an evolutionary release rather than a revolutionary release. The revolutionary features introduced with Release 2 (R.2), such as object libraries, blocks based on procedures and SELECT statements, and summary items in Forms and the Live Previewer and template support in Reports, are still supported in R.6.

This chapter examines the major new R.6 features for the Forms and Reports components of Oracle Developer. Other components are beyond the scope of this book, but you can get an overview of new features of these components by examining the New Features section in the Contents tab of the help system for the component you are interested in.

What if You Are Skipping Release 2?

If you are skipping from Developer R.1 (Forms 4.5 and Reports 2.5) to Developer R.6 (Forms 6.0 and Reports 6.0), you will find a number of new wizards, properties, Object Navigator objects (such as reports and popup menus in Forms and templates in Reports), layout objects (such as frames and tabs), and built-ins. While this upgrade path is not fully discussed in this chapter, it is useful to take a look at some of the most important new features of R.2 because they are all available in R.6 as well. If you are in the situation of upgrading from R.1 to R.6, you should round out your knowledge of new features by running through the "Quick Tour" (available in the Help menu of the Form Builder) and by reading the Release Notes. Also, if you can get your hands on a copy of the Developer R.2 help files, review the new features node of the Contents page in the help systems of Forms and Reports for a more complete discussion of the changes.

Changes in Forms from Release 1 to Release 2

In addition to reviewing the Quick Tour in Developer 6, it is worthwhile reviewing the Developer 6 Forms help topic "Form Builder 4.5 Runtime Behavior" (called "Runtime behavior, setting to Release 4.5" in the help index). This describes the differences between Developer Release 1 and Developer Release 2 Forms. The specific runtime behavior that changed with Developer R.2 was in the areas of validation, mirror items, the *Required* property, date and string format conversions, null values for list items, and the POST-CHANGE trigger. If you are converting forms from Developer R.1 to Developer R.2 or R.6, this help topic will inform you of these changes. If you have existing forms that require the Developer R.1 Forms 4.5 behavior, you can set the form module property, *Runtime Compatibility Mode,* to 4.5.

Developer Release 2 Forms included an enhanced developer interface and many more properties to manipulate. All features new with Release 2 carry over into Release 6. Some of the revolutionary features worth highlighting are the following:

- **Subclassing**   This object-oriented concept replaced the Developer R.1 concept of referencing. *Subclassing* means that you can reference an object from one form (Form A) into another (Form B). If the object in the master form (Form A) changes, those changes will take effect in the other form (Form B) when it is recompiled. You can also apply one object onto another object, which will allow them to share property settings. What makes subclassing different from the old concept of referencing is that you can change individual properties of a subclassed object without breaking the reference link.

- **Object library**   In Developer R.1 Forms, all objects were copied or referenced between one form and another form. Developer R.2 introduced a new Forms file type of *object library* (with an .OLB file extension) that stores the objects. You can drag and drop these objects from the object library to the form to copy or subclass them. The object library appears as a separate window with tab folders in the Form Builder. It opens automatically when you start up the Form Builder.

- **SmartClasses**   You can mark any object in the object library as a SmartClass. This makes the action of subclassing the object onto another object easier and faster because the SmartClass object will appear in the right-click mouse menu for a related object. For example, you could create a button item in your object library called TOOLBAR_BUTTON and mark it as a SmartClass. When you right-click on any button item in the Object Navigator or Layout Editor, the menu will contain an item for SmartClasses that has TOOLBAR_BUTTON as a selection. If you select that menu item, Form Builder will apply the subclass to the button item just as it would if you had opened up the Property Palette for the button and filled out the *Subclass Information* property. The properties of the object will be inherited from the object in the object library.

- **SmartTriggers**   SmartTriggers are a list of commonly used triggers for a particular object. These are also available in the right-click menus in the Object Navigator and Layout Editor. For example, if you right-click on a button item, the menu will contain an item for SmartTriggers that allows you to select the standard button trigger WHEN-BUTTON-PRESSED. If you select this menu item, the PL/SQL Editor will open and allow you to edit the trigger.

These concepts are keys to the effective use of Oracle Developer. Chapter 10 discusses some of these concepts further. Also, the Forms template system described in Chapter 11 provides examples of how they can be put to good use.

New Properties

Developer Release 2 Forms added a number of properties to support these new features. Another property worth mentioning is the block property *DML Array Size.* This property allows you to set the number of records that are sent to the database in one network trip. The default is "1", but if you set it higher, the form will construct an *array* (table of records) of records that need to be committed. This array is sent in one network hit to the database server. This process takes more memory, but can significantly reduce the number of DML (INSERT, UPDATE, and DELETE) statements that Forms creates. The best setting is the maximum number of records that require committing in one transaction.

Another new property as of Release 2 is the form property *Defer Required Enforcement.* This property is set to "No" by default. Setting the property to "Yes" postpones the validation on the item property *Required* until the entire record is validated. In previous releases of Developer, the *Required* property was checked as part of normal item validation. This stopped the user from freely moving out of a required item until the value was filled in. The new property allows you to present a friendlier interface with no extra coding.

CAUTION
Some utility programs from earlier releases such as the PECS (Performance Event Collection Service) form and the FFIGEN (Foreign Function Interface generator) form may not be available in early versions of the new release. Be sure to stay in contact with Oracle support through the online or telephone service if you need to use these utilities. In addition, the help system may mention a Forms Advanced Techniques *manual that was available only for Developer R.1. The information in this manual is now totally contained in the Form Builder help system. Using old utility forms and documentation may lead you astray because of the new and modified behaviors of Form Builder.*

Changes in Reports from Release 1 to Release 2

The main revolutionary concepts introduced in the Reports component of Developer Release 2 also carry over into Release 6. The same kind of enhanced developer interface was introduced with Developer Release 2 Reports. In addition, the following major features are worth mentioning:

- **Reports templates**   Templates allow you to start building your report with a particular set of layout properties. Templates assist in enforcing your report standards and allow you to concentrate on the report itself, rather than the particulars of a standard layout. Chapter 21 further explains the concept and use of Reports templates.

- **Live Previewer**   This new window runs the first page of your query and allows you to see data in a "live" mode as you make changes to the layout by dragging and dropping or resizing fields. It also allows you to change format masks, justification, and fonts through toolbar buttons.

- **Report Wizard**   This dialog steps you through the process of creating a report and allows you to bypass some previously labor-intensive steps. Chapter 18 and Appendix D further explain the Report Wizard.

New Properties

Developer Release 2 Reports added properties such as the *Line Stretch with Frame* property on boilerplate lines, which allows you to specify that a line will size to the frame.

Ref Cursor Query

Developer Release 2 introduced the ability to base a Reports query on a PL/SQL cursor variable instead of on a SQL query. A *cursor variable* (sometimes called a *ref cursor* because it is declared as a REF CURSOR type) points to a specific row in a query result set. Report Builder can base a query in the Data Model on a function that returns a ref cursor. Since you base the query on a function, you can embed complex logic into the query's data source. Chapter 24 contains an example and more information on this feature.

Conditional Formatting Dialog

Layout objects contain a property called *Conditional Formatting*. This powerful feature, new as of Release 2.1, allows you to specify printing conditions in a dialog, as shown in Figure 2-1. After you fill out and accept the dialog, Reports will create code to format the object, as shown in the following example:

```
function R_G_empnoFormatTrigger return boolean is
begin

  -- Automatically Generated from Report Builder.
  if (:empno BETWEEN '7300' and '7600')
  then
    srw.set_foreground_fill_color('cyan');
    srw.set_fill_pattern('solid');
  end if;

  return (TRUE);
end;
```

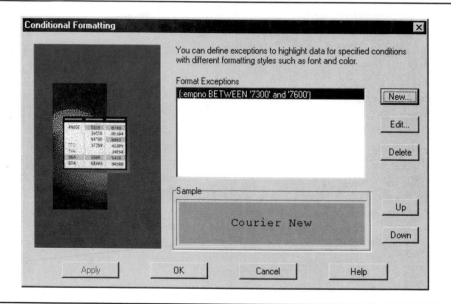

FIGURE 2-1. *Conditional Formatting dialog*

This code is automatically updated when you change the property. Although it may not be formatted to your standards, this code saves steps and thought when you just need to change the color of the text, fill, or border (or to hide the object).

TIP
Do not bother to reformat the code that Forms and Reports creates for you. Your reformatting effort will be lost if you ever decide to rerun the feature (such as a wizard) that created the code in the first place.

Web Preview

You can select **View→Web Preview→Generate to Web Browser** (when the Live Previewer is displayed) to view the report in an HTML browser or in a PDF reader (depending on how you set the menu items in the **View→Web Preview** submenu). This feature allows you to view a single page or multiple pages as they will appear when published on the Web.

Other New Features

Other developer-friendly enhancements were also added, such as the Layout Editor toolbar buttons for flush justification and for inserting a page number, or date and time into the layout. There were also PL/SQL enhancements—for example, SRW-packaged procedures such as SRW.SET_FONT_FACE that replace the SRW.SET_ATTR procedure functionality in a more user-friendly way.

Developer 6 Support for Oracle8

One new feature in Forms and Reports, as well as in other components of Oracle Developer R.6, is the support for Oracle8 objects and PL/SQL. The Oracle8 features are mostly transparent to the developer, but offer benefits when you are designing or running the form or report. Forms takes direct advantage of the Oracle8 DML returning value feature (discussed shortly), so you do not have to requery a block if a database trigger changes a value displayed in a form.

   The Oracle8 INSTEAD OF trigger attached to a view is useful to Form Builder. This trigger allows you to perform any DML on a view; you do not have to worry about key-preserved columns and their rules. The code you place in the INSTEAD OF trigger replaces the normal DML to the base tables.

Object Datatypes

Developer 6 allows you to access the Oracle8 large object (LOB) and binary file (BFILE) datatypes. These datatypes appear in the selection lists of both Form Builder items and Report Builder columns and fields. You can also access object columns in both components. For example, you can create an object type to represent an employee's salary history as follows:

```
CREATE TYPE person_t AS OBJECT(
    first_name      VARCHAR2(50),
    last_name       VARCHAR2(50),
    birth_date      DATE);
```

You can then create a table from this object type:

```
CREATE TABLE employee(
    emp_id          NUMBER NOT NULL,
    dept_id         NUMBER,
    person          person_t);
```

The resulting table contains standard, scalar columns (EMP_ID and DEPT_ID) as well as the object column of datatype PERSON_T, as this listing in SQL*Plus 8.1 shows:

```
SQL> set describe depth 3
SQL> desc employee
 Name                     Null?     Type
 ------------------       --------  -----------
 EMP_ID                   NOT NULL  NUMBER
 DEPT_ID                            NUMBER
 PERSON                             PERSON_T
   FIRST_NAME                       VARCHAR2(50)
   LAST_NAME                        VARCHAR2(50)
   BIRTH                            DATE
```

When you base a block on this table, the Data Block Wizard displays the PERSON object using separate columns, as Figure 2-2 shows.

You can select individual attributes of the object type the same way you select scalar columns. When you move the columns to the "Database Items" box, the names of object attributes include a qualifier that identifies the column name, as Figure 2-3 shows.

Form Builder treats the column object as if it were made of scalar columns, one for each attribute. Form Builder also supports REF columns that point to another object table. However, there is no support for collection types such as nested tables, VARRAYs, or VARARRAYs. You can, however, base blocks on tables that contain these types, although you cannot select the columns containing the collection type. You could not use tables containing objects at all in Developer R.2 except by "flattening" the objects into a standard table with a set of database packages called the *Object Iron*.

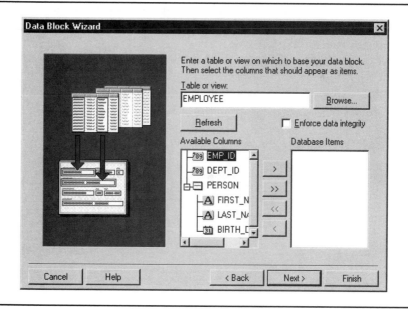

FIGURE 2-2. *Data Block Wizard selecting an object type*

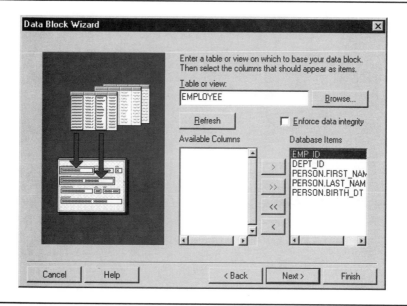

FIGURE 2-3. *Selected object attributes*

The LOV Wizard treats the object columns as if they were separate columns. Reports treats objects in a similar way. Figure 2-4 shows the Report Wizard Fields tab with the expanded PERSON object.

Developer R.6 also supports the database FLOAT datatype by mapping it to a NUMBER datatype. It does not support features such as stored procedures that return object values, collection types, and the NLS datatypes (NCHAR and NVARCHAR2).

PL/SQL 8

Oracle Developer R.6 supports calling PL/SQL 8 code in the database as well as PL/SQL 8 code written on the client side. However, the client-side implementation of PL/SQL 8 does not support the new PL/SQL 8 object features.

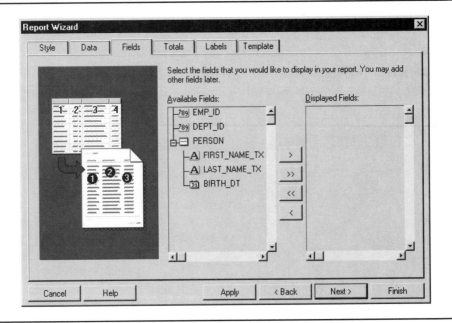

FIGURE 2-4. *Selecting an object in the Report Wizard Fields tab*

Form Builder New Features

As mentioned earlier, the new features offered by the Developer R.6 Form Builder are evolutionary in nature. The main areas of enhancements are in developer ease-of-use and in support of web deployment.

Ease-of-Use Features

There are many Release 6 features that are intended to make your work easier.

Interface

The Form Builder interface uses flat toolbar buttons, the standard in modern GUI applications. The Layout Editor toolbar contains the same buttons as in the Object Navigator for Run Form Web (to show the form in the Java Virtual Machine runtime) and Run Form Debug (to set the form into debug mode and run it), shown here:

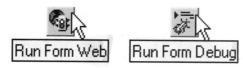

These buttons are new as of Release 6.

TIP
*The help topic "Using the keyboard in the editor" lists shortcut keys. Use the help system Find tab to locate this topic. If you have not used these keys before, you might discover that they can speed up your work. For example, instead of selecting **Program→Compile→All** to compile all PL/SQL in your form, you can simply press CTRL-SHIFT-K. All of these shortcut keys were available in Developer R.2 as well.*

Documentation

There is a new reference manual in Adobe Portable Document Format (PDF). This is available from the Oracle Information Navigator (OIN) window that opens when you select **Help→Manuals** in Form Builder. Figure 2-5 shows the OIN with an expanded Reference Manuals node.

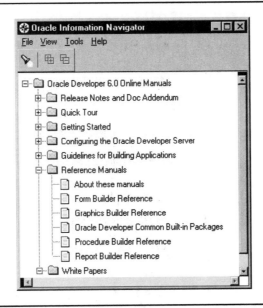

FIGURE 2-5. *Oracle Information Navigator Reference Manuals node*

The new manual, *Form Builder Reference,* lists, explains, and gives examples for built-ins, triggers, properties, options, and system variables. Much of this information is in the help system as well, but you may prefer browsing a document that is set up as a reference manual.

PL/SQL Editor Enhancements

The PL/SQL Editor received a functionality face-lift with Oracle Developer R.6. Windows users will find many new features that help in managing PL/SQL code. However, not all the new features are available on UNIX platforms.

SYNTAX PALETTE   The *Syntax Palette,* a window you can access through **Program→Syntax Palette**, is shown in Figure 2-6. It allows you to insert PL/SQL constructs and built-in declarations into your PL/SQL Editor code. After selecting the correct tab (PL/SQL or Built-ins), you choose a category with the poplist at the top of the tab and find the syntactical element. Clicking the Insert button pastes this element structure into your code. Some structures contain comments and lines in lowercase that you need to replace. This is handy if you forget the exact syntax or

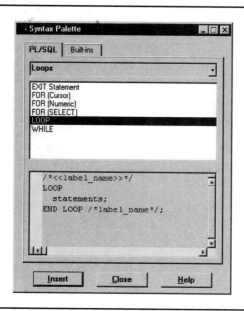

FIGURE 2-6.   *Syntax Palette*

need a reminder of all of the parameters for a particular Form Builder built-in. However, this will not in any way replace knowledge of the PL/SQL language.

FIND AND REPLACE IN PL/SQL   You can perform a search or search-and-replace operation on your PL/SQL code using **Program→Find and Replace PL/SQL** to access the dialog shown in Figure 2-7. This dialog allows you to construct conditional searches (using the Expression button) and look in some or all of the files open in the Form Builder session. After you click Find All to locate the occurrences, you can navigate to the code by double-clicking the Results line. You can also replace text strings using the Replace All button. This is a fast and easy method that is a big improvement over previous releases.

AUTO INDENTING   The enhanced editor will automatically indent to the same level as the line above when you press ENTER. The editor copies to the current line the tab or spaces you have used to indent the previous line. The default indent level is two characters (and Chapter 3 contains a tip for resetting the number of

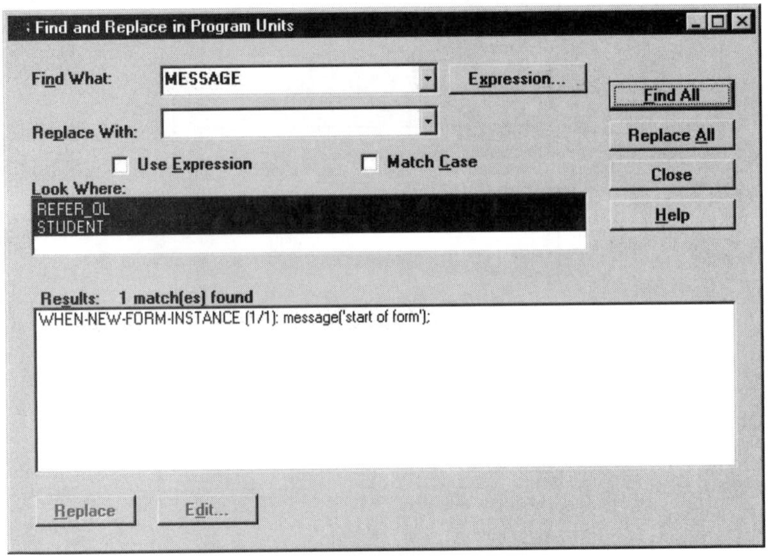

Find and Replace in Program Units

Find What: MESSAGE Expression... Find All

Replace With: Replace All

☐ Use Expression ☐ Match Case Close

Look Where:

REFER_OL Help
STUDENT

Results: 1 match(es) found

WHEN-NEW-FORM-INSTANCE (1/1): message('start of form');

Replace Edit...

FIGURE 2-7. *Find and Replace in PL/SQL dialog*

indent characters). The TAB key indents into the code body (instead of navigating to an editor button as in previous releases). Pressing SHIFT-TAB reverses the indent (or "outdents"). You can also use **Edit→Indent** and **Edit→Outdent** to perform these actions.

SYNTAX COLOR HIGHLIGHTING The editor automatically displays different colors for the code body, operators, comments, and character strings in quotes. This provides better readability for those who do not have difficulty differentiating colors.

TIP
You can open more than one PL/SQL Editor at the same time by finding an unopened program unit or trigger in the Object Navigator, holding SHIFT, and double-clicking on the program unit's icon in the Navigator. This has been a feature since Oracle Developer R.1.

LINE NUMBER DISPLAY   The editor displays the line number at the top of the edit area when you use the scroll bar. The following shows the right side of the Editor window as the mouse cursor is scrolling down the page on the program unit. At this point, line 141 is at the top of the edit area. This feature can help you find a line of code if a compiler message indicates the line number.

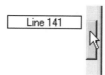

ENHANCED SELECTION AND TEXT HANDLING   The PL/SQL Editor also offers the following new features:

- The Editor window contains a gray border area on the right side of the window. If you drag the mouse cursor over this area while clicking the mouse button, the lines you drag over will be selected. Thus, you can select the entire line without having to worry about where the actual edit cursor is.

- You can select columns of text instead of complete lines, as shown in Figure 2-8 (where indent spaces are not selected). Just press ALT as you click-and-drag the mouse over the text you want to select.

- Once you select the text, you can drag and drop it to another location. This saves a cut-and-paste operation.

- If you drag and drop text while holding CTRL, you will copy the text.

- The Editor window allows you to split the views horizontally and vertically by dragging the bar on the top of the right scroll bar or on the left of the bottom scroll bar. This gives you areas that can scroll separately, as Figure 2-9 shows.

- You can print a program unit separately by loading it into the PL/SQL Editor and selecting **File→Print**.

- The editor provides multiple levels of undo (CTRL-Z) and redo (CTRL-Y). These operations are also available in the Edit menu.

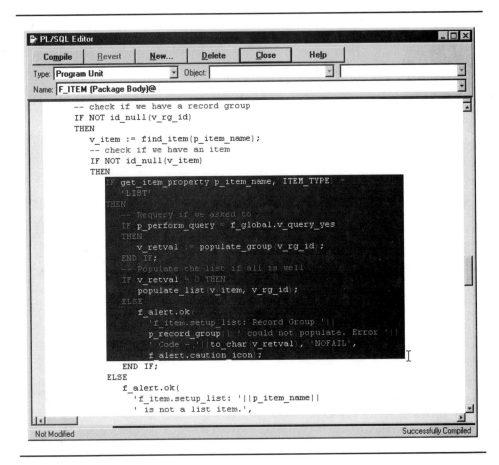

```
-- check if we have a record group
IF NOT id_null(v_rg_id)
THEN
   v_item := find_item(p_item_name);
   -- check if we have an item
   IF NOT id_null(v_item)
   THEN
      IF get_item_property(p_item_name, ITEM_TYPE) =
      'LIST'
      THEN
         -- Requery if we asked to
         IF p_perform_query = f_global.v_query_yes
         THEN
            v_retval := populate_group(v_rg_id);
         END IF;
         -- Populate the list if all is well
         IF v_retval = 0 THEN
            populate_list(v_item, v_rg_id);
         ELSE
            f_alert.ok(
               'f_item.setup_list: Record Group '||
               p_record_group|| ' could not populate. Error '||
               ' Code - '||to_char(v_retval), 'NOFAIL',
               f_alert.caution_icon);
      END IF;
   ELSE
      f_alert.ok(
         'f_item.setup_list: '||p_item_name||
         ' is not a list item.',
```

FIGURE 2-8.   *Selecting columns of text*

TIP
Use the poplists in the PL/SQL Editor window to navigate to a particular trigger or program unit. If the editor is open, it may be faster to find a program unit by selecting from the list than by drilling down to it in the Object Navigator.

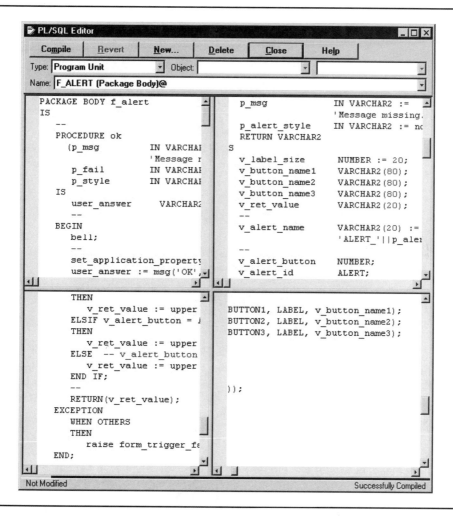

FIGURE 2-9. *PL/SQL Editor split views*

Hierarchical Tree Control

Form Builder now has a native hierarchical tree control! This is great news to many developers because it is an interface that users can easily relate to. It is a logical way to display data that is structured recursively or hierarchically. Figure 2-10 shows the NAVWIZ.FMB demo form that uses this control to show employees and their managers.

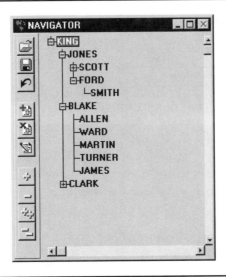

FIGURE 2-10. *Demo of the hierarchical tree control*

This control was available in the Oracle Developer Release 2 demo forms, but it was made of Forms objects and required much PL/SQL programming to manipulate. The R.2 version of the control is a native control with its own built-ins and triggers, which means that you do not need to write as much code. Chapter 25 contains an example of how to code and use this new control.

LOV Wizard

A feature that is new with Developer Release 6 is called the LOV Wizard. This wizard makes the job of constructing a *list of values* (LOV) easier. The dialog shown in Figure 2-11 appears when you create a new LOV and specify that you want to use the LOV Wizard. You fill out the subsequent dialogs for the query, columns, column display, LOV display, advanced properties, and which items you want this LOV attached to. The wizard will create the LOV and record group, if specified, set the correct sizes and other properties, and attach the LOV to the items. The wizard automates the many steps involved with creating an LOV manually. It virtually ensures that the LOV you create will work the first time. You can reload the wizard for an existing LOV by selecting the LOV node in the Object Navigator and choosing **Tools→LOV Wizard** from the menu.

Connecting to Multiple Data Sources

You can connect to multiple databases in the same Forms session using the EXEC_SQL built-in package. A demo form, called EXEC_SQL.FMB, includes calls to

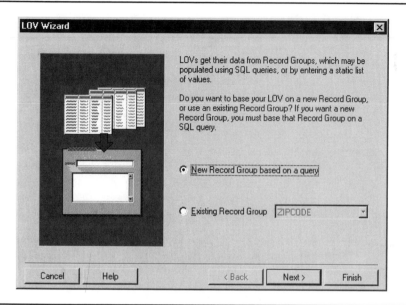

FIGURE 2-11.   *The LOV Wizard*

this package and a demonstration of a multi-database connection. Although the help file may state that EXEC_SQL is a separate .PLL library file (which was true in Developer 2), it is now a built-in package. This package is documented in the help file PDPKG.HLP located in the ORACLE_HOME/tools/doc60/us directory. You can also access this file from the main Forms help system by searching for EXEC_SQL. The Adobe Acrobat file OCA_INFO.PDF in that same directory contains information on the Open Client Adapter (OCA) that allows you to connect to ODBC data sources.

TIP
The PDPKG.HLP file contains documentation for other built-in packages such as ORA_FFI, the foreign function interface to Windows functions; TEXT_IO to read and write to files; LIST to maintain arrays of lists programmatically; and ORA_PROF, which allows you to time your code. This information is also available as the Oracle Developer Built-in Package Reference *(a .PDF file) in the Reference Manuals section of the Oracle Information Navigator (which you access using **Help→Manuals**).*

DML Returning Value

A new block property in the Advanced Database section called *DML Returning Value* overcomes a common problem that occurred with database triggers and forms before Developer R.6. As an example, this problem would occur if you have coded a database BEFORE UPDATE trigger on the EMPLOYEE table that converts the last name to uppercase using the following code:

```
:new.last_name := INITCAP(:new.last_name);
```

If the user commits a change to a record using a Form Builder module, the database trigger will convert the last name to lowercase with an initial capital letter on each word, regardless of what the user entered. If the user inputs "SMitH", the value in the table will be "Smith". The onscreen value might then be different from the database table value because the database trigger changed it. If the user wanted to make a change to the same record after the database trigger fired, a Forms message ("FRM-40654: Record has been updated by another user. Re-query to see change.") would appear, indicating that the screen value was not the same as the database value. The "other user" in this message refers to the database trigger.

Another typical example is displaying the last user who modified the record and the date that the modification occurred. A database trigger would normally update the name and date, but if the form were to display this value, the same message would appear when the form was committed.

The answer to this problem for situations such as these in Developer Releases 1 and 2 was to requery the form after the commit using the same query conditions as the last query (stored in the :SYSTEM.LAST_QUERY variable). This also required navigating to the proper record if the query were to return more than one record. The code to do this was not difficult, but required some thought and debugging time.

In Developer 6, if you set the *DML Returning Value* property to "Yes" (the default is "No"), Forms takes advantage of the Oracle8 returning-clause syntax for INSERT, UPDATE, and DELETE statements. After the statements complete, this syntax signals that the database should return values to the source that issued the SQL statement. Form Builder will automatically update the values on the screen to correspond with the values in the database if the *DML Returning Value* property is set to "Yes."

NOTE
If another user tries to make a change to the same record and the values on that screen are different from the values in the database, the Forms requery message will still appear, regardless of the DML Returning Value *setting.*

Forms Runtime Diagnostics

You can log all Forms events to a file in case you need to determine what is happening in a form. The resulting file shows all values retrieved into blocks on the screen as well as the code that executes. This facility is activated by a command-line option RECORD, as in the following listing:

```
ifrun60 module=student userid=scott/tiger record=collect log=student.log
```

In this example, the Forms runtime (ifrun60) runs the STUDENT.FMX file logging in as SCOTT/TIGER. It indicates that you want to record diagnostics into a file called STUDENT.LOG. When the form exits, you can examine the file and determine what events occurred. Consider that the STUDENTS.BUTTON item has a WHEN-BUTTON-PRESSED trigger with the following code:

```
set_item_property('STUDENTS.ID', VISIBLE, PROPERTY_FALSE);
```

If you run diagnostics on this form, this one code line will create the following trail within the log file:

```
# 3 - STUDENT:STUDENTS.ID
CLICK STUDENT STUDENTS BUTTON 1 MOUSE

WHEN-BUTTON-PRESSED Trigger Fired:
Form: STUDENT
Block: STUDENTS
Item: BUTTON

State Delta:
FORM STUDENT
  CURFIELD    BUTTON

Executing FIND_ITEM Built-in:
In Argument 0 - Type: String    Value: STUDENTS.ID
Out Argument 0 - Type: Integer   Value: 65538

Executing SET_ITEM_PROPERTY/SET_FIELD Built-in:
In Argument 0 - Type: Integer  Value: 65538
In Argument 1 - Type: Number   Value: 1401
In Argument 2 - Type: String    Value: NULL
In Argument 3 - Type: Oracle Number  Value: 5
In Argument 4 - Type: Oracle Number  Value: 0
```

```
# 4 - STUDENT:STUDENTS.BUTTON - MENU
FORM STUDENT
  BLOCK STUDENTS
    FIELD ID
      ENABLED     FALSE
      NAVIGABLE   FALSE
      QUERYABLE   FALSE
      UPDATEABLE  FALSE
END
```

This trace shows the built-in and the results. If there had been any errors, the error number and message would be recorded as well. This gives you a precise (and voluminous) picture of all events in the form and assists in debugging.

TIP
There is a similar trace facility in Reports as well. You can set the trace file name and settings using **Tools→Trace**. *This has been a feature of Reports since Developer R.1.*

File Filter Behavior

The dialog you see when you select **File→Open** in Form Builder contains a file filter poplist where you can specify the type of file you want to see in the list (.FMB, .MMB, .PLL, or .OLB). In Developer Release 2, you could specify an access preference called *Show* (using **Tools→Preferences**) so that this poplist would default to a certain file type. This preference is no longer available in Forms (although it is in Reports), so the filter always defaults to "All Files." If you only want to see files of a certain type, you can just select the file type in the poplist after the File dialog displays.

TIP
There are a number of shortcut keys you can use in the Form Builder. The shortcut key for a specific feature is listed next to its menu item. The following table shows the keypresses for some of the most common features or operations:

Keypress	Feature or Operation
F11	PL/SQL Editor
F2	Layout Editor
F4	Property Palette (select an object first)
CTRL-T	Compile the file
CTRL-S	Save the file
CTRL-O	Open a file
CTRL-W	Close the file

Popup Menu Features

Popup menus appear when you right-click on an item or canvas. You create these menus in Form Builder as objects in the form (not as part of a separate menu module). You then attach the menus to items or canvases using properties of those objects. The popup menu object was new with Developer Release 2. These menus have been enhanced in Release 6 to allow you to create check box, radio button, and image menu items. These are standard features of a normal menu as well. Chapter 28 contains an example of some of these menu characteristics.

New Cursor Icons

You can programmatically change the mouse cursor icon using the SET_APPLICATION_PROPERTY built-in using the following syntax:

```
set_application_property(CURSOR_STYLE, 'BUSY');
```

You would use this call if you were executing a long-running query or process and wanted the user to know that there would be a wait time. When the process is finished, you would change the cursor back, using the same call with the 'DEFAULT' icon name. If you need an icon other than the busy icon, you would substitute a different icon name. Table 2-1 shows these names. The "*" indicates new icons as of Release 6.

Chapter 27 contains a code sample that illustrates this built-in. The cursor shape does not imply any special functionality. If you want to do something (like resizing a column) after changing the cursor shape, you still need to write the code to do it.

Icon Name	Use or Meaning	Icon
*ARROW	An arrow shape even if the mouse cursor is over a text item	
BUSY	Waiting for a process	
*COPY	Drag and drop and copy	
CROSSHAIR	A specific point	
DEFAULT	The normal shape that changes into an Insertion icon when the mouse cursor is over a text item	
*DRAGGABLE	Shows that the item is available for a drag and drop operation	
*HAND	Hand shape	
HELP	Help question mark with arrow	
INSERTION	Mouse is over a text item	
*LINK	Drag and drop a link or shortcut	
*MAGNIFY	Magnifying glass for zooming in	
*MOVE	Drag and drop shape	
*NODROP	Item is not available for drag and drop	

TABLE 2-1. *Available Mouse Cursor Icons*

Icon Name	Use or Meaning	Icon
*RESIZEH	Resize horizontally	↔
*RESIZEUL	Resize the upper-left or lower-right corner	↖↘
*RESIZEUR	Resize the upper-right or lower-left corner	↙↗
*RESIZEV	Resize vertically	↕
*SIZECOL	Resize a column	←|→
*SIZEROW	Resize a row	↕
*SPLITH	Split horizontally	←||→
*SPLITV	Split vertically	↕

TABLE 2-1.   *Available Mouse Cursor Icons* (continued)

The new icons are not in the documentation as of this writing. Not all icons are available on all platforms, although all those shown in Table 2-1 are available on Windows and Motif. If the user has changed the default shapes for the system, the icons may appear different.

Some of these cursors (DEFAULT, BUSY, CROSSHAIR, MOVE, INSERTION, and HAND) work in web-deployed forms. There are eight additional icons (oriented around points of the compass) you can use for Web-deployed forms, as shown in Table 2-2.

Icon name	Use or Meaning	Icon
ERESIZE	Resizing right side	↔
NERESIZE	Resizing upper-right corner	↗
NRESIZE	Resizing top side	↕
NWRESIZE	Resizing upper-left corner	↖
SERESIZE	Resizing lower-right corner	↘
SRESIZE	Resizing bottom side	↕
SWRESIZE	Resizing lower-left corner	↙
WRESIZE	Resizing left side	↔

TABLE 2-2. *Additional Mouse Cursor Icons for Web-Deployed Forms*

Other New Features

There are a number of other features or changes that are worth special mention.

ASSOCIATE PROMPT   The Layout Editor contains a new button called "Associate prompt," which allows you to link a boilerplate prompt with an item. This is particularly useful if you are upgrading forms from Developer Release 1 to Developer Release 6 because (as of Developer Release 2) a prompt can become an item property. If the item's prompt is a property, you can manipulate it with the SET_ITEM_PROPERTY built-in. To use this feature, select the boilerplate text and the item that will be associated with it (using the CTRL-click key combination). When you click the Associate prompt button in the top toolbar, the boilerplate text will be placed in the item *Prompt* property.

ITEM BEVELS   Additional options for the item *Bevel* property are now available. Developer Release 6 adds a value of "Plain" that shows a border around the item (in client/server deployment). There are also values of "Inset" and "Outset" that were new as of Developer Release 2. The "Raised", "Lowered", and "None" values have been available since Release 1. Figure 2-12 shows the item bevels in both web deployment and client/server runtimes.

VISUAL ATTRIBUTE PROPERTIES   You can now programmatically set and "get" the visual attribute property values for items in individual rows separately. For example, you could programmatically determine what the font size is for a particular row (GET_ITEM_PROPERTY('EMP.EMPNO', FONT_SIZE)) and change just that property without having to reassign a visual attribute to it (as was necessary

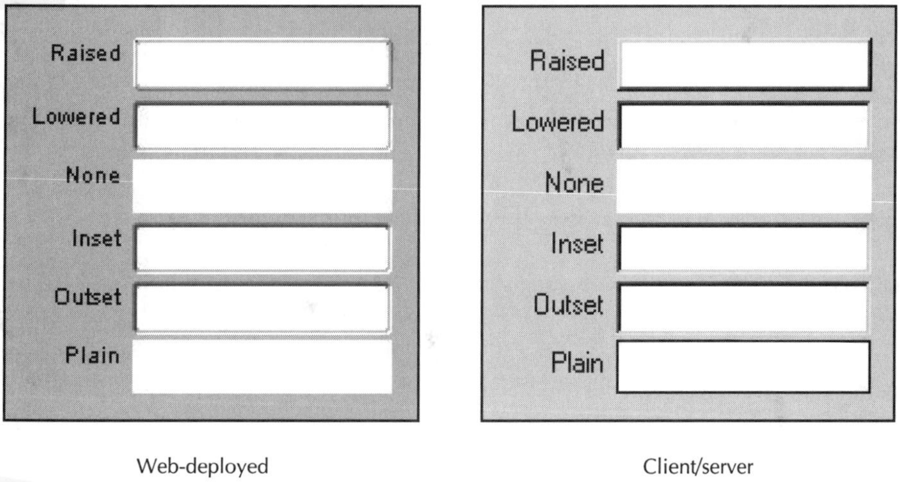

Web-deployed   Client/server

FIGURE 2-12.   *Item bevels*

in previous releases of Developer Forms). The GET_ITEM_PROPERTY and SET_ITEM_PROPERTY programmatic properties follow:

- BACKGROUND_COLOR
- FILL_PATTERN
- FONT_NAME
- FONT_SIZE
- FONT_SPACING
- FONT_STYLE
- FONT_WEIGHT
- FOREGROUND_COLOR
- WHITE_ON_BLACK

These properties are also accessible with the get and set built-ins for radio buttons, tab pages, canvases, and windows.

You can also programmatically get and set the property values for the current record attribute. The *current record attribute* is one that takes over the setting for a particular object when the cursor is in that row. As the cursor moves through the block from record to record, the current record attribute changes the way the items look for the row the cursor is in. The programmatic settings are available through item, block, and form built-ins (for example, GET_BLOCK_PROPERTY and SET_FORM_PROPERTY). The properties are named with a CURRENT_RECORD_ prefix with the same name as the other visual attribute properties.

ICON PATH The Windows registry contains a string value—UI_ICON—in the HKEY_LOCAL_MACHINE\SOFTWARE\ORACLE node that specifies the directory path where Form Builder will find icon files. Icons are used for iconic buttons, the hierarchical tree control, and window icons (that show in the top left corner of the window). Form Builder finds the icons in one of the directories stored in this registry value. As with other paths (except UNIX), you separate directories using a semicolon. For example, the value of UI_ICON in a Windows environment could be the following:

```
.;C:\FORMS;C:\APP\PROD\FORMS
```

The "." indicates the current working directory (the Start In directory in the Forms runtime or Form Builder shortcut properties). Be careful not to exceed 512 characters in this path when working under MS Windows (NT or 95 or 98).

NOTE
Some icons, such as the standard icons in the Form Builder menu toolbar, are read from the Forms runtime executable or library. These are also available for iconic buttons you create. For example, you can create a button with an Icon Filename *property of "exit". When you run the form, even if there is no EXIT.ICO (or EXIT.GIF on the Web), the icon will display because it is part of the Forms runtime executable. Finding the names of these icons is a matter of trial and error, but you can start experimenting by using the names of the icons in the ORACLE_HOME/devdem60/bin/icon directory.*

PROPERTY PALETTE VISUAL SELECTION POPUPS   There are now color, font, and pattern selection popups (or palettes) inside the Property Palette. In previous releases, if you needed to select a property value that required a font, color, or pattern, you would click the selection button next to a property value and see an LOV containing a list of the names of those objects. In Release 6, clicking the selection button for a color or pattern property will display the same color palette that you use to choose colors in the Layout Editor. After you make a selection, the name of that color (for example, r0g0b88) or pattern will be placed in the property value. You can also just type in the color or pattern name if you know it.

For a font property, if you click on the name of the font category (for example "Font" or "Prompt Font"), a More button will appear. Clicking that button will display the standard font dialog box where you can select the font, weight, and size. When you accept this dialog box, the appropriate properties will be filled in automatically. This is much easier than setting the individual font properties. The trick to remember here is to click on the heading to display the More button.

Web Features

Oracle Developer R.6 contains many enhancements to the multi-tier, server-based deployment environment for Oracle Developer. This book focuses on generic techniques and standards and does not offer a complete solution for working in the web environment. However, it is useful to examine some of these enhancements that are new as of Release 6 because web deployment is the current and future focus for Developer applications, and the new features will make your move to the Web easier and faster.

The Web Previewer
A new button in the Layout Editor and Object Navigator toolbars, called "Run Form Web," allows you to run the form locally (in client/server) in the *Web Previewer.*

This previewer offers the same kind of Java runtime engine (Java Virtual Machine or JVM) as you would use when running forms on the Web. The Web Previewer (implemented through a separate program file—IFWEB60.EXE) is only available (at this writing) on Windows NT, although there are plans to offer this feature on Win 95 and Win 98 in an upcoming release.

Before this release, you had to install and configure the application server, create the form and test it locally in client/server mode, and then copy it to the proper directory on the server (and possibly recompile for a new operating system). After those steps were completed, you could then run the form in a web browser that connected with the network version of the form. This method, while relatively straightforward, was a bit inconvenient.

The new Web Previewer removes all those extra steps for the development phase. You still have to fully test the form in the multi-tiered environment with the Oracle Developer Forms Server and your web listener, but the new run option allows you to get an idea of the look and feel of the form before the final testing stages.

If you want to use an HTML startup file with customized parameters (as Chapter 13 describes), you can enter the name of the file in the Runtime tab of the **Tools→Preferences** dialog.

TIP
To replace the standard Web Previewer splash screen, use the following parameter in your HTML startup file (substituting your new splash screen .GIF file for mysplash.gif):

```
<param name="splashScreen" value="mysplash.gif">
```

Java Support

Form Builder Release 6 offers support for Java components when you run the form on the Web. You can link into your form the functionality provided by Java code from a third party. You can also write your own Java code (called a *Pluggable Java Component* or PJC) to include in the form if you comply with the IView interface. This interface is defined in the help system (check for the Index topic "IView"). There are two ways to include Java components in your form: as a JavaBean control and as a replacement for a standard Forms item.

THE JAVABEAN CONTROL   The Layout Editor contains a new toolbar drawing button for a new item type, called a *Bean Area.* Drawing a Bean Area on your canvas creates an unseen item that will display a Java Bean when run on the Web. Basically, a JavaBean is a piece of compiled Java code that does something such as presenting a button or calendar control on the canvas. You need to specify the name of the bean in the *Implementation Class* property.

You can control the JavaBean at runtime using the Forms SET_CUSTOM_ITEM_ PROPERTY built-in. The trigger WHEN-CUSTOM-ITEM-EVENT fires when the user interacts with the control, and SYSTEM.CUSTOM_ITEM_EVENT indicates which event (such as "Spindown") took place. Figure 2-13 shows a demo form that uses a progress bar JavaBean. The Bean Area is only active when you run the form in the Web Previewer or in a true Forms Server Web environment.

JavaBeans allow you to supplement the set of standard Forms controls. Anything you can obtain or create in Java using the proper interface is a candidate for your Forms application. In this way, JavaBeans provide the same kind of extensibility to web-deployed forms as OCX and Active-X controls offer to the client/server environment.

REPLACING A STANDARD FORMS ITEM   Another way to include a Java component in your form is to use it to replace a standard Form Builder control such as a button, text item, check box, list item, or radio group. This will allow you to use the standard Forms functionality for the object (such as a WHEN-BUTTON-PRESSED trigger for button objects) and also take advantage of the additional features of the Java component. For example, suppose you want to use a Java object called

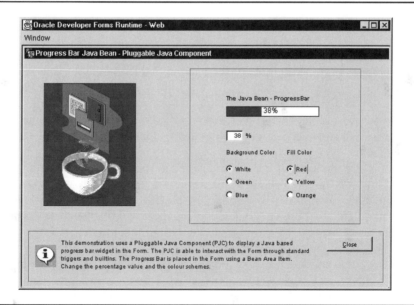

FIGURE 2-13.   *Demo form for progress bar JavaBean*

RoundedButton instead of your normal button object. This object renders buttons with rounded corners, as follows:

The end buttons are rounded more on the edge that does not face another button. The button object "senses" the buttons around it and renders itself accordingly. This functionality is built into the Java object. If you use the Java component's name in the *Implementation Class* property and set the *Item Type* property to "Push Button" as you would for a normal button, the normal button triggers (and properties) will be in effect. You are just replacing the normal Form Builder object with a Java component.

IMPLEMENTATION CLASS PROPERTY VALUE   The *Implementation Class* property specifies the name of the Java component (both types) that you are linking to your form. The name includes the directory structure (delimited with periods). The ORACLE_HOME/forms60/java directory is the home for all Forms Java code. The demos directory in this subdirectory path contains some sample JavaBeans. To use a demo JavaBean, you would qualify the bean name with oracle.forms.demos in the *Implementation Class* property (for example, oracle.forms.demos.ProgressBarPJC). The SOURCE directory under the demos directory contains the source Java code and a README file with descriptions.

New Look and Feel
Forms deployed on the Web now run in a multiple document interface (MDI) window. This mimics the Windows MDI and allows you to manipulate the outer runtime window separately. It also provides a way to open multiple forms within the same outer (MDI) window. You can specify (using the USESDI command-line parameter) that you want to use a single document interface for the Web or client/server.

   There is also a new look and feel that you can specify for the web runtime. You use the parameter lookAndFeel with a value of "oracle" to specify this. If you include this parameter in your startup HTML file (Chapter 13 discusses web-deployed forms and the startup file in more detail), the user interface will be displayed in an alternative way. Figure 2-14 shows a simple form running in the Java runtime environment using the Oracle look and feel.

   This new look and feel provides a much more "rounded" view of a form. The window border, scroll bars, buttons, poplists, LOV and alert windows, and items themselves all have rounded corners. There are also a number of color "schemes" that you designate with an HTML startup file parameter called colorScheme (with

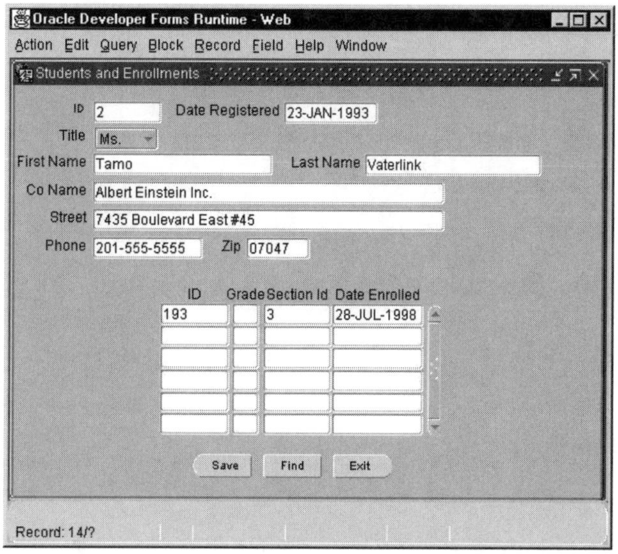

FIGURE 2-14.   *Form running with Oracle look and feel*

valid values of blue, khaki, olive, purple, red, teal, and titanium). The color schemes provide a certain set of coordinated colors as highlight and background colors. Figure 2-15 shows the rounded poplist and alert. The alerts also have animated icons (the bell in this alert "rings" when the alert is shown).

DISPLAYING THE NEW LOOK AND FEEL IN THE WEB PREVIEWER
To show the new look and feel using the Web Previewer, create an HTML file with contents as follows:

```
<applet code ="oracle.forms.engine.Main" width = 600 height = 500>
<param name = "JNIregistryPath" value = "file:D:\orant\FORMS60\java">
<param name = "lookAndFeel" value = "oracle">
<param name = "colorScheme" value = "khaki">
<param name = "serverArgs" value = "module=c:\forms\student_web userid=student/student">
</applet>
```

Substitute the location of your Forms Java code for the JNIregistryPath parameter. Substitute the path and name of your form (and your username/password) in the serverArgs parameter. (If you are storing the form in a directory in the Forms path, you do not need to specify the drive and directory name with the file name.) Navigate to the runtime preferences in the **Tools→Preferences** dialog in Form Builder. Fill in the

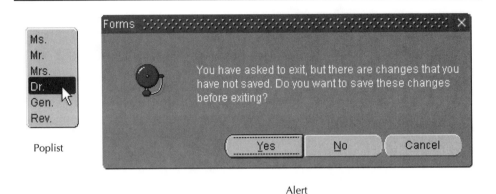

Poplist

Alert

FIGURE 2-15. *Rounded poplist and alert*

HTML File Name field with the name of the file you just created. When you run the Web Previewer, using the Run Form Web button, the new look and feel will appear. You can experiment with different color schemes as well.

Other Web Features
In addition to the interface enhancements, Oracle Developer Release 6 offers many new features on the Developer (application) Server side. These enhancements include an increased ability to scale to multiple clients, options for reducing the form startup time, reduced memory footprint for the application server, and installing the Forms Server as an NT service. There are, at this writing, plans (with the next version of Developer) to offer HTTP 1.1 support (beta in Release 6.0), which will allow you to deploy applications regardless of firewall restrictions. There are also plans for integrating the Forms Server with Oracle Enterprise Manager. Chapter 13 explains some of these new features in more detail.

Report Builder New Features
Some of the new Report Builder features parallel those in Form Builder. The new features of the Report Builder PL/SQL Editor are the same as in the Form Builder PL/SQL Editor, except that the Syntax Palette contains SRW built-ins for Reports. Reports' new documentation consists of a manual called *Report Builder Reference* in the Reference Manuals node of the ORACLE Information Navigator (**Help→Manuals**). This contains the sections on Reports built-ins, triggers, properties, and executables.

Report Builder offers the same flat toolbars as in Form Builder. It also contains the same EXEC_SQL built-in package. The major new features in Reports are also in the categories of ease-of-use and the Web.

Ease-of-Use Features

There are a number of evolutionary new features that assist you in designing feature-rich reports and distributing them in the correct formats to the correct locations.

New Demos

The Oracle demo reports are worth examining. They help with an understanding of the range of techniques that the tool offers. All demos come with source code that you can examine and use as a pattern for your own code. Oracle Developer R.6 contains new demo reports that show output in the client/server or web modes. There are sample reports that demonstrate many of the new features such as the PL/SQL Ref Cursor, Oracle8 object support, drill-down reports (client/server and Web), matrix with group report, and bookmarks on the Web. There are also samples of reports in different formats and a report based on Express data (if you have Oracle's Express product installed).

You can run the demo reports from the Benefits and Features icon in the Demos group of the Start menu. The Visualization tab contains a selection for "Reporting & Web page generation" that runs the demo reports. The source code for these reports is located in the ORACLE_HOME/tools/devdem60/demo/reports directory.

Report Sectioning

In Report Builder, you can define one to three sections, each with its own layout area. Figure 2-16 shows the three layout sections in the Object Navigator. The sections are called *Header* Section, *Main* Section, and *Trailer* Section (to correspond to similar objects in previous releases of Reports). These sections could just as well be called Section 1, Section 2, and Section 3 because they all have the same capabilities. Each has a Body and Margin layout area that you can lay out using the Layout Editor or the Report Wizard. If you want to use the Report Wizard to lay out a particular section, open the Layout Editor and select the particular section using the top toolbar buttons. The Report Wizard will create the layout in the selected area.

Another new feature of sections is that they have properties, as Figure 2-17 shows. This means you can specify a different orientation (portrait or landscape) or width and height for each section.

This feature is useful when you want to create different layouts within the same report. Each layout can have a different orientation (portrait or landscape) and different page sizes (height, width, and number of panels). There is an explicit page

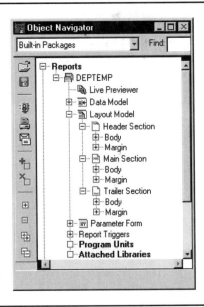

FIGURE 2-16. *Layout sections in the Object Navigator*

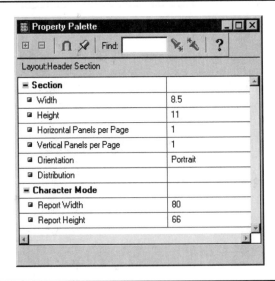

FIGURE 2-17. *Reports section properties*

break between each section, which helps you separate the parts of the report. You can also send the different sections to different destinations, as discussed next.

Multiple Destinations

Before release 6, if you wanted to send a report to more than one destination, such as email, the printer, and an HTML file, you had to run the report once for each destination. With Developer release 6, you can set up multiple destinations so the report (and its related database query and access) only runs once but is copied to different destinations such as the printer, an HTML file, a PDF file, and email. You can even send different sections to different sets of destinations.

The secret to this is the new property *Destination* on the Report module level and on the Layout Model section level (Header Section, Main Section, and Trailer Section). If you click on the *Destination* property button, you will see the dialog as in Figure 2-18. You can set up as many file, printer, or email destinations as you require. You need to have a MAPI-compliant mail system to send the printer output to an email attachment using the Distribute option. Reports will create an email with text attachment.

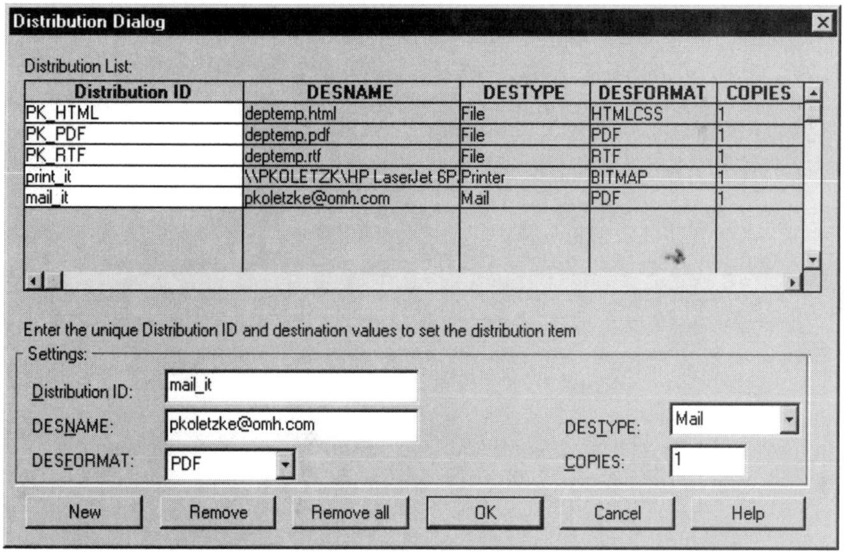

Distribution Dialog

Distribution List:

Distribution ID	DESNAME	DESTYPE	DESFORMAT	COPIES
PK_HTML	deptemp.html	File	HTMLCSS	1
PK_PDF	deptemp.pdf	File	PDF	1
PK_RTF	deptemp.rtf	File	RTF	1
print_it	\\PKOLETZK\HP LaserJet 6P	Printer	BITMAP	1
mail_it	pkoletzke@omh.com	Mail	PDF	1

Enter the unique Distribution ID and destination values to set the distribution item

Settings:

Distribution ID:	mail_it	
DESNAME:	pkoletzke@omh.com	DESTYPE: Mail
DESFORMAT:	PDF	COPIES: 1

New | Remove | Remove all | OK | Cancel | Help

FIGURE 2-18. *Distribution dialog*

TIP
*Output to a Rich Text Format (RTF) file if you want
to edit the report output using a word processor
such as MS Word.*

After you set up the distribution list, select **File→Distribute** (after clicking on the Object Navigator window to make it active). This will run the report and output it to the destinations you set up in the Property Palette. If you are running the report from the command line or from a form, you can turn on the distribution list by including the parameter and value DISTRIBUTE=YES.

Another option for distribution is to specify the distribution list in a file instead of the property. You create a list of the destinations in a file with a .DST extension. See the help system topic "Distributing a report to multiple destinations" for a link to sample .DST files. You then use the command-line parameter and value DESTINATION=*filename*.DST, where *filename* is the name of the file you created. You still need to issue the DISTRIBUTE=YES command-line parameter when you use this file.

TIP
*The Oracle Support web site, MetaLink, offers a
technical bulletin on this subject (68244.1 - Setting
up Distribution in Reports). It contains sample .DST
files and cautions such as not to mix bitmap and
character mode destination definitions within the
same report. You will receive an REP-32305 error
if you try to mix the modes.*

Generate to Text

You can output the report to a file that has values separated by *delimiters* (special characters). If you output a simple tabular report to a text file that is separated by commas, you will be able to open the file in Excel without conversion. The **File→Generate to File→Text** menu selection displays the delimited Output dialog, as Figure 2-19 shows.

In this dialog, you select the delimiter character (such as a comma) and the format mask that dates and numbers should use. You also specify the *cell wrapper*—the character that will surround the value. If you used a comma as the

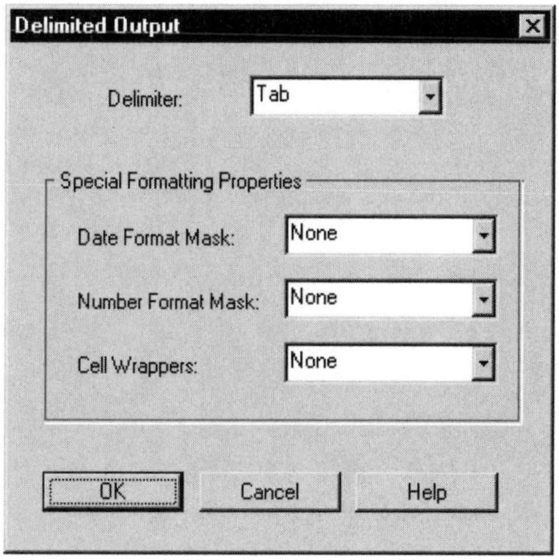

FIGURE 2-19.   *Delimited Output dialog*

delimiter and a double quote as the cell wrapper, a simple tabular report of
employee numbers and department names would look like the following sample:

```
"Empno","Department","7369","RESEARCH"
"Empno","Department","7499","SALES"
"Empno","Department","7221","SALES"
"Empno","Department","7788","ACCOUNTING"
```

Although the field prompt is displayed for each line of the output, you can
remove the prompts from the Layout Editor if you do not need them so they do not
print into the file. A help topic called "About delimited output" explains in detail
how the text is formatted into the output file based on the delimiter settings you set.

If you are running the report from the command line or from a form, you need
to supply parameters with values as shown in Table 2-3. You also need to use
the parameter and value DESFORMAT=DELIMITED. All parameters except
DESFORMAT=DELIMITED are optional. The default delimiter is a tab character.
The other parameters have no defaults.

Parameter	Use	Values
DELIMITER	The character between cells	tab (or \t) , (comma) . (period) space return (or \n) none
CELLWRAPPER	The character surrounding cells (front and back)	tab (or \t) " (double quote) ' (single quote) space return (or \n) none
NUMBERFORMATMASK	Format mask used for all number values output	Any valid number format mask
DATEFORMATMASK	Format mask used for all date values output	Any valid date format mask

TABLE 2-3. *Delimiter-Related Parameters*

Web Features

A few new features introduced with Oracle Developer Reports R.6 are directed toward web deployment.

HTML Page Streaming

A new feature called *HTML Page Streaming* provides a summary page in the report output that allows end users to navigate to any other page in the report. This overcomes the previous limitation that the entire report file had to be created and downloaded when the report was run. The summary page contains bookmarks or hyperlinks to the other pages of the report. This means that one report can be made of many files, but the files will be smaller and more manageable than if the report were output to a single file.

The technique to enable this feature includes setting the report module properties *Page Navigation Control Type* and *Page Navigation Control Value*. You also need to run the report with a command-line parameter and value of PAGESTREAM=YES. The help topic "HTML page streaming" further describes the details of this feature.

Chart Hyperlinks

There is a new property for a chart layout object called Chart Hyperlink. This property allows you to link each row in a chart (such as a pie section in a pie chart or a bar in a bar chart) to another HTML file or part of a file. The user can click on a section of the chart at runtime and navigate to another part of the same report or to another report.

You can fill in this property manually using the hyperlink uniform resource locator (URL) that identifies the link. You can also let the Web Wizard do the job. After creating a chart object, select **Tools→Web Wizard** and step through the dialogs, specifying the chart you want to link on the page that lists the available charts. This will create a value such as "#CT_1&<empno>" in the *Chart Hyperlink* property. In this example, "<empno>" represents the value of an employee number and the "#" indicates that there is a link to an HTML anchor in the same file. This is a useful technique to work with if you need to implement a drill down to details from a value represented in a chart.

PART
II

Basic Developer
Standards

CHAPTER
3

SQL and PL/SQL
Standards

Far along the world-wide whisper of the south-wind rushing warm,
With the standards of the peoples plunging thro' the thunderstorm;
Till the war-drum throbb'd no longer, and the battle-flags were furl'd
In the Parliament of man, the Federation of the world.
                              —Alfred, Lord Tennyson (1809–1892), *Locksley Hall*

n important part of your development standards is a plan for how you will standardize the SQL and PL/SQL code that you create. The coding standards for Oracle Developer Forms, Reports, and other components should correspond to your other coding standards for the database and other tools. There are some specifics, of course, based on where the code will be executed, but the general guidelines can be generic enough for all uses of SQL and PL/SQL.

This chapter discusses the areas you need to consider when developing a coding standard for your work with Oracle Developer Forms and Reports. Since PL/SQL is available in other components of Oracle Developer, the standards can also apply to those components. This chapter will also provide a sample for each standard. The standards are divided into two sections: SQL and PL/SQL. There are also some general standards that apply to both types of code. You can use these general standards as a starting point for other languages that you might use.

Some of the standards discussed in this chapter are variations and extensions of principles discussed in the book *Oracle PL/SQL Programming, Second Edition,* by Steven Feuerstein (1997, O'Reilly and Associates, Inc. In this book, Feuerstein discusses the reasoning behind many of the formatting decisions for both SQL and PL/SQL code. This chapter, however, will not reiterate this reasoning in detail. You will want to refer to Feuerstein's book for those details. Also refer to that book for explanations on the PL/SQL language in general, which this chapter assumes you understand.

Coding standards include a number of aspects, as follows:

- **Formatting** This set of standards governs the way that the code appears on the screen or page. It includes topics such as the amount and placement of white space and indention as well as which words use upper-, lower-, and mixed case.

- **Naming** Standards for coding must include how you name the user-definable elements of the code, such as variables, constants, cursors, and exceptions. The standards also must cover the names you give the program units themselves.

- **Organization** You need to set a standard for how the code is organized. Does it appear in packages only, or will you allow the developer to create individual procedures and functions as well? Do you promote the use of local procedures and functions to reduce the size of the trigger code?

■ **Documentation**   Part of the standards includes how you will use comments to explain how the code works. A standard header for each program unit and comments within the body of the code help those who read your code determine what it should do.

■ **Usage**   Developers should use language elements in a consistent way. For example, functions must always have one and only one RETURN statement at the end of the code body.

This chapter discusses these aspects as they relate to two languages, SQL and PL/SQL.

Why Coding Standards?

Coding standards evoke strong reactions from the programming community. If programmers have thought about coding standards at all and have come up with their own standards, they have very strong opinions about the way they format and name their code. If they have not thought about it, they will be annoyed that they have to comply with standards. Therefore, it is good to enumerate the benefits of a common way of formatting, naming, and organizing code.

Readability

The main reason that you need coding standards is to improve readability. If the code you write has a known and documented standard and all developers on the project use that standard, the code will be easy to read. Easy-to-read code means easy-to-maintain code. When you need to fix problems with or enhance existing code, the main activity is reading the code to determine its logic and the flow of control. Consistent formatting and naming assist the reader in determining the structure and intent of the code.

Therefore, adhering to a coding standard is important for each developer. Equally important is maintaining that standard throughout the organization or project. It is not enough that an individual developer creates and adheres to a standard. Code modules usually contain work by more than one individual. If each developer uses a different standard, the reader will need to shift back and forth between styles and might have to pause when the style shifts to figure out how it works. Therefore, consistency within the development team is another key to the success of a coding standard.

Documentation

The goal of all code is that it be self-documenting. That is, someone who is conversant with the language but who is new to the application should be able to examine the code without any documentation and be able quickly to determine its structure and intent. Naming standards assist with the readability because if you choose the right names, you should be able to read the code in a narrative manner. Granted, the syntax will be pretty specific, and may be grammatically incorrect for conversational speech, but the structure and intention should be perfectly clear.

Naturally, this goal is not always attainable, and there will be cases where you need to supplement the self-documentation with comments that explain the code further. It should never be necessary, outside of the code header, to write more than a few lines of comments in your code. More than that breaks the flow of the code and makes it more difficult to follow.

There will also be requirements for broader, higher-level system documentation to provide overviews of how the modules (forms and reports) work and interact. This is particularly important for complex forms. However, if you have standards that dictate not only how individual program units are written, but also how forms and reports are designed and how they interact within a certain application architecture, then the requirements for system documentation of any type are reduced. The standards imply a certain way that the system works and supply part of the documentation.

Enforcing the Standards

Setting standards is easy, but getting compliance is something else. We, as technical managers and project leaders, have many reasons why standards are essential. Developers have many reasons and excuses for not using standards. The main reasons follow.

Top 10 Reasons to Not Use Code Standards

1. The standards make no sense.
2. My personal standards are better.
3. The standards infringe on my creativity.
4. I don't need to write readable code because I won't be maintaining it.
5. I don't want to write readable code because I want to be the only one who can maintain it.
6. I am doing a prototype and just want to test the code.
7. I don't have time for writing code in a certain format.

8. I can't type well enough to format the code as I write it.

9. No one will notice until it is too late to standardize the code.

10. I will go back later and reformat the code to comply with the standards.

What Is the Answer?

There are no perfect answers to many of these. If you are a project manager, you must assume that developers will not adhere to standards. If you are serious about implementing standards, you must also implement a quality assurance (QA) process that will periodically check adherence to the standards. If there is no monitoring, it is virtually guaranteed that your carefully developed standards will be ignored.

Depending on your situation, it might also be useful to give a short presentation to developers on the benefits to the organization and to them personally of sticking to the standards of the project. You can also hold regularly scheduled code reviews that address, among other subjects, the standards compliance. Another idea is to make developers sign off on the standards once they have read and understood them. Smaller standards documents have a better chance of being accepted and used.

A somewhat expensive way to ensure that developers use common standards is to assign them the task of creating the standards—standards by committee. Depending on the developers, this could take a long time and have some psychological side effects (such as ill-will between members of the committee if their favorite standards are overridden), so you have to consider this option carefully. It can work with a small set of developers, though. If the developers themselves come up with the standards, it is quite likely that they will understand and adhere to them.

If you have a group of experienced developers, it is likely that each has a personal preference for coding standards. You might be able to maximize compliance to a common standard in the group by merging their standards. Everyone will have to change some aspect of the way they code, but each should be able to retain something of his or her own personal style as well.

 NOTE
There are third-party tools that will perform some of the QA functions by checking adherence to naming and programming standards in code. There are also tools that will reformat SQL and PL/SQL code to a certain standard. Check the Oracle web site for links to their partner products, or initiate an Internet search for Oracle programming.

If you work in certain industry sectors such as military, pharmaceutical, or government, standards are a way of life, and selling them to developers may not be necessary at all. Even these, and in many other sectors, the reasons for not using standards often seem to outweigh the benefits. Your main weapon to use to enforce standards is still education as to the benefits of standards in general and each standard you use in particular. It also helps to remind programmers that standards are a matter of habit and that they will, in time, become accustomed to the new standards.

The Tool Helps

Some of the new features of the Oracle Developer PL/SQL Editor can help programmers format and read their code. Two of these features follow:

■ **Color coding** The PL/SQL Editor highlights keywords in a different color. This helps you quickly determine the structure of the code, although it is still important to use indenting and upper- and lowercase consistently. It does not help those who have trouble distinguishing colors or those who do not have a color monitor.

■ **Automatic indenting** If you indent a line of code and press ENTER, the next line of code will automatically start on the same indent level. This saves a lot of time when you're writing code that has many levels of indenting. If you use TAB to indent a line, the next line will indent using a tab character. If you use space characters to indent a line, the next line will indent using space characters. As mentioned next, tab characters have drawbacks over spaces when used for indenting. The automatic indent will work with both indenting styles. Pressing SHIFT-TAB removes one level of indent.

TIP
To change the width of the tab indent, open the registry (see Chapter 29 for a technique on this) and add a string value under the node HKEY_LOCAL_ MACHINE\SOFTWARE\ORACLE called DE_PREFS_TABSIZE. Change the value to the number of characters that the tab key should indent. Pressing TAB will still insert a tab character. Therefore, if you change the registry value after embedding tab characters, the next time you open the editor, the new tab setting will take effect on the old code.

General Coding Standards

The following are standards you can apply to all code you write in Developer regardless of the language and tool.

Maximum Length of 30 Characters

The names for code elements that you create should not contain more than 30 characters. This is a restriction in SQL and PL/SQL, and the tools will enforce this standard.

Three Spaces for Indenting

Selecting the number of characters to use for indenting is important. Tab characters are easier to use because you just need to press TAB to indent one level. However, different tools interpret and display tab characters differently. For example, Windows Notepad may display a tab character as five spaces, but another tool may convert the same tab character into three or eight spaces. The difference between tools used to display the code can actually hinder readability. If another tool displays the tab character differently and readers are accustomed to seeing a certain indent size, they may need to take time to adjust to seeing a new indent size.

Consistency in the code is important, and this standard chooses to use spaces for indenting. The number of characters that you indent each level is arbitrary, but too many characters (five or more) will cause a multiple-level section of code to scroll too far to the right. If you adhere to the 80-character line limit to be discussed shortly, this will cause the code to wrap excessively as you reach deeper indent levels. A one-character indent does not provide a strong visual cue that there is an additional level. Furthermore, one of the beneficial aspects of indenting code is that you can follow a line starting with the first keyword in a structure (such as IF) to the last word in the structure (END IF). Both words should start at the same character location on the line. This allows you to clearly separate a structure section. A one-character indent, however, requires great care in lining up the start and ending characters. Figure 3-1 shows a code snippet that uses a one-character indent.

Oracle uses a two-character indent in many of its examples, and this is the default indent level you get when you press TAB in the PL/SQL Editor. (See the preceding Tip on how to change the indent width.) However, a three-character indent has been found to be clearer as far as showing the structure of the code and is the style promoted in Feuerstein's book. Figure 3-2 shows the Figure 3-1 code reformatted using three-character indents.

NOTE
As mentioned earlier, the PL/SQL Editor in Developer R.6 displays keywords in a special color. It also displays—each in a different color—operators, comments, and character strings in quotes. This color coding can help make the code easier to read, but does not completely substitute for code formatting standards.

```
FOR r_emp IN c_emp
LOOP
 IF v_list IS NULL
 THEN
  v_list := r_emp.last_name;
 ELSE      -- not the first time to add to the list
  v_new_name := ',' || r_emp.last_name;
   IF LENGTH(v_list || r_emp.last_name) <= 2000
   THEN
    v_list :=  v_list || r_emp.last_name;
   END IF;
 END IF;
END LOOP;
```

FIGURE 3-1.   *Code with one-character indents*

Uppercase for Keywords

The notes for each language specify how to determine a keyword and how the keywords are arranged. This is a subject of contention for programmers who are accustomed to coding in context-sensitive languages like C++ or UNIX-based scripting languages. Whatever your feelings are on this subject, you need to consider that the use of uppercase keywords is becoming a standard. It has been adopted at Oracle and is being promoted more and more from many sources, including various SQL and PL/SQL books.

```
FOR r_emp IN c_emp
LOOP
   IF v_list IS NULL
   THEN
     v_list := r_emp.last_name;
   ELSE      -- not the first time to add to the list
     v_new_name := ',' || r_emp.last_name;
     IF LENGTH(v_list || r_emp.last_name) <= 2000
     THEN
        v_list :=  v_list || r_emp.last_name;
     END IF;
   END IF;
END LOOP;
```

FIGURE 3-2.   *Code with three-character indents*

Combined with the indent level, the uppercase selection for keywords makes the structure and logic elements of the code perfectly clear. The following is a code sample from the previous example, this time using all lowercase:

```
if v_list  is null
then
   v_list :=  r_emp.last_name;
else      -- not the first time to add to the list
   v_new_name := ',' || r_emp.last_name;
   if length(v_list || r_emp.last_name) <= 2000
   then
      v_list :=  v_list || r_emp.last_name;
   end if;
end if;
```

While this may be easier to type, the code's logic structures are not as easy to determine. The following listing uses uppercase keywords:

```
IF v_list  IS NULL
THEN
   v_list :=  r_emp.last_name;
ELSE      -- not the first time to add to the list
   v_new_name := ',' || r_emp.last_name;
   IF LENGTH(v_list || r_emp.last_name) <= 2000
   THEN
      v_list :=  v_list || r_emp.last_name;
   END IF;
END IF;
```

In this example, the keywords pop out and clearly define the structures.

Lowercase for User-Defined Elements

The elements for which you use this standard are specific to the language. The discussion for each language explains this in the context of the language standards.

Maximum Line Length of 80 Characters

Too many characters on a line make the code hard to read. In the printed medium, typographers balance the font, size, and line length with the amount of space between each line. Long lines of text require more space between them to keep the reader's eye on track. Shorter lines can be closer together and still be easier to read. A case in point is the text in a newspaper, which is laid out in short columns with a small amount of space between each line. The text is easy to read because the lines are short. The printer can squeeze lines together because the reader's eye can quickly follow a short line from start to finish.

While you do not have control over the font, size, or line spacing of your code, you can limit the line width to an easy-to-read length, for example, 80 characters. This length will allow the reader to easily follow the code. When you use the PL/SQL Editor in Oracle Developer tools, you have control over the size of the window. The editor also allows you to split the screen both horizontally and vertically and scroll each part individually. You accomplish this by dragging the vertical or horizontal drag bars into the window. These drag bars are black bars located on top of the vertical scrollbar and to the left of the horizontal scrollbar. Figure 3-3 shows the windows after dragging both horizontal and vertical drag bars.

If you split the screen like this, you can view the right side of the code separately from the left side of the code and the top part separately from the bottom. However, this quickly becomes difficult to read, because you lose track of what part of the code you are looking at. A better solution is to size the PL/SQL Editor to the line length in your standards. Figure 3-4 shows the PL/SQL Editor sized to allow 80 characters per line.

An 80-character width is narrow enough so that you can still show other windows in the tool at the same time. The window size also gives you a visual display of the 80-character limit, enabling you to wrap the line before reaching it.

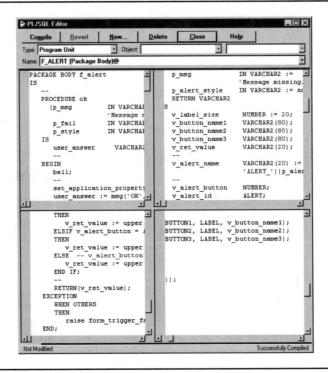

FIGURE 3-3. *PL/SQL Editor with split screen*

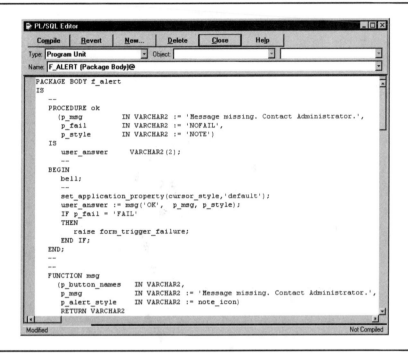

FIGURE 3-4. *PL/SQL Editor with an 80-character window*

If you need to reset the PL/SQL window width, you can store a trigger called
EDITOR_ WINDOW in your object library and subclass it to your template. This
trigger displays an 80-character line width. Figure 3-5 shows this trigger.

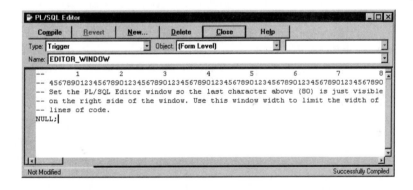

FIGURE 3-5. *EDITOR_WINDOW trigger used to manually set the PL/SQL
Editor width*

Normally, Form Builder will save the size of the PL/SQL Editor window between sessions. When you reopen the tool, the window size will be the same as when you last closed it. If you need to reset the window width, open this trigger in the PL/SQL Editor and set the width of the window so that only 80 characters show. You will then know when to wrap to another line when writing code. Chapter 5 discusses the window arrangement in the Form Builder and Report Builder in more detail.

TIP
*Remember that you can set up an external editor for your PL/SQL code in the tools. If you want to use another editor in Form Builder, for example, set the FORMS60_EDITOR variable in the registry in Windows (open REGEDIT and navigate to HKEY_LOCAL_MACHINE\SOFTWAREORACLE) to the program name. Start up Form Builder and open the Forms PL/SQL Editor for a particular program unit. Be sure the **Tools→Preferences** setting "Use System Editor" is checked. Then select **Program→External Editor** from the menu. Your editor will open with the program unit loaded. Make the changes, save the program unit, and exit the program to reload the PL/SQL Editor with the new code.*

Monospaced Font

SQL and PL/SQL code run independently of formatting in the editors such as font, color, and size. Still, if you have a choice, you should use a monospaced font, such as Courier New, that uses a single width for all characters. Proportionally spaced fonts (such as Times New Roman or Arial) can hide spaces and cause difficulties in lining up clauses. The Oracle tools enforce this standard by using a monospaced font in the PL/SQL Editor. If you use an external editor, be sure it is set up to display a monospaced font. Similarly, when you print code or include it in a document, select a monospaced font (like the examples in this book) for the same reasons.

One Thing per Line

Both SQL and PL/SQL languages use the semicolon (";") character as a command terminator. The end of a line has no meaning in these languages, and you can actually stack more than one command, expression, or clause on one line. In fact, if your editor were to allow wide enough lines, you could write all your code on one line.

The industry-accepted standard is to separate commands and even parts of commands with new lines. This allows the reader to grasp a single command or clause by reading a line (or multiple lines if the expression wraps to another line). This standard has variations for each language as discussed next.

Comments for Documentation

Comments in the code serve as online documentation to the reader. They document the logic and purpose of the program. Too many comments slow down the reader and detract from readability. You need to balance this with ensuring that the code is totally understandable. When in doubt, comment anything that has a degree of complexity or that may not be self-explanatory to a reader who understands the language. You will use two different types of comments: *header* and *inline.*

Header Comment

Each program unit should have a header that states its name, purpose, and history. The history section includes the names of developers who created or changed the code, and the dates for those actions. The header comment should also include additional information that is specific for each language, as discussed shortly. Use standard comment delimiters ("/*" and "*/") for header comments.

Inline Comments

Use inline ("--") comment delimiters within the code body. These comment delimiters allow you to comment out large sections of code that include inline comments using the standard delimiters. This is a common debugging technique. If you use the standard delimiter symbols in the body of the code, you will not be able to comment out large sections that include those delimiters, because you cannot nest that type of comment. For example, your code includes the following:

```
/*
   Test the counter.
   If it is over 10, reset it.
*/
IF v_ct > 10
THEN
   v_ct := 0;
ELSE
   /* the count was less than or equal to 10, so increment it */
   v_ct := v_ct + 1;
END IF;
```

If you need to comment out the entire IF conditional statement, you would need to place standard comments around two sections as follows:

```
/*
   Test the counter.
   If it is over 10, reset it.
```

```
*/
/* IF v_ct > 10
THEN
    v_ct := 0;
ELSE */
    /* the count was less than or equal to 10, so increment it */
/*    v_ct := v_ct + 1;
END IF; */
```

A better approach is to use inline comment delimiters as follows:

```
-- Test the counter.
-- If it is over 10, reset it.
IF v_ct > 10
THEN
    v_ct := 0;
ELSE
    -- the count was less than or equal to 10, so increment it
    v_ct := v_ct + 1;
END IF;
```

To comment out this section, you would only need one standard start and end delimiter for the entire section:

```
-- Test the counter.
-- If it is over 10, reset it.
/*IF v_ct > 10
THEN
    v_ct := 0;
ELSE
    -- the count was less than or equal to 10, so increment it
    v_ct := v_ct + 1;
END IF; */
```

Take Database Object Names into Account

Naming conventions for SQL and PL/SQL are part of an overall standard that also includes naming conventions for database objects. Database-object naming standards are fully discussed in the book *Oracle8 Design Using UML Object Modeling,* by Dr. Paul Dorsey and Joseph R. Hudicka (Oracle Press, 1999). Examples in this book use the column naming standards outlined in that book and repeated in Table 3-1.

If you adopt a naming standard such as this, the names you create for SQL and PL/SQL code units can use this same naming convention for variables or other objects. The table examples used in this book center around the pre-designed Oracle sample tables, so many examples will not use these extensions. This naming convention is a

Suffix	Description
_ID	Numeric primary keys
_CD	Character primary keys and any attributes that come from a restricted list of character values
_YN	Boolean
_DT	Dates stored to the nearest day
_TM	Dates stored to the nearest second
_TX	All other text formats not covered by CD and YN, including LONG variables
_CY	Numeric values representing currency amounts
_NR	All numeric fields not covered by ID or CY
_GR	Graphics, images, and large binary objects

TABLE 3-1. *Column Suffixes from* Oracle8 Design Using UML Object Modeling

powerful tool for making clear the use of columns and is one you should consider in your database naming convention. If you do use this naming convention, or one like it, your SQL and PL/SQL code should reflect the same convention.

SQL Coding Standards

Structured Query Language (SQL) has specific elements that require standards in addition to the general standards mentioned earlier. These standards apply to SQL code inside PL/SQL and SQL code outside PL/SQL. Therefore, if you create pure SQL scripts or code fragments to run in SQL*Plus or another tool, the SQL in those locations should comply with the standards you use for SQL within PL/SQL.

NOTE
One of the benefits of enforcing SQL standards is an optimization one. If the SQL engine finds a SQL statement that was already executed and is still in the database memory area, it will skip the parse for that statement and will use the same execution path as it used before. This saves a bit of time, but requires that the statements be exactly the same. SQL standards can help ensure this consistency and the ability to reuse the statement.

Upper- and Lowercase

Following the preceding general guideline, all keywords are written in uppercase. SQL does not really use structural words as much as verbs and clause keywords. Verbs such as SELECT, INSERT, UPDATE, and DELETE and clause keywords such as FROM, WHERE, ORDER BY, VALUES, and SET are all written in uppercase. SQL functions and words such as COUNT, MIN, MAX, SYSDATE, USER, NULL, and DISTINCT and subclause keywords such as AND, OR, NOT, EXISTS, LIKE, BETWEEN, DESC, and ASC are also written in uppercase.

Use lowercase for all column names, column aliases, table names, table aliases, user-defined functions, and other words that are not SQL keywords. In general, the rule is to use uppercase for all SQL keywords, clause keywords, and functions and to use lowercase for all user-defined elements.

White Space and Indenting

Since there are no real structures such as IF...THEN...END IF in SQL, you really only need to consider a single SQL statement when thinking about formatting. The standard is to left justify the keywords that identify clauses of the statement and left justify the expressions after that. This creates a block of code in two "columns." An example follows:

```
SELECT    emp.emp_id,
          emp.first_name,
          emp.last_name,
          empsal.annual_bonus
FROM      employee emp,
          emp_salary empsal
WHERE     emp.emp_id = empsal.emp_id
AND       emp.last_name LIKE 'Fran%'
AND       dept_id IN
          (
          SELECT    dept_id
          FROM      department
          WHERE     location = 'New York'
          )
ORDER BY last_name ;
```

Notice that the subquery appears indented under the predicate's AND clause because it is, logically, part of that clause. The parentheses that separate the subquery each appear on a single line to create a "container" for the statement.

Each column in the SELECT clause starts a new line. This means that the query can become quite long if there is a large number of columns. However, it also makes the statement easier to edit because adding a column or deleting a column requires editing only one line of the statement. If you decided to place three columns on each line in the SELECT clause, for example, and you had to delete one in the middle, your lines would be out of balance, some with three columns and some with two columns.

There is a three-space indent after the SELECT keyword so lists of elements after phrases like ORDER BY and GROUP BY will align correctly.

Although it is not part of this standard, some developers use the Oracle Designer standard that a comma precedes each column name (except the first) in a SELECT clause. This makes editing much easier because you do not have to worry about missing or extra commas when deleting or adding a column.

CAUTION
SQL statements will not run correctly if there are blank lines in the middle of the statement. If you want to add blank lines for readability, use an inline comment ("--") to fill the line.

Use the same kind of formatting for the FROM clause table list as you do for the SELECT clause column list. Each AND statement in the WHERE clause is placed on its own line. If you have multiple levels of OR and AND logic, make the order of precedence explicit by using parentheses. The following excerpt shows multiple levels:

```
WHERE last_name LIKE 'Stan%'
AND   (   first_name IS NULL
      OR  last_name IS NULL
      OR  (    salary > 1000
           AND commission = 500
           )
      );
```

When determining this formatting standard, you have to think about both clarity in the structure so you can easily reveal the order of precedence and brevity, so as much code as possible is displayed on the page. These often conflict, and you may need to compromise on both.

NOTE
If you are weighing the benefits of various ways to format SQL statements, think about starting your column list on the next line after the SELECT clause, indented three spaces. This will not separate the keywords as well, but the structure will still be visible and you will not need to type so many spaces before entering a column name.

Other White Space

In addition to the white space created by levels of indentation and the blocks of keywords and names, there is another important space to consider. Spaces between words or symbols on a line can improve the readability. In the preceding example, there is a single space surrounding comparison operators ("=" and ">"). This space helps separate the operator from the operands and assists the reader in distinguishing the intent of the expression.

Commenting the Code

SQL statements (in PL/SQL or in Forms or Reports properties) will use inline ("--") comments preceding the statement to explain the intention of the code if the statement is complex or contains logic that requires careful reading. The comment should consist of a sentence or two about the results of the statement and where the statement is used.

Database objects such as views may be used as the basis for forms and reports. These views contain the type of complexity or extra logic that would normally need a comment. However, since they are database objects, the comments will be written for the database object. The standard for database object commenting should be part of your database object standard.

Naming Conventions

The SQL that you use in Oracle Developer code consists mainly of keywords and the names of database tables and columns. You have no control over the keyword names, and the database object names are guided by a different set of standards. All SQL statements in Developer are inside the form or report module (except for the external query source file in Reports). Therefore, file names are not an issue with SQL files in Oracle Developer. There are names that you need to devise to provide *aliases* that act as pseudonyms or abbreviations for a table or column. You declare an alias by placing its name after the name of the column or table (with a space separating the two) in a SELECT or FROM list. For example, the FROM clause using an EMP alias for the EMPLOYEE table would be "FROM employee emp." Once you declare an alias in the SQL statement, you can use it in that same statement as a substitute for the object that you aliased. These aliases require a naming convention.

Table Aliases

Use table aliases for all multitable SQL statements. The table alias should be an abbreviation of the table using eight characters or less. When you create a table in the database, you should assign an alias and record that alias in your system documentation. If you use Oracle Designer, the table alias is a property of the table. There is no need (and no real space) for a prefix or suffix in a table alias.

The table alias should, therefore, be an abbreviation of the table based on a certain set of guidelines. For example, if you use a multiword table name, the alias could be just the first letter of each word. For example, the table SPMTS_EMPLOYEE_BENEFIT would use an alias of EB. A different guideline is to use an abbreviation of each word to make the name more explicit, for example, EMPBEN.

This alias follows the table for all of its uses. You use it as the block name for forms as discussed in Chapter 6. You also use it as the alias in all multitable SQL statements inside PL/SQL and outside PL/SQL.

The benefit of using table aliases is that there is less typing required to completely identify a column. For example, you can use EMPBEN.EMP_ID instead of SPMTS_EMPLOYEE_BENEFIT.EMP_ID.

Qualified Column Names

Another standard is to fully qualify the columns, using the *table_alias.column* syntax, in a multitable SQL statement. Therefore, even if a column appears in only one table, you must use the table alias as a qualifier. This eliminates any potential ambiguity, although it is superfluous for single-table statements.

Column Aliases

Column aliases are not as commonly used as table aliases, but are necessary if you want to provide a name to a complex (or even simple) expression (such as concatenated columns or arithmetic expressions or functions) in the SQL statement. For example, if you want to retrieve a column that computes PRICE * QUANTITY from the INVOICE_ITEM table, you use the SQL statement as follows:

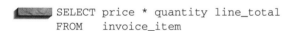

```
SELECT price * quantity line_total
FROM   invoice_item
```

The column alias, LINE_TOTAL, provides a name for the expression PRICE * QUANTITY. It is available for use in cursor records in PL/SQL. With Oracle v7.1 and later, you can use the column alias in the ORDER BY clause as well. The column alias name should comply with the standards you set for names of columns. Therefore, if you use column name suffixes, use the same suffix style for column alias names.

CAUTION
When creating table or column aliases, be careful of reserved words. It is easy to use a reserved word like TO or AND when you are just thinking of an alias name, because your attention is on the meaning of the alias. You will have a problem using reserved words for aliases at some point, and the error message may not help you identify the error right away. Also be careful not to use column names from another table in the FROM clause as aliases.

Organization of Code

SQL, by nature, is not stored by itself in the database or in Developer. The concept of the organization, or how to group the code is, therefore, not a concern. This is because all uses of SQL will appear as a single statement in PL/SQL or as a property, for example in the Report query, Form record group, or Form data source for a FROM clause query.

Sample Code

The following example is a sample of the principles described as applied to a SQL statement stored in a file. According to the standards, the code displays in a monospaced font, which makes the formatting easier to determine.

```
/***********************************************************************\
|| Program:     SHOW_COURSES.SQL
|| System:      Computer Training Associates
||
|| Description:
||   Show all courses if the instructor lives in ME and the course meets in
||   Sayles 210 or the course number is from Q0100 to Q0300. Show the cost
||   increased by $100 plus 10%.
||
|| Modification History:
||   ----------------------------------------------------
||     Date          By           Remarks/Reason
||   ----------------------------------------------------
||   19-Mar-2000    pkoletzke    Initial creation
||
\***********************************************************************/
SELECT    (crse.crse_cost + 100) * 1.1 new_cost
          crse.crse_id,
          sect.sect_id,
          NVL(crse.prereq_crse_id, 'None') prereq
FROM      course  crse,
          section sect
WHERE     crse.crse_id = sect.crse_id
AND       ( crse.crse_id BETWEEN 'Q0100' AND 'Q0300'
          OR sect.location = 'S603'
          )
AND       sect.inst_id IN
          -- subquery for all instructors who live in Maine
          (
          SELECT    inst.instid
          FROM      instructor inst,
                    zipcode  zip
          WHERE     inst.zip = zip.zip
          AND       zip.state = 'ME'
          ) ;
```

PL/SQL Code Standards

All PL/SQL code in forms, reports, and the database will use the following guidelines for formatting and organization.

Upper- and Lowercase

PL/SQL, like SQL, is case insensitive. The guideline here is the same as in SQL formatting: use uppercase for keywords such as BEGIN, EXCEPTION, END, IF THEN ELSE, LOOP, END LOOP, OPEN, FETCH, and CLOSE. Use uppercase also for PL/SQL functions and procedures such as NULL, RETURN, and RAISE and cursor attributes like %FOUND and %NOTFOUND. Scalar datatypes such as VARCHAR2, NUMBER, and DATE are also written in uppercase. Also use uppercase for the Boolean values, TRUE and FALSE.

Use lowercase for all variables, cursors, user-defined exceptions, user-defined datatypes, %TYPE qualifiers, user-defined procedures, and packages. Forms and Reports PL/SQL code uses lowercase for its built-in or prepackaged procedures such as SET_ITEM_PROPERTY, EXECUTE_QUERY, and SRW.SET_ATTR. Any SQL inside PL/SQL uses the standards discussed in the earlier section on SQL.

Use uppercase for built-in constants such as the Forms constants WINDOW_ STATE, VISIBLE, and PROPERTY_FALSE. A sample line of code follows:

```
set_item_property('EMP.EMPNO', VISIBLE, PROPERTY_FALSE);
```

NOTE
Some properties have more than one name. For example, the Displayed property on the Property Palette for an item is accessed either by the Forms constant VISIBLE or DISPLAYED.

Use uppercase for Forms object names within quotes (such as EMP.EMPNO in the example above). Use lowercase when referring to the object value directly, such as in the following code:

```
:emp.hire_date := SYSDATE;
```

White Space and Indenting

White space and indenting provide an important readability factor to your PL/SQL code. PL/SQL contains control structures such as IF...THEN...ELSE...END IF that you can think of as "containers" for lines of code. The structure keywords are left justified and in line with one another. All code under the structure is indented one level. For example, a PL/SQL block containing a conditional structure would look like the following:

```
BEGIN
    IF (    v_ct = 0
        OR LENGTH(v_list) = 0
        )
    THEN
        v_list := v_last_name;
    ELSIF (  v_total_rows = 1
        OR (    v_last_name IS NOT NULL
            AND  v_first_name IS NOT NULL
            )
        )
    THEN
        v_list := v_first_name || ' ' || v_last_name;
    ELSE
        v_list := v_list || ',' || v_last_name;
    END IF;
END;
```

Both THEN keywords are on lines by themselves and in line with IF and ELSE to set off the conditional clause from the executed code. If there are complex conditionals with multiple levels of AND and OR, use parentheses to make the order of precedence explicit and follow the same conventions for WHERE clauses in a SQL statement. In a loop construct, the WHILE or FOR clauses appear on the first line and the LOOP statement appears on the following line.

The example also shows the structure nesting (an IF...THEN...END IF structure within the BEGIN...END block structure). A similar formatting strategy applies to other PL/SQL structures such as FOR...LOOP and WHEN...THEN (in the exception section).

NOTE
To save space on the page and allow more lines of code to be visible, you may want to create a standard that allows the THEN keyword to appear on the same line as the IF keyword and conditional test in cases where the entire line will fit within 80 characters.

Other White Space

The same guidelines apply to PL/SQL code as to SQL code. Use spaces around operators such as =, >, <, and ||. If you need to present a comma-separated list on one line, use a space after the comma before the next item in the list, for example:

```
OPEN c_emp(v_emp_id, v_salary, v_location);
```

Readability is the main benefit from this type of formatting. With many editors you are able to press CTRL-RIGHT ARROW or CTRL-LEFT ARROW to advance the cursor a word at a time. If you have formatted spaces around your operators, the cursor will advance in a more orderly way with these key combinations.

Commenting the Code

Comments in PL/SQL are equally as important as those in SQL. Comments should explain the main sections of the program and any logic that is nontrivial in nature. As mentioned, you use "/* */" comments for header comments and "--" inline comments for comments in the code. The header comment should contain the same description and history sections as the header for SQL. Since the PL/SQL unit is executable, you also need to write a section that explains the usage of the code. An example header template follows:

```
/*************************************************************************\
|| Program:     <name of program unit>
|| System:      <full name of system>
||
|| Description:
||    <description>
||
|| Modification History:
||    -------------------------------------------------------
||      Date          By              Remarks/Reason
||    -------------------------------------------------------
||      <date>        <programmer>  <created or modified>
||
|| Global Variables:
||    <variable>
||        <description>
||
|| Usage:
||    <proc1>
||        <description 1>
||
||    <proc2>
||        <description 2>
||
\*************************************************************************/
```

This template is set up for PL/SQL packages and would appear on top of the package specification. It contains a description of each procedure and function in the package. The package body would contain a similar header with the Usage section containing only descriptions of the local program units. If the program unit were an individual procedure or function, you would omit those sections as well.

The same header template can be used for database code as well as for code in forms, reports, and libraries. Since you want to use the same standard header in all program units, you should save this template version of the header in a file or database package that all developers can access.

TIP

Store your comment header template in the database as a package specification called A_PACKAGE_HEADER (or some other name that sorts to the top or bottom of a list alphabetically). Grant EXECUTE privilege to PUBLIC. Then all developers will be able to open the Database Objects node in the Forms or Reports Object Navigator and navigate to the package specification so they can copy and paste the template for a new program unit. Figure 3-6 shows the Form Builder with the package specification loaded into the PL/SQL Editor.

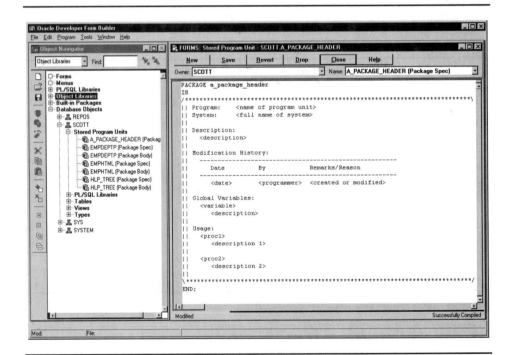

FIGURE 3-6. *PL/SQL Editor with header comment template*

Other Commenting

The package body, procedure and function will contain inline comments for the code to explain DML, cursors, or complex logic. Most of these comments will consist of a small number of lines because the main logic and purpose of the program unit is documented in the header.

Add inline comments for each clause in an IF...THEN...ELSE construct, as the following example shows:

```
DECLARE
   v_ct   NUMBER := 0;
   v_list VARCHAR2(2000);
BEGIN  -------------------- MAIN ------------------
   -- there would be some kind of loop around this IF statement
   IF v_ct = 0
   THEN       -- the counter has just been initialized
      v_list := v_last_name;
   ELSIF v_total_rows = 1
   THEN       -- we returned only one name
      v_list := v_first_name || ' ' || v_last_name;
   ELSE       -- v_total_rows > 1
      IF v_ct = 10
         v_list := v_list || ',' || v_last_name;
      END IF;    -- v_ct = 10
   END IF;       -- v_ct = 0
END;
```

In general, add comments wherever a construct starts and stops; for example, the END IF statement of an IF...THEN...ELSE construct should be commented to indicate which IF statement it completes. If you use nested IF constructs that are long, it may be difficult to easily follow the indent back to the start. The completion (END IF) comments will help readability because it will be easy to see which statement started the construct.

Naming Conventions

PL/SQL allows you to name a number of elements. You should also use a naming convention for database objects, and you want to ensure that this convention works well with your naming convention for PL/SQL elements. The objectives for naming PL/SQL elements are the same as for naming other elements. Each element has its own concerns and, therefore, its own naming convention.

Variables, Cursors, and Exceptions

One guideline for naming any element in PL/SQL is to avoid the names of database objects. You can do this pretty much across the board by using unique prefixes for PL/SQL elements. For example, if you do not use one-character prefixes for column or table names, you can distinguish variable names from table names by using one-character prefixes for variable names. Table 3-2 shows the names and prefixes associated with each PL/SQL element.

Parameters to cursors inside PL/SQL need to be named differently than parameters to the function or procedure itself. Cursor parameters still use a p_ prefix, but the name will be an abbreviation (three to six characters long).

If the variable is associated directly with a column, its name consists of the column name with a prefix. In combination with the prefix, this provides both a

Element	Prefix	Name	Example
Cursor	c_	Table alias of main table in query. (May need a modifier.)	c_emp (c_invalid_emp)
Exception defined by the user	e_	Noun describing the condition.	e_invalid_range
Global package variable used outside the package	g_	Associated column name or other variable name.	g_user_id
Parameter variable passed into a procedure, function, or cursor	p_	Associated column name or other descriptive variable name.	p_last_name
Record variable or cursor record variable	r_	Table alias of main table in query. If no table, use a short but descriptive name.	r_emp
Table variable—single column or table of records	t_	Table or record variable name.	t_name
Variable or constant used locally within package	v_	Associated column or other descriptive variable name.	v_emp_id

TABLE 3-2. *PL/SQL Element Names and Prefixes*

unique name that is easy to understand. If you use this scheme, you can be assured that you will not have conflicts or ambiguities between database objects and PL/SQL elements. You can add to this list, but be sure you do not select one-character prefixes used for other purposes, such as to identify a library package (as discussed shortly). When constructing suffixes that are not column names, be sure to be descriptive in order to make the purpose of the element clear.

CAUTION
When developing a prefix system for variables, it is important to avoid suffixes you would use for database tables and columns. If you inadvertently use a column name (like P_EMPNO) as a parameter for a cursor on a table that has a column of the same name, the PL/SQL interpreter will use the column value instead of the parameter value in the SELECT statement. The same effect occurs in other uses of SQL where you are using PL/SQL parameters in the SQL statement.

Program Units
The names you give to Oracle Developer program units (packages, procedures, and functions) are different from the names you give to objects in the database, which are covered by another naming convention. When you look at a piece of code, it is useful to know the source of a called program unit. If you know where the program unit resides, you can quickly locate it to examine its comments or code. Therefore, your naming convention should indicate where the program unit is located.

FUNCTIONS AND PROCEDURES   One standard, explained next, is that all procedures and functions appear in packages. Regardless of that standard, a single naming convention applies to procedures and functions (stand-alone or packaged). This convention is that functions are named as nouns because they return a value. Procedures are named as verbs because they perform an action. For example, a function that returns an employee's name based on an ID value would be called ID_TO_NAME or EMP_NAME. A procedure that inserts a record into the department table after checking for duplicates would be called ADD_ DEPT. Naming program units in this way makes reading the code much easier because the syntax is almost narrative.

CAUTION
Be careful of reserved words when naming program units. For example, if you name a packaged procedure COMMIT and call it within a procedure in the same package, you do not need the package name qualifier. Therefore, the call you issue will be the same as the SQL command COMMIT, and you may get unexpected results. One solution is to use a prefix for procedures and a different prefix for functions. Another solution is to name the procedure something other than a reserved word (like COMMIT_ALL).

DATABASE PACKAGES   As mentioned, you should create a separate standards document to define the names for database code. If your package names use the system abbreviation as a prefix, you will be able to distinguish them from Developer package names. You may also want to create an additional prefix to indicate a subsystem. For example, the SPMTS project has a number of subsystems (Data Migration, Batch Processing, and User Interface). The prefix for packages in the database would indicate the system and subsystem, for example, SPMTS_DM_, SPMTS_BP_, and SPMTS_UI_. The system may have common utility packages that all subsystems use; these would use no subsystem prefix. Subsystem prefixes allow developers to sort package names alphabetically and to quickly navigate to the required package.

Procedures and functions within the package need no distinguishing name because the package name always precedes those names and identifies the context.

FORMS AND REPORTS PROGRAM UNITS   You can attach a library (as a .PLL source or .PLX runtime file) to a form or report so the code is available as if it were written directly in the form or report. It is useful to be able to distinguish which code comes from a library and which code comes from the form or report. Library code is contained in packages that use the prefixes of the organizational level they represent. These prefixes include the following:

- **F_**   This is for code in a library that manipulates Forms objects only. For example, the F_ITEM package contains procedures that act on an item (such as hide or display). Appendix A contains more examples of F_ packages.

- **Fnn_**   This is for code in a library that is application specific but used by all forms. The "nn" denotes a two-character application alias. If your application were CTAR, the alias for this purpose would be CT and the full prefix would be FCT_. You can use more than one library to organize the code, but all packages use the same prefix.

Reports library code follows the same convention but uses the letter "R" instead of the letter "F" as a prefix. Package code that is specific to a form or report needs no prefix (such as STARTUP and UTIL). Using these conventions, you will be able to quickly identify the location of a package. Table 3-3 summarizes the package names.

It is important to name Forms and Reports program units differently than database server program units. If you have a procedure called F_BLOCK.QUERY_ALL in the form itself, in a Forms library, and in the database, it will be confusing as to which one is executed. Technically, Forms looks for code in the form first, then in attached libraries, and finally in the database. This order is not something you should count on, as it may change in a particular release of the product.

Therefore, the best strategy is to use a different naming convention for the packages in the form, in the library, and in the database. The actual procedure and function names can have the same names if needed because you always prefix the name with the package name. As mentioned before, all code should be contained in packages. This means that you only need to worry about the names of the packages themselves.

RENAMING PROGRAM UNITS   You may find yourself in the situation that you have named a package with a specific application prefix but also need to use it for another application. Since the convention is to use the application prefix for all code, you might be tempted to copy the package and rename the copy with the new prefix. However, this creates a maintenance problem because the code exists in two places. The solution is to create a stub (non-functional program unit) that contains the same program units with the same set of parameters as the original package. It will then appear as if that new package owns the code although it merely calls the code in another package.

This technique can also be used if you need to rename a procedure or package that has already been used by production code. In this situation, you would keep the original code intact and create a new package with the correct name. The code in this new package would call the code in the old package. It may make more

Package Naming Convention	Example	Location of Code
Prefix of system and (optionally) subsystem abbreviations	SPMTS_UI_UTIL	Database
Prefix of product	F_ALERT	Developer library file
Prefix of product and system	FCT_UTIL	Developer library file
No prefix	STARTUP	Form or report file itself

TABLE 3-3.   *PL/SQL Naming Convention and Location of the Code*

sense in this situation to move the code to the new package so, when you need to perform maintenance on the code, you will interact with the package that uses the desired name.

Code Usage

In addition to the formatting and naming standards, you also need to develop standards for how your developers will use PL/SQL. There are usually many ways to write logic that solves a particular problem. Without guidelines as to the best way to do this, the developer has to spend time thinking about the alternatives. With a standard in place, there will still be the potential for multiple solutions, but there will also be some form of guidance for the best one.

While the subject of "best practices" for the use of PL/SQL is a topic for a series of articles or white papers, or even another book, it is useful to examine some of the more generally accepted practices and techniques that can be part of your standards.

Standards for Organization of Code

This standard fits into three words: Always use packages. Packages offer a number of compelling advantages over stand-alone procedures and functions, as detailed in Chapter 7. The main benefits are in the areas of code organization, object orientation, publicly available objects, publicly restricted source, and better performance.

Standards for Functions

A few usage standards apply specifically to functions. One is that all functions contain only one RETURN statement. The following is an example of a function that uses more than one return statement:

```
BEGIN
    IF :f_salary < 500
    THEN
        RETURN (FALSE);
    ELSE
        RETURN (TRUE);
    END IF;
END;
```

Although this example is easy to read, you will create functions that are not so short and simple and may have more RETURN statements that are not as easy to find. An alternative coding for this function follows:

```
DECLARE
   v_return BOOLEAN := TRUE;
BEGIN
   IF :f_salary < 500
   THEN
      v_return := FALSE;
   END IF;
   RETURN (v_return);
END;
```

This method requires an extra variable, but ensures a single exit point from the routine, which is one of the marks of a well-constructed program. Larger examples of code would make the logic of the first, multiple-exit-point version of this code harder to follow. The single-exit-point method clarifies exactly which code will run. Anything before the RETURN statement can be executed, but anything after it cannot be executed.

Another guideline that will be a standard is that functions do not change data. It is possible to pass a function an IN OUT parameter and allow the function to modify the value of that variable. This situation is not desirable because the expected objective of a function is to take a value or values and return another value. The function's user will rely on only this objective and will not expect any of the passed values to change. This is a called a *side effect* because it is not the main or expected purpose of the function. Developers should avoid coding functions that produce this type of side effect by not using IN OUT parameters for functions.

Ordering Within the Package

Your standard also should include how to order the procedures and functions inside the package. The first thing in the package spec is the header comment. The comment lists all procedures and functions in alphabetical order. You then declare variables and other elements in the order mentioned in "The Declaration Section" later in this chapter. If the comment lists program units in alphabetical order, you can browse through and find the exact name. Then you can use the editor's search facility to find the exact declaration section. The same strategy applies to finding code in the package body. Once you know the exact spelling of the name, you can search for the body code.

The functions and procedures are declared next in the package spec. Placing these in alphabetical order is not as important as placing the header comments that document them in alphabetical order, because you will use the search facilities of the editor to find the program unit in the body.

TIP

If you have created Forms code that calls a package and need to add procedures or functions to that package, add them to the end of the specification. If you do not, you may receive a database error in the form (ORA-04062) that the package signature has changed. This will require you to recompile all libraries and forms that access that package. You can avoid this in most cases by adding the program units to the bottom of the package specification or by writing a separate accessor package. This package contains only the procedures and functions that you call from Forms code. The program units pass the call through to the base package. If the base package changes and the accessor does not, the calls from your forms should remain intact.

Implicit Cursors

Implicit cursors are SQL statements for which you do not declare a cursor. INSERT, UPDATE, and DELETE statements automatically open implicit cursors, but you have no control over those cursors other than to read the cursor attributes (such as SQL%ROWCOUNT). You can code a SELECT statement inside your PL/SQL body like the following:

```
DECLARE
    v_ename       emp.empname%TYPE;
    v_sal         emp.sal%TYPE;
BEGIN
    SELECT    ename, sal
    INTO      v_ename, v_sal
    FROM      employee
    WHERE     empno = 101;
END;
```

This code assigns the values from the query to the declared variables. It opens a nondeclared (implicit) cursor, performs the fetch, and closes the cursor. This syntax only works in embedded SQL such as this PL/SQL block. It also only works if there is one and only one row retrieved. You would need to write exceptions for NO_DATA_FOUND and TOO_MANY_ROWS to handle the common exception states that may result.

Your SQL standard should state that implicit cursors are to be avoided because you do not have control as you do with explicit cursors and, in theory, implicit cursors require two fetches from the table. The first fetch retrieves the row; the second fetch determines if there are any more rows that fulfill the conditions. If so, the PL/SQL engine raises an exception, TOO_MANY_ ROWS. With PL/SQL v.23, this effect is not a huge problem because implicit cursors have been optimized. The following code uses an explicit cursor to perform the same process. It only requires one fetch:

```
DECLARE
    CURSOR c_emp (
        p_eno    emp.empno%TYPE)
    IS
        SELECT    ename, sal
        FROM      employee
        WHERE     empno = p_eno;
    --
    v_ename        emp.empname%TYPE;
    v_sal          emp.sal%TYPE;
BEGIN
    OPEN c_emp(101);
    FETCH c_emp INTO v_ename, v_sal;
    CLOSE c_emp;
END;
```

Naturally, in both examples, you would code a parameter to the cursor or procedure instead of the hard-coded value 101. You would also code exception sections to handle the NO_DATA_FOUND and TOO_MANY_ROWS exceptions, at least.

The implicit cursor requires less coding than the explicit cursor, but it is less flexible because you have less programmatic control over the steps taken in retrieving data. Therefore, the standard should state that explicit cursors should always be used instead of implicit cursors for queries.

The Declaration Section

There is a standard for each part of the PL/SQL block that handles issues specific to that section. In the declaration section, there is a standard for the order of the elements. Each declaration appears on its own line, and the declarations appear in logical groupings. In other words, place together declarations of variables that are used together. An example follows:

```
DECLARE
    --
    v_emp_id                   employee.emp_id%TYPE;
    v_last_name                employee.last_name%TYPE;
    --
    v_salary                   employee_salary.salary%TYPE;
    v_new_total                v_salary%TYPE;
    v_raise                    v_salary%TYPE;
    v_standard_raise           v_salary%TYPE := 500;
BEGIN
```

In the PL/SQL block, there are two sections: one accessing the EMPLOYEE table to find a salary ID and the second to calculate and add a new record in the salary history table with the employee's raise. The variables for the first section are declared as a group. The variables for the second section are also declared as a group. This allows you to read the variable sections as a unit and relate them to code sections in the body.

Cursors must, by definition, be declared before the record variables that use them. For example:

```
DECLARE
    --
    CURSOR c_emp
    IS
        SELECT    empno, ename, sal
        FROM      employee;
    --
    r_emp   c_emp%ROWTYPE;
BEGIN
```

The declaration section uses inline comments "--" to separate the groups of declarations.

DATATYPES   Another standard dictates how datatypes are declared for the variables. This example uses datatypes left justified. This sets the variable names apart from the datatypes and allows you to quickly check the datatype. Be sure to leave enough room for the maximum number of characters in a variable name. Therefore, the datatype should start 32 characters after the start of the variable name. This allows you to use variable names of the maximum length without the need to reformat variables already declared.

This example also demonstrates another standard: If you are declaring a variable based on a database column, always use %TYPE and %ROWTYPE to datatype the variable. This gives you the most flexibility to change the size of columns after code has been written. It is unlikely that you will change datatypes of columns after writing the code since you need to evaluate and use special operators based on the datatype.

For example, you cannot perform an arithmetic addition on two character strings. If you used a database column of datatype NUMBER as a type for a variable declaration and used that variable in an arithmetic operation, that piece of code would break if you were to change the database column to a VARCHAR2 datatype and insert nonnumeric values in them. Using the flexible typing will save you if the database column size is changed. Changing a column size happens more often than changing a column datatype.

LOCAL PROCEDURES AND FUNCTIONS   Another standard to promote is making the body of the code short so it is easier to read. One way to do that is to move sections of the code that would make the code body longer into procedures or functions declared in that program unit. These procedures and functions are declared at the very end of the DECLARE section for the program unit and are available only to that program unit. The benefit is that they reduce the body to a single call instead of all the code that appears in the procedure or function. Consider using this technique even if the procedure or function would only be used once.

Another method to accomplish this task is to write the local procedures and functions at the top of the package body. This cleans up the program unit declaration section, but requires the reader to jump to the top of the block to check a called program unit in the middle of the program unit body. A variation on this arrangement is to place a declaration of the local procedures and functions in the top of the package body (formatted the same as if you were to put them in the package spec). Then place the globally-available procedures and functions that are declared in the package specification. Last, place the full code for the local procedures and functions. This sets the local code apart from the global code and allows you to quickly reach the global code. If you use local program units in the package body, be sure to provide documentation on them in the package body header comments.

CURSOR PARAMETERS   When you declare cursors that require a variable, always pass cursor parameters. It is possible to declare a procedure such as the following:

```
PROCEDURE add_department(
    p_dept_id department.dept_id%TYPE,
    p_location department.location%TYPE)
IS
    CURSOR c_dept
    IS
        SELECT    1
        FROM      department
        WHERE     dept_id = p_dept_id;
BEGIN
```

The problem with this method is that the body of the code may need to pass the cursor a value different from the parameter value. The way this is declared, you can only pass the cursor the value of the parameter. The solution is to use a cursor parameter as in the following example:

```
PROCEDURE add_department(
    p_dept_id department.dept_id%TYPE,
    p_location department.location%TYPE)
IS
    CURSOR c_dept(
```

```
            p_department_id department.dept_id%TYPE)
    IS
        SELECT    1
        FROM      department
        WHERE     dept_id = p_department_id;
BEGIN
```

Note the formatting of the cursor statement into multiple lines and the placement of the parameters in the procedure and cursor declarations. These placements are also used as standards.

HARD-CODING STRING VALUES   If you need to compare variable values with string values, use global constants. For example, you retrieve a value from the STATUS column of the EMP_HISTORY table. The status is either an "A" or an "I." When you write code to evaluate the status, you compare it with "A" to see if the history record is active. The problem is that whoever writes code to evaluate that status will need to know that the comparison must be with the string "A", not with the string "ACTIVE", "active", or "Active". In addition, if the data requirements change and you need to compare with a different value such as "Y", you will need to change the hard-coded value everywhere it is used.

A better solution, that should be a standard, is to create a package constant to represent "Active." Here is the code to accomplish that:

```
PACKAGE app_global
IS
    -- global constant to be used for the "active" status.
    g_active_status    CONSTANT VARCHAR2(1) := 'A';
END;
```

Each time you need to refer to the active status or compare with the active status, you would use APP_GLOBAL.G_ACTIVE_STATUS. For example, in a procedure where you have loaded the status value from a table into the variable V_STATUS, you would write the following to determine what the status was:

```
IF v_status = app_global.g_active_status
THEN
    -- the status is active, so process it accordingly
...
```

The developer creating the code does not need to remember the exact spelling of the active value. If the value for "active" ever needs to change, there is only one place that the change needs to be made—in the constant's declaration. This is a simple example, but the technique becomes more important when there are many codes that are not so easy to remember.

The Body Section

The PL/SQL code body requires some standards itself. One is how to format calls to procedures and functions that use parameters. The standard is to place all parameters on the same line as the procedure or function name if they fit within the line length limit. If they do not fit within the line length limit, place them on separate lines. An example follows:

```
BEGIN
    IF spmts_dept.name_to_id(v_dept, v_location) IS NOT NULL
    THEN
        add_department(v_dept, v_location);
    ELSE
        query_system_data(
            'DEPT',
            v_dept_id,
            v_location,
            v_user,
            v_timedate);
    END IF;
```

LOOPS   Another usage standard for the body section is to always use cursor FOR loops when traversing the contents of a table. You can use explicit OPEN, FETCH, and CLOSE statements, but the loop syntax is more involved.

Avoid the EXIT or RETURN statements to leave a loop. Construct your loops so the conditional logic is built into the WHILE or FOR syntax. Exiting in the middle of a loop breaks the guideline for a single exit point for code (as mentioned in the earlier section on functions). If you allow the loop condition to do the evaluation, the exit point will be the top (or bottom) of the loop structure.

GOTO AND USER-DEFINED EXCEPTIONS   The GOTO statement is available in PL/SQL, but like an EXIT statement in a loop, it breaks the normally ordered flow of control. While you may need to use it as a last resort, there are usually ways using IF constructs to avoid that statement.

User-defined exceptions can be as misused as the GOTO statement. Exceptions should be exceptional. User-defined exceptions should not be used to exit a piece of logic in the middle unless there is a true error or invalid state that is not normal. One guideline in making the decision about exceptions is to ask yourself if you could possibly code the logic using a normal conditional (IF) structure instead of a jump to an exception section. You can also ask yourself which method would make the code easier to read. Generally, jumping around in the code logic makes the code more difficult to read, but if the code is long and involved, an exception may be easier to read than an additional IF condition. If the code is short, an IF condition is better than an exception because you do not have to jump to another section when reading the code.

The Exception Section

The main standard for the EXCEPTION section is that you should always code a WHEN OTHERS exception to trap exceptions that are not otherwise handled. The OTHERS exception must appear as the last condition in that section.

Sample Code

The following sample PL/SQL package demonstrates the principles discussed in the preceding standards.

Package Specification

```
/*****************************************************************************\
|| Program:     SPMTS_UI_UTIL
|| System:      Computer Training Associates Registration
||
|| Description:
||   Commonly used utility procedures and functions. Called from the user
||   interface Forms and Reports modules.
||
|| Modification History:
||   -----------------------------------------------------
||     Date        By           Remarks/Reason
||   -----------------------------------------------------
||     19-Aug-1999  pkoletzke    created
||
|| Global Variables:
||   g_user_name
||       Initialized by the logon form. The default is the current username,
||       but a user may have logged in using a proxy account and this name
||       should be saved for audit purposes.
||
|| Usage:
||
||   course_id_to_name
||       Function. Pass in the ID and return the name of the course. If the
||       course is the parent without prerequisites, use that name. If other
||       than the parent, return the concatenation of all course names other
||       than the parent (the list of prereqs).
||
||   set_ui_user_name
||       Procedure. Pass in the username from the form and set the package
||       global variable to that name. This variable is used by the insert/update
||       trigger of each table to assign the audit column values (USER_CREATED,
```

```
||      USER_MODIFIED).
||
\*************************************************************************/
   --
   g_user_name all_users.username%TYPE := USER;
   --
   FUNCTION course_id_to_name(
      p_crse_id  ctar_course.crse_id%TYPE)
      RETURN ctar_role.name%TYPE;
   PRAGMA RESTRICT_REFERENCES (course_id_to_name, WNDS, WNPS);
   --
   PROCEDURE set_ui_user_name(
      p_user_name  VARCHAR2);
   --
END;
```

Package Body

```
/*************************************************************************\
|| Program:     SPMTS_UI_UTIL
|| System:      Computer Training Associates Registration
||
|| Description:
||   Commonly used utility procedures and functions. Called from the user
||   interface Forms and Reports modules.
||
|| Modification History:
||   -------------------------------------------------------
||    Date         By          Remarks/Reason
||   -------------------------------------------------------
||    19-Aug-1999  pkoletzke    created
||
\*************************************************************************/
   --
   FUNCTION course_id_to_name(
      p_crse_id ctar_course.crse_id%TYPE)
      RETURN      ctar_role.name%TYPE
   IS
      CURSOR c_crse(
         p_id    ctar_course.crse_id%TYPE)
      IS
         SELECT      name, parent_crse_id
         FROM        ctar_course
         CONNECT
         BY PRIOR    parent_crse_id = crse_id
         START WITH crse_id = p_id;
      --
      v_full_name  VARCHAR2(2000) := NULL;
   BEGIN
      FOR r_crse IN c_crse(p_crse_id)
```

```
    LOOP
       IF v_full_name IS NULL
       THEN
          v_full_name := r_crse.name;
       ELSIF r_role.parent_crse_id IS NULL
       THEN
          v_full_name := r_crse.name || ': ' || v_full_name;
       ELSE
          v_full_name := r_crse.name || '-' || v_full_name;
       END IF;
    END LOOP;
    --
    RETURN (v_full_name);
  END;
  --
  --
  PROCEDURE set_ui_user_name(
     p_user_name VARCHAR2)
  IS
  BEGIN
     IF p_username IS NOT NULL
     THEN
        g_user_name := p_username;
     ELSE
        g_user_name := USER;
     END IF;
  END;
  --
END;
```

CHAPTER

4

What Do You Base a Block on?

Nothing can be created from nothing.

—Lucretius (99–55 B.C.), *On the Nature of Things*

t is simple to build a block based on a single table. The native Oracle Developer drivers access Oracle database tables without any extra effort or extensive coding on the developer's side. In addition, through ODBC (Open Database Connectivity), you can hook forms up to a table in virtually any database. However, you may want to display information from multiple tables in the block. Using POST-QUERY triggers has traditionally satisfied this requirement. However, these triggers create unnecessary network traffic and may cause performance bottlenecks. When trying to performance-tune an application, one of the easiest techniques to improve query performance of a block is to remove POST-QUERY triggers from the block by using one of the techniques outlined in this section.

Once the information is queried into the form, you will often need to manipulate the data before updating it in the database. As long as you are only dealing with columns from a single table, it is relatively straightforward. Using Oracle8 and Developer Release 6.0, there are far more elegant solutions to these problems requiring less developer effort with better performance. An important part of your standards is information such as guidelines for what to base a block on. If these guidelines are documented, it will assist developers in making decisions about the best way to architect their forms.

There are many different sources you can use for your blocks. Some use methods that have been available in earlier versions of Oracle Developer; others are new with R.6. The following are things you can base a block on:

- Nothing (a control block)

- A table

- A view (updateable view, view with INSTEAD OF triggers, or non-updateable view)

- A procedure (PL/SQL table type or REF CURSOR type)

- A FROM clause query

- Transactional triggers

This chapter explains each of these and provides techniques or tips on how to implement them.

There are two categories to examine when determining what to base a block on. The first is the *data source*—where data is queried from. The second is the *data target*— where data in the form goes when the user issues a COMMIT in the form. There are block properties that manage both categories. For example, you set the property *Query Data Source Type* to the kind of object (such as a table) that you want Forms to use when querying. There is a corresponding property, *DML Data*

Target Type, that specifies what kind of object (such as a procedure) that you want Forms to use when issuing an INSERT, UPDATE, or DELETE statement to the database. Both source and target can be set differently in some cases, based on your needs and on the restrictions of the property value combinations (as documented in the help system). This chapter will focus on the data source but will also mention the data target in the implementation discussion.

Forms Query Text

Traditionally, basing a block on a table allows you to further modify the query by adding additional text to the *Query Data Source Name, WHERE Clause,* or *ORDER BY Clause* block-level properties. What is Oracle Forms doing when filling in these properties? It is building the following statement:

```
SELECT    <all of the database column items in the block>
FROM      <Query Data Source Name property>
WHERE     <WHERE Clause property>
ORDER BY <ORDER BY Clause property>
```

You have a number of options for manipulating the string that Forms passes as a query to the database. For example, the *WHERE Clause* and *ORDER BY Clause* properties can be manipulated at runtime using the SET_BLOCK_PROPERTY built-in. This allows you to manipulate the block's sorts and filters at runtime. This feature is used extensively in the Locator described in Chapter 15.

The *ORDER BY Clause* property can be used to change the sort order of records in the block and can also be manipulated at runtime.

CAUTION
When setting these properties, you are simply providing material that Forms will concatenate to form the SQL statement. Therefore, there is nothing to say that the table source must be a single table. For example, you can use "DEPT,EMP" as the value for the Query Data Source Name *property and "DEPT.DEPTNO = EMP.DEPTNO" in the* WHERE Clause *property. This allows you to select columns from either the DEPT or EMP table without the need for a view in the database. Using the properties in this way is not a recommended strategy because it is nonstandard and may confuse someone else trying to maintain the form. Also, in Form Builder release 6.0, there are alternative methods of having blocks return information from multiple tables simultaneously without resorting to such workarounds.*

Whether you will allow users to change the *Order By Clause* property at runtime is a GUI design issue. Normally, runtime specification of the ORDER BY clause is not necessary. Most blocks should have this property set when the block is created, particularly if a large number of records must be retrieved. Keep in mind that the *Order By Clause* block property alters the query statement sent to the database. By adding an ORDER BY clause to the query, there may be a significant performance impact to consider.

Basing a Block on Nothing (a Control Block)

Blocks may be created without a data source. When a block is not being populated from a database source, it is called a *control block*. Control blocks are used for items that are not explicitly associated with database objects such as buttons, total items, locator query criteria objects, and items for displaying messages. Control blocks can also be used to display values from items selected elsewhere. For example, if you are maintaining a list of selected items and you do not want to store a list of selected items in the database, they can be stored locally and populated in a control block.

Control blocks are almost always single record blocks. However, if you are displaying a list of items as mentioned above, your control block will display a number of records and may have a scroll bar. Any type of item may be contained in a control block.

Utilizing the GUI techniques described in this book, almost every form will have at least two control blocks. Each form has a "STUFF" block holding the authors' template null item and other template items (as mentioned in Chapter 11). Most forms also have a locator control block to hold locator query criteria items (as Chapter 15 describes).

Implementing a Block Based on Nothing

If you want to create a new control block, specify that you will be building the block manually when you click on the Create button in the Object Navigator. To create a control block from an existing block, set the *Query Data Source Type* property in the Database section of the block Property Palette to "None". By default, when a block is created, the *Query Data Source Type* property is set to "table" and the *Query Data Source Name* property is empty. This setting will also work for a control block. For the items in the control block, the *Column Name* property should be left as "NULL", although this will not create any problems if it is set to something else.

If you have many nondatabase items in your form housed in a control block, you might want to create multiple control blocks to organize the items. In very complex forms, you might have an additional control block for every base table block to house the control items for that block.

Basing a Block on a Table

Basing a block on a table involves associating the block with a specific table in the database and associating some number of items in the block with columns in the table. Additional non-base table items in the block are populated with POST-QUERY triggers. This is traditionally the most common mechanism for attaching a block to data stored in the database. Unfortunately, this method has some serious drawbacks. First, most blocks in production forms require the display of columns not in the base table. Therefore, most base table blocks have POST-QUERY triggers to retrieve additional information from the database.

This is a terrible design method. Recall that a POST-QUERY trigger executes every time a row is fetched into the block. Therefore, if a POST-QUERY trigger contains a cursor to retrieve information from the database, retrieving 200 records into this block entails 200 additional and unnecessary trips to the database. This same situation can be handled far more efficiently through a view discussed later in this chapter.

NOTE
No POST-QUERY trigger should ever contain a cursor.

The only time that a block should be based on a table is when there are no columns that need to be populated by triggers that access the database. Because of the POST-QUERY trigger restriction, basing a block on a table should be a rare occurrence (less than 10% of your forms).

Implementing a Block Based on a Table

When basing a block on a table, you should usually use the Data Block Wizard. This wizard is re-entrant so that if a column is omitted, rather than having to manually add it to the block, you can use the Data Block Wizard to add it. Just remember that, if you also rerun the Layout Wizard to add the item on the canvas, the wizard will reposition all the items in the block regardless of where you have moved them.

CAUTION
When running the Data Block Wizard, the Column Name *property for each database item is filled in. If you change the name of the item, it will still be pointing to the same column. If the* Column Name *property is "NULL", the item will use the Item Name as the name of the database column.*
Although the Column Name *property was null by default in the Data Block Wizard of Forms R.5, it is not null by default in Developer Forms R.6.0.*
Leaving the Column Name *property set to "NULL" is a better development practice. This way, if the name of a database column is changed, you can change the name of the item in the block accordingly (and update the column list in the* Query Data Source Columns *property). You do not need to change the* Column Name *property. Therefore, all the authors' item SmartClasses in the template have this property set to "NULL". (Chapter 10 explains the SmartClass feature.)*

When using the Data Block Wizard to implement blocks based on tables, the Wizard creates a block with the *Query Data Source Type* property set to "Table" and the *Query Data Source Name* property set to the name of the table. For each item, the *Database Item* property is set to "Yes" and both the *Name* and *Column Name* properties of the item are set to the database column name.

On a block that has been based on a table, you can navigate to that block using GO_BLOCK or GO_ITEM built-ins to any item in the block (that has the *Keyboard Navigable* property set to "Yes"). Onscreen, you can navigate to a block either by tabbing to any item in the block or mouse-clicking on any mouse-navigable item in the block. Buttons are mouse-navigable if the *Mouse Navigate* property is set to "Yes". Text items are always mouse-navigable so that there is no *Mouse Navigate* property on the Property Palette for these item types. Display items are never navigable either by mouse or keyboard so neither property (*Mouse Navigate* or *Keyboard Navigable*) appears on the Property Palette.

Querying data into a block is handled via the EXECUTE_QUERY built-in. This built-in operates only on the current block and does not accept a block name as a parameter. Inserting records into a block is handled by navigating to the first open row and entering values. You can also create a blank row using the CREATE_ RECORD built-in wherever the cursor is, leaving other records in the block intact.

Deleting the current record from the block is accomplished with the DELETE_ RECORD built-in. Modification to a block item can be handled by navigating to a specific record and changing the value of the item. To permanently apply your changes to the database, a COMMIT_FORM built-in is required.

NOTE
Inserts, updates, and deletes to records are not automatically posted to the database. If you make changes to records in a base table block and then query the database (even in the same session), those changes will not be reflected in the database unless you explicitly execute a POST or COMMIT_FORM.

Basing a Block on a View

A view does not contain data. It is just a text string storing a SELECT statement. When a DML command is executed with a reference to the view, the code is parsed in such a way as to take the view into account. You can base a block on a view in the same way you base a block on a table. The view can represent a master-detail relationship, a code description lookup, or any other type of SELECT statement that would make sense for your application. For example, here is the definition for a view based on the EMP table that joins the table to itself so it can show the manager's name and job title.

```
CREATE OR REPLACE VIEW emp_v
AS
    SELECT  emp.empno,
            emp.ename,
            emp.job,
            emp.mgr,
            emp.hiredate,
            emp.sal,
            emp.comm,
            emp.deptno,
            mgr.ename mgr_name,
            mgr.job mgr_job
    FROM    emp emp, emp mgr
    WHERE   emp.mgr = mgr.empno (+)
```

This view uses an outer join to retrieve all rows of the EMP table even if they have no value in the MGR column. If you base the EMP block on this view, you will not need to use a POST-QUERY trigger to query the manager information for each row;

the manager information will be retrieved as part of the same row in the view. Using a view in this way can save a significant amount of network traffic. This example assumes that you are not updating the manager information, although this would be possible by using INSTEAD OF triggers (described later) or some other mechanism.

You can use views in different ways—as updateable objects or as non-updateable objects. You can also take advantage of an Oracle8 feature that allows you to write database (INSTEAD OF) triggers for the view. Other than the extra step of writing trigger code, there is no difference in syntax for creating views that are in the category of updateable, non-updateable, or INSTEAD OF. However, the different uses require different design considerations and Forms techniques and each will be discussed separately.

TIP
If you need to sort the records in a block on a non-base table item that does not appear in the table or view that the block is based on, you can create a function in the database that loads the non-base table item and add that function's name to the ORDER BY Clause property on the block you wish to sort.

Updateable Views

An *updateable view* is a view created where one or more columns support DML commands. There is nothing special required syntactically to make a view updateable. The Oracle database decides for you which columns are updateable. To find out which columns are updateable, you can query from the system view USER_UPDATABLE_COLUMNS. The documentation on updateable views (in Chapter 3 of the *Oracle8 Application Developer's Guide - Fundamentals* manual) includes a very precise technical discussion of *key-preserved* (or *ROW ID preserved*) columns. In short, if your view is essentially querying from a single table with some extra display columns, then you can perform INSERT, UPDATE, and DELETE operations to columns in the base table as shown in the following code:

```
CREATE OR REPLACE VIEW emp_v
AS
    SELECT e.empno,
           e.ename,
           e.deptno,
           d.dname
    FROM   emp e, dept d
    WHERE  e.deptno = d.deptno
```

In this case, you can insert into this view as if it were the EMP table. However, you cannot insert into the DNAME column. Another way to think about this is that an updateable view is a view that contains a join between master and detail tables. You can update columns that are derived from the detail table (that contains the *key-preserved* columns) of this view. The view has to be constructed so that the foreign key column comes from the detail table (not the master table). In this example, the detail table is the EMP table. The master table is the DEPT table and the DEPTNO foreign key column comes from the EMP table. Therefore, you are able to update all columns from the detail table (EMP) but not from the master table (DEPT).

When creating an updateable view, it will always have the same number of rows as its core (detail) table unless you are filtering out the records using a WHERE clause. The previous code example could be modified to include:

```
AND e.deptno < 30
```

You can still INSERT, UPDATE, or DELETE records in the EMP table using the EMP_V view even though the number of records in the view is potentially less than the number of records in the table.

One very useful technique using updateable views is to embed a function in a view. To do this, you should first place the function into a database package. Next, in the package specification, use a PRAGMA RESTRICT_REFERENCES directive (Chapter 3 contains an example of this syntax). This function can then be embedded in the SELECT clause of the updateable view.

The example above could also be rewritten by creating a function called EMPNO_TO_DNAME and storing it in a package called K_EMP. The view definition would be changed as shown below:

```
CREATE OR REPLACE VIEW emp_v
AS
SELECT empno,
       ename,
       deptno,
       k_emp.empno_to_dname(empno)
FROM   emp
```

This view now operates in the same way as if you had a base table block based on EMP with a POST-QUERY trigger to look up the department name. However, since you are basing your block on the updateable view, the number of network round trips will be reduced. You can still update the columns from the EMP table but you cannot update the column based on the function. Usually, joining the tables will be more efficient than performing lookups using embedded functions. The reason both methods have been presented is to point out how every block with a POST-QUERY trigger (that contains a lookup cursor) can always be restructured as a block based on an updateable view. You can accomplish the lookup by rewriting the POST-QUERY trigger as a function that you place in the SELECT clause of the view. Using functions for lookups instead of POST-QUERY triggers requires no extra operations by the database and will require much less network traffic because all queries are performed on the database server before query results from the view are passed to the form. This demonstrates why POST-QUERY triggers with cursors should never be used.

CAUTION
When creating an updateable view and joining to a table based on an optional relationship, be sure to use an outer join to ensure that all records are retrieved.

Many developers assert that updateable views are more complex and actually slower than tables with POST-QUERY triggers. This is indeed possible if your updateable view is a multitable join. Even though the overall efficiency of bringing all of the records back is improved, the perceived performance by users may actually degrade. If this problem exists, the solution is not to go back to using a POST-QUERY trigger on a block. Instead, the updateable view should be changed. This can be done by using the same strategy to build the updateable view as was used to build the base table block and POST-QUERY triggers, namely rewriting the triggers as database functions. When this is done, you can build your updateable view to select all columns from the base table plus any additional formula columns. This mechanism will always be faster than a table-based block with POST-QUERY triggers. The only difference between the two methods is that rather than performing network round trips for every record, instead, the function calls are all happening within the core database query. This strategy can dramatically decrease the number of network roundtrips required by an application.

You should base most of your blocks on updateable views. Any time you have a table with a POST-QUERY trigger requiring database access, it should always be replaced by an updateable view. Not only will network traffic decrease (thereby improving performance) but you will also achieve better encapsulation of the code, which also improves the chances for reuse. The same view built in one context can be reused in reports or other system forms. Because of the reuse possibility, always include all columns from the core table in the updateable view.

Views with INSTEAD OF Triggers

A new feature in Oracle8 allows you to support INSERT, UPDATE, and DELETE operations on any view. This feature enables you to create a view on multiple tables and allow DML operations to be defined in any way desired. The benefit is the elimination of the limitations imposed by updateable views. The disadvantage is the need to write all of the programming logic for the view.

Although you cannot perform DML statements on a view that is not updateable, in Oracle8 (8.0 and 8i) you can write an INSTEAD OF trigger that will fire when DML is attempted on the view. The trigger code will take over when the DML is issued and can manipulate any of the base tables of the view.

NOTE
The term DML (Data Manipulation Language) technically refers to all operations that you can apply to a data set. It is distinguished from DDL (Data Definition Language) that includes statements to alter and create data structures. While DML operations in SQL include the INSERT, UPDATE, DELETE, and SELECT verbs, many sources use the term DML to mean only the INSERT, UPDATE, and DELETE verbs. You will find this term used this way in block properties such as the DML Target Type. *This book follows the latter usage.*

The following is an example of an INSTEAD OF trigger (the suffix identifies it as occurring instead of an Insert, Delete, or Update). For simplicity, this code does not insert or update the manager information in the EMP table, but logic for those DML statements could easily be added.

```
CREATE OR REPLACE TRIGGER emp_v_biud
   INSTEAD OF INSERT OR UPDATE OR DELETE
   ON EMP_V
   FOR EACH ROW
DECLARE
   v_message  VARCHAR2(100);
BEGIN
   IF INSERTING
   THEN
      v_message := 'Inserting an EMP record using EMP_V_BIUD';
      -- The manager record must already exist or the INSERT will fail
      INSERT INTO emp (
         empno,
         ename,
         job,
```

```
                  mgr,
                  hiredate,
                  sal,
                  comm,
                  deptno)
         VALUES  (
                  :new.empno,
                  :new.ename,
                  :new.job,
                  :new.mgr,
                  :new.hiredate,
                  :new.sal,
                  :new.comm,
                  :new.deptno);
      ELSIF UPDATING
      THEN
         v_message := 'Updating an EMP record using EMP_V_BIUD';
         -- Assumes the manager name and job are not updateable
         -- Also assumes the primary key value of EMP did not change
         UPDATE emp
         SET    ename = :new.ename,
                job = :new.job,
                mgr = :new.mgr,
                hiredate = :new.hiredate,
                sal = :new.sal,
                comm = :new.comm,
                deptno = :new.deptno
         WHERE empno = :old.empno;
      ELSE  -- DELETING
         v_message := 'Deleting an EMP record using EMP_V_BIUD';
         --
         DELETE FROM emp
         WHERE  empno = :old.empno;
      END IF;
EXCEPTION
   WHEN OTHERS
   THEN
      raise_application_error(-20001, 'Error: ' || v_message ||
         ' - ' || SQLERRM);
END;
/
```

The trigger defines INSERT, UPDATE, and DELETE statements for each operation that you allow on the view. It uses the :NEW and :OLD values available in row triggers to build DML statements for the EMP table.

CAUTION

INSTEAD OF trigger views should only be built by highly skilled developers. It can be very difficult to debug a complex application if a block based on an INSTEAD OF trigger view contains an error. Also, since you are not using an updateable view, the automatic check on the correct coding of the view is not available so you may believe that the view is correct when, in fact, it is not.

An INSTEAD OF trigger view can be used any time there is a complex block based on multiple tables and you want update capability but an updateable view is not sufficient. This is a very powerful technique that will not be required in most applications. If you need many INSTEAD OF views to support your applications, you should probably examine your database design and GUI standards carefully for potential problems.

Non-Updateable Views

It is common to need to view information from the database without the need for updates. You are essentially building an "onscreen report." As long as you do not need to update the information, basing your block on a view is the best strategy. The view can be as complex as necessary including joins, embedded functions, and so forth. To create a screen report, your block should, in fact, be based on a view. The block should not be based on a table with a POST-QUERY trigger calculating your additional block items since this causes unnecessary network traffic. Having the structure of the block encapsulated in a view also promotes reusability of the structure in other forms or printed reports.

An example of a common situation where you might base blocks on non-updateable views is a query on customer activity. Assume you have three tables where customer activity is stored, structured as follows:

- **Contact Structure**   To record telephone calls and human interactions

- **Letter Structure**   To store details of all correspondence activity

- **Financial Structure**   To track monetary activity

You can create a view that is a union of all three structures sorted by date in order to display a chronological record of all activity associated with a particular customer.

Implementing a Block Based on a View

You build the block as if it were based on a table. The Data Block Wizard includes the columns from the view in the same way that it would for columns from a table. The only difference is the database restriction that you cannot perform DML on non-updateable views. If you need to perform INSERT, UPDATE, and DELETE operations on the tables in the view, you can use one of two strategies mentioned above: an updateable view or an Oracle8 INSTEAD OF trigger. Otherwise, you will be using the view as a non-updateable view.

For an updateable view, the only change you need to make in the form (after creating a block on the view in the same way as if it was a table) is to set the *Query Only* property to "Yes" for the items from the master (key-preserved) table. This means that these columns will not participate in DML but they will participate in queries. There is nothing special you need to set when defining a block for a non-updateable view or a view with INSTEAD OF triggers.

CAUTION
If your view restricts the rows available using the value of a column (such as "WHERE EMP.DEPTNO > 30"), an update of that column value (such as "DEPTNO = 20") could make the row unavailable to the view. This effect, not unique to Forms work, may be undesirable so you may want to write application code to restrict the values for columns that restrict rows in the view.

Properties That the Data Block Wizard Sets

It is useful to know which item and block properties the Data Block Wizard sets specially for tables and views so you know what to change if you need to modify the block. Basing a block on a table or view using the Data Block Wizard sets the block property *Query Data Source Name* to the name of the table or view. The *Query Data Source Type* property remains at its default of "Table". The *Query Data Source Columns* property is set to the names of the columns in the table or view. Figure 4-1 shows the column names in the *Query Data Source Columns* property.

This column list identifies the column names and datatypes that are returned from a query to the table or view in the database. While this list is useful, it is not critical to the block mechanism if the block is based on a table or view. It is critical for blocks based on procedures, as discussed later.

The Data Block Wizard also fills the item property *Column Name* with the name of the column that supplies the data for the item. This is also optional in most cases

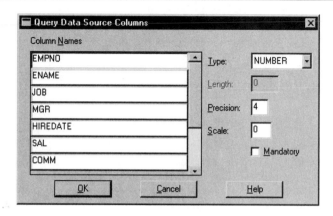

FIGURE 4-1. *Query Data Source Columns property*

because the Form Builder will use the name of the item as the name of the column when constructing the query or DML statement. For tables that use object columns (made of a number of elements) the syntax for the SQL statement uses dot notation to identify a column member. For example, the FIRST_NAME member of the PERSON object inside the EMPLOYEE table would be fully identified as EMPLOYEE.PERSON.FIRST_NAME in a SQL statement. The Data Block Wizard would construct an item named PERSON_FIRST_NAME and place the value "PERSON.FIRST_NAME" in the *Column Name* property of that item. The item name would not suffice as the column name in this case.

Another technique you can use in some circumstances is to base the source block on a view and base the DML target on one of the tables in that view. This allows you to directly update records in that single table. To accomplish this, set the *Query Only* property to "Yes" for all items in the block that are not associated with the table.

Basing a Block on a Procedure

Blocks can be based on PL/SQL procedures that return a REF CURSOR or PL/SQL table variable that contains one or many rows. You can also issue DML from the block to other procedures that will manipulate the records in the table based upon parameters that the block passes to the procedures. Basing a block on a procedure allows you to change everything about the query including the source or target tables. You can also use PL/SQL conditional and loop structures to manipulate values before returning them to the block. When the block issues DML statements, you can intercept them and use the same kind of logic to route the values the way you want. This gives you an enormous amount of flexibility and power beyond what is possible with SQL alone. It is useful to examine details on the two types of procedures that you can use to base a block on: a PL/SQL Table and a REF CURSOR.

PL/SQL Table Procedure

A block can be based on a procedure that returns a PL/SQL table. This is particularly useful when you want a block to display information that would otherwise require a very complex SQL query resulting in terrible performance.

As an example, assume you are using the data model shown in Figure 4-2. You want the block to have the employee names as the columns, one row for each calendar day, and each item in the block containing the total sales for that employee for that day. This requires a block to function as a crosstab report.

Trying to write a SQL query to support such a block would be a challenge to any developer. Once written, this query could take a long time to execute. One solution to this problem is to make the block a non-base table block with a complex client-side PL/SQL routine to populate the block one item at a time. A better approach is to make a PL/SQL procedure with a table as an IN/OUT parameter. This method is both relatively easy to use and easy to optimize performance.

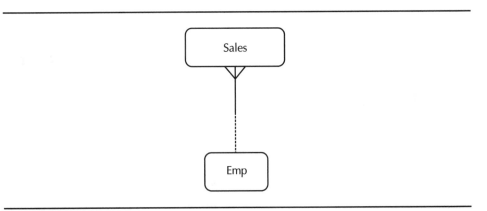

FIGURE 4-2. *Data model example*

REF CURSOR Procedure

A *cursor variable* (declared as a REF CURSOR datatype) points to a specific row in a query result set. When you want to perform a query, you declare the REF CURSOR and create a function that retrieves the rows into the cursor variable. A REF CURSOR is a pointer to a server-side cursor variable similar to pointers in C that are addresses to a memory location. The stored procedure returns a reference to an open cursor populated by the SELECT statement that is used as the data source for the block.

You can have one or more cursors stored in a PL/SQL procedure. You can then programmatically select which cursor is used to populate the block. The cursors must be pre-defined before runtime but you can modify the cursor using bind variables. You cannot define a REF CURSOR using DBMS_SQL so that the degree of flexibility is somewhat limited. A further limitation is that the REF CURSOR can only be a data source and not a data target, meaning that you cannot pass information back to the procedure through the REF CURSOR. For this reason, the effectiveness of REF CURSOR is limited. REF CURSORs are appropriately used with a block that may need to be based on one of several data sources, for example, in a multiple database environment, with the same table in different databases, or between development and test instances. You can programmatically switch between the two tables and quickly scan for differences. Everything that can be done using a REF CURSOR can also be done with greater flexibility using a FROM clause query as discussed later in this section.

The question remains of when to use a REF CURSOR instead of a FROM clause query. The answer is to use a REF CURSOR whenever you can. As you move from blocks based on tables or views to procedures that return REF CURSORs to blocks based on FROM clause queries, you increase flexibility. When a block is based on a table or view, you can modify the WHERE clause and the ORDER BY clause at runtime by setting block properties. With REF CURSORs, you can select from completely different queries and modify those queries using bind variables. With a FROM clause query, you can change the SELECT statement upon which the block is based at runtime. You should base your block on REF CURSORs whenever you only need the level of flexibility that REF CURSORs offer.

Implementing a Block Based on a Procedure

You can base a block on either type of procedure. The technique described next uses a cursor variable to retrieve rows into the block. The section called "Using a PL/SQL Table" describes the considerations for basing a block on a PL/SQL table. This technique shows an example of the join between the DEPT and the EMP tables.

The data requirement is simple enough that it could be filled with one of the other alternatives for block data sources, but is given so the requirement does not distract from the focus on the technique. There are two main focus areas of work: the procedure package and the form.

The Procedure Package

The cleanest way to create and manage the procedures you need for block data is with a package. You can name the package similarly to the table and it will implement an object-oriented-like set of methods used to access the table. The first step to creating the package is to declare type variables in the package specification as follows. (The comment header has been deleted to save space.)

```
PACKAGE empdept_maint
AS
    TYPE emp_t IS RECORD(
        empno       emp.empno%TYPE,
        job         emp.job%TYPE,
        hiredate    emp.hiredate%TYPE,
        deptno      dept.deptno%TYPE,
        dname       dept.dname%TYPE);

    -- For SELECT
    TYPE rc_empdept IS REF CURSOR
        RETURN emp_t;

    -- For the DML - a table of records
    TYPE t_empdept
        IS TABLE OF emp_t
        INDEX BY BINARY_INTEGER;
    --
    PROCEDURE slct(
        p_empqry IN OUT rc_empdept);
    --
    PROCEDURE ins(
        p_emprec IN OUT t_empdept);
    --
    PROCEDURE upd(
        p_emprec IN OUT t_empdept);
    --
    PROCEDURE del(
        p_emprec IN OUT t_empdept);
    --
    PROCEDURE lck(
        p_emprec IN OUT t_empdept);
    --
END;
```

This specification declares the types that are based on a record variable that represents the columns in the cursor, the REF CURSOR itself, and a PL/SQL table of records. The REF CURSOR is used as the return value for the SLCT procedure that queries the table. The PL/SQL table of records is used to pass values in and out of the DML and lock procedures.

NOTE
The DML and lock procedures must contain at least one table-of-records parameter because the form communicates to the procedures using arrays (tables of records).

The Package Body

The package body contains a procedure for each DML statement as well as one for the SELECT and LOCK statements. The following SLCT procedure used to query the records is excerpted from the package body.

```
PROCEDURE slct(
    p_empqry IN OUT rc_empdept)
IS
BEGIN
    -- This can be more complex and include conditional
    -- logic to select from one source or another.
    OPEN p_empqry
    FOR
       SELECT emp.empno,
              emp.job,
              emp.hiredate,
              emp.deptno,
              dept.dname
       FROM   emp emp, dept dept
       WHERE  emp.deptno = dept.deptno;
END;
```

You can also perform DML and lock statements for the form's records using other procedures in this package. The following shows an additional excerpt of the package. The INS procedure uses a loop through the record variable to check the records to be inserted. It checks that the department record that the employee record refers to is in the DEPT table (using a function not displayed here). It then inserts the EMP record using the values passed in from the form.

```
PROCEDURE ins(
    p_emprec IN OUT t_empdept)
IS
```

```
      v_message  VARCHAR2(100);
BEGIN
   FOR v_ct IN 1 .. p_emprec.count
   LOOP
      -- If the dept doesn't exist, insert it
      IF p_emprec(v_ct).deptno IS NOT NULL
      THEN
         IF dept_not_exists(p_emprec(v_ct).deptno)
         THEN
            v_message:= 'Insert of DEPT';
            INSERT INTO dept(
                     deptno,
                     dname)
            VALUES (p_emprec(v_ct).deptno,
                     p_emprec(v_ct).dname);
            -- Exception handling goes here. This might even
            -- be a separate procedure to do the insert.
            --
         END IF;
         --
         v_message := 'Insert of EMP';
         INSERT INTO emp(
            empno,
            job,
            hiredate,
            deptno)
         VALUES (
            p_emprec(v_ct).empno,
            p_emprec(v_ct).job,
            p_emprec(v_ct).hiredate,
            p_emprec(v_ct).deptno);
         -- add an exception handler here
      END IF;
   END LOOP;
EXCEPTION
   WHEN OTHERS
   THEN
      raise_application_error(-20002, 'Error: Inserting record ' ||
         'using EMPDEPT_MAINT.INS. Inform Technical Support. '||
         v_message);
END;
```

Other DML statements would follow the same pattern of looping through the table of records and performing the DML statement using the values in a row of the table of records. The following is the LCK procedure that locks all records in the table of records.

```
PROCEDURE lck(
    p_emprec IN OUT t_empdept)
IS
    v_empno      emp.empno%TYPE;
BEGIN
    FOR v_ct IN 1 .. p_emprec.count
    LOOP
        SELECT empno
        INTO   v_empno
        FROM   emp
        WHERE  empno = p_emprec(v_ct).empno
        FOR UPDATE;
    END LOOP;
END;
```

Forms Work

Once you have written and installed the PL/SQL package to support the block, you are ready to create a block based on the packaged procedures. In the Data Block Wizard, you select Stored Procedure in the Type page. On the Query page, enter the name of the REF CURSOR procedure (such as EMPDEPT_MAINT.SLCT). The columns in that REF CURSOR will appear after you click the Refresh button, as Figure 4-3 shows.

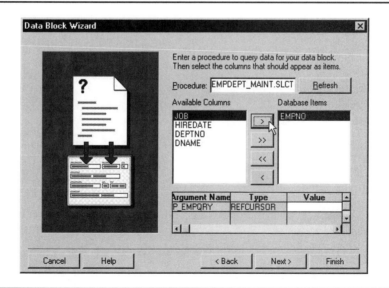

FIGURE 4-3. *Selecting columns from a query procedure*

You set the Insert, Update, Delete, and Lock pages that follow the Query page in a similar way using the names of the corresponding procedures in your package. The Data Block Wizard will assign the values for the block properties as shown in Table 4-1.

In addition, the Layout Wizard will create items based on the columns in the query procedure's REF CURSOR variable. When you compile the form, the compiler will create block-level procedures called INSERT-PROCEDURE, UPDATE-PROCEDURE, DELETE-PROCEDURE, and LOCK-PROCEDURE. These

Property	Notes and "Values"
Query Data Source Type	"Procedure"
Query Data Source Name	The name of the SELECT procedure (prefaced by the package name)
Query Data Source Columns	The list of columns in the SELECT procedure's REF CURSOR
Query Data Source Arguments	The name of the REF CURSOR declared as the main parameter of the SELECT procedure
DML Data Target Type	"Procedure"
Insert Procedure Name	The name of the INSERT procedure
Insert Procedure Result Set Columns	The list of columns from the table of records used as a parameter to the INSERT procedure
Insert Procedure Arguments	The name of the table-of-records parameter used for the INSERT procedure.
Update Procedure Name, Update Procedure Result Set Columns, Update Procedure Arguments	The same type of contents as the corresponding properties for INSERT
Delete Procedure Name, Delete Procedure Result Set Columns, Delete Procedure Arguments	The same type of contents as the corresponding properties for INSERT
Lock Procedure Name, Lock Procedure Result Set Columns, Lock Procedure Arguments	The same type of contents as the corresponding properties for INSERT

TABLE 4-1. *Block Properties Assigned by the Data Block Wizard*

contain code to call the procedures you associated with the block in the Data Block Wizard. The following is sample code from an INSERT-PROCEDURE trigger:

```
DECLARE
bk_data EMPDEPT_MAINT.T_EMPDEPT;
BEGIN
PLSQL_TABLE.POPULATE_TABLE(bk_data, 'EMP', PLSQL_TABLE.INSERT_RECORDS);
EMPDEPT_MAINT.INS(bk_data);
END;
```

These triggers are maintained by the Forms compiler. If you make a change to the trigger, it will be lost the next time the form compiles. This is why you do not need to worry about formatting this code even though Forms will not generate it according to your code formatting standards.

TIP
Always use the Data Block Wizard to populate the block properties when working with procedures for a block. The wizard will set the properties correctly based on the inputs you provide in the wizard's pages. You can try to set the properties manually, but it is possible that you or the Form compiler will miss something and you will get unexpected results. This can be avoided if you use the Data Block Wizard.

Queries
The Query-By-Example feature allows the user to place the form into Enter Query mode, enter query conditions in the items, and execute the query to retrieve rows from the database. When you base a block on a table, Forms Runtime creates a SELECT statement from the items in the block and constructs a WHERE clause based on query conditions that the user enters in Enter Query mode.

When you base a block on a procedure, Forms Runtime will not create the normal SELECT statement so query conditions the user enters in Enter Query mode will have no effect. However, you can write code to emulate some of the functionality of the Query-By-Example feature. The code requires a change in the SLCT procedure and a change in the form.

If you want to use additional parameters for the DML and lock procedures, you can follow the same steps for those procedures. When you are considering what query criteria to allow the user to use, be careful that the SQL statements that use those criteria are as efficient as possible. Otherwise, you can experience a degradation in performance over what you would see if the block was based only on a table.

CHANGING THE SLCT PROCEDURE   You need to pass parameters to the procedure that you can work into the query's WHERE clause. Consider that you want to allow the user to query by entering the first few characters of the JOB column. You would create parameters for the job value as shown in the following procedure declaration:

```
PROCEDURE slct(
    p_empqry    IN OUT rc_empdept,
    p_job       IN emp.job%TYPE);
```

You also need to add the parameter to the WHERE clause of the query in the SLCT procedure body as follows:

```
AND    job LIKE p_job || '%';
```

This code will retrieve records from the tables if the parameter value is in the first part of the job title value. You can construct other scenarios to fit the queries that you decide to support. You can also pass additional parameters and work them into the query in the same way.

> **NOTE**
> *If you change the procedure while the form is open, you may have to reconnect to the database or close and reopen Form Builder to be able to see the changes.*

CHANGING THE FORM   As before, you work in the Data Block Wizard. Select the block in the Object Navigator and choose **Tools→Data Block Wizard** from the menu. On the Query tab page, click the Refresh button and the new parameter will appear, as shown here.

Argument Name	Type	Value
P_EMPQRY	REFCURSOR	
P_JOB	VARCHAR2	

The new parameter will pop up in the arguments list. You have to supply a value for the argument in the Value column. In this example, the value column is the value that the user has filled into the JOB item, so you reference that value using the syntax: :BLOCK.ITEM (or :EMP.JOB in this example). This is the only step required in the form. Now, when the user runs the form, any value entered into the JOB item will be matched with the wildcard in the procedure's query.

CAUTION

If you receive an ORA-03114 error when accessing a procedure in an Oracle8i NT server from an Oracle Developer release 6 form, you should check with Technical Support for the availability of a patch for Oracle8 bug number 939287.

Using a PL/SQL Table

The first step in implementing a block based on a PL/SQL table is to create a package to hold the required procedure (as with the REF CURSOR). Then declare a record type and a PL/SQL table type. In the package spec, you may want to declare one or more variables that can be used to pass information to the PL/SQL procedure. Properties must be set the same way as for the REF CURSOR (as listed in Table 4-1), except, instead of using the REF CURSOR's columns and parameter names, you use the PL/SQL table's columns and parameter names.

As with the REF CURSOR, you should use the Data Block Wizard to load the properties since everything must be typed correctly or the block will not populate. Then, in the code to populate the block, assign the package variables with an EXECUTE_QUERY command on the block as usual.

When you use a PL/SQL table as the data source, you use the same procedures for INSERT, UPDATE, and DELETE as you do for the REF CURSOR. The additional DML procedures are a very powerful feature but they may be rarely used.

NOTE

The package for the PL/SQL table can reside either in the form (in a program unit or attached library) or in the server. Blocks built based on PL/SQL tables are usually placed client-side during development and then moved to the server for deployment, if appropriate. However, since you can base a block on a PL/SQL table that is local to the form, you can programmatically load that PL/SQL table from any source (database or not). Thus you can use Forms' built-in query mechanism to load a block based on data that you construct programmatically.

The only tricky part of this method is creating the PL/SQL table of records. Prior to using this method, you should build a trivial procedure that returns a small PL/SQL table to familiarize yourself with the necessary steps.

Basing a Block on a FROM Clause Query

You can also base a block on a query statement, called a *FROM clause query*. This is useful if you want to test a SELECT statement for a block or if you cannot create views easily because of database privilege restrictions or company policy. It is particularly useful for CONNECT BY queries when you need to change the START WITH clause at runtime. The effect of this technique is to create an unnamed query-only view in the form. Any SELECT statement that you can create is suitable source material for a block. The items you create in the block are based on the columns returned by the SELECT statement. Using a FROM clause query allows you to completely change the SQL statement upon which a block is based at runtime.

This feature implements the ability of SQL in Oracle7 and Oracle8 to include a SELECT statement in the FROM clause. For example, the following shows how a SELECT statement can be embedded in the FROM table list:

```
SELECT  e.ename, d.dname, s.salary, s.start_date
FROM    emp e,
        dept d,
          (SELECT  salary, start_date, empno
           FROM    emp_sal
           WHERE   saldate > SYSDATE - 90) s
WHERE   e.deptno = d.deptno
AND     e.empno = s.empno
```

This query in the FROM clause acts just as a view would—as a source for data and for joining with other tables.

FROM clause query blocks only allow queries. You cannot UPDATE, INSERT, or DELETE in them. Frequently, you can set a specific table as the DML target, depending upon the FROM clause query. Anything that can be done with a REF CURSOR can be done using FROM clause queries.

There is a performance impact to using FROM clause queries that REF CURSORs are not subject to. A FROM clause query is implemented as a SELECT from SELECT statement. Rather than using a table name for the SELECT statement, the query that supports populating the block is of the form:

```
SELECT  <all columns in block>
FROM    <Query Data Source Name property>
```

The *Query Data Source Name* property contains the SELECT statement used as the data source. Using FROM clause queries, you can easily create an application allowing you to view the contents of any columns in any table. If you are particularly ambitious, this capability could be used to build a rudimentary ad hoc query tool. With the exception of query-only blocks based on recursive tables, FROM clause query blocks are rarely used.

As mentioned earlier, FROM clause queries are somewhat more flexible. However, because they are implemented as "SELECT FROM (SELECT ...)" queries, they may take longer to execute. FROM clause queries should only be used when the application requires this level of flexibility and cannot be supported by basing the block on a table, view, or procedure that returns a REF CURSOR.

Implementing a Block Based on a FROM Clause

Creating a block from a SELECT statement is just a matter of changing a few properties from the usual values. There are two ways to do this. The hard way, which you will have to use in some cases, is to use the steps shown next.

The Hard Method

Although this method contains more steps and is more time consuming, you may need to use it if there is no table or view that you can use as a model for the block. The steps for the hard method follow.

1. Create the block manually and change its name to describe its purpose.

2. Change the block's *Query Data Source Type* property to "FROM clause query". This value is one of the allowed values for this property as the following shows.

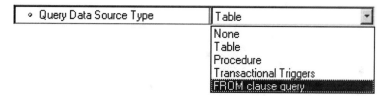

3. Change the block's *Query Data Source Name* property to the SELECT statement. You can optionally fill in the *Query Data Source Columns* with the names of the columns in the SELECT statement.

4. Create items with names based on the columns in the SELECT statement.

5. Flag an appropriate item as the primary key by changing the item's *Primary Key* property to "Yes".

6. Set the item properties for *Prompt, Data Type, Maximum Length, Canvas, Required,* and other properties to appropriate values.

The Easy Method

You can save much work in the layout and property-setting steps by creating a block based on a table using the Data Block Wizard for step 1. You would then perform steps 2 and 3, skip step 4, and clean up the appropriate properties and names in steps 5 and 6. This is much faster and you will be more likely to correctly set values for necessary properties. Remember that the Data Block Wizard adds a value to the *Column Name* property. Therefore, if you name a column in the SELECT statement differently from the column in the table you based the block on, you will have to change the *Column Name* property as well.

How Does the Query Work?

Although there are many more manual steps to complete this method, you have complete flexibility in constructing the SELECT statement that the form will use. When the form queries the database, it will construct a SQL statement with the following format:

```
SELECT    item1_column_name, item2_column_name, …
FROM      (SELECT statement in the Query Data Source Name property)
WHERE     (WHERE Clause property)
ORDER BY  (ORDER BY Clause property)
```

How Does DML Work?

There is a block property *DML Target Name* in the Advanced Database section that allows you to specify a data target for DML separately from the query source. If you leave this property blank, the form will use the name in the *Query Data Source Name* as the DML target. In the case of an updateable view or INSTEAD OF trigger view, this default behavior works because the query source is an actual object that can have DML issued to it.

In the case of a FROM clause query (sometimes misleadingly called a Sub-Query in the help system), the data source is a SELECT statement and issuing DML to a SELECT statement does not make sense. Therefore, you get an error message if you use a FROM clause query and do fill in the *DML Target Name* property. If you want to use DML on a block with a FROM clause query, you can specify a table or view name in the *DML Target Name* and turn off the DML for columns that the SELECT statement constructs. In the example, you would make the following changes in the form:

- Set the *DML Data Target Name* as "EMP". The *DML Target Type* is left as the default "Table".

- Set the *Query Only* property of the HIRE_TYPE item to "Yes" to indicate that this item participates only in the queries but not in the DML.

Programmatic Control

You can use the SET_BLOCK_PROPERTY built-in to change the DML target and the query source for the block programmatically as follows:

```
SET_BLOCK_PROPERTY('block_name', QUERY_DATA_SOURCE_NAME,
    'name_of_source');
```

In this example, *block_name* is the name of your block and *name_of_source* is the value (table or view name or SELECT statement) for the *Query Data Source Name* property. This is documented to work only if the value of the *Data Query Source Type* property is not "Transactional Triggers".

You can change the DML target using the same built-in with the same format but with the DML_TARGET_NAME property. This is documented to work only if the *DML Data Target Type* is set to "Table". Be sure to commit and clear the block before attempting to change any of these properties programmatically.

CAUTION
If you are typing a FROM clause query in the Property Palette, this can be done normally (SELECT... FROM ....WHERE...). However, if you are populating the property using a SET_BLOCK_ PROPERTY built-in at runtime, you must pass the query enclosed in parentheses. When you are typing the property in using the Property Palette, Forms adds the parentheses automatically. For example, if your query was "SELECT empno, ename FROM emp" you would pass the string "(SELECT empno, ename FROM emp)" to the SET_BLOCK_PROPERTY built-in.

Basing a Block on Transactional Triggers

It is possible to base a block on a view (or table) and then override the default INSERT, UPDATE, DELETE, and LOCK operations that Forms usually uses with any PL/SQL procedure written by the developer. This is effectively the same functionality supported through INSTEAD OF trigger views. However, if you provide this functionality within the application, you have failed to encapsulate the logic in the view (where it properly belongs) and instead are calling the code from within the application.

The only reason to use this functionality is if you are attaching to a non-Oracle database. This functionality may also be required as the shift to object-relational databases is made when these procedures would correspond to the associated methods in the object table. Further discussion of this topic is beyond the scope of this book.

Implementing a Block Based on Transactional Triggers

Set the *Query Data Source Type* and *DML Data Target Type* properties to "Transactional Triggers" and write the ON- triggers required to perform all SQL to the table or tables represented by items.

CHAPTER
5

Forms GUI Standards

...There is nothing for which we have no standard.
—Leo Nikolaevich Tolstoi (1828–1910), *War and Peace*

his chapter will discuss how a form looks and is designed as well as how that design can be implemented. To some extent, this entire book is a guide to using the Oracle Developer product in the best ways possible to create forms and reports with the desired look and feel. This chapter will explore some of the foundational principles of forms development standards to guide developers when building forms.

The importance of standards cannot be overstated. Without a formal, coherent set of standards, every form is a custom development project built from the ground up. Developers can spend hours deciding how to lay out the screen, what color to use, what GUI objects to use and so forth. One developer in an organization may end up with applications having a very different look and feel than those created by a second developer in that same organization. Code will be inconsistent, meaning that only the person who created the form will understand the development philosophy behind it.

The only way to create a consistent, well-designed application using multiple developers in a reasonable amount of time is to have a detailed, formal set of standards that are rigorously enforced. With such standards in place, a large part of any development effort should be straightforward. Developers should not be making decisions about how to perform common tasks but merely implementing the established set of standards. Simple master-detail relationships among blocks, reference value lookups, and navigation between forms should all have established standards, perhaps with supporting underlying template objects.

The only types of design decisions developers should make are for non-standard portions of a form. For example, in a payroll application, the routine used to calculate a paycheck would be specific to that application and needs to be custom developed.

The Forms Development Process

In order for forms to be efficient and to achieve user acceptance, it is critical to have an established set of GUI standards as guidelines. Forms developers should have an idea about the overall look and feel of the forms they create before beginning the design process. The goal is to allow users to easily manipulate forms to retrieve the desired information. The screen shown in Figure 5-1 illustrates how the effective use of GUI standards allows a lot of information to be shown on the screen in a clear and systematic way.

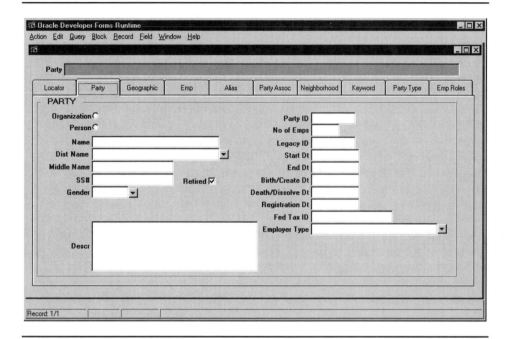

FIGURE 5-1. *Sample tabbed form*

In the authors' vision of the development process, a form goes through three phases:

- Non-functional storyboard
- Semi-functional prototype
- Production form

This applies to organizations creating forms in Oracle Developer as well as those generating forms using Oracle Designer. A description of each phase follows.

Phase 1—Non-Functional Storyboard

The first step for building the form is to create a storyboard of the entire form. A storyboard is a non-functioning (or semi-functional) prototype of a form that can be built very quickly to demonstrate the look and feel of the proposed application. Storyboards allow users to envision the look and feel of the application prior to its development.

The main function of storyboards is to communicate an understanding to the users of how the completed system will work. As little time as possible should be spent on these storyboards since it is highly likely that your vision of the system will change before going forward. There should be no button functionality added. The only working portions of these storyboard screens should be navigation buttons to move from one screen to another. Even this may not be necessary since a storyboard review can be done using printouts of the screens.

There are some advantages to this approach since users can jot down notes on each page. Having users review these initial storyboards is critical in helping them crystallize their thinking. New requirements or even previously ignored business areas may be discovered as a part of this process. This can be a valuable analysis phase tool. Since they can be quickly and easily built, storyboards can be used at a detail level to communicate back to a user what was elicited in a single interview.

The entire system should be storyboarded, including all of the reports that will be a part of the system being developed. As mentioned in Chapter 17, forms' and reports' functionality should overlap and should not be considered separately. Developers should go through as many iterations as necessary with users until users sign off on the non-functional storyboards. No code should be written until users are satisfied with the storyboards.

Non-functional storyboards can be created following a specific set of techniques, which are Developer-centric by definition. Creating these storyboards should take place concurrently with database design. Initial project storyboards should be built using Oracle Forms so that they can be fully developed into completed applications later in the process.

In building the storyboards, you need to select the appropriate template. This entails making a few decisions such as:

- Will the form use a tab canvas or not?

- Will there be a header area?

- Is the form used for navigation?

Once these decisions are made, the storyboards can be created as simple forms based entirely on control blocks and not even requiring a database to run. As the design of the system matures, the control blocks will be replaced by the appropriate base table blocks. At this point, the forms will either be built using Developer or generated using Oracle Designer, depending upon the development method selected.

This approach to storyboards fits in with the way the authors think about system design including generic models and overloaded items. Large, complex systems may be built with fewer tables and many fewer applications. For example, one of the authors encountered a system to support document workflow management with 600 tables and about the same number of Oracle Forms programs with limited functionality. When redesigned using generic modeling techniques, the new system had less than 100 database tables (many of which were already supported by pre-built reusable components) and only a dozen or so forms. In addition, the new system included more functionality than the old one and was much easier to maintain. This illustrates the benefits of using a generic approach to Forms development.

Using this generic approach leads to the development of fewer, but much more complex forms. Therefore, there is less incentive to move to Oracle Designer generation and fewer reasons for using automated testing tools. Additionally, this approach eliminates the need for an army of Forms developers to create large systems with hundreds of forms since fewer individual applications are necessary. However, depending upon the data modeling approach used, building applications this way may not make sense for every organization.

Phase 2—Semi-Functional Prototype

A semi-functional prototype is a working form built using all of your standard template reusable components. Blocks will be hooked to base tables, navigation between forms should be enabled, and reference value lookups should be included. During this phase, only the portions of the application that can be built quickly and cheaply should be created. No custom development should be done at this point.

The purpose of this prototype is to give users a sense of what the final application will do. It has been the authors' experience that until users can see how applications operate against real data, the quality of the user feedback is limited. It is expected that when users interact with the semi-functional prototype, significant changes will be suggested. Changes at this point in the process are still relatively inexpensive.

When the data model is complete and your storyboards have been approved by the users, it is useful to add an artificial stopping place to the development process before the major development phase begins. One of two steps should be taken next:

- In Oracle Developer, you can build prototype applications.

- In Oracle Designer, all phase II prototypes should be generated. It is beyond the scope of this book to include a discussion of the application generation process in Oracle Designer; see *Oracle Designer Generation* (Atkins, Dirksen, and Ince; Oracle Press, 1999) if you would like to explore the application generation process further.

Some portion of the data migration should have been done by this time so that real data is available in the database. If no real data is available, you can use an automatic sample data creation utility, which fills up the database with sample data. Sample data is not ideal but is adequate to give users a feel for how the applications will work when completed. Users like to see data. It is much easier to understand an application when users can see real data and they may take their review of the application more seriously. Even though the applications are not much farther along than the storyboards were, users must face the realization that these are close to what the final applications will look like. Any complaints or requests for changes must be addressed at this point in the process.

At this point, all base table blocks should be hooked to real database tables. Therefore, all base table items should be associated with their appropriate database columns. Many post-query triggers should be written so that all items in all query blocks populate with the appropriate information. You don't have to have all of the post-query items working for this review. However, the majority of them should be in place, especially where they are necessary for understanding the purpose of the block.

It is also a good idea to make a working LOV to demonstrate this functionality within the system. LOVs with many records should have the *Filter Before Display* property set to "Yes" to allow the user to type in a few characters and return the relevant records.

Even in this second phase of adding functionality, there is still a high probability that the system will change. You don't want to write complex routines at this point. For example, it is too early in the process to be able to aggregate business events to generate journal transactions for an accounting system or write database triggers that update inventory when sales occur in a retail system. At this point, user sign-off is meaningful since users should have a clear idea what the system will look like and how it will work. This is the last opportunity to make substantive changes before the system is fully developed.

Phase 3—Production Form

From the start, you will need to recognize that the production system that is completed is really Version 1 of the ultimate system. You should not try to make the system perfect at this point. It is more important to create a fully functioning system and then go back to make improvements. The phased implementation of the system will reveal any remaining critical problems. Like most software, the first version will need more work before the users are completely satisfied.

Guidelines for Forms Development

There are some important guidelines to keep in mind when developing forms. This section will describe some of the standards, techniques, and tips that the authors have gathered in their experience in using the Forms component of Oracle Developer in real projects.

The Size of the Form

One of the most important aspects of Forms development is managing the size of the forms you create. You can build an entire system using one form with dozens of windows, canvases, and blocks. There are a number of reasons not to do this. First, Oracle Forms, as a product, is not structured to accommodate this type of thinking. You cannot partition a form nicely by grouping blocks together or organizing canvases or windows into a hierarchical structure. The only method for grouping program units is to place them into packages. Trying to place too much functionality into a form causes the same kinds of code organizational problems as writing a long program with only global variables.

Second, performance will suffer with larger forms. The larger the form, the longer it takes to load. These performance impacts will occur each time the form is loaded. In a web environment, these larger forms will consume more memory resources, thus requiring a larger, more powerful application server.

Third, the Form Builder component of Oracle Developer is less stable with very large forms and will quit unexpectedly more often in the development environment. However, Forms is very stable in the runtime environment. Large forms are particularly problematic in a Windows 95 environment. It may not be possible to open and edit a very large form in a poorly tuned Windows 95 environment.

For all of these reasons, you should carefully manage the size of your forms. Usually, each window will be its own form (potentially with multiple canvases). Exceptions to this may be forms that call a pop-up window alert, multi-selection tool, or wizard-like object.

All code spanning multiple forms should be placed in libraries attached to the forms where appropriate. Even with the multitab environment illustrated in the form shown in Figure 5-1, forms will still have a tendency to get very large. The larger a form, the harder it will be to maintain and debug and the less stable the behavior of the Form Builder component of the product will be.

Screen Resolution and Monitor Size

There are two separate monitor types to be concerned with when developing forms: the development monitor and the monitor that the forms will be deployed on. These are two independent issues.

Screen Resolution for Development

If you have precisely defined your GUI standards, there is no reason to design applications on the same size screen as that used to deploy them. In fact, this is a bad idea. You should always develop on the largest screen possible. This way, you will have sufficient screen real estate to have the Object Navigator, Layout Model, Property Palette, and PL/SQL Editor all open at the same time. Given current monitor prices, all developers should be using 21-inch monitors running at 1600 × 1280 resolution unless this makes items too small to be easily seen. Developers should work at as high a resolution as is comfortable. With some video cards, it is now possible to support multiple monitors simultaneously. This would allow you to place the Layout Model on one monitor and the Object Navigator, Property Palette, and PL/SQL Editor on the other. The authors have not seen this technique implemented yet, but it would improve developer productivity.

Forms is inherently a multi-window product. Working on a lower resolution monitor requires repeated toggling from one open window to another. This is a slower and more inconvenient way to work. Given the current developer labor rates worldwide, it is easy to cost-justify the purchase of a 21-inch monitor to improve developer productivity and efficiency.

TIP
The higher the resolution you can build at, the lower your development cost.

Screen Resolution for Deployment

The higher the resolution for deployment, the easier it will be to lay out your screens. Over the years, the standard lowest resolution monitor to support has moved from 640 × 480 to 800 × 600 to today's 1,024 × 768 resolution. With some clients willing to invest in larger monitors, screens can be built at 1,280 × 1,024.

As the resolution increases, more screen real estate becomes available. Screen layout is easier and requires less precision. Fewer screens will be required resulting in more user-friendly applications developed for less cost. Unless you are building an application to support hundreds of users, it is almost always worthwhile to build the cost of monitors that support 1,024 × 768 into the budget. A complex system built for a small number of users should be designed for 1,280 × 1,024 resolution with every user given a 21-inch monitor.

It is important to recognize that screen resolution must go hand in hand with monitor size. The highest practical resolution for developing on various monitors is shown in Table 5-1.

Monitor Size	Resolution
15-inch	800 × 600
17-inch	1,024 × 1,168
20- or 21-inch	1,280 × 1,024

TABLE 5-1. *Suggested Screen Resolutions for Development*

The only place where screen resolution remains a problem is for public applications deployed on the Web. For these uses, applications must be adapted to the browsers and Java runtime engines utilized by most of the users.

Screen Real Estate

Conservation of screen real estate is extremely important in Forms design. Screen real estate is the developer's most precious commodity. It is very easy to lose lots of screen space by not being careful about where things go. The way to minimize wasted screen space is to think carefully about each item's placement.

There are two schools of thought about open space in a screen design. One faction believes that users are intimidated by many elements on a screen whereas others believe that you should try to fit as much information as possible on one screen to maximize the efficiency of user operations. In general, if a form is used very frequently, it makes sense to place more information on the form and spend some extra time training users. However, if the form is only used occasionally, you might want to leave more blank space in order to make the form appear less intimidating.

For example, in a multi-record block, don't leave space between items. A wise old moving man once told me about how to load a truck. You start at the back and fill it up from floor to ceiling in a layer. Then work forward, doing one layer at a time. Screens should be built the same way in horizontal layers starting at the top and working your way down.

As you identify each block or area, lay it out horizontally to maximize the use of screen space.

Instead of laying out fields with labels above, which wastes vertical space, place the labels to the left of the fields.

Here are some ways to maximize screen real estate:

- **Don't put titles on screens.** Put the title on the window. Unfortunately, many users are not used to reading window titles. If you are using window titles to save screen real estate, users will need to be trained to pay attention to window titles.

- **Space horizontal items carefully.** For horizontal items, stack the labels horizontally next to the item and move them two points away. The recommended space between horizontal items is 10 points.

For multi-record frames, it is important to decide how many rows are realistically needed. If the user will be looking at a large table, it is desirable to get as many records on the screen as possible. For example, in an employee list, seeing as many records as possible improves the usability of the form. However, if looking at attached printers for PCs where 90% have only one choice, 5% have two, 5% may have three to four, it doesn't make any sense to display 10 records on the screen. Blocks should only display as many records as are appropriate for the application. Having a multi-record block with 15 records when there are never more than two or three items in the block unnecessarily clutters the screen while providing no additional functionality.

If there is lots to look at, try to let the user see as much as possible on one screen. From the user's perspective, a crowded screen is usually better than a less useful screen or more than one screen. However, this is a stylistic decision. In SQL*Forms 3.0, the authors had the experience of encountering five screen applications which, through re-engineering, fit on one screen without the use of tabs.

For records with a long text item (for example, a note, comment, or description), a good way to handle this is to divide the screen into two parts, as shown in Figure 5-2. The top part displays the important items (all records). The bottom part shows the note, comment, or description associated with the selected item. This can be done by setting the *Items Displayed* property on the Property Palette to "1."

Field Placement
Proper field placement allows the developer to fit a lot of information on one screen. There are two basic types of layouts: tabular and form-like.

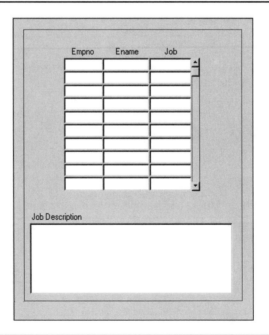

FIGURE 5-2. *Divided screen*

TABULAR LAYOUT   Figure 5-3 shows a screen designed with a tabular layout. Tabular layouts should be used whenever possible. They are neat, concise, and allow you to display a large number of records. Each field is stacked together horizontally and lined up at the top vertically. Labels are placed on top lined up with the left side of the field (or the right side if the field shows numeric information). If the label is too long for the field, elevate the label, drawing a line between the label and its corresponding field, as shown in the check box section on the right side of the form in Figure 5-3.

FORM-LIKE LAYOUT   Figure 5-1 is an example of a form-like layout. This layout is used when there is too much information to be shown in a tabular layout. Form-like layouts are more difficult to design. It is very easy to end up with a screen that is hard to read. That is why great care must be used in aligning fields from top to bottom. Notice how in Figure 5-1, most fields are either left-aligned or right-aligned with one another. This gives the form an orderly appearance that is easy for the user to work with.

   The screen shown in Figure 5-1 was designed for a display using 800 × 600 resolution. You should develop in the highest resolution possible, allowing you to fit even more information on the screen. This makes proper screen layout even more important.

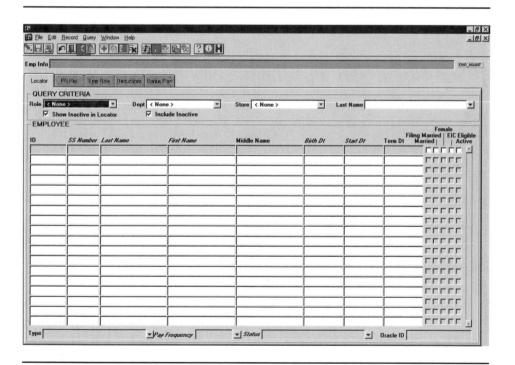

FIGURE 5-3.   *Example of a tabular layout*

Buttons

Buttons shouldn't be any larger than they need to be. They need to show the label plus a few extra points on each side. In a row of buttons, they don't all need to be the same size. For example, an Exit button doesn't need to be as large as an Execute Query button. With a multi-record block displaying three records, try to make it display five instead. This means getting 66% more information on the screen. It is important to get user input in laying out the screen. Take this input and go back to the Layout Editor to move things around as needed.

Putting buttons across the bottom of the screen minimizes waste of vertical space. Standard buttons only take up 17 points.

Poplists and LOVs

Poplists are a major space-saving device. Using a poplist, only enough space for one record to be displayed must be allocated. The poplist will then show as many records as needed when selected. A practical limit for poplists is 200 records. It is too cumbersome to scroll through a list of much more than this. However, there is a solution for this problem. If there are too many records to go into a poplist and a better search facility is needed, an LOV can be used (as mentioned in Chapter 16).

Logos

In general, logos and fancy graphics should be avoided. They take up a lot of space and have very little use. Certainly, internal forms within organizations do not need logos. People who work there don't need to see the company logo on every form. For forms going to outsiders, graphics and logos can be placed on a welcome screen rather than eating up memory, functionality, and space on the working forms.

If users require a logo on every screen, try to discourage them. If they insist, use a low resolution or line art graphic that does not require lengthy loading time on every screen. Chapter 25 discusses a strategy for loading image items at runtime.

NOTE
Just because you have sized a multi-megabyte image to a one-inch square does not decrease the length of loading time for the image.

Items: Fonts, Colors, and Properties

Determining the appropriate fonts and colors for your items is actually quite important. It governs how much room you will have on your screen. If you pick a 14-point font for your items when a 10-point font would have been adequate, you will be able to fit 10-20% less information on your screen. When you are trying to fit that last field on the screen, you will be very happy that you selected a smaller font.

Care should be taken when selecting fonts to make sure that they are large enough to be comfortably read by the system users on their computers. Prior to creating a GUI standard, you should build a prototype application and make sure that it is suitable for all users on the actual equipment where the system will be deployed.

Selecting the right height for an item is a matter of trial and error. One strategy is to make ten fields, each one a slightly (one pixel) different height. That way you can find the one that is exactly the right height at runtime. Make sure you test that letters with tails are not cut off on the bottom.

You will have to determine the correct height of a multiline item the same way as for simple text items. A two-line item is not twice the height of a one-line item. You want the multiline item to be exactly the right height to display the desired number of rows. If you don't size the multiline item correctly, it will appear as if an extra line could fit into the box, indicating incorrectly to users that they are looking at the entire contents of the textbox.

The width of text items is a little tricky because the standard proportional fonts (such as MS Sans Serif) use characters with different widths. For code items that are one to three characters wide, it is a simple decision to make the item as wide as necessary to accommodate any three letters ("WWW" is as wide as any character combination). For longer items, it makes little sense to make the item wide enough to accommodate all "W's." For items that are 20-30 characters wide, using all "W's" would result in an item that is over twice as big as necessary. For basic text items where you can reasonably expect a mixture of letters, you can use sequential numbers to estimate the correct width. For example, for a 20-character item, you should make it wide enough to fit:

12345678901234567890

Notice how much smaller it is than 20 "W's."

WWWWWWWWWWWWWWWWWWWW

It is probably still a little too big as the first 20 characters of this sentence only reach as far as the first 14 numbers, but it is better to err on the side of caution.

Color Palette

Restricting applications to the basic Windows 16 colors is not acceptable for a user-friendly application. Two hundred fifty-six colors provide adequate variety for a robust application and will likely appear more or less the same from client to client. If your application demands many subtle colors, you will need to test your GUI standards carefully on various systems to ensure that color selections are appropriate for all deployment machines. You should be particularly careful using colors to indicate meaning on screen since your system may be unusable by color-blind individuals.

For color of the text foreground and background, you will need to make sure that the text is readable both with the main color as background as well as with the color when the item text is selected. You will need to decide on what different kinds of colors you want. You can use different colors for editable items, non-editable items, and current record visual attributes. All text data is usually black.

The effective and consistent use of color on labels and fields helps to convey functionality to the user. Table 5-2 shows the colors used in the examples by item type.

As for suggested fonts, Times New Roman 12 point Regular can be used for data and Times New Roman 12 point Bold can be used for labels. These are good choices since this font is supported by most systems and programs.

Using the information shown in Table 5-2, users can look at the screen and determine essential functionality about it without knowing anything about the application system.

Object Type	Functionality	Color
Item	Enterable	White
Item	Display Only	Gray
Label	Mandatory	Blue/Underlined
Label	Optional	Black
Record	Current Record	Yellow

TABLE 5-2. *Colors Used to Convey Functionality*

Text, Labels, Lines, and Rectangles

Appropriate text, lines, and so on are dependent upon your chosen look and feel for the application. It is useful to place a frame around blocks and other logical groupings.

Using the label color to indicate required items is preferable to changing the color of the items themselves. It is less obtrusive to the visual flow of the application and it is just as easy for the users to recognize. For users who are color blind, you need to use an alternate cue in addition to changing the color of the label. Italicizing the label or adding additional characters such as an asterisk or greater or less than sign is another way to indicate a required field.

Forms Layout Editor Tips and Techniques

There are many ways to accomplish the same task in Oracle Forms. Different developers have different styles. This section will guide you through the process of building a form. Trying to use Oracle Forms without some experience or guidance is often not very productive. A senior developer working from a clean storyboard can lay out a form, create the necessary blocks, hook items to the blocks, and have the form production-ready in about 20 minutes per screen. A less experienced developer may need an hour or more to lay out the same screen. A junior developer who may even have several years of experience with the product but hasn't yet mastered the tricks and techniques may take four to eight hours to lay out the same screen. Using Oracle Forms efficiently, you can go from a base template to a partially functioning prototype of a complex application in half a day.

What are the differences between the developer who can create screens in 20 minutes and the developer who needs four to eight hours to lay out the same screen? Here are some of the reasons:

- The faster developer understands the function of the form from a business perspective. It is critical for developers to understand all of the items in the application before they begin coding. This can be enforced by having developers explain what the application does.

- Developers also need to have an idea of the cardinality (number of records) associated with each item. This greatly influences how forms are laid out.

Consider the example of a master-detail relationship between items such as equipment assigned to a person and components of that equipment. If a person has more than one or two pieces of equipment assigned to him or her and each piece of equipment has many components, you may want to have the master block display three to four records and have the detail block display as many as possible. If this is a scientific operation where each technician is assigned 20-30 pieces of equipment, you may not need to know about the associated components (or there may be very few). In this case, the master block should display as many records as possible and the detail block display only a few.

■ Good developers use an established set of GUI design standards so that they do not need to think about these while implementing a form. Ninety-nine percent of all forms design should not be creative. Most design decisions should have already been made as a part of the organization's established GUI design standards. These standards are frequently not the optimal way to lay out a form. Marginal improvements can be made to the layout or user-friendliness of the application. However, these should not be done. The difference between 20 minutes and four to eight hours of development time is justification for this. It is better for an organization to have numerous production-ready applications than to make one a little bit better.

■ Knowing the most efficient way to use Oracle Forms to accomplish given tasks is another advantage. Getting items and labels aligned properly and laying out a block quickly take some experience.

Miscellaneous Forms Standard Techniques

There are some techniques you can use, in addition to those explained in Chapters 25–29, to help enforce your Forms GUI standards, make your applications run more smoothly, and give guidance about some less obvious features and settings that you might otherwise not be aware of in Forms. While these are not all related to GUI standards, they all affect the way you would set up, use, or develop Forms applications.

Defer Required Enforcement Property

On the Form Module Property Palette for the form, set the *Defer Required Enforcement* property to "Yes." This will ensure that when you set the *Required* property on a column to "Yes," validation will only occur when the record is validated. If you don't set the *Defer Required Enforcement* property to "Yes," when a user enters a required item, he or she will not be able to leave the item without entering a value. This is particularly important for web-based applications, since not only do you encounter inappropriate form behavior, but you'll also generate unnecessary network traffic.

Setting Up Your Directory Structure

What directory structure should be used for a Forms environment? The answer depends on the number of forms in the system. If applications are built using the generic philosophy described by the authors, it is rare that even a very complex system will require more than 20-30 forms and a few dozen reports. In this case, one directory for all forms and a second for all reports are sufficient. Subdirectories for development, test, and production versions can be included in each.

In a more traditional development environment with several hundred forms and reports, you will need at least one additional structural layer of directories, as shown here:

```
Project X
    Forms
        Develop
        Test
        Production
        Template
            Reuse
            Icon
    Reports
        Develop
        Test
        Production
        Template
            Graphics
```

The additional directories are used for the template components. Under Forms, the various templates that the developers can select from are listed. Reusable components are stored in the Reuse and Icon subdirectories. In Reports, the template subdirectory holds the Reports templates that developers can select from with report graphics in the Graphics subdirectory. Form-level graphics such as company logos are also stored in the Reports Graphics subdirectory.

Search Paths

In a production environment, the forms directories should be placed in the FORMS60_PATH variable (in the Windows registry or UNIX environment). Reports directories should be placed in the REPORTS60_PATH variable. During development, you can create separate icons for Form Builder, each with a different Start In directory to support whether you are working with development, test, or production versions of the application.

When a form is calling another form, running a menu, or attaching a library, it will first look in the working directory. Next it will check the directory list in the FORMS60_PATH variable and finally it will look in the ORACLE_PATH variable directory list.

Arranging the Windows in Form Builder

The Forms Object Navigator window should be left open at all times and should fill the left one-third of your monitor from top to bottom. The remaining area of your screen should show the Layout Editor, except when writing complex code using the PL/SQL Editor window. Property Palette windows will cover a portion of either the Object Navigator or Layout Editor depending upon the task.

TIP
If you want to cut and paste between canvases, you must either have two Layout Model windows open or cut and paste objects within the Object Navigator.

Ordering Blocks and Items

When a form opens, the cursor will be positioned in the first navigable item in the first block in the Object Navigator. Blocks in the form should be ordered in the same way as they logically appear in the application. With a multitab application, Tab1 blocks should come before Tab2 blocks and so forth. In a multi-window application, blocks should appear in the same order as they appear in the logical order of windows.

The tab order of items on the screen corresponds to the order of navigable items in the Object Navigator. Items in the Object Navigator should be consistent with the tab order on the screen (left to right, top to bottom for compatible languages read from left to right).

Non-display and non-navigable items should be placed next to the items to which they are related, if any. For example, a button that activates an LOV next to an item should be placed next to that item. If you have an item which is a non-displayed companion to a displayed item (for example, employee ID and employee name), place the non-displayed item next to the name. Non-display and non-navigable items not associated with any item should be placed at the bottom of the block with buttons last.

Comment Property on Forms Objects

For complex coding in a form, there are frequently items created in the form whose function is not obvious without explanation. Developers should enter descriptive comments for these items using the *Comment* property in the item's Property Palette.

Key Shortcuts in the Development Environment

There are a variety of key shortcuts that developers should be familiar with to speed up common operations, as shown in Table 5-3.

In addition to the shortcuts shown above, you should use the Forms toolbar icons for Bold, Italic, Underline, and common alignment operations.

Key	Access Portion of Product
F2	Layout Editor
F4	Property Palette
F11	PL/SQL Editor
CTRL-L	Repeat Alignment

TABLE 5-3.   *Key Shortcuts in Oracle Forms*

CHAPTER

6

Forms Naming Conventions

The Universe is a trinity and this is made of name, form, and action.

—Upanishads (c. 1000–600 BC)

reating a naming convention for objects in your forms has a couple of benefits. First, those who read your code and who view the objects in the Form Builder will be able to quickly grasp the meaning of a particular object. This makes maintenance of your form easier because developers viewing the code can quickly find an object that needs their attention. The second benefit is that a naming convention frees developers from having to "rediscover" a way to name objects. On one hand, using such a standard requires less creativity on the naming side, although working with Oracle Developer Forms (Forms) offers so many other opportunities for creativity that this should not be missed. On the other hand, it offers structure to your work and does not require you to stop in the middle of a task to think about a name.

As mentioned in the other naming conventions chapters, the principle attributes you apply to naming conventions as well as other standards are the five Cs:

- **Consistent**   The way you name objects must be the same throughout the application. If you change the way you name objects within a form or even between forms in the same application, the reader will need to relearn the standard you are working with. It would be like speaking about a subject in a certain language and then switching languages without warning. Listeners would have to retune their ears for the new language.

- **Concise**   The names you give objects must be short. This eases the burden on the developer, who might need to type the name of the object many times into code. Even though most developers are fair to excellent typists, the fewer characters they have to type, the more accurate they can be. Also, short names ease the burden on the reader, who can more quickly scan the code or list of objects.

- **Clear**   While it may seem like an opposing principle to conciseness, the names you give objects must clearly transmit to the reader the purpose of the object. Names should describe the use and intent of the objects. It might be difficult to be both concise and clear at the same time, but your naming convention should state these objectives and offer suggestions for a solution.

- **Complete**   If you use naming conventions at all, you must use them for everything. This means that nearly your entire standard needs to be developed before any Forms work begins. If you left out a particular object from your standards, developers should bring that to your attention, and you will be able to come up with and communicate a standard before development of that object proceeds.

■ **Catchy**   The names you use should not be difficult to say. The naming convention should discourage the use of names that end in "ed" and "ing" because they are hard to pronounce and can be misinterpreted.

This chapter explores how you might come up with standards for the types of objects you need to create when developing a form module using Oracle Developer. It also suggests a convention for naming these objects. A Forms naming convention is part of your overall naming scheme that includes SQL and PL/SQL code, Reports, and database objects. This chapter will not mention the names you give to various code pieces like variables or cursors, as this is discussed in Chapter 3. Also, as the title of this chapter implies, there will be no mention of how to name Oracle Reports objects; Chapter 9 handles that subject. Therefore, to obtain a complete picture of naming conventions in Oracle Developer, be sure to also review Chapters 3 and 9. These chapters do not mention objects in other Oracle Developer components like Graphics Builder and Project Builder as these are out of scope for this book. Although the objects in those products are different, the principles of creating naming conventions discussed in this chapter extend to these objects as well. This chapter also does not mention database naming conventions—that is a subject for a database design book such as the Oracle Press book *Oracle8 Design Using UML Object Modeling,* by Dr. Paul Dorsey and Joseph R. Hudicka, Oracle Press, 1999.

Why Name Forms Objects?

Before discussing specific standards, it is useful to examine why it is worthwhile to name Forms objects in a certain way. Forms assigns default names for objects when you create them in Form Builder. Except for a few objects, such as table-based items, relations, and graphics, you will need to change the names of the objects. The reason is simple: the objects will make more sense to those reading the code and will be easier for them (and you) to find if they have logical names that adhere to specific known standards.

There are a few ways to find a particular object in Form Builder's Object Navigator. The first and fastest is to know the object's type and name. This allows you to use the Find item at the top of the Object Navigator. It also allows you to drill down in the specific object type and quickly find the name in the list. However, as your forms grow and you develop more and more items, you will lose track of the exact names of your objects. You can still find an object if you have adhered to naming conventions. You should know the type of object and be able to find the parent node in the Object Navigator by drilling down. If the objects are named by a standard, the object you are looking for should be easy to pick out once you have drilled down to its level.

TIP
You can use the Layout Editor to find an item as you do in the Object Navigator. Open the Layout Editor and display the canvas that contains the item. If you have named your canvases descriptively, this should be easy. Click on the object you want to modify or view. Press F3 to display the Object Navigator. The item you selected in the Layout Editor will be selected in the Object Navigator. If you press F4 instead of F3, you will display the Property Palette instead. If you right-click the item and select SmartTriggers from the list, you can create a new trigger or edit an existing trigger on the item. You can also use the Find item at the top of the Object Navigator if you know the first few letters of an object's name.

Naming Convention Considerations

When you are making decisions about what standards to create for naming Forms objects, you will need to consider the capabilities of the tool. For example, you cannot use object names that contain more than 30 characters. In addition, the tool forces all names in the Object Navigator to uppercase, thus creating a naming convention. Code you write can use any combination of upper- and lowercase for Forms objects, but the standard, as Chapter 3 mentions, is to use uppercase to refer to objects in quotes and lowercase to refer to objects in the code body.

Block Naming Considerations

The Data Block Wizard is worth using because it automates the time-consuming task of loading your block with items and providing each item with the correct property values. It also creates a link to the table upon which the block is based. The problem is that the block takes on the name of the table. Any code that the wizard creates, for integrity checking or block coordination, will use the name of the table. Therefore, if you rename the block after creating it with the Data Block Wizard, the form may not work or even compile properly because the code and links in the item property *Copy Value from Item* all use the old block name.

In Forms 4.5 (Oracle Developer R.1), you could change the block name in the New Block Options dialog just before accepting the dialog, and the block references would be created with that name. In Developer Release 2 as well as Release 6, the Data Block Wizard enforces the standard that the block name be the same as the table name. If this is not your standard, there is a way to bypass this action and use your own block names, as described in Chapter 26.

Other Considerations

Forms naming conventions should follow your GUI standards. If you develop forms in a certain way, it will affect your naming standards. For example, if your GUI standards state that you will use the tab canvas interface in all forms that require multiple canvases, you need a naming convention for the tab canvases and their pages. With that convention, you can create generic code that maintains the objects (for example, highlighting the tab labels) and place the objects and code in your template system. This code can be written to require generic names (such as TAB1, TAB2, or TAB3) or specific names (such as EMP, DEPT, or SAL). The naming convention would allow flexibility to add tab canvases or pages when required, and the code would work without requiring modification.

The code in your form will access local program units, program units in libraries attached to the form, code inherited from the template or object library, and database code. The code in the form should conform to the standards you set for SQL and PL/SQL, as discussed in Chapter 3. The decisions you make about naming conventions will need to take these standards into account.

General Conventions

When developing your naming conventions, you can make general statements about all objects in the form such as the following:

- Names for all objects will use 30 characters or less.

- Names will be singular (EMPLOYEE not EMPLOYEES) if database object names are singular.

- If the name consists of multiple words, an underscore character ("_") will separate the words.

- Names will be in uppercase. The tool enforces this.

- Names will not use numbered extensions unless the objects are in a series or there is some generic code that maintains them.

Regardless of the specific guidelines for the particular object, the names that developers use should at least comply with those standards.

NOTE
One naming convention to consider for database objects is to use words that are not more than five letters. Each object can be comprised of more than one word. For example, a table that represents the history of staff salaries would be called EMPL_SAL_HIST. Using this kind of name allows you to be both concise and clear. Whatever system you select for table and columns will affect the form's blocks and items.

Formatting

Another area to consider is the actual formatting of your standards. You need to create a "standard" for your standards so that they will be easily understood. Naming conventions are basically a hierarchical concept with overall standards (such as length of name and uppercase or mixed case) at the top and each object in the Object Navigator hierarchy under it. Therefore, an outline format is best for the standards document. You can number the outline entries in any way, but having a numbering system ensures that you can refer to specific standards by paragraph number.

A key deliverable when creating naming conventions is a list of objects that you will need to name. This list should be as complete as possible, but should be relatively easy to create if you write down the names of all objects (and subobjects) in the Object Navigator.

Suffixes and Prefixes

One decision you need to make before launching into the naming conventions for specific objects is whether to use suffixes or prefixes. One school of thought identifies Forms objects with a suffix or a prefix. For example, you would name blocks with a B_ prefix (for example, B_EMP) and canvases with a C_ prefix (for example, C_MAIN). This naming convention is a holdover from other (non-Oracle) tools that list different object types together. Oracle Forms does not usually list different object types together, so it is unnecessary to use prefixes (or suffixes) to identify an object type. If you refer to objects inside PL/SQL code, the context of the code always identifies the object type. For example, you will never be confused about the type of an object that is referenced in a SET_ITEM_PROPERTY call.

The only place that Forms lists different types of objects together in the Navigator is under the Object Group Children node. You can place a reference to any object except for an Attached Library into that node. In this node, the object types are distinguishable by icon, although sometimes the icons are hard to tell apart. However, this small potential confusion is not worth a compromise in the naming convention.

Prefixes or suffixes can be useful for two purposes. They can identify an item usage. You might create a non–base table item that displays a lookup value. This item has as its source a column in another table. The general rule for items is to name them the same as their source columns, but this item is not from the same base table as the rest of the block. Therefore, you would use a prefix to indicate that this is a non–base table item from another table. For example, if your block were based on the PRODUCT table and you needed to look up the price for a product based on the PRODUCT_PRICE table, you would create an item called DSP_PRICE (where DSP is defined in your standards as the abbreviation for DISPLAY) that displays the price for the product. A suffix would serve the same purpose, but would not be as easy to pick out of the Object Navigator list.

CAUTION

Naming items with a suffix or prefix that denotes the Item Type *property, such as text item or poplist, is risky if, after you have written code based on the item name, you change the item type to something else—like a radio group. At that point, you would need to modify the item name and the code that refers to it, or leave the item name with the wrong, and potentially confusing, item type designation. Also, if you use database column suffixes, as mentioned in Chapter 3, be careful that the suffixes you use for items are different so you can easily distinguish an item suffix from a database column suffix.*

Another use for suffixes and prefixes is to create objects that you will manipulate with generic coding. The code would apply a common action to a set of objects by processing a common prefix or suffix. For example, the canvases on all your forms contain image items that you want to load from image files. You name the image items based on the file name; image items called CO_LOGO_01 and CO_LOGO_02 in the IMAGE block would be loaded with a file called CO_LOGO.GIF. A generic library procedure loops through the IMAGE block, verifies that the item is an image item, and loads the image item with a file named the same as the item without the number suffix (and with a .GIF extension). This routine is totally generic and depends only on the item name. Chapter 25 contains details on this technique.

In most situations other than for item names, you will not need to use suffixes or prefixes.

NOTE
When developing your naming conventions keep in mind the way that the object names will sort in an alphabetized list. Prefixes will keep all similar objects together in such a list. Suffixes will not.

Naming Conventions for Specific Objects

The following section lists naming conventions you might use for objects in various Forms modules. The naming conventions for template forms and application-specific forms are the same, so the following discussion applies to objects in both uses of Forms files.

All naming conventions comply with the guidelines mentioned in the earlier "General Conventions" section.

Application Systems

While technically not a Forms object, applications systems need careful naming. The usual example of an application system name is an abbreviation such as SPMTS for a system called Stock Portfolio Management Tracking System. Since this name will be used in a number of other names, conciseness is important, and a maximum of six to eight characters should suffice.

Forms and Object Libraries

Since standard objects in the object library are named the same as they are in the form from which they are created, this section covers objects in both types of Forms files. Figure 6-1 shows the object types as they appear in the Object Navigator. Some objects in the object library will be used as SmartClasses, and the following sections list naming conventions for those objects separately.

Form Modules

The form module name should be the same as the file name without the extension. This will keep things simple for the reader. It will also eliminate questions when you use Forms built-ins to determine the form name. Some of the built-ins return the file name and some return the form name. If these are the same, you will never need to worry about which built-in to use.

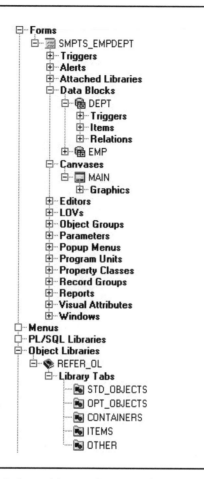

FIGURE 6-1.   *Form and object library objects in the Object Navigator*

Files

Name form files descriptively. While file-name length is governed by the operating system, 30 characters should be enough to describe the form, so the 30-character maximum applies. Setting a maximum number of characters will allow you to correctly size variables to hold the file name in PL/SQL variables within Forms.

Form file names should be lowercase. This is not so important in the Windows environment because the Windows file system is not case sensitive. However, if you develop a form on Windows and move it to a UNIX operating system for deployment on the Web, the upper- and lowercase use becomes important because UNIX is case sensitive. If you are not aware of this, you may be surprised when a form that you call from another form cannot be found because the file name is in a different case. You might say to yourself (or even to Oracle Support), "Gee, it worked in Windows, why doesn't it work on the Web?" The answer is that UNIX cannot find the file because it is looking for specific upper- and lowercase letters in the name. When you save a file for the first time in Windows, the default name is the name of the form module (if you have assigned it before saving). The name and the extension are in mixed case by default, so you need to pay attention when saving for the first time. After that, the file will always be saved as that same file name with the same case.

The files should have a prefix of the system name or abbreviation (eight characters or less) followed by an underscore, followed by the name of the main function that the form fulfills. The prefix will allow you to perform group operations on the files in case they are stored in the same directory as forms from other applications. If you decide that this is not important, consider some other naming convention, such as naming the form file the same as the main table supported in the form.

Forms source files should always use the default extension, .FMB, so you can tell them apart from code libraries, object libraries, and menus. If you need to make multiple versions of a form as a backup and you do not want to use version control software, copy the file into the same directory. In Windows, you can do this using CTRL-C and CTRL-V in the Windows Explorer or any file dialog. This will create another file with a "Copy of" prefix. You can change that name to the original file name with a version-number suffix (for example, SPMTS_CLIENT01.FMB).

For instance, a form for the Stock Portfolio Management Tracking System (SPMTS) that manages the client records is in a file called SPMTS_CLIENT.FMB. This form has a module name (displayed by the form module Property Palette) of SPMTS_CLIENT.

TEMPLATE AND OBJECT LIBRARY FILES Generic forms such as templates and object libraries use the company or department name or abbreviation as the prefix. For example, the standard template used for the Information System for Sales department would be ISSALES_TEMPLATE. If you use a customized version of the template for your application, use the application abbreviation as the prefix (for example, SPMTS_TEMPLATE).

TIP

As mentioned in Chapter 10, you should use a form (.FMB) file as the source for your object library (.OLB) file. Whenever you create or modify an object library object, you do so in the form and then drag it into the object library. Name your object library differently from the form you use to maintain it. While you can tell the files apart from the file extension, the Subclass Information *property in the form makes no distinction between subclasses from forms and subclasses from object libraries. The following shows the* Subclass Information *property for an alert:*

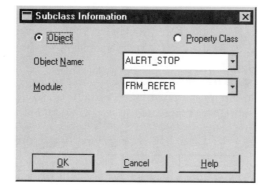

The Module setting does not denote the file type. If the files are named with a suffix denoting the type, you will not be confused as to the source of a subclass when looking at this property. For example, you can name the form that is the source of all objects in the object library REFER_FORM.FMB and the object library that stores the objects for subclassing REFER_OL.OLB.

Object library files should retain the default .OLB extension so you can determine the file type. Template files are the same type of file as normal Forms files and use the .FMB extension.

Triggers

You do not have a choice about how to name standard Forms triggers. All are multiple words separated by hyphens. The names indicate the events that cause them to fire, and the way you signal trigger code to fire for a particular event is to give it one of the standard Forms trigger names (like WHEN-NEW-FORM-INSTANCE).

CAUTION
While you can write triggers for property classes, this is potentially dangerous because the code is basically hidden and developers may become confused about which code is actually firing for an object with a property class. You will use the subclassing technique more than property classes, but it is still useful to state your position on triggers for property classes because it is a technique that developers can use.

User-defined triggers have user-assigned names, so you need a naming convention for them. User-defined triggers on all levels (form, block, and item) should use the same naming convention. User-defined triggers may not use hyphens, but may use underscores. This is a visual clue about whether the trigger is user defined or not. If it has more than one word and the words are separated by hyphens, the trigger is a Forms built-in trigger. If the trigger name is one word or multiple words separated by anything other than a hyphen, it is a user-defined trigger.

The convention to use for naming triggers is full descriptive words starting with a verb. For example, a trigger you create to show the contents page of a help file would be called SHOW_HELP_CONTENTS. The only way that a user-defined trigger will ever fire is if you issue a call to EXECUTE_TRIGGER in your code—for example, EXECUTE_TRIGGER ('SHOW_HELP_CONTENTS'). Normally, you can create the same effect by calling a package or procedure directly, and Oracle discourages the use of user-defined triggers. Still, they are useful for calling Forms code from menu items. Chapter 28 discusses menu code and provides some examples of this use of user-named triggers.

Alerts

The template form subclasses alerts from the object library. You will not need more than three alerts since the supporting library code allows you to change the message and all button labels. The three alerts have different *Alert Style* properties and display different icons in the upper-left corner. The names of the alerts can merely be the names of the alert styles: STOP, CAUTION, and NOTE.

Attached Libraries

Although this is a separate high-level node in the Object Navigator, you can only add the names of existing library files. The following section discusses library file names.

Data Blocks

Block names should be the name of the table or view that is the main source of the data. If the source for the block is a procedure, transactional trigger, or "FROM clause query," use the name of the table that is the main element in those types or a name that identifies the purpose of the block (such as EMPLOYEE_MAINTENANCE).

An alternative method for naming is to use the table alias. You assign a table alias (in your system documentation) to a table when you first create it. This alias is used in all queries that include that table. It can also become the block name using a technique described in Chapter 26. A short alias name as a block name has several advantages. The block name is easier to type into code; it is a fully descriptive word that is associated with the table whenever the table is used; and it corresponds to the way Oracle Designer generates Forms code (the block name is the table's alias property).

TIP

If you find yourself wanting to use updateable join-views as the source for a block, but your DBA does not grant you access to create views, use the "FROM clause query" value for the block property Query Data Source Type. *This will allow you to use a SELECT statement as the source for the items in the block. This is virtually the same as using a view as the source, except you cannot use the standard query-by-example feature. If you are allowed to create views, the updateable view is a flexible way to work with many tables in one block, but there are some restrictions.*

OTHER BLOCKS   Blocks that are not based on tables or data elements are normally called *control blocks.* The traditional name for a control block is, surprisingly, CONTROL. You may need more than one block for control (non–base table) items. The guideline is to name these other blocks by function. If the block serves as a container for toolbar buttons, for example, call the block TOOLBAR.

BASE TABLE ITEMS   Items are subobjects under blocks, but the naming convention is different. Just as block names are based on the database table or view, item names are based on database columns. With Developer Release 2 and later, you can actually name an item differently from the table column it is based on, but this only causes confusion later.

NOTE
There are actually two types of base table items. The first is based on an updateable column such as a column from a base table or an updateable column of a view. The second is based on a non-updateable column of a view. This type of column will have a different naming convention (such as a v_ prefix) in the view itself, and this name will be reflected in your item in the form. Chapter 4 explains how to set up a block based on an updateable view.

NON–BASE TABLE ITEMS   As mentioned earlier, non–base table items that are in the same block as base table items should have a prefix to characterize them. For example, if you look up the department name to display in the employee block, call the item DSP_DNAME (to denote that you are displaying the DNAME column from another table). A calculated column (for example, on PRICE * QUANTITY) would use the prefix CALC_ (for example, CALC_LINE_TOTAL). A summary column would use the prefix SUM_; for example, a total of all LINE_ITEM values in an order block would be called SUM_LINE_TOTAL.

BUTTON ITEMS   Toolbar buttons (if you use toolbars outside the menu system) are named as the built-in that represents the Forms function they execute. For example, a toolbar button that exits the form issues an EXIT_FORM built-in call and is called EXIT_FORM. A toolbar button that saves records (COMMIT_FORM) is called COMMIT_FORM. Naming the buttons as the built-ins they represent allows you to create generic coding to handle them, as Chapter 7 ("How to Handle Forms Functions" and "Which Level of Trigger") discusses.

Canvas buttons use prefixes based on their function. If the button displays an LOV on the item it is adjacent to, use a prefix of LOV and a suffix of the item name for which the LOV displays. For example, an LOV button for the ZIPCODE item would be called LOV_ZIPCODE.

If the button is an action button for functions like "OK" or "Cancel," name the button using the label of the button, OK or CANCEL. If your form contains many OK buttons, you might need a prefix to denote the canvas it appears on. Alternatively, you can create multiple control blocks for the buttons, each for a particular canvas, and name the blocks as TOOLBAR_*canvas_name,* CONTROL_*canvas_name,* or BUTTONBAR_*canvas_name,* where *"canvas_name"* is the name of the canvas on which the buttons are placed.

Some naming conventions use a PB prefix (for "push button") to identify buttons. In the case of buttons, as in the case of other items, this prefix is not required because the context of the item will identify its type.

RELATIONS   When you use the Data Block Wizard, Forms uses two words to name relations that link a master and a detail block: the name of the master block, an underscore, and the name of the detail block. If you use the table aliases as the names of the blocks—for example, DEPT and EMP—the relation name will be DEPT_EMP. The relation always appears under the master block node. If your block names are longer than 15 characters, the wizard truncates the master block name to 15 characters and the detail block name to 14 characters (so the total will be 30 or less, including the underscore separator).

There is no need to change the name of the relation, but if you do so after it has been created, Forms will rewrite the trigger and program unit code with the new name. If you create a relation outside the Data Block Wizard, use the same naming convention (*MasterBlock_DetailBlock).*

Canvases

There are different types of canvases: *content, stacked, toolbar,* and *tab.* Canvas names should be ten characters or less (excluding the suffix if there is a suffix). Each form should have a content canvas called MAIN (on a window called MAIN) that appears when users start up the form. The template contains this canvas, so all forms developed from the template will also contain this canvas. Your developers will then know that each form they create will have a standard canvas that they can start with. Some forms may need only the MAIN canvas. You can size this canvas for your standard monitor resolution and attach a standard visual attribute.

Other content canvases you create in addition to the MAIN canvas should use names that use the prefix of the window name and suffix of the contents or purpose of the canvas. For example, a form that contains three content canvases to display departments, employees, and salary history all within the MAIN window would use the names MAIN_DEPT, MAIN_EMP, and MAIN_SALHIST for those canvases, respectively. The names of the content canvases are independent of the name of the window in which they appear.

STACKED CANVASES   A stacked canvas appears on top of a particular content canvas, but is assigned to a window. Therefore, if you use many content canvases on a single window, the stacked canvases assigned to that window will appear on all of them. The stacked canvas name, therefore, should be based on a prefix of the window name and the word "STACK" and a suffix of the function or contents of the canvas. For example, if you use a stacked canvas to conditionally show a particular set of items and boilerplate lines for a salesperson's commissions, the stacked canvas in the MAIN window would be called MAIN_STACK_COMM.

You can also use stacked canvases to hide items or boilerplate objects. In addition, you can use stacked canvases to overlay a scroll bar on a multirecord block conditionally. These uses for a stacked canvas are named using the same convention. For example, the canvas to hide the manager's name item and prompt in the MAIN window would be called MAIN_STACK_HIDE_MGR.

TAB CANVASES AND TAB PAGES   Tab canvases appear on top of content canvases, too. Therefore, the same naming conventions apply to tab canvases as apply to stacked canvases, except that the prefix for a tab canvas is TAB.

Individual tab pages within a tab canvas are named PAGE*nn* by default (where *nn* is a number). Change these names to match the contents of the tab page. You can refer to the tab page name in code, so it is important to make the name short and descriptive. If you have a tab canvas with pages for Commission Plan, Bonus, and Annual Goal, the tab page names would be COMM_PLAN, BONUS, and GOAL, respectively.

If you use tabs that stack over existing tab pages, the tab canvas would use a SUBTAB_ prefix (for example, SUBTAB_EMP would pop up over the EMP tab page). The tab pages for these subtabs would be named descriptively as usual. Chapter 23 contains a technique for adding subtabs to a tab page.

TIP
Another standard that some developers use is to name windows, content canvases, and tab pages with the object name prefix and a number (for example, CANVAS_01 or PAGE01). This makes looping through and modifying all canvases in the form easier, but it makes finding a specific canvas in a long list very difficult.
If you find that you need to loop through all canvases, you can create a package variable to store the names of all canvases with a comma separator (for example, 'MAIN,DETAIL,QUERY'). Load this variable in the WHEN-NEW-FORM-INSTANCE trigger. Then write generic code to parse the variable extracting the canvas name and performing the action on it in the same kind of loop you would normally use. You need to maintain this variable as you add canvases, but your canvases will be named descriptively so you can find and use them more easily.

BOILERPLATE GRAPHICS Whenever you create a graphic object on the canvas, an object is inserted into the Graphics node under the canvas. All boilerplate graphics files, lines, frames, rectangles, circles, and other shapes that you draw with the Forms drawing tools become individual objects. You cannot manipulate these objects programmatically, although you can display and modify their properties using the Property Palette in Form Builder.

When you need to find a graphic object, just click it in the Layout Editor and it will be selected in the Object Navigator. Since finding a graphic object in the Object Navigator is the only operation in which a meaningful name would help, there is little payback for the time you would spend changing the names. If you do need to display the properties for a graphic object in Form Builder, use the technique mentioned earlier to click the object in the Layout Editor and press F4 to display the object's properties in the Property Palette.

Editors

Editors are useful only on items that contain values longer than the item allows. Editors offer search-and-replace capabilities and a scrollable text region with a prompt and title. You can replace the default editor that Forms supplies with one that you define. You then attach that editor to the item's *Editor* property. If you use an editor for more than one item, use the name of the domain (identifying a datatype and size) for the editor name. If you use the editor for only one item, name the editor with the name of the item. For example, you create an editor to allow easy entry of address items in two different blocks. The editor would be called ADDRESS. Another example would be an editor you define for a single item called DESCRIPTION. Call the editor DESCRIPTION to match the item name.

LOVs and Record Groups

These two objects are grouped together for this discussion because when you create an LOV with the LOV Wizard, the objects will be named the same. Change the record group and LOV names from LOV*nn* (where "*nn*" is a number) to a name that signifies the result of the query, for example, EMPLOYEE or ZIPCODE. Changing the name right after creating the object will not require you to change any other object or code. Forms maintains a link from the LOV to the record group even if you change the name. If you create a record group for a use other than an LOV (such as for use in populating a list item), name the record group by its contents (such as ACTIVE_EMPLOYEES). Programmatic record groups use the same naming convention as Object Navigator record groups.

Object Groups

It is not likely that you will be using object groups outside of the object library form unless you are subclassing a set of objects from one form to another. As with other objects in Forms, names of object groups should be short and descriptive (ten characters or less). Object groups can be named with plural nouns because they are groups of objects by definition.

For object groups in the object library, use prefixes to indicate whether the object groups are copied (COPY prefix) or subclassed (SUBCLASS prefix) into the template from the object library. You do not reference the names in code, but the prefix will indicate to those using the template what method was used to incorporate the object group from the object library.

For example, if you create an object group for the standard alerts that you will subclass into the template, the object group will be called SUBCLASS_ALERTS.

Parameters

Parameters are useful for passing values to another form that you call from the command line or from another form. Global package variables are another way to pass values, and Chapter 29 discusses this method. Parameters in forms can be named according to their function. No prefix or suffix is needed, but you should keep the name short to help the reader grasp the purpose and help the developer write code for the parameter.

For example, a parameter that you pass into the form to indicate whether it was called from a form in query-only mode would be called QUERY_ONLY_MODE.

Popup Menus

The same conventions apply to popup menus as apply to editors. Both are separate items that act on and supplement the features of a particular item (or, in the case of popup menus, a canvas). Therefore, the popup menu itself should be named the same as the item or canvas name. If the popup menu is applied to more than one object, use a name indicating the items it is attached to. For example, a popup menu that appears only on the EMPNO item should be called EMPNO. If the popup menu is attached to all items on the form, call it ALL_ITEMS.

MENU ITEMS   Individual menu items in the popup menu use names descriptive of their function. For example, an item for Cut should be called CUT. An item for Exit should be called EXIT_FORM.

Program Units

Program units follow the naming conventions of other PL/SQL code, as described in Chapter 3.

Property Classes

You will probably not use property classes because subclassing from the object library provides the same functionality and is more flexible. If you do use property classes, the names should describe the objects and function that they will be attached to. With property classes, the type of object you will attach it to is an important part of the name because the list of property classes will contain different types of objects. To quickly find a particular object type, you can scan through the list and look for a particular suffix (the object type) and prefix (the purpose).

For example, a property class that supplies the properties of canvas button items would be called CANVAS_BUTTON. A property class that designates the properties for text items used for display only would be called DISP_TEXT_ITEM. A property class that designates the properties for display items would be called DISP_DISP_ITEM. A property class for the properties of the MAIN canvas would be called MAIN_CANVAS.

Reports

Report objects in forms are just references to report files stored in the file system. You can base a report on a block, and this will open Report Builder to create a new report file. There are built-ins to manipulate the report object and call it easily from the form. The report object in the Object Navigator should be the same name as the report file. For example, if your report file were called DEPTEMP.RDF, the report object in Forms would be called DEPTEMP. Default names like REPORT2 and REPORT7 do not make sense.

Visual Attributes

Since visual attributes are used for a specific object's colors and font, the name of the visual attribute should denote the purpose of the visual attribute and the name of the object. For example, a visual attribute that changes the color of the record that the cursor is in would be named CURRENT_RECORD. The visual attribute for a standard canvas button would be called CANVAS_BUTTON.

Windows

Just as you have a standard canvas called MAIN, you will also have a window called MAIN to house the canvas. The MAIN window is the first one to be shown in all forms, so you can write generic code that sizes the window (or maximizes it) and that assigns a window title. This code can be built into the template so that the developer does not have to think about the mechanism.

If you add other windows to the form, they should be named in the same way as the canvases. In fact, the window can be named the same as the content canvas if the canvas is to appear in a separate window. For example, you create a canvas called NEW_USER that will appear in a window called NEW_USER. Since the window name may be used as a prefix for stacked canvases, the window name should be short so that the stacked canvas name does not become too long.

Object Library Tabs

The tabs in your object library should have short and descriptive names that identify the contents. For example, an object library with tab labels such as Standard Objects, Optional Objects, Items, Containers, and Other SmartClasses would have tab names such as STD_OBJECTS, OPT_OBJECTS, ITEMS, CONTAINERS, and OTHER, respectively.

SmartClasses and Subclassed Objects

Objects in the object library consist of object groups that are subclassed and copied into the template as well as objects used as SmartClasses for Forms objects. The object groups follow the naming conventions mentioned earlier. The SmartClasses follow the same naming conventions of property classes. That is, the name will contain a prefix of the purpose and suffix of the object type. For example, if you set up a SmartClass based on your MAIN window so you can apply its properties to other windows you create, the SmartClass would be called MAIN_WINDOW. You would use the name TOOLBAR_BUTTON for a SmartClass that is applied to all toolbar buttons and CANVAS_BUTTON for a SmartClass that is applied to buttons on the canvas. Chapter 11 contains more examples of SmartClass objects.

Libraries

As Figure 6-2 shows, libraries contain only Program Units and Attached Libraries, which you will name using the same conventions you used for those objects in forms. The library file name becomes the name of the library node in the Object Navigator, unlike the form, where you can (although it is not part of the naming convention) have a form name different from the file name. You will create libraries that are generic, application specific, and form specific. All have common naming conventions for the file names. All libraries use names that parallel the form standards, a prefix to denote the area, and the function name as a suffix. All library source files use a .PLL extension.

FIGURE 6-2. *Library objects in the Object Navigator*

Generic libraries use the company or department abbreviation as a prefix and the function or grouping of procedures as the suffix. For example, a set of utility packages that manage form objects as a standard for the IS-Sales department would be called ISSALES_FORMUTIL.PLL.

Application-specific libraries use the same type of suffix with a prefix of the application abbreviation. For example, the SPMTS system uses a library file that contains packages with utilities for its forms; this library is called SPMTS_FORMUTIL.PLL.

Form-specific libraries use the same name as the form. For example, the form SPMTS_USERMAINT.FMB file uses a library called SPMTS_USERMAINT.PLL.

Menus

Menu files can also be generic templates, application specific, or form specific. Menu source files use an .MMB extension. As with form files, you can use a different name for the menu module node and the menu file name, but the naming convention is to use the same name for both file and menu module.

The library naming convention applies to generic and application-specific menus. That is, generic menus use a prefix of company or department abbreviation and suffix of the function that the menu serves. Application-specific menus use the application prefix with the same suffix. Form-specific menus use the form name with an additional suffix of MNU. For example, a form-specific menu for the SPMTS_USERMAINT.FMB file would be called SPMTS_USERMAINT_MNU.MMB.

Menus contain a menu and items, as Figure 6-3 shows.

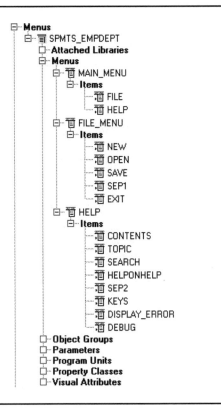

FIGURE 6-3. *Menu module objects in the Object Navigator*

Menus

The menu hierarchy uses menus as the highest-level object. The first (starting) menu is called MAIN_MENU. If you use the Menu Editor to lay out the menu, it will use a suffix of MENU for each menu node it creates. There is no reason to change this naming convention, although it is a bit redundant because the name contains the object type. The naming convention for menus at any level is to use a prefix of the menu label and a suffix of MENU. For example, the File menu is called FILE_MENU.

Menu Items

Menu items are named by function. If possible, use the name of the label because this will make the menu item easy to find. For example, the Exit item in the File menu would be called EXIT. If the label is long, use a meaningful abbreviation for the name. For example, the item labeled "Call User Maintenance Form" would be called CALL_USERMAINT.

Other Menu Objects

Menus contain attached libraries, object groups, parameters, program units, property classes, and visual attributes, and you name all of these using the same naming conventions you use in forms.

CHAPTER
7

Where to Put the Code
in Forms

An ounce of prevention is worth a ton of code.

—Anonymous

I t should be easy. You want to put some code in your form. You know what you want to do, and you know how to do it. The problem is that there are many choices for where to locate this code. Although you can write code that works regardless of your choice, if you put the code in the wrong place, you run the risk of the code performing in a less than optimal way and bogging down the network unnecessarily. You also run the risk of creating code that is not reusable and is difficult to maintain.

Part of your Oracle Developer Forms (Forms) programming standards should be dedicated to helping your developers decide where the code is placed in the application. This is not a decision that developers should have to spend time on while they are in the midst of programming. If you have standards and guidelines for this purpose in place, all the developers on your team will have a clear picture of where they should put the code and why they are placing it there. They should also have an idea of where to find other developers' code when it comes time for maintenance.

This chapter will provide suggestions about standards that you can use for determining where to put the code in your forms. Chapter 8 explains where you put the code in reports and Chapter 3 discusses SQL and PL/SQL coding standards in general.

Standards for Code Placement

There are a number of questions you need to answer when deciding where to put the code in Forms. Answering them will provide you with a set of Forms coding standards. Using standards for code placement will eliminate confusion about some decisions that developers need to make when locating their code. The code placement standards should answer a number of basic questions:

- Do you use packages or stand-alone program units?

- Which is better, database code or Forms code?

- How do you handle Forms functions such as EXIT_FORM?

- Do you write the code in a trigger or in a program unit?

- Does form-side code belong in the form or in a library?

- Which library do you write the code into?

- If you use object library code, should you copy or subclass it?

- Do you write the trigger on the form, block, or item level?

Clearly, some of these questions are interrelated, and answering one in a certain way will make other questions irrelevant. The following sections examine and present a sample standard for each of these questions. Armed with a standard, you will be able to place code so it is most efficient and flexible.

The assumption throughout this chapter is that even before writing the code, you first examine the database, form libraries, templates, and object libraries to see if anything exists that would accomplish the task at hand. If the existing code was developed using a set of standard naming conventions and documentation, it will be easier to find an existing routine.

Packages or Stand-Alone?

You need to decide on a standard for whether to use PL/SQL *packages* (a named group of procedures, functions, variables, cursors, and other PL/SQL objects) in your Forms code and in code that is stored in the database. The alternative to writing packages of code is writing individual functions and procedures. The decision will become part of your standards document. Generally, it is better to write code inside packages because there are many benefits to doing so.

NOTE
The Packages Standard
Use packages for all PL/SQL code.
The benefits outweigh the drawbacks.

Benefits of Packages

You need to consider the following benefits of packages when making the decision about using packages or stand-alone program units:

- **Organization of code** Packages act as containers for related routines. For example, you can place all procedures, functions, cursors, and variables that apply to your security system in a package called APP_UI_SECURITY. This benefit is particularly important when the application grows and developers need to access hundreds of stored routines. If you have an organized system for housing the routines, your developers will be able to find the necessary code more quickly and will probably not duplicate existing code as often. This is important on small projects, too, because small projects can become large projects, and if you create a system of packages at the outset, your application can grow into the structure. It also acclimates your team to the idea of using packages. Packages also enhance the process of browsing the database code since there will be a smaller number of code objects to scan.

■ **Object orientation** Oracle8 implements methods on objects using packages. Even if you are not using the object extensions in Oracle, with version 7 or version 8 you can write code that acts as an interface to database objects. For example, you can create a package containing INS, UPD, DEL, and SLCT procedures to perform the operations INSERT, UPDATE, DELETE, and SELECT, respectively. The benefit of this approach is that the procedures can perform whatever logic is necessary to implement complex business rules such as complex validation or loading rows into other tables. Normal SQL operations can only implement basic functionality, such as ensuring mandatory values, enforcing an allowable list of values, maintaining links from one table to another through foreign key columns, and cascading deletes to a child table.

Whenever you need to access or manipulate the table through whatever application, you do so through these procedures. While the table is a separate database object, the package could be named appropriately so the table and package would act as a single object. The package defines the published methods for accessing the table.

In essence, the package acts as an Application Programming Interface (API) and can contain routines other than the standard Data Manipulation Language (DML) operators, such as functions to translate a name to an ID or an ID to a name. You can also create packages for concepts like security that might use more than one database object. The "object" that the package supports, in this case, is not just a table, but an application module.

■ **Publicly available objects** One of the benefits of packages is that they give you the capability to store variable values that persist throughout the database connection session. This concept extends to cursors as well. If you create a variable of any datatype or a cursor in the package specification, any code, in Forms or otherwise, can read and write to these objects within the same session.

Thus, if you have a multiform application, a package variable set in one form is available in another form that the first form calls or opens. This same effect applies within a form. Normally, variable values set in one trigger's code are not available in another trigger's code. If the trigger sets the value of a package variable in the database or in the form or in a library attached to that form, the value is available to other triggers within that same form. For example, you can store a list of canvases in the form in a package variable so that, whenever you need to loop through the canvases in your code, you can read that variable for the canvas names.

A package defined within a form does not share its variables outside of the form, but if that form writes to a database package variable, that variable value will be available to another form in the same session. In addition, Forms libraries can share package variable data between forms if the CALL_FORM, OPEN_FORM, or NEW_FORM built-in call uses the SHARE_LIBRARY_DATA parameter. Chapter 29 discusses sharing variables further.

■ **Publicly restricted source**   Developers do not always need to know the internal code that comprises a particular procedure or function. If developers are granted access to the package, they will be able to see the specification that includes the calling interface with its parameter list and return values, but will not be able to see the actual code in the package body. This strategy also allows you to change the package body without requiring a recompilation of all forms that use the code.

Since you place all documentation about the intent and usage of the package code in the specification, developers using the packages only need to know the name of the package. The header comments can guide developers on which part of the package to use. When a development process is ongoing, this is a clear advantage because any documentation of the contents of the package will frequently become outdated. If you enforce the standard that developers document the procedure, function, or cursor in the package specification, those using the package can scan through the header and look for routines that will accomplish their task. These comment headers are critical when developers need to find a routine for a particular purpose.

■ **Increased performance**   Package code stored in the database has the additional benefit of being cached as a unit. Therefore, when you access a packaged piece of code for the first time, the entire package is loaded into memory on the server. Subsequent calls to the same code or other code inside the same package are retrieved from memory, which is much faster than from disk.

NOTE
In releases before Oracle8i, definer's rights, where each program unit executes with the privilege set of the user who owns it, applied to all program units. The invoker rights feature of PL/SQL in Oracle8i allows you to use the calling user's privileges to execute a program unit. If the program unit for which you define invoker rights is a package, all procedures and functions within that package will execute with the calling user's privileges. Packages make it easier to apply invoker rights to many program units. Invoker rights are defined by adding the "AUTHID CURRENT_USER" clause in the program unit declaration (for example: "CREATE PACKAGE spmts_employee AUTHID CURRENT_USER AS").

Drawbacks of Packages

The benefits of packages are compelling, but there are some drawbacks:

■ **Extra development steps** A few extra steps are necessary for creating and maintaining this organization. You have to maintain the package specification separately from the body. For database packages, if you create a packaged function that you will use in SELECT statements, you have to write a PRAGMA RESTRICT_REFERENCES command in the specification to state the purity level of the function. Chapter 9 of the *PL/SQL User's Guide and Reference* manual from the Oracle8 documentation set explains this further.

■ **Less access granularity** Access to every procedure or function in the specification will be granted if you grant EXECUTE privilege on the package. Therefore, you do not have individual control over which objects in the package are accessible since you grant at the package level.

TIP
If you need to have more control over access, you can create a package containing a subset of the procedures and functions in another package. You then grant the EXECUTE privilege to the subset package, not to the original package. You can use this method to reorganize package contents as well since the subset package can contain calls to any number of other packages.

■ **Additional object to handle**   Using packages requires that you create and follow standards for another type of object (packages) in addition to functions and procedures. This means your developers will need to think about which package is the appropriate location for their new procedure or function. This is not a problem if the developers just create procedures and functions outside the package. However, the extra level of organization you gain is worth the extra step of having to think about where a program unit should go.

■ **Additional development overhead**   There is a bit of overhead with creating a package for a single program unit such as a procedure. In practice, you may have a small number of packages that only have one procedure or function. The overhead, though, is merely an additional code piece—the package specification—that offers benefits itself (including code hiding and public variables). Also, the benefit of being able to add other procedures to that package later outweighs this small developer inconvenience.

These apparent drawbacks are controllable largely by providing training on the proper use of packages. The benefits do outweigh the drawbacks—particularly the first benefit of the ability to organize your code and reduce the number of stored program units.

Database Server or Form?

One question you need to ask early in the process of locating the code is whether the code is stored in the database or in the form.

NOTE
The Database Standard
If the logic you are creating acts only on the database and is application-independent (it must fire when the table or view is acted on regardless of the application), use a database trigger. If the code contains SQL access of database objects, write that part of the logic as database server code (packaged procedures and functions) and call it from the Forms trigger. If you are coding both database access and Forms code, split the code and place form-specific code on the form-side and call the database server code from Forms code. If you have complex logic to execute for a block data source, use views or procedures as the query source and DML target.

If you decide to write database code, the database server will execute the code. If you decide to write the code on the Forms side, there are two possibilities for where the code will be executed. In the Web environment, forms will be located on the application server, so the Forms code will execute there, not in the client browser. If you are deploying forms in a client/server environment, the forms will be located on the client side (file server or local PC) and all Forms code will execute on the client machine. Regardless of the environment, any Forms code can call database code or objects as well as Forms built-ins.

Placing code on the database server will cause it to do extra processing. Server hardware can be pretty efficient. If you find that the amount of code executing on the server is causing a slowdown, the solution (after tuning) is probably a hardware one: processors, memory, or disk space on the server. Implementation in this case is centralized—you only need to upgrade or replace one machine instead of many (client) machines.

Network *bandwidth* (the amount of data that the network can handle simultaneously) is a key issue with networks. This commodity is usually at a premium, and upgrading a network may be more difficult or costly than upgrading the server hardware. Therefore, a key determinant in placing your Forms code will be how you can use as little of the network as possible.

Forms code can be focussed toward two main targets: the form itself and the database. The form-oriented code must be located on the form side. The database cannot interpret commands like SET_BLOCK_PROPERTY. Database objects are another issue because you can place blocks of database-oriented code either in the form or in the database. It is best to place as little database code as possible in the form because of the network overhead.

The exception to avoiding SQL in the form is SQL that Forms creates implicitly. For example, if you call the EXECUTE_QUERY built-in for a database block, Forms will create a SELECT statement and issue it to the database. The same mechanism works when you commit a new, modified, or deleted record in Forms. This automatically created SQL requires no code and is an important benefit of using Forms. You would not want to circumvent this feature.

If your code accesses and manipulates database objects, it makes more sense to have the code reside on the database server. In this situation, you would call the server code from the client form. This greatly reduces the network traffic created by sending blocks of PL/SQL code or large SQL statements to the server. However, if the code manipulates form-side objects or performs other actions that the form can handle without calls to the server, the code should execute on the form. Code that contains Forms-specific calls, such as Forms built-ins, naturally needs to run on the client because the database PL/SQL interpreter cannot handle Forms built-ins. Forms has its own PL/SQL interpreter that will handle the built-ins as well as conditional and iterative logic. The only time that interpreter will access the database is when it makes a call to code or objects stored in the database.

How to Split the Forms Code

When examining your Forms code to determine if you are being most efficient, you can look for any DML statements, particularly SELECT statements. These are indicators that there is database code in the form that should be moved to the server. You should be able to replace the block of code that performs DML with a single call to a database package object. Here is an example of code you might initially write in the PRE-INSERT trigger of an EMP block in the form:

```
DECLARE
    v_found   BOOLEAN;
    --
    CURSOR c_empseq
    IS
       SELECT    empno_seq.nextval
       FROM      dual;
    --
BEGIN
    OPEN c_empseq;
    FETCH c_empseq
    INTO  :emp.empno;
    v_found := c_empseq%FOUND;
    CLOSE c_empseq;
END;
```

There is nothing wrong with this code, but Forms would send the cursor declaration and all cursor statements to the database for each row that was inserted. A better strategy is to write the following code as part of the SPMTS_EMP package in the database:

```
FUNCTION next_empno
    RETURN NUMBER
IS
    v_found  BOOLEAN;
    v_empno NUMBER;
    --
    CURSOR c_empseq
    IS
       SELECT    empno_seq.nextval
       FROM      dual;
    --
BEGIN
    OPEN c_empseq;
    FETCH c_empseq INTO  v_empno;
    v_found := c_empseq%FOUND;
    CLOSE c_empseq;
```

```
    RETURN (v_empno);
END;
```

This code uses an explicit cursor (instead of a SELECT ... INTO implicit cursor) because of the standard as discussed in Chapter 3. The PRE-INSERT trigger code would consist of only the following:

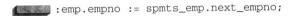

```
:emp.empno := spmts_emp.next_empno;
```

The new code reduces the cursor declaration and four other cursor commands to a single call. This single call reduces the network traffic and thus makes the code more efficient. Therefore, the standard dictates that cursor code is written in the database and called from the form.

Other Database Code Sources

There are other ways to use database code in your form besides calling the database code from your form's triggers. The following describes several of the alternative locations for database code.

Database Triggers

Another place you can write code is in a database trigger. You can write database triggers on tables and views (with Oracle8's INSTEAD OF triggers). You can specify that database triggers fire on standard DML operations—INSERT, UPDATE, and DELETE. If there is code that you want to execute each time one of these operations works on the table, whether or not it is from your form, use a database trigger. Once you use a database trigger, all applications will use the code because the trigger fires when the table is acted upon. Database triggers require no Forms code at all and are seriously worth considering. The book *Oracle8 Application Developer's Guide,* supplied online with the Oracle database, contains examples of and details about database triggers.

Blocks Based on Views

Normally, you base a block on a table, but you can also base a block on a view. If you construct your view as a single-table SELECT statement, you can perform DML operations on that view without restriction. If you construct the view as a join between a master and a detail table (with a foreign key relationship), you can perform DML on the detail table of the view. This is a very powerful feature of the form because you can construct virtually any display of the data and perform basic INSERT, UPDATE, and DELETE operations on certain parts of it. It also means that you can virtually eliminate POST-QUERY triggers that cause many network trips and require you to open and close multiple cursors for one query.

For example, you want to show the department name in a block based on the EMP table. If you write a POST-QUERY trigger that retrieves the department name from the DEPT table after each row is retrieved, you can write that name into a non–base table item. The problem is that the POST-QUERY trigger fires for each row in the query, and if many rows are returned, the extra retrieval of the department name can impose some overhead.

If you use a view on EMP and DEPT as the source for the block, you can define the view to contain the department name, and a single query in Forms will retrieve the required data without an extra network trip for each row coded into the POST-QUERY trigger. This can be more efficient. Chapter 4 contains a technique for a block based on a join view.

Views also allow you to provide complex column sources for your items. A view column can consist of a function that returns a value based on the contents of the row. For example, you might need to calculate an item for the line total on an invoice (PRICE * QUANTITY). You can do that with a formula item in the block, but this requires extra processing on the Forms side. You can offload that processing to the server by including a column for PRICE * QUANTITY in the view. Your form does not need to do the calculation, and that column is available for anyone else who uses the view. This is a simple example, but you may have a need for a more complex calculation or one that uses a function as a column source. These would be more efficient if they were coded on the database server.

You can also base a block on a query by setting the *Query Data Source Type* block property to "FROM clause query." You then write a SELECT statement in the *Query Data Source Name* property and use that as the source for the block's items. This feature has similar flexibility because you can specify join conditions and complex columns. The "view" in this case is constructed on the Forms side, although it is executed on the server. This means that if you have a large WHERE clause or large query, the entire text must be sent across the network to the server before rows are retrieved. It is much more efficient to code a view directly on the server. Chapter 4 provides an example of a block based on a FROM clause query.

Blocks Based on Procedures

You can also base your block on a procedure. The form can pass parameters to the procedure, and rows are retrieved using a REF CURSOR or table variable in the database. You can also perform INSERT, UPDATE, and DELETE operations to procedures. The benefit of this technique is that you can use complex code that is beyond the capabilities of SQL to retrieve the records. Also, the queries are potentially more efficient because they use array retrieval. You are not able to do query-by-example as easily, since you need to load arguments that are passed to the procedure as parameters. For the sake of efficiency, tables and views are better block sources, but the procedure is worth considering if you have a complex piece of logic to execute that SQL cannot handle.

Using a procedure as the data source is also useful if the logic can change. You can dynamically re-create procedures with any code you require. The form will not know the difference if the calling interface (parameter list) does not change, but the results can be very different based on the logic inside the procedure. The technique for basing a block on a procedure is explored more fully in Chapter 4.

The same standard of whether you put code in the database or in the form applies to these alternative locations for code. In essence, the question is the same: database or form? The answer is also the same, although there are variations on the actual code that you can place on the server.

Handling Forms Functions

Another standard you can set initially is how you will handle standard Forms functions. *Forms functions* are actions that Forms provides to manipulate the data on the form or navigate between objects on the form. Examples of Forms functions are the actions you see on the default menu, such as EXIT_FORM, HELP, COMMIT_FORM, and ENTER_QUERY. Depending on the design of your form, users can execute these functions using one of three actions: selecting a menu item (or menu toolbar button), clicking a separate button you have created on a canvas, or pressing a function key on the keyboard. If you need to replace or supplement a normal Forms function, you must be sure that all three actions will call the same code. This will make reading and maintaining the code easier.

TIP
The help system topic that lists KEY- triggers is called "Function Key Triggers." There is another list of Forms functions in the help topic for the DO_KEY built-in.

How to Handle Forms Functions

The default form menu contains menu items (and associated toolbar buttons in the Smartbar) that issue calls to the DO_KEY built-in. The DO_KEY built-in emulates the user pressing a Forms function key. For example, the **File→Exit** menu item issues a "DO_KEY('EXIT_FORM');". This causes an EXIT_FORM event as if the user had pressed the Exit function key (F10 on a PC). If there is a KEY-EXIT trigger, that will fire; if not, the form will execute the default exit function. Since the toolbar buttons use the same code as the menu items, the same effect occurs on those buttons.

NOTE

The Forms Functions Standard
You want to ensure that the same code you write to call a Forms function will be activated from the corresponding menu item, canvas button, or keypress. There are a few steps involved with this:

1. Write a form-level KEY- trigger for the Forms function that calls a procedure in the F_TOOLBAR library package.

2. Write menu item code if there is a corresponding menu item that issues a DO_KEY call with the function name as the parameter, for example, "DO_KEY('COMMIT_FORM');". If you define that the menu item also displays as a menu toolbar button, the button will use the same code as the menu item.

3. Write WHEN-BUTTON-PRESSED code on the canvas button (if one exists) with the same text as the menu item code.

You also need to write a form-level KEY-OTHERS trigger (with "NULL;" as the code) to disable all Forms functions that do not have explicit KEY- triggers. If you are using default Forms processing for a function (for example, to exit the form), write a KEY- trigger for it and call the standard Forms built-in (for example, EXIT_FORM).

One option for handling Forms functions is to create KEY- triggers for actions you want the users to perform and write a KEY-OTHERS trigger on the form level with code of "NULL;" to disable all other KEY- triggers. This allows you to control exactly which Forms functions the user will be able to execute. You may also want to provide buttons to execute the same actions as the enabled KEY- triggers.

Another option is to disable the Forms functions and programmatically execute the desired function when the user performs some action. For example, you might not want to bother the user about saving records by clicking a Save button or pressing the Commit function key. In this case, you would automatically commit the form, if a record were changed, when the user exits the form, queries a block, or navigates to a new master record.

CAUTION
If you use the KEY-OTHERS trigger to disable function-key presses, be sure there is at least a way for the user to exit the form. You may need to provide a KEY-EXIT trigger or button with WHEN-BUTTON-PRESSED code of "EXIT_FORM". Also, if you want the user to be able to tab back and forth through items on the screen, you will need KEY-NEXT-ITEM and KEY-PREV-ITEM triggers. Users may be accustomed to navigating from one record to another by pressing UP ARROW and DOWN ARROW. In that case, you would also need KEY-UP and KEY-DOWN triggers. In other words, think carefully about which of the Forms functions are actually desirable if you use KEY-OTHERS.

Form-Level Triggers

Another option for handling all three paths (menu, canvas button, and keypress) in the same way is to create a form-level trigger for each Forms function (for example, KEY-EXIT, KEY-HELP, KEY-EXEQRY, KEY-ENTQRY, KEY-DELREC, KEY-CREREC, KEY-COMMIT, and so on). Use the KEY-OTHERS trigger, as mentioned, or add a trigger with the code of "NULL;" to disable undesirable functions. For example, you can disable the KEY-MENU trigger so the user does not display the block menu. Each of these key triggers calls a procedure in the F_TOOLBAR package code in the generic library. For example, the KEY-EXIT trigger would call the F_TOOLBAR.EXITFORM procedure. Since these triggers are required for each form, they would be subclassed from an object library (as described in Chapter 11).

With this exit mechanism in place, the menu item and canvas button would each issue a "DO_KEY('EXIT_FORM');". This would emulate the keypress, and the KEY-EXIT trigger would fire. This trigger calls the library procedure F_TOOLBAR.EXITFORM. Thus, all three actions lead to the same code; if you need to change what happens when the user requests an exit, you just change the library code, and all forms inherit the change. If an individual form needs to do something special, you can replace or precede the call to the library procedure in the subclassed trigger with different code.

Table 7-1 summarizes the code involved with the EXIT_FORM example.

Component	Effect
Keypress (CTRL-Q on the PC)	Fires the KEY-EXIT trigger, which calls the generic library package procedure, F_TOOLBAR.EXITFORM.
Menu item and associated menu toolbar button (**File→Exit**)	The code is "DO_KEY('EXIT_FORM');". This fires the KEY-EXIT trigger.
Canvas button	The same code as the menu item.
F_TOOLBAR.EXIT_FORM	This procedure does everything you need to do before exiting (checks uncommitted records, automatically commits, asks the user for confirmation on the exit, and so on). It then exits the form.

TABLE 7-1. *Sample Forms Function*

In this example, any button or other code that you wanted to use would need to follow the same single-destination path. For example, you may want to create a button that exits the form on the main canvas. The WHEN-BUTTON-PRESSED trigger on this button would use the same DO_KEY('EXIT_FORM') call as the menu item used. This also means that if you need to issue an EXIT_FORM built-in anywhere in your form, you would use DO_KEY('EXIT_FORM') instead to maintain the single destination for the code.

Trigger or Program Unit?

The main decision here is whether you write the bulk of your code in the Forms trigger itself or in a packaged procedure that you call from the trigger. This is largely a matter of personal taste, but is one practice you need to put in your programming standards so developers do not need to think about this as they are coding. Code is executed only from triggers, but calling a local procedure from a trigger does not add to execution time.

NOTE
The Trigger Standard
Store all code in packaged procedures and place one-line calls to the procedures in the trigger. Name the procedures descriptively so you do not need to look at the trigger code but just open the package to access the code.

This means that if you decide to use the Program Units node in the Object Navigator to store the code you call in triggers, you will have two places to look for the code. One is the trigger, to see which package procedure or function is called, and the other is the package itself, to see the actual code.

This is the argument some developers use for placing code in the trigger itself. However, triggers are usually more difficult to find than program units whether you use the pull-down lists in the PL/SQL Editor or drill down in the Object Navigator. Although the PL/SQL Editor is the same for both triggers and program units, you cannot group triggers into one unit as you can group procedures and functions into packages.

On the other hand, using calls to a packaged procedure provides a cleaner-looking trigger because the trigger text can actually be a one-line call. If you name the procedure descriptively, you will not even need to open the trigger to see the code; you will be able to go directly to the packaged procedure in the Program Units node. In addition, without looking for another trigger, you will be able to view and edit other procedures in the same package in the same PL/SQL Editor session.

For example, a WHEN-VALIDATE-ITEM trigger on the EMP.EMPNO item level would call a package procedure called EMP.VALIDATE_EMPNO. This procedure could be used anywhere in the form that needs validation on an employee number value. In fact, if this were a useful procedure for a number of forms, the procedure would be placed in an application-level library and attached to the forms that need the procedure.

Form or Library?

If you decide that the code belongs in the form, you need to decide if it should be written in a library or in the form itself. If the code is something that other forms can use, a library is a logical place for the routine. The library can be attached to more than one form, and if the code in the library changes, all forms will automatically inherit the changes with no recompilation necessary. Libraries reduce the amount of local code and make the finished form a bit smaller.

NOTE
The Library Standard
Assume that all code you write is useful in other forms. After you write the code, step back and think if it is truly specific to the form you are working on. If you can't make a good case for not genericizing it, make it generic, test the generic version, and move it to a library.

Even if the code does not seem useful outside the form, you may want to take advantage of this flexibility of the library. For example, suppose you create a package procedure that loops through all buttons in a block and disables them. You could parameterize the name of the block and write the code so it loops through the items in the block whose name was passed into the procedure, checks if the item is a button, and if it is, disables that item. Nothing in the code would be written specifically for a particular form or block, so the code is a good candidate for a library. Even if there is only one form that uses the code, if the code is generically written, it will be available to other forms when required.

Generic Library Code Example

The following shows a generic procedure you would write to disable all items in a block. The procedure would be located in the F_BLOCK package of the library.

```
PROCEDURE disable_all_buttons(
    p_block_name IN VARCHAR2)
IS
    v_curr_item    VARCHAR2(30);
    v_block_item   VARCHAR2(61);
BEGIN
    -- validate the block name passed in
    IF id_null(find_block(p_block_name))
    THEN
        f_alert.ok('Error: The block name passed in (' ||
            p_block_name || ') is not valid. Contact the ' ||
            'administrator.', f_alert.g_fail);
    ELSE
        v_curr_item := get_block_property(p_block_name, FIRST_ITEM);
        --
        -- loop through all items in the block
        WHILE v_curr_item IS NOT NULL
```

```
      LOOP
         v_block_item := p_block_name || '.' || v_curr_item;
         --
         -- turn off the enabled property for the buttons
         IF get_item_property(v_block_item, ITEM_TYPE) = 'BUTTON'
         THEN
            set_item_property(v_block_item, ENABLED, PROPERTY_FALSE);
         END IF;
         v_curr_item := get_item_property(v_block_item, NEXTITEM);
      END LOOP;
   END IF;
END;
```

This procedure accepts a parameter of the block name and checks that a valid name was passed in. This makes the code generic and reusable for any block. If you wanted to make this procedure even more generic, you could add a parameter of the item type to be disabled. The test for item type in the middle of the loop would only disable certain types of items. The procedure would then be better named DISABLE_ALL_ITEM_TYPE. You could also extend the procedure to disable all items in the block if a NULL value were passed in as an item type. This is the way you work flexibility into your code: start simple and add more as required.

Regardless of your attempts to make a routine generic, all indications may point to the code being only for one form. For example, you might have a routine that validates a particular item in a particular block. The form in which these objects are housed is the only form that will address the needs of that block. Another example would be a procedure that only runs in one logon form when the user starts up the application. No other form would ever use that code, as there is a single point of entry. You would place the code for that function in the form itself.

CAUTION
Although placing code directly in the form makes the call more efficient because Forms does not need to look in an external file, you lose the ability to make changes to that code without recompiling the form. You also lose the ability to share the code with other forms. Therefore, try to use libraries as the repository of Forms code as much as possible.

Which Library?

If you decide that the code should be genericized and located in a library, you have to then decide which library to put it in. There are three levels of libraries, as follows:

1. A generic library As you create more and more Forms applications, you will create a toolbox of code that helps with normal chores. Appendix A describes an example of this type of library. The packages in this library are written to support specific objects, but are written totally generically so that they can be used for any project in the future. For example, the F_MENU package contains procedures to hide, show, enable, and disable a menu item. While these effects are not extremely difficult to code with native Forms built-in calls, the F_MENU package makes them even easier and provides meaningful error messages. Moreover, if the procedure is in the library, all forms with this library attached need not worry about the steps involved with the menu item properties. In effect, the library supplies a developer-friendly interface to the Forms built-ins.

NOTE

The Specific Library Standard
Place the code in the generic *library if it is truly nonspecific for any database. Use the* application *library if it contains references to database code in a specific application. Place the code in the* form-specific *library if it only be used by one form.*

The good part is that if you have a generic library, many of your developers do not have to learn the intricacies of Forms routines. An example of this is loading a poplist from a database query (as described in Chapter 25). There are a few steps involved with this, and with error handling included, this becomes a 70-line piece of code. If it is written into a single call, the Forms developer need not rewrite (and debug) those 70 lines each time a poplist needs to be loaded.

You can divide the generic library into two files: one library file for *nondatabase* actions and one library file for *database* actions. The nondatabase library would contain code to manipulate Forms objects (such as items, blocks, canvases, and windows). The database library would contain code to handle generic routines that were non–application specific (such as security, queries to a standard lookup table, generic routines to load a sequence value, and so on). Keeping the database code separate from the Forms-only code means that you can change the database and not be required to recompile the Forms-only library (which can become rather large). Appendix A describes the packages in a Forms-only generic library.

2. **An application-specific library** This library contains code that calls database packages for a particular application. For example, a packaged function that you might include in this library would be one that performs lookups on a particular reference table to derive a description from an ID. This function would call a database function that would query the table based on an ID and return the value of the description. For example, the procedure would return the project description from the PROJECT table if it were passed the project ID. The Forms library would call this function and manipulate the results in some way.

   This library would be attached to and available to all forms in all applications. It may use procedures and functions from the generic library, so you would need to attach that library to the application-specific library.

3. **A form-specific library** There may be code that is just too specific to make it generic to serve many forms and applications. You might want to include this code in a form-specific library and attach it to the single form. The benefit is that the form size is smaller than if the code were in the form itself, but the drawback is that the form needs to read a second file when it needs the code in that library. Another benefit is that you can change the library slightly and there is no need to recompile the form that uses it. You can also use this library to isolate calls to database procedures and functions. If the database code parameters change, you only need to recompile the library, not the form.

   Practically speaking, this type of library is not as essential as the other two. Any code that is a candidate for this library could also go into the form itself without adverse effects.

Table 7-2 shows the scope of the code in the three different types of libraries. The libraries themselves have no characteristics that distinguish their type, but the contents of the libraries point to one type or another.

Library \ Scope	All Applications	All Forms in One Application	One Form
Generic	Yes	Yes	Yes
Application-specific	No	Yes	Yes
Form-specific	No	No	Yes

TABLE 7-2. *The Scope of Library Code Availability*

Subclass or Copy from the Object Library?

As mentioned earlier, the first step when writing code is to determine if there is already code that can do at least part of the work. Someone may have already written a function to translate an ID to a name, for example, and you might be able to use this as is or incorporate it into your new code. Code reuse is an important goal in every project. The keys to finding an existing routine are *naming conventions* and *documentation*. If the packages and their contents are named descriptively, you will be able to find a particular code piece in short order. Documentation of the code in the package header will detail what the procedures actually do, so you can decide whether they have what you need.

NOTE
The Object Library Standard
Avoid storing program units in the object library. If you need form-level triggers that exist in an object library, subclass the triggers.

Consider that you have found an existing code piece that fulfills your requirements. You may need to decide how to use it. If it is a packaged procedure or function stored in the database or in a Forms library, you just reference the code in the trigger. If the code exists as a program unit or trigger in an object library, you have the choice of subclassing or copying the code into your form.

Subclassing Code from Object Libraries

While you can store program units in object libraries, code libraries (.PLL files) are better places to store code since the code units in an object library may not be easily modified. Object libraries can act as sources for program units that you need to copy or subclass into a form, but except for the initial setup of your template system, as described in Chapter 11, you will probably not need to do this.

Object libraries can also act as sources for triggers that you need to copy or subclass. Again, the setup of triggers in your form was probably accomplished when the template was created. There are triggers that may only apply to some forms, and if these are in the object library, it is best to subclass them. An example is a WHEN-TIMER-EXPIRED trigger. Not all forms in your system need that, so it is not included in the template. However, you have three forms that need to check the expiration of two different timers. The timer creation code exists in an application library. The three forms call that library code to initialize the timers, but all three need the trigger to process the expiration event.

While it is a simple matter to create that trigger in each form, it is even easier to subclass the trigger from the object library. In this way, the triggers will all have the same code, and if you do not change the code in any particular form, changing the object library will cause all forms to change the next time they are recompiled. Subclassing also maintains a link between the form and its source, in this case, an object library. The link establishes a commonality between all forms that use the same source.

Subclassing also allows changes. You can override the code in a subclassed program unit. If you do that, the Property Palette will show a broken inheritance symbol (an "x" instead of an arrow symbol) by the *Trigger Text* property to indicate that the text is overridden, as Figure 7-1 shows. The danger with inheritance is that if you make modifications to the inherited trigger and click the Inherit button by mistake, Forms will reset the trigger text back to the value from the source, and your changes will be lost. You can avoid the problem if you write your code in a local Forms procedure package and make a single call to that procedure from the trigger.

Chapters 11 and 12 contain examples of how you would use subclassed triggers from an object library.

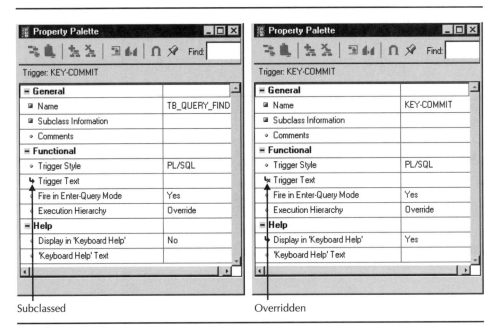

FIGURE 7-1. *Subclassed and overridden trigger text*

Which Level of Trigger?

You also need to decide at what level to place the trigger—form, block, or item. Figure 7-2 shows the location of these triggers in the Object Navigator.

CAUTION
You can also write triggers for property classes, as Figure 7-2 shows. The property class itself offers less flexibility than the SmartClass, and there is no real reason to use it in the current release of Oracle Developer. In addition, triggers on property classes can cause confusion because they are hidden one level under the item or block to which they are attached. Therefore, your standard should be to not use property classes in general, and to never use property-class triggers.

NOTE
The Trigger-Level Standard
Write block-level triggers for item and block events. This will greatly reduce the number of places you need to look for Forms code.

It is best to avoid item-level triggers such as single WHEN-BUTTON-PRESSED triggers because these require you to drill many levels in the Object Navigator. You can easily place the item-level trigger code at the block level and can place the code needed for all items in the trigger or in a single packaged procedure. This makes changing the code much easier because you can just open one trigger (or package) and edit the code for all the items at once. The trigger would contain conditional logic to sense which button was clicked and would act accordingly. For example, the following is a procedure contained in the F_TOOLBAR package. It is called by the WHEN-BUTTON-PRESSED trigger written on the block level. The buttons in the block are named with DO_KEY functions. For example, the Exit, Save, and New Record buttons are called EXIT_FORM, COMMIT_FORM, and CREATE_RECORD, respectively.

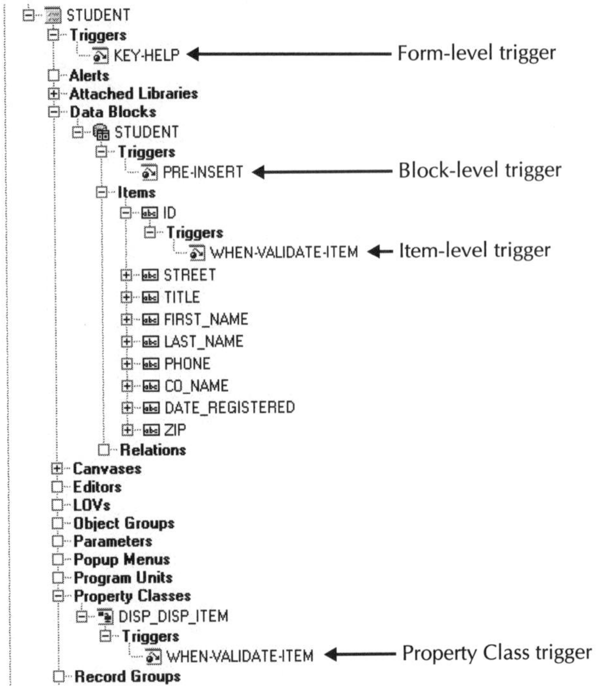

FIGURE 7-2. *Forms trigger locations*

```
PROCEDURE button_pressed
IS
    v_blockitem    VARCHAR2(61) := name_in('SYSTEM.TRIGGER_ITEM');
    v_itemname     VARCHAR2(30) := substr(v_blockitem,
                   instr(v_blockitem, '.') + 1);
BEGIN
    IF INSTR(',' || f_global.v_dokey_functions || ',',
       ',' || v_itemname || ',') > 0
    THEN
        do_key(v_itemname);
    ELSE
        execute_trigger(v_itemname);
    END IF;
END;
```

In this code, F_GLOBAL.V_DOKEY_FUNCTIONS is a variable that contains a list of the names of all functions that the DO_KEY built-in can execute. It is comma delimited—for example, EXIT_FORM,EXECUTE_QUERY,COMMIT_FORM, so the procedure easily can parse an individual name. If the item name of the button that was pressed is one of those functions, the code calls the DO_KEY built-in and uses the name of the item. This will fire a KEY- trigger to execute the proper code. If the button name is not a DO_KEY function, the code executes a trigger with the name of the item (for example, HELP_CONTENTS). This trigger would be written on the form level and would call the appropriate code to display the help system.

In addition to the benefit of being able to see all code for all buttons in the block in one location, there is an added benefit of the ease of adding a new button. If the new button is a DO_KEY function, you just need to add the button, name it with the function name, and move it to the right location on the canvas. The code is already written into the block trigger.

The alternative (individual button triggers) would require more work opening and closing nodes on the Object Navigator to find the correct trigger and potentially follow it back to the proper procedure.

Execution Hierarchy

You can define a trigger at a higher level and then code the same trigger on a lower level—for example, on an item level WHEN-BUTTON-PRESSED when there is already one on the block level. The lower-level code takes precedence unless you set the *Execution Hierarchy* property on the lower trigger's properties to "Before" or "After."

CAUTION
If you add triggers to a lower level than triggers in the template form (such as item level), be sure to set the trigger property Execution Hierarchy to "Before," "After," or "Override" based on whether you want your trigger to fire before, after, or instead of the trigger in the template that is on the higher level. Keep in mind, however, that the same trigger firing on different levels can be confusing to code readers because they need to follow the path up or down the form-block-item hierarchy with the order in mind.

Another Example

As another example of a high-level trigger, you can create a single WHEN-VALIDATE-ITEM trigger for all items in the form that calls a single packaged procedure. This procedure checks the :SYSTEM.TRIGGER_ITEM and performs a validation based on that. To maintain any validation anywhere in the form, you just need to open that package and manipulate that code. You do not need to create individual triggers on each item. This eliminates the need to navigate down to a trigger under an item inside a block to find the code.

NOTE
There are some triggers that apply only to certain levels. For example, the WHEN-NEW-FORM-INSTANCE, WHEN-WINDOW-CLOSED, and WHEN-TIMER-EXPIRED triggers fire only on the form level. Your decision about where to put those triggers has already been made.

The Options

Your standard can actually embrace any of the three following options:

1. **Form level**   Write all triggers for all events on the form level, and conditionally call a single procedure for each block. For example, if your form included blocks for EMP and DEPT, the logic in a form-level WHEN-VALIDATE-ITEM trigger would check the :SYSTEM.TRIGGER_BLOCK to see if it was EMP or DEPT and call a separate procedure for each to perform the validation on items in the block.

2. **Block level**   Write triggers on the block level to handle specific block and item actions. Use a single call to a packaged procedure in the trigger text. The procedure checks which item fired the trigger (using :SYSTEM.TRIGGER_ITEM) and calls other procedures to perform the action (like checking the item contents in a WHEN-NEW-ITEM-INSTANCE trigger). Forms events such as WHEN-NEW-FORM-INSTANCE would still be written on the form level.

3. **Item level**   Write triggers at the lowest level possible. If you need to validate an item, use the WHEN-VALIDATE-ITEM trigger on the item level. If you need to add a value to an INSERT statement, write a PRE-INSERT trigger on the block level. If you need to check which window the user closed, code a WHEN-WINDOW-CLOSED trigger on the form level. As in the other standards, you use a single call to a packaged procedure as the trigger text.

Mixtures of these standards can lead to confusion, so it is best to pick one as a standard.

The Development Process

The normal path for placing code is to write the code (database or form based) in the form trigger or package without worrying about where you will eventually place it. Junior developers often stop here, but this will not serve the application well in the long run. The real process should continue after you have tested the code and verified that it works the way you want it to. You are then ready to decide if you have it in the correct location or if you need to move it. This determination is the result of examining how the logic is used and of measuring your code against the standards. While it is possible that you may know the ultimate location before you even write the routine, it is also possible that you do not know where the code will go until you have written and tested it.

It is worth repeating that after you write and test the code, you are not finished. You have to go through the process, however brief or extended, of determining the best location for that code. You also need to determine if the code is generic or can be made generic enough to store in a library or publicly accessible database package.

Genericizing Code for the Library

If you decide that a package you have developed belongs in a library, you just need to drag and drop it into the library in the Object Navigator. Be sure you do not reference items using the bind variable syntax (:*block.item*). Instead, use the COPY and NAME_IN built-ins to assign items and reference the values inside items. For example, to assign the value of 100 to :EMP.EMPNO in library code, use the following:

```
copy('100', 'EMP.EMPNO');
```

To use the value of :EMP.EMPNO in an expression, follow this syntax:

```
IF name_in('EMP.EMPNO') = '100'
```

Both COPY and NAME_IN work only on character values. If your items are number or date datatypes, you must convert the value using the TO_CHAR, TO_DATE, or TO_NUMBER function. For example:

```
DECLARE
    v_today DATE := SYSDATE;
BEGIN
    copy(to_char(v_today), :emp.hire_date);
```

```
IF  TO_NUMBER(name_in('EMP.SALARY')) > 1000
THEN
. . .
```

Another key technique to genericizing code so you can put it in a library file is to remove all references to named objects in the form, replacing them with parameters that you pass into the form. Chapter 11 discusses generic code further.

CAUTION
Be sure to delete the local form package after saving the library file. It is not a good idea to maintain the same named package both in a library and in a form. This can lead to confusion, although Forms should look for the package in the form first.

General Guidelines

In summary, you can use the following as general guidelines for your more advanced developers:

1. As much as possible, implement data access and manipulation code as stored database server code. Forms should not use PL/SQL code that opens cursors or performs queries outside the default query and DML mechanisms.

2. Write code that is as generic as possible. If you create a form-specific utility that is reusable, put it in a library.

3. Use packages to organize and modularize the code.

4. Write Forms trigger code on the highest level, if possible.

If you spell out the general guidelines for the main decisions developers need to make and create a set of standards to assist developers in placing the code in the best place, you will speed up development. You will end up with forms that are coded for ease of maintenance and understanding.

CHAPTER

8

Reports Development Standards

By honor and dishonor, by evil report and good report...

—*The Holy Bible*, II Corinthians 6:8

I t is not possible to discuss development standards without also mentioning development philosophy. Oracle Reports is a flexible and powerful enough component of the Oracle Developer tool suite that it should influence the way you think about the reports needed for your system. The product has the ability to dynamically modify the query upon which the report is based and, to a limited extent, to dynamically modify the report layout. This enables system designers to satisfy a large, complex set of reporting requirements with a small number of physical reports.

The adoption of this flexible reporting style is key to the effective use of Oracle Reports. By applying this advanced functionality, the tremendous benefits of the product can be best realized. The implementation details of your report standards are actually a small set of information. A much more important issue is that of determining what reports (using this flexible, generic reporting philosophy) you are going to build.

This chapter will discuss reporting standards and how they are best implemented by a generic, flexible reporting approach as well as the benefits of using this approach. This chapter will also discuss how to do analysis of reports and the basic GUI standards for reports as they apply to the report templating philosophy discussed in Chapter 21. The reader is encouraged to look at Appendixes E and F concerning report audits and report specifications, respectively.

Genericizing Reports

It is important to build some level of genericization into the Data Model to support not only existing requirements, but also any similar requirements that may arise. The same principle can be applied to report design in supporting not only the current reporting requirements, but also the generation of many similar reports at runtime.

To effectively use generic report specifications requires the ability to modify the report during runtime. Flexible reports enable users to select appropriate breaks, sorts, filters, and (to a limited degree) fields that will appear on a report. It is even possible in some cases to specify, at runtime, the database table that the report will access.

Benefits of Genericizing Reports

Reports genericization actually decreases the amount of work required to specify the reporting requirements since the number of reports to build is greatly reduced. For example, if you are working in a full-featured reporting environment for a large, complex system with several hundred reports, genericization will decrease the number of reports to build and maintain by as much as a factor of 20. Even if only a limited number of reports have been specified, the number of generic reports needed will be roughly half of those necessary in a traditional system.

Other related benefits to genericization of reports include the greatly decreased cost of responding to data model changes due to the smaller number and more flexible nature of the reports created. In your report architecture, if you are careful about using views where appropriate, it is possible to support even drastic data model changes across the entire reporting system in a few weeks or even days. In a large, traditional reporting system with several hundred reports in production, supporting even a minor change in the data model usually requires months of effort.

Another benefit to genericization is the greater ease in accommodating new reporting requirements that inevitably arise during the course of system design. Frequently, these new reports simply require changing a few runtime parameters on an existing report structure.

Drawbacks of Genericizing Reports

Using a generic approach is not without cost. Generic reports are more difficult to build than traditional reports. They do not necessarily require more time, but do require a more skilled developer to create them. Traditionally, report development has been considered a less skilled task assigned to junior developers. Since reporting is a very important aspect of system design and requires greater creativity and skill than most screen application development, it should be assigned to more experienced talent. Using a generic approach, it is critical to have a senior-level developer with strong SQL and PL/SQL skills, as well as expertise with the tools being used to actually build the reports. Junior developers might design and build reports that produce the desired output but these reports may contain unmaintainable code and run inefficiently. It is not uncommon for a badly written report to take days to run rather than executing in seconds or minutes if it had been designed and built by a more skilled developer.

When to Genericize Reports

Thinking carefully about when to use generic versus specific reports is a worthwhile consideration. Some level of genericization should almost always be applied to a report. There is nothing new about this concept. Even the simple passing of a date range or a department ID to a report is a type of genericization. How far can the notion of genericization be pushed? There is no easy answer. It will depend upon the skill of your development team, development strategy, and specific reporting requirements. If you must supply hundreds of relatively simple reports, a generic approach is obviously indicated. If you have a handful of very complex reports, each requiring days or weeks of development work, genericization may not be appropriate. The more experience a team has with genericizing reports, the more often this technique will be used and the smaller the number of reports that will be needed. Reports will be more flexible as well. The data model itself also influences the degree of genericization needed. Generic, object-oriented data models will naturally lead to the development of more genericized reports. For example, in a system that one of the authors worked on, over 200 different correspondence letters were sent out in response to many different situations. The cost of developing 200 separate reports would have been enormous. Writing one, very flexible letter-writing report was a difficult task, but only needed to be done once.

The suggested strategy is to gather reporting requirements in the traditional way by assembling (potentially) hundreds of reports. These reports can either be existing legacy reports or pro forma copies of new reports. Then carefully work with the reports to determine which ones can be easily combined. If necessary, encourage users to accept a single report that is a union of two or more other reports to further decrease the total number of reports necessary.

Supporting flexible reports requires the use of various techniques including

- Lexical parameters
- Bind variables

The details of how to employ these techniques in the context of a flexible reporting system are covered in Chapters 17 and 20.

Setting the Report Standards

It is not simply the look, feel, and layout of a report that determine the standards. Until you have a sense about how to build reports, it is impossible to formulate a coherent set of standards. The design philosophy itself is the most important part of setting the standards. There are several factors that influence the creation of the report standards in a particular environment. Each will be discussed separately.

Printing Hardware

You cannot count on the fact that the way a report looks in preview mode will be the way it comes out of the printer. "WYSIWYG" (What You See Is What You Get) is really "WYSISoWYG" (What You See Is Sort of What You Get). If reports will be displayed over the Web and will allow remote printing, you will need to perform extensive testing before solidifying your standards. The actual output is a function of the Microsoft printer drivers. The way that printing is emulated on the screen may not be exactly the way that pages are printed. Characters may occasionally be truncated at paper edges or letters truncated within fields. As Windows has matured, this has become less of a problem. However, testing should include viewing physical reports printed on paper before a system goes into production.

The report standards you set should be very simple:

- Keep the number of different fonts and font sizes to a minimum.

- Avoid unnecessary use of background shading.

- Use italics (which are hard to read) sparingly.

- Use standard, commonly used fonts such as Arial or Times New Roman to avoid variations in the way characters are printed.

- Use blank spaces on the report to separate records, but don't waste space.

There have been specific instances where specialized hardware was used to print reports. In these cases, standards specific to a particular setting needed to be created. For example, an 11" × 17" line printer or an 11" × 17" high-speed dot-matrix printer required specialized standards. The concept should be to use relatively plain standards, wasting as little space as possible and maximizing the amount of information on each page.

An example of standards used in a four-level (Master-detail-detail-detail) production report is shown in Table 8-1, and a sample report as shown in Figure 8-1.

Where Do You Put the Code in Reports?

Code in Oracle Reports is much simpler than code in Oracle Forms because there is less coding to do and fewer alternatives for where to place the code. The vast majority of report code usually involves assembling the required data from various sources and applying the various filters that are specified. Most of this "code" should not appear in the report at all. All the required data assembly, including

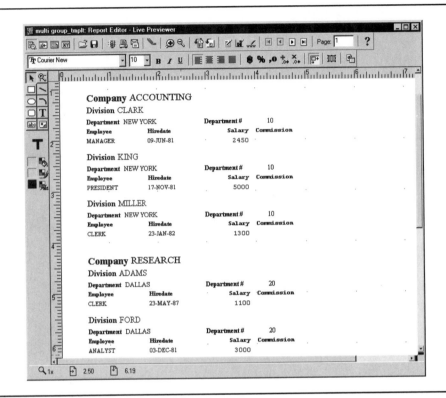

FIGURE 8-1. *Sample Master-detail-detail-detail report*

Report Element	Font	Style	Size
Report titles	Arial	Bold	14 point
Core data	Times New Roman	Regular	8 point
1st level breaks	Times New Roman	Regular	14 point
2nd level breaks	Times New Roman	Regular	12 point
3rd level breaks	Times New Roman	Regular	10 point
Data for all levels	Times New Roman	Regular	

TABLE 8-1. *Report Formatting Standards*

Report Element	Font	Style	Size
Labels for all levels		Bold	
Separation between horizontal data rows			0
Vertical separation between level 2 data			0.2"
Vertical separation between level 3 data			0.1"
Vertical separation between level 4 data			0.3"
Separation between fields			0.1"
Numbers and associated column levels		Right justified	
Dates, text fields and associated column labels		Left justified	
Page numbers		Upper right corner	
Date report is run		Upper left corner	
Filter parameters for report		Bottom of first page	

TABLE 8-1. *Report Formatting Standards* (continued)

the fields required by the filters, should be pushed back to the database as a view definition. This allows your report to be based on a simple SELECT statement from the view. In Reports itself, you are mainly concerned with layout and formatting. There are a few other places where code can be placed in a report. A list of these alternatives is followed by a separate discussion of each:

■ Attached libraries

■ Local program units

- The Data Model
- Report queries
- Report triggers
- Format triggers

Placing Code in Attached Libraries

It is possible to use the same generic attached library in your Reports template that you use in Forms. However, this is rarely done because, in most cases, complex PL/SQL code resides in either the form, stored procedures, or embedded within a view. Attached libraries are used for the rare reports when a function from the attached library is needed. For example, to display a comma-delimited list, you need to have separate functions to do this stored in an attached library. Most code should be in views in the database so that the need for attached libraries in reports is fairly small.

Placing Code in Local Program Units

Accessing server-side packages or isolated functions and procedures can be done by placing code in local client-side program units. With the exception of program units automatically generated by formula columns, not many program units are needed when writing reports. No program units that access the database should be stored locally in the report. Local program units that access the database cause unnecessary network traffic. If you follow this strategy, more program units will be in the database. However, during development, you might want to build local program units and test them. Once the report is completed, for performance optimization, program units can be moved to the server side.

Placing Code in the Data Model

Summary columns for performing sums, counts, and other aggregation functions are also a form of Reports coding that can be created in the Data Model. Discussions of formula and summary columns can be found in Chapters 18 and 19.

Within the Data Model, you can create formula and summary columns. You can create a formula column calculated by a function. When the formula column is created, the function used to populate it is actually stored as a program unit. Formula columns should be limited to client-side operations such as adding variables or concatenating two strings. Even these operations are better placed in a view, so that other forms or reports can easily reuse them. However, sometimes a specific operation is truly report-specific and can be placed within the report Data Model.

Summary columns should be used for totaling and subtotaling. These columns require very little overhead, and you should use them instead of creating views to support the same display. If you can use a summary column, you should do so.

Placing Code in Report Queries

Program logic can be embedded in report queries using server-side functions. You can create complex server-side PL/SQL functions that are accessed directly by the SQL statement or are embedded in views that the queries are based on.

NOTE
If you are going to access a function in a query, it must be stored in the server. You cannot access local functions in a report query.

Placing Code in Report Triggers

PL/SQL code can be placed in the report triggers BEFORE PARAMETER FORM, AFTER PARAMETER FORM, BEFORE REPORT, BETWEEN PAGE, and AFTER REPORT. These triggers are also discussed in Chapter 18.

There are five report-level triggers where you can place code, as follows:

■ **BEFORE PARAMETER FORM**   This trigger fires before the Parameter Form is displayed. Use this trigger for manipulating the display of objects in a Parameter Form.

■ **AFTER PARAMETER FORM**   This trigger fires after users click the Run Report icon (traffic light) on the Run Parameter Form but before the query is parsed. This trigger code can validate that what the user entered in the Parameter Form is correct. The advantage to using this trigger is that if the Parameter Form trigger returns FALSE, the user is returned to the Parameter Form. This is very useful because after the user inputs parameters, you can semantically validate the information. If there is an error in input, you can return to the Parameter Form, forcing the user to double-check the input values. If the user parameters are somehow invalid, you should deliver a message to the user explaining why. You can do this by using the SRW.MESSAGE built-in. However, this means that two alerts will be shown: one regarding the invalid parameter and the second showing that the AFTER_REPORT trigger failed.

TIP
Rather than returning FALSE in the AFTER PARAMETER FORM trigger, you can raise an SRW.PROGRAM_ABORT exception. All that this does is change the message of the second alert. An additional alternative is to write your message into a user parameter, so that your message will be displayed on the Parameter Form.

If you are not satisfied with these limitations, you can handle your user parameter checking through an Oracle Forms front-end and avoid using the Parameter Form at all.

- **BEFORE REPORT**   This trigger fires after the query is parsed and the first set of fetches is executed but before the first page is displayed. It is used for any pre-processing of the report such as:

  a. The implementation of security measures to provide validation that the user has sufficient privileges to execute the report with the current parameters

  b. The retrieval of information from the database that will alter the query

  c. The use of user-specified values in the Parameter Form to build a WHERE clause to fill in a lexical parameter used in the query

- **BETWEEN PAGES**   This trigger fires before the display of every page in the report except the first one. It does not fire before the first page or after the last page. For a three-page report, it will only fire twice. It can be used to pass printer codes to support changing page orientation in the middle of a report.

- **AFTER REPORT**   This trigger fires once after the report is successfully executed. This trigger can be used to send a message of successful report completion as well as to pass back the last page number in a multi-page report.

FORMAT TRIGGERS   Format triggers can be placed on any layout object. These triggers fire every time there is an attempt to display an object.

The first step in determining the appropriate placement for code in your report is to determine what information will be displayed in the report. You are better off doing as much of this as possible in the server by building functions and embedding them in views. Any report that fires a single access to a simple view will almost always outperform a logically equivalent report built using multiple queries or cursor-laden formula columns.

CAUTION

A query against a single view performs very well. However, if you use a view in the FROM clause of a query, the query becomes difficult (and maybe impossible) to tune. Views should be used with caution in multi-table queries.

This limitation does not apply if you use a simple single-table view with some additional functional columns. As an example, use a view based on the DEPT [no period] table to run a report displaying department names and the number of employees in each department. One approach would be to create a function called NUMBER_OF_EMPS, taking department number as an input parameter and returning the number of employees. Next, create a view using the following code:

```
CREATE OR REPLACE VIEW dept_v
AS
    SELECT deptno,
           dname,
           number_of_emps (deptno) no_of_emps
    FROM dept
```

In this case, you can join to DEPT_V without encountering any tuning problems because the query is based on a single table. In general, this single-table strategy should be used often for constructing report views. Queries should be based on single table views, if possible. This usually improves performance as well as the maintainability and reusability of the code. Creating views also has an additional advantage in that it is easier to find skilled SQL and PL/SQL developers than skilled Reports developers.

Format triggers can be used for two purposes. First, they can conditionally suppress the display of an object. For example, in a master-detail report with more than five details, you don't want to display the master or any of its details. In this case, you can attach the following trigger to the master repeating frame:

```
DECLARE
    v_return BOOLEAN
BEGIN
    IF :count > 5
    THEN
        v_return := FALSE;
    ELSE
```

```
        v_return := TRUE;
    END IF;
    RETURN (v_return);
END;
```

As another example, if a field is blank, you want to suppress the printing of its label. For this example, write the following code in the boilerplate format trigger:

```
DECLARE
    v_return BOOLEAN
BEGIN
    IF :field IS NULL
    THEN
        v_return := FALSE;
    ELSE
        v_return := TRUE;
    END IF;
    RETURN (v_return);
END;
```

The second use for format triggers is for populating a value into a field using SRW.SET FIELD commands. With these you can populate a field with a value when Reports would be unable to provide the calculation any other way. This is a function that is rarely used because in most cases, information can be displayed using normal query, formula, or summary columns.

CHAPTER
9

Reports Naming Conventions

He said true things, but called them by wrong names.

—Elizabeth Barrett Browning (1806–1861)

 ust as consistent naming conventions are important in forms and throughout a system, they are equally critical in reports. This chapter will describe the naming conventions for each of the report elements and objects as shown in Figure 9-1.

Naming the Report Itself

The Reports component of Oracle Developer uses an .RDF file extension to indicate that the document is a report; no special report-naming convention is necessary. Reports files should be named using the same style of descriptive names as is used for Forms described in Chapter 6. The Reports module will automatically take the name of the file. For example, a payroll summary report might be called PAYROLL_SUM.RDF. When you save the file as that name, the report node name in the Object Navigator becomes PAYROLL_SUM.

Naming Queries

Queries are the primary Data Model construct in the Reports component of Oracle Developer. However, once a query is named, that name is almost never used elsewhere in the report. One exception to this is that there are a few SRW built-in functions that allow you to manipulate some query properties such as SET_MAXROW. (This function will set the maximum number of rows retrieved by a query when it is executed.) The reason to name the query is so that when developers look at the Data Model, they can understand the report more quickly and easily. However, if the groups are descriptively named, almost the same purpose will be accomplished.

If you have multiple queries in your report, it is useful to name the query using one or more table names most closely associated with the primary rows in the report that the query is retrieving. All you need to do is name the queries clearly. For example, a query to support a master-detail report involving the DEPT and EMP tables could be called DEPT_EMP or simply EMP because one row per employee is retrieved.

SQL Naming Standards

For the SQL in your queries, you should follow the SQL standards described in Chapter 3. However, Oracle Reports includes the nicely integrated Query Builder. If your query is simple enough that it can easily be maintained in the Query Builder,

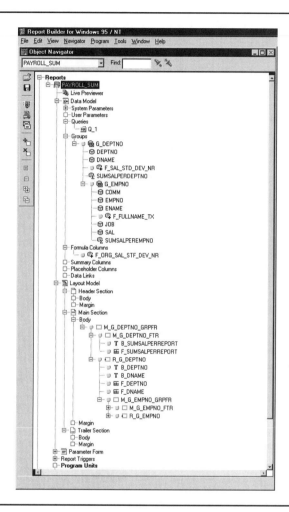

FIGURE 9-1.   *Oracle Reports Object Navigator*

there is no need to take the extra time to format your SQL beyond what the Query Builder does automatically.

Although the Query Builder is adequate to support most simple queries, there are some limitations. For example, the Query Builder does not support unions or other set operators. Another problem occurs when you have multiple queries with the same column being selected in each query. Every field that appears in the select list of a query in a report is global. There is no grouping of objects into "blocks" for naming purposes, as is the case in Forms. If you have a DEPTNO column in two separate queries, when the query generates the associated column name in the Data Model, the second instance of the column will automatically be called DEPTNO1 and the next instance, DEPTNO2, to enforce uniqueness. This is not an acceptable naming convention.

If you alias the fields in the select list of your queries and recompile them, the names of your fields can change. There are two possible solutions to this problem. In the first release of Oracle Developer v.6, in Reports, you can change the name of a column in a group after it has been created. This may not be possible in later versions and, moreover, this is not recommended, because there is no tie from the object name back to the query. Instead, alias the names of columns in queries in order to control uniqueness. You might also want to alias column names so that they are more easily identifiable. For example, if the name of the project were stored in a column NAME_TX, in the query this would be referred to as PROJ.NAME_TX. However, elsewhere in the report, it would simply be NAME_TX. You should alias the column as PROJ_NAME_TX in the query.

Naming Groups

It is important to name groups in a report. You should use the same rigor with naming groups as with database entities, namely, "Each row in this group contains information about a…" All groups should be given meaningful names.

Whenever each row in a group corresponds exactly with one row in a table, you should use that table name for the group. However, sometimes you may have a break group where each record does not correspond to any table in the database. In this case, you should view the group as a pseudo-table, and create a new name for it just as you would for any other table. Great care should be exercised when naming groups. Group names act as an important tool to assist developers in ensuring that columns in the query have been placed in the correct group. For simple reports, carefully naming groups will seem like a waste of time. But for complex reports, careful group naming can be helpful in debugging report logic. For example, in the case of a DEPT and EMP master-detail query, you would have one group called DEPT because each row corresponds to one department, and one group called EMP where each row corresponds to one employee. By default, Oracle will name the groups G_<*Name of first column in the group*>. For example, if you build a query on the DEPT table in the Oracle sample schema Scott, the group will be called G_DEPTNO if DEPTNO is the first column selected. This is not a suitable group name since it is not descriptive enough.

Columns in Groups

You need to set naming standards for three types of columns (base table, summary, and formula) as follows.

Base Table Columns

You should leave the base table column names in groups the same as their database columns. In a large, complex report, you may want to alias the columns in the query by adding a short group-alias prefix to each column name to help identify the group to which the column belongs. For example, In the DEPT EMP master-detail report, the DNAME column could be aliased as DEPT_DNAME. This makes it easy to see which logical group each field is in as you go through the Report Wizard. In a simple report with only a few fields, this is too much work for a limited benefit. However, for a complex report with dozens of columns and six or more groups, being able to easily identify which column is in which group can be useful.

Summary Columns

Summary columns should be named using the summary function followed by the name of the field being aggregated. For example, for a field that is the sum of all salaries, the name would be SUM_SALARY_NR.

Formula Columns

Formula columns should be named with an FC_ to indicate that they are formula columns followed by a meaningful variable name for the information being returned. For example, if Salary and Commission were added to determine Total Compensation, the name would be FC_TOT_COMPN_NR.

Parameters

Parameters are named the same way as in Forms. See Chapter 6 for details.

Naming Frames

Given that most frame creation will be done automatically either by the Report Wizard or by the Additional Default Layout tool, Oracle Reports already names all the frames created. The developer can either accept the Oracle Reports naming convention (detailed next), or manually rename all frames. Manually renaming all frames is not worthwhile, so you should simply use the default names detailed next.

Enclosing Frames

Enclosing frames are all named with an M_ preceding the name of the group they are enclosing. There are three types of enclosing frames used by Oracle:

- Frames around a whole report section are suffixed with _GRPFR.

- Headers are suffixed with _HDR.

- If summary columns have been specified for printing, Oracle attaches the suffix _FTR (for "footer" since they are at the bottom of the page).

For example, the frames associated with the DEPT group would be M_DEPT_GRPFR, M_DEPT_HDR, and M_DEPT_FTR, respectively.

If you need an enclosing frame surrounding a subset of fields in order to manipulate the layout, use an S_ prefix to indicate that the frame is a subframe, followed by the name of the group being surrounded by the frame. If you need multiple subframes, use a suffix indicating the location within the enclosing frame (Left, Right, Top, and Bottom), as shown in Figure 9-2. For example, a subframe enclosing the DEPTNO and DNAME fields would be called S_DEPT or S_DEPT_LEFT to denote its position in the parent frame.

Repeating Frames

Repeating frames are named with an R_ preceding the name of the source group. For example, the repeating frame for the DEPT group would be R_DEPT.

Naming Display Fields

Oracle uses an F_ followed by the name of the source column for naming display fields. Any fields created manually can be named using the same convention. If you have two display fields based on the same source column, you can use positional reference to distinguish one from the other.

Naming Program Units

See Chapter 3 for a discussion of naming program units.

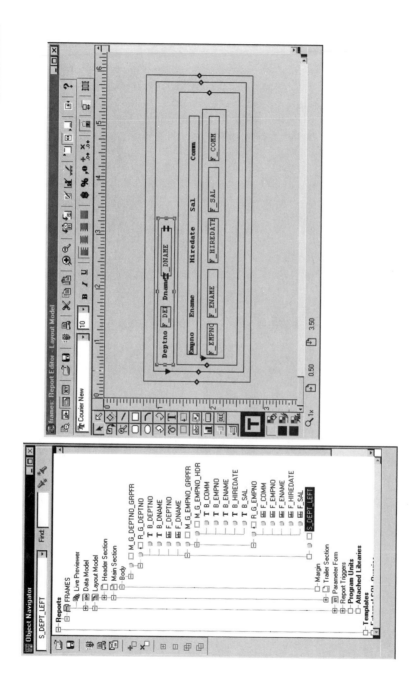

FIGURE 9-2. *Subframes within a report*

Naming Boilerplate Items

When created using the Report Wizard, text boilerplate objects are automatically named with a B_ followed by the name of the column being labeled. For example, if the label is called "Last Name," the Object Navigator will show B_LAST_NAME. Despite the unnecessary B_ prefix, this is an acceptable naming convention. In practice, other than for field labels and separator lines, additional boilerplate objects are not often used. It is not necessary to have special naming conventions for lines, boxes, and other drawing objects because Oracle Reports uses separate navigation icons for each of these, and you can always find the object by clicking it in the Layout Model. It is not necessary to rename the boilerplate objects that the Report Wizard creates.

PART
III

Forms Templates

CHAPTER
10

Forms Template Basics

...from so simple a beginning endless forms
most beautiful and most wonderful
have been and are being evolved.

—Charles Darwin (1809-1882), *The Origin of Species*

he best way to quickly incorporate a standard look and feel to your Oracle Developer Forms (Forms) applications is by using a template system. A template system also offers the quickest way to develop forms. With a template system in place, you can produce many more times the number of forms than you can produce without a template system in the same amount of time. The forms will incorporate a standard look and feel. They will also be easier to maintain and enhance.

This is not news to most developers who have spent any concentrated time with Forms. Developing forms without a template is just too difficult. The largest user of Oracle Developer—the Oracle development team that develops Oracle's ERP suite, Oracle Applications—knows this and has created an extremely rich template system (called the Application Object Library or AOL) that manages hundreds of forms in all areas of the product. Using templates when developing Forms applications is not really an advanced concept. It is The Right Way to develop forms.

This chapter focuses on the subject of Forms templates by discussing the place templates hold in Forms development. It also explains how the components of the template fit together and which object-based features of the product they exploit. Chapter 11 continues the discussion by explaining how to develop a Forms template system. Chapter 12 rounds out the discussion by explaining how to use a Forms template to build a basic form.

Forms and VRAD

Rapid Application Development (RAD) strategies shorten development time by packing the analysis, design, and development phases into a single, iterative prototyping process. The basic idea is to get a picture of the business requirements, then quickly prototype (or mock up) a working version of the software to show to users or to knowledgeable customers. The feedback from the initial demonstration of the prototype helps developers refine the design and produce another version, which can be used to get more feedback. The process of refinement and feedback continues until the application is approved. This requires cooperative and motivated business users as well as decision-makers who can maintain the focus on the end goal as the process progresses. The promise of RAD is that this process takes less time than other traditional software development methodologies for some projects.

It also involves the end users in the process from the earliest stage and, therefore, all but guarantees that users will readily accept and enjoy using the final product.

Since the application is the focal point for the RAD process, the key is familiarity with and maximum use of a flexible development tool. Oracle Developer Release 6 is well suited for RAD. The Forms component provides enough object-based features and such strong ties to the Oracle database that the authors call this process of iterative prototyping *"Very Rapid Application Development"* (VRAD).

Major elements that assist in the success of VRAD projects are the reuse of generic code and the enforcement of graphical user interface GUI standards. Forms allows the developer to take advantage of reusable objects and code in many different ways. Code reuse means that the developer can create libraries for program code, which can be shared by all parts of the application. In addition, common interface objects can be grouped together into templates or object libraries so all forms share a common user interface.

The template, as the embodiment of all object- and code-sharing techniques, is the key to the VRAD methodology.

What Is a Template Form?

A *template form* is a form that serves as the foundation for other forms. When you create a new form, instead of starting from scratch and adding objects to a blank module, you open a copy of an existing template form that contains prebuilt and pretested code and objects. The blocks and objects you create go into this form. The completed form automatically "inherits" the preestablished functionality and look and feel of the template. It leverages the work done to prepare the template and is the epitome of code reuse in Oracle Developer. There are many benefits and some drawbacks to using a template for developing Forms applications.

Benefits of Template Use

The benefits of using a template are numerous:

- **Object sharing** If you have been building forms with Form Builder for even a short time, you have noticed that your forms all tend to have the same sorts of objects in them. For example, you build LOVs and alerts in a certain way. All forms you create may require a calendar selection window for a date item. All forms need the same set of toolbar or canvas buttons. Developing these objects from the ground up for each new form is too much work. Maintaining forms built this way is also too much work. The template provides a way to share the common objects among your forms.

■ **Code sharing**   The code that supports the template objects is generic and reusable. It is easily shareable among your forms. In addition, you may have written a number of PL/SQL utility packages that support the code you need in many different forms. For example, code to call the help system is required by all forms. This code can be shared by using .PLL libraries in the template system. The base form you use as the template already has attached to it all commonly used libraries. This allows you to start coding without having to worry about whether a function you wrote in a utility library is available. A strong benefit to the template system is that it supplies frequently used code that has been fully debugged and proven.

■ **Standards deployment**   Since you establish GUI standards before you create the template system, you can work into the template system as many of your look-and-feel standards as possible. The template supports the standards. A diverse group of developers will be able to create Forms applications that have a standard look and feel because of the underlying elements provided by the template. Pre-determining sizes, fonts, colors, and placement of objects assists in the common look. Setting up common features such as a toolbar, menu, alert system, and LOV properties assists in the common feel. All this is the domain of the template. Another aspect of standards is that the creation of the template forces you to seriously think about and check the completeness of your GUI standards.

■ **Quick development time**   Templates also have the benefit of quick development time. When you're building applications, much of the development work is repetitive. For each form you create, you need to set up a standard item size and font and determine a layout strategy. There are major portions of each application that are similar to those of many other applications. The template speeds up this development time because of its built-in functionality and standards. The template enables developers to create simple applications in minutes and complex applications in a fraction of the time normally required. This benefit naturally follows the code and object sharing, because the less development and testing you have to do, the faster a form will go into production.

■ **Resource allocation**   Templates offer a clear benefit in how you allocate your pool of developers. Novice developers will be able to produce forms that comply with standards and contain complex built-in objects, because those standards and objects were already developed and included with the template. Without a template system, you would need to allocate experienced developers to create even the simplest forms, because those forms need some advanced functionality that the novice developer could not handle. The template system allows you to assign novice developers to the simple or medium-complexity forms. This frees the experienced developers to work on complex forms as well as on generic coding and common objects for the template system itself.

■ **Development guidance**   Many developers are not comfortable with the amount of latitude that GUI development gives them. They find themselves lost in a daunting list of possible triggers and options. Even a skilled C++ programmer will fight the tool, trying to force it to act exactly like a favorite C++ program. All developers will be more productive because of the guidance the template gives in how to properly create a form. If you have to add developers to a project already under way, those developers can be almost instantly productive because the template guides their work.

The time-saving benefits of the template allow you to concentrate on the application-specific business rules and needs. Figure 10-1 represents this effect. The template provides much in the way of native objects and code, and the main task you have as a Forms developer is to develop the customized application-specific code and objects to add to the template system functionality.

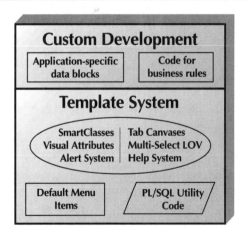

FIGURE 10-1.   *Template system and custom-development objects*

Drawbacks of Template Use

Template use does have some limitations that you need to plan for:

- **Skill stagnation** In a development environment that uses senior developers to build and maintain the template system, novice developers (particularly those new to Forms) will never get experience with advanced PL/SQL coding and generic objects. Since a template system supplies a large amount of code, complex generically written PL/SQL will not be needed as frequently outside of the template. When it is required, this type of code might be automatically assigned to a senior developer. Thus, junior developers would not obtain practice in anything but the most basic development work.

  To offset this effect, you can use novice developers to maintain, document, and write some of the library code for the templates. Senior developers should perform the code review, but while writing code to support the generic objects in the template, the novice developers will obtain additional experience with PL/SQL. It is also important that the novice developers have a detailed understanding of how the template system works so that they can extend or override it when required in their forms.

- **Learning curve** Another negative side effect of template use is the learning curve. Those new to the template environment, novice or not, need to learn how the specific template system works and how to extend it. They also need to be intimately familiar with the often-ignored, object-based features of Form Builder. In addition, they need to learn about all the objects in the template system so that they do not spend time reinventing something that has already been standardized in the template. There is no easy answer to this, other than keeping "developer friendliness" in mind when creating, modifying, and documenting the template files. If the template is easy to use from a developer standpoint, it will be easy to learn and remember.

These drawbacks are manageable and are not strong enough reasons to offset the benefits of using a template system.

What Do You Put in the Template?

The template contains standard objects and code libraries that make working with the form easier for both the developer and the end user. The template you use will contain objects and code that is customized for your application. There are some standard objects or code that you can include in the template system to make coding easier or to standardize look and feel. Some examples follow later in the chapter.

Everything you put in the template system falls into one of three main categories:

- Archetype objects
- Reusable components
- Generic code

It is useful to explore each of these categories further.

Archetype Objects

The *archetype* provides a basis or pattern for another object you create in the form. There are two main facilities for implementing this concept in Forms: subclasses and visual attributes.

SUBCLASSES   A *subclass* allows you to implement a type of inheritance from one object to another. Objects can share properties from the same parent object. When the parent object properties are modified, the child objects will update when the child form is recompiled or reopened in Form Builder. The section in this chapter called "Form Builder Features Used in the Template" explains this concept further.

VISUAL ATTRIBUTES   A *visual attribute* is a Forms object that manages a common look for objects such as windows, canvases, boilerplate graphics, LOVs, editors, alerts, items, and item prompts. A visual attribute works in a similar way to a subclass, but whereas a subclassed object can include any property from that object, a visual attribute only includes visual properties, as Figure 10-2 shows. You attach a visual attribute to an object using the object's *Visual Attribute Group* property.

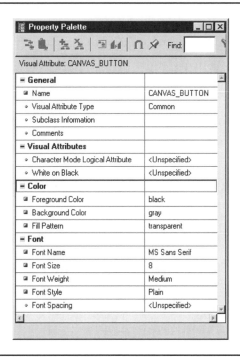

FIGURE 10-2.   *Visual attribute properties*

You can think about a visual attribute as providing a subset of the functionality that a subclass provides. Since it is attached using a separate property, you can use two "parent" objects to manage a particular object: the subclass master object and the visual attribute.

The visual attributes must be available locally in the form. Instead of re-creating all visual attributes for all forms, you can subclass them into the form from an object library. That way, one set of visual attributes can serve as the visual standard for all forms.

WARNING
Subclass and visual attribute attachments are maintained by name only. Therefore, if you change the name of a subclassed object in the master (reference) form, all references to it in other forms will break. When you open those forms, the reference will be unresolved and the object will revert to a default (and usually undesirable) state. This unresolved reference will also occur if the file with the master objects is not in the working ("Start in") directory or in the FORMS60_PATH.

TIP
You can actually use this reference behavior to your advantage if you have an application that requires different property settings based on a physical limitation such as monitor size, available fonts, color palette, or runtime environment (Web or Windows). In this situation, you can create a set of visual attributes and subclass master objects with settings specific to one physical environment. You would use this master file when compiling and working with Forms in that environment. For another environment, you would create a separate master file using the same names for the file and the master objects. These master objects would have different settings based on the different environment. When you open or recompile the form in that new environment, you would ensure that the new master file is the only one that is available. This way, you can use the same form source file and, with the different environmental master files, compile it into different code.

Reusable Components

Some of the functionality provided by the template is accomplished with pre-assembled groups of objects. The Oracle demonstration forms use the term "reusable component" for this type of object, which accurately describes its function. Essentially, a reusable component is a group of related objects and code that performs a certain task. Reusable components supply a feature in the template system that is self-contained, prewritten, and pretested. For example, presenting a multi-selection LOV requires a certain amount of code and a set of Forms objects that can be packaged together into a "Multi-Select LOV" component. In Forms, the easiest way to bundle objects into a reusable component is by using the object group. The object group is just a collection of Forms objects with a certain name. Object groups are explained in more detail in the section called "Object Groups." Other examples of reusable components follow.

HELP SYSTEM   Most Forms applications need to provide some level of end-user help. If the need is extensive, you should use some standard system for providing help such as WinHelp files or HTML files (as described in Chapter 14). These systems contain hypertext links, search capabilities, and even embedded graphics to assist users in finding the answer to a question. The forms objects needed for this system are minimal; you just have to create code to pass the name of the item that the cursor is in to a specially created file containing the help text. The template menu supports this with standard items in the Help menu to call Contents, Index, and Help-on-Help. The template form contains user-defined triggers that are subclassed from the object library and called by the menu items. The entire help system is included with the template system and requires no coding to implement in a particular form.

Another type of help system mentioned in Chapter 14 is the table-based help system. This displays the help text stored in a database inside a form or window in the same form. For example, if you use a window in the form to display help text, your object library could include a group of objects that query the help text from that table and that display the text in a context-sensitive way. The objects included with this system would be a window, a canvas, and a block that contains items for the help text and buttons. You would place these objects in the Object Group Children node under an object group node. Figure 10-3 shows such a set of objects under the SUBCLASS_HELP_SYSTEM object group. Although all of the objects are called "Help," the icons beside each one indicates a difference in object types (in this case, a window, a canvas, and a data block).

This object group becomes the reusable component. You then subclass the object group into the form from the object library so that changes to the help system will be easy to include in existing forms that are based on the template.

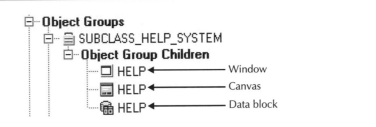

FIGURE 10-3. *Help system object group*

HELP ABOUT WINDOW   An additional help feature that you can include in the template is a Help About window. The Help About window displays the context information username, form name, date, database name, application name, item name, and so on. This is information that the user will need to provide to a help desk if there is a problem. Users expect to see this in the Help menu of Windows applications, and it is simple to create in forms. Depending on how often you expect this to be activated, you can place a dedicated modal window in the form (if it is requested frequently) or create a separate form (if it is requested infrequently). The template system contains the code to activate and display this window as well as the form or window itself. Supplying this feature after preparing the template requires minimal or no coding.

STANDARD TOOLBARS   You can create toolbar menu items that will appear in the multiple document interface (MDI) window. This toolbar will appear in all forms and over all windows in the form to provide a common interface to the user. If you include the toolbar menu items in the menu template, all forms will automatically pick up any changes made to the toolbar in the master form when you recompile the menu. You can include the code that the toolbar buttons execute in a library that is attached to the form, so the toolbar in all forms will act in the same way. You can include hooks into the toolbar system so the developer can add to or modify the subclassed objects.

ALERT SYSTEM   You cannot create a message box (alert) dynamically. Form Builder has no way to display a message box unless you first create an alert object in the Object Navigator. You can, however, create a generic alert system comprised of a set of alerts with no button labels or message. Code in a library calls the alert—passing it the button labels, message, and icon type—and returns the name of the button pressed. This saves a number of calls to Forms built-ins so you don't have to stop when coding a particular application and think about how to call the alert. This alert feature (described further in Chapter 27) is a totally generic part of the template system and is included automatically in your form when you use the template.

MESSAGE SYSTEM   You may want to replace the standard Forms hint line message system with one of your own. This could include alerts, a message item in the toolbar or on the canvas, or a separate window. This system would also contain ON-MESSAGE and ON-ERROR triggers to capture the standard Forms messages and errors and translate or just present them in another form. You could even display the DBMS_ERROR_CODE and the related text (DBMS_ERROR_TEXT) to show database errors.

Generic Code

There are two types of generic code needed in the template system:

- Utilities and object support
- Reusable component methods

This code is written in a form library module that is attached to the form or in an object library from which the code is subclassed.

UTILITIES AND OBJECT SUPPORT   The template system provides a set of utilities that you can call on to make Forms objects easier to use for the developer. These utilities can also provide a common interface to the user for common Forms functions such as committing a change.

You can organize the packages in your template library by feature or reusable component. For example, the F_ALERT package will support the alert system, and F_HELP will support the help system. You can also create generic code to support and facilitate using Forms objects. Therefore, you can code an F_ITEM package to support the item object in Forms and an F_BLOCK package to support the manipulation of blocks. A package like F_ITEM would contain procedures to accomplish tasks such as disabling items, enabling items, hiding or displaying items, and loading poplist items from a query. These procedures make the tasks easier to code as they require a single line of code instead of a number of lines of code. For example, the procedure to load a poplist from a query is about 60 lines of code if it is written correctly with sufficient exception handling. The call to the procedure is only one line. This saves the developer time because there is no need to code and debug this common operation.

The following is an excerpt from the F_ITEM package specification that contains the procedure just mentioned. Appendix A contains details on more of the packages in a sample template library.

```
PACKAGE f_item IS
/**********************************************************************\
|| Description:
||    Procedures that affect individual items (buttons, text items, list
||    items). All issue a message if the item is not found. The parameter is
||    the item name.
||    SETUP_LIST
||       Populate a list item from a record group. The parameters are the
||       record group name, the item name, and, optionally, whether or not
||       to perform the query again (if this is called more than once in
||       the same form and the data may have changed in between calls). Use
||       the f_global.g_query_yes and f_global.g_query_no package variables
||       to represent "Yes" and "No." The default is to requery.
\**********************************************************************/
    --
    PROCEDURE setup_list(
        p_record_group    IN VARCHAR2,
        p_item_name       IN VARCHAR2,
        p_perform_query   IN VARCHAR2 DEFAULT  f_global.v_query_yes);
    --
END;
```

An excerpt from the package body for this procedure follows. The F_ALERT package call in this code shows an alert containing an OK button and the text passed in through the parameter.

```
PACKAGE BODY f_item IS
    --
    PROCEDURE setup_list(
        p_record_group    IN VARCHAR2,
        p_item_name       IN VARCHAR2,
        p_perform_query   IN VARCHAR2 DEFAULT  f_global.v_query_yes)
    IS
        /*
        || Load an existing record group and poplist.
        || This loads the record group only if the query worked.
        || The third parameter is whether or not we want to
        || repopulate the record group.
        */
        v_rg_id      RECORDGROUP := find_group(p_record_group);
        v_item       ITEM;
        v_retval     NUMBER := 0;
    BEGIN
        -- check if we have a record group
        IF NOT id_null(v_rg_id)
        THEN
            v_item := find_item(p_item_name);
```

```
          -- check if we have an item
      IF NOT id_null(v_item)
      THEN
          IF get_item_property(p_item_name, ITEM_TYPE) = 'LIST'
          THEN
              -- Requery if we asked to
              IF p_perform_query = f_global.v_query_yes
              THEN
                  v_retval := populate_group(v_rg_id);
              END IF;
              -- Populate the list if all is well
              IF v_retval = 0 THEN
                  populate_list(v_item, v_rg_id);
              ELSE
                  f_alert.ok('f_item.setup_list: Record Group '||
                    p_record_group|| ' could not populate. Error ' || ' Code - '||
                    to_char(v_retval), f_alert.g_no_fail, f_alert.caution_icon);
              END IF;
          ELSE
              f_alert.ok(
                'f_item.setup_list: '||p_item_name||' is not a list item.',
                'NOFAIL', f_alert.caution_icon);
          END IF;
      ELSE
          f_alert.ok(
            'f_item.setup_list: '||p_item_name ||
            ' is not a valid name for an item.', f_alert.g_no_fail,
            f_alert.caution_icon);
      END IF;
  ELSE
      f_alert.ok('f_item.setup_list: '|| p_record_group ||
        ' is not a valid name for a record group.',
        'NOFAIL', f_alert.caution_icon);
  END IF;
  END;
END;
```

REUSABLE COMPONENT METHODS   The template system also includes
reusable component methods—code that supports a specific feature or function.
Reusable component methods provide the interface from the outside to an object
(such as an item) or to a reusable component (such as the calendar). The reusable
component methods provide the functionality for interfacing with the user and any
other code that supports the reusable component. An example of a reusable
component is the help system mentioned before.

The HELP block in this example includes triggers for items such as the OK
button, but does not include the code to display the window because this code is
not attached to a trigger in the block; it is written for a button outside the help
system. The code to call the help window is contained in a PL/SQL library that the
main form calls from a KEY-HELP trigger. This trigger fires when the user presses the

Help key or selects **Help→Help** from the menu. The package specification for this package follows:

```
PACKAGE f_help
IS
/***********************************************************************\
|| Description:
||    Procedures to apply to the help system. This help system implements a
||    help window that queries the help table based on the name of the window
||    that the cursor is in.
||    HIDE_HELP
||       Removes the help window and restores the cursor to its original
||       location. Assumes there is a DUMMY block with NULL_ITEM
||       in it. In case the return item does not exist,
||       the cursor returns to DUMMY.NULL_ITEM.
||
||    SHOW_HELP
||       Displays the help window and saves the cursor location. The help is
||       queried from the database into the HELP block. There is an ability
||       to provide item-level help although this implementation uses
||       window-level help. See comments in the body. The optional parameter
||       signals whether the show keys window should be shown after the
||       help window is hidden (as the result of a button click in the help
||       window). The parameters are the form name and the window name that will
||       be used to find the help row in the help table.
||
\***********************************************************************/
    --
    g_help_return_item    VARCHAR2(61);
    g_no_show_keys        VARCHAR2(20) := 'NO_SHOW_KEYS';
    g_show_keys           VARCHAR2(20) := 'SHOW_KEYS';
    --
    PROCEDURE hide_help(
       p_show_keys        VARCHAR2 DEFAULT g_no_show_keys);
    --
    PROCEDURE show_help(
       p_form             VARCHAR2 DEFAULT NULL,
       p_block            VARCHAR2 DEFAULT NULL,
       p_item             VARCHAR2 DEFAULT NULL);
    --
END;
```

In the KEY-HELP trigger, the form calls F_HELP.SHOW_HELP and passes it the parameters to make the text appear in the help window. The code for this package body follows:

```
PACKAGE BODY f_help
IS
    --
    PROCEDURE hide_help(
        p_show_keys     VARCHAR2 DEFAULT g_no_show_keys)
```

```
IS
BEGIN
   IF id_null(find_item(g_help_return_item))
   THEN
      f_alert.ok('Error: No item called ' || g_help_return_item ||
         ' exists. Contact the' || ' administrator.');
      go_item('DUMMY.NULL_ITEM');
   ELSE
      go_item(g_help_return_item);
   END IF;
   hide_window('HELP');
   -- If the show keys button is pressed
   -- in the help window show the key list.
   IF p_show_keys = g_show_keys
   THEN
      show_keys;
   END IF;
END;
--
--
PROCEDURE show_help(
   p_form       VARCHAR2 DEFAULT NULL,
   p_block      VARCHAR2 DEFAULT NULL,
   p_item       VARCHAR2 DEFAULT NULL)
IS
   v_pos          NUMBER;
   v_where        VARCHAR2(300);
   v_cursor_item  VARCHAR2(61) := name_in('SYSTEM.CURSOR_ITEM');
   v_form_name    VARCHAR2(61) := p_form;
   v_block_name   VARCHAR2(61) := p_block;
   v_item_name    VARCHAR2(61) := p_item;
BEGIN
   -- save the name of the item that the cursor is in
   g_help_return_item := v_cursor_item;
   --
   IF v_form_name IS NULL
   THEN
      v_form_name := get_application_property(CURRENT_FORM_NAME);
   END IF;
   --
   IF v_block_name IS NULL
   THEN
      -- the canvas of the button that was pressed
      v_block_name := name_in('SYSTEM.CURSOR_BLOCK');
   END IF;
   --
   IF v_item_name IS NULL
   THEN
      -- the item name of the cursor item (without the block name)
      v_item_name := substr(v_cursor_item,
```

```
              instr(v_cursor_item, '.') + 1);
       END IF;
       --
       v_where := 'FORM_NAME='''||v_form_name||
                  ''' AND BLOCK_NAME=''' || v_block_name ||
                  ''' AND ITEM_NAME=''' || v_item_name ||'''';
       set_block_property('HELP', DEFAULT_WHERE, v_where);
       go_block('HELP');
       execute_query;

       -- handle errors from no data found
       IF name_in('HELP.FORM_NAME') IS NULL
       THEN
           f_alert.ok('Error: No help text exists for this window. '||
                'Contact the administrator.');
           go_item('HELP.OK');
           execute_trigger('WHEN-BUTTON-PRESSED');
       END IF;
   END;
   --
   --
END;
```

This is generically written so it may be plugged into any form without modification.

TIP
The GO_ITEM and EXECUTE_TRIGGER statements in the preceding code sample are used to fire a WHEN-BUTTON-PRESSED trigger that is written on a button item. This technique is useful if you want to emulate the action of a user clicking a button. The technique allows you to maintain code in one place for the user clicking the button and for your program code performing the same action. While you would get the same effect if both the button trigger and the program code executed the same packaged procedure, the GO_ITEM and EXECUTE_TRIGGER calls make it clear that the code will perform the same action as when the user clicks that button.

WHERE TO LOCATE THE CODE   The archetype and reusable component code requires PL/SQL code to be available to the form. The best location for this code is a library file because the code is generic, not written for any specific form, but works only for forms (not database objects). You can divide the code into more than one library if it turns out that not all forms will need all the procedures. (Chapter 7 discusses some guidelines on where to place the code.) When you attach libraries to forms, the procedures and functions are immediately available as "extensions" to the Forms built-in packages.

Attached libraries cannot be subclassed from the object library or from another form. The only way to assure that the attached library is available is to add it to the template you use as a basis for the form. If the library is attached to the template, it will be attached to the form that you create from the template.

TIP

If you find you need to attach an additional library to your forms after you have created a number of forms from your template, you can open one of the existing libraries that is attached and attach the new library to it. After you save that library, the next time you open the form, the additional library will be attached automatically. For example, the template has Library1 attached to it, and you need to also attach Library2 to it and all other forms you have created from the template. You open Library1, attach Library2 to it (using the Attached Libraries node), and save Library1. The next time you open the template or another form built from the template, both Library1 and Library2 will be attached.

Form Builder Features Used in the Template

The Forms template system exploits many of the advanced features offered by Form Builder. While object-oriented programming (OOP) purists may complain about the level of object orientation in the tool, some features in Form Builder supply many of the same benefits that a fully object-oriented programming environment supplies. Forms libraries implement the OOP benefit of code reuse. Forms templates and object libraries supply the OOP benefit of object reuse and inheritance. The objective of OOP is to facilitate code reuse and high-speed development and maintenance. These objectives are also within reach of Forms developers. You can write generic code units and create generic objects that will modularize your Forms development environment. The template system provides the structure for these code units and objects. This section examines the main Forms features that the template system uses to accomplish VRAD.

Template Support

A template form is just a form that you use in a special way. Therefore, there is no need for extra object types or module types as there is for Reports templates. Form Builder mentions templates in the Welcome dialog, as Figure 10-4 shows.

This dialog offers a selection for "Build a form based on a template." If you select that option and click OK, the File Open dialog will appear. You can select a template .FMB file from that dialog, and the template file will load into Form Builder. You can get the same effect by just opening the template form file in Form Builder. The Welcome dialog option has two main benefits: Form Builder will rename the file to MODULE1, which signals you that this is a new form; and when you ask to save the file, Form Builder will not overwrite the template, but ask you for a new file name. This feature guards against the danger of overwriting your template file.

NOTE
Forms demonstration files include a sample template system comprised of a form, menu, and object library. The files all have the name STNDRD20 and are contained in the ORACLE_HOME/tools/ devdem60/forms directory. The Form Builder help system explains how these files are set up. This sample system is intended to get you started, but it is not a full solution.

The Welcome dialog is not only accessible when you start up Form Builder. If you want to use the template file feature again in the same Form Builder session, select

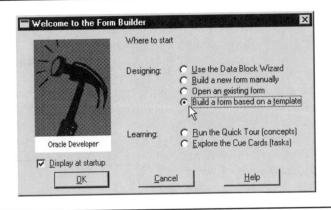

FIGURE 10-4. *Welcome dialog*

File→New→Form Using Template. You can specify that the Welcome dialog should not appear by using the Wizards tab of the Form Builder **Tools→Preferences** dialog.

TIP
*Set the file attributes on your template file to read-only using the Windows properties (accessible from the right-click menu in Windows Explorer). This will prevent you from accidentally opening and saving the file, but will not prevent you from using the Welcome dialog or **File→New→Form Using Template** menu selection. Make it a standard operating procedure to use this menu selection when starting a new form. Using the Object Navigator New or Create buttons will bypass the template feature.*

Subclasses

Subclassing is an important feature that was new with Oracle Developer Release 2. It takes the place of and improves on the reference feature supplied in previous releases. In Form Builder, you *subclass* an object to a new object using the *Subclass Information* property, as Figure 10-5 shows. Any object can be a master object that provides the subclass if the form or object library file that contains it is open in the Form Builder session. You can even subclass objects to other objects in the same form.

The subclassed (new) object inherits the nondefault properties of the master object. The Property Palette shows the properties that are subclassed using an arrow icon, as Figure 10-5 shows for the *Item Type* property. The Object Navigator shows that an object is subclassed using another arrow icon, as Figure 10-5 shows for the DEPTNO item in the left window. Default properties of the master object (property values that were not changed) have no effect (and no indicating icon other than a small round bullet as in the *Popup Menu* property shown in Figure 10-5). You can change any property, inherited or not, in the subclassed object. Changing a property of a master object will change that property—unless the value has been overridden—in the child object when the form is reopened or recompiled.

If you override (change) any property on the new object, the property will indicate the override with an "x" over the inheritance icon's arrowhead like this:

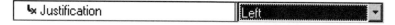

An overridden property will never inherit from a master object. You can revoke an override by selecting the overridden property and clicking the Inherit button, shown in Figure 10-6. This will reinherit the property value.

Subclassed item   Subclassed property

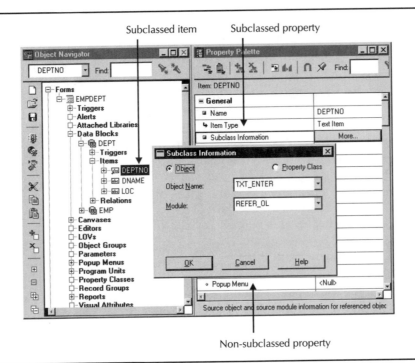

Non-subclassed property

FIGURE 10-5. *Subclass Information property*

For example, you create a button on a non-toolbar canvas called CANVAS_
BUTTON with certain values in the *Background Color, Foreground Color, Font
Name, Font Size, Width,* and *Height* properties and drag the button to the object
library of the template system. You then create a button object in a new form and
subclass it with the CANVAS_BUTTON object library object using the *Subclass
Information* property. The color, font, and size properties of the CANVAS_BUTTON

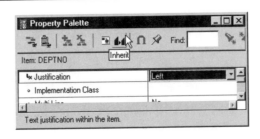

FIGURE 10-6. *Reinheriting an overridden property*

object will be inherited by the new button. If you change one of these properties on CANVAS_BUTTON, the property will change on the new subclassed object when you recompile or reopen the new form. However, if you override a property like the *Width* property, that value will stay the same regardless of what you do to the master object.

NOTE
Although you can only reinherit one property at a time, you can group items together and reinherit the same property for all items in the same operation.

Subclassing is a powerful facility, as it implements the concept of object inheritance. It is one of the main foundations for the template system. Most of the objects in the template are subclassed to take advantage of this inheritance.

CAUTION
When you subclass, the form or object library file that provides the master object for the subclass must be open in the same Form Builder session. However, when you open a form that contains subclassed objects, the master object file does not need to be open. Form Builder will resolve the reference to the object and the file by searching the file system. The master object file must be in a directory in the FORMS60_PATH or ORACLE_PATH (as written in the Windows registry) or in the working "Start in" directory for the Form Builder icon. Another aspect of this reference resolution is that the file name itself is stored as part of the reference. Therefore, if you rename a master object file, you will receive an error when you open another form that references an object in that file. The easiest solution for this error is to rename the master file to the original name.

Inheritance Levels

While you can only apply one subclass at a time to an object, subclass inheritance is multilevel. Therefore, if you create BUTTON1 and set its properties in a special way, you can subclass it to BUTTON2. BUTTON2 will inherit the nondefault properties of BUTTON1. You can also create BUTTON3 and subclass BUTTON2 onto it. BUTTON3 will inherit the nondefault properties of BUTTON2 in addition to

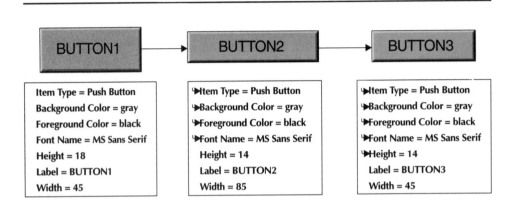

FIGURE 10-7. *Subclass inheritance example*

the subclassed properties that BUTTON2 inherits from BUTTON1. Figure 10-7 shows BUTTON2 inheriting properties from BUTTON1. The *Height, Label,* and *Width* properties are set explicitly for BUTTON2 and override the settings of the inherited properties. BUTTON3 inherits properties from BUTTON2. The *Label* and *Width* properties override the settings from BUTTON2, but the other properties of BUTTON3 are inherited from either BUTTON2 or BUTTON1. If the *Font Name* property were to change on BUTTON1, the *Font Name* properties of BUTTON2 and BUTTON3 would change as well.

Object Groups

One powerful but commonly overlooked Form Builder feature—the object group—is at the heart of the template system. An *object group* is a Forms object that is merely a named set of other Forms objects. The purpose of object groups is to allow easy subclassing and copying between form modules, because you can subclass or copy the group, and all child objects go with the group. You can create an object group the same way you create other Forms objects, using the Object Navigator Create button after clicking on the Object Groups node. Figure 10-8 shows an object group node with its children.

You can drag any top-level object in an object library into an object group except an attached library and the form module itself. You can include blocks but not items, for example, because the blocks are at the top level in the Object Navigator. Including a top-level object such as a block will include all its subobjects, such as items and triggers. The child objects are not copies of the base objects, but are references to the base objects. Therefore, if you delete a child object from an object group, the master object you dragged in to create the child will not

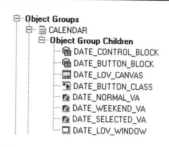

FIGURE 10-8. *Object group and children*

be deleted. However, if you delete the master object, the child object that references it will also be deleted from the object group.

Property References

If an object-group child object references another object that is not in the new form, the reference will be maintained, but will not be used. For example, you create an object group called MESSAGES in your master form and include a block called MESSAGE that contains an item called MSG_TEXT. In the master form, the item displays on a canvas called MAIN, but that canvas is not in the object group. You then drag the MESSAGES object group into a new form. Form Builder will ask if you want to copy or subclass using the following dialog:

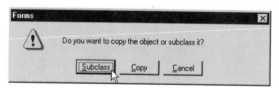

If the new form does not have a canvas called MAIN, the item will not be displayed but will maintain the reference to the canvas MAIN. The next step would be to change the *Canvas* property to reference the name of a canvas in the form. Alternatively, you can build (or subclass) the MAIN canvas into the new form, and the item will automatically show up on it.

Deleting Object Groups

When working with object groups, it is good to remember that the object group is a container. If you delete a subclassed object group, you are deleting a container and its contents. The container just contains references to objects that are actually created elsewhere. Thus, deleting a subclassed object group also deletes all child objects from the form (since the child objects are merely references). On the other hand, copying an object group into a new form will also create new physical instantiations of the child objects, not just references to the objects in another file. Therefore, deleting a copied object group will only delete the object group (the container) itself, not the copied objects.

Benefits of Object Groups

The key benefit of object groups is that you can more easily manipulate a set of objects as if it were a single object. You can also more easily share a set of objects between forms. Another benefit is even more important. If you add an object to the master of an object group, all existing forms that subclass (not copy) that object group will automatically gain the new object when they are recompiled or reopened in the Form Builder. This makes adding to the template system much easier.

For example, you have an object group called SUBCLASS_VISUAL_ATTR that contains all visual attributes you know you will need. That object group is subclassed into the template so that all forms built from the template will inherit the same set of visual attributes. While in development, you find that you need a few more visual attributes and want to add them to every form you have already created. With the object group in place, you just add the new visual attributes to the master form and include them as child objects in the object group that contains the visual attributes. The next time you open a form that has a subclass of the SUBCLASS_VISUAL_ATTR object group, the new visual attributes will automatically be there. The object group is subclassed, not the individual visual attributes. The following summarizes the steps you would go through to add a visual attribute to all forms. Assume you have an object group called SUBCLASS_VISUAL_ATTR in the REFER_FORM.FMB form file that contains all visual attributes and this object group is subclassed into all forms.

1. Add a visual attribute to the REFER_FORM file.

2. Drag the new visual attribute into the SUBCLASS_VISUAL_ATTR child node.

3. Save REFER_FORM (not required, but recommended).

When you open the existing form that has the object group already subclassed, the new visual attribute will be available. The same strategy applies to any other object type that you can include in an object library. This works for subobjects as well. For example, if you add an item to a block that is part of an object group, the forms that subclass that object group will automatically add the item when you open or recompile the form.

Drawbacks of Object Groups

Object groups have several drawbacks that are manageable but worth mentioning. Object groups are not well-known in the Oracle development community. Therefore, using object groups could confuse those who do not understand how they work. This is a manageable drawback since it just requires education for novice developers. Experienced developers should be able to understand the principles without much extra time or effort.

Another drawback occurs as a side-effect of the most powerful benefit. When you subclass an object group into a form, the object that is subclassed is the object group itself, not the individual child objects. Therefore, if you try to open the *Subclass Information* property for a child object of a subclassed object group, you will see the following dialog:

The only place that the subclass information is available is on the object group itself because that was the actual subclassed object. This can make it slightly frustrating to find the source of a specific object that you know is subclassed. The steps that you need to go through to navigate to the source of a specific subclassed object follow:

1. Verify that the object is subclassed by checking for the arrow symbol in the Object Navigator.

2. Check the *Subclass Information* property on the object itself to see if it was created without using an object library. If it was, you have the answer.

3. If you see the dialog just shown, look at the list of object groups in the form to see which ones are subclassed. Look for a logical match to the object type you are researching.

4. When you find a likely candidate, open its Object Group Children node to see if your object is there. If not, look for another object group.

5. Once you find the object group that contains the object, open its *Subclass Information* property and determine the module (file) that is its source.

6. Open the source file and find the object in the Object Navigator.

This seems to be a complex series of steps, but it does not take long. It helps if you know the object group name that the object contains. If you name the object groups descriptively, your job will be easier. For example, if you name an object group that contains visual attributes SUBCLASS_VISUAL_ATTRIBUTES, you will have a good clue for where to look when you need subclass information on a particular visual attribute.

Object Library

The concept of an object library was also introduced with Oracle Developer
Release 2 and is unchanged in Release 6. An *object library* is a separate file that
contains Forms objects that you want to subclass or copy. It is a special type of form
module file (with an .OLB extension) that you can create and open in Form Builder.
True to its name, an object library acts as a library for Forms objects.

When you open an object library, it appears in the Object Navigator along with
other objects (as Figure 10-9 shows). You can display the object library using the
menu option **Tools→Object Library** or by double-clicking on its icon in the Object
Navigator. This will open another window with a tab folder interface, as Figure 10-9
shows. You can open an object library file by using **File→Open**. You can create a
new object library file by using the Create button in the Object Navigator or by
using **File→New→Object Library**.

Form Builder remembers the last object library you had open when you closed
it, so this object library will be loaded automatically when you start the Form
Builder again. Object libraries should be located in the Forms path or in the current
working directory (called "Start in" in the Windows icon properties).

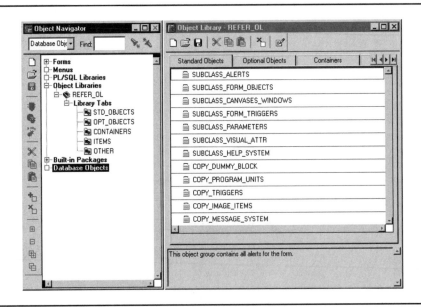

FIGURE 10-9. *Object library in the Object Navigator and Object Library window*

Subclass Inheritance in the Object Library

The *Subclass Information* property value is lost when you drag an object into the object library. For example, ITEM1 subclasses properties from ITEM2; that is, the *Subclass Information* property of ITEM1 references ITEM2. When you drag ITEM1 into the object library, the *Subclass Information* property becomes blank and the link to ITEM2 is lost. The properties values that were inherited from ITEM2 will be copied into the ITEM1 object library object. Thus, the object library flattens the subclass inheritance model. You cannot rely on a master object to supply properties to objects in the object library.

You can, however, use visual attributes to supply some of the properties to multiple objects in the object library. When you drag an object into the object library, the *Visual Attribute Group* property is preserved and the link to the visual attribute is maintained. Therefore, if you have a number of objects in the object library that use a single visual attribute, changing the properties on the visual attribute will change the corresponding properties for the objects that use it. This facility provides inheritance within the object library for the visual properties.

SmartClasses

One of the most powerful features of an object library is its ability to create SmartClasses to manage your archetypal objects. A *SmartClass* is just an object library object that you have flagged in a certain way. SmartClasses enable you to choose from a subset of the objects in the object library, even if the object library is not visible on the screen. To flag a SmartClass, click on the object in the object library and select **Object→SmartClass**. A check mark will appear next to the object name in the object library, as Figure 10-10 shows. The SmartClass will be available in the right-click menu immediately after you flag it (there is no need to save the object library file).

TIP
You can apply a SmartClass to a group of objects using the Object Navigator (not the Layout Editor). Group the objects as usual in the Navigator, and select the SmartClass from the right-click menu.

To use the SmartClass, right-click on the item in the Layout Editor or in the Object Navigator and select SmartClass. A list will appear with the names of all SmartClasses in all object libraries that are open in Form Builder. Only those objects that are of the same item type as the object selected will be displayed. Thus, if you have selected a button, you will only see SmartClasses associated with buttons. Figure 10-11 shows this action.

Although you can smartclass any object in the object library, only canvases, windows, and items will offer the right-click menu SmartClass selection. Chapter 11 discusses examples of which objects you might want to smartclass.

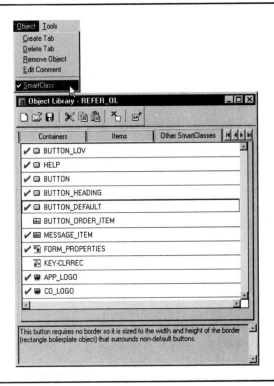

FIGURE 10-10. *Creating a SmartClass*

NOTE
SmartTriggers are "smart" in a different way than SmartClasses. SmartTriggers are just a list of triggers that appear in the right-click menu for an object in the Layout Editor or Object Navigator. The list of triggers is automatically narrowed down to the ones you would most commonly use for the object. For example, the SmartTrigger list for a button includes the WHEN-BUTTON-PRESSED trigger, which is the most common trigger you would use for a button. However, the list also contains the WHEN-NEW-ITEM-INSTANCE trigger, which you would rarely use for a button. There is also a selection for "Other" that displays a list of all triggers.

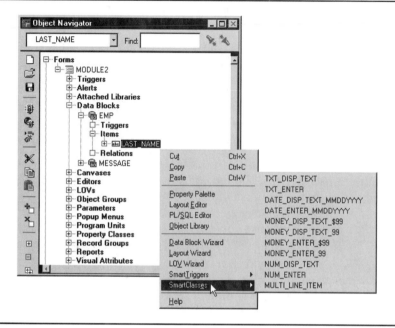

FIGURE 10-11. *Selecting a SmartClass*

Object Library Contents

Once the object library is created, you can drag and drop objects from an existing form into it. You can have more than one object library open at once. Each object library contains one or many tabs that help you organize the contents. Some objects in the object library are copied or subclassed into the template so that they will be available for use in every form you create. For example, you could create an object library with the following tabs:

■ **Standard Objects**   This tab supplies classes of objects that are placed into the template. These contain classes for alerts, help system, canvases and windows, triggers, visual attributes, parameters, and so on. Most of these are subclassed into the template and are designated as subclassed with a SUBCLASS prefix. Other object groups are prefixed with COPY to indicate that a copy is made in each form.

■ **Optional Objects**   There may be a set of objects that are not used in each form but need to be available for use in various forms. Examples are the

Calendar, Picklist, Navigator, Toolbar, and Wizard. These are not subclassed or copied into the template.

- **Containers** Containers for objects include windows and canvases. These are marked as SmartClasses and are also not copied or subclassed into the template.

- **Items** Standard archetype items are required for all forms. This tab contains items used mainly for data input. All are marked as SmartClasses and do not appear in the template. These SmartClasses are responsible for an important task: managing the size, font, and color of items in the form.

- **Other SmartClasses** This tab contains objects that are all marked as SmartClasses but do not fall into the other categories. Examples of objects in this tab are buttons, property classes, triggers, display items, nonvisible items, and image items.

TIP
You can navigate through the tabs in an object library by clicking on the tab (using the tab scroll bar if the tab is out of the window) or by clicking on the tab subnode under the object library in the Object Navigator.

You can add a comment to the object library object (shown at the bottom of the object library window), and you may delete the object. Most actions that you do with the object library can be performed with its toolbar or with the Object menu that becomes active when you click the object library window. Once you have created all objects in the library, you save the file using an .OLB extension.

Managing the Object Library Objects

Object libraries have many benefits, including the tab interface and SmartClass feature. Therefore, while you can always subclass from a form instead of from an object library, the best strategy is to always use object libraries as the master for subclassed objects.

However, you may not view or change properties of an object library object without dragging it into a form, making the change, and dragging it back to the library. The best strategy for using object libraries is to keep all objects in a related form and drag and drop them into the object library to create or update the library. For example, the object library REFER_OL.OLB would have a sister form called REFER_FORM.FMB. The form would contain all objects in the object library. When you need to modify or add an object library object, you would make the change or addition to the form itself and drag the new or changed object into the object library.

TIP
Oracle Designer (R.2.1 and later) supplies a utility called FORM2LIB.EXE. This utility creates an .OLB file from an .FMB file. Using that utility ensures that the .FMB and .OLB files are always in sync because you re-create the .OLB each time. Without the utility, you just need to keep track of which objects you changed so you can drag them back to the object library.

The code that supports the objects should go in a .PLL library. Trigger code for objects such as blocks and items are an exception. Triggers will be in the object library if the block or item that they are defined for is in the object library already. Therefore, there is no need to create separate object library entries for most triggers.

An easy way to place a comment on an object library object is to fill in the comment property on the object in the master form. For example, if you are dragging a window object into the object library from the form, the *Comments* property of that window will fill in the comments for the object in the object library when the drag operation occurs. If you place the comments on the object library object and not the form object, when you drag the modified form object into the object library, the comments you placed on the object library object will be lost.

Object library objects can be used as subclasses even if the object is not a SmartClass. You can fill in the *Subclass Information* property for any object with the source module and object. You can also subclass an object by dragging and dropping it from the object library into the form or Object Navigator. This action presents the same dialog for subclassing or copying and creates a new object in the form. Chapter 11 contains further details on the design and contents of objects in the object library.

NOTE
Subclassing information is lost when you drag an object into the object library. Therefore, if an item is subclassed from an object library and you drag it to the object library, the link to the master object (in the Subclass Information property) will be lost, but the item will retain the other property settings from the subclass.

Template System Architecture

The template system exploits these features to create a flexible and productive development environment. The following discussion focuses on a sample template system that the authors have used successfully. In practice, you would probably create more than one template for a development effort because there are different types of forms that require different types of base objects. Chapter 11 discusses some other template forms you may want to create.

The files that comprise the template system with the links between the files are depicted in Figure 10-12. Specifics on the files follow. As Chapter 6 mentions, you would probably prefix the file names discussed below and represented in Figure 10-12 with an application or company abbreviation.

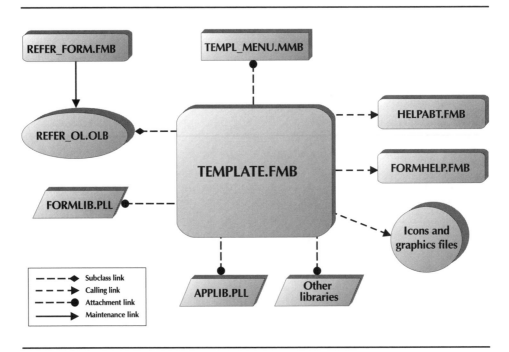

FIGURE 10-12. *Sample template form files and their links*

REFER_OL.OLB—The Object Library

This is the object library file consisting of Form Builder objects. It contains the tab folders described earlier. The objects are archetype objects (such as items and buttons) and reusable components (such as the calendar and help system) that are subclassed to the template or to an application form.

REFER_FORM.FMB—The Object Library Source

This file is used as the master file for the object library. It contains all objects in the object library. If you need to make a change to an existing object, you do so in this file because you cannot make changes in the object library itself. After making a change in REFER_FORM.FMB, you drag and drop the object into the object library, as Figure 10-13 shows. If you want to add an object to the object library, you add it to the form and perform the same drag-and-drop operation. The important principle is that these two files stay in synch because they have different purposes. One file (the form) maintains the objects and their properties. The other (the object library) is the master file for subclassing to all templates and application forms.

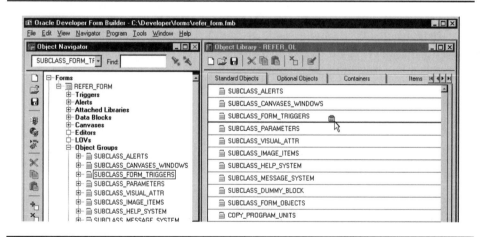

FIGURE 10-13. *Dragging an object group into the object library*

TEMPLATE.FMB—The Template Form

You use the *template form* as a starting point for creating other forms. The template form contains all standard objects that you need in all forms. Most objects are subclassed from the object library so you can maintain and add to them easily. For example, you need a set of visual attributes in each form to manage the look of items and canvases. This set is subclassed from the object library object group called SUBCLASS_VISUAL_ATTRIBUTES. Creating the template is merely a matter of dragging objects in from the object library and subclassing them. The following types of standard objects are in the template:

- **Standard objects** You subclass the main features of the form into the template from the object library object groups. Examples include the alert system, the help system, visual attributes, standard boilerplate graphics, windows and canvases, standard triggers, and parameters.

- **Attached libraries** These cannot be subclassed because you cannot store an attached library link in the object library. Therefore, you attach the library manually in the template or drag it in from another form. There may be more than one library to attach, depending on how you divide the code.

Two major features of the object library are the archetypal objects and the optional classes. These are included in the form on an as-needed basis, but are not part of the standard template. Therefore, the main activity in creating the template file is in subclassing object groups from the object library and attaching the code libraries.

Another task in creating the template is to subclass the form module itself by using a property class. This property class supplies common form-level properties such as the *Console Window, Menu Module, Runtime Compatibility Mode*, and coordinate system. The property class is subclassed from the object library, but needs to be manually attached to the form module (*Subclass Information* property) when you create the template because you cannot store a form module in the object library.

You use the Forms menu selection **File→New→Form Using Template** to open the template file and automatically rename it as a basis for a new form.

FORMLIB.PLL—The Template Code Library

This library is attached to the template. It contains packages that are used to support forms objects and classes. For example, there is a package that manages alerts. This package provides a friendlier developer interface to the alert system as well as support routines for block, item, and menu built-ins. It also contains procedures to manage the help system. This library contains no database calls to application tables or packages. This makes the file generic to any application. All packages in this library are named with an F_ prefix. Appendix A contains package specifications from a sample library. The comments from these specifications describe the procedures and functions of the major packages in the template code library.

APPLIB.PLL—Application-Specific Code Library
This library contains packages that use database calls for form-specific actions such as checking security or looking up a description in a specific table. Packages in this library use an "Fap_" prefix where "ap" is the two-character application alias.

Other Files
The template system uses a number of other files to supply more functionality:

- **Other libraries**   Optional classes may require code that is not in the standard library. Therefore, you may have to attach another library to support the interface for the reusable component. For example, the date-selection object group uses the CALENDAR.PLL library to supply code to display and assign a selected date. Since only some forms require this code, it is not part of the normal code library. The library is only attached to the form if the form uses the calendar component from the object library.

- **HELPABT.FMB—Help About form**   This is a standard help form that appears when the user selects **Help→About**. It displays general information about the system and about the form that is running. This is generic to all forms and all applications and only needs to have certain values passed to it from the calling form.

- **FORMHELP.FMB—Help Text Viewing form**   This form is used if you implement a help system using the table-based method described in Chapter 14. The form is completely generic, but is considered an extension of the template system because the code to call the form is in the template system, and the forms created from the template automatically include the help system.

- **Icons and graphics files**   If you are using iconic buttons or iconic menu items or loading image items with graphics files, you will need the source files for the images. These will be located in the Forms path or in the working directory (or another central location).

- **TEMPL_MENU.MMB—Template menu**   There is a default menu file attached to the template form that provides features included in the template. You can make changes in this file for your application, or copy it and attach the new version to the forms on a one-by-one basis.

How to Use the Template

Chapter 12 provides an example of how to build a form using the template system, but it is useful at this point to complete the picture of the template architecture by summarizing the major steps.

1. Install the Template

The first step is really the installation of the template files. While you are developing the form, all files must be available in the Forms or Oracle path stored in the registry (FORMS60_PATH or ORACLE_PATH in the HKEY_LOCAL_MACHINE\SOFTWARE\ ORACLE node). When the forms are run, only the PL/SQL library files need to be available because the contents of the object libraries will be copied into the runtime .FMX file. This is a one-time step.

2. Create a New Form

To create a new form, select **File→New→Form Using Template** or use the Welcome dialog to open a new form using a template. This will open the template file and rename it to a name such as MODULE1.

3. Add the Data Blocks

Use the Data Block Wizard and Layout Wizard to create the data blocks.

4. Apply SmartClasses

For each item, use the SmartClasses feature of the object library to attach a subclass archetype. This is easiest in the Object Navigator. Right-click on an item (or select a group of items and right-click), and select the closest subclass from the SmartClasses submenu.

5. Add Code and Objects

As you are adding objects, smartclass them as often as possible. If an object is created based on a SmartClass, you will be better able to change the properties and manage the common look and feel of that type of object. When you write code, use the code libraries as much as possible and code generically as much as possible (more on that in Chapter 11). Use the packages that are local to the form for customizing the form. For example, place startup code that is specific to the form in the local STARTUP package. Place code used throughout the form that is form specific in the local UTIL package. Remember that you can override any code in a subclassed trigger.

There is no explicit inheritance from a template to the form that is based on it. However, the template itself uses many subclassed objects. This means that the template is no different from a form created from the template. Both types of forms have the same subclassed objects. Therefore, if you need to change the template and all other forms that have been created from the template, make the change to the object group that is subclassed into all forms. This will cascade the changes to all forms when they are reopened in the Form Builder or recompiled. This exploits the power and benefits of the object groups.

Spending some time developing a template system like this is an important step toward the goal of VRAD. When you have a really functional and feature-rich template, you can quickly and easily create new forms with a large amount of prebuilt and debugged code, prebuilt and standardized objects, and a friendly user interface. The best part is that the template eases the burden of how to program the user interface and allows you to concentrate on the business-specific rules and data.

CHAPTER
11

Constructing the Forms
Template System

The liquid drops of tears that you have shed
Shall come again, transform'd to orient pearl,
Advantaging their loan with interest
Of ten times double gain of happiness.
　　　　　　　—William Shakespeare (1564–1616), *Richard III* (IV, iv, 321)

uilding forms using a template system is clearly the right thing to do. The time that the template development will require is many times less then the time it would take to hand-code the forms without the template. The question of how to create the template system remains. This is not a trivial task and requires careful thought. This task touches the heart of your standards because the template system must support the development of applications according to established interface GUI standards.

This chapter explains the process of creating a template system for Oracle Developer Forms (Forms) and provides techniques to use in thinking about how to structure the template. It also discusses how to approach genericization, which is the key to effective template work. Chapter 10 introduces template system basics, and this chapter builds on that. Chapter 12 explains how to use the template system to create a sample form.

The Process

Developing a fully featured template system is not a trivial weeklong effort. With each project that the template system is used for, the system will evolve and require periodic major or minor revisions. Initially developing the template system is a project and needs to be managed as such. The project will go through the standard software life-cycle phases of Analysis, Design, Build, and Test.

The Life Cycle

The Analysis phase is usually just a matter of determining what standards need to be worked into the user interface. If there are no interface standards, the template work can assist in the effort to create them because, as you are designing objects and code for the template, you will be making decisions about how the interface will look and feel. These decisions can form the basis of your interface standards.

The Design phase of creating a template is a matter of setting up the architecture of the template objects and code. (Chapter 10 provides an example of template architecture.) The Design phase is also spent planning where to use the standards you decided to implement in the Analysis phase.

The Build phase is where you actually construct the objects and code in a Form Builder file to support the standards and your template design. The easiest way to accomplish this is to create a *template prototype* that is a working form with blocks and items that are tied to database tables. This template prototype is the working place for your standard code and objects. When this is debugged and tested, you use this form as the source for code you put in the code libraries and object libraries.

One general issue when you're designing the template is how much flexibility to build into it. You have to temper the desire to add flexibility with the requirement that the template system be easy to understand and easy to use. If it does not fulfill the developer-friendly factor, no one will want to use it, or you will slow down the development process and miss one of the key benefits of using a template.

The Test phase is spent building a sample application using the template system and making notes on enhancements and bugs. Documentation about the template structure and use needs to be available during the Test phase, as this documentation will be tested as well.

The system is then ready for production use. However, you will find that every time you use the template, you will discover code that you want to change or objects that you want to add. Your template system becomes an evolving product, with each iteration being better than the last. Some enhancements that contribute to the evolution may be as simple as an additional component object that you can place in the object library for reuse when needed. Other enhancements may actually be improvements in the efficiency of the code or changes to the interface standards themselves.

NOTE
Keep in mind that your template system will always be evolving. Although you will establish as much of it in the initial releases as possible, so you can use it effectively, the features, functionality, and standards it implements will not be static.

Development Resources
In each of these development phases, you need to allocate the proper resources. The Analysis work can be done by anyone who is aware of GUI standards and is able to relate them to Forms. The analysts do not need to know low-level details on how to write generic code and objects. However, in all phases, the standards work must be tempered by a reality check to see if the standard can be implemented in Forms. In addition, there will be Forms-specific standards that need to be worked into the existing standards. Only experienced developers can perform these reality checks in the Analysis phase.

The Design phase requires experienced Forms experts who can create a structure for generic code and generic objects. The Build phase requires work on the Forms files themselves. Some of this work, particularly some of the PL/SQL coding and creation of predesigned objects, can be done by novice Forms developers under the guidance of experienced developers. Experienced developers will be in charge of ensuring that the template system is easy to use and well documented.

The Test phase needs to be completed by the developers who will be building the forms. Since novice developers should be able to create a form quickly using the template, they are the best testers. You will find out quickly how easy to use and well documented the template system is when you have a novice developer sit down and you give her or him the task of creating a form using the template. The Maintenance phase has the same resource requirements as the Build phase. Experienced developers will usually determine the best way to fix a bug or provide an enhancement based on findings from the Test phase or from enhancements that surface while building a production system. Novice developers may also be able to implement the required change or enhancement.

Where to Start

While all of this may seem like a daunting task and one that requires more time and effort than you want to invest, consider that the paybacks are well worth this investment. In fact, development of a template system will often pay for itself by saving development time in the first project for which it is used. Subsequent projects will actually be less expensive to produce because the majority of the template system has already been developed.

If your standards have been identified beforehand, the look-and-feel analysis will be faster. If the standards are not defined at all, you might find the process is not only slower, but also less efficient because you can get to a certain point in the design but be unable to go forward because there is no standard. While you can determine the standard on your own, this has ramifications for the work of others. You may find yourself scheduling one-hour meetings that drag out to four hours with only minor accomplishments (such as determining the proper font to use for text items). If the standards are in place, you can avoid this bottleneck, although when creating the template, you may need to supplement some standards.

Oracle and third-party software vendors sell Forms template systems. For example, the Oracle Applications ERP suite is bundled with a well-documented and full-featured template system, called the Application Object Library (AOL), that you can use to extend the Applications forms. When thinking about purchasing a template product, seriously consider the learning curve and how quickly you can work your standards into the product. If you are starting from scratch on standards and the template, the latter issue is not a serious consideration because the template development can help you develop the standards. The learning curve is an issue because the more fully featured a template system is, the deeper it is and the harder it is to learn. If you develop a template system on your own, this is not a problem, although the development time will be longer.

One way to design and build a template system is to start with a simple example. The Oracle Developer demo files STNDRD20.* in the ORACLE_HOME/ tools/devdem60/demo/forms directory contain a very basic template system that

can be used as a tool for learning the concepts of a template, but they will need
to be supplemented for real production work. The authors' web sites (listed in the
biographies in the front of the book) also contain samples.

The RAD Approach

Another strategy for creating a template system, assuming you have standards in
place, is to collapse the full life cycle steps of Design and Build mentioned before.
This is more like the Rapid Application Development (RAD) methodology used in
systems development. The main step in this approach is just to create the template
prototype with the proper look and feel. When you have this form working fully the
way you want it, you can think about how to package the objects in the object and
code libraries. This is the process of genericization (described later), where you
rework the objects so they may be shared among all forms. Although you can create
PL/SQL code within the template form during development, you would probably
want to place that code in a Forms library file when you are finished. This will cut
down on the size of the finished form and will provide a central location for your
code, making it easier to maintain and administer.

Using the RAD approach, you still need to go through the Test and Maintenance
phases, but since the entire approach is a spiral (iterative but moving forward), you
can also think about these phases as being collapsed into the new Design-Build
phase. Figure 11-1 summarizes the steps in the process of developing a template.

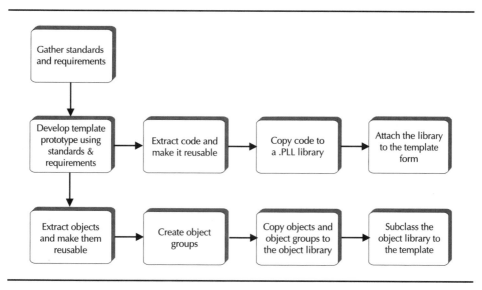

FIGURE 11-1.   *Template development process*

The steps are similar no matter which approach you use. With both the full life cycle approach and the RAD approach, you need to discover the standards and requirements and build a sample form before constructing the actual template files.

TIP
Another RAD-style approach to template development is to start with an existing production form that the users have approved and accepted. This gives you a head start into the Design-Build phase because standards are already in place.

Summary of Steps

Regardless of the exact method you use to create the template system, you will pass through the following steps, at some point in the development cycle:

1. Determine standards.

2. Design and build a template prototype.

3. Genericize code and objects.

4. Move objects into the object library.

5. Move code that supports the object library objects into a PL/SQL (.PLL) library.

6. Create the template from the object library.

7. Create a reference master form.

8. Document the reusable components and template use.

The remainder of this chapter will discuss the key concepts used to accomplish most of these steps. The actual standards you will be implementing with the template are discussed in Chapter 5.

Genericizing Objects and Code

Creating objects and code in a sample working form is the easy part of developing a template system. The harder part that follows is creating versions of the objects and code that you can use in any future form. This is the process of *genericization,* where you make the object properties and code more general (not specific to a particular form) and, therefore, more reusable. Genericization is the essence of reusable code. The more generic your code and objects are, the more reusable they will be. Developing reusability into forms is an art that requires experience and creativity. You have to think carefully about how the Forms components you use in one form can be reworked and reused to service future forms. You also have to think about how to make the objects you develop flexible enough to fulfill multiple purposes. There are different concerns you will need to address and techniques you need to apply when genericizing code and objects.

Genericizing Code

When you develop a PL/SQL procedure or function in a form, you usually add direct references to objects in the form and test the form thoroughly. The next step, which is often missed, is to reexamine this code in the light of making it more generic. The objective in genericizing code is to allow the same code to serve more than one form or more than one object in the same form.

In general, any code that supports a generic component (such as the calendar component) or supports generic tasks in Forms (such as looping through a block and setting all items to be non-updateable) should be genericized and placed in a PL/SQL code library file (.PLL). While you can place individual Program Units into the object library, the object library does not offer easy editing, compilation, or browsing of the code. Therefore, the best and most logical container for the code is the code library.

After genericizing the code into a library, you would attach it to the specific form that started the process. In the case of developing a template system, this form is the template prototype. After attaching the library, you can then remove the local version of the code from the form and be sure you are calling the library version. You are then ready to test the form with the attached library.

The library offers the best way to distribute generic code. However, the library compiler will not accept references to actual form object names, so you need to make these references more generic using the techniques of parameterizing and dereferencing.

NOTE
Appendix A contains the package descriptions from a sample PL/SQL library to give you an idea of the type of code that is appropriate for the library.

Parameterizing

Code you first create in a form will reference objects in that form explicitly. When you make the code more generic, you create procedures that refer to the objects using parameter values. This allows you to call the procedures for any object of the same type within the form. This is best explained with an example. You have a business rule that EMP record date columns cannot be updated if the related DEPT record has an inactive status (STATUS != 'A'). If the status is "A", you want to allow updates on the date items. When you create the form for the first time, you write a WHEN-NEW-RECORD-INSTANCE in the DEPT block with the following code:

```
IF :dept.status != 'A'
THEN
    set_item_property('EMP.HIRE_DT', UPDATE_ALLOWED, PROPERTY_FALSE);
    set_item_property('EMP.BIRTH_DT', UPDATE_ALLOWED, PROPERTY_FALSE);
    set_item_property('EMP.TERM_DT', UPDATE_ALLOWED, PROPERTY_FALSE);
ELSE
    set_item_property('EMP.HIRE_DT', UPDATE_ALLOWED, PROPERTY_TRUE);
    set_item_property('EMP.BIRTH_DT', UPDATE_ALLOWED, PROPERTY_TRUE);
    set_item_property('EMP.TERM_DT', UPDATE_ALLOWED, PROPERTY_TRUE);
END IF;
```

You test this and it works until you add another date column to the EMP table. You then need to remember to add the item and change the code in the DEPT block. Remembering to add the item may be easy, but remembering to change the code may not be so easy. If you did not change the code, the business rule would not be fully implemented.

The first solution is to come up with a flexible procedure that loops through the items in the block and changes the updateable property based on the status of the DEPT.STATUS item. The following code implements this solution:

```
DECLARE
    v_curr_item     VARCHAR2(30);
    v_block_item    VARCHAR2(61);
BEGIN
    v_curr_item := get_block_property('EMP', FIRST_ITEM);
    --
    -- loop through all items in the block
    WHILE v_curr_item IS NOT NULL
    LOOP
        v_block_item := 'EMP.' || v_curr_item;
        --
        -- Toggle the updateable property of the non-button, date
        -- items based on the value of DEPT.STATUS.
        IF get_item_property(v_block_item, ITEM_TYPE) != 'BUTTON'
            AND get_item_property(v_block_item, DATATYPE) LIKE '%DATE%'
        THEN     -- the datatype could be something like DATETIME or JDATE
            IF :dept.status != 'A'
            THEN
                set_item_property(v_block_item, UPDATE_ALLOWED, PROPERTY_FALSE);
            ELSE
                set_item_property(v_block_item, UPDATE_ALLOWED, PROPERTY_TRUE);
            END IF;
        END IF;          -- end of get_item_property
        v_curr_item := get_item_property(v_block_item, NEXTITEM);
    END LOOP;
END;
```

This makes the trigger generic with respect to the actual items in the block. No matter how many date items are added to the block, the code will handle the business rule correctly with no code changes. However, this code is still specific to a block. Therefore, if you added an EQUIP block to this form (for equipment owned by the department), the code would need to be repeated to loop through that block as well. The next genericization for this code is then to make it non-specific to any particular block. The code can be split out into a PL/SQL packaged procedure that has no references to a specific block. It is therefore able to serve multiple blocks. The next iteration of the code passes the name of the block to the procedure. This makes the procedure generic to the block. The procedure would be located in the UTIL package of the form's program units as follows:

```
PACKAGE util
IS
--
    PROCEDURE set_date_update(
        p_block            VARCHAR2,
        p_property_value   NUMBER);
--
END;

PACKAGE BODY util IS
--
    PROCEDURE set_date_update(
        p_block            VARCHAR2,
        p_property_value   NUMBER)
    IS
        v_curr_item    VARCHAR2(30);
        v_block_item   VARCHAR2(61);
    BEGIN
        v_curr_item := get_block_property(p_block, FIRST_ITEM);
        --
        -- loop through all items in the block
        WHILE v_curr_item IS NOT NULL
        LOOP
            v_block_item := p_block || '.' || v_curr_item;
            --
            -- Toggle the updateable property of the non-button, date
            -- items based on the value of DEPT.STATUS.
            IF get_item_property(v_block_item, ITEM_TYPE) != 'BUTTON'
                AND get_item_property(v_block_item, DATATYPE) LIKE '%DATE%'
            THEN       -- the datatype could be something like DATETIME or JDATE
                set_item_property(v_block_item, UPDATE_ALLOWED, p_property_value);
            END IF;          -- end of get_item_property
            v_curr_item := get_item_property(v_block_item, NEXTITEM);
        END LOOP;
    END;
--
END;
```

The WHEN-NEW-RECORD-INSTANCE trigger on the block calls this procedure as follows:

```
IF :dept.status != 'A'
THEN
    util.set_date_update('EMP', PROPERTY_FALSE);
    util.set_date_update('EQUIP', PROPERTY_FALSE);
ELSE
    util.set_date_update('EMP', PROPERTY_TRUE);
    util.set_date_update('EQUIP', PROPERTY_TRUE);
END IF;
```

In this code, the block name and property setting are passed into the procedure. This allows the procedure to serve additional actions as well as additional blocks. This procedure, once tested and debugged, could be placed in a library file because it has no direct references to Forms objects. The library could be attached to many forms, and each would be able to call this update property code.

Further refinements could be made on the procedure to make it even more generic. For example, you could pass in the datatype of the item as a parameter. This would allow you to use the same procedure to set properties of items with datatypes other than date. The name of the procedure would have to be changed to something more generic if this change were made.

The more you start thinking about how to genericize the code, the more ideas you will come up with for making it as flexible as possible. There is a danger in going too far, however. If the code has too many parameters, it may be difficult to understand or remember, and this would defeat a main advantage of using generic code.

Dereferencing

Code in the .PLL library cannot contain any direct reference to a bind variable (using the :BLOCK.ITEM syntax). *Dereferencing* in Forms work refers to the process of changing direct references for blocks, items, parameters, system variables, and global variables to indirect references. Direct references are only used when determining the value of an item and in assigning a value to an item. The two Forms built-ins you use to dereference bind variables in these operations are COPY (for assigning) and NAME_IN (for determining the value). For example, your code in a form contains the following assignment:

```
:emp.job := 'CLERK';
```

This will not work in a library because it has a direct reference to the :EMP.JOB item. If you wanted to place this code in a Forms library, you would change it to the following:

```
copy('CLERK', 'EMP.JOB');
```

This removes the bind variable syntax and allows you to place the code in the library. The drawback of this syntax is that there is no compiler check to see if the item actually exists. Therefore, if the item does not exist, you will not see an error until the form runs and reaches this line of code.

Determining the value of a bind variable uses the NAME_IN built-in. For example, your code could contain the following:

```
IF :emp.job = 'MANAGER'
THEN
    go_block('DEPT');
END IF;
```

The conditional statement determines the value of the JOB item, but it uses a direct reference to that item. To place this code in a library, you would change the conditional statement to:

```
IF name_in('EMP.JOB') = 'MANAGER'
```

The item name is placed in quotes (without the bind variable colon) so the library compiler will accept it.

NOTE
Both COPY and NAME_IN work only on character values. If your items are number or date datatypes, you must convert the value using the SQL TO_CHAR, TO_DATE, or TO_NUMBER functions. Some examples are "COPY(TO_CHAR(10), 'EMP.DEPTNO');" and "IF TO_DATE(NAME_IN('EMP.HIREDATE'), 'DD-MON-YYYY') + 30 > SYSDATE THEN..." Forms will do an implicit type conversion if you assign a character to a number or date item. For example, "COPY('01-JAN-2000', 'EMP.HIREDATE');" will load the string '01-JAN-2000' into the date item :EMP.HIREDATE. The string will be automatically converted to a date datatype by the item.

Genericizing Objects

Genericizing objects is somewhat easier than genericizing code since it is just a matter of setting properties. The idea is the same because you are creating an object for reuse. You still have to think about how the objects will be used. Since you want to be able to use the objects in many different forms. Objects in the object library will serve as archetypes to enforce standards and as reusable components to give developers a quick way to incorporate prebuilt and pretested groups of objects. When you develop the template prototype form, you are creating some of the objects that will be placed into the object library. The process of genericizing objects includes setting their properties to remove any form-specific references and bundling them together into object groups.

Creating Archetypes by Setting the Properties

As Chapter 10 explains, subclassing an object will force all the nondefault properties in the parent object to be inherited by the child object. This means that you have to be careful of the actual properties that are set in the objects you want to reuse. When you decide that an object in your template prototype is reusable, you have to examine all properties to see if there are any that should not be inherited to child objects.

For example, you want to create an archetype button item (called CANVAS_ BUTTON) that will be the parent for all canvas buttons in your forms. You determine the desired font and colors and create a visual attribute for those properties, as in Figure 11-2. You then attach the visual attribute to a button in the template prototype.

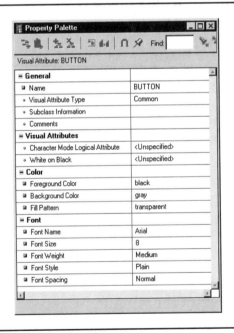

FIGURE 11-2. *Button Visual Attribute properties*

The properties of the archetype button will determine which properties are set when you use this object for subclassing. Any nondefault property will be subclassed to the child object. You would normally not want properties such as *Label, Canvas, X Position,* or *Y Position* to inherit to subclassed objects. Therefore, you need to reset these properties to the default by selecting the property in the Property Palette and clicking the Inherit button. Figure 11-3 shows this action on the *Y Position* property. The green square icon next to the property name will change to a gray circle icon (as in the *X Position* property in Figure 11-3) when the property is defaulted.

Any object that you subclass from this object will retain the setting of defaulted properties. For example, a canvas button that you subclass from this object will already be placed in a specific location on the canvas, and you would not want that to change when the subclass is applied.

NOTE
The rule of thumb when determining which properties need to keep their default values (so the objects that are subclassed from them will not inherit that property value) is that a property should be left with a default value if it may need to be set specifically for a particular instantiation of an object. The first time you encounter an object that will be a subclass, it is useful to look at each property and go through the decision process for that property.

There are some properties that may be subclassed in some cases and not subclassed in other cases. For example, for some cases you would choose not to subclass the *Width* property because each item that is subclassed will have its own specific width. However, in other cases you may want to subclass the *Width*

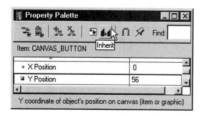

FIGURE 11-3. *Setting the* Y Position *property to default*

property if you want to create a more granular archetype. For example, you might always have an exit button in the lower-right corner of each canvas. That button would always have the same *Label, Height, Width, X Position,* and *Y Position.* Those properties would be specified on the subclass master itself so each button you create from it will have the same properties.

Another property to manipulate at this point is the *Name.* This property will become the SmartClass name if this object is an archetype. Select a name using the naming conventions you have decided on (see Chapter 6 for some guidelines). If you will only use this object as a SmartClass, the name does not matter.

Other properties to examine are those that have references to other objects in the form (such as *Canvas, Window, Synchronize with Item, Copy Value from Item, Previous Navigation Item, Next Navigation Item,* and so on). If it is possible that the objects that these properties refer to will not be in the child form that you subclass the object into, they should be set to the default. There may be occasions when you want to leave references to other objects in the archetype. For example, if all your forms will contain a canvas called MAIN on a window called MAIN, the *Window* property of the subclass parent can have a value of MAIN.

If the object that a subclassed property refers to is not in the form, there will be a compile or runtime error, but the Form Builder will not remove the invalid reference. This is a different behavior from versions of Oracle Developer before R.2. This behavior means that you do not have to worry about the order that you create or subclass objects in the form. Hanging references will resolve themselves if the referenced object is created.

Creating Reusable Components with Object Groups

Crafting the properties settings is the main action when you're genericizing archetypal objects. Creating reusable components for the object library is really just a matter of creating object groups that package a number of objects that are required for a particular function into a single unit.

For example, as part of your template prototype, you come up with a calendar window to allow the user to select a date or date range in a visual way. (This particular component is included with the Form Builder demos, so don't start from scratch if this is really a requirement.) The calendar is a perfect example of a reusable component because it can be written generically so that it contains no direct reference to a particular item or block in a particular form. The calendar window includes a canvas, a window, a number of items, and a set of buttons for accepting or canceling. Figure 11-4 shows the Forms demos calendar window.

All objects are contained in an object group, as Figure 11-5 shows. Since the data blocks own the items, those objects are implicitly included in the group. In addition to the objects, the calendar requires triggers and program units to advance

FIGURE 11-4. *Calendar window*

the calendar month and pass values back and forth to the block. The trigger code is attached to calendar objects and is included with the data blocks, but the program units are contained in a library that you attach to the form if you require the calendar. Attached libraries cannot be object group children. The entire CALENDAR object group is placed into the object library. The only action needed by the developer is to drag and subclass the object group into the new form, attach the PL/SQL library, and write triggers (such as WHEN-BUTTON-PRESSED triggers on date item buttons) to call the calendar.

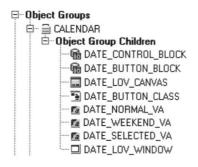

FIGURE 11-5. *Calendar object group*

The action of creating object groups for specific functional components is the same as with the calendar. Once you have created the template prototype, you need to examine it for potential reusable components. You then identify all the parts of the reusable component and drag each one into the component's object group.

Another Use for Object Groups

Another use for object groups is to store sets of objects that you can maintain centrally. For example, when starting a project, you may be able to guess that every form will require parameters (in the Object Navigator) for LOGIN_USER and LOGIN_TIME. You can include these in the object library and subclass them to the template so each form created from the template can use them. However, there may be additional requirements for parameters that come up during the development process. You can add the parameters to the object library and subclass them into the template at that point. However, if you had already created forms based on the initial template, those forms would not contain the new parameters. You would need to open each form and subclass the new parameters individually from the object library.

If you use a single object group for all your parameters, this process is much easier. The object group called SUBCLASS_FORM_PARAMETERS would contain the LOGIN_USER and LOGIN_TIME parameters initially. The object library would contain only the SUBCLASS_FORM_PARAMETERS object group, and the template would subclass that object group. If an additional parameter were required, you would add it to the object library maintenance form, drag the new parameter into the SUBCLASS_FORM_PARAMETERS object group in that form, and drag the object group back into the object library, which would refresh the object group in the object library. The next time you opened or recompiled a form created from the template, the new parameter would be available because it is part of the existing subclassed object group. Removing parameters would work the same way.

Therefore, the more you make use of object groups, whether it is for reusable components or for inherited Forms objects, the easier maintenance will be.

Object Library Elements

Creating the object library is the next step after genericizing objects and code. Since you have already identified the archetype objects and reusable components, it is just a matter of dragging them from the form and dropping them into the object library. The easiest way to understand what goes into the object library and how the library is arranged is to look at an example. Figure 11-6 shows the tabs of a sample object library.

The tabs arrange the object library objects into logical groupings of reusable components and sets of objects (Standard Objects and Optional Objects tabs) and

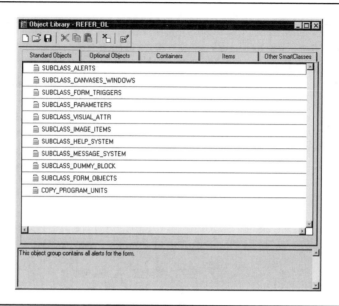

FIGURE 11-6.   *Sample object library*

archetype objects used as SmartClasses (Containers, Items, and Other SmartClasses). It is useful to examine the objects in each tab.

Standard Objects

This tab (shown in Figure 11-6) contains object groups that serve as reusable components and sets of objects that are used in each form. All groups are copied or subclassed into the template form. Therefore, you would not normally need to access the objects in this tab while building a form from the template. The object groups use a prefix of the method used to place them in the template (copy or subclass). The object groups on this tab are discussed next.

SUBCLASS_ALERTS

The template system uses a flexible alert system that can call an alert and pass it the button labels and message. Most of this alert system is in PL/SQL library code, but the code requires an alert without a message for each of the standard alert icons (Caution, Note, and Stop). This object group contains these three alerts because you cannot programmatically change the alert icon.

SUBCLASS_CANVASES_WINDOWS

The template form provides a sample window, content canvas, and content canvas with tabs. The canvases and windows are sized for the resolution that the system requires. This object group contains these objects.

SUBCLASS_FORM_TRIGGERS

The system you use to handle user keypresses, menu selections, and button clicks passes through the KEY- triggers written on the form level. (This code path is described further in Chapter 7.) Each KEY- trigger (such as KEY-EXIT) contains a single call to a procedure code in the PL/SQL library. The library procedure contains the actual logic. This strategy gives you a central location to maintain all code for Forms functions (such as exit, enter query, execute query, and commit). The trigger code is written into the triggers in the object library and, through this object group, subclassed into the template. All forms inherit these form-level triggers, but the developer can override or supplement the code on an as-needed basis. This object group is primarily for the KEY- triggers and other user-defined triggers that are called from the menu.

An example of an inherited trigger is the WHEN-NEW-FORM-INSTANCE trigger that executes a set of startup procedures. These procedures set up poplists and populate record groups, check the user's security level and disable items if necessary, read graphics files into the canvases, and set the window title from a table value. It turns out that all forms in the application will need to do this startup processing, although some of the routines, such as populating the record groups, will be different for each form. One way to make this procedure more generic is to call a common startup procedure that is stored in a library. If you have to modify the procedures that are executed when a form starts, you can do so in this library package and it will affect all forms. The forms, meanwhile, can also perform actions that are applicable to their particular situation. This gives you the best of both shared code and local code.

In this system, the WHEN-NEW-FORM-INSTANCE trigger calls a local PL/SQL procedure STARTUP.WHEN_NEW_FORM_INSTANCE. The STARTUP package can be copied or subclassed from the object library. Since you will be making changes to the code for each form, subclassing the package brings no advantage, so you can copy it as a local version of the object library code. The WHEN_NEW_FORM_INSTANCE procedure calls a library procedure for common startup routines (to check security, read graphics files, and so on) and then does form-specific actions such as setting up window sizes, checking the form version, checking login privileges, populating record groups, loading poplists, and assigning control block items. Placing some of the code in a library package allows you to add or change the startup code for all forms from a common location. It also allows you to run custom procedures for a specific form before or after the startup library code call. The path that this code takes is shown in Figure 11-7. The form in this diagram represents the template and all other forms that are based on that template. The object library, template, and library work together to automatically provide a large amount of functionality to the startup of the form.

The developer can override the code inheritance that the subclassed triggers offer. For example, a form-level KEY-COMMIT trigger is subclassed into the template from the object library and contains a call to a library procedure, F_UTIL.COMMITFORM. This procedure checks to see if the users have made changes and presents a confirmation dialog if they have. If there are no changes, another dialog displays with a message to that effect. This trigger works well for all forms, but a particular form needs to replace this message with an automatic commit instead of the dialogs. Since the trigger is subclassed from the template, it contains a call to the library procedure. If you replace that call with code that performs an automatic commit, the trigger will still be inherited from the object library, but the overridden code will be used instead of the object library code.

SUBCLASS_PARAMETERS

This object group houses all Object Navigator parameters (not programmatic parameters) that are required by all forms. Since this entire object group is subclassed, it is easy to add a parameter to all forms by just adding it to this object group and recompiling the existing forms.

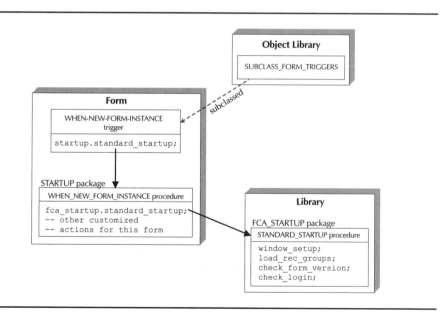

FIGURE 11-7. *Subclassed trigger and its related code*

SUBCLASS_VISUAL_ATTR

The visual attributes you use in your forms are one of the main methods of implementing a common look and feel. This object group contains all common visual attributes. Usually, you want to create visual attributes for display items, text items (and other input items such as poplists), buttons, canvases, LOVs, editors, and alerts. All these visual attributes are stored in this object group. In addition, you may need to create visual attributes to support reusable components like the calendar. However, these visual attributes are used for a specific purpose and will be packaged with the component object group.

SUBCLASS_IMAGE_ITEMS

This object group exemplifies an application-specific subclassed object group. The application that this template supports requires a company logo and an application logo on each canvas. The logo image files are read into image items when the form starts up. This object group stores the image items and their block. The subclassed image items are copied into the same block and assigned to another content canvas if there is more than one content canvas in the form.

SUBCLASS_HELP_SYSTEM

The help system can be implemented in a number of ways, as Chapter 14 describes. This object group holds all objects that this help system needs. For example, if you decide to implement table-based help and copy a window into each form with the mechanism to query the help table, this object group will hold the window, canvas, block, and items that the help system uses. This becomes a self-contained reusable component that is subclassed into the template.

SUBCLASS_MESSAGE_SYSTEM

This is another application-specific requirement. The design of the application that this template supports called for a message item at the bottom of the content canvas to show all messages to the user. The normal status and hint lines are removed (using the form-level property *Console Window),* and the objects in this component object group are subclassed into the template to provide the alternative message line. As in the image item group, if there are other content canvases, the message item is copied into the same block.

SUBCLASS_DUMMY_BLOCK

The DUMMY block is a control block that contains an item called NULL_ITEM (width and height of 0). This is a handy location, which you can move the cursor into, if you are changing properties on all items in a block. There is a restriction on setting some properties on the item that the cursor is in. Moving the cursor to this item in this block lifts the restriction and allows you to change any property in any item. Your code needs to include a routine for moving the cursor to this item and returning it when the property settings are complete. The DUMMY block and NULL_ITEM item are subclassed into the template from this object group.

SUBCLASS_FORM_OBJECTS

After forms have been created from the template, you may need to place an object in all forms. This object group is the catchall for objects that are required but that do not fit into any other object group. It is subclassed into the template even if it does not have any child objects so if a new object is needed in all forms and does not fit into any other group, you can just add it to this group and recompile all forms.

COPY_PROGRAM_UNITS

The template form contains some local program units that the developer needs to change for the specific form. These program units are copied into the template from the object library. Since these are just a shell for the developer to write form-specific code, the link to the template form is not appropriate.

There are two packages that are copied through this object group: STARTUP and UTIL. The STARTUP package contains procedures for PRE_FORM and WHEN_ NEW_FORM_INSTANCE. These are called from the PRE-FORM and WHEN-NEW-FORM-INSTANCE form-level triggers, respectively, to execute form-specific routines such as initializing poplists from database queries, automatically querying blocks that need to be populated, initializing control blocks, checking user security, and other application-specific tasks. There are other procedures in the STARTUP package that support the initialization of the form. If the CLEAR_FORM built-in needs to be called, the initialization procedures can also be called to reinstate the values for the objects.

The UTIL package contains ON_ERROR and ON_MESSAGE procedures that are called from the form-level ON-ERROR and ON-MESSAGE triggers, respectively. The trigger that each procedure is built for is apparent from its name. (Remember that built-in Forms trigger names contain hyphens and procedures do not.) These triggers replace the normal Forms error and messaging functions. They allow you to ignore some messages (such as the message that states how many records were committed) and replace others with a message of your own. You can usually decide how to handle the common messages on an application level. These can be written into the F_UTIL.ON_ERROR (or F_UTIL.ON_MESSAGE) procedure in the PL/SQL library. Some messages or errors will be specific to the form. The UTIL package in the form contains a default call to the library procedure, but you can handle any specific error code before that call if your form calls for handling outside the library procedure. The UTIL package also contains a POST_FORM procedure that is called from the POST-FORM trigger to clean up global variables and to perform last-minute validation.

NOTE
While you can place stand-alone triggers into an object library, remember that subclassed triggers cannot be moved to a different location in the Object Navigator. Therefore, if you store a trigger in the object library, you would have to copy it to the form instead of subclassing it in order to move it to the block or item level.

Optional Objects

This tab (shown in Figure 11-8) contains reusable components that you might use in a specific form but that are not general enough to include in the template. These are written as reusable objects that can be dropped and subclassed from the object library to the form. They are complete with the exception that a library may need to be attached to supply the code for the component. This tab contains reusable components that you might want to drag and drop and subclass into a form. The CALENDAR and STANDARD_CALENDAR (used to emulate the Oracle Applications template calendar) display a calendar for date selection.

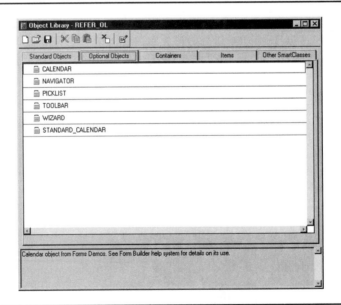

FIGURE 11-8. *Optional Objects tab*

There is also a toolbar object group in this tab that may not be used in every form, but that could be dragged into a new form when required. If you decide not to use menu toolbars and your application requires different toolbars for different applications, you can create a set of standard toolbars, each stored in a separate object group in this tab. The toolbar block, items, and triggers are stored in the object group.

Other standard object groups in this tab are from the Forms demonstration files. The NAVIGATOR displays a hierarchical tree navigator using Forms objects. It contains the code to expand and collapse the nodes and query the records into the tree. This object group uses Forms objects instead of the new hierarchical tree control available in R.6. This allows you to have more control over the events and appearance of the tree, but does not provide the ease-of-use and built-in functionality benefits of the hierarchical tree control. The other demonstration reusable components offered in this tab are object groups for the PICKLIST (multiple selection LOV) and WIZARD (that presents a series of easy-to-use dialogs for completing a record).

 NOTE
Remember to fill in the Comments property on the Object Group before you drag it into the object library. This property will copy to the object library object so you will not need to edit the comment in the object library itself.

Containers

As Figure 11-9 shows, this tab contains archetype objects defined as SmartClasses for windows and canvases. The sizes are defined so the window will fill the screen at a certain display resolution (such as 800×600). The content canvas is also defined to fill the window at the same resolution. Each full-screen window or canvas you create in a form subclasses these objects to maintain a consistent size. Since these are defined as SmartClasses (with the check mark icon), they will show up in the SmartClass right-click menu.

Items

This tab, shown in Figure 11-10, organizes the archetypes for items. There are variations on combinations of properties for item type (display item, text item, poplist, radio group, and check box) and purpose (display, data entry, money, numbers, dates, and multiline display). Generally, there are display-only display item (suffixed with DISP_DISP), display-only text item (suffixed with DISP_TEXT), and data entry (suffixed with ENTER) versions of items with prefixes of TXT (for text values), DATE (for date items), NUM (for numbers), and MONEY (for currency). The last category contains varieties with and without the "$" prefix to the format mask.

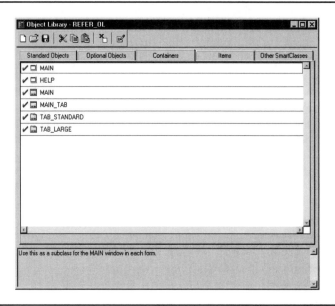

FIGURE 11-9. *Containers tab*

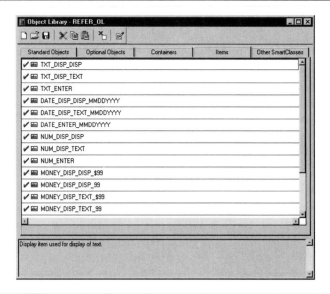

FIGURE 11-10. *Items tab*

The differences among these are mainly in the *Item Type, Data Type, Format Mask, Visual Attribute Group, Insert Allowed,* and *Update Allowed* properties. There is one SmartClass for a multiline item, so you can easily set the properties that you need to implement this type of item (*Multi-Line, Wrap Style,* and *Height*). The *Height* and *Visual Attribute Group* properties are set the same for most items. The objects in this tab are used to subclass a new item that is created on the form. These are also SmartClasses so they will be available in the right-click menu for this purpose.

The *Width* property for text items, display items, poplists, and multiline items is defaulted because the Data Block Wizard will size items based on their database column width. The SmartClass for the item should not be the source for the width property. If the item is a check box or radio group, setting the *Width* property in the subclass makes sense because these objects have a fixed width. You can create a SmartClass for the radio button itself; the radio group does not have physical properties except for the canvas name.

TIP

When you create SmartClass objects, it is important to temper the desire for completeness with the desire for conciseness. If you think about the range of SmartClasses you will need for items, the list can grow to be quite long. A long SmartClass list slows you down when you need to select a particular entry from the right-click menu.

Other SmartClasses

The last tab in the object library, shown in Figure 11-11, contains objects that are used for other purposes than for data items or containers. They are all defined as SmartClasses to subclass an object once you have created it. There are a number of button archetypes for different needs, for example, an LOV_BUTTON that you place next to an object that has an LOV defined. The button calls the LOV. There are also button archetypes for a standard canvas button, a button that serves as a heading above a column, and a help button. The properties that are set in each of these are standard button properties, but setting an explicit value for the *Height* and *Width* properties may actually make sense in the case of buttons because a consistent size creates a clean look.

There are also application-specific objects such as MESSAGE_ITEM, SORT_BUTTON, APP_LOGO, and CO_LOGO. These are used to subclass objects that are created in a new form for showing the message line, ordering a block, and displaying the application and company logo graphics. FORM_PROPERTIES is a property class that is applied to the form module itself. Since you cannot store a form module in the object library, this is the best way to manage the form properties

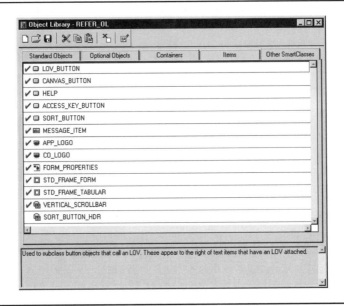

FIGURE 11-11. *Other SmartClasses tab*

for *Console Window, Menu Module, Current Record Visual Attribute Group,* and *Runtime Compatibility Mode.* The *Coordinate System* property is not available for the property class, so you have to set that manually. Figure 11-12 shows the dialog from the *Subclass Information* property of the form module.

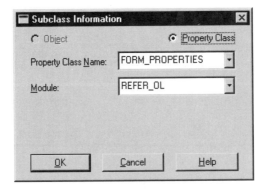

FIGURE 11-12. *Setting the form module* Subclass Information *property*

This tab also contains frame objects for form and tabular-style blocks, a block SmartClass that applies a vertical scroll bar of a standard width, and an object that is the starting point for the sort button system described in Chapter 26.

Other Template Tasks

After you create the object library and PL/SQL library by genericizing code and objects and saving them in libraries, it is time to complete the template system. The main tasks left are to create the reference form and template form, and to document the template use. You also need to create a menu template and to have a strategy for changing the template components during the development process.

The Reference Form

You cannot view or change properties of existing objects in the object library itself. You also cannot tell which subobjects are included with a particular object such as a block or object group. This is a limitation of the object library and means that you have to instantiate the object in a form to make changes to it or to view its properties and subobjects. An alternative to dragging the objects into a form is to maintain a separate form containing all objects from the object group. Everything in the object library is also in the form. This takes a bit of care because there is nothing that links the two files (form and object library).

However, the benefits of maintaining a reference form are worth this extra care. One benefit is that you can easily browse and modify all objects without the action of dragging the object into a form. This is particularly useful for object groups because the child objects are invisible in the object library. Another benefit of maintaining a reference form is that you can take advantage of some of the Object Navigator features such as applying one property value to objects by grouping the objects together and displaying and modifying the Property Palette for the group. This is, of course, possible with the object library, but it requires the extra drag and drop operation. If the objects are already in the form, you save that extra effort.

Creating the Reference Form

You can create a reference form by dragging all object groups from the object library into a new form. SmartClass objects also need to be instantiated by copying (not subclassing) into the reference form. For top-level objects such as windows, canvases, parameters, alerts, program units, and visual attributes, you can just drop the object into the appropriate node in the reference form's Object Navigator. For subobjects that you use as archetypes, such as items, you have to create a parent object, such as a block, to hold them. Name the block to indicate the tab in which the item appears. This will clarify the organization later. Figure 11-13 shows the sample reference form's Object Navigator with blocks and object groups. The items in the Items and Other SmartClasses tabs appear in the blocks called ITEM_TAB and OTHER_TAB, respectively.

The reference form will end up looking similar to the template prototype, but will have no sample data blocks or program units specific to any application.

Maintaining the Reference Form

You have to change the way you think about the reference form files. Think of the object library and the reference form file as a unit. Open both, make the change to the object in the reference form, and immediately drop it into the right place in the object library file. Once you get into this habit, it will be easy to do. If you do not drag the changed object into the object library right away, you may lose track of which objects have been changed in the form. The form will then be out of synch with the object library.

As mentioned in Chapter 10, Oracle Designer provides a utility, FORM2LIB.EXE, that creates an object library from a form file. You can use that to keep the files in synch because you would just delete the object library and re-create it from the .FMB file with this utility. Details on how this works can be found in the FORM2LIB.TXT file in the ORACLE_HOME/cgenf50 directory. If you do not have Designer, you need to use the manual method.

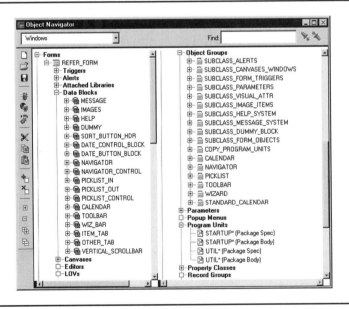

FIGURE 11-13. *Reference form blocks and object groups*

TIP
There is no easy way to reorder the objects on a particular tab in the object library. You can, however, use the Cut and Paste buttons in the Object Library window to reorder some types of objects. Cut the object, select the object you want to appear before the cut object, and Paste the cut object. Renaming objects in the object library is not possible except by renaming the reference form object, dragging the object into the object library, and deleting the old object.

The Template Form

Once all the preliminary steps are complete, creating the template form itself is relatively straightforward. You do not want to start with the template prototype form because the objects in it are not subclassed. The main step is subclassing the standard object groups from the object library. Some of the object groups are copied and some are subclassed; the prefix on the name indicates which operation to use (for example, SUBCLASS_ALERT_SYSTEM is an object group to subclass). The next step is applying the FORM_PROPERTIES property class to the form module. Open the form module properties and fill in the *Subclass Information* property to reference the property class from the object library as Figure 11-12 shows. The last step is to attach the required libraries to the template on the Attached Libraries node.

This will create the basic generalized template. If you decide to create style-specific templates, you will use this template as a start and add objects to it (as described later on) to create a style-specific template or project-specific template.

Documenting the Template Files

A certain amount of documentation is required so the developer knows how to work with a particular template. The documentation should assume that the reader understands the template architecture and how to build a form from a template. It does describe the specific actions needed with the objects in the template. For example, the instructions can tell how to copy and subclass a window or content canvas if needed.

The documentation should be written into a text file that is available in the same location as the template files. This allows the developer to keep the instructions open while working with the template. There can also be a separate file to document the PL/SQL libraries for developers; this will consist of the package headers that are extracted from the .PLL file and contain descriptions of all procedures and functions in the library. Documentation on the object library can also be contained in a separate text file. This only needs to describe the general contents of each tab. Since the standard objects are already included in the template, the main descriptions will be about the optional objects. SmartClasses should be intuitively named and should need no further explanation.

Overdocumentation is undesirable because it can slow down the development work. If you find that you have to write a large amount about a particular template system file or function in the file, your system may not be intuitive enough, and you may want to refine the design to make it easier to use. A one-page "cheat sheet" for each template file should suffice. This instruction list describes the basic features and outlines the steps you go through to create a form from the template. Use bullet points rather than complete sentences because they are quicker to absorb.

In addition, you may want to show screen captures of sample forms running to give the developer an idea of how the form will look. A simple ALT-PRINT SCREEN keypress will capture the screen to the Windows clipboard. You can then **Edit→Paste** the image into an image editor such as Paintbrush or a word-processing program such as Word. These files can be stored in a SAMPLES directory in the application file system.

The Menu Template

Your menu system is determined by the application design and how the user will navigate from one form to another. You may decide to not use a menu at all but to rely on buttons on the form to execute Forms functions and navigation. If the system is complex or you need to allow the user to execute a number of Forms functions, a menu system may be indicated. You also have to decide how the menu will work. One strategy is to use the opening form (the navigation form) to navigate to other forms in the system. When you exit from each form, you return to the navigation form. The menu for this form contains calls to the other forms in the system (or you place buttons on the screen to do that and remove the menu completely). The individual forms that the opening form calls attach a different menu that contains standard Forms functions such as Save (commit), Enter Query (if you are using that mode), Next Record, Help, Delete Record, Insert Record, and Exit.

Another decision you have to make is if you will use the menu toolbar. This is just a matter of setting the *Visible in Horizontal Menu Toolbar* property to "Yes" on selected menu items. You also have to set the *Icon Filename* property as the name of the icon file (without the file extension). The menu toolbar takes up space and, depending on how computer-aware your users are, may or may not be used.

Creating the Menu Template

Your design decisions will help you create the menu templates. If you are not using menus, the template is not needed. If you are using menus, you can devise a menu template that will be generic to all menus in the system. You can even place menus or menu items in the object library so you can build menus by dragging and dropping from the object library. You can also subclass menu items from the object library so the items inherit standard properties.

If you can determine a set of menus and menu items that are used for every application, you can store those in a menu object group that is copied into the object library. The template menu subclasses that object group. This gives you all the benefits that the template form gains from the object library subclassing.

Menu Code

One of the guidelines when working with menus is that the code should call KEY-triggers whenever possible. This gives you a central location for changes to the code. For example, if you have a menu item for exiting the form, it should contain the call: "DO_KEY('EXIT_FORM');". This will emulate the exit function keypress and fire the KEY-EXIT trigger. Whatever code you have in the KEY-EXIT trigger will fire as if the user had pressed the exit key. If you decided to include the menu toolbar button, that button would call the same code (because it is the menu item itself). If you created a canvas button for exiting the form, you would use the same call as the menu item. In this way, all possible ways of exiting the form will go through the same code. This gives you a central location for maintaining the code.

If your menu item does not issue a Forms function call but the form will need to call the same code, you can write a user-defined trigger on the form level. The trigger would contain a call to execute the user-defined trigger. For example, you want to display a Help About form from the menu to display details about the form. You would write a user-defined trigger in the form called HELP_ABOUT. This trigger would contain a call to a library procedure to call the Help About form and pass it parameters with details about the form that called it. The menu item would contain the following: "EXECUTE_TRIGGER ('HELP_ABOUT');". This would execute the form's trigger and provide a single calling point for code that is used in the menu and in the form. It also eliminates the need to attach a library to a menu. While you can easily attach a library to a menu, if the library changes, you will have to recompile the menu when you recompile forms that use the library. If there is no library attached to the menu, you do not need to recompile it. Chapter 28 contains more menu techniques.

NOTE
Other than the technique of calling forms code from the menu, there is little use for user-defined triggers.

Changing the Template Components

During development work, you continue to evolve the template system. After developing a feature in a form, you should step back and ask yourself if this feature is a candidate for inclusion in the template system. If so, you would need to genericize it and add it to the system. You might also want to make changes to existing objects in the template system. If you have to make a change to an existing object, you do so in the reference form and copy the object back to the object library. It is a similar process for adding and deleting. Adding an object requires you to follow the predetermined standards so that it blends in with other objects. After you create the object in the reference form, you decide if it should go into an object group or if it will be used as a subclass. If it should be part of an object group, you need to drop it into the object group node in the same form and then refresh the object group in the object library by dragging it to the object library. If it is an archetype (SmartClass) object, you can just drag it into the reference form.

Changes will be cascaded to forms that have the objects subclassed. This will occur the next time you open or recompile the form. If you have a number of forms that you need to recompile, you can use a command such as the following in a Windows command-line prompt to batch compile all forms in a directory:

```
for %f in (*.fmb) do start ifcmp60 userid=scott/tiger@db module=%f
```

If you want to include this command in a batch file, substitute double percent signs (%%) for the single percent sign (%). Chapter 29 contains a detailed discussion of this technique.

Copied objects will not automatically inherit the changes or additions, so you will need to open each form that is already created and copy the change. This is necessary, too, if you want to include a new object in the template that is not in an object group. If you have object groups that all objects can go into, there is no need to open each form and add the object manually.

Changing the Object Library

Be sure to close any open forms that subclass object library objects before making changes to the object library. Otherwise, updating an object library object that is subclassed may break the inheritance link on a property level between the form and the object library. For example, you make a change to the trigger code on a form-level trigger in the REFER_FORM.FMB file. When you drag the object group that contains the trigger back into the object library, the object library will contain the new code. If a form that subclasses that object group is open in Form Builder at the time, the inheritance link to the trigger text property for that trigger and all others in that object library will break, even if they were not broken before. This means you need to reinherit the text property of each trigger separately. If some text properties were overridden by intent, you have to remember this and not inherit the text property. The best rule of thumb is to save and close forms that subclass object library objects before you make a change to the object library.

Style-Specific Templates

Up to this point, the discussion has focussed on how to create and structure a template system with only one template file. While it is possible to create all forms from a single template, in practice, there are some basic form styles that you always build. These form styles should have a specific template to use as the basis for the form. This requires a bit more work to identify the styles and create separate templates. The payback is design consistency. For example, there are many different ways to lay out an administration form, even if you use a basic (not a style-specific) template. However, if you have designed an administration template, all forms of this style will look similar.

Therefore, in addition to one generic template, it is useful to include different styles of template in your template system. The supporting object libraries, PL/SQL libraries, and menus may be common for all templates. The only difference is the template file itself, which is the starting place for developing a form. You can think of each template form as supporting different application functions. Each of the functions uses a different style of interface and, therefore, requires a separate template form.

In constructing the template system, you develop template prototypes for the common categories of forms you have determined. Each of these will become a specific style template. The style-specific template file will be named with an abbreviation of its style, for example, TEMPLATE_ADMIN.FMB for the administration style template. You can store objects for all styles of forms in the same object library, but each style would use its own tab to organize the style-specific objects while keeping the tabs described before to serve all templates.

Other than the basic template, there are several styles of forms you can create, each of which requires a separate template, as follows:

- Tab interface
- Navigation
- Administration
- Locator
- Hierarchical tree
- Project-specific

Depending upon your GUI standards, you may or may not find these appropriate, but the basic idea of specific templates for specific applications remains the same. You would supplement these with online README files for each template style so the developer would have reference material to use when developing the form. You would also include a graphic image of a sample form that uses this template. These instructions would also include information such as what triggers need to be modified, what properties or which objects need to be filled in, and how to safely add or remove form elements. The following describes these templates on a very high level so you can get some ideas of the style of templates you can create.

Tab Interface

The tab interface is a familiar one to Windows users. It allows you to place many canvases and items on a single window and provides an intuitive and logical interface to navigate between sets of items. You can create a template with two tab canvases and the code to support them prebuilt. The tab template will support you organizing the data in any logical way. Based on the needs of a particular form, you would copy the tab canvases to make more space for items.

A variation on this template is a template with a poplist in the heading above the tab. The poplist allows the user to select query criteria or a specific dataset. This can be data from different tables or just subsets of data from the same table. The extra code to support the automatic query of the tables in the tabs would be built into the template.

Navigation Template

A navigator module is a top-level form used to navigate to other applications using a button for each called form. If the application is very large, the navigator might involve several canvases including top-level and subordinate canvases for each interest area, although it is unlikely that you will need more than one or two subordinate canvases. All this navigator form does is call other forms. The developer just has to change the labels on the buttons, enter the names and paths of forms that are called, and perhaps duplicate or delete a few buttons to correspond to the exact requirements of the application.

There is a block-level WHEN-BUTTON-PRESSED trigger that calls a form with the same name as the button. Therefore, the only development time required is to create buttons (by copying existing buttons and subclassing them from the object library) and to name them the same as the form they will be calling. The template also contains whatever code is required to display logo graphic files (as explained in Chapter 25). The form also can have security facilities built in to check permissions from a table and disable or hide buttons that represent forms to which the user has no access.

Administration Template

There are several choices for handling the administration of code tables that store code values (such as A for "Active" and I for "Inactive"). This supports manual maintenance of the codes and descriptions by developers or data administrators.

First of all, you have to decide on the table structure. Some developers use a "clean" approach, with a different table for each code description. However, this could result in a large number of tables. Other developers prefer to combine all code descriptions in a single table with different views to separate them. The single-table approach is more flexible because, as the needs arise for new categories of codes (such as sales status), rows can be added to the same table and a view constructed to implement the new code category. On the other hand, having separate tables for each category allows you to create foreign-key constraints from the table using the code to the code table itself. The database will enforce the validation of codes in the main table. There is extra program code required with each choice. In the end, this can be a matter of personal choice because, since code tables often hold a small number of rows (2,000 at most), performance is not an issue.

After making the decision on table structure, you have to decide on the screen layout. A good strategy is to have one single administration form that supports the maintenance of all administration functions. Each function (corresponding to a view in the single-table approach) appears on a separate tab canvas. Blocks are queried only when their respective tabs are selected. The object library would include an object group with canvases and items for several different kinds of code description tables (or views). Some may require date history flags or status flags, while others may be simple code and description views. When you build the form from this template, you make copies of existing tabs if you need to support more code tables. You also alter the base table names and column names to match the data source.

Another way to support this type of data administration is to create a single block with a flexible data source. The user selects the table that needs to be maintained, and the Forms code takes care of creating the SELECT statement (or parameters for a block based on a procedure) and populating and updating the proper table. The table structure and layout are stored in another table. The form looks up this table structure and changes the number of columns and the actual prompts based on the table that needs to be maintained.

This approach requires a high level of generic coding and an expert development team that easily grasps the concepts of reusability and dynamic Forms objects. The time spent on this type of application can pay back many times because you spend the most time on the template itself. Using the template, you should be able to build a maintenance screen that handles a project-specific set of tables in a day's time. Although the template will require a bit of time to create, it becomes a tool that you take from project to project.

Locator Template

This common type of application allows you to quickly and easily locate a specific record. For example, in a Purchase Order (PO) system, you can easily find a particular PO if you know the PO number. However, if all that you know is which department initiated the PO and that the PO was issued in the past two months, you will have problems. The Oracle Forms query facility is not sophisticated enough for a user who does not know SQL to easily support a query of this type.

Therefore, to make it easy for users to locate particular records, it is customary to build a separate forum that helps users locate those records based on arbitrary criteria. Such an application has an area at the top of the screen to set criteria and an area at the bottom of the screen to display query results. Double-clicking a retrieved record in the locator automatically opens the primary application associated with that record and retrieves the record into the application. A locator application can also act as a Reports front-end, passing flexible sorts, breaks, and filters to Oracle Reports for use as lexical parameters.

This type of form can be based on a style-specific template. The template contains a sample set of query items and a multirecord block below for the set of records returned from the query. The code built into the query and clear buttons is generic to any block. Since the query items are non–base-table items, it is easy to build a generic block and supplement it when you create the actual form. The base-table block would need to be customized for the particular use, but the layout would be preset and predesigned.

Hierarchical Tree Template

If your application design specifies the need for a number of forms that use the hierarchical tree control, you would create a template that contains the code and objects to support this interface. Although the query will be specific to the form, the properties of the hierarchical tree can be smartclassed from an object library object so there is consistency between the forms. Also, you can develop code that will handle the tree events in a similar way. For example, when a user clicks on an item node, a property window will open with details about the record. All of this fits into the template system's libraries and template form.

Project-Specific Templates

When thinking about which templates you need to support your application development, you can consider another level, that of the project-specific template. It may not be enough to construct template forms for a generic form or style-specific form because the project may require yet another level of template. This may take the form of a specific look and feel for existing templates or may incarnate as a completely new set of style-specific templates. The project-specific template may just be the same as the existing templates with additional logo graphics and boilerplate objects.

The project-specific object library can contain object groups that you can drag into forms when needed. Examples would be specific blocks that appear in more than one form, poplist items that are used in many forms, LOVs and record groups that reappear in many forms, and locator canvases to support particular tables such as EMPLOYEE.

CHAPTER
12

Building a Form
Based on a Template

Take thy beak from out my heart,
and take thy form from off my door!
Quoth the Raven, "Nevermore."

—Edgar Allan Poe (1809–1849), *The Raven*

nce you have created and tested the template system, you are ready to build a production form. The template system supplies most of the standard look and feel that you have designed, so all that is left is to add application-specific objects and code. This chapter explains the process involved with building a form using the template system once you have completed the necessary steps of storyboarding and designing the layout and functionality of the form. It is not intended to be a step-by-step tutorial, but is an examination of each step. The chapter also provides notes and tips on how each step should be performed. The process of building a form from a template consists of the following steps:

1. Install the template (a one-time task).

2. Create a new form.

3. Add data objects.

4. Apply SmartClasses.

5. Modify the template code.

6. Add other objects.

7. Add other code.

The example uses the sample template system described in Chapters 10 and 11. There are always many ways to perform specific operations in Oracle Developer Forms (Forms). This chapter presents some of the methods that the authors have found to be most efficient. Much of the form-development process, especially in creating the block and applying SmartClasses, is repetitive work done to a large number of objects. Therefore, small amounts of time saved for a particular operation can add up over the course of developing the entire form.

1. Install the Template

Installing the template for the development platform only needs to be done once. (Of course, whenever you make a change to a template file, you have to be sure to copy the file to the proper location.) You also need to set up the development environment properly so developers will know how to access the template system. In addition, you have to be sure that all developers can access the database code and database objects (such as tables) that support the template.

Locating the Template Files

For development, all Forms files (forms, object libraries, code libraries, and menus) must be located in a directory listed in the FORMS60_PATH variable. On Windows, this is a string value in the Windows registry under the HKEY_LOCAL_MACHINE\ SOFTWARE\ORACLE node. On UNIX, this variable needs to be set up and defined as an environment (shell) variable. The value of this parameter is a list of directories, each separated by an operating system–specific delimiter (for example, a semicolon in Windows). Be sure the list is not longer than the 512-character limit if you are working in Windows. Alternatively, for client/server deployments, you can place the forms files in the default (or "Start in") directory for the Form Builder or Forms Runtime icon. In Windows, access the *Start in* property (that indicates the working or default directory) through the right-click menu (Properties selection) on the program icon in Windows Explorer. Navigate to the Shortcut tab, and change the *Start in* property to the location of the Forms files. While it is possible to support most development activities by having the paths embedded in the form files, the authors do not recommend this strategy because it has limitations if you ever need to move the application to another system with different directory structures.

TIP
If the Forms runtime does not seem to be able to find a file in the current working directory, add the current directory to the path. To make this generic, use "." (no quotes) to represent the current directory.

For runtime, the .FMX file will contain compiled versions of all subclassed objects, so you only need to install the .FMX, .PLL (or .PLX), and .MMX files in the runtime environment.

The icon files (for menu items, iconic buttons, or hierarchical tree nodes) can be located in the "Start in" directory or in a directory listed in the registry under the UI_ICON parameter (in the same location as the FORMS60_PATH). Image files should be located in the "Start in" directory unless you are supplying a directory name as part of the file name. The image file locations apply both to runtime and to development environments.

NOTE
The Forms runtime also looks for Form Builder files (.FMX, image, and icon files) in the directories listed in the ORACLE_PATH registry value (or UNIX environment variable). The search order is the working directory, the FORMS60_PATH, and the ORACLE_PATH.

Setting Up the Development Environment

For a large project with more than three or four developers, the directories that contain the files should be located on a file server that is accessible to all developers. This helps reduce the danger of a developer using an older version of a template file. Developers still need to know how to point their development environment to the correct file server, but the directory structure will be part of the development standards document and should be specifically addressed in developer training. The drawback to a shared area is that, if a developer is accessing a form that uses an object library or PL/SQL library, there may be a lock on the file that will prevent updating it. This can be managed by announcing that a change will occur and being certain that all developers are logged out of the Form Builder when a template system file needs to be updated. There should be one person in charge of making changes to and updating the template files when the need arises.

If the project has few developers or is being developed remotely, you can store the template system files on each developer's machine. It is important to be sure that changes to template files are distributed to all developers so the base files do not become out of synch. Locating the template files on many machines is trickier than locating them on a common file server because of the communications involved. It is simpler to have updates made on the files, because there is no locking issue if each developer is only managing a local set of files. This strategy is also useful if the network that would be used to store the files is not always fast or reliable. Local copies of files will load faster than network copies.

Keeping Template Versions Straight

Set up a versioning system for the template. You can place a procedure in the common startup procedure that all forms call. This procedure can check the value of a parameter in the template form (TEMPLATE_VERSION_NUMBER) to check what the version number is. The procedure compares the version number with the value in a table to see if it is an updated version. The person who makes the changes to the template form updates the version number in the parameter and in the table. You can keep a separate version number for each PL/SQL library (as a package spec variable value in the F_GLOBAL package). You can also keep a separate parameter for the REFER_FORM.FMB (which you copy into REFER_OL.OLB). Menus contain the same type of parameters as forms, and you can handle menus in the same way.

If necessary, you can turn off this check with a system parameter (stored in a table) when the form goes into production. This is a handy technique to use even when in production, because you may have different runtime versions of forms that are copied to different servers. You can have a runtime form version parameter that the startup procedure checks to be sure that the user is running the proper version.

Setting Up Data Access

Just as developers need to have access to application tables and server code so they can check the code they write, developers also need access to the tables and server code that the template system uses. You can handle the template system code in the same way as the application code. That is, you can create public grants and synonyms, or private grants and synonyms, or a combination of public and private grants and synonyms. The code that the template system uses in the database may check system parameter (codes and switches) tables that are generic to the application. Therefore, while you may create these tables in the application table owner's schema, the tables may need to be located in another schema. You will want to coordinate this decision with the database administrator (DBA) in charge.

2. Create a New Form

The easiest method for starting a new form is to select **Form→New→Form Using Template** from the menu and to choose the template form (.FMB) file. This is a new feature of Oracle Developer R.6 that will open a new form based on the template and mark it as unnamed. Thus, if you try to save the file, you will not overwrite the template, but be prompted for a new name. Figure 12-1 shows a composite screen shot of the Object Navigator nodes after starting a new form based on a template. The plus signs indicate that there are preexisting objects under each node.

Another method you can use to create a form from a template is to open the template, rename it (using the form module properties), and save it with the new name. If you use this method, you run the risk of accidentally overwriting your template with the new form.

CAUTION
When saving a form to the file system for the first time, be careful of your use of uppercase characters in the file name. If you name the form module (using the Property Palette) before saving the file for the first time, the default name might be uppercase with a lowercase extension (for example, EMPDEPT.fmb). Operating systems such as UNIX are case sensitive and see the file EMPDEPT.FMX as different from the file empdept.fmx. Forms built-ins such as CALL_FORM, NEW_FORM, and OPEN_FORM use a form name parameter that is a quoted string. This string needs to match the upper- and lowercase of the file name if you are deploying on a UNIX server (using web-deployed forms or client/server forms). Therefore, it is important to use a consistent naming convention for upper- and lowercase in file names.

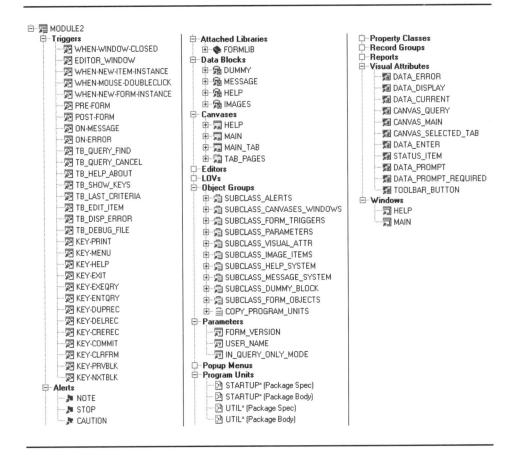

FIGURE 12-1. *Object Navigator nodes for a new form*

TIP
Remember to use the recently-opened-file list whenever possible. The bottom of the File menu contains the last four files you opened in Form Builder. It is much faster to select from that list than to select from a file dialog.

3. Add Data Objects

The process of adding data objects to a form that is based on a template is the same as adding data objects without using a template.

Using the Block Wizards

The best way to add data objects is by using the block wizards. Although this book assumes you have some production experience with Forms and, therefore, understand the major aspects of the wizards, it is useful to review the important points of each of the areas in the Data Block and Layout wizards.

The Data Block Wizard

You run the Data Block Wizard to create the block and the Layout Wizard to place the block items on a canvas. You can also use the wizards to modify the objects after creating them (using the Tools menu items). You run the Data Block Wizard by creating a block and selecting "Use the Data Block Wizard" from the dialog that appears. You can also select a specific block before clicking the Create button, but the new block will appear under the one you selected. Since the cursor navigates by default using the Object Navigator order, you have to be careful about where the block is placed in the Object Navigator.

After you decide whether this block is based on a procedure or a table (the Type Page), you fill in the table (or view or procedure) name on the Table Page (as shown in Figure 12-2), and click the Refresh button. You select the columns (be sure to select foreign-key columns if you need to use them in a master-detail relation even if you will not display them). You also decide whether to select the Enforce data integrity check box.

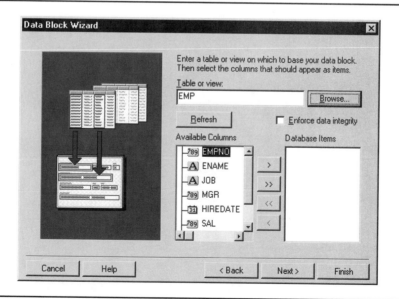

FIGURE 12-2.   *Data Block Wizard Table Page*

If you check the Enforce data integrity check box, Forms will create triggers to check that there is a value in items based on mandatory (not null) columns. Forms will also create triggers to check for violations of foreign keys (where the primary key value that the foreign key points to does not exist). The problem is that this code accesses database objects and is written into the form. Although the code is highly optimized, it will generate more network traffic than if the code were written in the database. Therefore, you can choose to check the integrity check box and move the resulting code to the database (after some changes such as removing references to form objects) if you are interested in the network traffic savings. Alternatively, you can leave the check box blank and write the integrity code yourself. It is useful to create the code at least once to see what kind of code you would have to write manually.

The next page in the wizard is the Master-Detail Page, as Figure 12-3 shows. If this is a master block, you can skip to the next page. If it is a detail block, you can let Form Builder create the relation with existing master blocks. Of course, this means that you have to create a master block first.

If you check the Auto-join data blocks check box, you will see a list of eligible master blocks when you click the Create Relationship button. The eligible master blocks are those based on tables that are on the primary-key side of a foreign-key column in the table you are using for the block. When you select the block, the join columns will fill in automatically. For example, if your form contains blocks based on the DEPT and LOCATION tables, when you create the EMP block, the master block list in this tab will only contain the DEPT table. The reason for this is that the

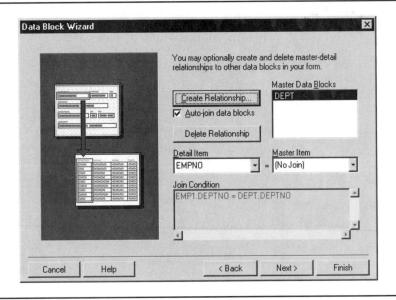

FIGURE 12-3. *Data Block Master-Detail Page*

EMP table only has a foreign key to the DEPT table, not to the LOCATION table. If you do not check the Auto-join data blocks check box, you can select any block on the form. In this case, you also have to specify the join columns.

The last page in this wizard (the Finish Page) lets you call the Layout Wizard automatically or just create the block without the Layout Wizard. If you choose the latter, you can go back to the Layout Wizard (by selecting it from the Tools menu) at any time.

TIP

*Turn off the welcome pages for Form Builder and the wizards (Data Block Wizard, Layout Wizard, Chart Wizard, and LOV Wizard) by using the Wizards tab in the **Tools→Preferences** window. After you have read them once, they will only slow you down.*

The Layout Wizard

The Layout Wizard places items on the canvas based on the columns you selected in the Data Block Wizard. The first page you reach in this wizard when you run it for the first time (after the Welcome Page) is the Canvas Page, where you select the canvas on which the items in this block will be placed. If the block will be split across a number of canvases, you will have to move the items after laying them out on a single canvas. With the Layout Wizard, it is not possible to lay out items in the same block on different canvases, even if you reenter the wizard. You can select an existing canvas name, and the items will be placed on that canvas. You can alternatively select a new canvas and specify the type of canvas (such as content, stacked, toolbar, or tab). You cannot apply SmartClasses or subclass objects in the wizard. Figure 12-4 shows the Canvas Page with a new content canvas selected.

The next page is the Data Block Page, as Figure 12-5 shows. After moving the items to be displayed to the Displayed Items area (be sure not to move the foreign-key items if this is a detail of a master block), you can change the item type by clicking on the item and changing the Item Type poplist. Changing the item type is useful at this point because, when you apply SmartClasses later on, the list of available SmartClasses will be filtered by item type. For example, if you know that an item will be a check box, you will save time later if you change it from a "Text Item" to a "Check Box" on this page. Later, when you apply the SmartClass, the list of available SmartClasses for that item will be reduced to the objects that have an *Item Type* property of "Check Box".

The next page is the Items Page, where you specify each item's prompt, width, and height (scroll to the right to see this). Figure 12-6 shows this page. It is useful to change the prompt at this point because you can access all prompts from one screen. It is easier to change the prompts for a number of items here than it is in the Layout Editor or Property Palette.

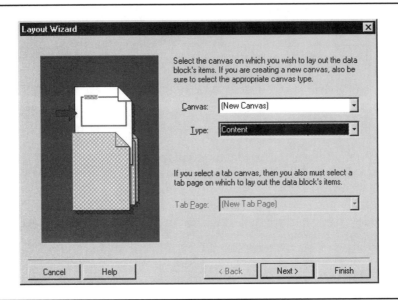

FIGURE 12-4. *Layout Wizard Canvas Page*

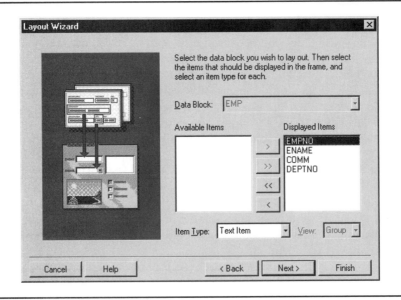

FIGURE 12-5. *Layout Wizard Data Block Page*

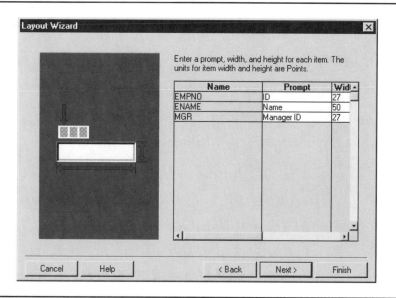

FIGURE 12-6. *Layout Wizard Items Page*

The next page is the Style Page, where you select whether this block will be laid out in a form style (one record and multiple lines per record) or tabular style (many records and one line per record). Based on your selection, the graphic at the left of the page will change to reflect how the block will generally appear, as shown in Figure 12-7. This is based on your design, but master blocks are usually form style and detail blocks are usually tabular style.

TIP
If you decide to rerun the Layout Wizard to add objects, the wizard will lay out the existing items as well (although it will not remove subclass information). Since you may have placed the items in a particular location, this may not be desirable. Therefore, rerun the Layout Editor only if you have major changes (for example, if you want to add additional canvases or all items need to be rearranged). Most changes that the Layout Wizard *would make for you are possible merely by changing properties on existing objects, such as the* Layout Style *frame property that allows you to change the block layout from form to tabular or tabular to form.*

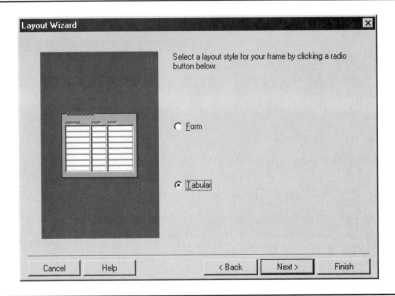

FIGURE 12-7. *Layout Wizard Style Page*

The next page is the Rows Page, where you specify the number of records to display in the block. Figure 12-8 shows this page.

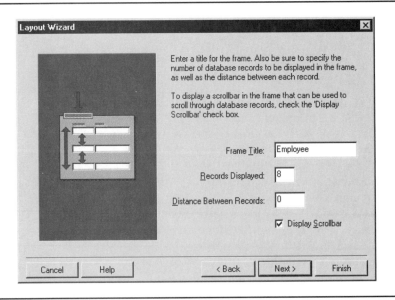

FIGURE 12-8. *Layout Wizard Rows Page*

FRAMES   Using the information on this page, Form Builder will create a *frame* that manages the items in the block. The frame is associated with a block and has a title and other properties that determine how the items within the frame are arranged. Figure 12-9 shows the layout properties of the frame. For example, resizing the frame border will rearrange the items within the frame if the *Update Layout* property is set to the default of "Automatically". If the *Update Layout* property is set to "Manually", the layout will not update until you click the Update Layout button in the Layout Editor toolbar or reuse the Layout Wizard for that block. You can also set the *Update Layout* frame property to "Locked" if you want to disable the automatic layout features. This is necessary if you split the block's items between canvases, because the automatic layout feature will move all items in the block to the frame's canvas regardless of where you placed them.

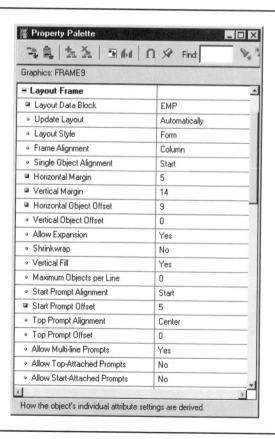

FIGURE 12-9.   *Layout Frame properties*

NOTE
Deleting a block in the Object Navigator will delete the block, items, triggers, relations, and associated code, but will not delete the associated frame. The next time you run the Layout Editor, the new block will lay out under the empty frame. Thus, it is best to delete the associated frame when you delete a block.

The choices that Form Builder makes for the automatic layout may not correspond to your own ideas, so you might want to delete the frame. If you want to keep the frame but hide it, set the *Edge Pattern* color to "none". You can determine a standard for the font and layout properties of the frame and create a SmartClass in the object library that will assign the correct values. This is useful to do if you decide to use the features of frames because you will not need to reexamine all the layout and visual properties of each frame you use. If you want to keep the frame but not use the autolayout feature, set the *Update Layout* frame property to "Locked".

NOTE
The Show Scroll Bar *property on the frame is the same as the* Show Scroll Bar *property of the block assigned to the frame. Setting the property for one object will set the corresponding property for the other object. However, there are more properties for the block to manage the scroll bar than there are for the frame.*

There are other properties that the block and frame share, such as *Number of Records Displayed*, but the value-copying between objects may not be automatic. For example, you can set the *Number of Records Displayed* property on the block and the frame property will not automatically update. The best strategy is not to use frames for layout purposes.

FINAL STEPS   Include a scroll bar if this block is multirecord. Otherwise, the scroll bar may not make sense unless you specify a scroll bar here and convert it to a horizontal scroll bar sized to look like a set of buttons, as follows:

These buttons look like Next Record and Previous Record buttons, but are really just a scroll bar that requires no code.

After setting the frame title, number of records, space between records, and scroll bar, you are finished with the Layout Wizard. Since this is the last page in the wizard, you can click the Finish button. The Next button will move you to the Finish Page that just explains the steps you need to take when the wizard is finished.

CAUTION
The Layout Wizard will place items below any other object on the assigned canvas and resize the canvas so that the items will fit. You will need to move the items and reinherit the canvas size properties after the wizard is through. Remember to perform these operations if you reenter the wizard.

Building a Block Manually

It is not necessary to create blocks with the Data Block Wizard. It is possible to create a block, set the properties for the data source and query source, and add all items manually. This is a time-consuming and difficult way to create a block, and it is better to take advantage of the Form Builder's automated way to create a block. If you need a block that is not based on a table, view, or procedure, you will have to create the block manually. It is possible to create a base table block and then change the *Database Data Block* property to "No". This will convert the block to a non–base table (control) block. This is a handy technique to use if the items in the control block are similar to items in a table (for example, for a find or locator form that looks like a table-based block but is really a set of control items).

TIP
To move objects from one canvas to another, group the objects in the Object Navigator and change the Canvas *property. If you want to move them using the Layout Editor, you will have to open one Layout Editor for each canvas and cut and paste between them.*

4. Apply SmartClasses

Once you have the main block items on the canvas, you need to apply SmartClasses so they can comply with your standards and can be managed by the template system files. The result of subclassing is to apply nondefault properties from the archetype (pattern) object that contains your standards. This operation is necessary for a small number of object types, such as items, canvases, and buttons. The general idea is to find the object, right-click it, and select a SmartClass from the right-click menu. This will fill in the *Subclass Information* property with the file name and object name of the source object, as shown in Figure 12-10.

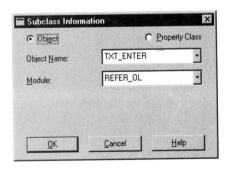

FIGURE 12-10. Subclass Information *property of SmartClassed item*

How to SmartClass

The SmartClass (as described in Chapter 10) is just an easy way of applying a subclass. The other way to subclass an object is to open its *Subclass Information* property and select the file name and object name. This is much less efficient than applying a SmartClass because there are more steps. The only steps involved with applying a SmartClass to an item are the following (both shown in Figure 12-11):

1. **Find the object in the Layout Editor or Object Navigator**   Finding an object in the Layout Editor is easier than in the Object Navigator because you can just open the canvas that the item is on; you do not have to drill down to the block and item or struggle with the Find box in the Object Navigator. Also, there is no need to select the object.

2. **Right-click the object and select the SmartClass**   Right-clicking the object will select it and display the menu. The SmartClass menu item in this menu contains the list of SmartClasses for the selected Item Type from object libraries that are open in the Form Builder.

   If you use the Object Navigator to apply SmartClasses, you can group objects and apply one SmartClass to the group. This is not possible using the Layout Editor (although, sometimes, you can use the Layout Editor if you first select the objects in the Object Navigator). When grouping objects, use the normal click, SHIFT-click, and CTRL-click operations. Always right-click on the last object selected instead of using other click operations. This will keep the other objects in the group selected, select the object you clicked, and open the menu.

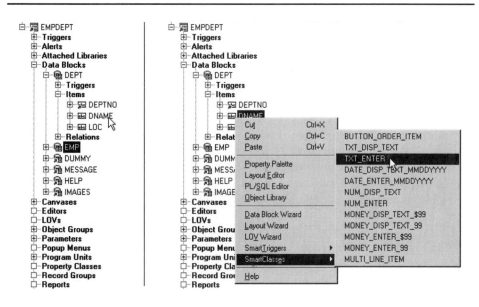

1. Find the object.   2. Select the SmartClass.

FIGURE 12-11. *Selecting an object and applying a SmartClass*

To apply the SmartClass, the object library containing the SmartClass object must be open in Form Builder. It need not be showing in a window, but the name should appear under the Object Libraries node as follows:

NOTE
Remember that you do not need to reload object libraries when you close and reopen Form Builder. The object libraries that are open in your Form Builder session will automatically be open the next time you open Form Builder.

Which SmartClass to Choose

When you created the template system (as Chapter 11 describes), you created SmartClasses based on the template prototype. You also named the SmartClasses descriptively. Therefore, the question of which SmartClass to choose should be a simple matter. You need to select the SmartClass that most closely matches the purpose for the object. For example, if the object is a text item, your SmartClass list will show text item SmartClasses, as in Figure 12-11. The SmartClasses are named by their purpose. You already know what the purpose of the item is because you have storyboarded and designed the form. Therefore, if the item you are subclassing were an entry text item, you would choose the SmartClass TXT_ENTER. If the object were a non–entry text item, you would select TXT_DISP_TEXT.

If the SmartClass for a particular purpose does not exist, create the object in the form, copy it into the REFER_FORM.FMB file, include it in the appropriate object group, and refresh that object group in the object library.

You may want to add SmartClasses to your object library to handle different item widths. Although the Data Block Wizard approximates the size of the item from the size of the database column on which the item is based, the font you choose for the item's SmartClass may require an item width that is more or less than this default. If you create a separate SmartClass for each of the common character widths you will need (such as 1, 2, 5, 10, 20, 25, 30, 50, 100 characters), you will be able to manage the *Width* property from the object library. It takes some experimentation to come up with the correct width for an item based on the font, but once this process is complete, you will not need to guess at item widths. Chapter 5 contains a discussion on how to determine item widths.

The only problem with creating a separate SmartClass for each item width is that your list of SmartClasses will grow in size. Each item type (display text item, entry text item, display item, and so on) will have a full set of widths. When you display the SmartClass list for a particular item type, Forms displays only the list of SmartClasses applicable to that item. Therefore, one drawback of maintaining a long list of SmartClasses is a manageable concern.

CAUTION
If the SmartClasses you intended for the object do not appear in the list, it is possible that the Item Type *property is set incorrectly.*

SmartClassing Other Objects

All objects that have visual representations—items, canvases, windows, LOVs, and editors—should be subclassed. Subclassing provides centralized control of your

Forms objects and enforcement of look-and-feel standards. The examples up to this point have applied to items. Other objects follow the same process. The difference is that, for objects other than items (and canvases), you cannot use the Layout Editor to find the object. There are a few notes worth mentioning about SmartClassing specific objects.

Canvases

Canvases often need to be different sizes from the master object. Remember that you can override specific properties including the width and height. Therefore, select a canvas SmartClass that is named as closely as possible to its purpose in the same way you select SmartClasses for other objects. Then override the properties as required.

Windows

Whenever you need a new window, you can copy an existing window or create one from scratch. Use the duplicate function (CTRL-D) so the copy will share the same SmartClass as the original window. As with other objects, if there are properties that do not conform to the standard of the SmartClass, you can override them. If the property changes will be useful to a number of forms, consider creating a new SmartClass.

TIP

When copying objects that are subclassed, use CTRL-D (duplicate) instead of CTRL-C and CTRL-V (copy and paste). The duplicate function will retain the Subclass Information *property value (the SmartClass assignment).*

Blocks

There are very few properties for blocks that are reusable. However, all multirecord blocks in your forms should have scroll bars of the same width. Therefore, it is useful to create a SmartClass for blocks that sets the *Scroll Bar Orientation* property to "Vertical" and the *Scroll Bar Width* property to a standard width (such as 11 points). If you need a horizontal scroll bar, you could create another SmartClass for that purpose.

Removing a SmartClass

You cannot change the *Subclass Information* property for an object that is subclassed using an object group. This is because the object group is the object that is subclassed, not the individual object. Also, there is no way to remove a SmartClass using the right-click menu. You can remove subclasses for objects, one at a time, by opening the *Subclass Information* property and setting the object name to NULL as follows:

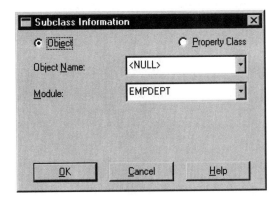

5. Modify the Template Code

Once you subclass the data objects, you need to customize the template code for the specific form. When you created the template system, you decided on common actions for the keypresses and menu selections and coded these into the library and template. You also identified the common set of startup routines that would need to be run for each form. This step in the process modifies startup code and forms functions that need to be customized for the particular form. Of course, other than the startup code (explained a little later), the template code may suffice, so you would not need to change any other code.

Subclassed Triggers

The code to modify (in the sample template system) is contained in subclassed triggers and copied PL/SQL program unit packages. The code design of the template system designates that all calls are contained in form-level triggers. The menu, menu toolbar, canvas buttons, and user keypresses all go through these triggers. The triggers contain only a single call to a program unit procedure; the package that contains this procedure is either in the PL/SQL library or in the form itself. Therefore you should not need to modify the triggers themselves except on the rare occasions where you need to supplement or replace the library code call for one form only. Table 12-1 shows the code in some of the form-level triggers. (In this and other chapters in the book, some of the code is abbreviated for reasons of space. For the full text of the packages and procedures, please refer to the sample files on the authors' or publisher's web sites. See the authors' biographies at the front of the book for the addresses.)

There are three main types of form-level triggers in this system: built-in Forms events triggers, such as WHEN-NEW-FORM-INSTANCE and ON-ERROR; built-in KEY- triggers, such as KEY-EXIT and KEY-HELP; and user-defined triggers for menu item and button calls, such as DO_KEY_EDIT_ITEM and DO_KEY_HELP_ABOUT. The code for these three types is located in the form program units and the PL/SQL library.

Trigger Name	Code
WHEN-NEW-FORM-INSTANCE	`startup.when_new_form_instance;`
PRE-FORM	`startup.pre_form;`
POST-FORM	`util.post_form;`
ON-MESSAGE	`util.on_message;`
ON-ERROR	`util.on_error;`
KEY-COMMIT	`f_toolbar.key_commit;`
KEY-CREREC	`f_toolbar.key_crerec;`
KEY-DELREC	`f_toolbar.key_delrec;`
KEY-DUPREC	`f_toolbar.key_duprec;`
KEY-ENTQRY	`f_toolbar.key_entqry;`
KEY-EXEQRY	`f_toolbar.key_exeqry;`
KEY-EXIT	`f_toolbar.key_exit;`
KEY-HELP	`f_help.show_help;`
KEY-PRINT	`f_toolbar.key_print;`
DO_KEY_EDIT_ITEM	`f_toolbar.key_edit_item;`
DO_KEY_HELP_ABOUT	`f_toolbar.help_about;`
DO_KEY_SHOW_KEYS	`f_util.show_formkeys;`

TABLE 12-1. *Form-Level Trigger Code*

NOTE
Remember that the term function key *in Forms signifies a keyboard keypress that activates a Forms function. These keypresses are not necessarily keyboard function keys such as F1 or F2. For example, CTRL-Q is a Forms function key that represents the Exit function. The key list is available by using the Forms runtime **Help→Keys** menu option.*

There are several packages that contain the procedures for these triggers: STARTUP, UTIL, F_UTIL, and F_TOOLBAR. F_UTIL and F_TOOLBAR are stored in the template PL/SQL library. They contain code that will be the same for all forms. If you need to modify the code for a particular form, you can replace or add to the call in the trigger itself or modify the library if the modification would apply to all forms. The package specifications for F_UTIL and F_TOOLBAR are shown in Appendix A.

NOTE
A number of form-level triggers contain the command "NULL;", which turns off the functionality: KEY-MENU, KEY-CLRFRM, KEY-PRVBLK, and KEY-NXTBLK. You can code a KEY-OTHERS instead with the command "NULL;" or a call to an alert that displays an error message. This will turn off the functionality of all forms function triggers that do not have an explicit trigger written. Be sure to create key triggers, particularly KEY-EXIT and KEY-NEXT-ITEM, for all required forms functions, to ensure that the user can perform any necessary actions.

Why Copy the Program Units?

The STARTUP and UTIL packages are written locally as program units in the form. These packages are copied instead of subclassed from the object library into the template. The reason is that, even though you can also subclass program units and retain the ability to modify them, there will be less confusion over whether they are subclassed or copied. The problem with subclassing program units is that the Object Navigator shows the subclass symbol. This may imply to an unsuspecting developer that the code is the same as the template, but it may or may not be the same. You can tell if a subclassed program unit's code has been modified by looking at the program unit's Property Palette. The inheritance symbol will show as broken (with an "X") if the code has been modified. Copying the code into the template (and form) from the object library sidesteps this question altogether. Since there is no subclass symbol in the Object Navigator, you can count on the code being different from the template. You will document the changes you make to the package code in the package spec header comments, so the reader will be able to tell what has been modified from the template code. There are specific changes you need to make for each of these packages.

STARTUP Package

As shown before, the PRE-FORM and WHEN-NEW-FORM-INSTANCE triggers call procedures in the STARTUP package. The specification for this package follows.

```
PACKAGE startup IS
/*****************************************************************************\
|| Description:
||    This package contains procedures that are run when the form starts up. Some
||    procedures are also recalled when a form is cleared and needs
||    initialization.
||
|| Usage:
||    PRE_FORM
||       Called from the PRE-FORM form-level trigger to initialize objects before
||       the form appears. Be careful of the restrictions of this trigger. For
||       example, you cannot call navigation built-ins in a PRE-FORM trigger.
||
||    WHEN_NEW_FORM_INSTANCE
||       Called from the WHEN-NEW-FORM-INSTANCE trigger. Non-restricted so you
||       can do any kind of navigation or initialization here.
||
||    INITIALIZE_FORM
||       Called from the WHEN_NEW_FORM_INSTANCE procedure to populate form items
||       such as poplists and default values. You can also call this procedure
||       after the form starts in case you have to clear the form. Use the
||       p_process parameter only for the form startup with the parameter value
||       STARTUP. No parameter value is required for reinitialization.
||
||    SETUP_OBJECTS
||       Called from the WHEN_NEW_FORM_INSTANCE procedure to set the window
||       sizes and enable-disable buttons.
\*****************************************************************************/
    --
    PROCEDURE pre_form;
    --
    PROCEDURE when_new_form_instance;
    --
    PROCEDURE initialize_form(
      p_process  IN VARCHAR2 := 'REINIT');
    --
    PROCEDURE setup_objects;
    --
END;
```

It is worth examining each procedure in more detail because this is the main code you need to modify when starting a form.

PRE_FORM
The code for this procedure follows.

```
PROCEDURE pre_form IS
BEGIN
   --
   -- **** BLOCKS and ITEMS
   --      Poplist items that are queried automatically with their Record Groups
   --      sample value: 'EMP.DEPTNO:DEPT_RECGRP,EMP.MGRNO:EMP_RECGRP'
   f_global.v_auto_query_lists := NULL;

   --      Blocks that will automatically query when the form starts
   --      sample value: 'EMP,DEPT'
   f_global.v_auto_query_blocks := NULL;

   --      Blocks that need to be loaded with default values
   --      sample value: 'EMP,DEPT'
   f_global.v_auto_default_blocks := NULL;

   -- **** WINDOW
   --      Window title for the MDI frame
   f_global.v_mdi_win_title := ' ';

   -- **** HELP ABOUT FORM
   --      Version number, descriptive name, author, message
   f_global.v_form_version := '1.0';
   f_global.v_form_description := 'Departments and Employees';
   f_global.v_form_author := 'Peter Koletzke and Dr. Paul Dorsey';
   f_global.v_form_message := 'Show a department and its employees.';

   -- **** MENU ITEMS
   --      All menu items are normally enabled. If you want to disable
   --      some based on Normal or Query mode, add them to the list here.
   --      If they are not in the list, they will not be touched.
   --         Q=query mode only
   --         N=normal mode only
   --         B=Both (the default)
   --         X=Neither
   f_global.v_show_menuitems :=
      'MAIN_MENU.FILE:N,'||
      'QUERY_MENU.LAST_CRITERIA:Q,'||
      'QUERY_MENU.CANCEL:Q,'||
      'MAIN_MENU.ADMIN:N,'||
      'MAIN_MENU.SETUP:N,'||
      'MAIN_MENU.MAINTENANCE:N,'||
      'MAIN_MENU.WORKFLOW:N,'||
      'EDIT_MENU.DUP_FIELD:N,'||
      'EDIT_MENU.RECORD:N,'||
      'EDIT_MENU.NAVIGATE:N,'||
      'EDIT_MENU.CLEAR_BLOCK:N';
   --
   initialize_form('STARTUP');
END;
```

The inline comments explain the details, but, as a summary, there are three main sections to this procedure:

- ■ **Global variables for form startup**   The developer fills in the variable values based on the blocks and items in the form. The variables are single (scalar) values that contain lists delimited by commas and semicolons. The variables store the names of poplist items and the record groups that will be queried to load them with values; blocks that will automatically query when the form starts; blocks that will be navigated to when the form starts to load them with default values; and the MDI window title.

- ■ **Global variables for the Help About form**   The Help About form is a small form that is called from the **Help→About** menu item. It indicates context information about the form (date and time, form name and description, author, and version). This information is all loaded into global package variables when the form starts up.

- ■ **A global variable for menu items**   The menu items enable and disable based on whether the form is in query mode or normal mode. This variable stores a list of menu items (including toolbar menu items) and flags, each with the behavior it will have in query mode and normal mode. A library procedure uses this variable to automatically disable and enable items.

- ■ **A call to initialize_form**   This call passes the parameter value "STARTUP" to indicate that it is being called from the PRE-FORM trigger.

The F_GLOBAL variables are created and stored in the FORMLIB library. If you were to call one form from another and share the library data, you would need to create form parameters for the values instead of package variables because the called form would overwrite the calling form's global variable values.

INITIALIZE_FORM

The code for this procedure follows. There is no code you need to change in this unless you want to disable or supplement the processing.

```
PROCEDURE initialize_form(
      p_process   IN VARCHAR2 := 'REINIT')
IS
BEGIN
   -- For startup only, set up the form's objects
   IF p_process = 'STARTUP'
   THEN
      startup.setup_objects;
   END IF;
```

```
--  Customize the following for things that should happen
--  when the form starts up or is re-initialized after
--  an "undo."
--
--  Populate the list items from a query using the list.
--  uses f_global.v_auto_query_lists assigned above.
f_item.setup_all_lists;

--  Populate the blocks using the list variable.
--  The cursor ends up in the first block in the list.
--  uses f_global.v_auto_query_blocks assigned above.
f_block.query_all;

--  Visit each block so the default values will be shown.
--  Not needed if you did the block queries above.
--  The cursor ends in the first block in the list.
--  uses f_global.v_auto_default_blocks
f_block.default_all;
--
END;
```

This procedure uses the global variable values set up in the PRE_FORM procedure. It calls the following procedures:

- **SETUP_OBJECTS**   This is described later in the chapter.

- **SETUP_ALL_LISTS**   This procedure from the F_ITEM library package loads all poplist items from record group queries. This provides dynamic loading of poplist values from the database. The list of poplist items and record groups is loaded in the PRE_FORM procedure. When you add a new poplist and record group as a source of values, you just need to add the names to the variable, and this procedure will automatically load them when the form starts.

- **QUERY_ALL**   This procedure from the F_BLOCK package queries the blocks that are listed in the variable assigned in the PRE_FORM procedure. As with the poplists, all you need to do to add a block to this procedure is to include its name in the list variable.

- **DEFAULT_ALL**   This procedure from the F_BLOCK package moves the cursor to each block named in the list assigned in the PRE_FORM procedure. When the cursor moves to a block, the default values for that block are populated. Therefore, if you want to display the default value for any block when the form starts, just include its name in the variable that this procedure uses.

SETUP_OBJECTS

This procedure is called from the INITIALIZE_FORM procedure. The code follows.

```
PROCEDURE setup_objects
IS
BEGIN
    --
    --  Set up buttons and menu for non-query mode.
    f_util.change_mode(f_global.v_normal_mode);
    --
    -- Give the MDI window a title
    --
    -- Use this when returning from called form
    -- if you want to reset the MDI title.
    set_window_property(FORMS_MDI_WINDOW,
        TITLE, f_global.v_mdi_win_title);
    --
    --  Maximize the MDI frame
    f_window.max_the_window('FORMS_MDI_WINDOW');
END;
```

This procedure calls the following procedures:

- **CHANGE_MODE** This procedure (in the template library) sets the buttons and menu items in the menu to Normal mode. This would, for example, disable the Cancel Query and Last Query menu items because they are not appropriate in Normal mode. When the form goes into Enter Query mode, the same procedure disables other buttons (such as Exit and Duplicate Record) and enables the query buttons.

- **SET_WINDOW_PROPERTY** This procedure sets the title of the MDI window based on the variable you set in the PRE_FORM procedure.

- **MAX_THE_WINDOW** This procedure (also in the library) maximizes the MDI window. It is written in a library, so if you decide to base the MDI window size on actual points or pixels later on, you can change the library procedure and all forms will use the new setting. This procedure works for document windows (inside the MDI frame) as well.

WHEN_NEW_FORM_INSTANCE

This procedure consists of one call to a library procedure as follows.

```
PROCEDURE when_new_form_instance
IS
BEGIN
    fca_startup.standard_startup;
END;
```

The startup procedures that are common are handled with this single call to a library procedure, STANDARD_STARTUP, which calls all other procedures. This allows you to add startup functionality without recoding any of the forms. The STANDARD_STARTUP procedure could contain the following:

- Setting up the sizes of other windows

- Checking the form version number

- Checking the user privileges

- Setting up global variables that indicate the user's privileges in this form

- Closing the calling form (if this form was called using OPEN_FORM)

- Setting up the window titles based on a value in a table

You can also place in this routine some of the procedure calls that are made in the INITIALIZE_FORM and SETUP_OBJECTS procedures discussed earlier. The rule of thumb is that if you want to make a call standard to all forms, put it in the STANDARD_STARTUP procedure. If it changes from form to form, leave it in the INITIALIZE_FORM or SETUP_OBJECTS procedure.

Startup Code to Modify

Out of all the code shown or described, the only part that really needs modification is the PRE_FORM procedure, because the variable values drive all the other procedures. If you wanted to make this table-driven, you could load the values into a table and assign them in the PRE_FORM procedure. This would save the developer from having to open the code at all when using the template. It would also be more flexible and easier to make changes because the values are not written into the form code. However, this requires database queries and a small amount of extra processing on the server side to retrieve the values.

UTIL Package

While the STARTUP package contains the template code that you will most likely need to modify when you are creating the form, you may also need to modify the UTIL package. This would be necessary if you have a special requirement for error or message handling. The template UTIL package is a relatively small amount of code, as the following specification listing shows:

```
PACKAGE UTIL
IS
/***************************************************************************\
|| Description:
||   Procedures to handle common events that might be slightly different for
||   each form.
||
|| Usage:
||   ON_ERROR
||      Called from the form-level ON-ERROR trigger. This normally calls the
||      library procedure F_UTIL.ON_ERROR, but you can test for your own error
||      codes before passing the control to that procedure. For example, if you
||      wanted to check for a FRM-40809 and this was not handled in the library
||      procedure, you would change the body to:
||
||         PROCEDURE on_error
||         IS
||            v_code     NUMBER       := ERROR_CODE;
||            v_text     VARCHAR2(100):= ERROR_TEXT;
||            v_type     VARCHAR2(10) := ERROR_TYPE;
||         BEGIN
||            IF v_code = 40809
||            THEN
||               message('Error: The operating system command did not work. '||
||                  'Please re-enter the text');
||            ELSE
||               f_util.on_error;
||            END IF;
||         END;
||
||
||   ON_MESSAGE
||      This is called from the ON-MESSAGE form-level trigger. The use and
||      modification is the same as ON_ERROR except that this captures message
||      states instead of error states.
||
||   POST_FORM
||      Handles any processing required when the form exits.
||
\***************************************************************************/
   --
   PROCEDURE on_error;
   --
   PROCEDURE on_message;
   --
   PROCEDURE post_form;
END;
```

The package body follows:

```
PACKAGE BODY util
IS
    --
    --
    PROCEDURE on_error
    IS
    BEGIN
        f_util.on_error;
    END;
    --
    --
    PROCEDURE on_message
    IS
    BEGIN
        f_util.on_message;
    END;
    --
    --
    PROCEDURE post_form
    IS
    BEGIN
        f_util.reset_variables;
    END;
    --
END;
```

These procedures all call corresponding procedures in the F_UTIL library package. There are notes in the F_UTIL package comments on how to change the ON_ERROR and ON_MESSAGE procedures that are called from the ON-ERROR and ON-MESSAGE triggers, respectively. The idea is that you have one master message and error-handling procedure in the library. This can be written using different error-handling styles (discussed further in Chapter 27), such as displaying the Forms message without the message number (as shown in the UTIL package spec comments before), querying the error text from a table, logging the error in a log table, or just reading text from a package variable. Using a local package gives you a chance to override or supplement the standard error handler in the library. Of course, if you end up capturing the same error or message codes in each form, those codes should be written into the library error handler.

Another operation that you can modify in this package is the POST-FORM trigger code. The POST_FORM procedure does whatever cleanup is needed—resetting global package variable values that are only needed in the form or setting context variables so the next form has access to information about the calling form. The set of procedures you execute here will be application specific. If there is a common set of routines, you can create a library package procedure that is similar to the STANDARD_STARTUP procedure discussed earlier. This procedure, STANDARD_SHUTDOWN, would call all procedures needed to close the form down.

Figure 12-12 shows the poplists for Type, Object, and Name.

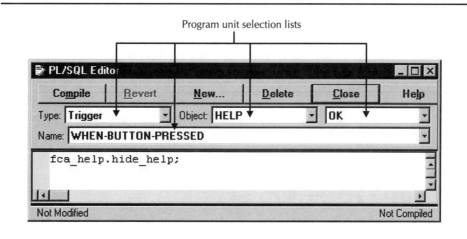

FIGURE 12-12. *PL/SQL Editor selection lists*

TIP
*Use the pull-down lists in the PL/SQL Editor window
to navigate to a particular trigger or program unit. If
the editor is open, it may be faster to find a program
unit by selecting from the list than by drilling down
to it in the Object Navigator.
Figure 12-12 shows poplists for Type (Trigger,
Program Unit, or Menu Item Code), Object (two
pulldowns for the block, menu, item, or program
unit name), and Name (trigger or program unit
name). You can also quickly access a program unit
for an item (button or text item), by selecting PL/SQL
Editor from the right-click menu in the Layout Editor.
If the object has a trigger, the PL/SQL Editor will
display with the code loaded into it.*

Adding Reusable Objects and Code

A general rule of thumb for work based on a template is to pay attention to the code
and objects you add to a form and ask if they are suitable for the template system.
Some objects and code may not appear to be reusable until later in the project.
Others will be useful to more than one form. This is not a shortcoming in the
template system you developed as much as a reality that it is not possible to identify
all reusable objects at the outset of a project. As the project ages, working reusable
objects into predeveloped forms may be more effort than it is worth, but it is a
process worth considering.

6. Add Other Objects

The next two steps in the process—adding objects and adding code—are familiar to
those who work with the Forms component of Oracle Developer. Therefore, it is not
worthwhile to spend time on the specific process, but it is useful to discuss what is
different because of the template system.

The major decisions about the objects that you need to add will already have
been made in the storyboarding stage. When you are creating the form, you should
not be making major design decisions. The time to plan what will be in the form was
earlier in the process. The development work itself may sound a bit boring as a
result. However, there still is some creativity involved because not even the most
detailed specification can make all the decisions that a Forms developer will need
to make when creating a form. There are two kinds of objects to add: preexisting
reusable components (object groups) and other new objects you create from scratch.

Adding Reusable Components

Reusable components are existing groups of objects with prebuilt functionality. If you have determined the main types of reusable components you need for a template system beforehand, you just need to drag and subclass these into the form. Examples of reusable components are the Calendar, the Toolbar, the Multiple-select LOV Picklist, the Navigator, and the Wizard. When you create the template system, you start with a number of reusable components in the object library. After you drag and subclass the object group into the form, you may need to attach a PL/SQL library that contains the supporting code. Some may require extra manipulation or modification. For example, the wizard offers a different presentation style for a data block. You need to move objects around to other canvases, create extra canvases, and write code for the navigation buttons. There are other reusable components, such as the calendar component, that require no other manipulation. This is complete and requires nothing more than attaching the library and creating calls to the code in your form.

Adding Other Objects

The form design completely determines what other objects you will need. The main guideline is to subclass everything possible (using SmartClasses if they are available). Items, canvases, windows, LOVs, editors, and popup menus are all visually represented and must have inherited properties so you can manage the standard visual aspects. You should not need to create alerts because the flexible alert system handles that need; but alerts require subclassing as well because they are displayed.

If you need to create nondisplayed objects, such as parameters, triggers, program units, and record groups, be sure to consider whether they are candidates for reuse. If so, include them in the template system and subclass them into the form. Visual attributes will usually be eligible for reuse, so if you create a visual attribute locally in a form, consider whether it could be reused and include it in the subclassed object group of visual attributes if it is appropriate. You will rarely need property classes and should not promote their use because subclassing fulfills the need that property classes were created for. Therefore, you do not need to subclass property classes unless you have a good reason (such as the form properties use mentioned in Chapter 11) to use them in multiple forms.

This is the stage where you add control items, control blocks, and buttons on the canvas. Buttons in the toolbar can be managed by the menu system (Chapter 28 discusses a technique for menu toolbar design). As mentioned, you should subclass as many of these extra objects as possible by using SmartClasses when they are available. There are some specific techniques you might use to assist in this effort.

Duplicating Objects

The easiest way to create a new object with similar properties as an existing object is to copy the existing object. Selecting the object and pressing CTRL-D will copy the object and its property values (including the *Subclass Information* property). If you duplicate an item in the Object Navigator, the *X Position* and *Y Position* properties will also copy exactly. This means that the item will overlay the existing item, and you will not see much change in the Layout Editor. If you duplicate the item in the Layout Editor, the position properties will be modified so that the new item will be offset slightly and will be more easily visible. Pressing CTRL-C and CTRL-V will also copy the object, but the *Subclass Information* property will be lost. You can use this technique to copy an item to a different block, but duplicating and dragging to the new block will preserve the subclass and save the time it would take to reapply the subclass.

When duplicating objects, be sure to select an object that is as close as possible to the desired object. That way, you will have fewer properties to change after you copy the master object. For example, if you need a new item that will hold number data, duplicate an existing number item in the block. Since the datatype of the item is managed by the subclass, you can always apply a different component to the object, but you will avoid that process if the item you duplicate already has the correct subclass.

Duplicating Properties

If you need to create an object without copying, remember that you can copy properties by selecting them (using click, SHIFT-click, and CTRL-click) in the Property Palette and clicking the Copy Properties toolbar button in that window, as shown next:

You then navigate to the object that will receive the properties, and click the Paste Properties button in the Property Palette, as shown next:

TIP
When you are using the Property Palette, you can set the value of a property that has a poplist for its values by double-clicking the name of the property. This will cycle through the list of values in the poplist. If the list is long, click the property name and press the key for the starting letter of the text you want to appear as a value. This will automatically select the value. If there is more than one value with the same starting letter, keep pressing the same letter until the correct value appears.

7. Add Other Code

The last step in creating the form from the template is to add code to support the objects and functionality for the application. This is largely a matter of following the form design provided by the storyboard, keeping in mind where the code should be located (as Chapter 7 explains). One interaction with the template system files is that the code you write should use the library code whenever possible. Genericizing code enhances the reusability, as Chapter 11 mentions. However, even the most generic code is useless as a vehicle for reusability if no one takes advantage of it. Developers should know about the kinds of utilities available in the PL/SQL library. They should also know how to search the code libraries by looking at the header comments. In fact, developers might want to keep a printed or online version of the package specifications as reference material. The calling syntax is available by looking in the Attached Libraries node under the package specification, as Figure 12-13 shows.

The rule of thumb for Forms function calls is that whenever you call Forms functions such as EXIT_FORM or ENTER_QUERY, use a call to DO_KEY(*function_name*), for example, "DO_KEY('EXIT_FORM')". This fires the KEY- trigger, which contains calls to library code. The idea is that all Forms function calls go through the same call path (the KEY- trigger). This makes code maintenance easier. Be sure to think about how the code will execute because you may want to break this rule of thumb. For example, you do not want to use a "DO_KEY ('EXIT_FORM')" call in the code body of a KEY-EXIT trigger because this will loop—the DO_KEY inside the trigger will call the KEY-EXIT trigger again, and the loop will continue with no actual exit.

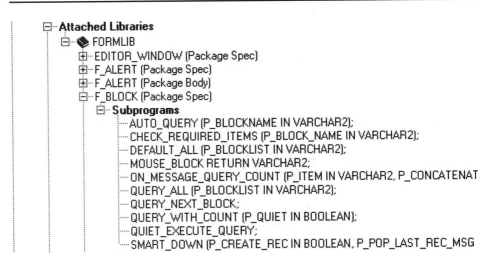

FIGURE 12-13. *Package Spec in the Attached Libraries node*

CAUTION

Be careful of the Execution Hierarchy *property on the trigger. If you create a trigger on a lower level that also exists on a higher level, you could have both triggers fire, or one could override the other. For example, you could write a block-level KEY-EXEQRY trigger that does processing specific to the form. If you set the* Execution Hierarchy *property to "Before", the trigger will fire before the form-level KEY-EXEQRY trigger. This is a more advanced feature that not many developers are aware of; use it sparingly because it makes your forms more difficult to understand and maintain. In general, triggers should be implemented on the highest level possible.*

PART
IV

Advanced Forms Topics

CHAPTER
13

Deploying Forms
on the Web

Out flew the web and floated wide;
The mirror crack'd from side to side;
"The curse is come upon me," cried
The Lady of Shallot.

—Alfred, Lord Tennyson (1809–1892), *The Lady of Shallot*

he Internet changes everything," goes the Oracle tagline. In the current era of information systems, the Internet even changes what users are asking for. Users are asking for new applications to be deployed on the Web, and those implementing the technology agree. The potential of the Internet is an attractive one that offers improved efficiency in business processes, new market opportunities, and new ways to retain customers. Often the requirement for this technology is so strong that those implementing the technology have no opportunity to fully evaluate it before building the system. Therefore, developers and designers in the trenches everywhere are being led into an environment that they do not know. This is nothing new. With each advance of technology, there is always a transition period where people with old development skills are learning new development skills and applying them immediately to mission-critical projects. The difference in this era is that the shift into the new environment has numerous business benefits, and users themselves are aware of, and are actually demanding, the technology.

Oracle responded to this trend by releasing the Oracle Developer Server as the key component that allows Oracle Developer applications to be run in a web environment. The Oracle Developer Server is a suite of processes that run on a multitier environment. It can allow an application to be run on an application server machine but to present a user interface in a browser. The Oracle Developer Server manages the communications between the web server listener product, Oracle Application Server, the client, and the database server. Often these three pieces reside on different servers, and this creates a multitier environment. Since the Oracle Developer Server uses Oracle Developer code, IT shops that are accustomed to creating and maintaining Oracle Developer applications will not have to learn a completely new tool or find developers who know the new tool if they want to deploy their applications on the Web. Another benefit is that Oracle has optimized the Java applet that Oracle Developer Server uses, so developers do not need to worry about tuning this part of the runtime environment for the best use of the network.

Web technology in the Oracle Developer world is relatively new and underused. However, Oracle Applications (Oracle's ERP suite that includes "prepackaged" applications such as Financials and Manufacturing), the largest user of Oracle Developer, uses the Web as its sole runtime environment. The Oracle Developer Server deployment of Forms, Reports, and Graphics applications has come of age, and the future of Oracle Developer lies in its ability to be run on the Web.

NOTE
The Oracle Developer Server can run Oracle Reports applications in client/server as well as in web environments. You can take advantage of the scheduling, caching, and batch engines that the server offers in either environment.

Web-deploying a Forms application is also still referred to in the user community as "Web Forms," although this term is no longer used by Oracle, except in a few places in the help system and release notes. While the official Oracle term for this feature is *Oracle Developer Server,* this chapter will compromise between the user and the Oracle terms and use *web-deployed forms* when referring to Forms applications running on the Web.

Oracle is heavily promoting web deployment. In the fall of 1997, *PC Magazine* voted Oracle Web Developer Suite (which included Oracle Developer) as Editor's Choice for web database development tools. Web-deployed forms are clearly here to stay.

The perception goes something like this: "You can web-enable your client/server Oracle Developer applications and obtain identical functionality by simply recompiling the source files." This representation is not totally accurate because, as is true with any new environment, there are some things that work in one environment and do not work in another. Early reviews by developers using the product were mixed because of some performance issues with the early versions. There was also confusion on the developers' side about the new environment— partially because of the architecture, partially because of interface changes that are inherent in the Java environment, and partially because of the special requirements for Java and browser versions. In the current release of Oracle Developer, great strides have been made to increase performance and to eliminate some of these special requirements, but some of the confusion still exists.

This chapter starts by discussing one of the aspects that cause this confusion: the three-tier architecture that web-deployed forms run in. Although this chapter is intended to just get you started, it provides direction on where to go for more information. The chapter then offers some general advice for successful work in this environment. It finishes with a discussion of techniques and considerations that you will need to work into your application design because "the Internet changes everything," including what you put in your forms and how your forms work.

This chapter specifically discusses the Form Builder (Forms) component of Oracle Developer. The methods and techniques for deploying Reports and Graphics applications on the Web are different enough that they would require their own treatment, which is not within the scope of this book. This chapter (and this book, in general) does not claim to provide a full discussion of Web technology. It does not discuss non-Oracle solutions to the question of how to deploy forms on the Web, such as the windows-terminal solution that the Citrix MetaFrame Server offers. This chapter also intentionally skips the critical steps of installing and configuring the Oracle Developer Server because these steps are in the realm of web administrators or system (or database) administrators rather than in the realm of developers. However, the standards and advanced techniques that are the main objectives of the book may all be used on the Web. Chapter 2 mentions other new features in Oracle Developer R.6.0 that help make web-deployed forms run more efficiently.

The Web-Deployed Forms Environment

In essence, web-deployed forms run in a three-tier environment that is really just an evolution of an old environment—that of two-tier or client/server. Client/server architecture consists of two logical machines: a client and a server (although you can run both client and server processes on the same machine). The client runs the runtime software and accesses the Forms files on the local machine or on a file server. The client is "fat," that is, it must have enough hard disk space and RAM to store and run the Developer Forms runtime files and the forms. The server runs the database management system, which also accesses the data files (usually on the database server). Figure 13-1 shows the components of a simple Forms runtime client/server environment. In this model, the client machine accesses application runtime files on its disk system (or on a file server disk system). The runtime program operates on the client machine. This communicates with the database server for its data needs.

The web-deployed forms three-tier (or web-enabled client) architecture consists of three tiers: a client, an application server, and a database server. Normally, each tier is located on a separate machine. (It is possible to run the tiers on one or two machines, but maintenance and performance optimization are easier if the tiers are on separate machines.) Figure 13-2 shows the components of the web-deployed forms three-tier architecture.

The Java Virtual Machine

The client runs a browser and, in the case of web-deployed forms, the browser runs a Java Virtual Machine (JVM) supplied by JInitiator. *JInitiator* is the Oracle version of a Sun Microsystems browser plug-in. The plug-in (written in Java) extends the capabilities of the browser so it can present the interface to a form running on an application server. JInitiator takes input from the client as well, but most of the processing, such as validation and trigger code, executes on the application server or database server. It contains the results of network optimizations that Oracle has built into the code.

JInitiator contains the same functionality as AppletViewer (an earlier version of the Oracle JVM). Both JInitiator and AppletViewer are pure Java solutions and rely

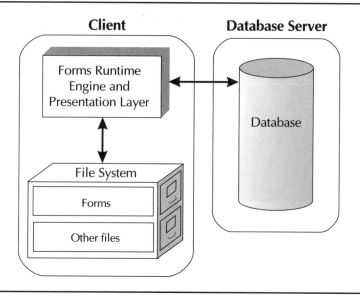

FIGURE 13-1. *Client/server Forms runtime environment*

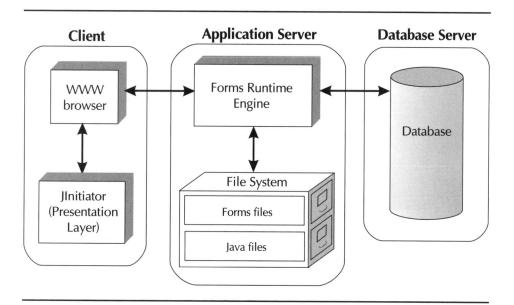

FIGURE 13-2. *Three-tier web-deployed forms architecture*

heavily on Sun's Java implementations. As of this writing, Oracle has certified the Microsoft Internet Explorer (IE) Release 5.0 as a stand-alone environment for web-deployed forms with no plug-in (JInitiator) requirement. This certification is not yet available for older versions of Developer Forms and for some operating systems, but Oracle is working on extending the certifications. Until a particular operating system is certified, it will require JInitiator or AppletViewer.

In addition, JInitiator offers some benefits over the native (IE 5.0) browser support, such as *on-demand JAR files,* which load Java class archive files when required instead of at startup, and *persistent JAR file caching,* which saves JAR files onto the disk so they can be used from a local installation instead of from a network installation. This saves download time. JInitiator offers the level of support required to run Oracle Applications on the Web.

The Middle Tier

The Forms runtime engine running on the middle tier (application server) accesses the file system on the server (or another networked location) and presents the user interface layer in a Java applet on the client tier. The application server in this environment is essentially the same as the client tier of the client/server environment. It runs the runtime engine and accesses the file system for Forms files and the database for data. It is critical to remember that the form presented in the client's browser is actually running on the middle tier with only the presentation layer revealed on the client's side.

The client is considered "thin" from a software standpoint because it does not need to store the Forms runtime programs or the Forms application files. The application server stores the runtime files and a Forms runtime engine (shown in Figure 13-2). There are other web components that also run on the middle tier to start a runtime session: the Forms Server and the HTTP listener (Oracle Application Server or any other web server such as Netscape Enterprise Server, Microsoft Internet Information Server, or Apache). The Forms Server and the HTTP listener are not used while a form is running, although the Forms Server is used to start the form. The database server runs the database software to manage the database files the same way it does in the client/ server model.

The only real difference between the client/server and three-tier models is that the three-tier client is split on two machines: the middle tier (application server) and the client. The database server is the same in client/server and in three-tier. The Forms modules run on the application server, but the presentation layer that would normally be viewed on the same machine is sent to the client browser. This allows multiple users to share the same files and runtime engine and allows an application server connected to the Internet to service client machines anywhere in the world.

The Web-Deployed Forms Runtime

There are a number of components to the web-deployed forms runtime environment. The best way to understand what the components are responsible for and how they work together is to examine the lines of communication during the two main runtime events: requesting the startup HTML file and running the form.

Requesting the Startup HTML File

The first step in starting a form is the client request, via a URL (uniform resource locator), to the application server for a startup HTML file. The *startup HTML file* contains special HTML tags that start the JVM. The following is a sample file for the Developer demo application.

```
<HTML>
<HEAD>
    <TITLE>Oracle Developer Server and Oracle JInitiator</TITLE>
    <X-CLARIS-WINDOW TOP=25 BOTTOM=608 LEFT=4 RIGHT=927>
</HEAD>
<BODY BGCOLOR="#FFFFFF" BACKGROUND="web_bkgd.jpg">
<P>
<TABLE BORDER=0><TR>
    <TD WIDTH=234>
        <P><IMG SRC="web_anim.gif" WIDTH=230 HEIGHT=300 ALIGN=bottom></P>
    </TD>
    <TD>
        <P>
        <OBJECT classid="clsid:9F77a997-F0F3-11d1-9195-00C04FC990DC"
          WIDTH=700
          HEIGHT=550
          codebase="http://mymachine/jinit117151.exe#Version=1,1,7,15,1">
        <PARAM NAME="CODE"       VALUE="oracle.forms.engine.Main" >
        <PARAM NAME="CODEBASE"   VALUE="/web_code/" >
        <PARAM NAME="ARCHIVE"    VALUE="f60all.jar, oracle_ice-4_03_1.jar" >
        <PARAM NAME="type"       VALUE="application/x-jinit-applet">
        <PARAM NAME="serverPort" VALUE="9000">
        <PARAM NAME="serverArgs" VALUE="module=start60.fmx userid=scott/tiger">
        <PARAM NAME="serverApp"  VALUE="default">
        <COMMENT>
        <EMBED SRC="" PLUGINSPAGE="http://mymachine/jinit_download.htm"
            WIDTH=700
            HEIGHT=550
            type="application/x-jinit-applet"
            java_code="oracle.forms.engine.Main"
            java_codebase="/web_code/"
            java_archive="f60all.jar, oracle_ice-4_03_1.jar"
```

```
        serverport="9000"
        serverargs="module=start60.fmx userid=scott/tiger"
        serverapp=default>
    <NOEMBED></COMMENT>
    </NOEMBED></EMBED>
  </OBJECT></P>
  </TD>
</TR></TABLE>
</P>
</BODY>
</HTML>
```

The username and password are hard-coded into this sample file, but you can omit the userid parameter and its values, and the form will prompt for the login. This file shows the *static startup file* that does not require the Forms Server to be installed as a cartridge. All values and parameters required are hard-coded into the file. There is also a *dynamic startup file* that you can use if you install the Forms Server as a cartridge. This file accepts parameters from the command line (URL) and plugs them into the placeholders % parameters in the file. The following is an example of a dynamic startup file from the web demo directory.

```
<HTML>
<HEAD>
<TITLE>Oracle Developer for the Web</TITLE>
</HEAD>
<BODY>
<P><BR>
Please wait while the Forms Client class files download and run. <BR>
This will take a second or two...</P>
<P><!-- applet definition (start) -->
<applet codebase="%Codebase%"
        code="%Code%"
        archive="%Archive%"
        width=%Width%
        height=%Height%>
<param name="serverHost" value="%ServerHost%">
<param name="serverPort" value="%ServerPort%">
<param name="serverArgs" value="Module=%Module%">
</applet>
<!-- applet definition (end) -->
</BODY>
</HTML>
```

TIP
There are other examples of HTML startup files in the online Oracle Developer documentation (from Oracle Information Navigator (OIN), select Guidelines for Building Applications and Working with Template HTML Files) *and in the demonstration files (in the ORACLE_HOME/tools/devdem60/web directory). There is also a file (JINIT-TAGS.HTM) that describes the parameters for JInitiator in the ORACLE_HOME/tools/doc60/us/odcfg60 directory. Browse the* Configuring the Oracle Developer Server *manual in the OIN for extra information on the HTML startup files.*

The format of the HTML startup file is slightly different when you are running in Internet Explorer without JInitiator. The following is a sample file that you can use in this environment. The parameters are explained in the Oracle white paper *Client Platform Support for Microsoft Internet Explorer 5.0 — Release 6.0* available on the Oracle web sites.

```
<HTML>
<BODY>
<APPLET CODEBASE="/web_forms/"
   CODE="oracle.forms.engine.Main"
   ARCHIVE="f60all.jar"
   WIDTH="800"
HEIGHT="600">
<PARAM NAME="serverPort" VALUE="9000">
<PARAM NAME="serverArgs" VALUE="module=grid2.fmx userid=scott/tiger">
<PARAM NAME="lookAndFeel" VALUE="oracle">
<PARAM NAME="colorScheme" VALUE="olive">
</APPLET>
</BODY>
</HTML>
```

The web listener on the application server determines that the URL indicates a standard static HTML file, retrieves the HTML from the file system, and sends it to the client browser. Figure 13-3 diagrams these steps.

NOTE
Java parameters in the HTML startup file are not case sensitive.

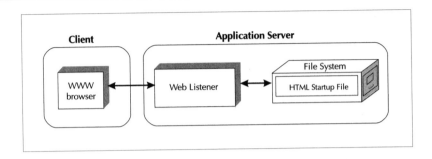

FIGURE 13-3. *Form startup HTML file request*

Running the Form

The next set of steps handles the startup of the Forms runtime and the form itself. The tags in the HTML file indicate that JInitiator will be used to display the form through the standard plug-in extension mechanism provided by the browser. They also indicate the Java class files that are required by the Java applet and that the applet start a connection with the Developer Forms Server listener (through the serverArgs and serverPort parameters). This information in the HTML file is sent to the web listener, which passes the request for a connection to the Forms Server Listener so that the Forms Server Listener can establish the connection with the client.

The Java class files are retrieved from the application server (if they are not cached on the client machine) and sent to the client browser. The browser starts the Forms client applet session as a separate window or as a window embedded in the browser. The Forms client contacts the server to request a runtime session. The Forms Server Listener then starts up a Forms Runtime Engine. These steps are shown in Figure 13-4.

The Forms Server Listener breaks the connection between the web listener and browser and sets up a TCP/IP socket connection directly from the Forms Runtime Engine to the browser. The form running in that session accesses forms and other files in the file system and communicates with the database through a standard SQL*Net or Net8 connection. The Forms client session is a child process of the browser session. These steps are shown in Figure 13-5.

The Benefits

Moving to a new environment is not something to be taken lightly. However, the benefits of web-deployed forms are compelling enough to make it worthwhile to make that move. The main benefit is in the aspect of centralization. The distribution of the application is centralized, as all forms run from the application server's file system. Maintenance is also centralized; to roll out new versions of your application, all you need to do is change the files on the application server. The

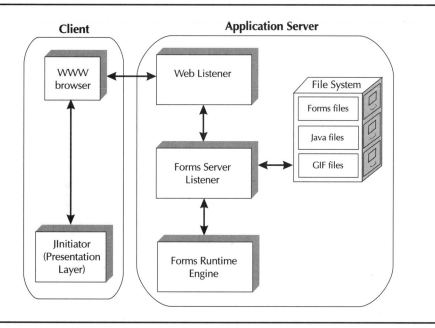

FIGURE 13-4. *Downloading the Java class files and starting JInitiator*

maintenance of Java class files and the client JVM used by this architecture is centralized as well.

The client install is automated. If users connect to your application and do not have JInitiator loaded locally, the application server redirects the users to a URL where they can download the files. Maintaining the current version is also automated, because the server senses the version of JInitiator and redirects the users to the same location if the locally installed version is out of date.

Administration of the runtime environment is centralized. This allows you to scale to a higher number of users by adding or upgrading the application server. Also, an application running on the Web is available outside normal corporate networks, although in the initial production release of Developer R.6, it must still be within a firewall (unless you have defined a port address that bypasses the firewall). The current version limits the deployment to intranet (companywide) and extranet (between cooperating companies) applications. Subsequent versions will support HTTP 1.1 protocols and allow you to go through firewalls. This feature is available in a beta version with the first release of Oracle Developer R.6. This will open the Forms web environment to the entire Internet.

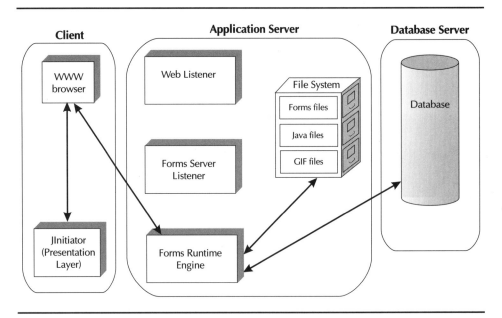

FIGURE 13-5. *Forms Runtime Engine communicating with the browser and the database*

Another important benefit is response time. While many developers experienced serious performance problems in earlier versions, the problems were mainly in the initial startup of the JVM. In Developer R.6, this largely has been mitigated, and there are many more options for tuning the startup files (as mentioned in the "Techniques and Considerations" section later).

In support of the improvements, an Oracle white paper, "Oracle Developer Server: How to tune for the deployment of Internet applications," reports that web-deployed forms show a marked improvement over client/server and Windows terminal environments. The study cited in this white paper measured the average bandwidth and average number of packets for data entry, validation, query, and navigation activities. Web-deployed forms excelled in all categories, with scores of between 100 and 500 percent less bandwidth or fewer packets required. Appendix G provides some hints on how to find the Oracle white papers online.

The Development Environment

Generally, the development environment for web-deployed forms is a client/server environment. Developer Release 6 Forms Builder offers a Run Form Web button that you can use to run the file in the Forms applet client. This client is a JVM that runs in a client/server environment and uses the same Java classes as the web environment JVM uses. This allows you to check the look and feel of the form as it would look on the Web. In addition to this test, you should periodically move the form to the application server, recompile it (if it is a different operating system), and run it from your browser. This process will ensure that the application server components handle the form in the same way that the client JVM does and that all objects will be handled in the same way.

Another potential development technique is to save and run the form on the application server. If you are running Windows NT, the .FMB and .FMX files you are working with can reside on the server, and you can access them through the file server network. If you are running an X-terminal or X-terminal emulator for a Solaris server, Form Builder will reside on the file server, and you will run a terminal session to access it. The forms files themselves can then be saved to the (development) application server so you can run the file immediately after compiling it in the X-terminal Form Builder.

This is really the same strategy as the client/server method, except that you are not developing on the client and do not need to have the Form Builder installed locally. The terminal strategy eliminates the need to copy the file to the application server for occasional testing.

Oracle Information Navigator Documents

There is documentation that can assist in your search for more information on this new environment. Some of the best sources of information are documents and technical white papers from Oracle. Appendix G lists some of these white papers. As the technology matures, you will see more and more white papers from users. Recent user conferences (for the International Oracle Users Group - Americas (IOUG-A) and Oracle Development Tools User Group (ODTUG)) have presented more papers giving user experiences and advice about web-deployed forms. (Search the user group web sites at www.ioug.org and www.odtug.com.)

The Oracle Information Navigator (OIN) is available in the Windows Start menu group Oracle Developer 6.0 Doc and also from the Form Builder **Help→Manuals** option. OIN contains the following manuals:

- ■ **_Guidelines for Building Applications_**   This HTML manual contains the essential Chapter 2, _Deploying Applications on the Web_. This is over a hundred pages long, with an excellent description of the architecture, details on how to set up and troubleshoot the servers (Forms, Reports, and Graphics), and the important section "Guidelines for designing Form Builder Web applications" (section 2.2.2). Read and "memorize" this section, as it contains published "feature restrictions." Chapter 4 (section 4.6) discusses performance tuning in this environment. This manual also contains Appendix A, *Working with Template HTML Files,* which explains the startup HTML file. Appendix B, *Including Application Specific Settings,* describes application class files.

- **Configuring the Oracle Developer Server**   This manual contains steps for setting up the Forms Server and contains more information about the startup HTML file. It also explains details of the JInitiator parameters and options.

- **Release Notes and Doc Addendum**   These files contain information that is not included in other sources. It is useful to check these for known limitations or work-arounds to Forms features. The files are a separate installation option in the Oracle Installer and may not be automatically installed with other Forms products.

- **Form Builder Reference**   This manual is available in the Reference Manuals node. It contains all reference information about the Form Builder objects, properties, built-ins, variables, and extensions. When creating a startup HTML file, you need to know the Forms command-line parameters (found in the topic "Forms Runtime Options").

- **Developer Forms help system**   There is some documentation in the help system on web deployment, but many of the help system topics refer and link to the online HTML manuals.

Most manuals available in the OIN are installed into the ORACLE_HOME/tools/ doc60/guide60/us subdirectory (although other languages may install into a different subdirectory of GUIDE60). Some have Adobe acrobat (.PDF) versions in addition to the HTML versions that OIN manages.

TIP
Load the file FBREF60.PDF (in the guide60/us directory) into Adobe Acrobat directly if you have problems with word searches when launching the Form Builder Reference *from the OIN.*

General Advice

There are some general words of advice that apply to your work in web-deployed forms. The technical tips discussed later support and explain this advice.

Design for the Web

You cannot always deploy the same forms on client/server and on the Web. It is not practical to design a form for client/server and expect to run it the same way on the Web. Therefore, if your deployment environment is the Web, you have to design for it. The main concerns are in how the Forms runtime system handles the visual elements and mouse actions. There are additional concerns in optimizing the forms to minimize network traffic from the client to the application server.

Developers accustomed to client/server development need to think of how the application server runs the forms. That is, it runs the form on the application server middle tier and presents the interface on the client. Application code executes on the application server, but the user interface objects such as text items and poplists will generate network traffic anytime the user acts on the object. There is no network traffic created if the user is just typing into a text item, but any navigation out of the item will create network traffic as a set of triggers fires. The "Techniques and Considerations" section later on contains some strategies for reducing network traffic and optimizing performance.

One key success factor to a project that uses web-deployed forms is being sure that you can implement the design using this technology. Therefore, in client/server applications or even in web applications with other products, you may want to hire a GUI designer to analyze and create an interface design. With web-deployed forms, this can be a key failure factor, as the designer can easily ignore the many limitations of the technology in favor of a friendly and pretty user interface.

You may need to make some compromises in your design standards, if you have them, for client/server forms deployed on the Web. For example, a typical background color for client/server forms is gray, but the standard on the Web for most pages is white. Therefore, you may want to consider breaking tradition and using a white background. In addition, some traditional design elements such as toolbars and menus are not normal features of web applications, and you might want to think about how to execute the functions they offer with canvas buttons.

TIP

Read Chapter 6—Designing Portable Applications—of the Guidelines for Building Applications *online manual (**Help→Manuals** in Form Builder). This chapter contains hints on how to consider platform-specific elements when designing forms. It lists platform-specific restrictions for Windows and Motif. It also discusses how to design forms for character mode. If you need to support web-deployed forms and client/server forms, this kind of advice is invaluable.*

Test for the Web

It almost goes without saying, but is important enough to state, that you should frequently test the application code you create on the Web (with the Run Form Web button at least) during the development process. It is a good idea to try a form on the Web before starting development, so you can be aware of the differences that will affect your design. Examine all types of items you will create. Test how complex you can make a form and have it operate efficiently. Check the action of GUI objects like buttons, check boxes, poplists, and radio groups.

Partition Your Code

As mentioned in Chapter 7, placing as much code as possible on the database server is standard practice in most modern development efforts. It is important when you're deploying in the web environment for the same reason: any database-access code that is located on the client side (which is partially running on the application server) will create network traffic between the database server and that application server. The application server is already handling a number of functions and processes to support the Forms Server and Forms Runtime, and the fewer network transactions it has to handle, the faster it will work.

Know What "Thin Client" Means

The perception that you will be able to run web-deployed forms on a "thin client" with a minimum amount of memory and system resources is not an accurate interpretation of the term as Oracle currently uses it. *Thin client* refers to the client requirement for installed software and, since the only software required to run in this environment is a browser (and, for some platforms, the applet), the term applies. Web-deployed forms use files on the client, and the more memory available on the client, the better the Forms will run.

The JVM running on the client requires enough memory to run the browser and the applet. In this case, the more memory, the better Forms will run (up to a point), because the need to swap memory to the hard drive will be diminished. Fortunately, the need for memory does not diminish the main benefit of centralization. The runtime JVM, JInitiator, is a plug-in for the browser, and uploading the correct version of the files can be maintained through the startup HTML file. The centralization of runtime form files is still a reality. The centralization of maintenance and administration is also effective because of the architecture and features.

Set User Expectations

It is a good idea to get user buy-in to this technology early in the development cycle. This means that you have to have a web-deployed forms environment working that they can use to test the applications, but you will need that anyway for testing forms in development. If you create prototypes, be sure to show them using web-deployed forms. If you are not using the embedded MDI window feature of Developer R.6, stress to users that these applications run outside the browser in an external viewer. Early user buy-in will improve your chances for success.

If your users are accustomed to a particular application running in a client/server environment, you may or may not be able to sell them on running that application on the Web, because it will act and look different from what they are used to. If you used some of the restricted features like WinHelp or any other Windows API with a presentation layer, you will have to forego web deployment until you can redesign the application and take the restrictions into account.

TIP
If the benefits of web-deployed forms are compelling enough reasons for you to move existing client/server applications to the Web, you have to sell users on the slightly different look and feel of applications running on the Web. The problem is that the users may perceive the change as only a difference in the startup process and slight changes in the runtime look. If you use the "Oracle Look and Feel" as described and demonstrated in Chapter 2, the application will look very different. Implementing this change only requires a command-line parameter (lookAndFeel=oracle). However, it drastically changes the form presentation layer and it may be enough that users perceive this as a completely different (and better) operating environment.

Recompile the Form

If your application server middle-tier machine uses a different operating system than the development environment, you need to recompile the file from .FMB to .FMX in that operating system. This is required because the form runs on the application server and uses the Forms runtime executable on that machine. Therefore, the form file it runs must be compatible with the Forms runtime for that operating system. The best way to ensure that is to recompile the file on the server.

Simplify Your Forms

Forms that have a small number of GUI items work very well. In contrast, forms with many items on one canvas can be problematic. Performance is reasonable with a limited number of users (based on the power of the application server) and a dedicated server with a basic level of memory (3–10 megabytes (MB) per concurrent user in R.2 and 1–6MB in R.6). Oracle has tested memory usage on the application server of a small form to be 1–2MB per user. They can support between 100 and 500 users per CPU and have proven the viability of web-deployed forms with up to 5,900 concurrent users.

CAUTION
If you use the strategy of creating many forms instead of one large form, the initial startup of each form will be faster, but moving from one form to another may be slower because a new form needs to start up. If the functions on the other form are rarely used, dividing the form may be better. Most of the time, the form would load quickly. But when you call another form, there would be a longer delay than usual, because a new form is starting. This wait may be less objectionable to users than the initial startup wait, so this strategy may prove useful.

Use a Certified Client JVM

As of this writing, Oracle has certified Microsoft's Internet Explorer Release 5.0 for running web-deployed forms without JInitiator. Users are also reporting that web-deployed forms work correctly in Netscape's recent versions (with the latest JDK) even without JInitiator. Currently, JInitiator, AppletViewer, and Internet Explorer 5.0 (with no plug-in) are the only certified clients. But Oracle is focusing a large amount of effort on improving this technology, so it is worth checking the currently certified method. The general word of advice is to use whatever Oracle certifies as the correct JVM. You should also install the latest version because there are frequent bug-fixes and enhancements. Doing otherwise may work most of the time for your application, but you may run into a limitation down the road.

NOTE
An Oracle white paper, available as of this writing, explains when various platforms are slated to receive certification. Appendix G provides some guidance on how to find Oracle white papers.

Set Up the Infrastructure

Web-deployed forms require much more in the way of network support. Administrators will need to set up a web listener and configure the Developer Server process on the application server. If the application will require multiple Developer Server processes, the administrator may need to set up additional servers and configure the load-balancing options. The document to start with when administering the Forms Server is the *Configuring the Oracle Developer Server 6.0* document that is available (as mentioned before) in the Oracle Information Navigator in the Windows Start menu.

TIP
Speed up your form testing by creating a form shell. This is a form with one text item and a button that executes a CALL_FORM to the form named in the text item. You keep this form running as you are developing and use it to test forms that you have compiled. This saves the time it takes to open the Forms Runtime executable each time you need to test a form. Instead of running the form from Form Builder, you press CTRL-C to compile the form, enter the name in the form shell, and click the button to run it. This technique is particularly useful when you use the Web Previewer (Run Form Web button) as this runtime environment takes more time to start up. However, be aware that you can only run one Web Previewer at a time, and, if the Web Previewer is running, you cannot run a form in client/server mode through the Form Builder.

Techniques and Considerations

There are some known feature restrictions with web-deployed forms due to the current state of the Java language. There are also some features that work differently or not at all; some of these are documented and some are not. If you are moving existing forms to the Web or if you are designing new forms, it is good to keep the limitations in mind. There are two things to remember when designing Forms for Intranet deployment in general:

- **Web-deployed forms run on the middle-tier server** and present only the user interface to the client.

- **This is a Java environment,** not a Windows environment. The look and feel is different between these two environments.

The remainder of this chapter discusses techniques to use and considerations to keep in mind when using web-deployed forms.

Operating System Concerns

There are a number of considerations that arise because the operating environment is Java and the operating system for the Forms runtime resides on the application server middle tier. Since web-deployed forms run in a Java environment, the application server will process any calls to the operating system that your form makes. This affects the following features or extensions to Forms.

FFI

Foreign Function Interface (FFI) code extends the abilities of Forms by allowing you to call functions in external libraries (DLLs in Windows). Since "external" means the host operating system, FFI calls in web-deployed forms will be sent to the application server. If you are trying to call Windows DLL routines like calling WinHelp to show a help file, the call will be executed on the server, but the client will not see the results.

This implies, too, that if you do use an FFI that does not require displaying something, the operating system might be different on client/server and web-deployed forms. For example, if you use an FFI call to a DLL that performs a complex calculation, you would create the DLL in Windows and register it to the FFI appropriately. However, if your deployment operating environment were a Solaris platform, the DLL would need to be recompiled under that operating system.

Another example of a call to a DLL is the button hint feature introduced with Developer R.1. This relied on an FFI call to a DLL that would not work in web-deployed forms because it displayed on the client. Fortunately, Developer R.2 and R.6 use the *Tooltips* property on items and canvases to implement this feature, and these work in web-deployed forms.

OLE and DDE

Object Embedding and Linking (OLE) and Dynamic Data Exchange (DDE) have the same concerns as the FFI except that they are Windows specific. This means that even if you are using an OLE object that does not display, you cannot use it at all if your application server is running in a non-Windows operating system. For example, OLE is not available on Solaris, and you do not even have the option of recompiling for the new operating system.

OCX and VBX

OCXes (also called ActiveX) and VBXes (16-bit versions of OCXes) are Windows extensions written in a standard way and compiled into libraries. You can embed these in your form, capture events like button presses, and set properties programmatically. Since OCXes are usually display-oriented (such as the grid control that allows you to resize columns), they will not work in web-deployed forms—the form is running on the application server and cannot show the OCX in the client. You can use a JavaBean instead of an OCX if you can find or build one with the same functionality.

HOST

HOST calls in Forms create a separate session in the host operating system. In web-deployed forms, the HOST call will run the session on the application server. Therefore, if you want to perform some action on the client machine, you cannot do it with HOST. In addition, if you are using HOST in client/server to display something in the client, this will not work in web-deployed forms—the client browser cannot interact with the application server's environment.

User Exits

The user exit library extension must be compiled in the application server operating system and located in an accessible location on the application server. If the user exit has any display aspects, they will not appear in the client browser.

Windows Registry

The client Windows registry, like the system editor, is not available because Forms runs on the server. Changing or reading the registry using FFI calls to Windows DLLs will not work if the middle tier (application server) is running under a non-Windows operating system like Solaris.

Printing

Printing from Forms is possible, but you have to realize that the printing will occur on the application server, not on the client machine. If the application server can access the client machine (through a network file system or other mechanism), you should be able to print from the application server to the client's printer. In addition, if you select **File→Print** in the applet window, you can print the screen on a client printer.

TEXT_IO

The TEXT_IO package provides functions that read and write files to the host's file system. As mentioned, in web-deployed forms, the host is the application server, so calls to TEXT_IO will access files on the application server. If the application server can see the client machine and has proper permissions, through a shared file system or other mechanism, it should be able to write files back to the client's file system.

Using the System Editor

Your forms can use a system editor, specified in the *Editor* property of an item, that normally calls an executable defined by the SYSTEM_EDITOR registry value. Since, in web-deployed forms, the form is running on the application server, the system editor is a program on the server. Calling this will, at best, open an editor on the server, not on the client. The work-around is to use a standard Forms editor. The client JVM supports this.

GET_APPLICATION_PROPERTY

If you have forms that will be deployed in different platforms (such as Web and client/server), you might have to write code that is different for each environment. You can check the runtime environment with the GET_APPLICATION_PROPERTY (USER_INTERFACE) call. This will return a value of "WEB" if the form is running under web-deployed forms. This is needed only if you have specialized code pieces that need to be run only in one environment or the other.

WEB.SHOW_DOCUMENT

WEB.SHOW_DOCUMENT, a Forms built-in, can connect to another URL and run another web application, or just show a web page in the browser.

TIP
WEB.SHOW_DOCUMENT opens another possibility for accessing the client machine. You can write HTML, Java, or JavaScript to execute a particular function on the client (like downloading a file to the client machine). Then call WEB.SHOW_ DOCUMENT with the URL of that function.

Reducing Network Traffic

Reducing network traffic is the name of the game for tuning web-deployed forms. Most of the tuning effort required is between the application server and client, as this is the most complex connection and the one that is most unfamiliar to Forms developers. It is useful to review some guidelines for reducing database server network traffic.

TIP
The Oracle white paper "Oracle Developer Server: How to Tune the Deployment of Internet Applications" contains detailed information about how to take advantage of the new application tuning features of Developer R.6.

Tuning Application Server to Database Server Traffic

The standard guidelines for optimizing a Forms application apply between the application server and database server. The techniques you use in client/server to reduce traffic to the database server are the same on the Web. You want to store as much code as possible on the database server and make a single call to that code from the form. You can also use array DML on the block to send a set of records to the database at the same time. Adjust the value in the block property *DML Array Size* to allow Forms to send information for more than one record to the database when Forms issues a DML statement. Chapter 27 discusses this property a bit more.

Another suggestion is to physically locate the application server close to the database server. This is important because the features of web-deployed forms that reduce network traffic between the client and application server are not available between the application server and database server. Two of these features are Event Bundling and Message Diff'ing. While you cannot modify their behavior significantly, it is useful to know how they work so you are aware of the kind of tuning that the Forms runtime provides.

EVENT BUNDLING   *Event bundling* is a facility used internally by the Forms Runtime engine to reduce network traffic. It is not a technique that you can control, but is something to be aware of when creating a form. Event bundling caches the triggers that execute together (for example, when the cursor leaves an item) and sends them to the application server as a group. The triggers still fire in the proper order, but the number of network round-trips is reduced. There is nothing you need to do on the form side to take advantage of this feature.

MESSAGE DIFF'ING   Another tuning feature that is automatically provided (although you can't modify its behavior significantly) is *message diff'ing*. Message diff'ing is an algorithm that uses the properties of existing items on the screen to draw new items and requires fewer messages to the application server to draw those new items. Normally, for each item on the screen, Forms sends a message from the server with instructions on how to draw it. Message diff'ing checks if there has been a similar item already drawn, and if so, only sends a reference to that item ("draw one like this") with any changes that the new item requires. When Forms needs to draw a new object, the message diff'ing algorithm sees if the last item drawn is the same type; if so, it does not ask the server how to draw it. While this feature currently requires that all objects of the same type be grouped together in the Object Navigator, a future release of Oracle Developer will not depend on the Object Navigator order. Other tuning strategies you can use now to take advantage of message diff'ing follow:

- **SET_ITEM_PROPERTY calls**   If you use a number of SET_ITEM_PROPERTY statements, they should be grouped by type: for example, text items first, buttons next.

- **SmartClasses**   Use SmartClasses to allow similar items to adopt the same properties. This allows the message diff'ing algorithm to work better.

Optimize the Class File Loading

The initial load time of the Java applet can be a sore point with users because it seems longer than the form startup in client/server environments. Part of this time is spent in loading the Java class files on the client side. You can optimize this task using the following tips. The following list refers to JAR (Java class archive) files that are collections of the Java classes used to render objects. You can create and open and manage these files using an archive utility such as WinZip. Most classes are named descriptively, so you can check whether a particular function is in a particular JAR file.

- JAR files are cached if you use JInitiator. This helps reduce the initial download time to a minimum. Use the ARCHIVE parameter in your starting HTML file to load one or more JAR files. For example: PARAM NAME= "ARCHIVE" VALUE="f60web.jar,icons.jar". The F60WEB.JAR file contains all but the LOV classes and is the one to use if you want to load all common classes when starting up.

- The default cache on the client is 20MB. Compare that number with memory as the application is running (using a system monitor such as the Windows NT Task Manager), and ensure that you have enough cache space available in memory. Increasing physical memory will help if you are running out of memory and swapping to disk. Freeing memory by closing other applications will also help.

- If JAR files are housed on different application servers in a load-balancing arrangement, the same JAR files could be downloaded from different servers because the classes are cached relative to the server. Therefore, locate the JAR files centrally if you have a load-balance configuration.

- A deferred-load feature allows you to embed references to other JAR files within a JAR file. The referenced files will not load immediately, but will wait until the class in that file is required. This deferred loading means that the form can display faster initially, although other classes that are required will be loaded as needed. Oracle supplies a number of JAR files with different contents, but you can create your own JAR files (using an archive utility such as WinZip) that contain references to other files.

- Store the .GIF icon files for buttons in the JAR file. This saves download time.

- If you are using JavaBeans, store them in the JAR file as well to speed up the download.

- Sign only the classes that need signing. *Signing* determines whether the source of a file is valid. This is required if the class file needs security to open a socket on a server other than the one from which it was loaded. Developer R.6 pre-signs only those classes that require security. If you create your own JAR file, you have to obtain the signature on your own. See the Sun web site for more information on JAR security.

CAUTION
Regardless of the tuning benefits mentioned, creating your own JAR files is a bit difficult and is normally unnecessary. The JAR files supplied with Oracle Developer will serve you well for most situations. In addition, Oracle discourages modification of the supplied JAR files. If you find that you need to modify the contents of a JAR file, it is best to create your own JAR file. That way, if Oracle upgrades a supplied JAR file, you will not have to redo your JAR file work.

Reduce Bandwidth

The key factor that differentiates web-deployed forms from client/server forms is their use of the network. Anything you can do to reduce network traffic will speed up the way the forms load or run. The following points address this principle.

- Reduce the number of boilerplate text objects, and use the prompt property instead. Boilerplate text is another object that needs to be rendered.

- Reduce the number of boilerplate graphics. Lines and rectangles are optimized, but other types are not.

- If your form contains many windows, allow the user to navigate to those other windows by clicking an OK or Done button instead of by pressing TAB to navigate through items. If the user does not need to change anything in those items, it is a waste of time to have to navigate to them. In addition, more triggers will fire as you navigate through items (such as POST-TEXT-ITEM and WHEN-NEW-ITEM-INSTANCE). If the user can skip to the next window with a button, the network traffic required by the item triggers will be eliminated.

- Use a simple startup form with just a few items on it. An example would be a logon screen with only a few items and graphics. This loads faster.

- Define a splash page using the splashScreen parameter of the HTML startup file (for example: <param name="splashScreen" value="co_logo.gif">).

This gives the user something to look at while the applet is loading and can help the user's perception of the load time.

- Hide objects not initially required. Set the canvas property *Raise on Entry* to "Yes." Set other objects' *Visible* property to "No."

- Tab canvases load all objects for the entire set of tabs at the same time. Set the *Visible* properties of all items to "No" to counteract this. Set them back to "Yes" when you navigate to a particular tab.

Other Tuning Tips
Here are some other techniques you can use to tune the runtime environment:

- Timers generate extra network traffic, as a packet is sent each time that the timer expires. Instead of using timers, use JavaBeans with the same functionality.

- Avoid MOUSE-UP and MOUSE-DOWN triggers, as these require extra processing on the server. Both triggers are handled by the same Java event. The Java event sends a message to the Forms Server regardless of the situation (MOUSE-UP or MOUSE-DOWN). The Forms Server needs to determine which one (MOUSE-DOWN or MOUSE-UP) is appropriate when this Java event occurs. Therefore, if you have a MOUSE-DOWN trigger but no MOUSE-UP trigger, the Java event will occur even in a MOUSE-UP situation. This is extra work for the Forms Server if you are not using that trigger.

- Item validation generates application server messages and processing. Use Java plug-ins instead of standard Forms widgets to do validation. For example, you can replace a text item with a Java item that already contains validation code. This moves the validation code to the Java class on the client and minimizes the application server messaging and processing. The extra code may require extra time to load the form, but this disadvantage may be less important than the savings in validation time.

- Use fewer displayed items on each canvas. Many items on a canvas means that there are many objects to initialize, and this will take more time to display than a canvas with fewer items.

- If possible, use the OPEN_FORM built-in and leave the form open instead of using NEW_FORM. Multiple forms open at the same time take more memory on the client. If another user has the same form open, it will share the memory on the server that is used by the program units. (No data portions or variable values of the form are shared.) However, if the user returns to an open form, the load will be faster than if the form had to be loaded again. NEW_FORM closes the calling form and releases the memory on client and server, but requires more startup time.

Design Differences

Web-deployed forms require different design decisions because of the different runtime environment.

Button and Menu Icons

Button and menu icon files use the .GIF format and are located in a directory in the Forms path. As mentioned before, you can download the icon files using a JAR file to save access time.

NOTE
Since menus and toolbars are not standard web application functionality, you might want to provide the functions they fulfill using other methods, such as canvas buttons or automatic links to other forms.

Fonts

It is not reasonable to expect Forms to use the same fonts, or in some cases, colors, in client/server and the Web—these are different environments. The differences in fonts could cause sizing issues; the difference in colors could cause unexpected displays. Both problems are solvable by reworking the form in Form Builder. You can also change the registry.dat file, which contains font aliases from Java fonts. In R.6, this file is located in the ORACLE_HOME/forms60/java/oracle/forms/registry directory. Font sizing and aliasing is documented in the *Guidelines for Building Applications*, Chapter 2, paragraph 2.2.2.4. Appendix B, section B-4, of that document contains information on how to change the registry.dat file.

NOTE
The standard MS Sans Serif font used in many Windows applications becomes the Dialog font in web-deployed forms. Arial becomes Helvetica. Both web fonts are different from the Windows fonts in size and shape, but are close approximations. Courier New and Times New Roman fonts in Windows translate to similarly named fonts on the Web.

Buttons Colors

On client/server, buttons are usually gray by default because the Windows Control Panel Colors applet manages the color of all buttons on that machine. In web-deployed forms, the Control Panel Colors applet is not in control, so buttons may be a different color (usually the color of the canvas). However, you do have control over the button colors. Create a visual attribute and attach it to the buttons. Better still, create a button SmartClass with the visual attribute attached to it in the object library, and subclass the button using that SmartClass.

TIP

As mentioned before, web-deployed forms look different from client/server forms. Be sure you run a test form on the Web early in the development process so you and your users can see how it works and looks. Test the MS Sans Serif font under a web-deployed form's runtime. You may find that 10-point looks better than 8-point.

Different Key Mappings

You will also not use the same function keys on the web as on client/server Forms. The standard file used in web-deployed forms to map keypresses to Forms functions is FMRWEB.RES (located in the FORMS60 directory). This contains key mappings for the Solaris environment. There is another file, FMRPCWEB.RES (in the same directory), that maps keypresses to Forms functions using the same keys as in client/server. Using that file (by renaming FMRPCWEB.RES to FMRWEB.RES) instead of FMRWEB.RES will provide you with the same key mappings on the Web and client/server. Both are plain ASCII text files that you can edit.

MDI Windows

In Developer R.6, web-deployed forms run in an MDI window by default, just as they do in client/server. If you want to run Forms so a separate window opens for each window and there is no MDI window, use the single document interface (SDI). You specify this as a server argument (serverArg parameter) in the startup HTML files, usesdi=yes. You can also embed the MDI window inside the browser window by using the serverArg parameter separateFrame=False.

TIP

As mentioned before, another serverArg parameter you can use is lookAndFeel=oracle. This provides your forms with the Oracle look—rounded buttons and scroll bars.

Limitations and Work-Arounds

There are some known limitations, some documented and some not. Some have fixes or work-arounds you can apply.

Triggers That Don't Fire

There are a few triggers that do not fire in web-deployed forms. Avoid using these even though they work in client/server applications. These triggers are WHEN-MOUSE-LEAVE, WHEN-MOUSE-MOVE, and WHEN-MOUSE-ENTER. These don't fire because of a limitation in Java.

Magic Menu Items

Avoid using magic menu items such as Cut, Copy, or Paste, because they do not work in web-deployed forms. Use CUT_REGION, COPY_REGION, and PASTE_REGION instead. The CTRL- key combinations (CTRL-X, CTRL-C, and CTRL-V) do work in web-deployed forms, however.

Drag and Drop

The drag-and-drop technique, as demonstrated in the Developer R.1 demo forms, does not work in web-deployed forms. This is because the WHEN-MOUSE-MOVE, WHEN-MOUSE-ENTER, and WHEN-MOUSE-LEAVE triggers do not work on the Web.

Maximizing the Window

The call to SET_WINDOW_PROPERTY for maximizing or minimizing the Forms MDI window does not work in web-deployed forms. Therefore, you have to resize the window by supplying the correct X and Y sizes and locating the form at position 0, 0 by using SET_WINDOW_PROPERTY. Minimizing the MDI window also does not work in web-deployed forms.

Maximizing an internal window (non-MDI window) in web-deployed forms also maximizes the window. However, the window title is not absorbed into the menu bar as it is in client/server. This means that if you use the extra canvas area that results from the window title disappearing in client/server, your layout may need to be adjusted when you move the form to the Web because that extra canvas area does not appear when you minimize the inner window.

Canvases

In releases before R.6, stacked canvases sometimes required explicit SHOW_VIEW and GO_ITEM calls to display, even though they might not require this in client/server. There may be other strange behaviors with stacked canvases that can be fixed if you use SHOW_VIEW to explicitly display the canvas. Another thing to try is to increase the space between stacked canvases if one is being automatically hidden. Be sure to check the forms on the Web, because you may not see these as issues in a client/server environment.

System Mouse Variables

You can use the system variable :SYSTEM.MOUSE_BUTTON_SHIFT_STATE to return a character string in a mouse trigger indicating which shift key was clicked (ALT, CTRL, or SHIFT). The help system states that the values returned in these variables are operating-system specific. Since web-deployed forms run in a Java environment, you might expect the values to be different and they are. In the client/server Windows environment, the strings returned by this variable are "Ctrl+", "Alt+", and "Shift+", indicating that the corresponding button was pressed when the mouse button was clicked. On the Web, the values are "Control+", "Alt+", and "Shift+".

Another system variable, :SYSTEM.MOUSE_BUTTON_PRESSED, returns a character string indicating which mouse button was pressed. The normal values (in client/server) are "1", "2", and "3" for the left, middle, and right mouse buttons, respectively. On the Web, only the left button returns a value.

TIP

As mentioned before, use the GET_APPLICATION_ PROPERTY(USER_INTERFACE) built-in function to determine the operating system in which the form is running. For example, if you are running on the Web, this function will return "WEB." If you are running in MS Windows, the function will return "MSWINDOWS32." You can test for the operating system and conditionally execute procedures that the particular operating system requires.

Another variable, :SYSTEM.MOUSE_BUTTON_MODIFIERS, provides an operating-system-independent value. You do not need to test the GET_APPLICATION_PROPERTY when checking the mouse button modifier keys. The values returned by this variable are "Shift+", "Caps Lock+", "Control+", "Alt+", "Command+", "Super+", and "Hyper+". Look up MOUSE_BUTTON_MODIFIERS in the help system for more information. If you are creating new forms (not just converting existing client/server forms to the Web), you can use this variable.

CHAPTER
14

Forms Help Systems

Small projects need much more help than great.

—Dante (1265–1321), *De Vulgaris Eloquio*

sers want an easy-to-use, searchable, full-featured help system that is available at the touch of a key or the click of a mouse. They will compare the Forms applications you develop with off-the-shelf applications that often include extensive online help systems. This raises the users' expectation for a readily available help system in your application. As an application developer, you need to provide online help systems to fulfill these expectations.

This chapter reviews the native Oracle Developer Forms (Forms) help facility. It also presents techniques and details of two options you can use to implement a help system for your Forms application:

- **Table-based help**   In this system, you create a table to store help text, a help form or window to display the text, and the Forms code to access the table and display the help text in the form.

- **WinHelp**   You create a .HLP file that contains the help text using a help-authoring tool. You also write Forms code that calls the Windows API (WinHelp) to load that file and jump to the proper place in the file.

This chapter also describes the technical requirements, development processes, and special considerations necessary for creating help systems to support Oracle Forms in a client/server environment and on the Web.

Before examining the technical details, it is useful to examine how to make the decisions about what level of help you need to implement.

How Much Help?

One of the first decisions you need to make when designing a help system for your Forms application is what level of help you will provide. This can range from none (a common choice) to a fully context-sensitive, multiple-level searchable system that includes links from one topic to another. *Context sensitivity* means that the first topic displayed, when the user requests help, is one that pertains to the item or block that the cursor is in.

To What Level?

This discussion will focus on the following levels. Keep in mind that these are relatively arbitrary divisions, and there are many levels between them.

1. **No help system**   This solution is the easiest for development but potentially the costliest from a support standpoint. Providing no help at all may cause the system to fail in user acceptance testing.

2. **Block-level help**   This option has help text associated with each block but no text associated with an individual item.

3. **Item-level help**   This means that each item as well as each block has help text associated with it.

4. **"The Works" help**   This is searchable, multilevel, graphical, and hypertext linked.

When you decide which level you need and what the content will be, you will weigh a number of factors:

- **The end user's business knowledge**   You need to consider how easily the end users will be able to understand the business reason for the processes in the form. If they need some help with the basic business practices, the help system should provide reference material, not only for the items they are filling in, but also for the actual result and intent of the information.

- **The end user's computer knowledge**   If the end users are not accustomed to computer applications, they may need more assistance in navigating and using the application. The text you write in the help system should take into account that there may not be a high level of comfort with mouse actions, menus, and windowing environments in general. A "Getting Started" section of the help system might be required for these purposes.

- **The frequency of use**   If users access the application frequently, they will probably need less actual online help than if they only access it a few times a month. If the use is infrequent, the help system should be written as if every user is accessing the application for the first time.

- **The application's intuitiveness**   Although you may strive toward creating the ultimate in intuitive applications, the form may involve a complex business operation that just cannot be represented intuitively. In this case, you need a more extensive help system to assist the users with difficult processes.

- **The amount of training given to end users**   If the end users receive formal training and a printed manual that supplies most of the details, an extensive online help system might not be required.

- **The number of end users**   If there is a small number of end users, it is possible that no help system is needed at all. A help desk or an IS support person could provide the assistance needed without undue drain on his or her time.

- ■ **The development cycle** While you can produce help systems quickly using some of the techniques in this chapter, there still may not be time and money available for the effort. This might be a mistake in project planning, but it can be an important factor in certain situations.

- ■ **Quality of other documentation** If the users have access to operations manuals or other user documentation, your online help system may not need to be very detailed.

- ■ **User turnover** The stability of the user community is another factor to consider when determining the extent of your help system. If the turnover rate is high, you will have new users accessing your application frequently and your explanations of functionality may need to be detailed and aimed at a lower level of business knowledge.

- ■ **Internet deployment** If your application's audience will access the application from the Internet (as with customers in an e-commerce application), it is likely that you will never know the user's level of experience. Web audiences will rarely be satisfied with an application that is less than completely intuitive. If the application is hard to use, users will give up rather than look for help. This places more of a burden on the application than the help system, but it may be necessary to build hooks into the help system from error or warning messages so the user can get more help if a particular operation is not performed correctly.

- ■ **Culture of the organization** If your users are accustomed to a particular level or style of help system, your decision on how much help to provide will be guided by the existing help. In essence, you may have a standard in your organization, whether or not it is formally declared.

How Much Content?

As mentioned earlier, your decision about the depth of the actual help content can be based on the users' business skills, the users' technical/computer skills, and the amount of training or outside documentation available. Essentially, a help system is only one part of an overall documentation strategy. You need to consider the entire picture of what documentation you will provide when making the decision on the help system content.

One strategy you can consider for providing actual content is to allow a knowledgeable set of users to provide and insert the text. This gives a user's slant on the wording and content and offloads a tedious task from the IS staff. This idea requires a set of trusted users and only works in selected circumstances.

The techniques discussed in the rest of this chapter describe the different techniques for providing help and how far each technique will carry you through the help levels.

Native Forms Help

While Forms Runtime (deployed on client/server networks and on the Web with the Developer Forms Server) does not provide much in the way of a native help system, there are a few features that will give you item-level help. The *hint text* is text that appears in the hint line at the bottom of the window when the user presses the Help key (F1) or chooses **Help→Help**. This hint line is specific to the item the cursor is in and is therefore context sensitive. Here is an example.

```
The name of the company that employs the student.
Record: 120/268
```

You can define this text on the item's Property Palette using the *Hint* property in the Help section. There is also a property in the Help section called *Display Hint Automatically* that indicates whether the text will appear automatically without requiring the Help keypress. If this property is set to "Yes" (the default), the text will appear as soon as the cursor enters the item. If it is set to "No," the user needs to press the Help key (or choose from the menu) for this to appear.

The hint text is quick and easy to develop, but it is passive and easy to ignore. It is also limited to a single line of 255 characters. If the user presses the Help key when the hint text is visible, Forms will display the properties that apply to that item, as shown in Figure 14-1. This is obviously of interest only to developers and will confuse most users.

The other capability that Forms has in its native feature set is *tooltips.* These are small boxes that pop up when the mouse cursor pauses over an item or canvas that has a value in the *Tooltip* property. Tooltips do not have the passive problem of hint text. The user must hold the mouse cursor on the item or canvas. However, the tooltip has the same single-line limitation as hint text. Shown here is a tooltip as it would appear under a text item:

```
Date Registered  24-FEB-1993
Last Name        Wilson
                 The student's last name as given on the invitation.
```

The native Forms help features are the easiest way to create a help system, because they only require you to enter help text into properties of the items. This type of help is extremely basic. If you decide to have any help system at all, the native features will probably not suffice. This means you need to explore how to create your own help system using table-based help or WinHelp.

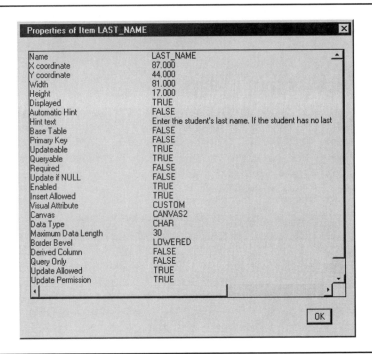

FIGURE 14-1. *Forms item help window*

Table-Based Help

The table-based help system stores help text in a table. A form or window in your application queries this text when the user requests help and provides a more detailed type of item-level help. With a primitive search facility, this strategy can even approach "The Works" type of help system. The help window can show as much text as you want on as many lines as you want and can include crude types of formatting such as line feeds and tabs. Storing the text in a table means that changes will be immediately available to all users. It also provides a central location for help text that does not require recompilation of the form (as do the native help features).

Another benefit is that programming a help system in Forms uses a familiar development environment and allows you to add features with the Form Builder. The look and feel of a table-based help system may not exactly parallel the standard Windows help that users are accustomed to (see "Other Table-Based Help Systems" later in this chapter for an exception). However, you can make the help form intuitive enough so that users will have no problem making the transition to a different type of help.

A table-based help system is portable, so you could deploy the same application files in a client/server environment as well as on the Web. While there is extra network traffic and server processing involved in table access, these will probably not be heavy since using one record at a time you can access only the primary key value.

The best way to explain how to implement a table-based help system is to examine the components of a sample system as described in the following section. A fully working sample of this system is available on the authors' web sites (as mentioned in the author biographies in the beginning of this book).

Components of the Help System

The sample system consists of four major components:

- **Help table**   This stores the text that appears in the help form. The table holds a record for each topic displayed.

- **Help form**   This form appears when the user presses the Help key or clicks the Help button. The text displayed reflects the form, block, and item that the cursor is in.

- **Help Library package**   Your application forms call the help form using a packaged procedure. You store this package in a .PLL library attached to the calling form.

- **Help Text Maintenance form**   The easiest way to manage the help table is through a form. This can be fairly simple, since only developers or trusted users will run it. Of course, the help records may be created by any other method such as SQL*Plus, SQL*Loader, or IMP (Oracle's import utility).

Help Table

The table that stores the text is essentially one column called TEXT, of VARCHAR2(2000) datatype. The primary key is a concatenation of the FORM_NAME, BLOCK_NAME, and ITEM_NAME. There is also a column called DESCRIPTION that acts as a display name for users. The table structure follows:

```
SQL> describe HELP_TEXT
Name                          Null?     Type
----------------------------- --------- ----
FORM_NAME                     NOT NULL  VARCHAR2(30)
BLOCK_NAME                    NOT NULL  VARCHAR2(30)
ITEM_NAME                     NOT NULL  VARCHAR2(30)
DESCRIPTION                   NOT NULL  VARCHAR2(40)
TEXT                                    VARCHAR2(2000)
```

A single help topic is easiest to read if it is not too long, and the VARCHAR2(2000) should provide plenty of space. If you are running Oracle8, you can increase this size to 4000, if needed. If you are using an earlier version of Oracle, you can convert this column into a LONG (that will hold up to 2 gigabytes (Gb) or 2,147,483,648 bytes), but you will not be able to search the text inside that column unless you use Oracle Context.

Storing the whole topic in one record has many benefits over storing it in multiple rows per topic. One benefit is that you need to manage fewer rows. There is no need to worry about line numbers for each line of text, and queries need no ORDER BY or multiple row result sets. Another benefit is that you can use a multiline text item to display the text. This item allows the use of copy and paste to insert text from another Windows editor or word processor.

The application form calls the help form and passes it parameters containing the primary key values—form, block, and item names—from the cursor location. The Help Form queries the table using these values when it starts up. This system provides item-level help.

If no record fulfills this search condition because help text has not been written for the current item, the form queries the table again using the form and block names and "GENERAL" as the item name; this is considered block-level help. If there is no block-level help, the form queries once again on the form level (with block and item names of "GENERAL"). The relationships between the columns and query levels are represented in Table 14-1.

Help Level \ Columns	ITEM_NAME	BLOCK_NAME	FORM_NAME
Item level	<cursor item>	<cursor block>	<current form>
Block level	GENERAL	<cursor block>	<current form>
Form level	GENERAL	GENERAL	<current form>
General level	GENERAL	GENERAL	GENERAL

TABLE 14-1. *Values of Item, Block, and Form Columns for Different Help Levels*

Help Form

The help form appears when the user presses the Help key or selects Help from the
Help menu of an application form. You could also provide a canvas button or
toolbar button with a WHEN-BUTTON-PRESSED trigger or a Help menu item
button with the PL/SQL code

```
do_key('HELP');
```

This would fire the KEY-HELP trigger on the form level as described in the "Help
Library Package" section later in the chapter. The text in the HELP_TEXT table
displays in a multiline text item, as Figure 14-2 shows.

The multiline text item accepts the contents of the TEXT column in the table and
displays it in a scrollable region. You can set the *Maximum Length* property of the
item to match the database column length (2000 in this example).

The Help Form provides three features that are useful in a help system:

- **Context sensitivity**   The calling form passes parameters representing the
  cursor position (form, block, and item) to the Help Form. When the Help
  Form starts, it queries the help table based on these parameters so that the

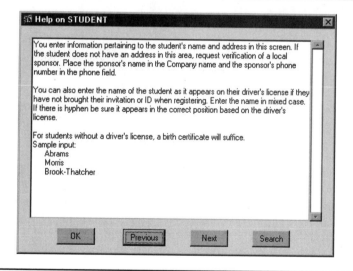

FIGURE 14-2.   *Help Form*

initial text displayed refers to the cursor location in the calling form. If no help text applies to that location, the Help Form follows the strategy described earlier to search other levels. If no help text is found, an alert appears with an error message.

■ **Multiple levels** The Next and Previous buttons show the user different levels of help for the cursor item. For example, if item-level help is displayed, the Previous button will display block-level help. The Next button from block-level help will display the item-level help.

■ **A search facility** The Search button on the form pops up a dialog window, shown here, that allows you to perform a word search on topics in the help system:

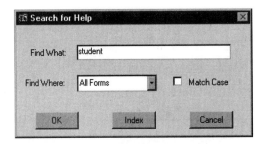

The user can enter a word or phrase in the Find What text item. Checking Match Case will perform a case-sensitive search. The Find Where poplist contains static values for All Forms, This Form, and This Block. The poplist narrows the search to topics in the calling form or block. This will speed up searches if the help table is quite large. The OK button starts the search and displays a *list of values* (LOV) of topics showing the DESCRIPTION column for all records that contain that word or phrase in the TEXT column.

The mechanism for this customized search is code in the WHEN-BUTTON-PRESSED trigger on the button that constructs a SQL statement with a WHERE clause based on the contents of the Find What item. The code also uses the Find What and Match Case items to add to the WHERE clause. It then loads the SELECT statement with this special WHERE clause into the LOV's record group using the POPULATE_GROUP_WITH_QUERY built-in.

Choosing one selection from the LOV loads that record into the form. To browse for topics in the list, the user presses the Index button and an LOV appears with all topics. This would be handy if the user were knowledgeable about the workings of the Forms LOV Find box, as it would allow a quick search for any word or phrase in the TEXT column.

Help Library Package

A library file contains a package called F_HELP with a single procedure (CALL_HELP) that creates the parameters and calls the Help Form. This package can appear in your standard utilities library or in an application-specific library. You attach this library to your form and write a KEY-HELP trigger on the form level with the following code:

```
f_help.call_help;
```

The procedure creates the FORM_NAME, BLOCK_NAME, and ITEM_NAME parameters from system variables indicating the cursor position (:SYSTEM.CURSOR_ ITEM, :SYSTEM.CURSOR_BLOCK, :SYSTEM.CURRENT_FORM), and then passes all parameters to the Help Form.

The library module makes it easy to add the system to existing forms. The only work is in attaching the library, creating the KEY-HELP trigger, and ensuring that the library is available in the Forms path (stored in the FORMS60_ PATH or ORACLE_PATH variables in the registry) or in the current directory when running the form. If you are using a template-based system, you can place the trigger in the template form or object library and attach the library to the template. In this way, all forms you create from the template will be able to access the help system without extra coding.

CAUTION

This sample help system depends on system variables, such as :SYSTEM.CURSOR_ITEM. This means that, to show help for the proper item, you do not want the cursor to move when the user clicks the Help button and navigates to the help form. If you set the Mouse Navigate property on the Help button to "No," the cursor will not move to the button, so the system variable :SYSTEM.CURSOR_ITEM will be correctly set.

Help Text Maintenance Form

The maintenance form assists in entering and updating the help text table. Figure 14-3 shows a sample session. The user types in a form name or selects one from an LOV that contains a list of all forms that currently have help text. There are also similar LOVs for block and item names. If the user clicks the Recall button, an LOV will appear showing a list of all topics (the DESCRIPTION column in the HELP_TEXT table). Selecting one of these will query the record onto the form so it can be edited.

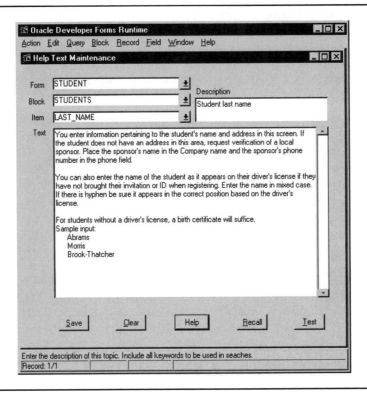

FIGURE 14-3. *Help Text Maintenance form*

This form contains standard editing features. The Help button calls up a window with text on how to use the form, as Figure 14-4 shows. This window is itself an example of another method for coding help systems: *embedded help text*. For this system, you place the text directly in the form and display it in a window with a scrollable, stacked canvas. This method may be best for some applications because it is simple to create, the access time is minimal, and there is no database or file retrieval needed. However, it is quite inflexible; you must edit and recompile the form using the Form Builder if you want to make changes to the text.

The Query Mechanism

The calling form uses a form-level KEY-HELP trigger to call the packaged procedure that passes parameters for form name, block name, and item name to the help form. The calling form issues a CALL_FORM command to open the help form, which is a modal call that places the focus in the help form and requires the user to exit the

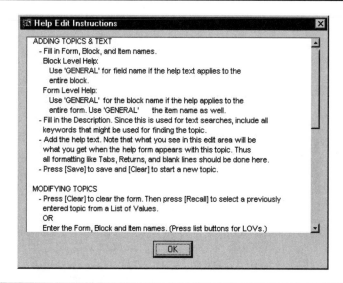

FIGURE 14-4. *Hard-coded Help Text window*

help form before continuing work in the calling form. The following code is the declaration in the package specification:

```
PACKAGE f_help
IS
--
    PROCEDURE call_for_help(
        p_formname IN VARCHAR2 DEFAULT NULL,
        p_blockname IN VARCHAR2 DEFAULT NULL,
        p_itemname IN VARCHAR2 DEFAULT NULL );
--
END;
```

An excerpt from the package body for CALL_FOR_HELP follows:

```
--
IF p_formname IS NULL
THEN
    v_formname := name_in('SYSTEM.CURRENT_FORM');
ELSE
    v_formname := p_formname;
END IF;
--
```

```
-- Assign block and item name variables using
-- system variables if they are passed in as NULL.
--
-- Add the parameters to the list & assign values
-- (v_pl_id is a PARAMLIST datatype)
--
add_parameter(v_pl_id, 'FORM_NAME', TEXT_PARAMETER, v_formname);
add_parameter(v_pl_id, 'BLOCK_NAME', TEXT_PARAMETER, v_blockname);
add_parameter(v_pl_id, 'ITEM_NAME', TEXT_PARAMETER, v_itemname);
--
--  Call the form with the parameter list
--
call_form('FORMHELP', NO_HIDE, NO_REPLACE, QUERY_ONLY, v_pl_id);
-- Get rid of the parameter list until next time
destroy_parameter_list(v_pl_id);
```

The help form contains default parameters corresponding to those passed into it from the CALL_FORM. A procedure in the help form, called by the WHEN-NEW-FORM-INSTANCE trigger, queries the table based on the parameters. If no records are returned by the query, the form queries the next level of help. An excerpt from the UTIL.GET_HELP_TEXT procedure called from the help form's WHEN-NEW-FORM-INSTANCE trigger follows:

```
PROCEDURE get_help_text
IS
   v_alertbutton    NUMBER;
   --
   v_retval         NUMBER;
   --
BEGIN
   --
   -- Load control fields with parameter
   -- values. These will in turn be copied into
   -- the Help block in a PRE-QUERY trigger.
   --
   :control.item_name := :parameter.item_name;
   :control.block_name := :parameter.block_name;
   :control.form_name  := :parameter.form_name;
   --
   --Load the control fields and execute the query.
   --
   IF util.query_help('ITEM') != 0
   THEN
      -- No help records on field level. Try BLOCK.
      IF util.query_help('BLOCK')!= 0
```

```
        THEN
            -- No help on block level. Try FORM.
            IF util.query_help('FORM')!= 0
            THEN
                -- No help at all so try GENERAL.
                IF util.query_help('GENERAL') != 0
                THEN
                    bell;
                    v_alertbutton := show_alert('ALERT_NOHELP');
                    exit_form;
                END IF; -- end of 4th if form_failure
            END IF;      -- end of 3rd if form_failure
        END IF;          -- end of 2nd if form_failure
    END IF;              -- end of 1st if form_failure
    --
    -- Set the window title based on the form name
    set_window_property('W_HELP', TITLE, 'Help on ' ||
        :control.form_name);
    -- load the parameters with current HELP values
    util.post_help_query;
END;
```

For example, if the cursor is in the LAST_NAME item and the user activates the help form, the form will query the table for text written for that level. If there is no help, Forms raises an error with an FRM-40350 message code. An ON-MESSAGE trigger written on the form level of the help form checks for this code and raises a form_trigger_failure exception. The main code for this trigger follows:

```
DECLARE
    v_errcode      NUMBER(7)      := MESSAGE_CODE;
    v_errtype      VARCHAR2(5)    := MESSAGE_TYPE;
    v_errtext      VARCHAR2(80)   := MESSAGE_TEXT;
BEGIN
    IF v_errcode = 40350 then
        -- This is the no data found error after the
        -- execute query. The failure will be tested
        -- in the calling procedure.
        raise form_trigger_failure;
    ELSE
        -- show the normal forms error number and message
        message(v_errtype || '-' || to_char(v_errcode) || ': ' ||
            v_errtext);
        raise form_trigger_failure;
    END IF;
END;
```

This causes a form failure state that is processed by the UTIL.QUERY_HELP procedure as excerpted here:

```
    v_retval   NUMBER := 0;

BEGIN
    --
    -- Execute the query. PRE-QUERY copies CONTROL
    -- values into HELP block.
    go_block('HELP');
    execute_query;
    --
    -- ON-MESSAGE raises a failure if no records returned
    IF FORM_FAILURE
    THEN
        v_retval := 1;
    ELSE
        :control.help_level := p_help_level;
    END IF;
    --
    go_block('CONTROL');
    RETURN v_retval;
    --
END;
```

The called procedure returns a value to the calling procedure, which requeries if there were no rows retrieved. The next query is based on block-level help (where the ITEM_NAME parameter is set to the value of "GENERAL"). If no help row exists for block-level help, the form looks for form-level help. If there is no form-level help, the form issues a message in an alert.

At the end of the WHEN-NEW-FORM-INSTANCE trigger, either a help record will display on some level, or the error alert will display.

NOTE
If your application requires multilanguage support, you can add a column to the help table to specify the language for a particular topic. When displaying the help topic, use the language (set in a global variable when the application starts) as one of the query conditions. This is particularly important for web applications that may have audiences with various language needs.

Enhancements to This System

If you end up using a system like this for your application, consider normalizing the help table into many tables. If you have a table each for forms, blocks, and items, you can link these together with ID key columns and provide the actual names of those objects in only one row in one table. This allows you to change the names more easily because the HELP_TEXT table keys are not based on names, but IDs. If you share the help table among a number of applications, add a table for the application name and ID as well.

Another enhancement you might want to make to the Help Form is to disable the Next and Previous buttons if there is no help topic in those directions.

Your users may not be comfortable with concepts like forms, blocks, and items. The query system depends slightly on that, but you can provide other terms that could do the same thing. The query mechanism would always, by default, load item-level help, but you may want to call items "fields" or "input boxes." If your forms use graphic rectangles to group items together, you can refer to "regions" or "groups" as a higher level. You can also group items by window. This makes more sense to users because they can see a title on the window but would not necessarily distinguish the blocks or groups within the window.

If you do use alternative groupings of items, you have to come up with a way to translate the cursor location into a particular group. For example, you might want to provide item-level help but also allow the user to click the Previous button and view window-level help. You would need to rework the sample system to be able to pass it the window name (or title if you reuse the same window for many canvases and reassign the title for the other canvases) as a parameter. If you use arbitrary groupings like region, you probably need to store the form, block, and item names in a table that maps these to the corresponding region.

If you decide (based on the factors mentioned at the beginning of this chapter) that you only need block-level help or window-level help, you can rework the sample system to provide only these two levels. However, you might want to leave the table design the same in case you want to add item-level help later.

Using a Help Window

Another method for displaying table-based help is to use a window in the same form. This has the obvious benefit of not requiring a separate form, which means you do not incur the overhead of a CALL_FORM opening and displaying another form. In some web environments, opening a window is significantly faster than displaying another window in the same form.

The drawback of this strategy is that you need to have help-related objects located in each form. You can soften this drawback if you create an object group called SUBCLASS_HELP_SYSTEM in your object library that contains the block, canvas, and window used for displaying help. You then subclass this SUBCLASS_HELP_SYSTEM object group from the object library into your template as described in Chapter 10. This essentially subclasses the object group into all forms you create from the template and allows you to make changes (add objects, remove objects, and modify objects) to the help window objects in a central location—the object library.

Even if you use a subclass from the object library, you will need to recompile all forms that use the help system if you make a change to any of its objects. If you create an automated batch compile script as described in Chapter 29, this is not a major drawback. You can also use Project Builder to compile a set of forms. In addition, weigh this drawback against how likely you are to make changes to the help system after a number of forms are developed. The likelihood of changes is great only if you have never completed a project using the help system. Even with your first help system project, you would probably work out the help system mechanism in advance and make very few changes once you started developing forms for the application.

The embedded help window works the same way as the separate form version. The query and search mechanisms work the same way as in the separate form method. The main difference is that you do not need to create parameters and use CALL_FORM to start up another form. Another difference is that the cursor needs to leave the item it was in and navigate to an item on the help window. This means that validation will occur for the item unless you code around this situation by programmatically setting the item property ITEM_IS_VALID to TRUE, calling the help window, and when the help window is dismissed, setting the same property to FALSE (if it was changed).

Other Table-Based Help Systems

You can likely think of other ways to format a table-based help system. Oracle has created a demo form implementing table-based help that looks like standard Windows help, as Figure 14-5 shows. This is documented in the Form Builder file under the topic "Online Help class." The help documentation describes how to create a set of help tables and packages to store the help text. (Run the DEMOS60.SQL script to create the help and other demo objects, not D2KHELP.SQL as mentioned in the help file.) There is also a facility to load data from the repository if you are using Oracle Designer. There is also a help editing form for maintaining the help text. The help form itself, D2KHELP.FMB, is located in the ORACLE_HOME/tools/devdem60/demo/forms directory.

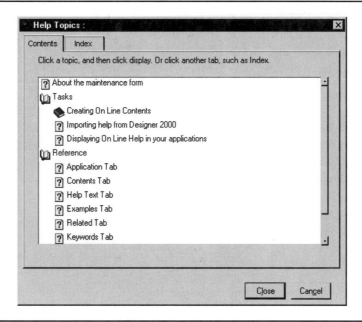

FIGURE 14-5.   *Table-based help form demo*

WinHelp Help System

As mentioned earlier, the table-based help system allows you to add virtually anything in the way of features to the help system engine. However, there is a price to pay in development time to add those features. Also, although you can create a Contents page that closely parallels the look and feel of the Windows help files that the users are accustomed to a table-based help system will not have embedded links and graphics, and will never reach the same level of sophistication.

To reach that level of sophistication, you can use the same facilities that Windows programmers use to provide help in their applications. You can create your own Windows Help files and call them using Forms code. This will give you the power of the Windows help engine—*WinHelp*—although you will not be able to add to its features. This type of help will give your users "The Works" type of help with a familiar interface that contains hypertext links and a searchable list of topics.

No WinHelp on the Web

The limitation on WinHelp systems is that they are not available for web deployment (if you are using web-deployed forms). Windows help displays on the machine that is running the form. In the case of web-deployed forms, the machine running the form is the application server, so calls to Windows help (if the server is running Windows) will execute and display on the application server, not in the client browser. Thus, WinHelp help systems are not viable for web-deployed Forms applications.

TIP

You can provide both table-based and WinHelp styles of help for the same application if it will be deployed on both client/server and on the Web. You can determine the runtime environment using the Forms built-in GET_APPLICATION_ PROPERTY(USER_INTERFACE). If this function returns the string "Web," the form is running on the Web and you can call table-based help. If it returns a value like "%WIN%," it is running under Windows and you can use WinHelp.

What's This?

There is a variation on WinHelp called "What's This?" help that displays a popup box showing context-sensitive help text. This popup box appears when you click a question-mark button and click on an object in the window. The cursor changes to an arrow and question-mark symbol between clicks. This style of help is part of the WinHelp engine, but must be coded specially into an application.

This is very difficult to code in Forms because there is no way to put a form into a suspended mode until the special mouse cursor is clicked on an object. It is easy to change the mouse cursor using the SET_APPLICATION_PROPERTY built-in, but you also need to prevent other code from firing until the cursor changes back. In general, the added functionality will probably not outweigh the time and effort required to add the feature. Also, there are other easier ways to do context-sensitive help as described in this chapter.

Working with WinHelp

The Forms code needed to implement a WinHelp system is relatively small, but you need to know some details about the way the WinHelp engine works if you are to be effective in integrating it with Forms.

The WinHelp Engine

WinHelp is the program (or "engine") that reads and displays a file compiled into a special format and named with a .HLP extension. WinHelp is responsible for presenting a window with a standard menu and toolbar. This system contains all the features you are used to when viewing a Windows help file. An application program calls WinHelp to display the help file when you choose an item from the Help menu or press the F1 key. The text appears in a resizable window that has a function toolbar. You can search on topic keywords by clicking the Index tab and typing the topic. You navigate between topics using Previous (<<), Next (>>), Back, and the History window (available from the Options button). Depending upon the help file, there may be embedded graphics or icons, and often there are links to other topics. When you click on a graphic or specially colored word or phrase, the topic referenced by those words will appear. Other than the buttons and Contents window, help files look and act much like HTML pages in a web browser.

The WinHelp engine supplies all these services and features for applications in the Windows environment. This engine is available to you as a programmer by calling the WINHLP32.EXE program file or by accessing the Windows API function WinHelp. WinHelp performs its work correctly if you supply the correct calling parameters and a properly formatted and compiled help file. Therefore, one key component to success with WinHelp is the help file itself. Appendix C contains a description of some of the major concepts of WinHelp systems.

Developing a Help File

The help file is a compiled binary file you create from a rich-text format (.RTF) file that contains special codes. You can insert the special formatting in the text file manually (not recommended) or with the assistance of a help-authoring tool (recommended). These tools are available as commercial products and as shareware products. The shareware help-authoring tools may be serviceable enough for your needs, but if you have an extensive help project, it would be wise to invest in a product that includes technical support. Look in the Windows Software Development forum of your favorite online service, or search for "WinHelp" or "Help Authoring" on the Internet.

You create text for the authoring tool either with an existing word processor or with the help-authoring tool's own editing environment. After you create the text, you use a separate help compiler program to compile the .RTF file into the binary (.HLP) file. Help-authoring program documentation often discusses the Windows help system at great length, and it is worth looking there for details on how to create a help file. Also, Windows programming tools such as C++ often have sample files and documentation on help authoring. In addition, Oracle Designer generates .HLP files automatically from repository definitions (as described later in the chapter).

How to Integrate WinHelp and Forms

After you create the source file and compile it into the .HLP file, you can call this file from Forms and pass it various parameters such as the starting topic. Much of the complexity of your help system will be in the help file itself, as you can incorporate more or fewer WinHelp features in the file. Regardless of the depth to which you go in the help file, you need to have an easy-to-develop system for calling WinHelp and displaying the file in various ways. You can call WinHelp directly as a program using a call to the HOST built-in and pass it the name of the help file with command-line parameters. Alternatively, you can use the Oracle Developer *foreign function interface,* a method for calling Windows API and other DLLs from PL/SQL code. The foreign function interface provides better integration to the operating system and has less overhead than the HOST call. The built-in package, ORA_FFI, supplies the procedures, packages, and datatypes that comprise this interface. Chapter 29 discusses the foreign function interfaces further.

The Forms WinHelp system consists of three parts as follows:

- **A help file**   You write the help source file (.RTF) in a third-party help-authoring tool and compile it into a .HLP file.

- **A PL/SQL package**   A package called F_HELP in your Forms library contains a procedure, CALL_HELP, that issues a call to WinHelp with the proper parameters.

- **A toolbar button, menu items, and keypress trigger**   These act as the initiators of the help request and allow the user to call for help in various ways.

The first of these is discussed in the preceding section on developing a help file. The last two require Forms-specific work.

The PL/SQL Package

You call WinHelp using a PL/SQL package written with the foreign function interface. The ORA_FFI package provides a way for the Forms developer to call functions in Windows DLLs that have a published call interface. For a WinHelp call, you use a PL/SQL dispatcher package to call a function called WinHelpA in a Windows DLL called USER32.DLL. This package contains a procedure that uses a special syntax to register the call to the Windows DLL and to provide a PL/SQL interface to the rest of your Forms code. If you are not used to it, working with ORA_FFI may seem a bit "foreign," so you might want to use some sample code to get started.

NOTE
The Developer Forms demos include a library—
D2KWUTIL—that has a procedure called
WIN_API_SHELL.WINHELP. This procedure
contains most of the features of the code described
in this chapter.

When you call WinHelp from Forms, you pass it parameters of the help file name, the command that specifies how the file will appear, and a value for the command if it needs one. For example, you can pass WinHelp parameters for the help command (HELP_KEY) and for the value (the name of the item that the cursor is in). The help file contains a topic with a keyword of the name of the item on the form. Forms calls WinHelp with these parameters (including the file name), and when WinHelp starts, it executes the command HELP_KEY (which is actually an integer value). This command tells WinHelp to jump to the keyword of the topic passed in as the value; this produces context-sensitive help. You use other WinHelp calling commands the same way—by passing the file name, the command (as a number), and the value for the command.

The code excerpted next appears in a packaged procedure in a Forms library that you attach to your forms. This procedure, called F_WINHELP.CALL_HELP, accepts parameters for the WinHelp command, the data that the command needs, and the name of the file. The file name is an optional parameter that is assigned a default of the form name and a .HLP extension. This means that you would name your help file the same as your form, and the package would take care of deriving the name of the proper help file.

As mentioned earlier, you might want to call WinHelp to get context-sensitive help. This is simply a matter of using other system variables, such as :SYSTEM.CURSOR_ITEM, to determine the cursor location.

The package specification contains the following code:

```
PACKAGE f_winhelp
IS
    --
    g_help_context        CONSTANT NUMBER := 1;
    g_help_quit           CONSTANT NUMBER := 2;
    g_help_contents       CONSTANT NUMBER := 3;
    g_help_helponhelp     CONSTANT NUMBER := 4;
    g_help_setindex       CONSTANT NUMBER := 5;
    g_help_key            CONSTANT NUMBER := 257;
    -- other help command constants are declared here too.
    --
```

```
PROCEDURE call_help(
   p_command  IN NUMBER,
   p_data     IN VARCHAR2,
   p_helpfile IN VARCHAR2 := :system.current_form||'.HLP');
   --
END;
```

The code passes commands using constants such as G_HELP_CONTENTS from the package specification. These correspond to commands that WinHelp expects to see. Table 14-2 contains some of the common command strings and their descriptions. Setting up constants allows you to use the command name in the package instead of having to remember the command numbers. The P_DATA (command value) variable is 0 unless otherwise described.

Help Command String	Description
HELP_CONTEXT	Shows topic with Context ID number in p_data.
HELP_QUIT	Exits the help file. Call this from POST-FORM.
HELP_INDEX	Shows Contents Topic.
HELP_CONTENTS	Same as HELP_INDEX.
HELP_HELPONHELP	Shows Help On Help (WINHELP.HLP).
HELP_SETCONTENTS	Same as SETINDEX.
HELP_SETINDEX	Sets the Contents Topic as p_data.
HELP_FORCEFILE	Forces the file you are passing parameters to be the one in p_data.
HELP_KEY	Finds the topic with keyword in p_data.
HELP_COMMAND	Executes the help command in p_data.
HELP_PARTIALKEY	Finds a topic with the keyword in p_data or shows a window with multiple matches.

TABLE 14-2. *Help Command Keywords*

The package body contains an initialization section to register the WinHelp function for use in PL/SQL. This initialization (the BEGIN section at the end of the package body) follows:

```
BEGIN
    v_opsys := get_application_property(OPERATING_SYSTEM);
    IF v_opsys != 'WEB'
    THEN
        v_libname        := 'USER32.DLL';
        v_functionname   := 'WinHelpA';
        --
        lh_USER := ora_ffi.find_library(v_libname);
        -- register function
        fh_WinHelp := ora_ffi.register_function(lh_USER,
            v_functionname, ora_ffi.PASCAL_STD);
        ora_ffi.register_parameter(fh_WinHelp, ORA_FFI.C_INT);
        ora_ffi.register_parameter(fh_WinHelp, ORA_FFI.C_CHAR_PTR);
        ora_ffi.register_parameter(fh_WinHelp, ORA_FFI.C_INT);
        ora_ffi.register_parameter(fh_WinHelp, ORA_FFI.C_CHAR_PTR);
        ora_ffi.register_return(fh_WinHelp, ORA_FFI.C_INT);
    END IF;
```

The actual body of the CALL_HELP procedure calls other dispatcher functions local to the body and is, itself, relatively simple, as the following listing shows:

```
PROCEDURE call_help(
    p_command   IN NUMBER,
    p_data      IN VARCHAR2,
    p_helpfile  IN VARCHAR2 := :system.current_form||'.HLP')
IS
    v_hwnd_l       PLS_INTEGER;
    v_helpfile_l   VARCHAR2(512) := p_helpfile;
    v_command_l    PLS_INTEGER;
    v_data_l       VARCHAR2(512) := p_data;
    v_rc           PLS_INTEGER;
BEGIN
    v_hwnd_l := TO_NUMBER(get_item_property(name_in(
        'SYSTEM.CURSOR_ITEM'),WINDOW_HANDLE));
    v_command_l := TO_NUMBER(p_command);
    v_rc   := i_WinHelp(fh_WinHelp,  v_hwnd_l, v_helpfile_l,
        v_command_l, v_data_l);
END;
```

You can then call WinHelp through the PL/SQL code as follows:

```
f_winhelp.call_help(f_winhelp.g_help_contents, ' ');
```

This will send WinHelp the proper command to display the Contents tab.

Menu Items and Toolbar Buttons

You need to provide a standard interface for your help system so users can quickly and easily load the help file. The interface consists of two categories: Menu Items and Toolbar Buttons.

The Help menu contains the following items:

- **Contents**   This calls WinHelp and loads the Contents help topic.

- **Help on Help**   This calls a standard Windows help file that describes how to use WinHelp.

- **Topic**   This shows a context-sensitive help topic.

- **Search**   This shows the help search window so the user can select or find a keyword in the system.

The menu item code for each of these contains code such as that shown earlier.

You need to attach the form library that contains the F_WINHELP package to the menu. In addition to these menu items, you can specify that the menu item display also as a toolbar button, or you can include a Help button on the canvas. The canvas help button issues a call to do_key('HELP'). This automatically fires a KEY-HELP trigger at the form level, which contains another call to CALL_HELP. If you want to use context sensitivity in your help system, you include a keyword in the help file for the name of every item (in the form of BLOCK.ITEM) on your form. You do not need to write a separate topic for each item—just attach each keyword (item name) to a topic appropriate to the item. For block-level help, you would write one topic and use all item names in that block as keywords. In this example, the form-level KEY-HELP trigger would be simply

```
f_winhelp.call_help;
```

The package uses a different version of CALL_HELP (not shown), which obtains the file name from the package variable, the command from the fact that this procedure invokes a keyword search, and the command value from the name of the item the cursor is on. The complexity is in the code, not in the call interface. Therefore, you can spend time on the initial package and use it everywhere you want in your forms with minimal effort.

Other Help Alternatives

Other than the table-based and WinHelp systems detailed earlier, there are a few other ideas that you might want to consider when determining what type of help system to create.

HTML-Based Help

The preference for help systems that serve applications deployed in a web environment is currently to use *HTML help* (hypertext markup language help). Both Microsoft and Oracle are moving away from the WinHelp engine and toward HTML used for web pages. This would make the help files more universal, as all platforms and sources could read the same file with their specific web browsers.

NOTE
The future of help systems may lie in Java help. Since you can hook JavaBeans into your form, you can obtain or build a bean that will function as a help engine.

Microsoft has a free product called HTML Help (available on Microsoft's web site) that allows you to create HTML files for use in help systems. These files have an embedded navigation tree that sits to the left of the help text and allows the user to jump to any topic easily. The files are compiled to make them faster to load. All help files are addressable by using a single URL. HTML Help is closely integrated with the Internet Explorer browser and Active-X technology. Although this product contains many user-friendly features, it ties you to a particular browser, and this strategy might not be viable in your environment.

CAUTION
Remember that, when you deploy your Forms applications on the Web using the Oracle Developer Server, you are giving up the option of using WinHelp. This is because the application is running on the application server, so any calls to the WinHelp DLL or executable will result in the help file being shown on the application server machine with unpredictable results (at best). Therefore, the main choice for a help system in web applications other than a table-based help system is an HTML help system that can be displayed in a web application.

You need to run a browser to call this type of help from Forms. If you are working in a client/server environment, this means you have to call the HOST built-in to run a browser. You start the browser with a command-line parameter of the location of the HTML file (either on a web server or from the local file system). If you are running on the Web (web-deployed forms), you can issue a call to the WEB.SHOW_DOCUMENT built-in to connect to the HTML file on the server. The benefit of implementing HTML help is that it is a fully featured ("The Works") help environment that contains graphics, fonts, colors, hypertext, hypergraphics, context sensitivity, and multiple levels. It is also platform independent, unlike the WinHelp solution.

Converting HLP to HTML
Many commercial help-authoring tools contain a facility to save the help files in HTML format. There are even conversion programs that create HTML files from .HLP files while preserving the graphics and links. This means that you could create a WinHelp file and run it through the conversion utility if you needed to support an Oracle Designer WebServer Generator application or if you were deploying Forms on the Web. This would also allow you to maintain both client/server and web versions of your help system. However, be prepared for the number of files to increase dramatically when you're using the HTML style of help. A WinHelp help system is normally one file or a small number of files that contain all topics and embedded graphics files. When you convert that system to HTML, there will probably be one file for each topic as well as one file for each embedded graphic file.

Designer-Generated Help Systems
Oracle Designer, a separate product from Oracle Developer, provides a help-system generator that parallels two of the options described in this chapter (table-based help and WinHelp). The table-based help facility extracts text defined in the *User Help Text* property for many of the Designer elements that comprise the form module definition. When you run the Form Generator to create .FMB and .FMX files in Designer, the generator will load the help text into a table. At runtime, the user activates the help system and displays a help form that is similar to the one described in this chapter. You can also explicitly load the help table from a Help Generator menu option.

Alternatively, you can generate WinHelp files from the same definitions in Designer. The Help Generator offers a dialog window that allows you to generate either table-based records or WinHelp files. You set a generator preference on the application or module level to specify which type of help you want to use. The form you generate from Designer will automatically contain the correct code to call the help system in a context-sensitive way. The WinHelp files created in this way are more basic than those you would create in a third-party tool, but depending upon the level of help you have decided to use, may do the job. The Designer front-end acts as the help-text maintenance form and allows you to edit the text.

Why Use Designer-Generated Help?

If you are using Oracle Designer to create final production forms or even initial prototype forms that you will modify with Oracle Developer, the table-based help generator will automatically load the help table or create the help file. It will also, without any additional code, insert the correct triggers and program units into your form to call the help system in a context-sensitive way. Getting bug-free code that works the way you want it to with virtually no effort is quite desirable. This is what Designer's Help Generator does. However, this only works if you have created the module and other definitions with help text for your form. Depending on the complexity of the form, this may not be an insignificant task. If you are not using Designer for anything else, it is probably not worth the effort just to generate the help system. It is beyond the scope of this book to go further into this option, but the Oracle Press book *Oracle Designer Handbook, 2ⁿᵈ Edition*, by these authors, contains a more detailed explanation. Another treatment of the Help Generator may be found in the Oracle Press book, *Oracle Designer Generation*, by Atkins, Dirksen, and Ince.

CHAPTER
15

Locator Forms

Attempt the end and never stand to doubt; nothing's so hard but search will find it out.
—Robert Herrick (1591–1674), *Seek and Find*

 n many systems, you are working in an environment with thousands, millions, or even tens of millions of records. You need to find a particular one. How should this be accomplished? If you happen to know the unique identifier for the row, it is simple to query the correct record. However, what if you don't know the object identifier?

Oracle provides a limited record-locating facility within Oracle Forms. In any block, you can set the form in "Enter Query" mode, and select one or more attributes. Then when you execute the query, it will bring back all of the records meeting your query criteria. This built-in query facility (a limited implementation of query-by-example, or QBE) is great for testing and prototyping but is not particularly user-friendly and is functionally limited. You cannot easily enter ranges of values to perform queries such as returning sales that occurred between a particular date range or to specify a list of values. You cannot easily return all projects where the Status is either "Open" or "Pending." You cannot easily exclude values, restrict the query to only projects that are not closed, or query by columns that are not base table items in the block, such as a list of all invoices that purchased machinery as one of their detailed items.

Frequently, the requirements for locating an item are more sophisticated than what basic Oracle functionality can provide. On an application that one of the authors worked on, it was necessary for a payment check from a customer to be credited to the appropriate account. However, checks often were received without the accompanying contract numbers. Time had to be spent figuring out which account the check should be posted to. Searching for checks expected at the same approximate time of the month or for approximately the amount indicated needed to be done. Other complex factors may be required to narrow a search such as this. Because of these types of requirements, you can create a dedicated Locator form, solely for the purpose of finding the appropriate object. This locator acts as the first tab of a multi-tab application, as described later in this chapter.

 NOTE
Users refer to places where data is selected or entered as "fields." Forms Developers would implement these fields as "items" using the Forms component of Oracle Developer.

A *locator* is composed of two blocks. The first is a series of data items where the user enters his or her query criteria information. The second block is a multi-record block displaying all records meeting the criteria specified in the first block. Figure 15-1 shows a simple locator to support finding an employee. Note that, in this system built for a retailer, you can query by the store the employee works in, the employee's

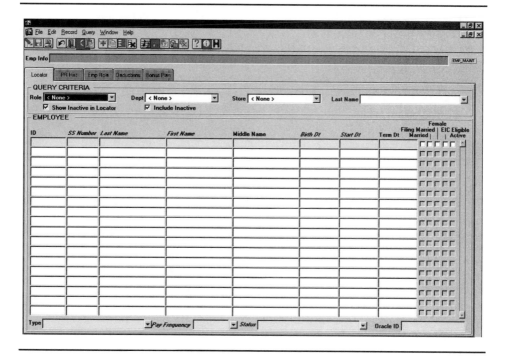

FIGURE 15-1. *Example of a locator application*

role in the organization, the employee's department, and his or her last name. This company only has a few hundred employees so this simple locator is sufficient.

The poplists in the query criteria area allow users to select from valid values for these fields. When users click on the Role poplist shown in Figure 15-1, they will see a list of valid roles to select from. The button next to the Last Name field opens an LOV showing all employee last names. Users can also type the first few letters of a last name in the Last Name field.

The user fills in one or more criteria and clicks on the Execute Query button. Employees meeting the selected criteria are displayed on the bottom half of the screen. To edit information associated with an Employee, the user double-clicks on the record to select that Employee.

Careful thought must be given to the selection of criteria necessary to locate a particular object. There are no obvious rules to determine what to query. A number of factors may influence your decision:

- The number of records you are selecting from

- How often the locator facility is used

- Specifics about the organization using the locator

If there are only a few hundred records in the whole table, sorting chronologically or alphabetically is usually sufficient. There is no need for a sophisticated locator when the user can scroll through a list of all of the items and make a selection. If you have ten million records and you only have the capability to query by status, then too many records will be returned by a query. The more records you have, the more sophisticated a locator you will need.

If the Locator is only used a few times a month, it doesn't matter too much that the user will have to scan through a few hundred records. If the locator is used by 25 operators 50 times per day, reducing the time spent locating a record by even a few seconds is worth the effort. The time savings alone will pay for the development costs of a more sophisticated locator quite quickly. The authors have encountered a system where there were two locators with the same level of sophistication built into each. One worked with a set of a few thousand records and was rarely used. The second locator supported millions of records with frequent use. System resources would have been more wisely spent making the second locator more sophisticated and limiting the first one to a few simple filter options.

How the users prefer to search for objects is the most important factor to consider in creating a locator application. You must ensure that users are querying by criteria that make sense to them.

Users are often unfamiliar with a locator-type application. They often don't understand how it works until you actually show them. So, rather than trying to perform a detailed analysis, it may be more useful to build a rapid prototype and let users play with it. After this exercise, they will be better able to tell you what search criteria they need.

Design of the Locator Items

For locators, you can use a relatively small set of different types of objects:

- **Single Field Numeric Items**   These items are mainly used for numeric IDs. Implementation involves adding to the *WHERE Clause* property on the results block where ID=:LOC.ID or something similar to this, where LOC is the locator block and ID is the search column.

- **Single Field Character Items**   These items are used to perform tasks such as name searches. Typically, the user types in the first few characters and the locator concatenates the % wildcard character to it. For example, if the user types in "FRE" and presses the Search button, he or she would get back "FRED, FREDERICK, etc."

- **Poplists and LOVs**   These are described in the next section.

■ **Range Items** This type of item can be used for text, dates, or numbers. The user enters information into two items. These are most commonly used with age ranges and date ranges. Examples might include contracts initiated between a certain date range or a range of alphanumeric contract identifiers.

When searching on a character field, you usually want your search to be case-insensitive. You can do this by converting both the search criteria and the compared value to uppercase or lowercase. Unfortunately, this requires a full table scan through the queried table to retrieve the appropriate records. The traditional solution is to place a redundant column in the database that is an uppercase conversion of the text field. Then you can perform an uppercase conversion of the query criteria and search against the redundant column.

With Oracle8i, this strategy is no longer necessary since you can directly index a function of a column without explicitly creating the redundant column.

TIP

When you create an index on a function of a column, Oracle creates the redundant column internally. There is still an equivalent storage impact but creating an index on the function of a column better encapsulates the logic and makes for a cleaner developer interface.

Poplists and LOVs

Poplists are used to select a single value from predefined lists of values. These are used in a wide variety of situations for selecting everything from a small list of values (such as filtering by the color of an object) to larger lists. With any item where you use a poplist or an LOV for selecting a value for data entry, you would use a poplist or LOV for query purposes. For further discussion of poplists and LOVs, see Chapter 16.

NOTE

Poplists are frequently used in a locator when filtering by a Boolean item. This is because you must be able to filter by whether a value is TRUE, FALSE, or NULL. A filter criterion for gender must be able to include M, F, or no filter.

Both poplists and LOVs can be used in pairs. For example, you might have two poplists, one for department and one for employee, in a locator that returns projects. If you select the department without the employee, the locator will return all projects supervised by anyone in that department. If you filter solely by employee, the locator will return all projects supervised by that employee. It does not make sense to filter by a department and an employee who does not work in that department since no records would be returned. Therefore, you can make the department and employee list include the following functionality:

- If you select a department and the value of the employee LOV/poplist is inconsistent (the employee doesn't work in that department), then the Employee LOV/poplist is assigned a "null" value.

- If there is already a value in the department LOV/poplist and you activate the LOV/poplist for the employee object, then only employees who work for the selected department are displayed.

Check Boxes

You usually use two check boxes in the locator query criteria as Figure 15-1 shows. The first is to show inactive results (records whose inactive flag is checked). It is not customary to provide the capability of selecting only inactive records. The user must either select all records or only active records. If the user clicks on an Inactive check box, the locator will not filter out inactive records. The second check box allows the user to query by values that are no longer active. For example, past projects are given a status of "Canceled." This is no longer a valid status and has been marked "Inactive" as the reference value. Typically, in a poplist, users will only see valid values. For the query criteria, if this check box is checked, any poplist with the query criteria will return the inactive as well as the active values.

Implementing Locator Query Criteria

The first step in implementing Locator query criteria is to create a block called LOC. This is where all locator objects are placed. Next, place query items into the locator using the consistent set of naming standards for your organization. The implementation of each type of item is discussed in the following sections.

Implementing the Locator

The basic strategy for implementing the locator is to allow the user to select some number of query criteria and click the Execute Query button on the toolbar. The Execute Query button fires the EXECUTE-QUERY trigger at the form level. This calls the EXECUTE_QUERY procedure within the menu package. The P_EXECUTE_QUERY procedure checks to see if the cursor is in the query criteria or query results block. If the cursor is in either of these blocks, then the EXECUTE_QUERY procedure calls the LOC_WHERE procedure. The LOC_WHERE procedure builds a complex WHERE clause based upon the values entered in the query criteria and attaches that WHERE clause to the results block using the SET_BLOCK_PROPERTY built-in to modify the *WHERE clause* property of the results block. Then, LOC_WHERE executes the query for the results block. Therefore, all complex coding is placed into the LOC_WHERE procedure.

Implementing Simple Numeric and Simple Character Items

The code for numeric and character items is very different. All locator query criteria require building a large WHERE clause and attaching it to the query results block. The procedure T_LISTVAR.F_QUOTE automatically places single quotes around a string. The procedure T_LISTVAR.F_BUILD_AND_STRING takes the original WHERE clause and concatenates it with the new WHERE clause criteria. The Filter on Inactive area assumes that the underlying table flags inactive records using an ACTIV_YN field. The following code example shows filtering by last name.

```
-- Filter on Last Name --
--
IF :loc_emp_maint.disp_emp_id IS NOT NULL
THEN
    v_cur_clause := 'LAST_NAME_TX LIKE ' || f_listvar.add_quote(
        '%' || :loc_emp_maint.disp_emp_id || '%');
    v_where_clause := f_listvar.build_and_string(v_where_clause, v_cur_clause);
END IF;


--
-- Filter on Inactive --
--
IF :loc_emp_maint.inactiv != 'Y'
THEN
    v_cur_clause := 'EMP.ACTIV_YN = ''Y''';
    v_where_clause := f_listvar.build_and_string(
        v_where_clause,v_cur_clause);
END IF;
--
-- Set the block property and execute the query
set_block_property('EMP', DEFAULT_WHERE, V_WHERE_CLAUSE);
go_block('EMP');
execute_query;
```

Note that this code can easily be made simpler by building a few generic routines that replace much of the above code. For example, a routine to build an equality portion of the WHERE clause for a simple character item is shown below:

```
PROCEDURE set_equal(
    p_inout_where IN OUT VARCHAR2,
    p_in_column VARCHAR2,
    p_in_text VARCHAR2)
IS
```

```
      v_cur_clause  VARCHAR2(200);
BEGIN
   IF NOT text_is_null(p_in_column)
   THEN
      v_cur_clause := p_in_column ||' LIKE ''' ||
         RTRIM(p_in_text)||'%''';
      p_inout_where := f_listvar.build_and_string(
         p_inout_where, v_cur_clause);
   END IF;
END;
```

This procedure is stored in the template library in a package called 'F_LOC,' then when the developer wants to query by a text item, he or she need only write one line of code that calls this routine. For example, the above department filter could be replaced with the following:

```
f_loc.is_equal(v_whereclause, 'LAST_NAME',
   :loc_emp_maint.disp_emp_lname);
```

A similar routine to support filtering by date ranges is shown below:

```
PROCEDURE from_to(
    p_in_disp VARCHAR2,
    p_inout_where_ IN OUT VARCHAR2,
    p_in_column VARCHAR2,
    p_in_from_dt DATE,
    p_in_to_dt DATE)
IS
    v_cur_clause VARCHAR2(200);
    FUNCTION date_string (
       p_in_dt DATE)
       RETURN VARCHAR2
    IS
    BEGIN
       RETURN 'TO_DATE(''' || TO_CHAR(p_in_dt, 'DD-MON-YYYY') ||
          ''',''DD-MON-YYYY'') ';
    END date_string;
BEGIN
    IF p_in_from_dt > p_in_to_dt
    THEN
       f_alert.ok('Error: The ' || p_in_disp || ' FROM value is ' ||
          'greater than the TO value you entered.', f_global.g_no_fail);
    END IF;
    --
    IF p_in_from_dt is not null
       AND p_in_to_dt IS NOT NULL
    THEN -- From/To filled in
```

```
        v_cur_clause := p_in_column || ' BETWEEN ' ||
            date_string(p_in_from_dt) || ' AND ' || date_string(p_in_to_dt);
        p_inout_where := f_listvar.build_and_string(p_inout_where,
            v_cur_clause);
    ELSIF in_from_dt IS NOT NULL
    THEN
        v_cur_clause := p_in_column || ' > ' || date_string(p_in_from_dt);
        p_inout_where := f_listvar.build_and_string(p_inout_where,
            v_cur_clause);
    ELSIF in_to_dt IS NOT NULL
    THEN
        v_cur_clause := p_in_column || ' < =' || date_string(p_in_to_dt);
        p_inout_where := f_listvar.build_and_string(p_inout_where,
            v_cur_clause);
    END IF;
END from_to;
```

Note that you are building a WHERE clause that is assigned to the *WHERE clause* property in the results block. You also have example code to support individual items and range items. Once the locator query block is built, creating the code to generate the complex WHERE clause only requires a few minutes of coding.

Querying from Another Table

For simple and range items, as long as they are within the base table or view of the query, the code is the same every time. However, you may occasionally want to query by things outside of the base table. For example, you might want to issue queries for: "Find sales where at least one of the items purchased was a tool," or "Show the maintenance to be performed on equipment over five years old." Querying of this type cannot be done with genericized code. Explicit custom code must be written to support this level of functionality. The following code allows us to retrieve sales where a specific type of credit card was used. In this example, the sales are stored in the PYMT table, not in the base table for the queried block.

```
-- Filter on Card Company Name --
--
IF :loc_sale.card_name IS NOT NULL
THEN
    v_cur_clause := 'sale_id IN (
        SELECT p.sale_id
        FROM   pymt p
        WHERE  p.ref_card_co_cd = ' ||
        f_listvar.add_quote(:loc_sale.card_name) || ')';
    v_where_clause := f_listvar.build_and_string(v_where_clause,
        v_cur_clause);
END IF;
```

Note that, in such cases, you use a subquery from another table instead of from the same table as the table's block.

Querying by Generic Items

When embracing generic modeling, occasionally you will need to do something different. Even variable names will need to be selected from the database. The portion of a data model, drawn in both ERD and UML notations in the following illustration, shows events of various types on a project.

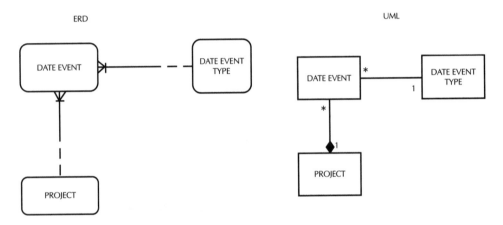

In this example, there are events of various types on a project. This model can support all workflow events on a project such as "Approval," "Initiation," or "Completion." The traditional approach is to have several date columns in the PROJECT table, one each for Approval Date, Initiation Date, and Completion Date. By moving the dates into their own table, there can be any number of different dates associated with a project. For this type of structure, you would use the user interface shown next for the date query criteria.

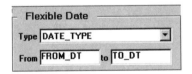

All of this code is hand-written using only the ADD_QUOTE and BUILD_AND_ STRING template library functions, available from the authors' web sites. Depending upon which of the two date fields are filled in, the procedure builds the appropriate subquery.

The code to support this part of the locator follows:

```
-- Filter on Flexible Date Range --
--
IF :loc_merch_move.date_type IS NOT NULL
THEN
    IF :loc_merch_move.from_dt IS NOT NULL AND
       :loc_merch_move.to_dt IS NOT NULL
    THEN
        v_cur_clause := ' MERCH_MOVE_ID IN (SELECT '||
            ' mmd.merch_move_id FROM merch_move_date mmd, ref_date rd ' ||
            'WHERE mmd.merch_move_dt BETWEEN  ' || f_listvar.add_quote(
            to_char(:loc_merch_move.from_dt, 'DD-MON-YYYY')) ||
            'AND ' || f_listvar.add_quote(TO_CHAR(:loc_merch_move.to_dt,
            'DD-MON-YYYY')) || 'AND mmd.ref_date_cd = rd.ref_date_cd ' ||
            'AND rd.name_tx = ' || f_listvar.add_quote(
            :loc_merch_move.date_type) || ')';
    ELSIF :loc_merch_move.from_dt IS NOT NULL
    THEN
        v_cur_clause := ' merch_move_id IN (SELECT ' ||
            ' mmd.merch_move_id FROM merch_move_date mmd, ref_date rd ' ||
            'WHERE mmd.merch_move_dt > ' || f_listvar.add_quote(TO_CHAR(
            :loc_merch_move.from_dt, 'DD-MON-YYYY')) ||
            'AND mmd.ref_date_cd = rd.ref_date_cd ' ||
            'AND rd.name_tx = ' || f_listvar.add_quote(
            :loc_merch_move.date_type) || ')';
    ELSIF :loc_merch_move.to_dt IS NOT NULL
    THEN
        v_cur_clause := ' merch_move_id IN ( ' ||
            'SELECT mmd.merch_move_id FROM merch_move_date mmd, ' ||
            'ref_date rd WHERE mmd.merch_move_dt < ' ||
            f_listvar.add_quote(TO_CHAR(:loc_merch_move.to_dt,
            'DD-MON-YYYY')) || ' AND mmd.ref_date_cd = rd.ref_date_cd '||
            'AND rd.name_tx = ' || f_listvar.add_quote(
            :loc_merch_move.date_type)||')';
    END IF;
    v_where_clause := f_listvar.build_and_string(v_where_clause,
            v_cur_clause);
END IF;
```

You can have as many of these flexible selection items as needed so that users can select by three or four criteria. You could even make a multi-record control block and loop through the block in order to generate the appropriate code. To date, the authors have never found a need to do this.

The check box to support "Show Inactive Values" requires no code in the procedure. The record groups that populate the poplists and LOVs are built to support the check box as in the following example:

```
SELECT  ' < None > ', NULL ref_move_cd
FROM    dual
UNION ALL
```

```
SELECT  name_tx, ref_move_cd
FROM    ref_move
WHERE   activ_yn IN (DECODE(:stuff.incld_inactiv_yn,
        'Y', 'N', 'Y'), 'Y')
ORDER BY 1
--activ = 'Y' or (activ = 'N' and incld inactiv = 'Y')
```

You can modify the default WHERE clause using the following code:

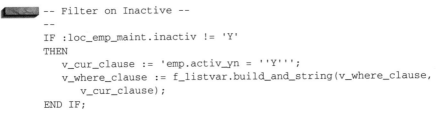

```
-- Filter on Inactive --
--
IF :loc_emp_maint.inactiv != 'Y'
THEN
    v_cur_clause := 'emp.activ_yn = ''Y''';
    v_where_clause := f_listvar.build_and_string(v_where_clause,
        v_cur_clause);
END IF;
```

Locator Results Block

The locator results block is a standard base table block with as many items as will fit horizontally. This block is usually only used for viewing information with the editing of that information done elsewhere. However, if the table only has a few columns and they can all be displayed in the query results block, it can also be used to edit the information. The naming of the block requires no special naming conventions.

Sorting the Results Block

There are several alternatives for sorting in the results block:

■ **Hard-code a specific ordering.** This is usually enough.

■ **Allow the user to perform ascending or descending sorts** by any column in the display. This means that you may end up having to sort by a non-base table column. To support this, you should create an updateable view and allow the user to order by any column in the view. For the user interface, you can place small sort buttons next to each item, which are named the same as the item. They are attached with the suffix ORDER_BY and the associated template code takes care of the rest. The changing of the button label causes the appropriate Up/Down arrows to be selected from Wingdings (Label font for button). Chapter 24 explains how to create a variation on this system of sort buttons. Chapter 25 provides a technique for using symbolic characters as button labels.

CHAPTER
16

Multi-valued
Selection Objects

Guess if you can, choose if you dare.

—Pierre Corneille (1606–1684) *Heraclius* (IV, iv)

There are many instances where you need to assign a value to an item and this value will be selected from a finite set of values. This can be as simple as selecting whether a record is active or not, specifying the gender or marital status of an individual, or selecting the appropriate value from thousands or even millions of records. This chapter discusses a number of objects you can use to display these values. All of these objects, with the exception of the lists of values (LOVs), have something in common. They each include a display value and the actual stored value. For example, with a check box, the user sees the box as checked or unchecked. Programmatically, this is either "Y," "N," or some other value. For a radio group, the user sees a set of circles and labels, one of which is selected. Programmatically, this is a single value, which corresponds to the selected item. List items (poplists, combo boxes, and T-lists) all include a list of paired values—one in the database and one that is displayed. The user interface for each of these objects is shown in Figure 16-1.

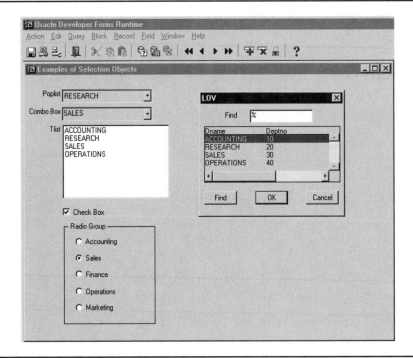

FIGURE 16-1. *Selection object user interfaces*

This duality of display and stored values is important to keep in mind. As a programmer, you do not usually have access to the displayed values, but only the underlying data values. You cannot write "If check box 1 is checked" in the program or "If radio group 1, Item 3 is selected…" You can use the GET LIST ELEMENT LABEL built-in to retrieve the label of a list element record but you will need to know the number of that record. All you immediately know is the underlying data value. From there, you need to determine which element this is by querying the database or walking through the record group. You can retrieve the displayed value in the list item but it is not very convenient.

An LOV is somewhat different from the other objects discussed in this chapter. It is made up of any number of columns (like a virtual table), one or more of which are displayed and any number of which are not displayed. When a row is selected, the LOV values can be assigned to any item in the form.

A number of factors go into selecting the appropriate GUI selection object. If there are only two valid values ("Active" and "Inactive"), a check box can be used. With only a few items to select from, you might want to use a radio group or a poplist. Any list that contains more than a few hundred records requires the use of an LOV because its improved search capability and flexibility become much more important as the number of items in the list increases.

Check Boxes

Check boxes use very little screen real estate and are intuitively obvious. They require no user training. Check boxes can only be used for two-value items since the box must be checked or unchecked as for Yes/No or True/False indicators. Frequently, an item may be nullable. This means that the item really has three values—Yes/No/Null. If Null is meaningful, then you cannot use a check box as the user interface. For example, with a gender item, depending upon the context, it may or may not be a nullable field as demonstrated in the following examples:

- In an Employer Human Resources database, it is likely that the gender of employees will be known.

- If you are dealing with a Contacts database for an organization where information comes in on printed forms, gender may not be known and a check box cannot be used.

If you are going to build a locator query form as an "Employee Finder" and list people of one or the other gender, even if the attribute is two-valued and can't be nullable, you cannot use a check box because you might want to retrieve men, women, or both. You should also consider the issue of gender neutrality. With the gender flag on Employee, does "checked" represent Male or Female? Although this is the logical interface, this may be a sensitive issue.

The visual appearance of a check box is governed by the operating system. As a result, check boxes can look different in different deployments. In MS Windows 3.1, check boxes appeared as small white squares filled in with an "x" when selected. In MS Windows 95 or 98 and MS Windows NT, the check box is a small square with a check mark showing when selected. In UNIX, the check box appears as a depressed button-like object when selected. The MS Windows interfaces are clear and user-friendly. The UNIX check box item is less obvious. You need to look carefully to see if the button is depressed or not. If you want to emulate the MS Windows check box look in a UNIX environment, you could create your check box object using a small field or button that, when selected, looks similar to that of the Windows 3.1 check box. This can be easily handled using WHEN-MOUSE-CLICKED triggers and changing either the value in the case of a field, or the label in the case of a button.

Implementing Check Boxes

In the template, there are only two SmartClasses for check boxes, one with initial value "Y" and one with initial value "N." Note that "Y" and "N" are used and not T/F. This is because Boolean is not a datatype within the database.

Check boxes are often used in multi-record blocks with one or more check boxes next to each other. This makes label placement without wasting screen real estate difficult. The solution to this is to move the label up several pixels and connect the label to the item with a black line. Several other options were explored, such as placing the labels vertically or on an angle. Vertical placement of labels tends to waste more space and can be difficult to read. Labels placed on an angle caused the characters to lose readability. Note the placement of the check box labels (Married, Female, EIC on the right side of the form) in Figure 16-2.

Check boxes can be based on base table columns. The most common use for check boxes is to attach them to mandatory base table items. Note that, just as on any field, the initial value on a check box is not assigned this value until the cursor moves to the record. Even if the initial value for the check box is the checked value, until the record for that check box is active, the check box will always appear unchecked. This can sometimes be disconcerting to users, particularly on single record blocks. You might want to use a GO_BLOCK on the WHEN-NEW-FORM-INSTANCE trigger to navigate to the blocks with check boxes in order to instantiate the initial values.

Check boxes should only be used for two-value items with valid values that are static and not likely to change in the future. The most common place to use check boxes is for an active (Y or N) item or another, similar flag item. Careful thought should be given to using check boxes for items such as the status of an application as "Pending" or "Complete." It is possible that a third status may be desirable at some future point in time. Whenever a two-value, not-null field is desired, check boxes are usually the best choice. However, there have been many applications that

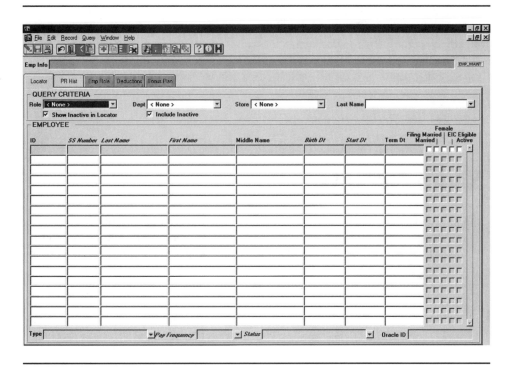

FIGURE 16-2. *Placing labels*

required redesign near production when developers mistakenly used a check box when it was not appropriate.

You should also specify whether you want the check box checked or unchecked if a value other than "Y" or "N" is passed to it. The authors' template SmartClass will also inherit the *Checkbox Mapping of Other Values* property. This property's value is "Unchecked."

In naming check boxes, as with any other item, the naming convention states that the name of the check box is the same as the database column, so if the name of the column is ACTIV_YN, then the check box is named ACTIV_YN.

Assigning a value to a check box can be accomplished just as with any other variable. You can assign the active Y/N flag to be "Y" without the user having to click on it. For example, use the following to assign the value "Y" to the ACTIV_YN item:

```
:emp.activ_yn := 'Y';
```

The WHEN-CHECKBOX-CHANGED trigger can be used to perform actions whenever the user clicks on the check box. This trigger fires after the value has already changed. Assume that a check box has "Y" as the checked value and "N" as the unchecked value. If you wanted to trigger the execution of a procedure called "my_proc" based on this action, the code is written as shown below:

```
IF :emp.activ_yn = 'Y' THEN
    my_proc;
END IF;
```

Radio Groups

A radio group consists of a set of one or more buttons. Since check boxes can handle two-valued items, radio groups usually have three or more buttons, each representing a separate value. It is the whole collection of radio buttons that forms the item. In a radio group, only one value can be selected at a time. If you want to simultaneously select multiple values in a group, you would use a collection of check boxes because you really require multiple items, not multiple values of a single item.

Radio groups are not often used because they are used for at least three values (since a check box is usually used for two values). By designing the user interface with radio groups, you are hard-coding values for radio groups in the database. You cannot easily change the allowable values without modifying the application. Radio groups should only be used when you are sure that the values will not change over time. You can change the value if you map the hard-coded value to a lookup table. You would have to manage that with some code that loads and queries the data correctly, but it is possible.

There are two places where you would commonly use a radio group. The first place is as a hard-coded set of range filters. An example of this would be a query screen used to retrieve Employee records by age. The relevant ranges are "Under 20," "21–30," "31–40," "41–65," and "Over 65." Keep in mind that even these ranges may need to be changed. For example, for many years, 65 has been used as the most common retirement age. Now, due to changes in demographics, that number has been changed to 62 or 67 in many organizations.

The second and most common use for radio groups is in a user interface on a table with an exclusive OR relationship. This can occur if an object is of one or more types and you display a separate stacked canvas depending upon the value of the radio group. For example, a customer can be an organization or a person. If you select organization, you would get one set of items and if you select person, you would get a different set of items. When records from this table are queried, you need to determine the value of the radio group. In the example above, if the record represents an organization, the value of ORG_ID is not null. If the record represents a person, then PERSON_ID is not null. Thus, the value of the radio group can be set using the following function that can be called from the SELECT list in an updateable view:

```
decode(org_id, NULL, 'PERSON','ORG')
```

This assumes that you have a radio group with two radio buttons with the values PERSON and ORG.

If the table can hold more than two kinds of objects as shown in the ERD in Figure 16-3, then you can nest the DECODE function in the SELECT list of the view, as shown below:

```
decode(contact_id, NULL, decode(CUST_ID, 'EMP', 'CUST'), 'CONTACT')
```

An example screen from an application that supports both individuals and organizations is shown in Figure 16-4.

In the authors' experience, radio groups are not often used. Even with the situation described above, this structure could be modeled generically so that you could add a new type of customer by adding data to a reference table. Types of customers would be stored in the database in a small table. A poplist or an LOV would be used to query the database and select valid customer types. There is no easy way to add radio group values at runtime.

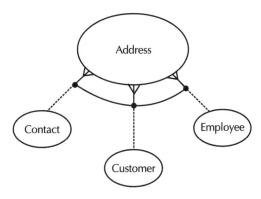

FIGURE 16-3. *ERD showing an "exclusive OR" relationship*

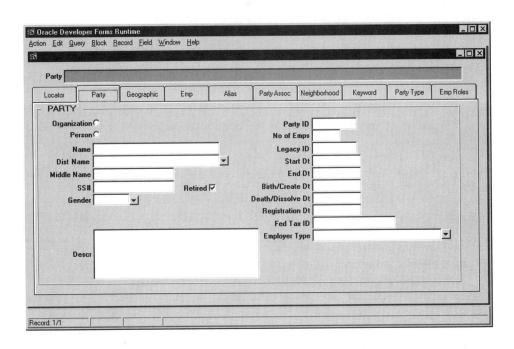

FIGURE 16-4. *Application that supports data entry of persons or organizations*

Implementation of Radio Groups

The authors use radio groups so infrequently that a single SmartClass for the radio group and a second SmartClass for the radio group item is sufficient. Alternatively, you can store a radio group in your object library and drag and drop it into your forms when needed.

One useful feature of radio groups is that the radio group items can be placed anywhere on the same canvas. Creating radio groups is not difficult. In the Layout Editor, when you create a radio group, two objects will be created in the Object Navigator—a radio group and a single radio button within that group, as shown in Figure 16-5.

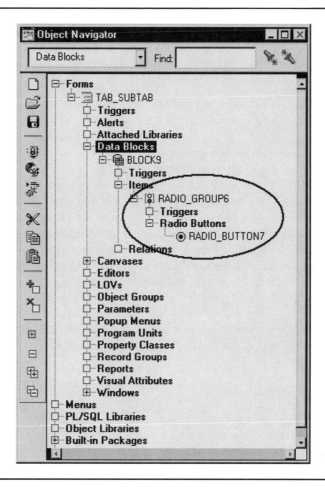

FIGURE 16-5.   *Object Navigator after creating a radio group*

The fastest way to create additional buttons and to set up the radio group is to follow the steps below:

1. Click on a radio button in either the Layout Editor or Object Navigator and duplicate it as many times as needed by pressing CTRL-D.

2. Select the radio group and set the *Data Type* property. This is only set once for the whole group.

3. Select individual radio buttons and set the *Radio Button Value* property on each. Also set the Prompt properties. Radio buttons have both labels and prompts, which both display text that will appear near the radio button. The *Label* property on radio groups is included for consistency with earlier versions and should no longer be used.

4. Set the *Initial Value* property of the radio group, if desired. The initial value of the radio group indicates what the default value of the radio group will be.

Radio group naming conventions should follow those for any other item. If a base table column is attached to a column STATUS_CD, then the name of the radio group will be STATUS_CD. For actual radio group items, use the exact value for the button. If it is numeric, you cannot start a name with a number, so add a "VAL_" prefix to the selection value to form the button name. For example, if the value of a specific radio button is ORG, then the name of that radio button should be ORG. If the value of the radio button were 5, then the name would be VAL_5.

Radio groups should only be used for a very small and stable number of values. This is not to say that there is any formal rule. You could have an onscreen questionnaire with dozens of different items in a single radio group. However, the authors have rarely built one with more than five or six.

Assigning a value to a radio group can be done just as with any other variable. You can assign the status to be "OPEN" without the user having to click on it, as shown in the code below:

```
:dept.status := 'OPEN';
```

This code will programmatically assign a value to the radio group. The value you assign must be the value of one of the radio buttons.

Triggering activity based on a radio group selection can also be accomplished. Most commonly, this is used to store some information about the record in another place. This is done with the WHEN-RADIO-CHANGED trigger. This trigger fires after the value has already changed. If you want to trigger an event when status is changed to "CLOSED," then you would use the code shown below:

```
IF :my_block.status_cd = 'CLOSED' THEN …
```

List Items

There are three types of list items: poplists, T-lists, and combo boxes, as shown in Figure 16-1. In the past, poplists and combo boxes were used in many applications built by the authors. T-lists were used infrequently. Several poplists (Role, Department, Store, and Last Name) are shown in Figure 16-2. When the user clicks on the poplist down arrow, a list of possible values appears and whatever is selected will be displayed.

When the user presses the key for the first letter of an item in the list, the selection will jump to the value with that first letter. If the user presses that key again, the selection will move to the next item in the list with the same first letter.

A combo box is similar to a poplist with a small space between the field and the button. The user can also type in an entry in a combo box, although the new value will not subsequently appear in this item for other records.

A T-list appears as a rectangular box and displays a fixed number of values, as shown in Figure 16-1.

You can either hard-code valid values for list items or assign them at runtime through a record group using the POPULATE_LIST command. Chapter 25 contains a tip for dynamically populating list items from a query. Since record groups can be populated from the database, this allows you to populate a poplist from the database.

Implementing Poplists

List items can get their values from two different sources:

- Hard-coded values entered through the *Elements in List* property.

- Values populated from a record group. The record group can either be built at design time as a static list of values populated from a query or built programmatically at runtime.

TIP
You can delete a hard-coded list element by using either the BACKSPACE *or* DELETE *key and navigating to a different element.*

Populating Poplists from a Record Group

Chapter 25 contains a tip for dynamically loading a poplist from a query in a record group. It is useful to examine some extensions to that technique in the context of how to use poplists. Once the record group is created, you can insert the contents of the record group in the poplist. The record group used to populate a poplist must be exactly two columns and the data value must match the declared datatype of the poplist. The authors got into the habit of always putting a TO_CHAR on numeric columns to ensure that applications worked smoothly. Since Forms is not strongly typed between screen and database items, you can have a character poplist linked to a numeric database column.

Typically, when using a poplist, you want to include the option of "no selection." From a user's perspective, this is simple to do by including "none" as an explicit option. You can perform a UNION ALL with an explicit null value as in the following example:

```
SELECT    '<null>' dname, NULL deptno
FROM      dual
UNION ALL
SELECT    dname, deptno
FROM      dept
ORDER BY 1
```

Notice the ORDER BY on the query. All queries populating poplists should have an ORDER BY clause on the record group query to explicitly declare the sort order on the display items. When writing the query for a record group, if the columns are not base table columns or if they are functions, they should be aliased so that the column mappings don't use system-defined names. It is hard to know what a system-defined name refers to. This can make debugging difficult.

Assigning a value to a poplist can be done just as with any other variable. For example, you could assign a status to be "OPEN" without the user having to select it in the poplist, as shown in the code below:

```
:problem.status := 'OPEN';
```

This code will programmatically assign a value to the list item. Triggering activity based on a list selection can also be accomplished. The syntax for retrieving the value of a list item is the same as in the previous radio group example. Code triggered by selecting a value should be attached to the WHEN-LIST-CHANGED trigger.

A Limitation of Poplists

When considering whether to use a poplist for a particular purpose, be aware of one limitation. You cannot include a value for display that is not in the list elements (valid values). While you can define a value in the *Mapping of Other Values* property that displays if an undefined value is retrieved from the database, this may not represent the data in the way that you want. This limitation can be a problem with inactivated values. For example, your form contains a block based on the CUSTOMERS table. This block contains a poplist (loaded from a record group query on the COMPANIES table) that is used to select a company name. One of the columns, called ACTIVE, in the company table indicates whether the company is an active company for the list. Your poplist record group query would contain a WHERE clause to restrict the records to only active companies—"WHERE ACTIVE='Y'". However, the CUSTOMERS table may contain records that refer to an inactive company. If you have a poplist on the COMPANY_ID item in the CUSTOMERS block and that poplist was loaded from the active companies query, customer records that referred to an inactive company would not be displayed.

Lists of Values (LOVs)

From a functional perspective, LOVs, as shown in Figure 16-1, are not much different from poplists and radio groups. However, from a developer's perspective, an LOV is very different. One implementation of it can consist of five separate objects:

- The display value

- The data value

- A button to call the LOV

- The LOV itself

- A record group to populate the LOV

The user sees the display field with a button next to it on the screen. When the user clicks the button, the LOV is displayed. The user will see a list of the display column values (the data item column or any other can also be displayed). When an item is selected, the display information is passed into the display item and the data is passed into the data item (which may or may not be displayed). For example, when selecting an employee, ID may or may not be displayed but the name would be displayed. Clicking on the button brings up a list of employee names and IDs. When an employee name is selected, the name is copied into a display field and the ID into a data field. If this record is to be displayed, you will need a POST-QUERY trigger to populate the name. A better solution is to base the whole block on an updateable view and the Employee name would be populated by the view on the server side.

One advantage of using an LOV is that you can display as many columns as desired. Poplists are limited to one column for display and one column for the data value. Since the display item is not populated using the LOV when the record is queried, you don't need to worry about which record group is being accessed for display or modification. It is possible to have LOVs dependent upon values in other items. For example, with little difficulty, a multi-record block with a department LOV selection can be followed by an employee LOV selection where the EMP values are restricted to the department selected.

LOVs have a built-in search capability on the first column in the LOV. If the allowable list of values is very large (more than 10,000), you can suppress automatic querying until the user has typed in the first few characters of the item they want retrieved and have this filter applied before values are displayed. This is accomplished by selecting "Let the user filter records before displaying them" in the LOV Wizard when creating the LOV or by setting the *Filter Before Display* property in the LOV itself to "Yes."

If you are querying from a recursive tree structure, you can create the LOV so that when the button is clicked, you will only see the top level of the tree. Item selection automatically navigates to child records of the selected record, making it possible to use LOVs to select from a list of records that may include millions of records.

All of this flexibility does not come without cost. It takes a few seconds longer to create an LOV than it does to create a poplist. However, with the new LOV Wizard as part of Release 6.0 of Oracle Developer-Developer Server, the additional development cost of an LOV over a poplist is negligible.

Implementation of LOVs

The challenge of implementing LOVs is to minimize the amount of time required to create them.

A new feature of Release 6 is the easy-to-use LOV Wizard. This wizard walks you through the process of building the LOV easily and efficiently. The only limitation is that when you are selecting return values, the name of the returned item (block name.item name) must be 31 characters or less. If your item name is longer than 31 characters, the LOV Wizard truncates the item name without warning.

From a developer's perspective, to mimic the functionality of a poplist, you only need to run the LOV Wizard, create two fields and one button, and write one line of code, as shown here:

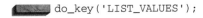

```
do_key('LIST_VALUES');
```

TIP
If you want to have a column in your LOV that you don't want to display, you can set its Display Width *property to "0." In this way, you can use the column as a return value source but not display it to the user.*

CHAPTER
17

Integrating Forms and
Reports

Let's get together...yeah, yeah, yeah.
      —Hayley Mills and Hayley Mills, *The Parent Trap,* Walt Disney Studios, 1961

he Oracle Developer Forms (Forms) and Reports (Reports) products were traditionally thought of as independent components of Oracle Developer. Forms is used to create screen applications, and Reports supports printed reporting requirements. Unfortunately, even system designers view these two types of applications (screen and printed reports) separately. This is a mistake. Screen applications and report applications should be considered together when you are designing a system, for a number of reasons.

First, there are system requirements that may be met by either a screen application or a printed report. The system designer must decide whether to support a given requirement using a screen application, printed report, or both. For example, you might use a locator form (as described in Chapter 15) to easily find records and view particular objects in the database. This means that numerous reports with hundreds of pages including extensive lists of one type of object or another (purchase orders, customer lists, and so on) may no longer be necessary. Conversely, if you are going to keep PDF (Adobe Portable Document Format) versions of all written correspondence, then there may not be a reason to have applications capable of regenerating a letter. You can't count on being able to compartmentalize forms and reports requirements.

The second reason, as discussed in Chapter 8, is that it is extremely effective to use forms and reports together to build flexible reporting systems. It is critical that the project technical architect has a thorough understanding of both Oracle Forms and Oracle Reports. Otherwise, one or more of the following situations will occur:

- You will end up with a sub-optimal system design because your system will include the same functionality in two places.

- You will have many extra reports with limited functionality.

This chapter discusses the techniques and built-ins required to call Reports from Forms. Calling Forms from Reports will not be discussed.

Calling Reports from Forms

There are two built-ins you can use to run a report from a form. Traditionally, the command used has been RUN_PRODUCT. This command can still be used. However, there is now a slightly easier command to use that works specifically for calling a report from forms: RUN_REPORT_OBJECT. This command is a function and not a procedure.

The RUN_PRODUCT command should be familiar to most developers. You simply pass the report file name as a parameter. Using the RUN_REPORT_OBJECT built-in function requires some preparation. First, you need to create a report object in the Reports section of the Form Builder Object Navigator. You can either base this report object on an existing report, or have Oracle Forms automatically build a simple report based on the block. In the report object, there are several common properties: Destination Type, Destination Name, and Destination Format can be used in lieu of setting these parameters in a parameter list.

You can pass a parameter list to RUN_REPORT_OBJECT as the second parameter to the command.

NOTE
In the help file, the ability to pass a parameter list using the RUN_REPORT_OBJECT built-in is not mentioned.

The actual syntax for RUN_REPORT_OBJECT involves passing two parameters. The first is either a report name or report ID. The second (which is optional) is the parameter list name or ID. You should always use the RUN_REPORT_OBJECT command since there are many useful features associated with it that can be utilized. Specifically, you can ascertain the status of the running of a report without having to use an odd work-around.

In earlier versions of Oracle Reports, there was no easy way to find out if a report had completely executed from the Forms component of Developer. In the past, this required the report to write to a global variable or to make a database update (when completed) that the form would query to check the status of the report. Now, if you are using the Reports Server, the form can interrogate the status of the report using the REPORT_OBJECT_STATUS command. This will indicate whether a report is in one of the following states: finished, running, canceled, opening, enqueued, invalid job, terminated with error, or crashed.

Another useful function for this feature is the ability to programmatically cancel the report from the form. If you run an asynchronous report that is taking a long time to run, you can use the CANCEL_REPORT_OBJECT command to stop the report from running.

An additional built-in, COPY_REPORT_OBJECT_OUTPUT (also only available if you are using the Reports Server), can be executed after a report has finished running to copy the cached output to a local file.

Passing Information to a Report

If you want your reports to respond to information from the form, there are a few alternatives. You can pass the information to a database object in a table by assigning information to server-side package variables or you can assign information to client-side package variables and have the report retrieve this information.

NOTE
The parameters you pass to reports are created programmatically and need not exist in the form's Object Navigator. They do need to exist in the called report's Data Model node under User Parameters.

Handling Parameter Lists

The best alternative is to pass the information directly to the report using a parameter list. A *parameter list* is essentially a record variable insofar as it is a series of variables with values. Parameters must be of standard scalar types (Date, Character, Number). A parameter cannot be a PL/SQL record or PL/SQL table. To pass a parameter to a report, first create the parameter list using the CREATE_PARAMETER_LIST command, and then add parameters and their values to the list.

You can change the value of an existing parameter by using the SET_PARAMETER_ATTR command. You should develop a uniform way of handling parameter lists. The algorithm used by the authors is as follows:

1. Check to see if the parameter list currently exists. If so, delete it.

2. Create the parameter list.

3. Add parameters and their values to the list.

The creation of the parameter list occurs immediately before the calling of the report, as shown in the following sample:

```
DECLARE
    v_pl_id   PARAMLIST;
    v_pl_name VARCHAR2(10) := 'my_list';
    v_rep_id  REPORT_OBJECT;
    v_rep_tx  VARCHAR2(100);
BEGIN
    -- delete parameter list if it currently exists
    v_pl_id := get_parameter_list(v_pl_name);
```

```
    IF NOT id_null(v_pl_id) THEN
        v_pl_id := destroy_parameter_list(v_pl_id);
    END IF;

    -- create parameter list
    v_pl_id := create_parameter_list(v_pl_name);

    -- add parameters
    add_parameter(v_pl_id, 'where_clause_tx', TEXT_PARAMETER, 'deptno = 10');
    add_parameter(v_pl_id, 'make_text_file_yn', TEXT_PARAMETER, 'Y');

    -- run report
    v_rep_id := find_report_object('my_report');
    v_rep_tx := run_report_object(v_rep_id, v_pl_id);
END;
```

In addition to passing text parameters, it is also possible to pass an entire record group of data to a report. This works well for relatively small datasets.

Bind Variables and Lexical Parameters

There are two primary ways to take information from user parameters and incorporate them into an Oracle reports query:

- Bind variables
- Lexical parameters

Each will be discussed separately.

Bind Variables

A *bind variable* is passed as a substituted value to the query. The syntax for using a bind variable is a colon (:) followed by the name of the user parameter being used as a bind variable. For example, if you have a numeric user parameter called P_DEPTNO, the Oracle query is the following:

```
SELECT  empno,
        ename
FROM    emp
WHERE   deptno = :p_deptno
```

If the value of P_DEPTNO is 10, the report will return a list of employees associated with department 10. The value of the P_DEPTNO parameter can be passed from a form as discussed in the previous section, set using a Reports parameter form, or set programmatically in one of the report's triggers.

NOTE
Parameter values cannot be adjusted using format triggers because the value of the parameter is locked during the execution of the report.

CAUTION
Queries with bind variables are sometimes parsed differently from queries with no bind variable and may use an entirely different optimization or execution plan if a hard-coded variable is replaced with a bind variable, even if the same value is passed through the bind variable. Do not assume that a query with hard-coded values will have the same optimization or execution plan as a query with bind variables.

When you are using bind variables, the datatype is assumed to be character. When you are passing a character value, the value of the character string should not include quotes unless the string itself has quote characters as part of the string.

TIP
You don't need to create user parameters for your bind variables in the Reports Object Navigator before you access them when writing your query. If you reference a bind variable that does not already exist to the text of your query, Oracle Reports will automatically create the user parameter for you.

You should use bind variables whenever you are trying to pass a single value to a query.

Lexical Parameters

A *lexical parameter* holds any portion of a SQL statement. It is used to alter any part of a report query at runtime. Lexical parameters (also called "lexical references") are much more flexible than bind variables since you are not simply passing a value to a variable. Instead, you are passing a string that can substitute for a portion of the query. In fact, you can pass the entire query as one large lexical parameter. Normally, you only pass a portion of it, usually a WHERE clause. The syntax for lexical parameters is an ampersand (&) followed by the name of the user parameter.

For example, if you wanted to have the ability to pass an additional portion of a
WHERE clause to a query, you could use the following code:

```
SELECT   ename
         dname
FROM     emp,
         dept
WHERE    emp.deptno = dept.deptno
         &p_where
```

Then you can add additional WHERE clause elements to modify the query.
For example, you can pass the string "AND deptno IN (10, 20)." When the query
executes, the clause is added to the query and only employees from departments
10 and 20 would be listed. Note the use of the AND keyword within the lexical
parameter since it is necessary to substitute the string value of the lexical parameters
for that portion of the query. You must keep this concept of string substitution in
mind when using lexical parameters. In the following example, you are passing a
string value to your query in a bind variable, as in the following code:

```
AND dept.loc = :p_loc
```

In this example, to find all employees working in New York, the bind variable
P_LOC would have to have the value "NY" (without quotes). To exchange the bind
variable for a lexical parameter of the same name, you would use the following code:

```
AND dept.loc = &p_loc
```

In this case, the lexical parameter would have to have the value 'NY' (the single
quotes surrounding NY are part of the value).

Lexical parameters can substitute for any part of your query. The only restriction
is that the names and datatypes of the columns selected cannot change. When
working with lexical parameters, keep in mind that the defined initial value of the
lexical parameters must be valid when Oracle Reports compiles the query. For
example, the following query would be invalid if the initial value of P_WHERE
were null.

```
SELECT   dname
FROM     dept
WHERE    &p_where
```

If you want to use a lexical parameter in this context, you must give it a default
value that does not affect performance and also does not logically modify the query.
In this case, you can use the initial value "1=1".

Lexical parameters can be used to support filtering of non–base table columns by
modifying both the FROM and the WHERE clauses. For example, in the following
query, the initial values of P_FROM and P_WHERE are NULL and "1-1", respectively.

```
SELECT ename
FROM   emp &p_from
WHERE  &p_where
```

You can use the preceding query to filter by location by passing the values shown in the following table to the lexical parameters.

Parameter	Value
p_from	,dept
p_where	emp.deptno = dept.deptno and dept.loc = 'NY'

Lexical parameters can be used to change which columns are displayed. For example, assume that you wanted to have the choice of whether to display just the base salary or total compensation (SALARY + COMMISSION) in a report. You could use the following query:

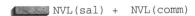
```
SELECT ename,
       &p_disp_sal salary
FROM   emp
```

The initial value of P_DISP_SAL would be SAL. If you wanted to display total compensation, you would change the value of p_disp_sal to the following:

```
NVL(sal) + NVL(comm)
```

CAUTION
When you substitute display columns, you need to make sure that the values they return are no larger than the original column will allow.

CAUTION
New with Developer Release 6—you can manually increase the width of a column using the column's Property Palette in the Data Model. If you rewrite your query after changing a width, the width will revert to the original value. Therefore, you should not rely on this behavior. To ensure that a text column is sufficiently wide, either select from a large column in the table or artificially increase its width using LPAD or RPAD.

You can use lexical parameters to substitute for any part or all of the query. Use lexical parameters whenever you want to have the ability to flexibly modify a query at runtime and the modification being made cannot be supported by a simple bind variable. The most common use for lexical parameters is to support a complex WHERE clause built on a Forms front-end so that you can add additional components to the WHERE clause, as shown in the following example where p_where is the lexical parameter:

```
SELECT  ename, dname
FROM    emp, dept
WHERE   emp.deptno = dept.deptno
        & p_where
```

Performance Implications

There is a potential performance impact when you are working with lexical parameters. A report created by use of a lexical parameter will run just as fast as a report built with a bind variable the first time it is executed. However, as queries are executed, they are stored in the shared SQL area. If the same query is rerun using a bind variable with a different value, Oracle will not have to reparse the query. With lexical parameters, anytime that there is even a small modification in any of the lexical parameters, the query is reparsed. Bind variables do not have that problem because the bind variable name, not the value, is stored in the shared pool. Usually, the passing of the query is a relatively small proportion of the total execution time.

PART
V

Reports Topics

CHAPTER
18

Reports—An Overview

It shall be a vexation only to understand the report.

—*The Holy Bible,* Isaiah 28:19

he Reports component of Oracle Developer is one of the most fully featured, powerful reporting tools on the market. You can build just about any report that you can imagine using Oracle Developer Reports (Reports). The tool is particularly robust in a client/server environment, but also works well in batch mode or in a web environment using Oracle Developer Server.

Its productivity is unsurpassed. A skilled Reports developer can produce standard, relatively sophisticated production reports at a rate of one or two per day. Under a time deadline, one of the authors created nine relatively simple production reports in one day.

One of the most powerful though rarely used features of Reports is its ability to dynamically specify major portions of the report at runtime. This feature allows developers to build flexible reporting systems that reduce or even eliminate the need for ad hoc query tools.

All this power and flexibility comes at a price. To someone unskilled with Reports, building reports with this product can be incredibly frustrating. Figuring out how to work with the Layout Model tool is very difficult for the novice user. The flexible reporting capabilities are exploited through the use of *lexical parameters* (strings of text that can be defined and incorporated into query text at runtime). Few developers have taken the time to understand these easy-to-use features. Many developers are unaware of the importance of the built-in PL/SQL packages required by many of the more complex features of Reports. To users who lack a thorough understanding of these features, Reports is merely another report writer, neither easier to use nor more fully functional than other PC-based report writing tools. However, for those who take the time to understand this product, there is no better development tool for production reporting on the market.

There are few limitations with Reports. The authors have used Reports to support company phone books with very complex reporting requirements as well as complex industrial reports with embedded graphics. The goal of the Reports section of this book is not just to teach you how to create basic reports but also to take full advantage of the most powerful features of Reports.

Report-writing tools tend to fall into three categories:

1. Tools that are easy-to-use but relatively limited

2. Tools that support power users in the construction of relatively complex reports

3. Production reporting tools that are capable of creating any report, but can only be used by skilled developers

What has been lacking in the industry is the so-called "organization-wide" reporting tool that can be used by both novice developers and end users for ad hoc reports as well as by IS professionals for complex production reports. The way to create this organization-wide reporting tool is to start with a fully featured production reporting tool and to create an easy-to-use "wizard" on top of the product for building simple reports. Oracle has now implemented this vision in Reports, attempting to give us the best of both worlds. Clearly, Reports' strengths lie in building complex production reports. However, with the new developer interface, Reports can also be used for a reasonable percentage of power-user reports as well, with the added advantage that a skilled developer can take these simpler reports and finish them using the more sophisticated parts of the product. This represents an important step forward for the industry, in that Reports makes it possible for developers and end users alike to create reports using the same tool organization-wide.

Even though the Report Wizard makes Oracle Reports as easy to use for creating standard reports as any of the other popular products that support end-user reporting, Oracle has chosen not to position the Reports component of Oracle Developer as an end-user tool. With respect to end-user access, Oracle suggests that developers create parameterized reports and make these available to users.

Before Reports 2.5, Oracle had a rocky history with developers who write reports. Many people believed that there were other report writers on the market that were easier to use, more powerful, or both. However, that perception of poor quality and lack of power in the Oracle development tools has been unjustified since version 2.5. The Reports component of Oracle Developer is so powerful and easy enough to use that it should silence the last of the critics.

The core functionality of Oracle Reports has not significantly changed since version 2.5. The difference is that reports can be built much more quickly, easily, and with less frustration with Reports than in any earlier version of this product. Much of what Oracle has done in this latest version has been to improve its usability for development. The Oracle development team for Reports was very much aware of the difficulties in using the 2.5 and earlier versions. Many of the changes in this product reflect Oracle's response to developer demands for an easier to use, more convenient, and intuitive product. The Oracle Reports interface for developers has been greatly improved, and numerous features have been added that decrease the time needed to learn how to skillfully use the product.

An additional improvement in Reports is that functionality in the product has been extended by including a Reports Server that speeds performance and adds scheduling and support for a three-tier architecture.

For those using another reporting tool, this chapter should convince you to consider giving Reports a chance. It will acquaint you with the new features in the current version that have an impact on the ease and speed of developing reports. For more detailed information, an overview of the improved Report Wizard can be found in Appendix B.

Report Builder Architecture

The Reports component of Developer is divided into two relatively isolated interfaces, which also correspond to the way that you build a report. In the first part of the tool, Report Editor—Data Model, you define the query or queries necessary for building the report, as well as placing this information in one or more logical groups. Then, in the Report Editor—Layout Model, you specify how those groups of information are physically laid out in the report. There are two additional interfaces in the product: the Parameter Form Builder and the Live Previewer. With the Parameter Form Builder, you can build a simple front-end that allows runtime control of user parameters. However, for complex control of user parameters, Oracle Forms should be used. In the Live Previewer, you can see how the report will be physically laid out when it is executed, and make adjustments to the report's appearance. The work areas of the Report Builder is shown in Figure 18-1.

In Reports, you will usually have two windows open on the screen: the Object Navigator and the Report Editor. The Report Editor is a window that you can toggle to display one of the following interfaces:

- Data Model
- Layout Model
- Parameter Form
- Live Previewer

The buttons that toggle between each of these interfaces are available on the toolbar so that you can easily switch between the different areas of the tool. Given the inevitable limitations of screen real estate, this is a helpful feature that improves developer productivity by decreasing the time spent managing multiple windows on the screen.

Data Model

As in Forms, Reports separates the logical groups of the data from the physical layout of the data. However, in Reports (unlike Forms) the separation between the logical and the physical is complete. In Reports, you build logical groups and

Reports Product Work Areas

Parameter Form:
User-specified
Input
Parameters

Data Model:
Queries
and grouping
of data

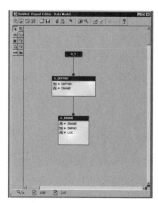

Layout Model:
Organization
and layout
of data

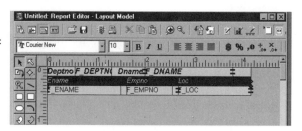

Live Previewer:
Pro forma
final display
of report

FIGURE 18-1. *Oracle Reports product architecture*

columns that you connect to layout frames and objects. In Forms, the logical groups are blocks; in Reports, they are *groups.* Groups are based on queries. You organize the data retrieved by a query into one or more groups. Groups within a query are strict, hierarchical, master-detail partitionings of data. In general, these logical partitionings will correspond directly to break groups in a report.

For example, suppose you want to create a classic master-detail report displaying names of employees who work in a particular department. You would write a single query to bring back the information, as shown:

```
SELECT all dept.deptno, dept.dname, emp.empno, emp.ename
FROM    dept.emp
WHERE   emp.deptno = dept.deptno
```

If you wanted to build a traditional master-detail report, you would put department information in a parent group and employee information in the child group. These groups usually (but do not necessarily have to) correspond to tables in the database. The specifics of building the query and creating the groups will be discussed in Appendix D.

It is important to understand that once a query has been used to create groups, its job is complete. There are very few places for the developer to be concerned with the query after the groups have been created. The purpose of the query is to create groups that will correspond to the data that you need to put in your report.

Layout Model

Objects in a report layout are organized via *frames.* Frames in Reports are much more flexible than the concept of bands used by other reporting tools. For every repeating frame in the Layout Model (that displays rows of data), there must be a group. However, there may be groups that are not associated with any frames. For example, in producing some complex reports, detail groups may be needed even though none of the information from those groups appears directly on the report, since it is only used to calculate summary information.

Parameter Form

Parameters are variables for your report that users can change at runtime immediately prior to the execution of the report. You can use system parameters to specify aspects of report execution, such as the output format, printer name, mail ID, or number of copies. You can also create your own parameters to change values in SQL or PL/SQL at runtime. For example, a parameter could replace single literal values or entire expressions in a query.

Live Previewer

The Live Previewer allows you to run the report and show the data as it will appear in the report itself, and provides an easy way to modify the way your report looks. The Live Previewer also allows you to see the changes you make immediately. Working in the Live Previewer, you can do all of the following:

- Align columns

- Resize columns

- Move columns

- Insert page numbers

- Edit text

- Change colors

- Change fonts

- Set format masks

- Insert a field

- Insert HTML file link

- Insert boilerplate objects

Advanced and Underused Features

Oracle Reports includes some powerful features that are rarely used by developers. Two are mentioned here briefly as examples of the possibilities for building sophisticated reports quickly and efficiently: lexical parameters and built-in PL/SQL functions. More details will be discussed in later chapters in this section.

Lexical Parameters

Perhaps one of the most powerful and rarely used features of Reports is lexical parameters. A *lexical parameter* is simply a text string that can be incorporated into the text of a query. This allows complete control over a query at runtime. This feature can be used to create a flexible reporting system.

To do this, you build a form as a flexible reporting interface front-end. Users choose the report they want to run. Then, through a series of poplists, multirecord blocks, and check boxes, they specify the report, sort criteria, and fields on which they want to break, along with a set of complex filter criteria. The form then builds the appropriate lexical parameters to modify the base report query, which then runs the report according to the user-specified criteria. In such a system, reports can be built to support one or more levels of user-specified breaks. If the breaks are not used, their display is suppressed through the use of format triggers. This procedure can also be used to allow users to specify the columns they want displayed.

Such a flexible reporting system can largely supplant the need for an ad hoc query tool without an organization having to worry about users creating reports that are not the reports they intended, as is frequently the case with ad hoc query tools. In these systems, you can also make it possible for users to save and retrieve their report settings, thus enabling them to run standard reports quickly, even those requiring complex settings.

Lexical parameters are, arguably, the single most important feature in Reports. While building a comprehensive reporting system for a client, the original report analysis estimated the required number of reports to be 200. Using lexical parameters and a flexible front-end, the reporting requirements were satisfied with 12 reports. An added benefit became evident when the database structure changed significantly three times during the course of the project. Each time, it was possible to rewrite and test the entire reporting system in about three days. At another client site where this style of flexible reporting was also implemented, the users' needs were not well defined. They made many modifications, asking for numerous additional reports beyond the original specifications. However, because of the flexible nature of the reporting system, in all but one case, all that needed to be done was to show the users how to use the system that had already been built to create their new report. In only one case was an extra column added to one of the reports. Everyone building production reporting systems should be using lexical parameters and a flexible Forms front-end.

Built-in PL/SQL Functions

Oracle provides a set of PL/SQL functions to support additional functionality in Reports. These functions are delivered in a PL/SQL package called "SRW" from "SQL Report Writer" (a historical reference to the name of Oracle's original reporting tool) that every Reports user should be familiar with. This package extends Reports much as the Forms-specific built-in PL/SQL commands extend Forms. Some examples follow:

- **SET_MAXROW** This is the procedure to change the maximum number of rows in a query.

- **GET_PAGE_NUM** This is used to get the current page number in the report.

- **SET_FIELD_NUM**   Data returned in a specific field can be overwritten for number fields.

- **SET_FIELD_CHAR**   Data returned in a specific field can be overwritten for character fields.

- **SET_FIELD_DATE**   Data returned in a specific field can be overwritten for date fields.

A complete list of SRW functions can be found in both the Reports documentation and the online help.

Report Wizard

The Report Wizard is Oracle's latest implementation of an automatic report generator. Some of this functionality existed even in Reports 2.5, but the sophistication and depth of the Report Wizard goes far beyond the last version. However, the Report Wizard does not replace the need to understand how to build a Data Model or how to manipulate the Layout Model manually.

Currently, only relatively simple reports can be created using the Report Wizard. Any modification beyond the defaults requires that developers fully understand how to use the tool. Even as the Report Wizard becomes more sophisticated, developers should not become completely dependent on the Report Wizard. It is important when dealing with generators or wizards to know not only how to use the generators, but also how to build reports manually.

One of the potential uses of the Report Wizard is as an ad hoc query tool for users and novice developers. With a relatively small increase in sophistication (that is, by next release), the Report Wizard could easily support that level of user. An additional advantage would be that after a user has attempted to build a report, if the report requires greater sophistication than the Report Wizard can accommodate, the IS professional helping the user need not discard the work already done by the user, but can simply modify the generated report. However, as mentioned earlier, Oracle does not consider Reports as an end-user tool.

The Report Wizard shows up in two ways. It is automatically invoked the first time the report is generated, and it will walk you through the creation of a report. If you bring up the Report Wizard manually, after a report has already been created, by selecting **Tools→Report Wizard,** you can access each part of the Report Wizard through a tab interface, as shown in Figure 18-2. A full walk-through of the Report Wizard can be found in Appendix D.

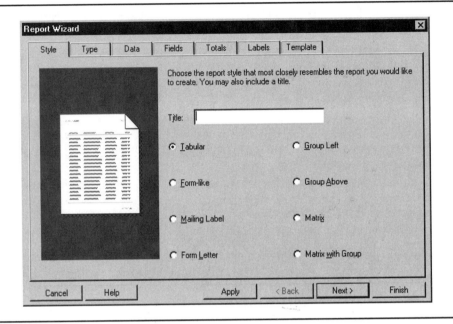

FIGURE 18-2. *Report Wizard tab interface*

Data Model

You can use the Report Wizard alone to build the Data Model only if the report has a single query and a straightforward single-group structure or is a simple master-detail or matrix report. It is also possible to base a report on a record group built in Oracle Forms and passed to Oracle Reports. For any reports containing formula columns, complex layouts, or multiple queries, you will need to use the Report Editor—Data Model that is discussed in detail in Chapter 19. The following section will provide you with a short overview of the Data Model to enable you to build most simple reports.

Building the Query

The first thing you specify in the Data Model is the query. The query can be as complex as you like, involving joins, unions, or "group by." To build queries within Reports, a developer must be a skilled SQL programmer. There are a number of different ways to get a query into the Data Model. You can create queries using the Query tab in the Report Builder Wizard or in the Data Model Editor directly by clicking on the SQL icon. Once the query is created and compiled, Reports will automatically generate a group. A *group* is a collection of columns. A group in Reports more or less corresponds to a block in Forms. It is these groups that form the foundation of the report, not the query. The queries build the groups, and then the groups are used to populate the report. The only function of queries in Reports is to create the groups. This distinction between queries and groups is important to keep in mind when building the Data Model for a report.

The benefit of this distinction is that you can tune a report by changing the queries that generate the groups, perhaps going from two or three queries to a single query, or shifting from using a complex query to a simple query using a view, without having to change (other than superficially) the rest of the report.

In the Data Model, it is easy to *link* multiple queries together. Linked queries are a way of including multiple queries in the same physical report. Linking queries creates one logical, although potentially complex, set of data that your report will be based on. However, linking multiple queries together effectively creates correlated subqueries. For every record fetched from the master query, a separate instantiation of the detail query is created.

Usually, performance can be increased by reducing the number of queries, ideally, to one. Of course, it is not always possible to do this.

However, when you look at the Data Model, recognize that all you're trying to do is to retrieve the information for your report. As long as the same information is getting into the same groups, the queries can be crafted in such a way as to optimize performance.

Query Builder

Query Builder is a point-and-click SQL writing tool that can and should be used to build all but the most complex queries. You can quickly select tables, click columns for inclusion in the query, and add WHERE conditions. One of the most useful features of Query Builder is that it reads referential integrity information out of the data dictionary (assuming that appropriate constraints have been defined) and automatically joins tables. The Query Builder is accessible from both the Report Wizard and the Data Model. In the Report Wizard, Query Builder is accessed from the Data tab and in the Data Model when you create or edit a query, as shown in Figure 18-3.

Complex queries can also be built quickly and easily. Another useful feature of Query Builder is that you can make direct edits to the text of your query in the Data Model. Then, if you click on the Query Builder, it will bring your query into the Query Builder graphical syntax. Of course, there are some limitations to this feature. The Query Builder is not capable of supporting all SQL queries. For example, if you create a complex query involving a UNION ALL and then try to bring it into the Query Builder, you will get an error because it cannot be imported. However, for most queries, the Query Builder is an excellent tool and a great timesaver.

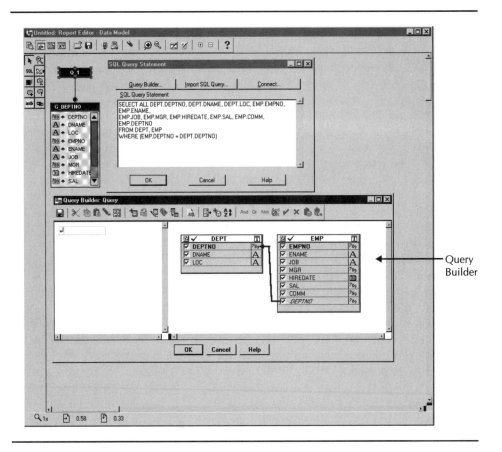

FIGURE 18-3. *Query Builder as accessed from the Data Model*

One of the best features of Query Builder is that it gives developers a quick visual representation of the query and greatly facilitates the debugging of complex queries. Also, for those developers who are "keyboard challenged," it allows you to create queries quickly by simply pointing and clicking the mouse.

Groups

When columns are selected in a query, they are automatically placed in a single group. This group of fields is what Reports works with to create the report layout.

Repeating frames in the Layout Model correspond to groups, not queries. A single query, however, may spawn more than one group. There is always the *main data* group; but it is also possible to have one or more *break* groups. If you create two groups, one is the main data group and one is the break group. These groups are created either through the Report Wizard or in the Data Model. Each method will be discussed separately.

Creating Break Groups in the Report Wizard

To create groups in the Report Wizard, you must first select one of the Report Wizard styles that uses a group (Group Left, Group Above, Matrix With Group). The Groups tab then becomes available. Every time a column is selected and brought over from Available Fields to Group Fields, a new break group is created. If the columns need to be combined into a single break group, you must drag columns into the same level, and the empty levels disappear.

Creating Break Groups in the Data Model

To create a break group in the Data Model, simply click and drag the column outside of the main query group. If you drag the column below the query group, that makes the group you were in a break group for the new group created below, as shown in Figure 18-4. What is the significance of having multiple breaks in a chain? For the break groups above, this forces a master-detail relationship between upper and lower groups. One row in each group will be created for each unique combination of all the columns in the group. For example, if you put all the departmental information into a group, there will be one row for each department. There will automatically be a logical master-detail relationship between the two groups with DEPT information above and EMPLOYEE information below. You can have as many break groups as you need. However, typically having more than three or four in any report makes the report almost impossible to read. In practice, there are almost never more than four groups for any particular query.

Summary and Formula Columns

Summary and formula columns allow the display of information that is not part of the base queries. The information may already be based on retrieved information (as is always the case in summary columns), may take already retrieved information as passed parameters (as is usually the case in formula columns), or, rarely, can be completely independent of anything else in the report. *Formula* columns are PL/SQL functions that return a value for display. *Summary* columns are special cases of formula columns that allow quick creation of commonly used functions, such as sum totals, minimums, maximums, averages, and counts of not null fields.

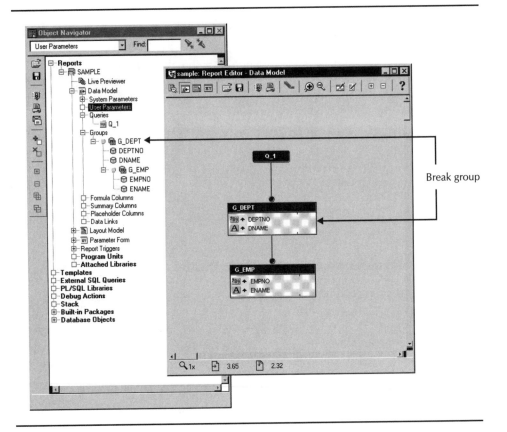

FIGURE 18-4. *Data Model break groups*

Summary Columns

Summary columns are simple aggregations of a single report column, as shown in Figure 18-5. The column that you are aggregating must be in a child group to the group where the summary column is placed. For instance, in the DEPT/EMP example, you cannot place a summary column that calculates the number of departments in the employee group.

However, this constraint does not mean that summary columns can't be used in formulas or displayed at a lower level—for example, with data from the employee

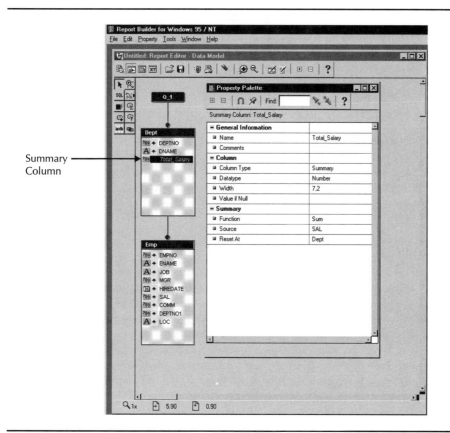

Summary Column

FIGURE 18-5. *Summary column and its Property Palette*

group. In looking at employee records, each record may take one or more pages. One of the lines in the employee report shows the number of employees in the department, total salary budget for that department, and what percentage of the total salary budget for that department a specific employee receives. Formula and summary columns calculate all department information residing in the DEPT group, but can also be displayed with the employee information. This is yet another example of the separation between the logical and display models, which is one of the most powerful features of Oracle Reports.

A summary column can be built in two ways:

- ■ **Using the Report Wizard Totals tab**   You can specify the field and aggregation function that you wish to calculate. If specified here, that field will then be aggregated in every group above the level of the field, including the report itself. If you do not want all those summary columns, you can delete them later.

- ■ **Using the Report Editor—Data Model**   You create a summary column by clicking on the Summary Column button on the left-hand toolbar and then clicking on the group where you want to place the column. If you want the summary calculated for the whole report, click in the gray area outside any group.

If you manually build your summary columns, you need to specify a function to be applied to the data. Reports will default to sum. In the Property Palette, you then need to identify the *source* column that you want to perform the operations on. The source column must be in a group below the level where the summary column is defined. In the DEPT/EMP example, if the summary column is placed at the report level, all fields will be available for aggregation. If placed in the DEPT group, then only employee fields will be available for selection.

The *Reset At* property must be specified next. For normal summaries, *Reset At* should always be set for the group in which the summary column resides. If you want the total column to be a running total, then specify *Reset At* for the page. It is not unusual to have multiple summary fields differing only by the value of the *Reset At* property. In the same report, a departmental total, a running total for the whole report, and summary totals at the bottom of each page may be shown by specifying different values for the *Reset At* property.

Formula Columns

Formula columns are used to calculate and display information that is not easily retrievable from the database. To some extent, this becomes an issue of style—whether calculations are done in the base query or as formula columns. In general, formula columns are less efficient. However, they make for clarity in the report, and that is frequently worth the small cost in performance.

Formula columns that involve processing of columns already retrieved from the database move processing from server to client, which, depending upon the relative speed and loads on the server and client machines, is frequently desirable. For example, a formula that adds two or more columns together for display is usually better as a client-side formula. However, any formula that uses a cursor will involve extra and perhaps numerous round-trips to the database server.

No matter what the relative performance of the client or server, network traffic should always be avoided if performance of the report is a consideration.

Therefore, in general, it will be rare to have cursors in formula columns. You should also be careful of implicit cursors. Note that anytime you make a call to SYSDATE, you are initiating a database query. However, if the database is small and performance is not an issue, having formula columns with cursors in them may create a report that is easier for a developer to understand and maintain.

Simple formula columns include numeric or string manipulations on information already retrieved from the database, where all activity is local on the client machine. These types of formula columns can be used with no performance penalties. The developer can decide to run them on the client machine, Reports Server, or wherever the database resides.

Other useful places to use formula columns include column values coming back from the database that you want displayed as if they were one value, such as inventory numbers, department names, or department codes that may be concatenations of other fields. Rather than having multiple objects in the Layout Model connected through anchors, for fields with a leading or trailing indicator ("+" or "-"), it is easier to create one formula column in the Data Model that is a concatenation of all the display fields. Then it is only necessary to have one object in the Layout Model that displays that formula column.

Formula columns cannot be built in the Report Wizard. You can use the Define Columns feature to create a formula column in the Query Builder, but these columns are limited to aggregate functions in SQL statements. There may be performance implications to this action as well, as discussed in Chapter 19. The only way to create a formula column is in the Report Editor—Data Model. Click the Formula Column icon. Then click whatever group the formula will belong to. To figure out where the formula column belongs, you need to consider the frequency with which formula columns will appear. Using the DEPT/EMPLOYEE example, it is necessary to understand what each group represents. For the DEPT group, each row represents a department. Each row in the EMPLOYEE group represents an employee. Here are three examples:

1. A formula column that concatenates various name fields for display: Such a formula would go in the EMPLOYEE group because the name belongs to the employee, as shown by F_FULLNAME_TX in Figure 18-6.

2. A more complex formula that shows the standard deviation of the salary for each department: You might be tempted to put the formula in the EMPLOYEE group because you are calculating employee information. But since this formula should only be calculated once for each department, it should go into the DEPT group, as shown by F_SAL_STD_DEV_NR in Figure 18-6.

3. A formula that displays the salary standard deviation for all employees in an entire organization at the top of a report: This formula need only be calculated once. This is referred to as a *report-level* formula, and the object is not placed in a group, but rather outside the groups in the open space of the Data Model, as shown by F_ORG_SAL_STD_DEV_NR in Figure 18-6.

The placement of the formulas in these simple examples is easy, but placing the formula in the correct group in a complex report may be a more difficult task. If you think a little about the process, you will be able to place formula columns appropriately.

Layout Model

The Report Editor—Layout Model is where you have precise control of the report layout and display. For even relatively complex reports, it is not necessary to use the Layout Model. Almost all tasks necessary for basic reports can be accomplished

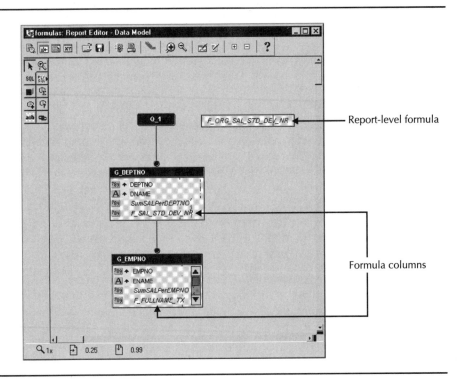

FIGURE 18-6. *Data Model showing report-level formula column*

easily by use of the Live Previewer. This section will give a short overview of how to use the Live Previewer to perform simple manipulations of your report layouts. A detailed discussion of the features of the Layout Model can be found in Chapter 20.

Live Previewer

The Live Previewer, shown in Figure 18-7, enables you to make changes to the Layout Model and immediately see their impact. Some changes to the layout can even be made right in the Live Previewer. For simple reports, the existence of the templates and the Live Previewer together means that it is not even necessary to understand

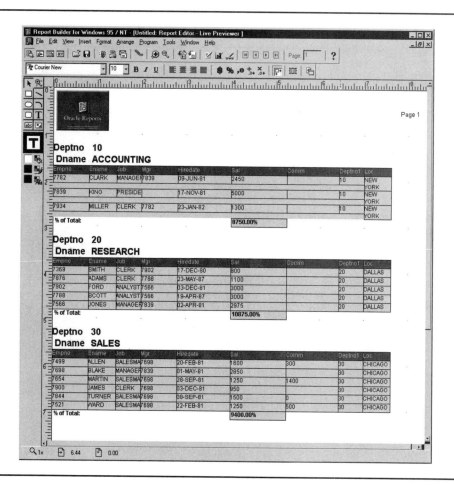

FIGURE 18-7. *Sample report in the Live Previewer*

the complexities of frames in the Layout Model. The Live Previewer helps novice developers create simple reports. However, for complex production reports, it is still necessary to understand how frames work in the Report Layout Model.

Using the Live Previewer, you can easily perform simple editing tasks, including changing font sizes, selecting frames so that you can change the spacing between frames on the Property Palette, changing the size of objects, and controlling formatting. This section will include brief descriptions of how to accomplish these tasks in a simple report.

Changing Font Sizes and Types

To change font sizes and/or types in the Live Previewer, select the desired column in the report. Click the down arrow button next to the font name and/or size on the toolbar. Then select the new font type or size from the pull-down poplists. The change will be immediately visible on the screen in the Live Previewer.

Changing the Size of Objects

To change the size of objects, click to select the object. Drag the select handles to adjust the object to the desired size. Notice that you cannot increase the vertical size of a group.

Controlling Formatting

You can use the $, %, Commas, and Add decimal place and Remove decimal place buttons on the Live Previewer toolbar (see Figure 18-7) to control the formatting of money, percent, commas, decimal places, and significant figures after the decimal place, respectively. The following is a list of the buttons and their functions.

- **Currency ($) button** Adds the dollar sign to the selected numbers.

- **Percent (%) button** Adds the percent sign to the selected numbers.

- **Commas (,0) button** Inserts commas after every three digits from the left of the decimal point.

- **Add Decimal Place button (+)**   Inserts one digit after the decimal place for every time the button is clicked.

- **Remove decimal place button (x)**   Removes one digit after the decimal place every time the button is clicked.

Working with Frames

While the Live Previewer is quite useful for some layout changes, you can modify frames themselves only in the Layout Model or Object Navigator. *Frames* are used to enclose objects and protect them from being overwritten or moved by other objects. For example, a frame might be used to enclose all the objects owned by a group, to surround column headings, or to surround summaries. When you use the default layout for a report, Report Builder creates frames around report objects as needed. You can also create a frame manually using the Layout Model.

Frames come in two varieties:

- **Enclosing (nonrepeating) frames**   Enclosing frames group similar objects together and enforce their relative positions in the layout. Frames may or may not be visible when the report is run. To make a frame visible, change its line width and color using **Format→Line Width** to change width and the Color icon at the bottom left of the toolbar to change line color. Enclosing frames should surround multiple objects. If a nonrepeating frame surrounds a single object, it is superfluous and can often safely be deleted if there are no triggers attached to that frame.

- **Repeating frames**   Repeating frames do more than simply group objects together. Repeating frames correspond to groups in the Data Model, and as you might expect, one of the properties on the Property Palette is the group with which the frame is associated. Each repeating frame must be associated with a group from the Data Model, but you might have groups in the Data Model that are not associated with a repeating frame. Within the repeating frame, you must only have objects from its associated group or objects from a parent group. Objects from a child group can also appear inside that repeating frame, but only if they reside entirely within an associated repeating frame for their own group. Because a repeating frame repeats objects inside the frame that it encloses over and over again, it is necessary to know how to display the multiple objects, that is, down the page in columns, or across the page in rows. The indicator for a repeating frame is circled here:

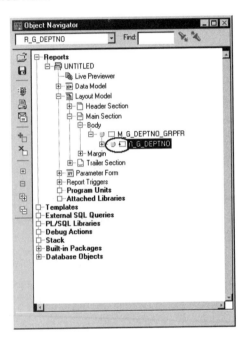

Object Navigator

The Reports Object Navigator, shown next, is similar to the one in Forms. Obviously, some categories will be different because reports contain different objects than forms. However, not only are objects grouped differently, but the Object Navigator also functions slightly differently in Reports than it does in Forms. Specifically, drag-and-drop can only be used in very limited areas in Reports.

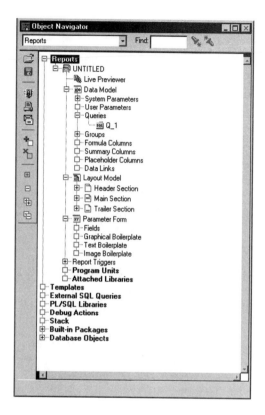

The highest-level object in the Reports section of the Object Navigator is the name of the report. Unlike Forms, the name of the report in the Object Navigator must be the same as the name of the report file. Specifically, the only way to change the name of a report is to save it to a file with that name. The following discussion explains the high-level nodes in the Reports Object Navigator.

Live Previewer

Although this is a node in the Object Navigator, the Live Previewer is not really an object. If you double-click the button, it will open the Live Previewer described earlier.

Data Model

This section shows the logical structure of the report. All the information from the Report Editor—Data Model is displayed here.

TIP

You should not use the Data Model section in the Object Navigator to do anything more than view the query structure. Modifying the query structure is handled more efficiently in the Data Model itself.

- **System Parameters**   This section contains the values of system parameters, such as the number of copies to print and report print orientation (landscape or portrait).

- **User Parameters**   User parameters are used primarily to store and manipulate information at runtime, such as bind or lexical parameters, or to allow users to define input parameters, such as date ranges.

- **Queries**   The Queries section contains the queries and their query text. Groups associated with queries are not found in the Queries section. Instead, these are stored in a separate Groups section.

- **Groups**   The Groups section stores the groupings of the report objects, database columns, formula columns, summary columns, and placeholder columns. Note that the database columns associated with the group are referred to as "fields" in the Report Wizard.

- **Formula Columns**   This section is where you will find calculated columns that are defined at the report level. As mentioned earlier, if a formula column is associated with a group, it will be stored as a sub-object of that group.

- **Summary Columns**   This is where report-level summary columns are found. As with formula columns, summary columns associated with a group are stored as sub-objects of that group.

- **Placeholder Columns**   This is where report-level placeholder columns are found. Placeholder columns will also be discussed in more detail in Chapter 19.

- **Data Links**   When you join multiple queries in a report, the join condition is stored in the Data Links section. This will be discussed in more detail in Chapter 19.

Layout Model

This is where all information and objects pertaining to the physical layout of the report are found. The four sections (Header, Trailer, Body, and Margin) refer to four distinct places to specify where you want information to print.

- **Header**   The header consists of one or more pages that are printed before the report proper. The type of information you might want to place here is a report title page or a chart that summarizes the report. When building a flexible reporting system, the report header is an appropriate place to display the selection criteria that were used in creating the report.

- **Trailer**   The trailer consists of one or more pages that print after the report itself, usually used (when used at all) for nothing more than an "end of report" blank page, but also used for a report summary or chart.

- **Body**   The body is where all the main report objects are placed.

- **Margin**   The Report Layout only governs the part of the pages designated for the main data portion of the report. The margins can be used to specify page headers and page footers.

NOTE
Page Headers and footers are not specified in the Header and Trailer sections, which refer to whole pages at the beginning and end of the report.

Parameter Form

This is a limited-functionality input screen tool that can automatically pop up when the report is run. Here, users can type in values or select from poplists to specify the values for system and user parameters. The Parameter Form can be helpful when running a report repeatedly during the development/testing process.

Report Triggers

This is where code is placed for any or all of the five possible report-level triggers associated with a report. Note that these are described in the order in which they fire in a report, rather than the order they appear in the Report Builder menu.

- **BEFORE PARAMETER FORM**   Any parameters passing to the report have already arrived when the report starts. There is nothing you can trigger before the first step in report execution. If you want to take parameters passed to the report and manipulate them so that they appear differently in the Parameter Form, this is where modifications can be made. For example, when you want to pass a department number but show the name of the department selected, use a BEFORE PARAMETER FORM trigger.

■ **AFTER PARAMETER FORM and BEFORE REPORT**   These two triggers are fired one after the other. No event occurs in between them. However, the way that the Reports product behaves when the triggers fail is quite different. If the AFTER PARAMETER FORM trigger fails (returns "False"), the report will be put back into the Parameter Form. It is useful to place code here to check whether values in your parameter are valid. Even though the BEFORE REPORT trigger is executed before the query runs, if this trigger fails, it won't fail until Reports tries to display the first page of the report. This means that even if something goes wrong in the BEFORE REPORT trigger (meaning that you may not want to run the query at all), it will run anyway. Therefore, you don't want to have code that could conceivably abort the report before it is executed placed in the BEFORE REPORT trigger. This code should be placed in the AFTER PARAMETER FORM trigger.

Keep in mind that anything placed in the AFTER PARAMETER FORM trigger will fire before the BEFORE REPORT trigger. You can manipulate information from the Parameter Form before it gets to the report. For example, this strategy can be used to prepare lexical parameters for a query. In fact, since you can write any PL/SQL code here, you can perform any level of basic or sophisticated validation checks on your parameters before sending them to the reports.

■ **BETWEEN PAGES**   This trigger fires before all pages except the first one. It will not fire after the last page of a report. If a report only has one page, it will not fire at all. You can use this trigger to send specific control characters to the printer to change the paper orientation or to do double-sided printing.

■ **AFTER REPORT**   This trigger fires after the report has printed or, in the case of a screen report, after the report is closed following viewing. This trigger can be used to update a global variable if you are returning the number of pages in a report. It can also be used to delete a temporary table used to print the report.

Program Units

This is the same as the section in Forms, where you can place client-side functions, procedures, and packages that will be called within the report. You can also create a package and store package variables that can be accessed anytime in the report. For example, if you need to have access to a global variable updated by format triggers while a report is running, the best implementation of such globals is with a package variable.

Attached Libraries

Similar to Program Units, Attached Libraries (as in Forms) can attach external PL/SQL libraries that can be called from within the report.

Templates

Oracle Reports allows you to apply prebuilt templates. This section is where you create or modify existing templates. Templates in Reports not only can include common objects in reports such as logos, report headers, page numbers, and dates, but templates are also "smart" insofar as they contain the default property settings that govern the generation of the report. Specifically, fonts are specified for both data and labels. You can specify different fonts for primary data frames as well as group by frames. Oracle provides several attractive looking templates and also gives developers the ability to create and save their own templates.

These templates will help to greatly decrease the time spent fine-tuning the layout of reports. Until now, there was a common tendency to stay close to default layouts in order to minimize development time. Report templates will allow developers to easily specify and reuse relatively complex layouts. This will be discussed in more detail in Chapter 21.

External SQL Libraries

If you are going to use the same query in a number of different reports, you can store it either in a file or in the database. That query can be called as the query text in any number of reports. This is the section where such queries are created and maintained.

PL/SQL Libraries

This is the same section as in Forms where you create and maintain external PL/SQL libraries.

Debug Actions and Stack

The Debug Actions and Stack nodes pertain to the debugging actions. Consult the Oracle Developer documentation for a description of these features. You can debug PL/SQL code in the report as the report is running by displaying the PL/SQL

Interpreter window and setting break points. The Debug Actions and Stack nodes will then contain information for the debugging process.

Built-in Packages

Just as in Forms, this area shows the basic syntax for all available built-in packages. This is often a quick and easy way to find the syntax for a particular command.

Database Objects

This is also the same node as in Forms. It allows you to have access to tables, columns, and other database-level objects.

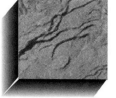

CHAPTER
19

The Reports Data Model

Data is a lot like humans: It is born. Matures. Gets married to other data, divorced. Gets old.
One thing that it doesn't do is die. It has to be killed.

—Arthur Miller (1915–)

As mentioned in Chapter 18, when a report is designed with the Reports component of Oracle Developer, it is built in two main steps. In the first step, you define the queries and declare the logical structure of the information. In the second step, you decide how that information will be physically formatted in the report. This chapter will discuss the first step, which is accomplished in the Report Editor—Data Model.

The Reports Data Model is where you specify what information is needed to create the report. This includes summary information and any calculated fields. The Data Model is not simply the set of information, but also is the logical structuring of that information, including its hierarchical organization. For example, a master-detail report is represented as two linked groups of information in the Data Model.

Almost all of the information that goes into a report is represented in the Data Model. But there are some exceptions, such as specific system-level fields like page numbers, titles, and date, that can be placed on reports without being represented in the Data Model. For complex reports, it is possible to include information that is calculated outside the Data Model and displayed in the layout. However, with the exception of page numbers and today's date, 99 percent of the time everything that appears in the report is based on information in the Data Model.

As mentioned in Chapter 18, unlike the Forms component of Oracle Developer, there is a precise separation between the logical Data Model and the physical layout of information in Oracle Developer Reports (Reports). In Forms, blocks are mostly logical groupings. The physical layout is set up on canvases and windows. Items are simultaneously both logical and display constructs. However, in Reports, there is a very clear delineation between logical objects and display objects. This is a fundamental difference between how Forms works and how Reports works. In Reports, there are *display* objects and *logical* objects that must be linked. In Forms, block items serve both roles. This adds a little more complexity to building Reports. However, it also allows for a more natural organization.

Crafting the Query—Keep It Simple!

The core of any report is one or more SQL queries. Most reports will be based on a single query, as indeed they should be. In addition to its obvious simplicity, a report based on a single query will usually have the best performance. The Report Wizard is only capable of creating single-query reports. However, occasionally, the only way to make a report is with multiple queries. In addition, it is possible to have multiple queries in a report that are completely independent and then have them associated with independent layouts. This effectively provides the ability to display multiple logical reports in the same physical report either side by side or one preceding the other. This flexibility is one of Reports' greatest strengths.

Query Builder

Queries can be built either in the Report Wizard or in the Data Model of the Report Editor. In each of these, there are three methods by which to build. The SQL query can be typed in, copied from a file, or you can use the Query Builder. The Query Builder can be accessed either through the button on the Data tab of the Report Wizard, or by choosing the SQL button on the left-hand toolbar of the Data Model screen. When creating the first version of the report, it is fastest to use the wizard. As long as the report is relatively simple, you can reenter the wizard and modify the Data Model. However, if the report is complex, requiring a nontrivial Data Model, you will need to build your query directly in the Data Model.

To use Oracle Reports effectively, you need to be an expert in crafting SQL queries. Novice developers without a great deal of SQL knowledge can easily use Oracle Reports to build a report that runs by using Query Builder to construct the query. However, those same developers may build a report that takes hours to execute rather than one that could run in minutes with a little more thought given to the report design. Some of the common techniques you can use to write better reports will be described next.

Multiple Queries

In the Data Model, you can have more than one query. Queries can either be unlinked or linked. *Unlinked queries* are used to build additional independent reports placed in the same physical report. For example, a report summarizing revenues on the left side of the page could share a page with a report summarizing expenses for that same time period on the right. Or, you could show the income statement for a division followed by the balance sheet. These are completely independent report queries that are displayed on the same physical report.

Linked queries are a second method of including multiple queries in the same physical report. Linking queries creates one logical, although potentially complex, set of data that your report will be based on. When you link two or more queries, you are effectively building a correlated subquery, since for every row fetched in the master query, you generate a new instantiation of the child query with a new bind variable value. In fact, this is much worse for performance than a correlated subquery, because for every new instantiation of the subquery, you are creating and opening an additional cursor, which is passed to the database over the network. The performance implications of this are profound. For small tables, of course, it doesn't make much difference.

It is useful to try to keep the number of queries small. However, in some cases the use of multiple queries is unavoidable. For example, when combining two or more reports into a single report, there must be one query for the first report and one for the second, which follow each other. In this case, two different and independent queries are returning information to the report. You should be careful about having too many independent queries in the same report, particularly if it is going to include a large number of pages. However, if the report fits on one page, it is usually acceptable. In one situation experienced by the authors, there was a specific report in which multiple queries were used: it was a one-page report with four separate summary queries that appeared on one page. This type of report can be built so that it only takes a few minutes to run, is stable, and works well.

CAUTION

Multiple independent queries should not be used when a report is very large and complex.

In another situation, an internal telephone book was built for a large government organization. The Data Model included six consecutive independent queries; this report also included OLE objects brought in from Microsoft Word. The resulting report was nearly 100 pages long. In this case, creating and managing the report was very difficult and caused problems. The report had to be split into six different reports running separately, using an Oracle Forms front-end.

If you have independent queries, it is better to use a small number of queries and only combine them into a single report for small simple reports. For complex reports with three or more independent queries, it is safer to handle multiple queries in separate reports.

One of the common mistakes that novice report developers make is creating extremely complex data models with many queries all linked together. Such a strategy can destroy report performance. The key to good report performance is to minimize the number of cursors involved in the report. In all but the most unusual cases, it is best to create a report with a single query that goes to the database one time and returns the appropriate information. This may mean using outer joins or embedded functions in queries (discussed later in this chapter). If you are not careful about report construction, report performance can suffer dramatically. Oracle Reports gives you great control over how information is retrieved from the database. However, this control means that you now have the ability to retrieve information in profoundly inefficient ways if your query is not properly written or the design of your database is not well optimized. It is important to understand the nuances of Oracle Reports in order to build efficiently.

Simple master-detail reports can almost always be crafted from a single query. Using the simple example of a master-detail report based on the DEPT/EMP tables, the output of this report is shown in Figure 19-1.

You can use two methods to build this report:

■ Using two queries—one a simple "SELECT FROM dept" and a second a simple "SELECT FROM emp"—and then linking the two queries as shown in Figure 19-2.

■ Using a single query that returns information from both DEPT and EMP tables and that joins the two tables as shown in Figure 19-3.

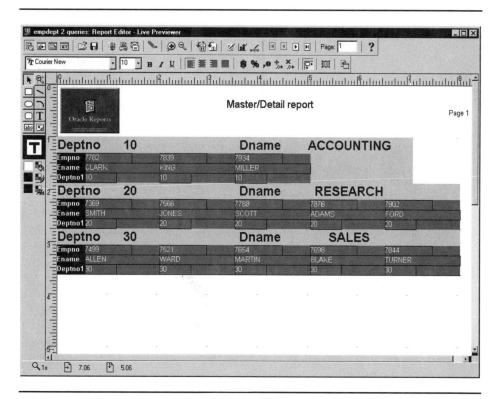

FIGURE 19-1. *Live Previewer view of a simple master-detail report*

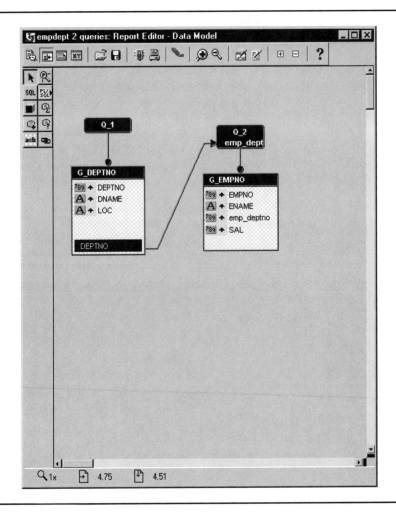

FIGURE 19-2. *Data Model with two linked queries*

Crafting this report with two queries rather than one will more than double the amount of time required to run the report. For each department row that is retrieved, a whole new query is created for the employee table and sent to the database for processing.

Sometimes multiple queries may be needed to generate groups correctly. This occurs most often when you need to use GROUP BY in order to get the top-level group, but ungrouped data is needed for the detail group. This happens with a

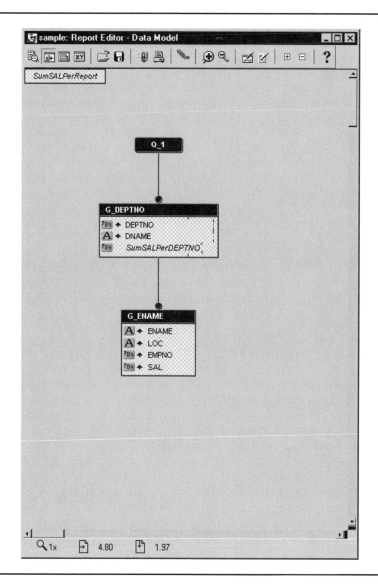

FIGURE 19-3. *Data Model for Dept/Emp report with a single query*

database that is not entirely normalized, although you may also need multiple queries in correctly formed databases. Continuing the DEPT and EMP example, if you want to have a single-query report sorted by the number of employees in each department, you would need to create a PL/SQL function that will return the number of employees in the department. That function is stored in the database. Then, when you write the DEPT query, you can select the function as one of the columns in the query that makes the summary column a base query object.

Another way to handle this report is with two separate queries. The first query would return the department information and would be written as follows:

```
SELECT    deptno,
          dname,
          COUNT(*) no_of_emps
FROM      dept, emp
WHERE     dept.dept.no = emp.deptno
GROUP BY  deptno, dname
```

The second query would be written as

```
SELECT    empno, ename, deptno
  FROM    emp
```

The final step would be to link the DEPT and EMP queries. This gives you the appropriate Data Model with the departments sorted by the number of employees in each department. You might think that you should be able to just use a summary column that simply counts the number of employees. But you can't sort on summary columns because they are calculated on the client side after the row is returned.

You can have as many queries in a report as you need. It is possible to have one master query that has multiple child queries. A child query can, in turn, be a master query for another child query.

There is no way to create a linked query in the Report Wizard. This can only be done manually in the Report Editor—Data Model. To link two queries, you have two options:

- Click the Data Link button. Click and drag from one query header (the oval box at the top of the query) to the other. Reports will make a guess at the appropriate join condition, by querying the foreign-key relationships between the tables from the database. If the queries are simple, one-table queries, it will guess correctly. However, if the query is complex, it will frequently guess wrong. In any case, depending upon the environment, it takes a little while to complete the join. Automatic joins should always be checked by looking at the Property Palette for the join arrow to make sure that the join was created correctly.

- Rather than clicking and dragging from one query header to the other, you can click and drag from the column in the *parent* query to the column in the *child* query that you want to join. This requires no database searches and happens immediately.

When you link queries, by default Oracle Reports uses an *equi-join*. However, non–equi-joins are also possible on those rare occasions where they might be useful. The authors have never found a reason to use non-equi-joins in a production environment and have only seen them in academic exercises.

Using Views

Because information is only being displayed and not updated, you can use views in the Data Model that are very complex. The Oracle SQL language's ability to embed functions in *views* is a powerful, yet often underused, feature.

In general, you should use views with most reports. Specifically, in large systems supporting many reports, a number of views centralize much of the business logic and code, and greatly decrease the overall cost and maintenance of the system. Even relatively simple things should be made parts of views. For example, you can add a department name column to the Employee view.

View construction should be considered as a critical step in building the reporting function for an application. In general, views are not built to support single reports. The idea is to take the designs for all your reports and think through the appropriate views to build in order to support those reports. Identify common objects and functions that will be used in multiple reports, and build single views to accommodate that functionality. The views can be designed and built by more senior developers, which enables junior developers to easily use those views to build the necessary reports.

Writing all reports against views also isolates the reports from the physical tables to some extent. If the data model changes, all that needs to be done is to modify the views so that all reports will run again.

One caution with respect to using views is that joining views to views or joining views to other tables can sometimes cause serious performance problems. In a project that one of the authors was involved with, there was a complex view that had several unions. Information was returned very quickly until it was joined to any other table, at which point it was not possible to avoid a lot of full-table scans. Rewriting the report using formula columns that accessed the view achieved adequate performance. You should make sure that queries against the view perform properly before using views in Reports. By doing this, you will ensure that performance problems will not arise due to these views and queries.

Aliasing Column Names

One of the less convenient features of Reports is that all column names are global. Recall that in Forms, if you want to specifically refer to an item, you uniquely identify it by *BLOCK.ITEM_NAME*. This allows a complex form to manage several hundred different items easily. In Reports, you might expect that columns could be referred to by a *GROUP.COLUMN* name. Unfortunately, all column names in Reports are global. The impact of having global column names is that, for example, by selecting the DEPTNO column in both the EMP and DEPT queries, the DEPTNO field name will be automatically aliased to DEPTNO1 in the second query. Even worse, over time, if you modify and regenerate the queries, you may find that the aliases will change, wreaking havoc on your already-written PL/SQL code. As a result, the best strategy is not to allow Reports to ever assign column names arbitrarily. The way to prevent this is by explicitly aliasing the column names in the query.

CAUTION
It is worth repeating that changing the query text so there is more than one column with the same name in the report can invalidate PL/SQL code that refers to the columns by name. It is best to always alias columns in the queries that you construct.

Selecting PL/SQL Functions Within Queries

One of the features of Reports (and Oracle's implementation of SQL in general) that is often neglected is the ability to select a function as part of a query. For example, you can have a function that returns the total value of a purchase order or the number of employees in a department.

Anytime you have a formula that requires database access, that function should be stored in the database. The goal is to minimize network traffic. Calculations performed in the client are fast. Calculations performed in the server are very fast. However, network round-trips are relatively slow. If you implement a function that relies on a database query using a formula column, the report will always run slower than if the formula were stored in the database.

To be able to store and access functions in the database, you need to follow these steps:

1. Place the function in a package in the database.

2. In the package specification, you need to use a special syntax with the command PRAGMA RESTRICT_REFERENCES that will tell the database that the function "writes no database states" (WNDS). Without the PRAGMA syntax, Oracle will not allow you to use the function in a SQL statement or view. The following code example demonstrates the correct syntax.

```
PACKAGE my_package IS
   FUNCTION f_dname(
      p_empno IN NUMBER)
      RETURN VARCHAR2;
   PRAGMA RESTRICT_REFERENCES(f_dname, WNDS);
END;
```

NOTE

If the SELECT list of a query including a function is selected in Reports, that function must *be stored in the database. Reports queries will not find the function if it is stored locally in the report or in an attached library.*

Utilizing functions in queries is not the same as using them as formula columns in the Data Model. There are serious advantages to putting functions in the SQL query. There is no case where using a formula column that relies on a database query provides any significant advantages other than ease for the developer and readability in the report. There are certain serious disadvantages to using formula columns; specifically, you can't sort on formula columns, but you can sort on a function column in a SQL query.

It is true that if your function does not require additional round-trips back to the database, you are shifting some CPU cycles to wherever the report is being executed (client or report server). In the rare instance where the database server is more heavily loaded than the report server, there may be some justification for the small benefit of having functions executed by the report. However, by having the functions in the server in packages and/or views, they are much more easily shared by other reports and forms.

TIP

Server-side storage of functions can have a profound impact on report performance. With a simple report that might take several hours to execute, by moving the database intensive functions to the server, report performance can usually be greatly improved.

Outer Joins

One of the reasons that multiple queries are often used and linked is that if two tables are joined using a simple equi-join, data that should be printed in the report may be missed. For example, in a standard Dept/Emp report, if you join DEPT and EMP, the report will not display departments that have no employees whereas a report with two linked queries will display all departments. However, if you use the appropriate outer join, you can also display departments that have no employees.

Of course, outer joins take longer to execute than queries without outer joins. But a report with an outer join will usually run much faster than the same report using linked multiple queries.

Temporary Report Tables

A technique that is used all too often is to build a temporary table that is populated with the data for a major portion of the report. A relatively simple report can be written to format and display the information in the temporary table. Every time the report is run, the temporary table is repopulated. Such a strategy should almost never be employed.

There is little reason to use that strategy. Extracting and storing all that information in an Oracle table is an extremely time-consuming and costly process. It is rare that a report is so complex and convoluted that it cannot be run without the use of a temporary table. Many existing reports use temporary tables unnecessarily.

One example where a temporary table required significantly improved performance was a large mailing-label report. In this report, several sets of labels, each meeting complex search criteria, had to be retrieved. This system contained a list of several hundred thousand names. Users wanted to be able to specify random subsets from this long list. This was implemented using stored procedures on the server that would accept the query criteria from a Forms front-end. Then, using the DBMS_SQL built-in package to execute dynamic SQL in a PL/SQL procedure, the random subset of names was generated and written to a temporary table. This example illustrates how complex a report needs to be to justify the use of a temporary table. If, while writing any report, you are thinking of using a temporary table, think again. If you can avoid using a temporary table, your report will probably run much more quickly.

In using summary and aggregation tables, there are times when temporary tables are needed to get reports to run with acceptable performance. For example, in a summary table where every row in the table represents a particular month's sales for a particular customer, a temporary table greatly improves performance in writing reports that show total customer sales over a period of time. However, this summary table is built once a month, independent of report execution. Any report could query from that table.

TIP

The number of rows retrieved in any query can be limited through the Maximum Rows To Fetch *property on the query. This is helpful when testing reports being run against very large tables. It can also be used for reports that, by design, only retrieve a specific number of records. For example, for a report that returns information concerning the top 25 customers by sales, simply order by sales in the query and limit the maximum number of rows to 25. This property can also be changed at runtime using the SRW.SET_MAXROW procedure.*

Non-Query Fields

It is sometimes necessary to display information on a report that is not explicitly stored in the database. Such information might be

- **Aggregated information**　For example, the number of people in a department or the total sales for a given period

- **Calculated information**　For example, the total compensation of an employee, which is the sum of salary and commissions

- **A string function**　For example, the first name concatenated with last name

Reports gives you the ability to make complex formula columns. This gives the developer great flexibility; but if incorrectly used, the resulting objects can adversely affect the performance of the report. Reports provides three different types of non-query columns: summary columns (as discussed in Chapter 18), formula columns, and placeholder columns.

Formula Columns

Formula columns are user-defined columns based on PL/SQL functions. They are useful—however, take care when using cursors in formula columns. Every time that formula is executed (which means one time for every row of that type in the report), another query is fired off to the database. An alternative that almost always enhances performance is to place the formula in the database as a function and make it part of the base query, thereby reducing network traffic.

In the Report Wizard's Query Builder, there is a Define Columns icon. Define Columns applies functions to columns in the base query that are sent to the server. Formula columns, on the other hand, are calculated in the client. When using Define Columns, you are limited to the type of columns you can define within the SELECT list of a SQL statement. On the other hand, with formula columns, you can write complex PL/SQL functions. Of course, you always have the option of storing and accessing PL/SQL functions on the server so that any calculations performed on the client using a formula column can also be performed on the server by using a defined column that calls a stored function. However, there may be performance and resource ramifications to consider. In general, performance can be greatly improved by careful placement of the code, specifically on the client (middle tier) or on the database server side. The most dramatic improvement can be seen with formula columns that use cursors, which may be fetching many rows from the database in order to determine a calculated value. Such code should always be stored and executed on the server. In one example, a report that required 12 minutes to execute using a formula column containing an embedded cursor ran in only 40 seconds after that code was moved to the server.

Indicator Formula Columns

Another trick with formula columns is to use them as indicators. For example, to have a departmental report display the number of men and women in each department, make two formula columns in the employee group, one for men and one for women. The value in the column for men is 1 if the employee is a man, and 0 otherwise. Likewise, the value in the column for women is 1 if the employee is a woman, and 0 otherwise. A simple summary count field can then be used in the master group to ascertain the number of men and women.

Placeholder Columns

Placeholder columns act as global variables in the Data Model. They can be used to keep track of certain values that you may want to print on your report. Formula columns in concert with PL/SQL package variables can perform the same functions. Choosing Placeholder or Formula columns in this context is essentially a matter of development style.

A good use of these columns is as placeholders when creating default layouts. Create extra placeholder fields with no labels to help position fields correctly in a report. This will be discussed in more detail in Chapter 20.

Placeholder columns are also best used when you will be populating an object on the screen using an SRW.SET command built-in function. The placeholder column generates an associated field in the Layout Model. In the format trigger on the Layout field, you invoke the appropriate SRW.SET command. This is done to populate the placeholder column. This is a powerful but rarely needed feature. An example of its use is a report that starts on a specific page number. The desired starting page number is passed in as a parameter and uses an SRW.SET command to add the starting page number to the logical page number for display. This technique could also be used for some complex accumulating function where information in a package variable is being periodically updated as the report runs, and it is necessary to display the contents of that package variable. The code is shown next:

```
FUNCTION upd_page_num
    RETURN BOOLEAN
IS
    v_tempnum NUMBER;
BEGIN
    srw.get_page_num(v_tempnum);
    srw.set_field_num(0, v_tempnum + ( TO_NUMBER (:p_start_page) - 1));
    globals.page_numbers := v_tempnum + TO_NUMBER (:p_start_page) - 1;
    RETURN (TRUE);
END;
```

Report-Level Objects

When building reports, you frequently need data objects (such as summary columns) that are not dependent on groups or even queries. Such objects are *report-level* objects. Report-level objects can be stored in several places. The best place to put them, if possible, is in the Data Model.

In the Data Model, report-level objects are columns that do not belong to a query. However, there are limitations to placing objects here. Data Model objects cannot be manipulated while the report is running. If you want to manipulate variables directly while the report is running, you should define the report-level objects as package variables. Package variables are defined in a package that is created under the Program Units node of the Object Navigator. Package variables can be freely updated and retrieved while the report is running. For example, you could use package variables for complex calculation of page numbers or other accumulating calculations not easily handled by the standard Reports functionality.

Some common objects that you might create as report-level objects are grand total summary objects and titles or footers for reports that are programmatically determined. To create report-level objects in the Data Model, create a formula, summary, or placeholder column outside of any group.

You can also create report-level objects as user parameters, but this is necessary only if you need to manipulate them from outside the report. This outside manipulation can be specified in one of two ways:

- By the user on the parameter form when the report is run

- Set prior to the report being called and passed to the report in a parameter list through a RUN_PRODUCT or RUN_REPORT_OBJECT command from Forms, or passed from the command line when the runtime version of Reports is called

TIP
If you are trying to pass parameters to Reports from a product outside the Oracle environment, you are limited to the number of characters available on the command line—256 characters in some operating systems. This severely limits the amount of information that can be passed to a report. If you need to pass large amounts of information to a report from an application outside the Oracle environment, you may need to place the information into a database table or a text file that can be retrieved by the report as soon as it opens.

Groups

Chapter 18 discusses basic information about the creation of groups. The report layout does not operate directly on queries, but instead works on the group. The group acts as an intermediate staging area for the data in between the query and the layout. Groups define the master-detail relationships within the data. Thus, you may return the information in a query and then break that single query into any number of master-detail groups.

Defining the groups correctly in the Data Model is a key step in the development of the report. If the groups are not laid out correctly, the report can perform badly or return unpredictable information.

Initially, when you generate a query in the Data Model without using the Report Wizard, Reports places all the columns from the query in a single group. It is then up to you to split the columns into their appropriate groups. For example, using the simple Dept and Emp report, all columns from the department table would go into the parent group, whereas columns from the employee table would go into the child group. Note that formula and summary columns must be placed in the appropriate groups. For example, if you are creating a summary column to calculate the average salary for all the employees in a department, you would place this summary in the DEPT group. If you were calculating the total employee compensation (salary + commission), this summary would be placed in the EMP group.

For summary columns, not only do you need to place them in appropriate groups, but you must also specify the rules for where the summary columns are reset. The reset point for a summary column is almost always at the group in which you place the summary column. The only exception to this is when you are creating cumulative summaries. For example, if you were displaying a running total of salaries across the entire organization, the reset point for the summary column would be the report. The reset point can be set on the summary column Property Palette by changing the *Reset At* property. This governs the point at which the summary is set back to zero. Your options are the Report (that is, it is never reset), Page, or any of the groups at or above where the summary column is set.

If you have multiple queries that are linked, the groups also become linked. For example, in Figure 19-4, on the left, there are two linked queries (Q1 and Q2) with groups A & B and C & D, respectively. The effect of linking these two queries generates a master-detail chain starting with the groups in the master query and ending with the groups in the child query. The group structure of the two queries on the left and the single query (Q3) on the right are equivalent.

The group linking structure in a report need not be linear. Consider the example of a report where, for a project, it is necessary to show the people assigned to the

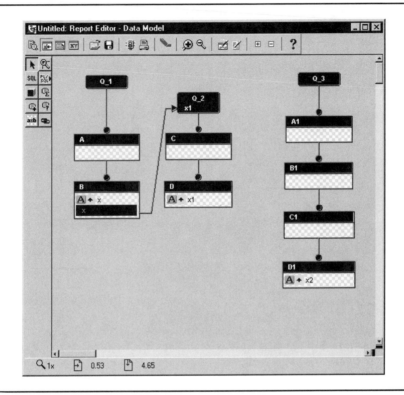

FIGURE 19-4.   *The effect of linking queries on group relationships*

project with their associated responsibilities. In addition, the costs associated with the project need to be viewed. The Data Model would look like this:

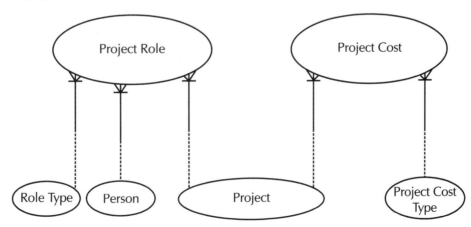

The query model would be set up as shown in Figure 19-5.
The effective group master-detail structure is shown as follows:

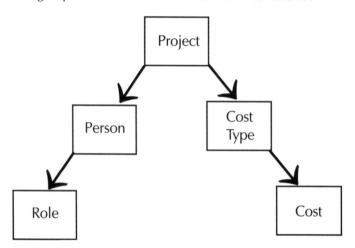

Break Columns

When you create groups, the columns in the group all have little blue arrows displayed next to them in the Data Model. These arrows indicate that the column has been marked as a *break order* column. There are two significant functions of the break order column. The first, and most important, is that it indicates the unique identifier of the group. Frequently, you will add nonprinting columns to a report in order to guarantee uniqueness in a break group. Suppose, for example, that in the Dept and Emp report, you are creating a master-detail relationship between DEPT and EMP and only put DNAME in your DEPT group. If there happen to be two departments with the same name, they would automatically be combined. Even if you put DEPTNO in the DEPT group, if it is not marked as a break column, it will not be used as the unique identifier column. Therefore, departments with the same name will still be combined.

When designing a report, it is important to look carefully at what columns are marked as break columns. By default, Oracle marks all columns as break columns. However, this places unnecessary ORDER BYs into the SQL query passed to the database and can affect performance. Leaving all the columns in a group marked as break columns is a sloppy development practice.

TIP

Set the Break Order *property of all nonbreak columns to "None." This will give you slightly better performance.*

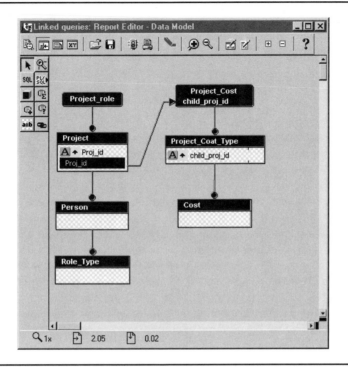

FIGURE 19-5. *Query model example*

The second function of break columns is as a sort order on the break group. They will not affect sorting in the detail group. This must be handled using an ORDER BY in the base query. The sorting is done by the order in which the columns appear in the group.

Specifying Groups

In general, groups correspond to print areas on your report. The identification of a group is much more complex than it seems. It is not always easy to specify the queries and their groups. Part of the problem is that groups don't necessarily correspond to tables in the query. Usually they do. However, frequently, the number of groups is different from the number of tables in the query or queries generating the groups.

A key concept is that groups must be *named.* The name of the group should be the real world object (usually a table) that this group is storing information about. The name of the group should correspond to the word completing this sentence: "Each row in this group is displaying information about a . . . ." In the Dept/Emp report, the appropriate names for master-detail groups are "DEPT" and "EMP," respectively. It is not usually difficult to create an appropriate name for the group. If you are having trouble, it is a good indication that the data model is flawed. However, depending on the report layout, the information in that group will not necessarily be attributes of that object's table. For example, in a Dept/Emp report, next to each employee, the name of that employee's department can be displayed. It is still an EMP group displaying information about employees, but DNAME is not an attribute of EMP.

You may actually have more groups in your Data Model than areas on your report, but this is very rare. The only time you should have extra groups on your report is when you are choosing not to display the lowest level of detail on the report, but are still returning this detail to the report for complex calculation purposes. You should rarely have the fields representing the columns in a group not displayed, unless they are the lowest level of detail in the group. A common mistake is to have extra groups at the highest level of aggregation in joined queries. As in the earlier example of a project report displaying the personnel associated with a project as well as associated costs, this obviously requires two queries. It would be tempting to set up the two queries as shown in Figure 19-6.

However, in this case, the project group in the second query is not necessary.

Group Filters

One of the most interesting features in the Data Model is the ability to filter information in a group. This can be done using the group Property Palette and setting the *Filter Type* property. For each group, you can specify one of three filter types:

1. **First**   This has the same kind of effect as specifying the maximum rows for the query, except this is a specification for the group. You specify a number of rows to view with the *Number of Records* property.

2. **Last**   This will hide all rows except those at the end of the query. You specify a number of rows to view with the *Number of Records* property.

3. **PL/SQL**   This will allow you to place a complex filter on the group.

When this capability was first added to the product, it appeared to be an exciting feature that would be very useful. However, in practice, it is rarely used.

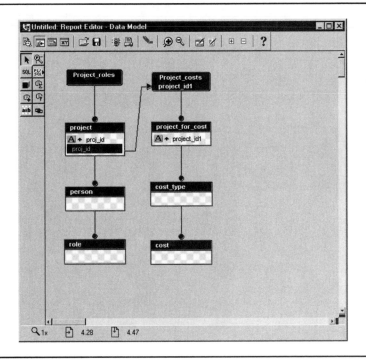

FIGURE 19-6.   *Query model with unnecessary group*

CHAPTER
20

The Reports
Layout Model

I was framed.

—Al Capone (1899–1947)

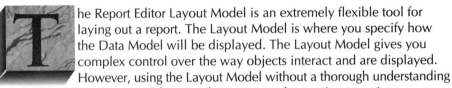he Report Editor Layout Model is an extremely flexible tool for laying out a report. The Layout Model is where you specify how the Data Model will be displayed. The Layout Model gives you complex control over the way objects interact and are displayed. However, using the Layout Model without a thorough understanding of how it works can be one of the most frustrating and annoying experiences you can have as a developer.

The Layout Model operates very differently from similar functions in other reporting tools. Many reporting tools, especially those advertised for end users, employ a banded structure. They have predefined horizontal areas (*bands*) where the different physical sections of the report are specified. Such a concept works fine for most reports. However, horizontal banding is inherently restrictive. Sometimes this limitation makes it virtually impossible to create a complex report. Oracle Reports uses a fundamentally different approach based on two very important underlying concepts:

- **Complete independence of the Data Model and the layout** First, you create the Data Model. Then the layout is created separately. The Data Model should be complete before you create the Layout Model. The idea is to construct a default layout quickly to validate that no more information is needed in the report. You must return to the Data Model for more information. An important reason for the Data Model to be complete before working on layout manipulation is that beyond default layout creation, adding new objects is tedious. You should use the Report Wizard to generate as much of your report as possible. The more of your report that can be generated automatically, the better. Most reports can be created using only the Report Wizard and Additional Layout Default tool (discussed later), requiring almost no manual manipulation in the Layout Model.

- **Using frames** Rather than using fixed horizontal bands, you can specify any number of rectangular regions in the report called *frames*. Frames group objects in the report layout. They also govern the layout behavior of the report, controlling print direction, master-detail relationships, and page breaks. The key to the Layout Model is in understanding how frames and objects work and interact.

CAUTION
A key limitation to the default layout utility is its inability to specify the format mask for a column before performing a default layout. If this were possible, virtually all reports would require no manual work in the Layout Model.

All of this flexibility enables you to create almost any report imaginable—but it comes with a price. To provide all of this flexibility, you must correctly set a number of properties within each frame. Incorrect property settings can cause unpredictable results and hours of frustration. Therefore, it is important to understand how frames work and how they can be used to create complex reports.

Because frames and objects can be placed anywhere in the report layout, when the report is printed, Reports must use precise rules to control how objects interact in the report. Frequently, if an object has so much data that it wraps to a second or third line, objects below it must move down to make space. Of course, objects must appear next to their associated labels, so they cannot be moved arbitrarily. The governing of object placement on the screen is called *anchoring* (discussed later in the section "Anchors: Keeping Things Where They Belong"). When run, the report will apply default anchoring to all of the objects in the layout. This default anchoring can be overridden by using explicit anchoring. One feature of Developer is that you can see the default anchoring that Reports applies to objects. You do this by making the Object Navigator the active window, selecting **Navigator→Navigator Options,** and checking the Anchoring Information box in the Layout tab, as shown in Figure 20-1. This will show you all of the explicit anchors that you have manually inserted as well as some of the default anchors that Oracle generates.

One additional feature that makes Reports such a powerful reporting tool is its use of the PL/SQL language. You can write complex PL/SQL procedures governing whether or not objects or groups of objects are displayed. You can also write PL/SQL functions that can return data, which is then displayed in the report.

Oracle Reports is not as flexible as a 3GL such as C++. There are limits to what can be accomplished in the Layout Model. For example, you cannot programmatically create objects or frames at runtime. You can only alter objects in a limited fashion. However, unless you are trying to write your own ad hoc query tool, Reports should be able to handle any reporting needs.

This chapter will demystify the Layout Model so you can really exploit the extraordinary strengths of the Reports product. Even if you are an experienced Reports user, this chapter will provide some useful tips and techniques that you may not have discovered.

Working with the Layout Model

Once you understand the way objects can be manipulated and what properties can be changed, you will be able to create the reports that you want. The principal point to understand with respect to the Layout Model is that you will not perform most actions in the Layout Model. The combination of the Additional Default Layout tool (discussed further below) and the Reports templates means that the number of times you will need to create or manipulate objects in the Layout Model is small.

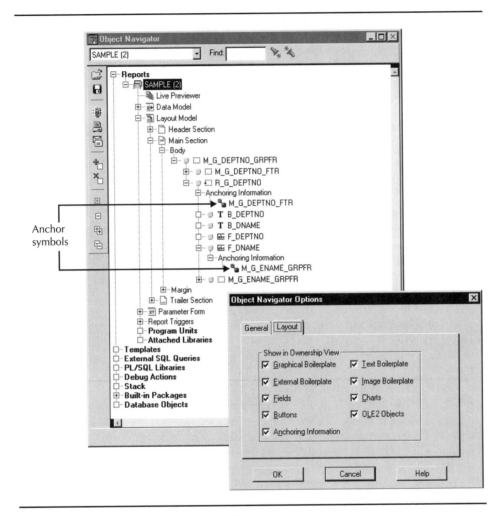

FIGURE 20-1. *Object Navigator options*

You should avoid manually performing the following actions in the Layout Model:

■ **Creating repeating group and layout objects**   This task is more easily performed using the Additional Default Layout tool.

■ **Creating a field**   Fields are usually most easily added by deleting the whole frame and regenerating it using the Additional Default Layout tool. You will still need to manually add summary fields and fields placed in margins or in header or footer sections of the report.

■ **Setting manual anchors**   You can place enclosing frames around objects to get anchoring to work correctly. Anchoring is discussed later in this chapter.

Actions that you will sometimes perform in the Layout Model include the following:

■ **Setting the *Format Mask* property for fields**   There is no way to create a format mask using the Report Wizard. You cannot specify a default format mask with a template. You will have to select your object either in the Layout Model Object Navigator or Live Previewer and apply the format mask. Note that you can apply some common format masks using the toolbar icons in the Live Previewer (Add/Remove precision past the decimal point and similar functions).

■ **Creating labels**   Most labels will be generated correctly by the Report Wizard. Occasionally you will need to create your own.

■ **Using enclosing frames around objects**   This will make the anchoring algorithm (as described later in this chapter) perform correctly.

■ **Setting properties on some objects**   The most common property to set is *Maximum Records per Page* on a repeating frame. This is usually set to 1 to enforce that each record appears on its own page.

■ **Setting the *Keep With Anchoring Object* property**   For fields and/or frames, setting this property will sometimes avoid orphaning headings.

■ **Placing format triggers on objects**   The most common use of formatting is to suppress printing a frame, header, or field.

Now that Reports includes the Live Previewer, there is a subset of actions that can be performed in the Layout Model that can also be performed in the Live Previewer with the advantage of instantaneously seeing the impact of any changes made. For this reason, the following actions are best done in the Live Previewer:

■ Setting *Format Mask* properties (there are now special icons on the Layout Model toolbar to make common numeric format mask changes)

■ Changing column widths

■ Changing the *Font* and *Font Style* properties of text objects

■ Changing object colors

Working with Frames

As mentioned briefly in Chapter 18, frames come in two varieties, *repeating* frames, which are associated with groups in the Data Model, and *enclosing* frames, which influence the anchoring of the objects within the frame and visually group objects in the report.

Repeating Frames

Repeating frames are always associated with exactly one group. Every object in that repeating frame must either be from that group, or from a parent group, or must be a report-level object. The symbols for repeating frames are shown in the following illustration:

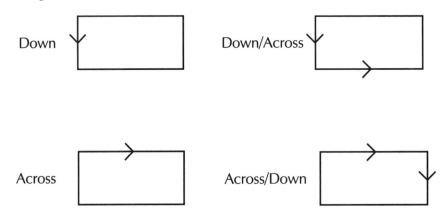

If you put an object into the repeating frame from a group that is a child to that group or an object from a group in an unconnected query, you will get the following error message when you try to run the report:

Field <field name> references column <column name> at a frequency below its group.

Repeating frames are always associated with exactly one group. Every object in that repeating frame must either be from that group, or from a parent group, or must be a report-level object. If you put an object into the repeating frame from a group that is a child to that group or an object from a group in an unconnected query, you will get an error message when you try to run the report. To explain this restriction, consider the Data Model shown in Figure 20-2 and its associated Layout Model shown in Figure 20-3.

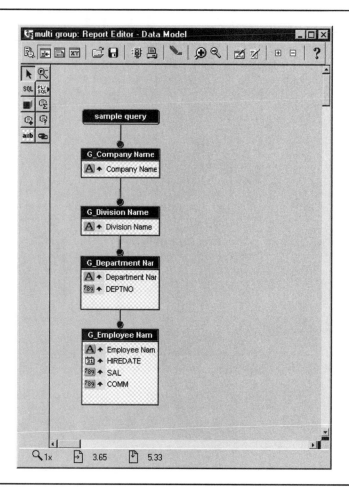

FIGURE 20-2.   *Sample Data Model with multiple groups*

If you have a repeating frame based on the Department group, any objects from the department group can obviously be placed in that repeating frame. However, any object from the division group, company group, or any report-level object could also be placed in the repeating frame, as shown in Figure 20-3.

Since this frame will print once for each department, it makes no sense to place an object from the Employee group in the Department frame because there are many employees in each department. In the Department frame, you could print the name of the company or the division next to the name of each department, or you could show the total salary for all companies with each department, even though

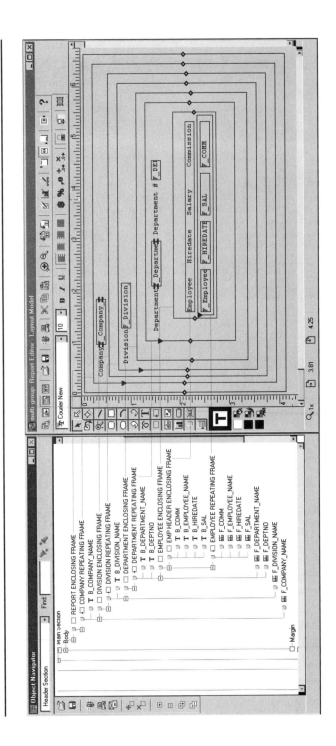

FIGURE 20-3. Sample Layout Model with multiple groups

that may or may not make sense in the context of a specific report. Practically, this is almost never done. All columns in a frame should come from that frame's group. This makes it possible for the frame layout to be created using the Report Wizard or the Additional Layout Default tool.

There is no problem with including a field that logically belongs in a higher group as a field in a lower-level group. For example, if you put the Dname column in the Employee group, it simply shows the name of the department for each employee. That value will be repeated for every employee in that department. If you want to display the information in both master and detail frames in the report, then the field must be placed in both groups. This is easily accomplished by selecting the column twice with an alias in the query. Rather than creating an additional object in the Data Model, you could simply create an additional layout object manually and attach it to the same source column. However, if you create the additional object in the Data Model, this enables you to create your layout objects automatically rather than creating them by hand. In the case of a formula or summary column, create the formula or summary column at the highest level and mirror its value through a formula column that simply returns the value of the summary or formula field.

Print Direction

After you have specified the group that the frame will be based on, you need to decide how you want the information to be laid out on the page. Specify the *Print Direction* property in the repeating frame's Property Palette. Since there is a repeating frame, it is assumed that multiple records will be returned from the group. If you know that the group will only return a single record, then setting the *Print Direction* property is irrelevant. There are four different options that can be selected:

- ■ **Down**   The frame will be repeated down the page until the bottom, at which point records will continue printing on the next page. This is by far the most common layout option. The remaining three options are infrequently used.

- ■ **Across**   The frame will be repeated moving from left to right across the page. When there is no more room, the process is repeated across on the next page. This option is most frequently used for reports with multiple columns of similar data, for example, multiyear budgets where each column represents a year's worth of data. You also use this option for a matrix report.

- ■ **Across/Down**   The frame will be repeated across the page until there is no more room, at which point it is repeated underneath on the same page like a text word-wrap. This can be useful in a situation where you have multiple observations on a specific test sample. The repeating frame holding the observations would be given the print direction across/down.

■ **Down/Across**   The frame will be repeated down the page until there is no more room, at which point it is repeated at the top of the same page. This is useful for mailing labels.

Vertical and Horizontal Elasticity

Elasticity refers to how objects can expand or contract in response to varying amounts of information contained in the data to be displayed. The *Vertical Elasticity* and *Horizontal Elasticity* properties can be applied to frames and data fields in either the Layout Model or the Live Previewer by right-clicking on the frame or field and changing the settings in the Property Palette. You can set either of these properties to "Contract," "Expand," "Fixed," or "Variable." You do not apply elasticity to boilerplate objects—lines, rectangles, static text, and so on.

Expansion or contraction on an object only takes place on one side of the object. With respect to horizontal elasticity, expansion and contraction only take place on the right. For vertical elasticity, expansion and contraction only take place from the bottom of the object. This is important to remember. For example, if there is blank space at the top of the frame, that space will remain no matter what the elasticity option, whereas blank space at the bottom of the frame may disappear.

There are four options for each direction of elasticity:

■ **Contract**   When the report is run, the object must be no bigger than its size in the Layout Model. If there is blank space available, the object can become smaller, but it will not be allowed to get larger. If there is too much information to fit in the frame, it will truncate.

■ **Expand**   When the report is run, the object must be at least the size shown on the Layout Model. If there is too much data to be accommodated by the existing frame or field, it will be expanded to the right for a horizontal expand or down for a vertical expand.

■ **Fixed**   The size in the Layout Model is exactly the same as the size on the report when it is executed. There is no symbol for fixed size.

■ **Variable**   The frame or object is free to expand or contract as much as necessary to accommodate the data to be displayed in the object.

Symbols for each elasticity type are illustrated here:

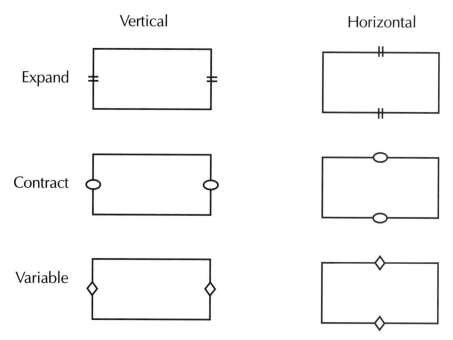

Having the elasticity set incorrectly can cause all sorts of problems that are difficult to diagnose. The most common settings to use for a repeating frame are *Horizontal Elasticity* "Fixed" and *Vertical Elasticity* "Variable." This allows the frame to expand downward as much as is necessary. If you make a repeating frame (particularly a master repeating frame) "Fixed" in the print direction that the child frame is trying to expand, you will get unpredictable results. Fixing a frame's horizontal or vertical elasticity can frequently be helpful. If you are working with a preprinted form where things must be laid out precisely, using fixed formats makes sense. Enclosing frames use fixed elasticity about half of the time. If they are surrounding boilerplate text or fields that don't wrap, then fixed elasticity makes the layout somewhat easier to understand. Recall that if you use Variable or Contract elasticity, what you see in the Layout Model can be very different from what you see in the Live Previewer due to the extra space in the objects, which may disappear as the frames expand or contract.

Fields

Most fields are commonly fixed both vertically and horizontally. The amount of information in the field is known along with the amount of information coming from the field. This information will show up in a specific place in the report.

NOTE
If you specify a width for the field smaller than the database size in the Report Wizard, when Reports creates the field, by default it will generate it with a setting of Vertical Elasticity "Expand," which would allow word wrapping within the field.

For comment and description fields, *Horizontal Elasticity* "Fixed" and *Vertical Elasticity* "Expand" are most commonly used. This combination is also frequently useful for a field if you want to have a field of indeterminate length and need to be able to place another object just to the right of the displayed information. A specific example of this will be given in the section "Anchors: Keeping Things Where They Belong."

Horizontal Elasticity and *Vertical Elasticity* "Variable" settings for fields are rarely needed.

Frames

The *Horizontal Elasticity* and *Vertical Elasticity* properties of most frames are set to "Fixed" and "Variable," respectively. Repeating and enclosing frames must have the *Vertical Elasticity* property set to "Variable" in order to accommodate information in any repeating/down objects or objects in the frame that expand down. If you find yourself getting only one or two records per page, it is likely to be because you have set a frame with *Vertical Elasticity* "Fixed."

TIP
If you create a frame manually in the Layout Model, by default it will be fixed both horizontally and vertically. Be sure to change the elasticity selection if necessary.

Frames that are used to group fields and their labels are usually fixed in both directions. Other settings for frames are used in matrix reports, which are discussed in Chapter 23 but are otherwise infrequently used.

Repeating frames are frequently fixed in both directions, unless one of the fields inside has vertical expansion. In that case, the frame should have its

Horizontal Elasticity property set to "Fixed" and *Vertical Elasticity* property set to "Expand."

The "Contract" and "Expand" elasticity settings are less frequently used. However, there are some exceptions that will be discussed in the following examples.

Example Elasticity Settings for Fields and Frames

A few examples where elasticity is used in a nonstandard way are listed next.

■ *Horizontal Elasticity* **"Contract"** and *Vertical Elasticity* **"Fixed"** Ordinarily, horizontal contraction is not necessary for a field. This can be used in a report where a dotted line connects two fields. The *Horizontal Elasticity* "Contract" setting allows the field to be only as wide as is necessary to display the data. In addition, you should place an extra space on the end of the field so that there is a small gap before the dots begin. In the example shown in Figure 20-4, the F_Name object has the Property Palette settings of *Horizontal Elasticity* "Contract" and *Vertical Elasticity* "Fixed."

■ *Horizontal Elasticity* **"Fixed"** and *Vertical Elasticity* **"Fixed"** This setting can be used for a repeating frame, as shown in Figure 20-5. This configuration is used quite frequently for preprinted forms. You can also use it for objects that have at most one or two detail records, so that each master block takes up the same amount of space. The Employee repeating frame has its Property Palette set to *Horizontal Elasticity* "Fixed" and *Vertical Elasticity* "Fixed."

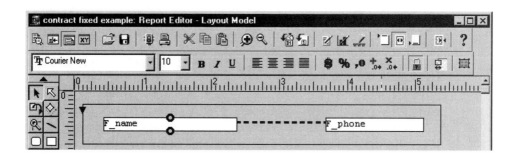

FIGURE 20-4. *Example of* Horizontal Elasticity *"Contract" and* Vertical Elasticity *"Fixed"*

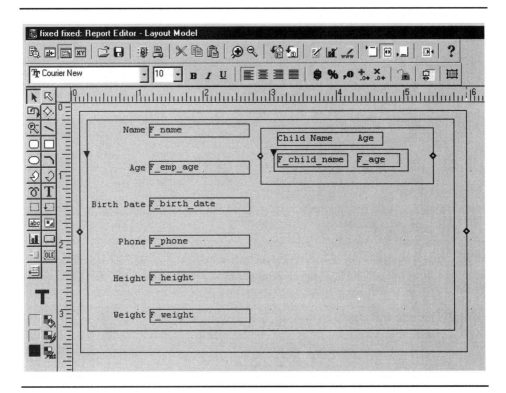

FIGURE 20-5. *Example of* Horizontal Elasticity *"Fixed" and* Vertical Elasticity *"Fixed" frame*

■ *Horizontal Elasticity* **"Fixed"** and *Vertical Elasticity* **"Variable"** This setting is a useful trick for an enclosing frame surrounding boilerplate text, as shown in Figure 20-6. In general, objects automatically anchor to objects above them. If you place an enclosing frame with these settings around boilerplate text and then put a format trigger on the boilerplate to suppress its printing, the frame will collapse and all objects below it will move up. If you simply suppress the printing of the boilerplate text, objects anchored to it will be positioned as if the boilerplate had printed, leaving white space where the boilerplate text would have been.

Flex Mode

Flex Mode is a great feature that allows you to work more easily with frames. Flex Mode can be turned on in either the Layout Model or the Live Previewer by clicking the Flex Mode icon, as shown in Figure 20-7. With Flex Mode turned on, when you

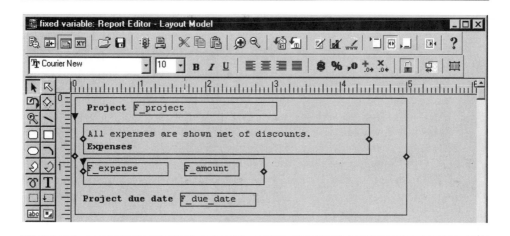

FIGURE 20-6.   *Example of* Horizontal Elasticity *"Fixed" and* Vertical Elasticity *"Variable" frame*

move or resize an object, all other objects in the layout will move accordingly. If a field is in a frame and you move the field, the frame will expand to accommodate the movement. When moving fields, you can only move the objects along a single axis, either horizontally or vertically. This makes sense since otherwise Reports wouldn't know how to move the associated objects. You can always move first horizontally, reselect the object, and then move it vertically.

Confine Mode

Confine Mode keeps all objects inside their parent frames. However, it does not prevent the overlap of sibling frames, which can cause badly laid-out reports. Confine Mode can be activated only in the Layout Model view by clicking on the toolbar icon that looks like a lock, as shown in Figure 20-7.

Furthermore, Reports does not seem to have difficulty with the intersecting frames that are not logically incorrect. However, this does allow you to create some bizarre layouts. In general, you should always keep Confine Mode turned on, except when moving an object (usually a boilerplate object) from one frame to another.

Reports 6.0 has taken a different approach from earlier versions. It will attempt to create a report even if you have done something highly illogical, such as having a child frame overlap a parent frame. If even one pixel of the child frame overlaps the parent frame, Reports will treat the child frame as if it is not inside the parent frame. If you move things around with Confine Mode turned off, you should verify that your layout is still correct in the Object Navigator.

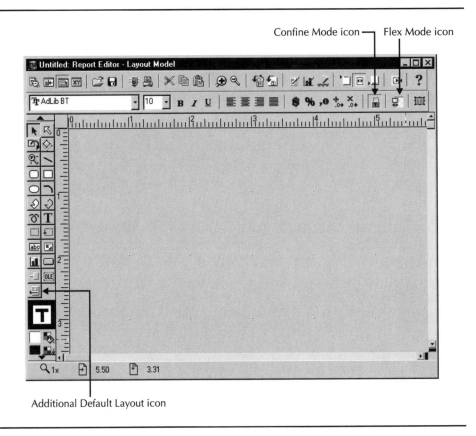

FIGURE 20-7. *Flex Mode, Confine Mode, and Additional Default Layout icons*

Additional Default Layouts

The feature that most effectively minimizes manual use of the Layout Model is the Additional Default Layout tool. Learning how to use this tool effectively will save you hours of time that you would otherwise spend modifying your report layouts by hand. Typically, when starting out with the Oracle Reports product, a developer would spend less than an hour crafting the report query and the remainder of the day working with the Layout Model. After you learn how to create reports effectively, the time spent using the Layout Model significantly decreases. By using the Additional Default Layout tool, you can create the layout for each group individually. This method is usually used for creating a single group. However, this is not to say that you cannot generate your entire report using the Additional Default Layout. To use this feature, click on the Additional Default Layout icon on the lower left of the vertical toolbar, as shown in Figure 20-7.

Drag out to define an area where you want the generated layout to be placed. This area must be large enough to accommodate the entire layout. If you are generating a child group, you should build it inside the parent repeating frame. After specifying the area for the layout, you are presented with a modified Report Wizard. You cannot modify the query, but you can select the groups and columns that you want to generate. Typically, to refine the layout of a report, a group is created, viewed in the Live Previewer, deleted, and then modifications are made to the Data Model or field widths are modified in the Report Wizard before regenerating. This process is repeated until the layout is correct. Using this strategy can greatly decrease the time spent using the Layout Model.

Adding Fields

At the end of your report, you discover that there is a field missing. How do you add a field to the report? The way that most developers do this is to readjust everything by hand to make room for the new field. This can be very time-consuming. Instead, the entire frame containing the space where the new field will be placed along with any objects it contains should be deleted and re-created using the Additional Default Layout feature. This is by far the easiest way to accomplish the task of adding a field to a report. However, this method only works well if you are building your report relying on the Report Wizard and templates.

There are rare occasions where adding a new field manually is necessary. To do this, you need to create the necessary space by turning on the Flex Mode feature and moving either an object or a handle on a frame. Double-check that you are in the right group, and then create the new field and assign it to a source that is the same as the group you are in. You can assign, as a source, a column from a higher-level group, but this is not recommended. If you assign an invalid source (often a column from a group at a lower level of the query group), you will get an error message saying that the field references a column at a level below its group.

Moving Objects

In general, the method for moving objects around on the screen is the same as that for adding fields.

CAUTION
Until you know what you are doing, moving objects can be tricky. You should rerun your report frequently to ensure that you haven't corrupted your report layout. Remember to save the report frequently. You can also use Undo (in the Edit menu) to reverse the last action.

If objects are generated correctly the first time by the Additional Layout Default tool and the Report Wizard, they don't need to be moved. If fields are in the wrong order, move them in the Data Model and then redo the layout using the Report Wizard. If fields are not laid out appropriately for a form, add placeholder columns and regenerate the layout using the Report Wizard. There are few times that you will need to manually move objects. You can also move objects in the Live Previewer.

TIP
Don't turn off the Lock button. This keeps most objects from moving outside of their logical groups. This does not work for sibling frames, but will protect you from most mistakes.

If you must move a label from one frame to another, turn off the Lock button, move the label to its new location, and turn the Lock button back on, being careful to ensure that the label is completely enclosed by its new parent frame. Oracle Reports is usually smart about moving things to their appropriate logical groupings. However, you should still verify that any object you move is correctly positioned logically within the Object Navigator. In previous versions of Reports, you needed to frequently use Move Backward/Move Forward selections in the Arrange menu of the Layout Model to correctly position objects after movement. Sometimes in the old version, you were unable to move objects within the right parent frame. The workaround was to cut and paste the objects and then reposition them. These tactics do not seem to be necessary with the current version of Reports, but may be useful if you are still having difficulty positioning objects correctly.

Layout objects sit within a logical hierarchical structure. Parent repeating frames enclose child repeating frames. Objects within a repeating group must be within the repeating frame. Objects within an enclosing frame must be subordinate to the enclosing frame. Objects that are all within the same place in the hierarchy are within the same *layer* in Reports. Oracle Reports has improved over time with automatic placement of objects within their correct layers. If you move an object in the Layout Model, it will automatically be repositioned into the appropriate logical layer. The most common exception to this occurs when you create an enclosing frame around some existing objects. You might think that this frame would enclose these objects. This is not the case. Instead, the frame will be created in the same layer as the objects. To logically reposition the frame, you need to move the frame up in the logical tree either by selecting **Arrange→Move Backward** or by pressing F8. When performing this operation, look closely at the Object Navigator to see when the frame has been moved to its appropriate logical position. Automatic positioning of objects in the correct layers is usually handled appropriately by Reports. But when manual objects are created, you should double-check to see that they are in the correct layer. If not, move the object into the correct layer using one of the following menu/function key options:

- **Arrange→Bring to Front** or F5
- **Arrange→Send to Back** or F6
- **Arrange→Move Forward** or F7
- **Arrange→Move Backward** or F8

Anchors: Keeping Things Where They Belong

The placement of objects in a report is fundamentally different than the placement of items in Oracle Forms. When you place an object on a screen, that is its placement. In a report, it is expected that the position of objects placed will be adjusted based on the way other report objects expand or contract. Simple, banded report writers handle this by placing objects in horizontal bands across the screen, which expand or contract as necessary. In Reports, you are not restricted to building reports with simple bands. Instead, you can use a rich selection of rectangular objects that expand and contract either vertically or horizontally. Oracle Reports users expect the product to provide appropriate layouts. To accomplish this, objects automatically anchor themselves to each other. In general, an object anchors itself to its nearest neighbor that might expand or move toward it. The default anchoring algorithm is based upon identification of each object's best "pushing" object. The details of this algorithm can be found in Reports Help under the listing "Body Algorithm." However, if the report does not lay out as expected because objects are overriding each other, you can change the way that objects are anchored either by setting an explicit anchor or by placing an enclosing frame around the objects that are not laid out correctly.

You can use anchors to position a child object relative to its parent both vertically and horizontally. The parent object will show the anchor symbol in the Layout Model. Anchors help you define the relative position of objects since some layout objects may change sizes when the report is run. The positioning is based on the size of the objects after the report is run. By default, Reports will anchor objects in a way that seems the most reasonable. Each object is anchored to its nearest neighbor to the left or above. As mentioned earlier, you can display some of the anchoring information by selecting **Navigator→Navigator Options** and turning on *Anchoring Information* on the Layout tab. You can override the default anchoring by selecting the anchoring tool from the Layout Model's vertical toolbar and clicking on part of the child object. Then click on the part of the parent object where you want the child object anchored. Notice that you must anchor from a specific part of the parent and child objects. This is only important if either parent or child is not fixed in either horizontal or vertical direction. Usually, anchoring one corner to another corner is the best strategy. However, it is almost impossible to draw the anchors this way. Typically, you can draw anchors any way, and then right-click to bring up the Property Palette. Change the percentage field to "0" or "100" on both sides.

Example of an Anchor

Why is it necessary to override default anchors? It is possible to produce hundreds of reports and never need to override the default anchors. However, sometimes there is just no other way to make fields behave properly. An example to illustrate this is a first name field and a last name field that you want to appear on the screen next to each other no matter what the size of the first name field, as shown in Figure 20-8.

You can anchor the end of the first name field to the beginning of the last name field with an appropriate space between the two fields. This gives the illusion that there is only one field printing. A better solution is to make a formula column to concatenate the two fields with a space, thus eliminating the problem.

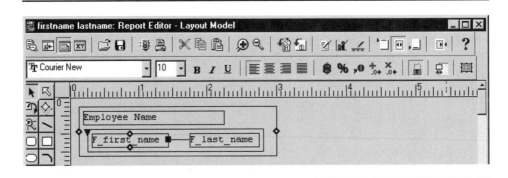

FIGURE 20-8. *Anchors in the Layout Model*

If you find yourself needing lots of anchors, you are probably not crafting your report carefully. Explicit anchors should almost always be avoided. Even in the preceding example, anchors can be avoided by creating a formula column in the Data Model that concatenates the first name with a space and then the last name, or by concatenating the columns in the query. This makes the report design cleaner and easier to maintain. When you are designing forms, think of alternate strategies to avoid excessive use of anchors.

Format Triggers

There is only one kind of trigger associated with a layout object, namely, a format trigger. A format trigger is a Boolean function. If the function returns "True," then the object will be displayed. If the function returns "False," the object is not displayed. This is useful in many contexts. For example, in a master-detail report, there is no need to display the master if no details are present.

You can put a format trigger on the frame surrounding the objects in the master group either on the repeating frame itself or on the frame that surrounds the repeating frame, and suppress printing if there are no detail records. The way to tell that there are no detail records is to make a summary column (NO_OF_RECORDS) in the master group that is a count of its associated detail records. Then write the following formatting trigger for the group:

```
IF no_of_records = 0
THEN
    RETURN FALSE;
ELSE
    RETURN TRUE;
END IF
```

When this code is executed, if there are no child records, the printing of the parent master frame and all of its enclosed objects will be suppressed.

CHAPTER
21

Using and Building Reports Templates

That you may take back a true report to him who sent you.
—*The Holy Bible:* Proverbs 22:20–21

 s mentioned in Chapter 10, an Oracle Developer Forms template is essentially a partially built form. You can make any .FMB file a template in Forms. As a result, this gives you the flexibility to put in triggers, objects, and libraries at whatever level of complexity you choose. An Oracle Developer Reports template works very differently.

A Reports template is a special file with objects that are copied into a report based on preselected properties and information governing the way that a layout is created using the wizards. When a template is applied to an existing report, Reports tries to make the appropriate decisions about which objects should be recopied and how to lay out the report. Unfortunately, the Reports architecture does not include explicit "changed" flags on every object. Therefore, reapplying a template to a report sometimes leads to unexpected behavior in the product.

TIP
Only apply a template to an overall report once. Make additional applications of the template only using the Additional Default Layout tool on the toolbar in the Report Editor—Layout Model. If you are going to change the template upon which a report is based, manually check each aspect of the application of the template to make sure you have achieved the expected result.

This chapter will discuss the following topics:

- Reports template structure

- Building a sample template

- Setting report template standards and putting together a set of templates necessary for a Reports production environment

Reports templates are an extremely valuable addition to Oracle Developer. For the first time, you have the ability to generate elegant reports very quickly. You can even create sophisticated reports requiring little manipulation in the Layout Model. Almost all manual manipulation in the Layout Model should involve nothing more than specifying an Additional Default Layout and generating it using a template. The only exception to this occurs when you need a FORMAT trigger on a frame or object.

If you don't have a set of report templates to support report development, you are not utilizing one of the most important productivity enhancements of the product. With earlier versions of Reports, you could build complex reports quickly, but making them look elegant required extensive manual manipulation. Now such manual intervention is unnecessary—with a template, you can generate sophisticated reports. If you find yourself performing a significant amount of manual manipulation of reports, you are not taking full advantage of Reports templates.

Overview

One of the big differences between Reports templates and Forms templates is the ability to use referenced objects in Forms templates. If your GUI standards change, you can make that change quickly and easily in Forms and have the change reflected in existing forms. With Reports, once you generate a report based on a template, there is no link back to anything in that template. You cannot make a change that will propagate through to multiple reports. The only way to share anything in Reports is either through database objects such as functions and procedures in packages, or through libraries that can be attached to multiple reports. These are the only ways to make changes to more than one report simultaneously. However, if you build your report entirely through the Report Wizard, you can generate a large percentage of your reports. These reports can then quickly be regenerated using a different template.

Reports templates really serve two purposes. In one sense, they serve the same function as Forms templates. You can predefine elements common to all your reports. You can specify various triggers, add user parameters, attach libraries, as well as put common objects in your report layout. The other purpose of Reports templates is to control the way that the report layout is generated through the Report Wizard or the Additional Default Layout tool. You can specify the fonts and many other properties used in fields, labels, and groups.

A number of sample report templates are shipped with Reports. However, most of these are only suitable for demonstrations of the product features and are not intended for production use. For example, many have a photo of the Oracle corporate office as boilerplate.

Limitations

Reports templates have some limitations:

- You cannot place objects in the Body section of the Template Layout Model. This is not a particularly troublesome restriction, but it does force you to place titles, page numbers, dates, and any other template objects in the margin area.

- You cannot create global objects in the Template Data Model. This restriction can be accommodated by creating user parameters and package variables in your template.

- There is no longer any way to specify default Header and Trailer objects in the report template, although this functionality existed in Reports 3.0.

Template Structure

There are several sections in the template that correspond to the sections in a report:

- Data Model
- Layout Model
- Report Triggers
- Program Units
- Attached Libraries

However, these sections are not all the same as the sections for a report. In addition to these sections, there is also a Property Palette for the whole report. If you want to change the default settings in the template's Property Palette, then every report created with the template will have the new settings. The most likely parameters you will change are the *Height* and *Width* of the page. If you are printing in Portrait rather than Landscape format, you will need to change the height and width settings in the Layout Model—Section Property Palette.

Template Editor—Data Model

In a template, by using the Data Model, you are able to specify default system parameters and user parameters. Therefore, it is possible to set defaults for system parameters. For example, you can specify having the report run in preview mode by setting the DESTYPE *Initial Value* property to "Preview" in the Property Palette.

NOTE
A description of the other system parameters can be found in the online help under the topic "System Parameters." You will not find descriptions listed under the individual parameter names in the help system.

You can add user parameters to support the use of lexical parameters or bind variables. You can add any common parameters to the Data Model that you want to have in all reports, such as date ranges or numbers of records. These parameters will automatically be placed in every report generated using this template. Keep in mind that user and system parameters are the only things you can specify in the Template Editor—Data Model of a report template. You cannot create default template queries or include any other objects you would create in the Data Model of the report.

Template Editor—Layout Model

The Layout Model section of the template is the core of the report template. This is where you specify properties that influence the way that the Report Wizard and Additional Default Layout tool generate report layouts. Using a report template, you can specify general properties for any report. You also have the ability to define specific settings for each of the different report types (Tabular, Group Above, Matrix, and so on). You can specify the look of the different visual attributes used for break groups in a master-detail report; for example, you can make the master font size larger than the detail font size. You should set your report level defaults in the Body section, as shown in Figure 21-1. However, for specific report types or specific levels within a report, you might want to have different formatting for different levels. For example, in a master-detail-detail report for Departments, Locations, and Employees, the Department font size can be set to 20 points, Locations to 15 points, and detailed employee information to 12 points.

In the Template Editor—Layout Model, you can only place new objects in the Margin section of the template. In earlier versions of Reports, you were able to place objects in the Header and Trailer sections of the template; however, that functionality has been removed from the product. When you apply a template to a report, any margin objects in the template will be copied into the report.

The body of the report in the template works differently than the margin. You do not have the ability to create any new objects here. Rather, you make changes to properties of objects in the Object Navigator and passively view the impact of those changes in the Layout Model. You can select and modify existing objects in the Layout Model and bring up the Property Palettes to change them, but you cannot create or delete objects in the Layout Model.

Once you have created the defaults in the Main section of the Layout Model, you can *override* the defaults in the Override section. The Override feature allows you to change the default settings for the properties associated with each report style. This must be done separately for each report style. When you specify sections in the override area for specific report styles, they will automatically inherit the properties you set in the Main section.

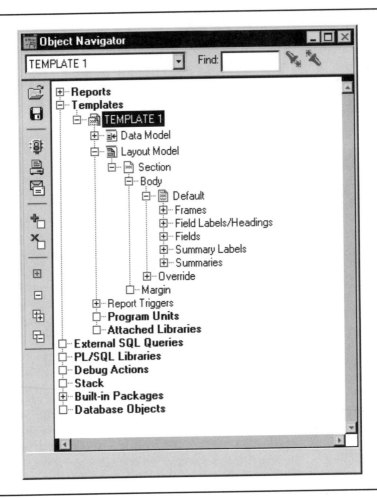

FIGURE 21-1. *Object Navigator template Body section*

When creating templates, you are working in two areas: the Object Navigator and the Template Editor—Layout Model. The most convenient way is to work in the Object Navigator while keeping the Layout Model open to see the effect of changes made in the Object Navigator.

Section

The first area you can manipulate under the Template Editor—Layout Model is the Section Property Palette. This is where you specify a number of properties, including the *Height* and *Width* of a page. Unlike all other template properties, the Section properties cannot be overridden. This is a limitation in the product, since you might want to have a Group Left report based on 11″ × 8½″ (landscape orientation) size paper. To accomplish this, you will need a separate template.

Body

In the Body section, you describe how you want the Layout Editor to work by specifying things such as font sizes and colors for different kinds of objects. If you are creating a complex multilevel master-detail report, you can tell the Report Wizard how each level should be laid out. This feature enables you to build elegant and sophisticated looking reports very quickly. Within the Templates–Layout Model–Body–Default section, you can specify the parameters for how everything in the report will be laid out. In the Templates–Layout Model–Body–Override section, you can change these settings for specific report types and specific parts of specific report types (that is, the master frame can be different from the detail frames).

BODY–DEFAULT SECTION The Property Palette for the Default section governs the behavior of all frames. For example, you can set the amount of horizontal space between fields using the *Interfield (Horizontal)* property. Anything set here can be overridden in the Override section in order to change a particular frame for a specific report type (that is, master-detail-detail).

Within the Templates–Layout Model–Section–Body–Default area of the Object Navigator, you can set properties governing the way that objects are laid out within a repeating group. This governs how a section of a report will behave. For example, space between frames and fields can be set using the Default Property Palette. The amount of space between records in a repeating group, a useful property, is unfortunately not available for setting within a template.

There are five categories of properties you can set in the Default section:

■ **Frames** This Property Palette governs the visual properties of four frame types (Section, Headings, Fields, and Summaries) and how these frames are created, as shown in Figure 21-2. Each time a section of a report is created by the wizard, each of these four types of frames will be shown (three if there are no summaries).

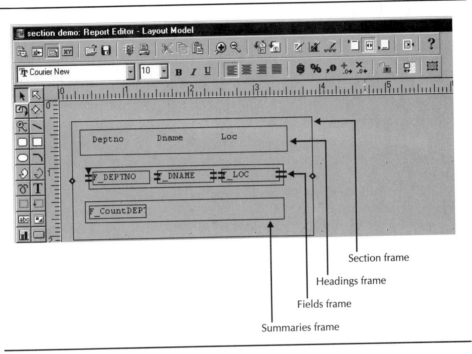

FIGURE 21-2. *Template Layout Model frame types*

- **Field Labels/Headings** This Property Palette allows you to specify the visual appearance of data labels and column headings. There are three different subheadings (Character, Number, and Date) that you can set. Each of these has its own Property Palette. In practice, the only difference you may want between the three might be the *Character Justification* property. Usually, "Left" is used for Character Field Labels and for Headings and Date, and "Right" is for Number Field Labels and Headings.

- **Fields** The same three subsections (Character, Number, and Date) are available for Fields as for Field Labels/Headings. These Property Palettes are used to set the visual properties (such as *Font, Color,* and *Fill Style)* for each type of information. You cannot specify a *Format Mask* here.

- **Summary Labels** The same properties are available for Summary Labels as for Field Labels/Headings.

- **Summaries** You can specify visual properties of Summary data fields for Character, Number, and Date types.

Since most reports are usually master-detail, you will probably want to have each level of the report look slightly different. There are several strategies you can employ to accomplish this. You can either have the default settings apply to the detail and override the master, or vice versa. It is somewhat more intuitive to have the default govern the detail and override the master. The reason for this is that there will be some reports that are not master-detail and that will assume the default.

OVERRIDES   *Overrides* allow you to specify template properties for specific types of reports (and even for different break levels of those reports) that will replace the properties you set in the Default section. In the Templates–Layout Model–Section–Body–Override section, you can specify particular properties for each report type and, where appropriate, for different break levels within each report type. By default, the Override section will use settings from the Default section. Any of these Default properties can be overridden and applied to any type of report or break level within a report.

The properties set in the Body–Default area can be overridden for a specific report type in the Override area Property Palette under each report type. For example, to override the settings for Tabular reports, bring up the Property Palette for the Templates–Layout Model–Section–Body–Override section in the Object Navigator and make the desired changes.

Overrides allow you to specify what parameters you want to set for each type of report, even if they are differ from the overall default settings. One disadvantage to these overrides is that they have to be set separately for each type of report. You cannot specify how master records work in general. For example, you will need to specify master properties for Group Left and Group Above reports separately, even if they have the same properties. One useful and interesting aspect of the override capability is that the properties from the default section Property Palette for each section are available as well as the properties from the Frames, Field Labels/Headings, Fields, Summary Labels, and Summaries sections. This allows you to override any property specified in the Default section.

A limitation is that you cannot override or have different margin objects for each type of report, since they are set once for the entire template. If you want to use different margin objects for different report types, you will have to make a different template for each type of report.

The properties in the Override section are inherited from the Default section with the traditional object-oriented behavior. Specifically, if you change a property in the Default section, it will be inherited in the Override section. You may want to explicitly set a property in the Override section that has the same value as the property in the Default section. The reason for this is that even if the property were changed in the Default section, it would not be overridden for a specific report. An example is setting frame distances in a mailing-label report. These might be the same as the distances for the default, but even if they were to change in the default, you would not want them changed for a mailing-label report. You accomplish this similarly to the way you do it in Forms. Set the value of the property on the inherited object to something different from the default. Then set it back to the original value. This will break the link to the Default section and fix that value in the Override section to the value entered.

Report Triggers

Report triggers have already been discussed briefly in Chapters 8 and 18. In a template you can create specific default report triggers. What happens when you apply a template containing triggers to a report? If the trigger in the template does not already contain code in the report, Oracle Reports copies (not inherits) the code in the trigger from the template. The impact of this can be seen if the template is changed and reapplied. It will not change the code behind the report trigger, because now the trigger already has code behind it. This is one reason not to reapply the template.

Note that this is different from the way Oracle Designer generates triggers. In Designer, in every trigger, you are allowed to have a generated portion of code as well as a manually created portion of code. The code trigger section in Reports is not that sophisticated. The rule is that if there is no code behind the same trigger in the report when the template is applied, then the template code will be copied to the report. Under no other circumstances will the template interact with report triggers.

The report triggers that you write do not have to compile cleanly. The report triggers may be code fragments. If there are parts of the code that must be modified for each report, having the trigger not compile may actually be useful. It forces you to modify the code as you build the report, in order to resolve the compilation errors.

Program Units

Program units behave similarly to report triggers. If you put a program unit in the template and apply that template to a report, it will copy that program unit into your report as expected. If you have an existing program unit with the same name, it will remain unchanged. If the program unit comes into the report through application of the template and you make modifications to the program unit and then reapply the template, all your changes will be unaffected.

CAUTION
If you remove the template from the Report Wizard declaring that the report is not based on a template, it will remove the program units in the template, even if these were modified.

Attached Libraries

As of this writing, the Attached Library functionality in templates is still limited. If there is an attached library in the template when you create a report based on that template, it will attach the library to the report. However, if you delete that attached library in the report and then rerun the Report Wizard applying the template with the attached library, Reports will not bring it back. If you go from a template with an attached library to one without an attached library, it will not remove the old attached library.

If you create a report based on a template with an attached library, it will bring in the attached library. However, if you decide to change templates or delete the attached library, the program may not act the way you think it should. In testing a few different circumstances, there were some instances where Reports did or did not attach the library, or aborted the program. When you are doing anything other than creating a report the first time using the template, check to see if the appropriate libraries are attached.

Building a Sample Template

This section will describe all the activities necessary for the creation of a working Reports template. This template supports the way in which the authors build production reports and should provide a framework for you to build your own Reports templates.

Before building a template, you must be an experienced Reports builder. The goal is to build a tool to increase your report building productivity. Without a clear idea of how to build reports, you will not be able to create a useful template.

An important point to recognize about templates is that you can create a single template to handle multiple kinds of reports. With a single template, you can support different kinds of reports (tabular or form) because the template allows you to specify parameters for each type of report.

The first step is to create a new template by clicking on "Templates" in the Object Navigator and clicking the Create button.

Data Model

Within the Templates–Data Model section of the Object Navigator, some settings need to be changed.

System Parameters

These are the basic system parameters for a report that include a set of defaults. If you are working in client/server mode and generating reports for printing, you will want to change the destination type (DESTYPE) *Initial Value* property to "Preview" to see reports on the screen before printing. Set the DESTYPE *Initial Value* property to "Printer" if you want reports to go directly to the printer. If you want to generate reports for web use, specify the DESTYPE *Initial Value* property as "File," the DESFORMAT *Initial Value* property as "PDF," "RTF," or "HTML," and DESNAME *Initial Value* property as the default path to the file where report outputs are stored. You can override the default value of any of the system parameters to suit your individual reporting needs. These should all be set to your desired options for the template.

User Parameters

A list of user parameters from outside the report can be placed here. These parameters can either be set at runtime using the Parameter Form or passed from Forms through a parameter list. Finally, they can be set through the command line if you are calling reports from another product. There is no limit to or restriction on the datatypes (character/date/numeric) and numbers of user parameters. The parameters suggested here are used by the authors when building a small number of reports. These parameters are passed to the report dynamically at runtime. The available parameters are

- **DISPLAY HEADER (HEAD_DISP)**   This is the title of the report. Make this a character variable field with maximum length of 1,000 characters and an initial value of "sample report title."

- **start page**   The default value is 1, indicating what page number the report will start with.

The remaining user-defined parameters are for dynamic report creation:

- **FLEX_FROM**   This is to add tables in the FROM clause of the query.

- **FLEX_WHERE**   This is for additions to the WHERE clause.

- **break1**   This is for flexible user-selected break columns in the report.

- **break2**   This is for flexible user-selected break columns in the report.

- **break1_disp**   This is for labels for the break columns.

- **break2_disp**   This is for labels for the break columns.

- **FLEX_DISP**   This is a long (2,000-character) display field that carries a narrative description of the flexible criteria passed to the report.

Layout Model

There are only a few objects that you may want to add to the layout. Page numbers, dates/times, and report run titles are the most common objects to add. These must be placed in the report margin. If the Template Editor is not open, right-click anywhere within the Templates section of the Object Navigator and select the Template Editor, as shown in Figure 21-3. You will see the default fonts for the way objects will lay out. Click the Margin button to get to the margin layout area shown in Figure 21-3.

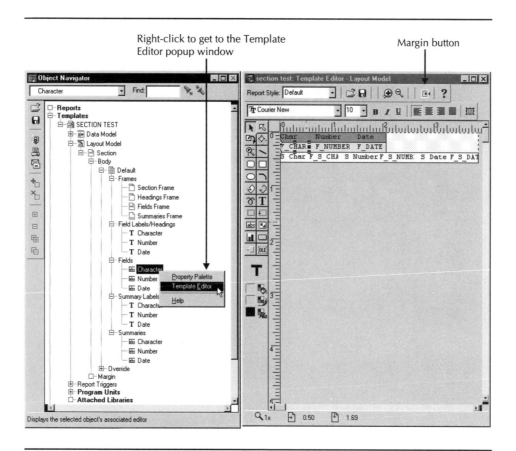

FIGURE 21-3. *Report Template Editor*

Date/Time

To place a date in the upper-left corner of your report, open the Layout Model for the report. Click the Insert Date and Time button on the top toolbar. This will bring up the Insert Date and Time Wizard, where you can select a date or time format, as shown in Figure 21-4. The DD-MM-YYYY format is commonly used.

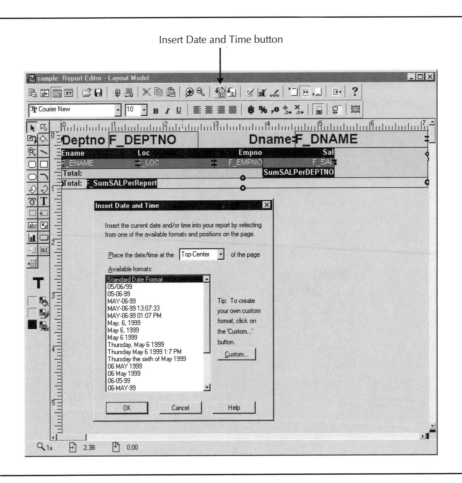

FIGURE 21-4. *Insert Date and Time*

Report Title

Rather than hard-coding the report title, you can pass the title of the report as a user parameter. This allows you to use the same report layout for multiple reports.

The object F_HEADER takes up most of the width of the top margin. The source is the sample report parameter HEAD_DISP. The title for a particular instance of a report is passed from the form. If the title is static for a particular report, simply make that title the initial value for the HEAD_DISP parameter. Its *Horizontal Elasticity* property should be set to "Fixed" so that extra long titles won't run into the date on the left or the page number on the right. The *Vertical Elasticity* property can be "Variable."

Page Number

One way to handle page numbering is to use the default page numbering supported by Reports. For most reports, this is sufficient.

To use the default numbering, follow these steps:

1. Open the Template Editor—Layout Model by right-clicking anywhere in the template area of the Object Navigator and selecting "Template Editor."

2. Click on the Margin button on the top toolbar. You will see a change in the toolbar and a thick line around the body of the report.

3. You can use the Insert Page Number button on the toolbar to bring up the Insert Page Number Wizard and specify the appropriate options.

Following these steps will generate some boilerplate text in the specified location. Note that this procedure will embed the value of a field—in this case, in the Page Number field. When your report runs, it will display "Page" <page number>. Note that the text in the boilerplate object is "Page &<PageNumber>." This technique works anywhere in a report. In any text field, you can embed the value of any report field by prefacing the field name with an "&." This can be useful because boilerplate text can be printed on any angle, whereas text fields can only be printed horizontally. It is also easy to create boilerplate text by hand without using the Wizard.

Report Runtime Parameter Display

The final margin field used in the sample template appears in the lower-left corner of the page, below the body. It is used to show a narrative describing the user parameters passed to the report and is printed only on the first page. Make this field extend all the way across the bottom of the page, as shown in Figure 21-5. The *Horizontal Elasticity* property is set to "Contract"; *Vertical Elasticity* is set to "Variable." The source is FLEX_DISP. In this case, a black line border is used on the field.

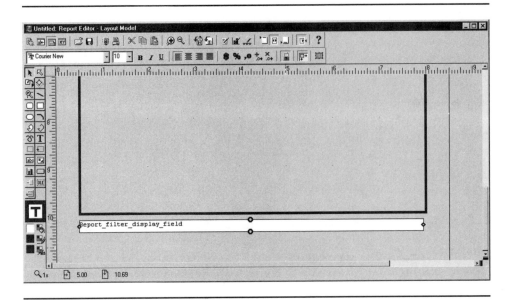

FIGURE 21-5. *Report runtime parameter display*

The following FORMAT trigger is placed on the field to suppress its printing entirely if there is no information being passed:

```
...
    v_return BOOLEAN := TRUE;
BEGIN
    IF :flex_disp IS NULL THEN
        v_return := FALSE;
    END IF:
    RETURN (v_return);
END;
```

Program Units and Attached Libraries

All general PL/SQL functions and procedures that you use for reporting can be placed into program units and attached libraries. You should place all the procedures described earlier in an attached library rather than storing them as program units. The reason for this (in addition to the odd behavior of templates with respect to this section) is that once a report is instantiated from a template, there is no object inheritance from the report to the template. If you change the template, the report will not automatically change. Functions and procedures stored locally in program units in the template will be copied to each report you instantiate. If you later find an error in one of these procedures, you will have to update it manually in every report that was built using the template. By placing all this code in an attached library, all you need to do is to change the code in the library and recompile. All the reports using that library will automatically be updated.

Changing Template Default Settings

For each type of report in the Report Wizard, you can modify the layout settings to make the report look the way you want it to after generation. To do this, navigate to Templates–Layout Model–Section–Body–Default. When you click on Default, you will see Frames, Field Labels/Headings, Fields, Summary Labels, and Summaries. You can change the default fonts as well as control the visual attributes for both normal data and summary columns.

The following instructions change the visual attributes to those that are used in the sample template:

- To change the format of default labels for data, expand the Default node in the Body section. Under the expanded Field Labels/Headings node, right-click on Character and change the font properties to "Arial," *Font Style* to "Bold," and *Size* to 10 points.

- In the Fields–Character section, change the font properties to Times New Roman/10 point.

- In the Summary Labels character section, change the font properties *Character* to Arial/Bold Italic/10 point.

- In the Summaries section, change the font properties *Character* to Times New Roman/Bold/10 point.

You should now save your template and build a simple report based on the newly created template using the Report Wizard. If you change your template and rerun the Report Wizard, the changes you made may or may not be reflected in your report. The reason for this is that Reports is trying to maintain any post-generation changes that are made. But there is no internal "changed" flag on each object. Oracle Reports tries to make logical decisions about what should be overridden and what should not.

If you want all your changes to be reflected, delete all the objects in the Layout Editor and regenerate the layout every time you make a change to the template. The reason you may want to just delete objects in the Layout Model and not start over is that, for a complex report, you go through a lengthy process of defining the Data Model. Then you can make a number of attempts to generate the appropriate layout by using different report templates or by changing column widths. You may notice that some of your labels are incorrect, or the fields may not be wide enough. It may be easier to use the Report Wizard to regenerate the layout than to manipulate it in the Live Previewer or Layout Model.

There are many other properties that you can manipulate. However, the ones mentioned earlier are the only ones necessary to change from the default settings.

Once you specify the defaults, you can set properties independently for all the different types of reports. For example, the most common type of report is Group Above. Since the sample template includes up to two levels of breaks through the break columns, you must set the appropriate default font sizes for those break groups.

1. Open the Property Palette for Templates–Layout Model–Section–Body–Override–Group Above–Section (Level 1). In the Field Labels/Headings section, change the Font size to "14 point" and the Section (Level 2) Font size to "12 point."

2. For a master-detail-detail report that will be based on this template, there will be three levels. When you go into the template in the Layout Model–Section–Body–Override area, click Group Above. Then click the Create icon three times to make three sections.

3. Within Section (Level 1), change the Field Label/Headings and Fields font sizes to 14 points. In the Summary Labels and Summaries area for Section (Level 1), change all the Character, Number, and Date datatypes to 14-point font size.

4. Change the Level 2 Field Labels/Headings for all datatypes to 12-point font size.

5. Don't change the Summaries *Character* "Font Size" for Level 2 because the Summaries font at Level 2 will be at the bottom of the column for the Level 3 objects and should look the same.

6. In the Templates–Layout Model–Section–Body–Default area, change the *Inter-Field (Horizontal)* property to ".1" (rather than .174).

These are the only changes you need to make. It would be useful to be able to change the *Vert. Space Between Frames* property for the repeating frames, but the template does not give you control over that property. You can make this change manually after the report is generated.

Finally, you can add a black line that will separate the Level 1 sections of a report from the Level 2 sections of a Group Above report. You accomplish this by setting the *Borders* property in the Layout Model–Section–Body–Override–Group Above–Section (Level 1)–Frames–Section Frame area to "Bottom Only."

Setting Report Template Standards

There is no one correct strategy for creating report templates. However, to maximize report development efficiency, some basic strategies are useful.

When setting GUI standards in the sample template, the old question of whether to perform significant post-generation modification or to make sacrifices to accommodate what the product can generate arises again. Because of templates, you can make much nicer looking reports with the default layout. However, to minimize the amount of manual work done in the Layout Editor, you need to be careful about the GUI standards you set.

In general, relatively traditional visual reporting standards make for reports that are easier to maintain, easier for users to read, and that allow more information to be displayed on a page. Fancy highlighting, contingent formatting, and some lines on a report can add little if anything to the usability of the report and can greatly increase development time. As in Forms, you should try to set standards that do not greatly increase the development time of the report. There are always key managerial reports that mandate very precise formatting and control. Keep in mind that such sophistication comes with a price.

In addition, you must recognize that while building production reports, half of the time you will be using the Report Wizard to lay out the whole report. The other half of the time, you will be using the Additional Default Layout tool to build a portion of the report. This means that you will need several templates. For example, you might have up to four levels in a Group Above report. If you specified a 4-level Group Above report in the Override portion of your template and try to apply the template to a 2-level master-detail report, the template will apply Levels 1 and 2 only. However, you may want to apply the bottommost levels of detail, not the topmost. Also, in a complex environment, you may want to lay out your report frames one at a time. For this reason, it is useful to create a number of different report templates. For a 4-level Group Above report, you would want a total of six templates:

- 4-level

- 3-level

- 2-level

- Individual template for Level 1 of each of the other multilevel reports (4, 3, and 2)

It is possible to include Override settings for more than one type of report in the same template. However, in practice, this can be confusing to maintain. It is better to have a different set of templates for each type of report that the Report Wizard generates. To satisfy the major portion of reporting needs, you will require the six Group Above templates mentioned earlier, four different Mailing Label report templates for common label sizes, and one template for Matrix reports. A simple Tabular or Form-like report uses the same 4-level template as a Group Above report since you can use the Default settings from those reports. Group Left and Matrix With Group reports are not created frequently enough to make creating templates for these specific types useful. If needed, the existing templates could be adapted to these report types with small manual modifications.

CHAPTER
22

Building a Production
Report

Report me and my cause aright.

—William Shakespeare (1564-1615), *Hamlet* (V, ii, 353)

his chapter will integrate all the report development processes discussed in earlier chapters and walk through the building of a fairly complex report using the Report Builder component of Oracle Developer. This example will illustrate a number of important principles about report writing. You will not only use the Report Wizard, but will also have to build part of the report by hand.

Both the strengths and limitations of the Query Builder will be discussed, along with some of the thought processes that should go into building a complex report. This report is modeled after an actual production report. It is more complex than an average report.

This example will use the demonstration tables shipped with Oracle Developer Release 6. The Demo tables can be installed using the Windows Start menu and selecting Install Demo Database Objects from the Oracle Developer Release 6.0 Demos program group. This will create a small number of sample tables and other database objects. The user will have to be created first and granted appropriate privileges to create tables. By default, the utility will create the tables in the SCOTT schema. Unfortunately, different production versions of Oracle Developer Release 6.0 have shipped with slightly different versions of the demo database. As a result, you may find that some of the tables and columns have different names from those used in this chapter. An export of the exact version of this demo database can be found on the authors' web sites.

In this tutorial, you will build a report that is probably more complex than the reports that most developers have to build. This tutorial demonstrates that Oracle Report Builder allows you to efficiently build even the most complex reports. Straightforward reports can be brought to production in an hour or less. One experienced developer was able to create nine production reports in one day. Some of these reports were also quite complex.

This tutorial is not simple. However, it will demonstrate some of the more powerful features of the tool not evident in the creation of simpler reports. Many reporting tools would be completely unable to build this report.

Preparing to Build the Report

The first step in building any report is knowing exactly what kind of report you want to build. You should have a picture on paper or at least in your head of what the final report will look like. In this case, it was determined that the structure of the report would look like the one shown in Figure 22-1.

Notice that this is a master-detail report where the master has two independent details. In this case, a list of products is being shown. For each product, the report shows how many were purchased by each customer as well as how many were sold by each salesperson. This report is based on a Data Model including a master group with two detail groups, shown diagrammatically in the following illustration. The Report Wizard cannot directly generate this entire report. However, the Report Wizard can generate a substantial portion of it.

Example report structure

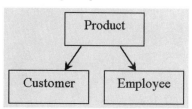

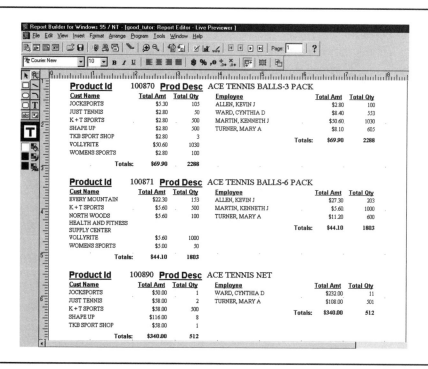

FIGURE 22-1. *Master detail-detail report*

First, you can generate the Product/Customer master-detail portion of the report. What is the Data Model to support this report? The following illustration shows the relevant subset of the report ERD.

Report Data Model

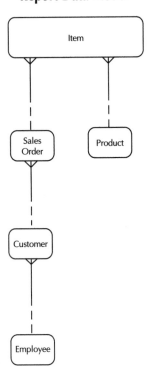

It is a good idea to include the relevant portions of the ERD in the report documentation. The portion of the Data Model shown in the preceding illustration is actually a common level of complexity for a report. The only difference in creating production reports is that you will probably use views rather than going directly against base tables in a production system.

At this point, you need to lay out, in some form, what the query groups will be, as shown in Figure 22-2.

Notice that there are five groups in two queries. The PROD group is the master group, and the CUST and EMP groups are the detail groups. SALE and EMP_SALE carry the detail transaction level information used to produce summary counts and dollar figures. Also notice how different the structure of groups in the query is from

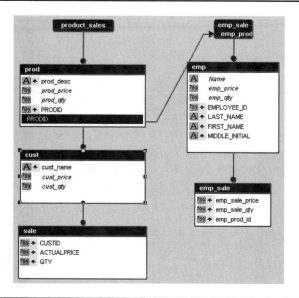

FIGURE 22-2. *Report query group*

how the entities are laid out in the Data Model. There is nothing to say that the way information is grouped in the report must be similar in structure to the grouping in the underlying Data Model. At this point, you are ready to build the first part of the report.

Step 1: Select the Report Style

With the Report Builder open, select **File→New→Report** from the menu to create a new report. Select the Report Wizard option from the following dialog. If you see the "Welcome to the Report Wizard" page, click Next. (Uncheck the check box on this page to keep it from reappearing each time you start the Report Wizard.)

The Report Wizard shows up in two ways. The first time the report is generated, it will walk you through the creation of a report. If you display the Report Wizard after a report has already been created by selecting Report Wizard from the Tools menu, you will have access to each page in the Report Wizard. (See Appendix D for more details about the Report Wizard.)

On the Style tab, you have the ability to select one of several report styles. These report styles govern the layout of the report. Descriptions of these styles can be found in Appendix D. For this tutorial, select Group Above.

Step 2: Connect to the Database

If you are not already connected to the database, click the Connect button. Connect to the user that owns the sample tables.

Step 3: Build the Query—Selecting Tables

First you need to build the Customer query. Click the Query Builder button, hold down CTRL, and select the CUSTOMER, ITEM, PRODUCT, and ORD tables in the Select Data Tables window. Click the Include button. Close the Select Data Tables window. Note that the tables may be automatically joined, as shown in Figure 22-3. This join information is taken from the referential integrity constraints in the database. You may need to join some of them manually. Use the Query Builder to create a join between two tables by clicking and dragging from the foreign key column in the child table to the primary key column in the parent table. You could also click the Set Table Relationship button (button showing two tables with an arrow connecting them) on the toolbar and type in the relationships. The joins required for this tutorial are

- ITEM.PRODID = PRODUCT.PRODID

- ITEM.ORDID = SALES_ORDER.ORDER_ID

- ORD.CUSTID = CUSTOMER.CUSTID

In Figure 22-3, the tables have been moved to make the lines look clearer; however, each time you return to this window, the picture will be redrawn using a default algorithm.

Step 4: Build the Query—Selecting Columns

Select the following columns for your report by clicking the check box beside the column name. From the PRODUCT table, select PRODID and DESCRIP. From the CUSTOMER table, select CUSTID and NAME. From the ITEM table, select ACTUALPRICE, QTY, and ITEMTOT. You will see check marks next to the selected columns, as shown in Figure 22-3. Click OK to generate the SQL Query Statement.

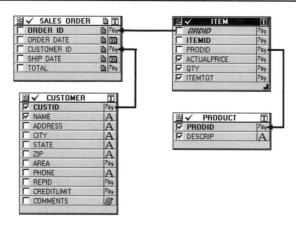

FIGURE 22-3. *Table layout of Query 1*

Step 5: Build the Query—Modify SQL Code

A problem with Reports is that all column names are global. In the SQL Query Statement, the name of the Customer Name column is "Name" and the name of the Product Description is also "Name." Product Description will be called "Descrip." These are not clear column names. Later on in the creation of our report, it will be useful to know what these refer to. Therefore, you should alias the names by modifying the generated SQL code by adding the alias "Cust_Name" after Customer Name and "Prod_Desc" after product description. Click Next.

Step 6: Build the Query—Selecting Fields for Breaks

Declare the fields (columns) for the master group by moving the PRODID and PROD_DESC columns to the right-side box. By default, this generates two break groups. Click and drag PROD_DESC on top of PROD_ID. The mouse cursor icon will change to a hand, and the Level 2 group will disappear when you release the mouse button.

Create a second level by moving CUSTID and CUST_NAME right and dragging CUST_NAME up into the CUSTID group, as shown in Figure 22-4. Click Next.

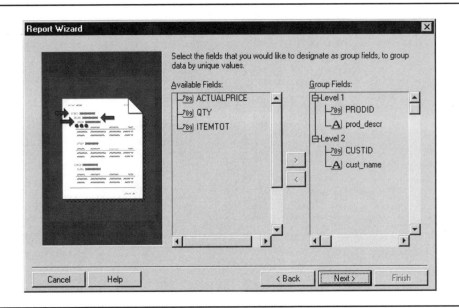

FIGURE 22-4. *Selecting fields for break groups*

Step 7: Display Decisions

Decide what will be displayed in the report. In this case, select all (using the double right-arrow button). If the fields are not in the right order for display, you can drag and drop them into the desired order in the window. The order in which these fields appear is the order in which they will appear in the report. Click Next.

Step 8: Summary Columns

Specify that you want to generate a sum on ITEMTOT and QTY. Click Next.

Step 9: Labels

At this point, you could change the report labels or field widths. For this example, leave the labels as they are. Click Next.

Step 10: Template Selection

For this example, select No template. Click Finish.

Step 11: Add a Query

You cannot use the Report Wizard to add additional queries. To add the employee information, create another query manually in the Report Editor—Data Model by clicking on the SQL button and then on a blank space on the Data Model screen. You will see the SQL Query Statement window. Click Query Builder and select the CUSTOMER, EMPLOYEE, ITEM, and SALESORDER tables. You don't need to click PRODUCT since you will be using the product group from the first query. Click Include and Close.

   If you have referential integrity in your database, the tables will join automatically. If not, you will need to create the joins manually as shown:

- EMPLOYEE.EMPLOYEE_ID = CUSTOMER.REPID

- CUSTOMER.CUSTID = SALESORDER.CUSTOMER_ID

- SALESORDER.ORDERID = ITEM.ORDERID

Step 12: Select Columns

In the Query Builder, do the following:

- From the EMPLOYEE table, select EMPLOYEE ID and LAST NAME, FIRST NAME, and MIDDLE INITIAL.

- From the Item table, select QTY, ACTUALPRICE, ITEMTOT, and PRODID so that you will have something to join to the other query, as shown in Figure 22-5.

- Click OK. Then click OK in the SQL Query Statement window.

Step 13: Alias the Column Names

To avoid the problem of Reports automatically naming columns to prevent duplication, alias these columns in the query code by displaying the query properties for Q2 and adding the alias names after the following column names:

- ACTUALPRICE aliased as EMP_SALE_PRICE
- QTY aliased as EMP_SALE_QTY

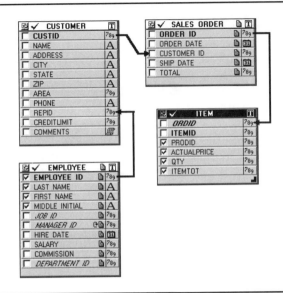

FIGURE 22-5. *Table layout for Query 2*

■ PRODID aliased as EMP_PROD_ID

■ ITEMTOT aliased as EMP_ITEMTOT

Step 14: Create Break Groups

In the Data Model, SHIFT-click EMP_SALE_PRICE, EMP_SALE_QTY, and EMP_PROD_ID, and drag these three fields down to create a separate group.

Step 15: Rename Groups and Queries

Display the Property Palette for each of the groups, and rename them as shown in Figure 22-2. Rename the queries using their respective Property Palettes with the names shown in Figure 22-2.

Step 16: Create Summary Columns

Make summary columns for EMP_ITEMTOT and QTY in the EMP group just as the Report Wizard did in the CUST group. To do this, click the Summary Column icon and click within the EMP group. A new column called CS_1 will be created.

Double-click the column to display the Property Palette. Change the *Name* property to column "EMP_PRICE." Change the *Source* property to "EMP_ITEMTOT." Change the *Reset At* property to "EMP." This will make the column sum the prices for each EMP group. Make another summary column in the EMP group. Change its name to EMP_QTY, *Source* to QTY, and *Reset At* to "EMP."

Step 17: Link Queries

Link the two queries by clicking on the Data Link icon (two hooked paper-clips or chain links). Click and drag from the Product Sales query header to the Emp Sales query header. If you have appropriate referential integrity in your database, Report Builder will usually select the appropriate join. In this case, you want to join the PROD_ID in the product sales query to EMP_PROD_ID in the EMP_SALE query. If you do not have the appropriate referential integrity, you can join the two queries by clicking on the Datalink button and first clicking on PRODID in product sales and dragging over to EMP_PROD_ID in EMP_SALE. You can view the actual joining condition by double-clicking on the arrow connecting the two queries to display the Property Palette.

You have now completed the Data Model and can begin to work on the layout. Save your work at this point.

Step 18: Create the Report Layout

Click the Layout Model button. Click and drag over the entire generated layout to select it. Delete the entire layout. Click the Additional Default Layout button and select an area approximately 7½" wide by 2" high. An abbreviated Report Wizard pops up. Click Style and select Group Above.

Step 19: Select Groups and Modify Settings

For the Groups tab, select only PROD and CUST, and click Down for each of these, indicating that they will repeat down the page.

For the Fields tab, select everything except the Sum, ITEMTOT, ACTUAL_PRICE_PER_REPORT, and SUM_QTY_PER_REPORT.

For the Labels tab, you can change the labels, if desired. For example, change the labels for the price (ITEMTOT) fields to "Total Amt" and quantity fields to "Total Qty." Click Finish and run the report in the Live Previewer.

Step 20: Change the Layout by Using the Live Previewer

When the report prints, the product description area is too narrow. This can be changed right in the Live Previewer by clicking on the field and dragging it to the appropriate width. You can also modify the labels in the Live Previewer. To change labels in the Live Previewer, click the label and alter the text.

Step 21: Add Information to the Report

Create an area for the employee information by clicking in the blank space under F_PROD DESC in the Layout Model. The large frame around it is selected. You cannot drag down on the bottom to expand the area because there is another frame surrounding the frame you want to enlarge. Oracle Report Builder has a useful feature to handle this. Click the Flex Mode button. Now you can click the bottom handle and resize the frame. Slide the bottom handle down approximately 1 inch to provide enough room to insert the employee information.

As you are preparing to lay out the employee information, notice that it is stored in three different fields: Last Name, First Name, Middle Initial. It is customary to want the name to appear in the format Last Name (comma) First Name (space) Middle Initial, for example, "Smith, John A." A function can be written to do this.

Step 22: Create a Function

Click the Data Model icon. Create a formula column by clicking the Formula Column icon and clicking in the Emp group. Double-click the new column CF_1 to display the Property Palette. Change its name to "Full Name," its Datatype to "Character," and width to 220. In the Comments property, you can add a descriptive comment such as "Employee Full Name" for documentation purposes. Click the PL/SQL icon to display a PL/SQL editing window. Here, you can enter any arbitrarily complex PL/SQL program. In this case, a simple function can be added:

```
Function Name Formula return char is
BEGIN
    RETURN :last_name || ',' || First_name || ' ' || :middle_initial;
END;
```

Click Compile to ensure that the code has been entered correctly with colons at the beginning of each variable name and a semicolon at the end of the line.

Step 23: Add the Employee Information

Click the Additional Default Layout button. Click and drag the additional default area within the open space beneath F_PROD DESC field. The Report Wizard will pop up.

For Style, select Tabular. For Groups, select the EMP group using the Down> button. For Fields, select NAME, EMP_NAME, EMP_PRICE, and EMP_QTY. On the Labels tab, change labels for EMP_PRICE and EMP_QTY to "Total Amt" and "Total Qty" just as for the Customer group. Change the label for NAME to "EMPLOYEE." Change the width of the NAME column to 15 for better use of space.

Step 24: Apply the Template

Click the Template tab. The template file will default to the last one selected. You may select any template from the list provided, or apply any template file you have created. The templates used to create this report can be found on the authors' web sites.

Click Finish. This will create the Employee portion of the report. If the Employee and Customer sides of the report do not line up, click and drag over the entire unaligned portion of the report to adjust it, if necessary.

TIP
Start the click/drag area outside of any
frame to avoid selecting that frame.

You may need to turn off Snap to Grid in the View menu to align the employee information with the customer information.

Step 25: Add Totals

The totals shown under customers would also be useful in the Employee area of the report as well. The easiest way to do this is to duplicate (select all items, press CTRL-D) the three fields in the Layout Model and drag them into the appropriate place.

Step 26: Fine-tune the Report Layout

Click the Live Previewer to look at the current status of your report. You will probably want to add some space between products. Identify the repeating frame associated with the Product group and place space between each frame. In the Object Navigator, under Layout Model, find the R_PROD frame. You can also select it from the Layout Editor. It will have the repeating frame symbol (that displays an arrow). Double-click the repeating frame to display its Property Palette. In the repeating frame section, change the property *Vert. Space Between Frames* to ".2". Press ENTER to save the property value. The Live Previewer will show the effect immediately. Also, so that products do not break at the bottom of the page, set the *Page Protect* property on the R_PROD frame to "Yes."

Step 27: Complete the Report

In the Live Previewer, SHIFT-click each of the four amount fields. Click the Currency button to format these fields as currency fields. Click the Add decimal place button twice so that information is represented as dollars and cents. If you have followed this tutorial correctly, the completed report should look something like Figure 22-6. Depending upon the template you used, the fonts and colors of the fields and labels could be different.

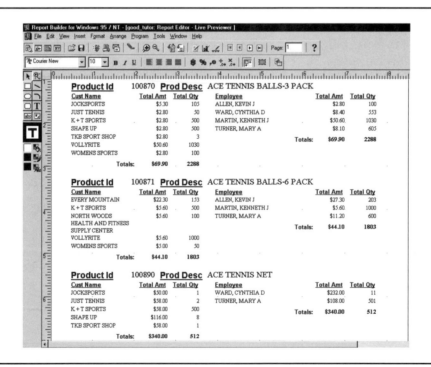

FIGURE 22-6. *Master detail-detail report*

PART VI

Developer Tips and Techniques

CHAPTER
23

Interview Questions

It is better to know some of the questions than all of the answers.
—James Thurber (1894–1961), Saying

he chapters in Part VI will describe techniques you can use with the Forms and Reports components of Oracle Developer. These methods for working with Developer are presented in different formats. Some are questions and answers such as those used in Chapter 23 formatted as interview questions. Chapters 24–29 present a variety of techniques as short tips, some as lengthier discussions of the techniques, and others as step-by-step recipes for performing specific tasks.

Oracle Developer Expertise

There is a great need in the industry for assessing the level of skill of a developer. There are numerous certification programs run by Oracle and other companies that attempt to assess developers' knowledge. Most of these tests address detailed knowledge of the product features, but do not measure problem solving ability or true in-depth knowledge about how to use the product to build real applications.

This chapter lists questions testing knowledge of Oracle Developer that would probably be acquired regardless of development style or GUI standards. Someone working within Oracle building prepackaged Oracle applications might have very different experiences with the product than someone working at a company building custom applications. This is not to say that one style of development is superior to another.

Correct answers to the questions presented in this chapter should reflect how much time a developer has actually spent working with the Forms and Reports components of Oracle Developer. The questions are divided into Beginner, Intermediate, and Advanced categories for both Forms and Reports.

About the Interview Questions

Even the beginner questions in this chapter are not trivial. These questions were not intended to find out if someone attended a three-week training course and learned specific material about Oracle Developer. These questions were written to test a candidate's sophistication and depth in using the product. If the interviewees can answer most of the beginner questions, you can assume that they can use Developer fairly well but may take a relatively long time to build a complex form or report—if they are able to build it at all. Unfortunately, many developers who present themselves as knowledgeable about Oracle Developer are likely to have difficulty answering some of the beginner questions presented here.

The intermediate and advanced questions clearly go beyond the basics of Developer. Correct answers to the intermediate and advanced questions indicate that the developer should be able to competently handle most complex requirements.

Oracle Forms Interview Questions

It is difficult to think of good interview questions to test knowledge of the Forms component of Oracle Developer. There are many different styles of Forms development. There are hundreds, if not thousands, of facts and techniques that must be mastered before individuals can consider themselves Oracle Forms experts. We have intentionally omitted questions about web-enabling applications since the intention was to test more broadly used components of the Developer tool suite.

All the questions and answers in this chapter assume the use of the standard sample Oracle schema Scott (Tiger is the password) and the DEPT and EMP tables contained in that database. You can calculate your score using the points assigned for each section and check your rating at the end of the chapter. If you want a list of questions alone, see Appendix B.

Forms Beginner Questions—Basic Product Functionality (5 points each)

The following section includes beginner-level questions about the Oracle Forms portion of Developer.

Forms Beginner Question 1

1. In building a form, you forgot to add the scroll bar when you created the block using the Data Block Wizard and the Layout Wizard. How can you add it now?

Answer to Forms Beginner Question 1

This question tests whether the interviewees have ever built a block manually without using the Layout Wizard. On the block Property Palette where you want the scroll bar to appear, set the *Show Scroll Bar* property to "Yes." Set the *Scroll Bar Canvas* property to the canvas where the associated block appears. If the canvas is a tab canvas, you will also need to set the *Scroll Bar Tab Page* property to the appropriate value along with any other relevant scroll bar properties.

The simplest solution is to select **Tools→Layout Wizard** and navigate to the page that shows the Display Scrollbar check box. Selecting that check box will add the scroll bar and set the appropriate properties.

Forms Beginner Question 2

2. You want to create a multirecord block with overflow items at the bottom, as shown in Figure 23-1. All these items are in the same block. How do you make some items appear multiple times and others only once?

Answer to Forms Beginner Question 2

There are several complex answers to this question involving control blocks and copied values. While technically correct, they are not the best solutions to the problem. The simple and elegant answer should be to set the property *Number of Items Displayed* to "1" for each of the two overflow items (in this example, salary and commission).

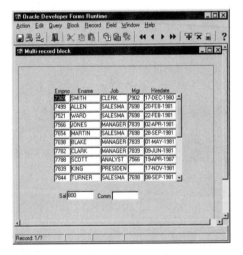

FIGURE 23-1. *Multirecord block with overflow items*

The *Number of Items Displayed* property for the other items should remain as the default "0" so that the number of items displayed will default to the *Number of Records Displayed* specified for the block.

Forms Beginner Question 3

3. When you created a block using the Data Block Wizard, you forgot to attach it to its parent block. How do you add a parent-child relationship to two blocks that already exist?

Answer to Forms Beginner Question 3

Navigate to the Master block (DEPT in this case) in the Form Builder Object Navigator and create a new relation by clicking on the Relations node and then the Create button. Enter the join condition to the detail block, as shown in Figure 23-2, or you can re-enter the Data Block Wizard and fill out the Master-Detail tab for the detail block. This creates the relation with the appropriate properties.

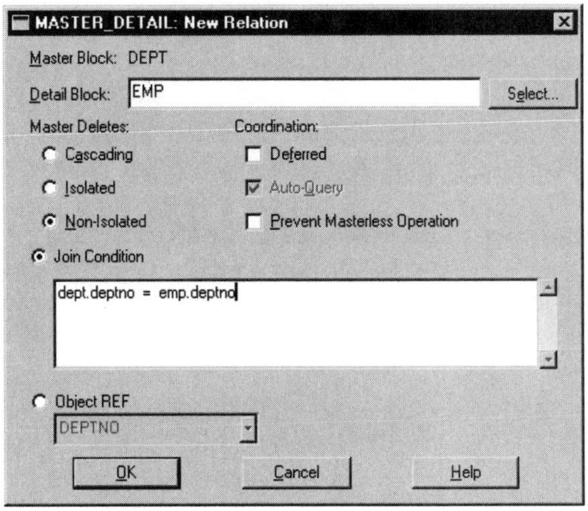

FIGURE 23-2. *Entering a join condition*

Forms Beginner Question 4

4. You want to create a poplist or LOV to show a list of departments from the database. What are the steps necessary to do this?

Answer to Forms Beginner Question 4

These questions have not been slanted toward any specific GUI standards. Development styles may vary from place to place. Some shops may use both poplists and LOVs, or only one or the other. If the interviewees know how to create either of these items, consider their answer correct. Both will be discussed.

Poplist method:

a. Create a record group in the Object Navigator or in code in a program unit using the CREATE_GROUP_FROM_QUERY built-in.

b. Create the item with a type of List Item.

c. In the code to populate the poplist (for example, in the WHEN-NEW-FORM-INSTANCE trigger) or in a procedure called by the WHEN-NEW-FORM-INSTANCE trigger, you must populate the record group using the POPULATE_GROUP built-in.

d. Populate the poplist using a POPULATE_LIST built-in procedure.

LOV method:

With Forms R.6, LOVs are very easy to build. You can simply invoke the LOV Wizard and follow the step-by-step instructions. LOVs can be invoked in several ways. You can have the LOV attached to an item and invoked through an access key or a button on the toolbar. The authors recommend placing a small button next to the item to simulate the appearance of a poplist and invoking the LOV using a SHOW_LOV command. If the developers are not aware of the new LOV Wizard, they might describe building the LOV manually using the following steps:

a. Create the record group. In a poplist you must have exactly two columns in the query. Using an LOV, you can have any number of columns in the record group.

b. Create the LOV and base it upon the newly created record group.

c. For the LOV to display a value after selecting OK, you must specify the return column for the appropriate LOV column. To invoke the LOV, create a trigger button next to a field with the SHOW LOV command.

This question tests whether the interviewees have ever worked with lists of values queried from the database. Anyone who has built a few forms should be able to answer this question.

Forms Beginner Question 5

5. You want to display the list of employees in a block and show the name of the department each employee belongs to, as shown in Figure 23-3. How can this be accomplished if you also want to allow INSERT, UPDATE, and DELETE on the records?

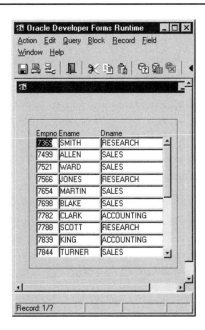

FIGURE 23-3. *Employee block showing department name*

Answer to Forms Beginner Question 5

The traditional way to do this is to place a POST QUERY trigger on the Emp block including the following code:

```
DECLARE
    CURSOR c_dname_tx IS
    SELECT dname
    FROM    dept
    WHERE   deptno = :emp.deptno;
BEGIN
    OPEN c_dname_tx;
    FETCH c_dname_tx INTO :emp.dname;
    CLOSE c_dname_tx;
END;
```

This method has the disadvantage of firing off a separate cursor for each row retrieved in the block.

A superior method (although one you are unlikely to see from any but the most experienced developers) is to use an updateable view. To do this, create a view joining the DEPT and EMP tables. This will automatically be updateable for the EMP table but not the DEPT table. Base your block upon the view and set the *Query Only* property of the DNAME column to "Yes." This method has the dual advantages of improved performance and the creation of a reusable view for other forms and reports. Chapter 4 contains a detailed example of a block based on an updateable view.

If the interviewees are experienced with Forms, they may mention that it is possible to select multiple objects in the Object Navigator and to smartclass them all simultaneously.

Forms Beginner Question 6

6. You left out one of the five date items in your block. The block has been laid out with triggers included so you do not want to delete it. List the steps necessary to add an item to the block.

Answer to Forms Beginner Question 6

For anyone who knows the Oracle Forms product, this should be an easy question. The answer you are likely to get is to create an item in the Object Navigator. By default, this will be a database item. Change the item's *Data Type* property to match the database object with the appropriate *Maximum Length*. Change the *Visible* property to "Yes," set the prompt to an appropriate label, and specify the canvas on which the item should appear. On the selected canvas, position the item appropriately.

A better answer is to select a similar column in the Object Navigator or Layout Model. Duplicate the item and change its *Name* and *Prompt* properties to the desired values. This method would save a few steps. Depending upon the development environment, the interviewees might also mention that they could smartclass the item to set its properties appropriately.

Forms Beginner Question 7

7. When the user clicks the Save button, you want an "Are you sure?" message to pop up where the user can select "Yes" or "No." What are the steps necessary to accomplish this?

Answer to Forms Beginner Question 7

This answer involves the creation of an alert. Create an alert called "SAVE" in the Object Navigator. On the alert Property Palette, name the alert and type the desired message in the *Message* property window. Fill in the *Button 1 Label* and *Button 2 Label* properties and two labels. In the WHEN-BUTTON-PRESSED trigger on the Save button (or whatever is doing your save function) you can place the following code:

```
BEGIN
    IF show_alert('SAVE') = ALERT_BUTTON1
    THEN
        commit_form;
    END IF;
END;
```

Forms Beginner Question 8

8. You have the following POST-QUERY trigger code in your form:

```
DECLARE
    CURSOR c_avg_sal_nr
    IS
        SELECT  avg(sal)
        FROM    emp
        WHERE   deptno = :dept.deptno;
BEGIN
    OPEN c_avg_sal_nr;
    FETCH c_avg_sal_nr INTO :dept.avg_sal_nr;
    CLOSE c_avg_sal_nr;
END;
```

You want to move the function with the cursor to the database. How would you rewrite the code to do this?

Answer to Forms Beginner Question 8

This is a straightforward exercise. Take the reference to the form and pass that as a parameter to the function. Rather than trying to write directly into the item, have the function return a value and assign that value to the item.

First, the function must be placed in the database, ideally in a package so that it can be used in queries or views. The code for the package is shown next:

```
PACKAGE emp_util
IS
    FUNCTION avg_sal_nr(
        p_deptno dept.deptno%TYPE)
        RETURN NUMBER;
END;

PACKAGE BODY emp_util
IS
    FUNCTION avg_sal_nr(
        p_deptno dept.deptno%TYPE)
        RETURN NUMBER
    IS
        CURSOR c_avg_sal_nr(
            p_dept dept.deptno%TYPE)
        IS
            SELECT   AVG (sal) avg_sal_nr
            FROM     emp
            WHERE    deptno = p_dept;
        v_casr c_avg_sal_nr%ROWTYPE;
        v_found  BOOLEAN;
    BEGIN   ---------MAIN--------------
        OPEN c_avg_sal_nr (p_deptno);
        FETCH c_avg_sal_nr INTO v_casr;
        v_found := c_avg_sal_nr%FOUND;
        CLOSE c_avg_sal_nr;
        RETURN casr.avg_sal_nr;
    END f_avg_sal_nr;
END emp_util;
```

The code in the post query trigger becomes a single line, as shown next:

```
:dept.avg_sal_nr := emp_util.avg_sal_nr(:dept.deptno);
```

Forms Beginner Question 9

9. You want all the dates in all your forms to use the same format mask DD-MON-YYYY. What is the best way to do this?

Answer to Forms Beginner Question 9

Create a single date field with the appropriate format mask. Place this field in the object library and flag it as a SmartClass. Then, as you create the date fields in your form, subclass them off of that SmartClass. If the interviewees are experienced with the Forms component of Developer, they may mention that it is possible to select multiple objects in the Object Navigator and smartclass them all simultaneously.

Forms Beginner Question 10

10. When your form opens, you want a block such as EMP to query automatically. How can you do this?

Answer to Forms Beginner Question 10

In the WHEN-NEW-FORM-INSTANCE trigger or in a procedure called by the WHEN-NEW-FORM-INSTANCE trigger, use the following code:

```
go_block('EMP');
execute_query;
```

Forms Intermediate Questions (10 points each)

The following are intermediate-level questions about the Forms component of Oracle Developer.

Forms Intermediate Question 1

1. You want users to be able to type in an employee ID. If the employee ID is valid, it should automatically populate an adjacent item with the name of the employee. If the ID is not valid, the user should get an error message. How do you accomplish this?

Answer to Forms Intermediate Question 1

The developer needs to write a WHEN-VALIDATE-ITEM trigger. This trigger can be placed at the item, block, or form level if you add some extra code to trigger this when the system cursor item is the appropriate field. Most people will place the trigger at the item level. Assume that the two items are in a block called CONTROL, the ID item is called IN_EMPNO, and the text item storing the employee's name is called OUT_TX. The code should look something like the following:

```
DECLARE
    CURSOR c_valid_emp(
       p_empno emp.empno%TYPE)
    IS
```

```
   SELECT    ename
   FROM      emp
   WHERE     empno = p_empno;
BEGIN
   OPEN c_valid_emp (:control.in_empno);
   FETCH c_valid_emp INTO :control.out_tx;
   IF c_valid_emp%NOTFOUND THEN
     :control.out_tx := 'Not a valid employee number.';
   END IF;
   CLOSE c_valid_emp
END;
```

As discussed in Forms Beginner Question 8, it would be better from a performance perspective to rewrite this code as a database function.

Forms Intermediate Question 2

2. In the previous question, you were asked about giving a user the capability of typing in an ID and having the form return the name of an employee. You want to use this same feature in many places on different forms throughout the application. What is the best way to make this functionality available to other forms?

Answer to Forms Intermediate Question 2

Assuming that you have already created this functionality to support question 1 on the IN_EMPNO and OUT_TX items, replicating this functionality in multiple places is very simple.

Create an object group from the IN_EMPNO and OUT_TX items. Store this object group in an object library so that it can be copied or subclassed easily into any number of forms.

Forms Intermediate Question 3

3. In a multi-tab application with a master block on the first tab and different detail blocks on each of the other tabs, when you query the first block, it takes a long time because you are also querying all the child blocks. How can you prevent querying of the child blocks and only do so when individual tabs are selected?

Answer to Forms Intermediate Question 3

There are two steps to this answer:

1. When you create master-detail relationships using the Form Builder Data Block Wizard, the child blocks are automatically queried anytime you query the master. You must find the relation to the child block in the Relations node of the Object Navigator of the parent block, display its Property Palette, and set the *Deferred* property to "Yes." Also set the *Automatic Query* property to "Yes." Setting the *Deferred* property to "Yes" in the child block means that when the parent block is queried, the child block will not automatically query. Setting the *Automatic Query* property to "Yes" means that you do not have to perform an explicit EXECUTE_QUERY command to populate the block. Instead, you only need to navigate to the block.

2. Assume that your child block is named 'EMP' and it appears on tab page 2 (called "EMP"). At the form level, create a WHEN-TAB-PAGE-CHANGED trigger, including the following code:

```
IF :system.tab_new_page = 'EMP'
THEN
    go_block('EMP');
END IF;
```

This question tests whether the interviewees have worked with tab canvases or blocks split across multiple canvases or windows. If they have, then this question should be easy to answer.

Forms Intermediate Question 4

4. You have a multi-record Employee block and a poplist to select a Department so that only employees in that department are shown, as in Figure 23-4. How can you do this?

Answer to Forms Intermediate Question 4

The best way to do this is to create a "fake" master-detail relationship between a poplist and a control block. Use the following steps:

a. Create a poplist called "DEPTNOLIST" within a control block called "CONTROL."

b. Populate the poplist with a record group containing the department names and department numbers of all the departments on the poplist.

c. Create a WHEN LIST CHANGED trigger with the code shown here:

```
go_block ('EMP');
execute_query;
```

d. In the EMP block Property Palette, change the *WHERE clause* property to "deptno = CONTROL.DEPTNO_LIST."

FIGURE 23-4. *Multirecord block with poplist*

Forms Intermediate Question 5

5. A junior developer created some required items in your form by setting the *Required* property to "Yes" in the Data section of the Property Palettes for each item. Users complain that as soon as they click in the items, they cannot move the cursor without entering something. The junior developer changes the *Required* property setting to "No." Now when users try to leave or save the form without entering something in the formerly required items, they get the error message "FRM-40508: ORACLE error: unable to INSERT record." What is a more user-friendly way to support required items in Oracle Forms?

Answer to Forms Intermediate Question 5

This question tests depth of Forms knowledge and keeping up with changes in the product. The problem of not letting the cursor move out of a required field is a holdover from pre-Windows applications. Currently, it is normal in a Windows environment for users to click in and out of required fields until they are ready to declare a specific record complete. Oracle Forms provides the option of making required field enforcement not happen until the record is validated. This is done by setting the *Defer Required Enforcement* form module property to "Yes."

Forms Advanced Questions (20 points each)

The following are advanced Forms questions requiring in-depth knowledge of the product.

Forms Advanced Question 1

1. Your form has a multirecord block used to select employees, as shown in Figure 23-5. In the first item, you select a department. Once a department has been selected, you can select employees in the second item. How can you build your form so that once a department is selected in the first item, users will only be able to see employees from the selected Department in the second item? (Hint: The things that look like poplists are really items with buttons next to them that display LOVs.)

Answer to Forms Advanced Question 1

This can be accomplished with poplists, but not as easily as with LOVs.

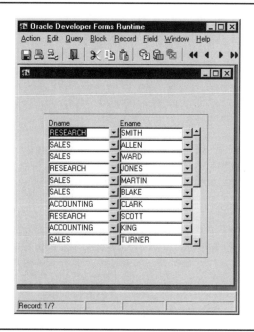

FIGURE 23-5. *Multirecord selection block*

Using an LOV, the button for the first column, DEPT, will display an LOV that shows departments based on the simple record group query:

```
SELECT    deptno, dname
FROM      dept
ORDER BY dname
```

The LOV for the second column is based on the following record group query:

```
SELECT    empno,ename
FROM      emp
WHERE     deptno=:emp.deptno
ORDER BY ename
```

Because the answer is so simple, this appears to be a relatively straightforward question. However, you are only likely to get this simple answer from someone who has been working with Oracle Forms for a while.

Forms Advanced Question 2

2. You want to create a multitab canvas and also include subtabs. How can this be accomplished?

Answer to Forms Advanced Question 2

This question is deceptive. It would be very simple to answer if Oracle Forms included the functionality such that a tab canvas could reside as a display item on a page of another tab canvas. However, this is not the case. Tab canvases behave more like stacked canvases and can only reside on content canvases. However, you can have multiple tab canvases visible at the same time with one on top of the other. This is the way this question can be handled.

You also need to make sure that the subtab canvas appears on top of the primary tab canvas when it is visible, or you won't be able to see it at all. You need to create an appropriate tab canvas in one position, and the subtab is simply another tabbed canvas small enough to fit entirely on a single page of the main tab canvas page, as shown in Figure 23-6.

Execute a SHOW_VIEW('subtab') command (where 'subtab' is the subtab name) on the page where you want the subtab to appear. You will need to use a HIDE_VIEW command on all the pages where you do not want the subtab to appear.

If there are items other than the subtab on the main tab page and you navigate to those items, the subtab will disappear. To prevent this from happening, place a SHOW VIEW('subtab') command on the WHEN-NEW-BLOCK-INSTANCE trigger in the block containing the items on the tab page where the subtab appears.

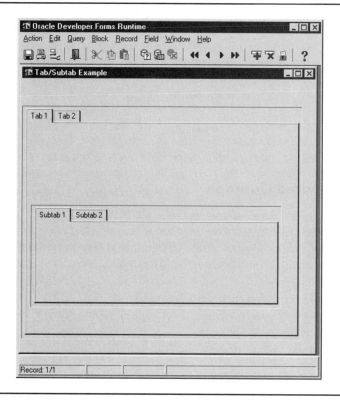

FIGURE 23-6.   *Tab canvas with subtab*

This is a very difficult question. If the interviewees haven't gone through the exercise of making subtabs work, they probably won't be able to think through this answer. If they haven't used subtabs but can think through most of the parts of the answer, give them full credit.

Forms Advanced Question 3

3. Junior developers approach you with the following problem: They are trying to create a stacked canvas with some items on it. They have used the SHOW_VIEW command to make the stacked canvas appear. When the form is run, the canvas appears and quickly disappears. What is wrong and how can it be fixed?

Answer to Forms Advanced Question 3

This question tests whether the interviewees have worked with stacked canvases. Stacked canvases cannot be displayed if the item that the cursor is in is beneath the stacked canvas. If that item is beneath the stacked canvas, it will cause the stacked canvas to disappear as soon as it is displayed. This is why the stacked canvas appears for an instant before disappearing. The solution is either to navigate to an item on the stacked canvas, which by definition is not under the stacked canvas, or to navigate to an item explicitly not beneath the stacked canvas. In the authors' Forms template, there is a special navigable item (NULL _ITEM) on the primary canvas with 0 height and 0 width appearing at position 0,0 for this purpose.

Forms Advanced Question 4

4. This question assumes you are using a LOCATION table in addition to the EMP and DEPT tables. You want to be able to select a location in a poplist and only see employees at that location, as shown in Figure 23-7. Note that there is no location ID in the employee table. How can you accomplish this?

Answer to Forms Advanced Question 4

This is the classic problem of having a block filtering on a column that is not in the base table. There are several solutions. Given the simplicity of this example, you can create an updateable view, base the block on that view, and use a simple

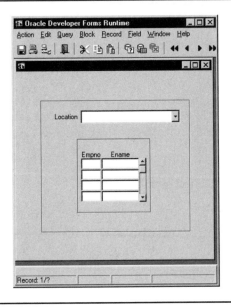

FIGURE 23-7. *Example of selection poplist*

WHERE clause. This solution will not work for more complex filtering problems and is less than ideal since, even if you don't filter on a particular criterion, you will still incur the overhead of querying from that view.

A better solution is to filter by a subquery. For example, in this case, you would use the following code:

```
DECLARE
    v_where_tx VARCHAR2(2000);
BEGIN
   IF :loc IS NOT NULL
   THEN
      v_where_tx := 'DEPTNO IN ' ||
         '(SELECT deptno ' ||
         'FROM dept ' ||
         'WHERE loc = ''' || :dept.loc || ''')';
   ELSE
      where_tx := NULL;
   END IF;
   --
   set_block_property ('EMP', default_where, v_where_tx);
   go_block ('EMP');
   execute_query;
END;
```

Note that this is the same strategy used in the Locator described in Chapter 15.

Forms Advanced Question 5

5. You have a form where you want to select a person from a list activated by a button (as if in an LOV). The database contains a few hundred thousand names so that scrolling through a list of names is not a viable option. You need to use a separate locator window with some selection criteria to help find a specific person. This same functionality will be required in multiple forms.

a. Should you create this functionality as a separate form or as a Locator object group in an object library?

b. How would you accomplish this using the selected strategy?

c. What are the pros and cons of each strategy?

Answer to Forms Advanced Question 5

a. The answer to this question is a matter of opinion and programming style. You have some type of functionality that cannot be implemented by a small widget. You can either build it as an object group and subclass it into each form where it is needed, or build it as a separate form to which you can pass information. Either answer is correct.

b. To use the object group approach, create an object group with all the locator objects, place the locator object group into your object library, and access it as needed in your forms. You will need to have a special function to invoke the locator passing the name of the field where you want the Employee ID returned. Otherwise, manual modification to the form would be required each time this functionality were used.

Using a separate form is a bit more complicated. You need to use a CALL FORM command. The called form will have to write its results information to a global or package variable in a shared package. The calling form can then retrieve this.

From the developer perspective, there is little difference between the implementation of these two approaches. The functionality is invoked by calling a procedure in both solutions.

c. Using the form approach, your core application will load more quickly since it would be smaller. The Person Finder would only be loaded when it is invoked. The disadvantage is in incurring this load overhead every time the locator is called. The converse is true for the object group approach. The underlying form will be larger and therefore load more slowly, but invoking the Person Finder will be faster.

The best choice in an individual case depends upon the frequency with which the Person Finder is accessed. If it will rarely be called, the form approach is a better option. If the Person Finder is called often, the object group approach is better.

Oracle Reports Interview Questions

All questions in this section refer to the following report: Using Oracle's sample tables in the Scott schema, create a master-detail report showing the names of the departments and the names of employees in each department. Departments should be listed even if they have no employees.

Reports Beginner Questions—Basic Product Functionality (5 points each)

The following section includes beginner questions about the Reports component of Oracle Developer.

Reports Beginner Question 1

1. Write the SQL query for the master-detail report described earlier.

   a. On paper, draw the Data Model and groups for the report.

   b. If you were to use the Report Wizard to generate a default layout, how would it look? Draw the frames and place the report objects, labels, and data fields in each frame, where appropriate.

Answer to Reports Beginner Question 1

There are two ways to write this query. The best answer is to use a simple query with an outer join, as shown next:

```
SELECT ALL dept.deptno,
       dept.dname,
       emp.empno,
       emp.ename,
       emp.hiredate,
       emp.sal,
       emp.comm
FROM dept, emp
WHERE emp.deptno (+) = dept.deptno
```

You can also create this report using two queries, one from DEPT and one from EMP and link the two queries in the Data Model. This is not as efficient as the first solution because each department now executes a separate employee query.

a. This is a very simple Data Model to create. You must be sure that there are two groups, one on top of the other. Bonus points can be given if the groups are named. Columns must be in the right place, as shown in Figure 23-8.

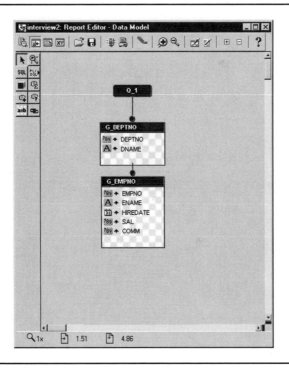

FIGURE 23-8. *Data Model for simple master-detail report*

b. Figure 23-9 shows the answer with the frames spread apart to make the diagram readable. If the interviewees can't correctly identify the two repeating frames and place the appropriate fields in the right places, then they do not know how to use the basic functionality of Reports. Don't worry if they forget the enclosing frames. What really counts are the two repeating frames with objects in the appropriate places. If, when answering this question, they look bored and draw everything correctly, hire them!

Reports Beginner Question 2

2. For each frame in the Layout Model, what would be the settings for the *Vertical Elasticity* and *Horizontal Elasticity* properties and the repeating direction for the repeating frames?

Answer to Reports Beginner Question 2

The *Horizontal Elasticity* property for all frames should be set to "Fixed." *Vertical Elasticity* for all frames can be "Variable" except for the Employee label header frame. This frame should have its *Vertical Elasticity* property set to "Fixed."

This question is testing understanding of elasticity. Don't worry whether the interviewees know what Reports will create. If they tell you that the *Vertical*

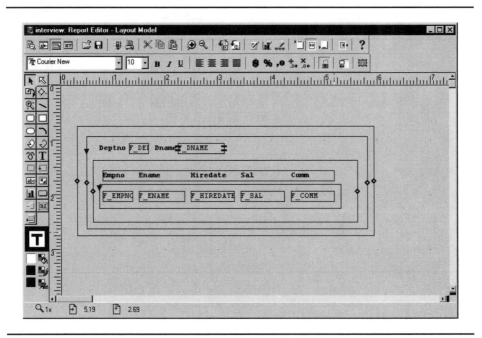

FIGURE 23-9. *Layout model for simple master-detail report*

Elasticity on the repeating frames should be "Fixed" or (even worse) set to "Contract," they do not understand the Reports elasticity properties.

The *Print Direction* property for each of the repeating frames should be set to "Down."

Reports Beginner Question 3

3. Each department must start on a new page. How can this be accomplished?

Answer to Reports Beginner Question 3

The correct answer is to set the *Maximum Records per Page* property on the Dept repeating frame to "1."

It is also possible to set the *Page Break After* property to "Yes" on the employee enclosing frame if there is something for it to break after. By inserting a line or object below the Employee enclosing frame and setting the *Page Break After* property to "Yes", this will force a page break between that object and any object anchored to it. If there is no object to anchor to, this strategy won't work. If you elect to place a line in the frame, you can make it white so that it will not show up on a white page. (White works better than selecting "No Line" since you will still be able to see the line in the Layout Model.)

The first answer is still a better choice, but the second method indicates some detailed knowledge of the product.

Reports Beginner Question 4

4. Rather than have each department listing start on a new page, how can you create a 1" separation between each department?

Answer to Reports Beginner Question 4

There are several ways to create this separation. The best way is to set the *Vert. Space Between Frames* property to "1"" on the Dept repeating frame.

You can also place a 1" vertical white line in between each Department to force them to be spaced an inch apart. This will work and the report will look almost identical to the report created using the first method when it prints. However, using this strategy, you might end up with a blank page at the end of the report if the white line ends at the bottom of the last page.

Also, it will be hard for someone maintaining the report to determine that this is the mechanism because the white line might be easy to miss.

Reports Beginner Question 5

5. You want to display total compensation (salary and commission). How can you modify the existing report to support this?

Answer to Reports Beginner Question 5

The best way to modify the report to display total compensation is to modify the query by adding the following to the SELECT clause:

```
NVL(sal, 0) + NVL(comm, 0) tot_comp_nr
```

At this point, you can add the field in the Layout Model. Be sure that the field is added in the right place. Wiping out the existing layout entirely and re-creating it after modifying the query is the best strategy if there are no manual layout modifications.

Another way to modify the report is to make a view with the same expression (sale + comm). This is also a good answer.

A third alternative is to make a Total Compensation numeric formula column added to the EMPLOYEE group, as shown next:

```
RETURN NVL(sal, 0) + NVL(comm, 0);
```

Reports Beginner Question 6

6. Page numbers must appear in the upper-right corner of each page of the report. Describe how to make a page number appear in the upper-right corner of the report without using the Report Wizard.

Answer to Reports Beginner Question 6

There are several ways to get the page numbers to appear in the desired location. One solution is to create a field in the Layout Model and declare its *Source* property to be "Page Number."

Another way is to embed the page number in boilerplate text using an "&" followed by the field name. Because this is a system field, you need to write "&<page number>". If the interviewees omit the < >, this is not a serious error.

Reports Beginner Question 7

7. You run the report and the page number only appears on the first page of the report. How can this be fixed?

Answer to Reports Beginner Question 7

There is a property on each report object called *Print Object On* that defaults to "First Page." Change this property setting to "All Pages." Don't worry about whether the interviewees know the exact name of the property. It is enough if they know that this property exists.

Reports Beginner Question 8

8. A report that has been successfully running has to have a field added. After adding the field, running the report generates an error message that "The xxx field references a column xxx at a frequency below its group." What happened and how can you fix the problem?

Answer to Reports Beginner Question 8

Every user of Oracle Reports has seen this error message. This means that you have an object that can't logically be printed in the frame in which it is placed. For example, if an Employee Number field is placed in the DEPT repeating frame, this makes no logical sense and the error message is displayed when the report is run.

The solution is to delete and re-create the object in the correct place, or to unlock the layout, move the object to the correct place, and relock the layout. You must verify that the object is in the right place on the Object Navigator by using the Move Forward and Move Backward capability to move the object, if necessary.

Reports Beginner Question 9

9. You want to use a DD-MM-YYYY format for displaying HIREDATE (for example, 17-JAN-1999). How can this be accomplished?

Answer to Reports Beginner Question 9

In the Layout Model, open the Property Palette for the Hiredate object, and set the Field *Format Mask* property to the MM-DD-YYYY setting. The interviewees should know that this is called a "Format Mask." What is important is that they use the Layout Model object and not try to set anything in the Data Model.

Reports Beginner Question 10

10. You need to create a report-level summary showing the total number of employees in the whole organization with no department-level summaries. How can this be accomplished?

Answer to Reports Beginner Question 10

There are several ways to get the report-level summaries. The most clever way is to use the Data Model to create a summary column that is not enclosed in any group (very important!) in the layout. Next, set the Summary *Function* property to "Count" with *Source* set to "Empno." Selecting Empno to count demonstrates the best programming practices. If the interviewees select Commission, the report will only count "not null" values. Selecting Ename is only acceptable if this column is declared as "not null" in the database, but is not good practice. Because the data model in our example includes an outer join if you place a formula column that returns some number and use a count function on that, it will count the null employees.

Reports Intermediate Questions (10 points each)

The following are questions testing knowledge about Reports at the intermediate level.

Reports Intermediate Question 1

1. If the name of the department appears at the bottom of the page and there is no room for even one employee (an orphaned department header), how can you make the department header move to the beginning of the next page?

Answer to Reports Intermediate Question 1

This problem is harder than it may initially appear. Unlike earlier versions of the product, when you create the default Group Above report, the Reports component of Oracle Developer no longer places a frame around master objects. There are two steps to this answer. First, you must set the *Keep with Anchoring Object* property on the enclosing frame to "Yes." However, this alone will not solve the problem, because the enclosing frame will anchor to exactly one of the Department Number or Name fields or their labels. You want to keep the Employees with the entire header and not just one label or field. The only way to do this is to create an extra enclosing frame to surround all the headers, as shown in Figure 23-10.

Reports Intermediate Question 2

2. You want to write a report listing the names of employees from a particular department by passing this information from Oracle Forms. How can this be done?

Answer to Reports Intermediate Question 2

To create a report with information passed from Oracle Forms, first, create a parameter list in Oracle Forms and pass this list to Oracle Reports through the RUN_PRODUCT or RUN_REPORT_OBJECT command. In Reports, you will need to

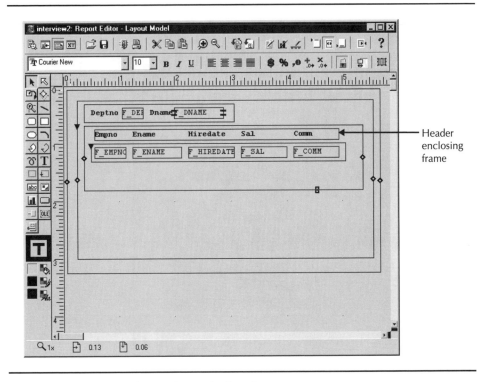

FIGURE 23-10. *Enclosing frame for headers*

define a user parameter. You must incorporate this parameter into the query using a bind variable or lexical parameter. For more details about integrating forms and reports, see Chapter 17.

Reports Intermediate Question 3

3. Two independent sets of information need to be displayed on the same page. For example, show all the departments on the top and employees on the bottom, as shown in Figure 23-11. What is the process required to accomplish this?

Answer to Reports Intermediate Question 3

Create the first query in the Data Model using the Report Wizard. Go back to the Data Model and add the second query. In the Layout Model, make a second layout underneath the first one by using the Additional Default Layout tool.

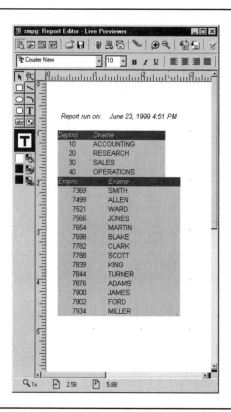

FIGURE 23-11. *Two reports displayed on the same page*

A second solution is to use the new sections feature and place each query in a different section (Header, Main, and Trailer). However, using this method, each section would have to start on a new page.

Reports Intermediate Question 4

4. You have a report with three independent parts. You want each part to start on a new page. How can you accomplish this?

Answer to Reports Intermediate Question 4

On the enclosing frame surrounding the first and second sections, set the *Page Break After* property to "Yes." Alternatively, you can set the *Page Break Before* property on the second and third sections to "Yes." Setting the *Maximum Records per Page* property to "1'" on the repeating groups is not a correct answer. If the sections are small, an entire section could appear on the remaining portion of the page with the previous section. You can also use the new sections feature of R.6.

Reports Intermediate Question 5

5. Draw the Data Model and Layout Model to support a basic matrix report where the rows are departments, the columns are locations, and each cell contains a count of employees, as shown in Figure 23-12.

Answer to Reports Intermediate Question 5

Intermediate users of Oracle Reports should be able to write out the answer to this question as shown in the Data Model and in the Layout Model in Figure 23-13. The Data Model should show two intersecting, overlapping repeating frames with the fields in the correct positions. This will verify that the interviewees understand the mechanics behind how a matrix report is constructed and not just rely on the Report Wizard. The interviewees should also draw the groups and objects correctly in the Layout Model.

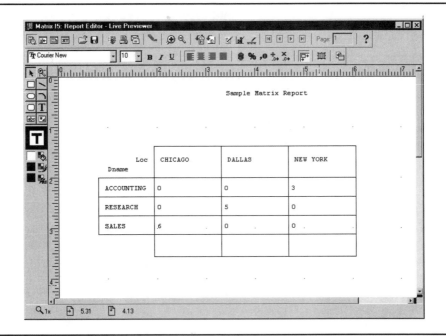

FIGURE 23-12.   *Sample matrix report shown in the Live Previewer*

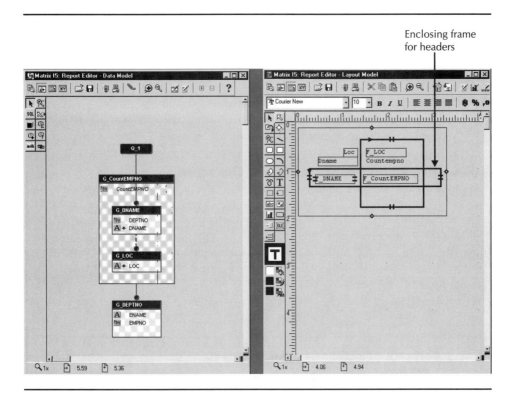

FIGURE 23-13. *Data Model and Layout Model for basic matrix report*

Reports Advanced Questions (20 points each)

The following are advanced questions about the Reports component of
Oracle Developer.

Reports Advanced Question 1

1. You need to create a report that is a master with two independent details.
   For example, a Project may be associated with people and equipment.
   What would the Data Model and Layout Model for this report look like?

Answer to Reports Advanced Question 1

This is a good example to demonstrate the power and flexibility of Oracle Reports.
The Data Model and layout for this example were built in 10 to 15 minutes to create
the screen shots in Figures 23-14 and 23-15. Few report products can support this

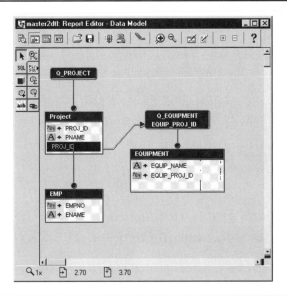

FIGURE 23-14.   *Sample Data Model of master with two details*

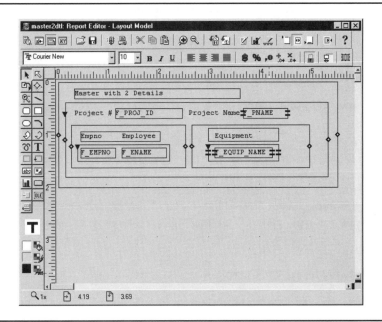

FIGURE 23-15.   *Sample Layout Model of master with two details*

type of report at all, and no other report writer could support it more easily than Oracle Reports.

To build this, the most efficient way would be to build the first query and layout using the Report Wizard. Next, use the Data Model and manually build and attach the second query. Use the Layout Model to increase the size of the Project repeating frame, and use the Additional Default Layout tool to create the equipment layout. The only manual work required in the Layout Editor is expanding the project frame. The detailed steps for this process are discussed in Chapter 22.

Reports Advanced Question 2

2. You want to create a report that returns the top N Employees (N is a parameter passed to the report). How do you do this?

Answer to Reports Advanced Question 2

This is a technical question. The answer will indicate whether the interviewees have created this common type of report. Even though this requires a precise piece of information, it is a fair question for advanced users.

The trick is to know about the query property called *Maximum Rows to Fetch*. However, you want to set this property programmatically using the SRW.SET_MAXROW command in the AFTER PARAMETER FORM trigger. Set the *Maximum Rows to Fetch* property to the number of rows in the parameter. In addition, you will need to place an ORDER_BY clause in the query so that the first ten records fetched will be the correct records.

Reports Advanced Question 3

3. You want to start a report on a page other than "1." How can you do this?

Answer to Reports Advanced Question 3

This is a difficult problem because there is no way to reference the logical page number in boilerplate text or to create any Data Model object that will make this work. This must be accomplished using an SRW.SET_FIELDNUM command or a format trigger on the layout field in the margin of the Layout Model. The details of this technique are explained in Chapter 24. If the interviewees know the answer to this question, you have probably found skilled Reports developers.

Reports Advanced Question 4

4. For the report data model shown in the following illustration, and data shown in the Big Projects and Little Projects database tables that follow, what is the required SQL query? What does the report Data Model look like?

Question 4—Data Model

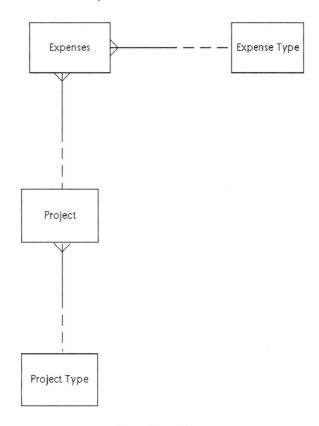

Question 4 Data

Big Projects

Exp Type	Total Amt
People	$10,000
Equipment	$20,000
Misc.	$ 5,000

Little Projects

Exp Type	Total Amt
People	$5,000
Equipment	$7,000
Misc.	$2,000

Answer to Reports Advanced Question 4

This should be a simple question, but many report developers find it difficult because the data model for the report is very different from the database Data Model. Novice or even intermediate users of Oracle Reports would have difficulty with this, but experts should have no trouble getting the correct answer.

The required SQL query for the Projects and Expenses report is as follows:

```
SELECT      projt.proj_type_cd,
            projt.name_tx,
            expt.exp_type_cd,
            expt.name_tx,
            SUM(exp.amnt_nr) tot_amnt
FROM        project_type projt,
            project proj,
            expense exp,
            expense_type expt
WHERE       projt.proj_type_cd = proj.proj_type_cd
AND         proj.proj_id = exp.proj_id
AND         expt.exp_type_cd = exp.exp_type_cd
GROUP BY    projt.proj_type_cd,
            projt.name_tx,
            expt.exp_type_cd,
            expt.name_tx
```

The Data Model should appear as in Figure 23-16.

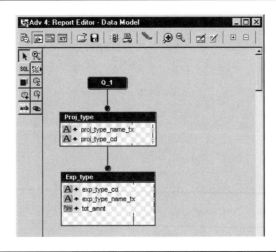

FIGURE 23-16. *Project/Expense Data Model*

Reports Advanced Question 5

5. You want to create a one-page report that folds horizontally in the middle so that the top half of the page is right side up and the bottom half is upside down, as shown in Figure 23-17. How can this be done in Reports?

Answer to Reports Advanced Question 5

This is a question that few people know the answer to. The two critical pieces of information are as follows:

a. Using the Rotate button, you can rotate boilerplate text but not fields in Oracle Reports.

b. By using an "&," you can embed field values in boilerplate.

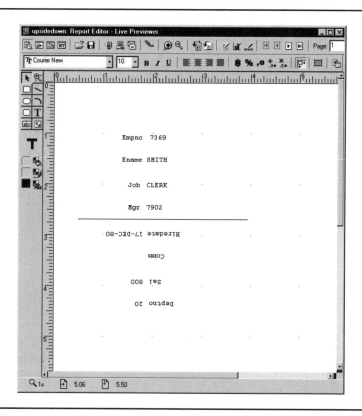

FIGURE 23-17. *One-page report with horizontal fold*

This is more of a trick than in-depth product knowledge. You build half of your report in the normal way. For the upside-down part, build labels and invert them. Next, create the fields. Create a boilerplate text item for each data field and invert. The resulting layout will look like the report shown in Figure 23-18.

Any developer who is aware of this information must be experienced with Oracle Reports. If the interviewees don't know the trick but are able to figure it out, this is an indication that they truly understand the product. Give the interviewees hints to test the problem-solving skills if the answer is not forthcoming.

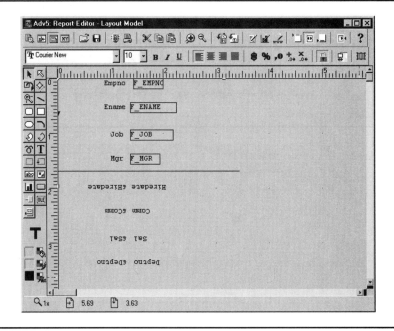

FIGURE 23-18.   *Layout Model for report with inverted portion*

Scoring Your Answers

Add up your points on the questions for each section. A score of 200 points is a perfect score in each of the Forms and Reports sections. Find your rating on the following table:

Score	Rating
Under 25 points	May have taken one class about Oracle Developer, but probably hasn't done any significant development work
25–50 points	Junior Developer
50–100 points	Mid-Level Developer
100–150 points	Senior Developer
150–200 points	Oracle Developer Guru (or they read this book!)

CHAPTER
24

Reports Tips & Techniques

I know a trick worth two of that.

—William Shakespeare (1564–1616) *Henry IV, Part I*

 he Reports component of Oracle Developer is a complex product. After working with it for a number of years, you will learn many useful tricks and techniques that can speed up your future report development. This chapter will present some specific Reports features and shortcuts that the authors have used to create production reports.

Page Breaks

It is important to be consistent in the way that page breaks are handled in your reports as part of enforcing your GUI and coding standards. Oddly enough, you will rarely set page breaks with the *Page Break Before/Page Break After* properties. These properties can be set using the Property Palette for any object in the Layout Model and are used only in special circumstances. The most common properties for controlling page breaks are the following:

- **Maximum Records per Page** This property is only applied to repeating frames. Normally, this property is left blank, which instructs Reports to put as many records as possible on the page. If you want to specify that you have exactly one record per page, then set the *Maximum Records per Page* property to 1. You might think that specifying the *Page Break After* property on the repeating frame would have the same effect, but it does not (see the explanation of *Page Break Before/After* later in this list).

- **Page Protect** Setting the *Page Protect* property to "Yes" forces everything in the regular or repeating frames to stay on the same page. The algorithm used is the following: Reports tries to print the frame entirely on the current page. If it is at the top of the page, it will print. If it is not at the top of the page, Reports looks to see if the whole frame can fit on the page. If so, it will print. If not, a page break is inserted and then the report is printed. When should you use *Page Protect?* With the Emp/Dept frame example from Chapter 19, if you have very small departments, more than one will be placed on the same page. If one department is too large to fit in the remaining space on the page, using *Page Protect* will force the large department to start printing on the next page.

■ **Keep With Anchoring Object**   This property can be set on any layout object. Setting the *Keep With Anchoring Object* property to "Yes" forces the object and its anchoring object to appear on the same page. If Reports would otherwise put a page break between the two objects, the break is then placed before the first object to keep objects together. You will use this property most frequently to keep group headers from being orphaned at the bottom of the page. If you are showing Departments and Employees, it doesn't make sense to put the department header at the bottom of the page only to repeat it at the top of the next page in order to display its employees. It is even worse to have a column header appear at the bottom of the page without any data. The *Keep With Anchoring Object* property is similar in behavior to Microsoft Word's "Keep with next" in the Line and Page Break settings, except that in this case, rather than being set for the top object, in Reports this property is usually set for the bottom object.

If a repeating frame is contained inside a regular frame and then a regular frame is placed above that with the header information, you would need to set the *Keep With Anchoring Object* property on the repeating frame in addition to the frame surrounding the repeating frames. However, what this does is effectively the same as setting the *Page Protect* property to "Yes" on the frame surrounding all the objects discussed. If you only want to prevent the header from being orphaned, you must not have a regular frame surrounding the repeating frame, so that the anchoring object for the repeating frame is the header itself. Header objects should be placed in an enclosing frame.

■ **Page Break Before/Page Break After**   The *Page Break Before* and *Page Break After* properties only control anchoring objects. These properties can be set on any object in the Layout Model. To use the *Page Break Before* and *Page Break After* properties effectively, you have to know where objects are anchored. Setting the *Page Break After* property to "Yes" moves all objects that are anchored to the object where the property was set to the next page. Even though they appear below the object in the Layout Model, sibling objects are not automatically moved to the next page. In general, when using *Page Break After*, you need to explicitly set anchors to make sure that the objects you want moved are child objects. This property can be useful in the case of a report with multiple parts that follow one above the other in the same report (such as two separate queries or two distinct layouts). You can set *Page Break After* to "Yes" on the frame surrounding the entire top layout when the report is run. The bottom layout is now a child object and moves to the next page. Alternatively, you can set the *Page Break Before* property to "Yes" on the bottom layout. In Figure 24-1, the *Page Break After*

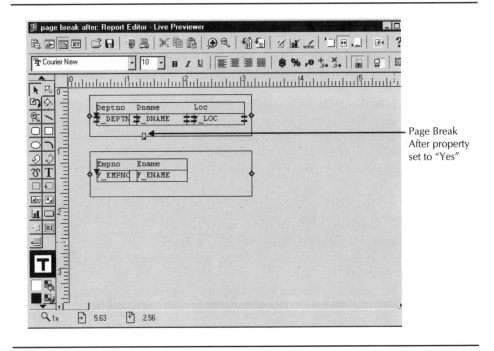

FIGURE 24-1. *Using the* Page Break After *property*

property is set to "Yes" on the frame surrounding the department layout. This caused the Employee report to start on its own page.

The *Page Break Before* and *Page Break After* properties are rarely used except in multipart reports.

Another option for setting page breaks is on the format trigger for the object, which could be used to send a hard-page-break code directly to the printer. This method then makes your reports hardware specific.

Flexible Page Breaks

Chapter 17 discussed integrating forms and reports. The notion of passing portions of the underlying SQL query to a report is relatively straightforward. However, trying to flexibly pass columns, and even breaks, to a report requires a bit more thinking. The idea is to allow the user to be able to flexibly select the break. As mentioned in Chapters 17 and 18, recall that lexical parameters are used to perform simple character substitutions in the SQL query embedded in the report that allow you to build the query for the report on the fly. One of the uses of this technique that is infrequently used is specifying breaks on the fly. The following are the steps required to perform this task:

1. Create a user parameter in the Data Model node of the Object Navigator called P_BREAK. The *Datatype* property should be "Character" with an *Initial Value* of 'x' (x enclosed by single quotes).

2. Build the query using P_BREAK as a lexical parameter. For example, to flexibly pass the break column to a report based upon the Employee information in the Scott schema shipped with Oracle Developer, create the following query:

```
SELECT &p_break break_col, empno, ename
FROM    emp, dept
WHERE   emp.deptno=dept.deptno
```

3. Create a query with two groups—one with the break column and the other with the remaining columns. You can also use lexical parameters to add to the FROM and WHERE clauses to allow breaks in additional tables.

4. Create a standard master-detail report layout and run the report.

If you pass the value DEPTNO to the P_BREAK parameter, the report will break on Department. Passing of parameters for the break column is best handled through an Oracle Developer Forms front-end.

If no breaks are required for a report and no information in the break area should be printed, the following steps are required:

1. Enclose all break columns in an enclosing frame.

2. Place a FORMAT trigger on that frame so that if the value of P_BREAK is "no break," it will not print the break information. Use the following code for the trigger:

```
FUNCTION M_1 FORMAT TRIGGER
   RETURN BOOLEAN
BEGIN
   IF :p_break = '''no break'''
   THEN
      RETURN (FALSE);
   ELSE
      RETURN(TRUE);
   END IF;
END;
```

3. At runtime, pass the literal 'no break' (including the quotes) to the break parameter.

If you want to have more than one break group, simply create two break parameters, two break groups, and two break frames in the Layout Model.

For any column or break group that you don't want to use in any report, simply have a form pass a null value, which you can then delete in a FORMAT trigger on enclosing frames, and suppress the printing of the unneeded object(s).

TIP

The obvious thing to do is to call the breaks P_BREAK_1 and P_BREAK_2, but doing this will make it difficult to remember which is the inner and which is the outer break. Instead, use names like P_BREAK_INNER and P_BREAK_OUTER.

This is a powerful technique that allows you to dynamically select which columns a report can break on. If you want to break on numeric or date information, you can either use a modified break column of the appropriate type, or you can use a TO_CHAR function to convert the data value to character. If you are breaking on a numeric column, you should recognize the impact this may have on your sorts since it will sort numbers based on their initial characters rather than numeric values. For example, 1, 10, 11, 2, 22, 300, 4… This may not produce the desired result unless you left-pad the value with spaces.

Control of Page Layout on a Form-Style Report

When you specify a Form-style report, the Report Wizard lays out each field, one next to the other, across the first line from left to right going down the page. This is usually not the way you want your report laid out. It is more likely that you would want one object on each line with the date in the upper-right corner. A developer could spend hours getting the report to look right by manipulating the layout manually. However, there are effective ways to make use of what the Reports Layout generator does by default that give developers sufficient control of the report layout to minimize having to do the layout by hand. There are two methods by which you can precisely control the fields:

■ **Setting the field widths** When working in the Report Wizard, change the width of the fields to force each of the fields to wrap onto a separate line, as shown in Figure 24-2. For example, if you want to put more than one object on a line, you can change the width to 50. These sizes will change depending upon the font selected. By manipulating the widths of the data fields on the Labels tab of the Report Wizard, you can achieve the desired layout. The disadvantage to this method is that field widths are too wide. You may need to adjust the widths of the fields manually in the Layout Model after using the Report Wizard.

■ **Adding placeholder columns** The alternative to changing field widths is to add placeholder columns to your groups to add space and force the line wrapping to occur in the right places, as shown in Figure 24-3. You will need to remove the default labels of the placeholder columns. This preserves the original width of the fields, but tends to clutter up the Data

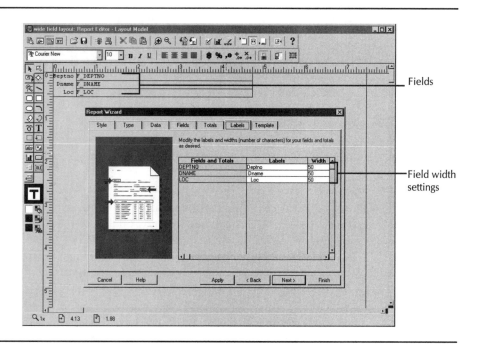

FIGURE 24-2. *Sample field width settings*

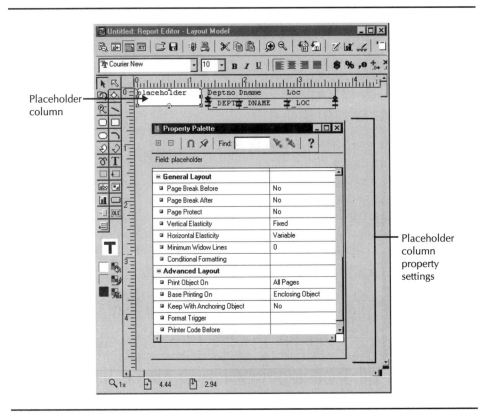

FIGURE 24-3. *Placeholder column and its properties in the Layout Model*

Model. If you want to use this technique, before beginning layout, go into the Data Model and pin the Placeholder icon by double-clicking on it. Then you can quickly add as many columns as you might need to the Data Model. They can always be deleted later. In the example in Figure 24-3, the interfield gap has been reduced to 0 in **Tools→Preferences** so that the fields could be aligned. Also note that a fractional width (2.5) was used for one of the placeholder fields, as shown in Figure 24-4.

Either of these methods will control where fields are placed by the Report Wizard. The placeholder method is more efficient in that it not only preserves the original width of the data fields, but also provides the ability to precisely control the exact placement of all objects on the screen. If you are only going to create the report once, it is probably slightly less work to use the first method. However, by

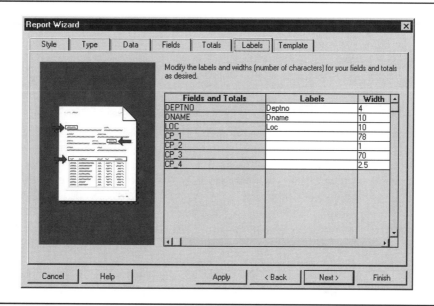

FIGURE 24-4.   *Setting placeholder column widths in the Report Wizard*

using placeholder columns, you minimize the amount of modification needed after
the Report Wizard finishes.

Complex Centering of a Report

The following is a useful trick for centering a report. In addition to being useful, this
technique also serves to illustrate that you sometimes have to be sneaky in
developing reports. If you can imagine something that you want Reports to do that
seems reasonable, it is almost always possible. However, sometimes the solution to
the problem is not obvious. For a particular run of a report, you might be unsure
how wide a horizontal repeating group will be. For example, the group might be
one, two, or three columns wide depending upon the situation. Additionally, you
want the report to be centered on the page. There is no mechanism in Reports that
allows you to do this directly. The solution is to put a field to the left of the report
frame that will expand or contract to move the report over to the right so that it is
centered on the screen. Use a horizontal variable field that you programmatically
pad with spaces (probably in a BEFORE REPORT trigger), explicitly anchoring the
left edge of the report frame to the right edge of the variable field. Discovering tricks
like this is what makes for highly productive Reports developers.

TIP
The new Stretch to Frame *property allows you to extend the boilerplate line based on the frame width.*

Strategies for Using Dot Leaders

In this context, dot leaders refer to a repeated string of leading characters, usually periods, connecting two fields of information as used in a table of contents or in a phone book with a name and phone number that display with dots or periods leading from one field to the next. Dot leaders make matching two pieces of information across a page much easier.

There are two ways in which you can display dot leaders. The most accurate, but quite involved, method is to create a table that stores the exact pixel size of every letter with the font you are using. You have to experiment by trial and error to figure out the width of each character. You then read each record as it is returned and select the sum of all the letter sizes from the table. You now have the length of each field and can display the exact number of dots required to fill the space between the fields.

You can see how this method can take some time and effort. There is, however, another way to display the dots. You create the layout with all the data fields in the desired locations. Then you create a text field that is long enough to span the distance from the start of the leftmost field to the end of the rightmost field that you want to display dots between. Completely fill the text field with periods (or another leading character). The text field should be positioned so that it overlays the data fields. This can be accomplished by selecting the text field and the leftmost data field and using **Arrange→Align Objects**. Align the objects to "Each Other," selecting Horizontally "Align Left" and Vertically "Align Top." Next, select each of the data fields individually. This may be tricky because the text object is on top, but you can move it around and shrink it a little if you need to get to the fields underneath. You can also easily select multiple fields by CTRL-clicking them in the Object Navigator. On each of the fields, put a fill color of white and select **Arrange→Bring to Front**. It is very important to also go to each field's Property Palette and, under General Layout, to set the *Horizontal Elasticity* property to "Variable." The dots will now display between the fields.

Make sure that the dot text field is long enough on the ends so that if the field is short, there will be enough dots to fill the space left when the data field shrinks. You may also want to place a blank text field, with a white fill color, to the left of any of the fields that have the dots leading up to them. This will ensure that a set amount of space displays before the field, thus creating consistent spacing.

You will need to explicitly anchor the columns to the top of the frame to prevent the fields on the right from moving horizontally. This way is much easier and faster than the letter sizing method; however, it isn't quite as accurate. Accuracy in this case refers to the number of dots between the fields. In this second method, you can get partial dots or an uneven amount of space between the last dot and the beginning of the field text.

Managing Reports with Forms

Very large reports have problems. If you have a very large report with many parts, frames, and embedded objects, the report file itself can become corrupted and unreadable. The best and most efficient way to handle very large reports is to break them into separate reports and to use a form to manage running and printing them.

You can use the form to run the various parts of the report in order, if need be, or to only run one section of the report. This task is quite simple using the RUN_ PRODUCT or RUN_REPORT_OBJECT Forms built-ins and their various settings parameters. You can do many things this way, such as:

- Skipping the preview of the report

- Setting the form to run continuously through all parts of the report

- Passing continuous page numbers from report to report (discussed further in the next section)

Passing Page Numbers to a Report

As mentioned earlier, you can pass page numbers to a report from a form. This makes using a form to manage reports even more efficient and attractive because it gives you the ability to support a multipart report. If you are breaking your report into multiple parts, you may want to start the sections of your report on specific page numbers to achieve consistency throughout the sections.

To pass page numbers to the report, follow these steps:

1. Set a user parameter in the report and a variable in the form that either the user sets at each runtime or that has an initial value.

2. In the report Data Model, create a placeholder column outside of any group in the model.

3. In the report Layout Model, place a field on the layout where the page number will display with the placeholder formula column as its source. Your column must have a specified source for this technique to work. If you do not attach a source to the column, even though the value of the *Source* is "Null," the code below will not cause a value to display.

4. Write a FORMAT trigger for the field. The FORMAT trigger will override the original field source unless the trigger returns "false." The FORMAT trigger code is shown next:

```
FUNCTION F_PAGENOFormatTrigger
    RETURN BOOLEAN IS
    v_temp_nr NUMBER;
BEGIN
    srw.get_page_num(v_temp_nr);
    srw.set_field_num(0,v_temp_nr + (TO_NUMBER(:p_start_page_nr) - 1));
    globals.page_numbers := v_temp_nr + TO_NUMBER(:p_start_page_nr) - 1;
    v_temp_nr + TO_NUMBER (:p_start_page_nr) - 1;
    RETURN(TRUE);
END
```

The code uses the SRW.GET_PAGE_NUM function to get the true page number. Then it uses the SRW.SET_FIELD_NUM function to set the page number based on the value passed into the report. The function is initialized to zero, and then the value is calculated. The parameter P_START_PAGE_NR is the number supplied by the form. The global package variable is used to pass the number back to the form.

For continuous logical page numbering in different physical reports, use a global session variable that is stored in a database package that can be picked up from the form. You can see an example of this in the code in the previous section. The global package variable GLOBALS.PAGE_NUM is a variable defined in a database package called globals. This number is calculated the same way as the value used in the report. Note that there is a slight inefficiency in this procedure since it is updating a global parameter in the database for each page in the report. You can eliminate this inefficiency by storing the page number in a local package variable and only passing it to the database global once in an AFTER REPORT trigger.

Alternating Page Headings

In the publishing world, odd page numbers print on the right side, and even numbers print on the left side. In reports, you have the ability to alternate page headings by reading the page number. This can be very useful when you are writing reports that are published, such as a book.

Create two sets of fields and frames on the layout where they should appear, one for odd-numbered pages and another for even-numbered pages. On each frame, write a FORMAT trigger that uses the SRW.GET_PAGE_NUM function to get the page number. If the page number is odd, return TRUE in the trigger on the odd page header and FALSE in the trigger on the even page header. Return the opposite value in each header if the page number is even. An example follows:

```
    ...
    v_page_num NUMBER;
BEGIN
    srw.get_page_num(page_num);
    IF MOD((Page_num + (TO_NUMBER(:start_page) - 1)), 2) != 0
    THEN
        RETURN(FALSE);
    ELSE
        RETURN(TRUE);
    END IF;
END;
```

This code declares a variable PAGE_NUM to place the page number returned by the SRW command GET_PAGE_NUM. Then it uses the MOD function to determine if the page that the report is on is odd or even by reading the current page plus the starting page.

Counts of Record Subsets

Counts of record subsets refers to a report that categorizes information, counts the number of records returned for each category, and displays the count instead of the data itself. You can also use this method to return sums of amounts for a category.

In the detail group of the report, you create formula columns that are of "Number" type for each category. Each formula contains an "IF" statement for its category. If the conditions are met, then you return a one (1); if they are not, you return a zero (0). Then, in the master group of the report, you create summary columns corresponding to each of the formula columns. Define each summary column as a sum, and then set the source to the appropriate formula column from the detail group. This gives you, in the summary colunns, the count of the number of records returned that fit into each category.

An example of the code follows:

```
BEGIN
    IF :occ_code = '0110'
    THEN
        RETURN 1;
    ELSE
        RETURN 0;
    END IF;
END;
```

Basing a Query on a Function

You can base a query on a REF CURSOR Query. There is a sample demo report called REFCURSOR.RDF that shows this principle. The file is located in the ORACLE_HOME/devdem60/demo/reports directory. You can use the following steps to re-create a report with a similar query based on a REF CURSOR. There is a preparation step of creating a package with the function that returns a REF CURSOR datatype. This package contains a function that determines whether the employee is in a department that has an ID of 40 (for Operations) and awards that employee a 30 percent raise instead of the normal 20 percent. While this particular example could be coded with pure SQL, the sample code demonstrates the principles of using a REF CURSOR Query.

The Package

The code that runs the query and returns the REF CURSOR is in a database package. A sample follows:

```
PACKAGE emp_qry
IS
/****************************************************\
|| The REF CURSOR returned by the function provides
|| the data for this query. The query decides
|| whether the employee is in a department that has
|| an ID of 40 (Operations) and awards those
|| employees a 30% raise instead of a 20% raise.
\****************************************************/
   --
   TYPE r_comp IS RECORD
       (deptno emp.deptno%TYPE,
        ename   emp.ename%TYPE,
        hiredate emp.hiredate%TYPE,
        sal      emp.sal%TYPE,
        total_sal emp.sal%TYPE);
   --
   TYPE comp_rc IS REF CURSOR
      RETURN r_comp;
   --
   FUNCTION emp_sal(
      p_deptno NUMBER)
      RETURN comp_rc;
END;

PACKAGE BODY emp_qry IS
   --
   FUNCTION emp_sal(
```

```
      p_deptno NUMBER)
   RETURN comp_rc
IS
   c_emp      emp_qry.comp_rc;
   v_raise    NUMBER;
BEGIN
   IF p_deptno >= 40
   THEN
      -- Operations Dept only
      v_raise := 1.3;
   ELSE
      v_raise := 1.2;
   END IF;
   OPEN c_emp FOR
      SELECT   deptno,
               ename,
               hiredate,
               sal,
               v_raise * (sal + nvl(comm, 0)) total_sal
      FROM     emp
      WHERE    deptno = p_deptno
      ORDER BY ename;
   RETURN c_emp;
END;       -- end of emp_qry
END;
```

Other Steps

After creating the package just shown, run Report Builder and complete the following steps.

1. Create a user parameter for P_DEPTNO. Set the *Datatype* property to "Number".

2. Draw out a REF CURSOR Query in the data model.

3. Fill in the *PL/SQL Statement* property in the PL/SQL Editor using a function that returns the cursor variable that runs the database function. Here is an example:

```
FUNCTION QR_1RefCurDS
   RETURN emp_qry.comp_rc
IS
BEGIN
   -- Be sure to create a p_deptno parameter first.
   RETURN emp_qry.emp_sal(:p_deptno);
END;
```

After compiling this function, you'll see a group with columns in the Data Model.

4. Close the PL/SQL Editor.

5. Create a standard Report Wizard tabular layout.

When you run this report, the query will load with records from the database function that returns a REF CURSOR.

Performance Optimization in Reports

There are many ways that you can improve report performance using both general strategies and specific techniques. This section will discuss some of the most important ways to make your reports run more quickly and efficiently.

Use a Small Number of Queries

As mentioned in Chapter 19, multiple linked queries in a report can cause large numbers of cursors to be executed in order to run the report. There is some overhead associated with the execution of each query, which should be kept to a minimum. The ideal situation is to create only one query to be sent to the database to retrieve information. Keep in mind that one of the most expensive development resources is the developer. You don't want to spend weeks creating the ultimate, elegant report as long as performance is adequate. If reports are not carefully written, performance can be terrible. As an example, one of the authors saw a novice developer use a separate query for each field in all his reports. Each query also contained a formula column with a cursor going back to the database to retrieve the information to be displayed. One of the authors encountered a single-page report that required over 100 queries to be executed. This created a maintenance as well as a performance nightmare. With more careful thought, the same report was rewritten using three queries, thus performing faster.

Avoid Using Formula Columns Requiring Database Access

With the exception of report-level formula columns that are only executed a single time, you should avoid using formula columns requiring database access in your reports. It is acceptable to create the formula columns with embedded functions until your report is running. You may want to leave these columns in the reports during development, and then move the formula columns to the database for performance optimization.

Using a formula column with a cursor in a multirecord frame will always degrade report performance. However, if the database is small enough, performance may not be an issue.

To avoid using formula columns with cursors, you can turn them into database functions stored within packages in the database. You can then either call these functions directly in your SQL statement, or create a view with the functions embedded in the view and write your query selecting from the view. The view approach is a better alternative since it more tightly encapsulates the information.

Don't Retrieve Detail Records from the Database That Won't be Displayed

You should not bring back unnecessary records from the database if they will not be displayed. For example, consider creating a summary-level Departmental report (using Dept/Emp in the Oracle sample Scott schema) displaying the number of employees in each department. You could create a master-detail report retrieving all employees, and use a summary variable to count the employees in each department. In the Layout Model, create a single repeating frame based on the department group. Such a report would work, but would not be efficient. It is much more efficient to use a GROUP_BY in the query and only retrieve one record for each department.

There are instances where it is inconvenient to display all groups in a query. However, you should usually restructure the query to avoid unnecessary retrieval of records.

Tune Your SQL

The factor with the greatest influence on report performance is a slow SQL query. If the query does not run quickly in SQL*Plus, it cannot run any faster in Reports. You must carefully tune your reports to improve performance. All the standard techniques should be used, including

- Indexing
- Hints
- Database tuning

All these techniques are important for improving report performance. With a slow running report, you can extract the query and test it by running it in SQL*Plus. If the performance is still slow, the problem has been identified. At this point, the developer, in conjunction with the DBA, must tackle the problem of improving query performance. A full description of SQL tuning techniques is beyond the scope of this book. There are several books on the market dedicated to this topic, including *Oracle8 Advanced Tuning & Administration* (Oracle Press, 1998) by Eyal Aronoff, Kevin Loney, and Noorali Sonawalla; and *Oracle Performance Tuning Tips & Techniques* (Oracle Press, 1999) by Richard J. Niemiec.

Beware of Bind Variables, Changing Database Versions, or Moving from One Database to Another

The execution plan of a query is automatically determined by the Oracle Optimizer. Various factors can cause this plan to change.

The SQL in an Oracle report may be well tuned; however, the addition of a bind variable can cause a change in the way the query is executed. Similarly, if you move from one version of your database to another, the execution plan of specific queries may change significantly. Moving from one database to another can also cause changes due to differences in the init.ora parameters or in whether tables have been analyzed.

Starting with Oracle8, you can specify the execution plan for a query and not allow the Optimizer to alter this plan. For a particularly problematic report, this is a good strategy to use.

Avoid Unnecessary Use of Graphics

Graphics images can add a great deal of overhead to the printing of a report and may even affect its execution. For example, if every other page of a report displays a different image, the report may run very slowly. If performance is a concern, you should use graphics minimally. If graphics are necessary, use the lowest possible resolution to keep the graphics-image storage size small. Using a 24-bit, high-resolution image to represent a black-and-white line-art logo is unnecessary overhead.

Printer Performance

In examining the length of time a report requires to run, it is easy to forget about how long the report may take to print. Using many graphics images or nonstandard fonts that a printer must represent as bitmaps can (depending upon the printer) significantly affect print speed. This is not usually a problem, but with older equipment or in cases where high-speed printing is essential, the printer performance should be taken into consideration when creating the reports.

CHAPTER
25

Forms Item Tips and
Techniques

The one fact that I would cry from every housetop is this:
the Good Life is waiting for us—here and now!
... At this very moment we have the necessary techniques,
both material and psychological, to create a full and satisfying life for everyone.
—Burrhus Frederic Skinner (1904–1990), Walden Two

 here are probably a thousand techniques that you need to know to be an effective Forms developer. The product is so deep and broad that you end up using many of these every time you work with Oracle Developer Forms (Forms). Since this is a book aimed at an advanced developer, you should already know at least half of these. This book has provided you with another large set of techniques up to this point. The rest of the chapters in this book provide you with many more.

Depending on the complexity and contents of the technique, there are several formats used in these chapters. Some techniques are formatted as *recipes* that explain the objective, list the preparation steps and "ingredients" required for the technique, and then provide the steps involved with carrying out ("cooking") the solution. Other techniques are formatted as discussions of problems, requirements, and explanations on how to fulfill the requirements. Some techniques are formatted as short tips that put a different spin on a familiar technique. The chapters are divided into categories by the major Forms topics:

- Items
- Blocks
- Form modules
- Menus
- System concerns

Other sources, such as *Oracle Developer Starter Kit,* by Robert Muller (Osborne/McGraw-Hill, 1999), will provide you with the basic techniques you need to get started with the tool, such as creating Forms objects and code, working with the debugger, defining keys in Oracle Terminal, and providing security systems for your applications. Most of the techniques discussed in this chapter go beyond the basics. This chapter discusses the first topic in the above list: techniques for Forms items such as the hierarchical tree control, dynamic poplists, system-assigned ID values, image item loading, access keys, and characters as button icons.

Hierarchical Tree Control

Hierarchical, or recursive, data is quite common in business because data is often related to itself in a parent-child manner. Organizational charts (org charts) show hierarchies within the staff of a company. Employees, company departmental structures, and sales territories can all be represented as hierarchical structures. You can identify hierarchical data when you see a link to itself within a table. For example, a manager employee number in one record of the EMP table links to the employee number of another record. When you design a form, you need to consider the best way to present this hierarchical data to the user.

Oracle Developer Forms Release 6.0 offers a new type of control: the hierarchical tree control. This functionality was actually available in earlier releases as a reusable component made of Forms objects such as items and canvases. However, the new hierarchical tree control is a true native Forms "widget" with properties, built-ins, and triggers to support it. The control allows you to present a tree interface such as that found in Windows Explorer or the Form Builder's Object Navigator. Users find this type of control quite intuitive if they are familiar with the data. The user can view hierarchical data by expanding and collapsing nodes to reveal or hide child data. After setting up the recursive query, you have little else to do other than program what happens when the user selects, expands, or collapses a node.

The following recipe provides the basic steps for loading data into this control, manipulating it with built-ins, and responding to its triggers. After you start using the hierarchical tree control, you will find many more techniques and tricks to apply to it. Figure 25-1 shows a simple implementation of the hierarchical tree control. The

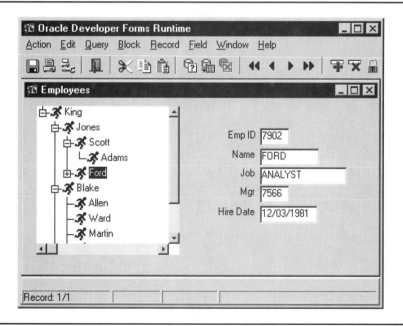

FIGURE 25-1. *Hierarchical tree control*

user selects an employee from the hierarchical tree on the left and the employee record is queried into the block on the right. The tree control gives the user an intuitive method for finding an employee.

Preparation

After you have determined that this control will work for your interface needs, you have to work out the SELECT statement that will return rows in a recursive loop. The standard SELECT statement clauses you use for this are START WITH to indicate where the query will start the loop and CONNECT BY to indicate the actual parent-child link. In addition, a recursive query will generate a pseudo-column called LEVEL that indicates where the record is in the hierarchy.

A sample SELECT statement that would return employee information in a hierarchical order follows:

```
SELECT     level,
           ename,
           empno
FROM       emp
START WITH mgr IS NULL
CONNECT BY PRIOR
           empno = mgr;
```

If you want to preview this statement with the indenting in a way similar to the hierarchical tree control, use the following:

```
SELECT     level,
           empno,
           mgr,
           lpad(' ',level * 2) || ename ename
FROM       emp
START WITH mgr IS NULL
CONNECT BY PRIOR
           empno = mgr;
```

The results of this query will look like the following:

```
LEVEL      EMPNO       MGR ENAME
------ --------- --------- ---------------
     1      7839           KING
     2      7566      7839   JONES
     3      7788      7566     SCOTT
     4      7876      7788       ADAMS
     3      7902      7566     FORD
     4      7369      7902       SMITH
     2      7698      7839   BLAKE
```

3	7499	7698	ALLEN
3	7521	7698	WARD
3	7654	7698	MARTIN
3	7844	7698	TURNER
3	7900	7698	JAMES
2	7782	7839	CLARK
3	7934	7782	MILLER

Spending time on the query will pay off when you start to create the objects in the form.

TIP
Consult the "Hierarchical Queries" section of Chapter 5 in the Oracle8i SQL Reference *for more information on SELECT statements that return hierarchical data.*

Ingredients

The only real ingredients you need for creating the hierarchical tree control are the program specifications or storyboards that indicate how the form should look and act. You also need a working knowledge of how the hierarchical tree control works. After building a few samples based on this recipe, it is useful to examine the Forms help system starting at the topic in the Index tab called "hierarchical trees - about." There is a Related Topics button that shows a list of all topics that covers the hierarchical tree object. Read about each of these and examine the examples. This will be useful when you start to use the control more fully.

Steps

The steps involved with creating a hierarchical tree control after preparing the query are as follows.

1. Create a nonbase table (control) block with a *Number of Records Displayed* property of "1". The tree control must be the only item in this control block.

2. Draw a hierarchical tree control in the Layout Editor by clicking its button and drawing a box on the canvas. Be sure this is in the control block.

3. Set the properties of the tree control. You can resize and recolor the object in the Layout Editor, but the most important property is the *Data Query* property. This is where you put the SELECT statement that you designed in the preparation stage. There is further discussion about this in the next section, "On the Query."

4. Write a trigger to populate the tree from the query. You can do this at any time in the form but a logical point would be the PRE-FORM trigger when you are setting up other items in the form. If your tree control was called CONTROL.EMP_TREE, the trigger would use the following code:

```
ftree.populate_tree('CONTROL.EMP_TREE');
```

All tree procedures and functions are stored in a built-in package called FTREE. Therefore, all calls to tree built-ins must start with "FTREE."

On the Query

The SELECT statement must include five columns in the following order:

- **Initial State**   This indicates whether you want the node expanded or collapsed. The values to use for this column are "1" for expanded, "–1" for collapsed, and "0" for showing the record on the same level as its parent record. You can use a DECODE function to set this initial state based on the LEVEL or some other criterion.

- **Node Tree Depth**   This is the position (rank) in the hierarchy. You use the LEVEL pseudo-column for this purpose. A top level record will be assigned a level of "1".

- **Node Label**   The label is the displayed value that you see in the hierarchy. If the value of the column you are selecting is a code or ID, use the name or description column for the label.

- **Node Icon**   You can assign an icon to the node that will show next to the label. The icon name should not contain the extension or the directory path. You can use a DECODE here, too, if you want to display different icons on different nodes. The icon must be located in the current working directory or a directory listed in the UI_ICON string value in the registry (for Windows) or in the environment (for UNIX).

- **Data Value**   This is the actual value of the node that you will use when the node is selected. This would usually be a code or ID that represents the node label.

The following is a sample query with all five columns based on the query in the preparation step:

```
SELECT decode(level, 1, 1, -1),
       level,
       INITCAP(ename),
       'tbrun',
       empno
```

```
FROM    emp
START WITH mgr IS NULL
CONNECT BY PRIOR empno = mgr
```

This query will use the initial-capped version of the employee name as the label and the EMPNO column as the actual value. It will expand the level 1 node and collapse all other nodes. The tbrun icon will be displayed next to each label.

Using a Record Group

You can also use a record group as the data source for the hierarchical tree by filling in the *Record Group* property instead of the *Data Query* property. The advantage to using a record group is that it is an object that can be shared by many hierarchical trees, if you have them, within the same form.

Additional Steps

If you want to add a block to display the details of a record, create the block with items and add code to a WHEN-TREE-NODE-SELECTED trigger on the CONTROL block as in the following example:

```
go_block('EMP');
set_block_property('EMP', DEFAULT_WHERE, 'EMPNO=' ||
    ftree.get_tree_node_property('CONTROL.EMP_TREE',
    :SYSTEM.TRIGGER_NODE, FTREE.NODE_VALUE));
execute_query;
```

This sets the *WHERE Clause* property of the block to the value of the selected node. When the query executes, this WHERE clause returns the row that matches the EMPNO with the node value that is also the EMPNO. If you are allowing the selection of multiple nodes, you will have to store the IDs selected in a variable and use this to construct a list for the WHERE clause of the block.

Other steps you can take once the hierarchical tree control is created are to make it generic for a specific table query and place it in the object library. This allows you to reuse the specific table tree later. You can also make the tree control even more generic by not coding a query at all, but leaving that property null. You would then write a generic procedure in the PL/SQL library to load the *Data Query* property with a new query that is passed to the procedure. The following code would load a hierarchical tree object with a query:

```
ftree.set_tree_property('CONTROL.EMP_TREE', FTREE.QUERY_TEXT,
    'SELECT decode(level, 1, 1, -1), level, INITCAP(ename),' ||
    '''tbrun'', empno FROM    emp' ||
    'START WITH mgr IS NULL CONNECT BY PRIOR empno = mgr');
```

Other Tree Properties

There are some other properties in the tree's Property Palette that you can set to modify the behavior of the control:

- **Allow Empty Branches**   If you set this property to "Yes", the tree control will show nodes that have no child nodes with a + or – expansion symbol even though there are no child nodes. The default is "No", which means that the lowest level child nodes (leaves) will not display the + and – expansion symbols. The following shows how a leaf node (Adams) would look if this property were set to "Yes".

- **Multi-Selection**   Set this to "Yes" (the default is "No") if you want the user to be able to select more than one node using SHIFT-click or CTRL-click. The following shows a multiple selection.

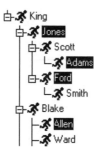

- **Show Lines**   If this property is set to "Yes", the default, there will be lines drawn that link the nodes to sibling nodes and to the parent. The following shows how the nodes would look if this property is set to "No".

■ **Show Symbols**   If this property is set to "Yes" the control will display + and – expansion symbols next to each node. If you set this to "No", the nodes will display as in the following illustration. You will not be able to expand or collapse nodes manually, although you can do this programmatically.

Built-Ins and Triggers

This should give you a starting place for working with the hierarchical tree control. If you want to explore the control further, examine the help system, as mentioned, and look for specific built-ins and triggers that manage the hierarchical tree. A list of these built-ins and trigger follows.

Built-ins

Prefix the following with the package name, FTREE, when you use them in code:

GET_TREE_PROPERTY	This queries the properties of a particular tree.
SET_TREE_PROPERTY	This assigns a value to a property of a tree.
GET_TREE_SELECTION	Use this to get a list of the selected nodes.
SET_TREE_SELECTION	Use this to set the selection (highlight) of a particular node.
GET_TREE_NODE_PROPERTY	This queries the properties of a particular node.
SET_TREE_NODE_PROPERTY	Use this to set the properties of a particular node.
GET_TREE_NODE_PARENT	Use this to find the parent node for a particular node.
FIND_TREE_NODE	This finds the next node that has a data value matching a particular string.
POPULATE_TREE	This loads the values into the tree from the query or record group assigned to the tree.

ADD_TREE_DATA	This adds a data set of records under a particular node.
ADD_TREE_NODE	This adds a single data element under a particular node.
POPULATE_GROUP_FROM_TREE	This loads the data from a tree into a pre-existing record group.
DELETE_TREE_NODE	This removes a data element from the tree.

Triggers

There are a number of triggers that fire when hierarchical tree events occur as follows:

WHEN-TREE-NODE-ACTIVATED	This fires when the user double-clicks the node or presses the ENTER key when the node is selected.
WHEN-TREE-NODE-EXPANDED	This fires when the user clicks on the + or – expansion icon to expand or collapse the node.
WHEN-TREE-NODE-SELECTED	This fires when the user clicks on a node label to select it.
:SYSTEM.TRIGGER_NODE	This is not a trigger, but is an included system variable that you can use to determine which node fired the trigger. Look in the help topic for one of the triggers listed above to see a description of this variable.

CAUTION

As with all new features, stay in touch with Oracle Support online for current patches. You will be able to track when problems are fixed, such as a problem in an early release of Developer 6 under UNIX, which did not properly load the :SYSTEM.TRIGGER_NODE variable.

NOTE
The hierarchical tree control has a specific set of actions and may not work exactly the same as other tree controls that you are accustomed to. For example, the WHEN-MOUSE-DOUBLE-CLICK trigger, which you would expect to fire when the user double-clicks a node, does not fire on this control.

Dynamic Poplists

Often a poplist is used to populate a code or ID item that would not make sense to the user. The poplist displays the readable description of the value that will go into the column. For example, the department number is required in the employee record, but the user may not know the number. The user should know the name, so it is better to allow them to select from a list of department names and assign the value associated with the name.

The basic definition of a poplist item includes static values in the *Elements in List* property. However, you will usually want to load your poplist with values from the database. This strategy allows you to change values using a simple table update without affecting the form definitions. It also allows you to change values based on the security access or business function of a particular user. You can also base the values list on the values entered in other items in the same record. In addition, loading the poplist dynamically from a table is easier than inserting values in the poplist *Elements in List* property. Shown here is a poplist that was dynamically loaded from a query.

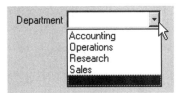

Dynamic poplist loading is most appropriate for code tables and lookup tables with a few (less than 100) rows. It is not always a substitute for LOVs because only one value is displayed, but is an interface style that GUI users are accustomed to.

CAUTION
There are some limitations with poplists that you should keep in mind when deciding whether to use them. Chapter 16 discusses these limitations in detail.

Dynamic Poplist Recipe

The following recipe uses the department table as a sample source for the query.

Preparation

You need to create a packaged library procedure called F_ITEM.SETUP_LIST that loads the poplist from a record group. This procedure (part of the sample library described in Appendix A) loads the record group with data using the POPULATE_GROUP built-in. It then loads the list item from the record group with the POPULATE_LIST built-in. Placing these calls in a procedure hides the minimal complexity of this operation. It also allows you to perform extensive error checking (such as whether the item is a list item and whether the record group populated correctly) that would be tedious to code each time you wanted to set up a dynamic poplist item.

Ingredients

The following are the two ingredients needed for the poplist recipe:

A Poplist Item	This should be subclassed from an object library object so it contains the correct visual properties.
A Table to Load into the Poplist	It is best to work out the query you will use to retrieve records for the poplist beforehand in SQL*Plus or another query tool. This will let you concentrate on the data itself and ensure that you are getting what you want.

Steps

After ensuring that you have the proper ingredients, you can use the following two steps to create the poplist:

1. **Create a record group** in the Object Navigator with the query that you have determined will retrieve the values and their descriptions. For example, a record group called DEPT would be based on the following query:

```
SELECT   dname, to_char(dept_no)
FROM     dept
ORDER BY deptno
```

There must be two and only two columns retrieved. The first will be the label shown in the list; the second will be the value stored in (or retrieved from) the block's table. The other important guideline is that both columns in the query must be character columns. Therefore, if you are retrieving a number or date column, you need to convert it to a character using the TO_CHAR function (as shown earlier).

If the value column is a date or number column, you can set the *Data Type* property of the poplist item to the appropriate type even though the poplist query is retrieving a character datatype. This is a little more efficient than leaving the poplist as a character type because Forms only performs an implicit conversion (from character to number, for example) when you load the poplist with values. There is potentially more overhead when Forms performs the implicit conversion when data is retrieved or updated from the form to the database (if you leave the poplist as a character type, but the column is something else).

The description column can be any length, but the value must be shorter or the same length as the *Maximum Length* property value on the poplist.

NOTE
Instead of creating the record group in the Object Navigator, you could create the record group programmatically as part of the SETUP_LIST procedure. You would change the SETUP_LIST procedure to call the CREATE_GROUP_ FROM_QUERY built-in before calling the others. This means that you could pass the SQL statement and item name to the SETUP_LIST procedure.

2. **Call the SETUP_LIST procedure** from the code in your WHEN-NEW-FORM-INSTANCE trigger. Using the template described in Chapters 10 and 11, put this code in the STARTUP.WHEN_NEW_ FORM_INSTANCE procedure that is called by the WHEN-NEW-FORM-INSTANCE trigger. The call passes the name of the record group and poplist item to the procedure as in the following example:

    ```
    f_item.setup_list('DEPT', 'EMP.DEPTNO');
    ```

These are the only two steps required after you have done the preparation and assembled the ingredients. When you test the form you might receive a compile message such as "FRM-30351: No list elements defined for list item. List POPLIST." If you make any changes to the *Elements in List* property, this message will not appear. The values there will be replaced by the dynamic loading mechanism anyway. You can also change this value and save the item as a SmartClass that you apply to poplist items. In any case, this is just a warning message and the item will work fine regardless of the message.

CAUTION
If you are querying a block that contains a dynamically loaded poplist, the form will not display a record if the value is not in the poplist value set and you have not defined a value for the Mapping of Other Values *property. This can lead to confusion on the user's side, so be careful that the values in the table you are querying are always represented by the values you load into the poplist. Of course, this effect can also be used to your advantage. It provides a way to filter out records, but this is not a standard method and may confuse developers who will be maintaining the form. Beware of this effect with other types of items that require a* Mapping of Other Values *property value such as check boxes, radio groups, and other list items.*

System-Assigned ID Value

One of your database design standards might be that every table uses a system-generated ID number column as a primary key. This allows you the best link from a foreign key table and standardizes an important element of the table design. In this situation, the easiest way to create a unique number to fill this ID column is with an Oracle sequence generator. This technique discusses a generic method for automatically assigning a value to this column when the user inserts a row into a form.

Naming conventions for database objects can assist in making the code you write more generic. Consider, for example, a table called STUDENT (alias STU) that contains a primary key ID column. Your naming convention says that the table alias is the prefix for the ID column, so the primary key column would be called STU_ID. Your naming convention also states that the sequence generator from which you query for ID numbers when inserting new rows is called STU_ID_S. These names are important for making this solution generic.

Forms and Sequences

You can assign the next value of a sequence generator to an item by placing its name (with a ":SEQUENCE." prefix) in the *Initial Value* property. For example, if you wanted to assign the STU_ID item with the next value from the STU_ID_S sequence, you would fill in the *Initial Value* as ":SEQUENCE.STU_ID_S.NEXTVAL." Anytime the user adds a record, the form will query the sequence and load the value into the item.

The problem is that this query happens each time the cursor navigates to a new record whether or not it will be completed and committed. A better solution is to query the sequence only when a row is actually inserted.

Using a Database Trigger

Another option is to assign the next sequence value in a BEFORE INSERT row-level database trigger. The problem with this is that the form will not know about the new value until the trigger fires. If the form does not have an item for this column, there is no problem with this method and it is probably the cleanest one to use. If the item is in the form and the block property *DML Returning Value* is set to "Yes", the new value will update the form item automatically. However, this update will come after any detail blocks that require the value have been committed.

For example, if you insert a new student record and new enrollment record (a detail of the student table) in the same transaction, the enrollment record needs to know the ID of the student record so that its foreign key column can be populated. A database trigger fires too late for this action. Therefore, the database trigger is not a viable solution if the form contains detail blocks.

If it is possible that a record can be inserted from a source other than your form, it is useful to also have a database trigger to populate the ID column. The trigger code could check if there is an ID passed into the INSERT statement. For example, if the form generated the number and used it in the INSERT statement, the trigger would not need to get the next sequence number if there was a value for the ID.

Using a PRE-INSERT Trigger

The PRE-INSERT form trigger fires before the INSERT statement is sent to the database. Therefore, if you fill the ID item with a value in this trigger, all the block coordination mechanisms will ensure that the value is populated in the detail blocks. You could write a function in the form that declares, opens, fetches, and closes a cursor to query the sequence for the next number. However, this method requires the form to send a number of lines of PL/SQL code to the database.

You can also write the same function on the database side and use a one-line statement in the PRE-INSERT trigger, such as the following:

```
:student.stu_id := spmts_student.next_id_number;
```

This is the best method because there is only a one-line call to the database and the code is executing on the tier where the sequence is located. There is a further refinement that will make this an even better solution. You can use dynamic SQL to query a particular sequence based on the table alias. This means that one function can service many sequences and fill the ID columns for many tables.

The assumption here is adherence to the naming convention for naming sequences. The code you use in the PRE-INSERT trigger looks the same, but you pass the table alias to the function and the function creates the cursor on a sequence that contains the table alias. The call would look like the following:

```
:student.stu_id := sys_util.get_nextval('STU');
```

The package body follows (with the comments from the package specification). For brevity, the error checking has been simplified.

```
CREATE OR REPLACE
PACKAGE BODY sys_util
IS
--
/********************************************************************\
|| Program:     SYS_UTIL
|| System:      SPMTS
||
|| Description:
||   Utility procedures and functions
||
|| Modification History:
||    ------------------------------------------------------
||      Date         By            Remarks/Reason
||    ------------------------------------------------------
||      09/20/1999   hfujimoto     created
\********************************************************************/
   g_lang_behavior          CONSTANT INTEGER := DBMS_SQL.V7;
   --
   FUNCTION get_nextval (
      p_tab_alias VARCHAR2)
      RETURN NUMBER
   IS
      v_return_nbr    NUMBER;
      v_sql_string    VARCHAR2(2000) := 'SELECT ' || UPPER(p_tab_alias)
                                     || '_ID_S.NEXTVAL FROM DUAL';
      v_cursor        INTEGER;
      v_feedback      INTEGER;
   BEGIN
      v_cursor := dbms_sql.open_cursor;
      dbms_sql.parse(v_cursor, v_sql_string, g_lang_behavior);
      dbms_sql.define_column(v_cursor, 1, v_return_nbr);
      v_feedback := dbms_sql.execute(v_cursor);
      v_feedback := dbms_sql.fetch_rows(v_cursor);
      dbms_sql.column_value(v_cursor, 1, v_return_nbr);
      dbms_sql.close_cursor(v_cursor);
      RETURN(v_return_nbr);
   EXCEPTION
      WHEN OTHERS
      THEN
```

```
            raise_application_error(-20010,
                'Error in sys_util.get_nextval. '||SQLERRM);
            RETURN(NULL);
        END get_nextval;
    --
    END;
```

Loading Image Items

Your standards require boilerplate graphics to display the company logo and project logo on each canvas. Your forms contain many canvases so you will need to load the graphics onto each canvas. One option is to place each graphic on a stacked canvas and ensure that the stacked canvases are visible each time navigation to another content canvas takes place. Since your forms have complex navigation paths, you decide the stacked canvas idea has pitfalls and choose to place the graphics on each canvas. The problem is that the graphics are stored as objects on the canvas and the more boilerplate graphics, the larger the size of the form.

The solution is to load the logo graphics from the file system (using the READ_IMAGE_FILE built-in) whenever the form starts. The following describes a generic procedure that you can place in your library that will require no extra coding in each form.

Loading Image Items Recipe

There are two main components to this solution: the items and the procedure.

Preparation

The main preparation is in creating the procedure that loads the items. This procedure is located in the generic library (FORMLIB.PLL) and is called from the STANDARD_STARTUP routine that is called from the PRE-FORM trigger. (Chapter 12 describes this procedure further.)

The procedure body code follows:

```
PROCEDURE setup_image_items(
    p_block     IN VARCHAR2 := 'IMAGES',
    p_type      IN VARCHAR2 := 'GIF',
    p_extension IN VARCHAR2 := 'gif')
IS
    v_curr_item    VARCHAR2(30);
    v_block_item   VARCHAR2(61);
    v_block        VARCHAR2(30) := p_block;
    v_block_id     BLOCK := find_block(v_block);
    v_filename     VARCHAR2(30);
BEGIN
    IF NOT id_null(v_block_id)
```

```
THEN
   v_curr_item := get_block_property(v_block_id, FIRST_ITEM);
   --
   -- loop through all items in the block
   WHILE v_curr_item IS NOT NULL
   LOOP
      v_block_item := v_block||'.'||v_curr_item;
      --
      -- turn off the mouse navigable property if this is a button
      IF get_item_property(v_block_item, ITEM_TYPE) = 'IMAGE'
      THEN
         -- chop off all before the last _
         v_filename := lower(substr(v_curr_item, 1,
            instr(v_curr_item, '_', -1) - 1)||'.'||p_extension);
         read_image_file(v_filename, p_type, v_block_item);
      END IF;
      v_curr_item := get_item_property(v_block_item, NEXTITEM);
   END LOOP;
END IF;      -- end of IF NOT id_null for block
END;
```

This procedure loops through all image items in the IMAGES block, strips off the
number in the name of the item, and loads the file with that name into the image
item. The files should be located in the Start in (working) directory, or in a directory
in the FORMS60_PATH or ORACLE_PATH in the Windows registry. For forms
running on the Web in a UNIX environment, the paths are stored as environment
(shell) variables.

Ingredients
The objects that you will need for this technique follow:

The IMAGES Block and Image Items	The image items are called APP_LOGO_01 and CO_LOGO_01. These are included in the template so that they will be available to all forms.
The Image Files	These files are located in the file system.
The Image Item SmartClasses	The object library contains SmartClasses of the image items so you can inherit the *X Position*, *Y position*, *Width*, *Height*, and some of the image properties.

The SETUP_IMAGE_ITEMS Procedure   This procedure is located in the generic library as described earlier.

Steps

The main canvas already has image items from the template. If you add a content canvas, follow these steps:

1. Copy the image items from and into the IMAGES block using the Copy and Paste commands in the Object Navigator.

2. Change the names of the new items to end with the next number after the items you copied. For example, if the items you copied were APP_LOGO_02 and CO_LOGO_02, the new items would be APP_LOGO_03 and CO_LOGO_03.

3. Change the item property for *Canvas* to the name of the new canvas.

The procedure will take care of the rest. The time-consuming step is in the one-time setup of the template objects and the library procedure.

Access Keys for Text Items

In forms that require heavy data entry, users find it easier to use the keyboard for many operations. When you design forms in this category, you need to consider how the user can use the keyboard to navigate from one item to another and to activate buttons. It is easier to move the cursor by pressing keys when your hands are on the keyboard than by reaching for, moving, and clicking the mouse. Your forms can be used more efficiently if you take this into consideration.

Forms implements the Windows concept of *access keys* that allow the user to move the cursor to an object by pressing a key combination. For example, if you press ALT-A, the Action pull-down menu will be activated. The menu access keys (also called *hot-keys* or *shortcut keys*) are familiar to any Windows user who prefers the keyboard to the mouse.

Forms extends the concept of menu access keys to other objects and allows you to define an access key for radio group buttons, buttons, and check boxes. There is no access key concept, however, for other items such as text items, list items, and image items. There is a technique you can use to supply access key functionality for those objects so you can make your forms "ALT-key accessible."

Defining an Access Key

Access keys are easy to define for the supported objects. The property list for radio group buttons, command buttons, and check boxes includes a property called *"Access Key"* in the Functional group, as shown in Figure 25-2. You just type a single letter, number, or character as a value for this property. When the form runs, the user can press this character with the ALT key to make the cursor move to and activate the item.

You can use the characters A–Z in lower- or uppercase; the ALT- keypress will work with either. In other words, character access keys are case-insensitive. Some other characters also work; for example, you can define an access key of a single quote and one for a double quote. Although these two symbols are normally on the same key, the ALT-' and ALT-" combinations will act as two separate keypresses. Therefore, you could have two buttons activated using the same key—one using a SHIFT keypress and one without. There are some other eccentricities, so if you use something other than a letter character, test the effect with and without the SHIFT key.

If there is a menu item access key defined the same as a button access key, the menu item will take precedence. Menu access keys are the first uppercase letter in the menu label or the first letter after an ampersand. They display as an underlined character in the name of the item. For example, the menu label "Action" has an underlined "A" and is activated with ALT-A. The menu with a label of "E&dit" has an underlined "d" and is activated with ALT-D.

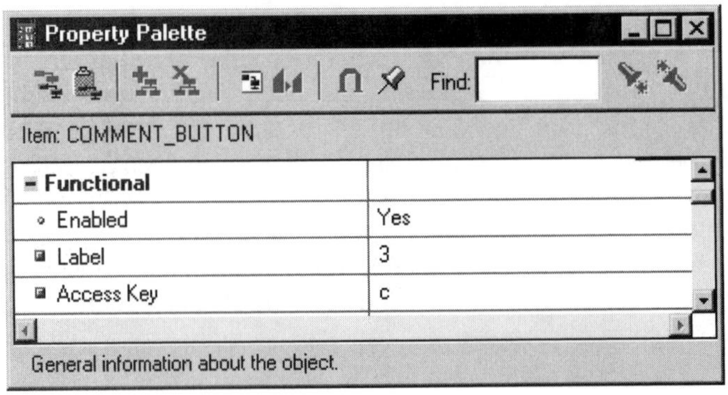

FIGURE 25-2. Access Key *property*

While running the form, the access key for an item moves the cursor and activates the item as in the following radio group.

Activating the item has a different effect depending on the object type. Basically, whatever would happen when the user clicks the object with the mouse cursor will happen when the access key is pressed: the menu item will be selected; the button will be pressed (and the WHEN-BUTTON-PRESSED trigger fired); a radio button will select its value; and a check box will toggle from checked to unchecked or unchecked to checked. Although you can define an access key for the radio group item (that contains the radio buttons), it has no effect.

If the item's label includes the access key letter, the character in the label will be underlined when the form is run (although not in the Layout Editor), as shown in the illustration above. If the character is not in the label, the access key will work anyway, but the user will not know which key to press. The underline is a standard convention that indicates the access key.

NOTE
Another rule with access keys is that the item must be displayed (the Visible *property set to "Yes") and assigned to a content or stacked canvas that is showing at the time the access key is pressed. If the object is on a toolbar canvas, the access key will work if the toolbar canvas is attached to the current window (not the MDI window).*

Recipe for the Text Item Access Key

The problem is that access keys are not available for text items and you might want to allow the user to press a key combination to navigate directly to an item. This would be useful on a canvas that contains a large number of items, only some of which are required. Instead of pressing the TAB key to move from one item to the next, the user can press an access key.

Since text items do not have an access key property, the secret to this technique is to create a button (called for this discussion an *access key button*) in the same block for each item that requires the access key. The button has *Height* and *Width* properties of zero and *Visible* property of "Yes" so that the access key will work but you will not see the button. WHEN-BUTTON-PRESSED trigger code automatically transfers the cursor to the text item with a similar name.

Preparation

As usual, a library procedure does the work. The main preparation is to write this simple procedure. The procedure assumes that the button has the same name as the item that the cursor is moving to, but with a _PB suffix. Therefore, the ENAME item would use a ENAME_PB button as its access key button. The procedure just determines the name of the button that was activated and moves the cursor to the item of the same name without the _PB suffix. The procedure (as excerpted from the F_ITEM library package) follows:

```
PROCEDURE access_key IS
     v_button    VARCHAR2(80) := :system.trigger_item;
     v_go_item   VARCHAR2(61) := substr(v_button, 1,
                                 length(v_button) - 3);
BEGIN
     IF NOT id_null(find_item(v_go_item))
     THEN
        go_item(v_go_item);
     ELSE
        message('Error: ACCESS_KEY failed to move to item called ' ||
                v_go_item||'. Notify Technical Support.');
        raise form_trigger_failure;
     END IF;
END;
```

The other preparation step is to create the block with the text items you want to access with keypresses.

Ingredients

The main ingredients are the text items you want to assign access keys to and the procedure. You also need to create a WHEN-BUTTON-PRESSED trigger on the block level with the following code:

```
f_item.access_key;
```

This code will fire when any button in the block is clicked (or activated with an access key). If there are other buttons in the block, you need to add a conditional statement to check the suffix as follows:

```
IF substr(:system.trigger_item,-3) = '_PB'
THEN
    f_item.access_key
ELSE
    -- the code to handle other buttons
END IF;
```

If the other buttons in the block use item-level WHEN-BUTTON-PRESSED triggers, you do not need the ELSE clause because the item trigger will override the block trigger.

TIP
When creating a trigger for a button, using the Object Navigator, an LOV will be displayed with the list of potential triggers for that item. If you use the self-reducing feature of LOVs, you will be able to select a specific trigger more quickly than by scrolling to find the name. For example, click the Create button to display the triggers' LOV after selecting the Triggers node under the form module. When the LOV displays, you can press the keys WNF to reduce the list to the WHEN-NEW-FORM-INSTANCE trigger. While the number of keys required to reduce the list varies with the trigger name, in time, you will learn these shortcut keys and be able to select a trigger name quickly. Also, be sure to check the SmartTriggers list (from the right-click menu) for the most commonly used triggers for a specific object type.

Steps

The following steps explain how to create an access key button for a single text item called ENAME that you want to move to using an ALT-N keypress.

1. **Create the access key button.**   This button is located on the same canvas as the item you are accessing. It has *Width* and *Height* property values of "0" and an *Access Key* property of "n." Select a letter that will be in the item's prompt. Be sure the *Visible* property is set to "Yes". The only other properties to attend to are the *X Position* and *Y Position*. You have to be sure the button is within the canvas borders. Also, since the button has no height and no width, you will not be able to see it. However, some displays might show a blank spot on the screen so you may want to place the button in the corner of an item or somewhere that the blank spot will not be a concern.

   Once you create an access key button with the proper settings, you can place it in the object library so you can subclass the main properties whenever you need to create another button. The *Access Key* and *Canvas* properties will be specific to the form, so you do not need to specify those for the object library version of the button.

2. **Create a prompt with an underlined letter.** This is a bit involved because you cannot mix normal and underscored characters in the same prompt item. Thus, you have to assign the *Prompt* property for the item using a standard font.

Then, add boilerplate text to the canvas with the letter that you will underline in the same font. Select the text and click on the Underline button in the Layout Editor toolbar. The letter will be underlined as follows:

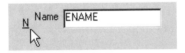

The only task left is to move the underlined character on top of the normal character. Select the text and use the arrow keys on the keyboard to position it. You may find it useful to zoom in to see the placement more easily. The result will be an underlined letter as follows:

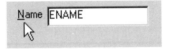

Other Ideas

You can use this access key technique to have an access key display another canvas. For example, add an access key button called EMP_CANVAS_PB to the first canvas. Then add a nonbase table item on the EMP_CANVAS with 0 height and 0 width. The access key for the button will then move the cursor to that text item on the EMP_CANVAS. If the user will interact with an item on the second canvas, you can just name the button with the name of that item and a _PB suffix.

Another way to make this system more flexible (to move to any block and any canvas) is to store the name of the item you are navigating to in the *Label* property of the access key button. For example, the ENAME_PB button would contain the *Label* property value "EMP.ENAME". You would change the code in the ACCESS_KEY procedure to:

```
go_item(get_item_property(name_in('SYSTEM.TRIGGER_ITEM', LABEL));
```

In this case, the names of the access key buttons do not have to be anything special.

Characters as Button Icons

Instead of using icon files for buttons, consider using character symbols. This eliminates the problem of distributing icon files and saves the Forms runtime from having to find them on the disk when running the form.

To use characters as icons, define the *Label* property of the button as the symbol you want to represent. Assign a symbol font as the font. For example, the following button was defined with a label value of "3" and a font of Monotype Sorts 12 point. The checkmark symbol is the 3 character in this font family. Other symbol fonts such as Symbol and WingDings contain symbols that you can use as icons. Be careful that the font you are using is installed on the machine that will run the form (in the case of web deployment, this is the Java runtime environment, which may or may not have the specified font). However, this may make your form less portable between operating systems unless you select a font that looks the same in both operating systems.

NOTE

Another important property to set for buttons is the Tooltip *property that appears in the Help section of the Property Palette. The text you place here will become the tooltip for the button. When the mouse cursor rests over a button, this hint will appear in a small box under the button. This works in both client/server and web deployment environments without any code or extra files. You can use the* Tooltip *property to define tooltips for items as well.*

CHAPTER
26

Forms Block Tips and Techniques

He was not merely a chip of the old block, but the old block itself.
—Edmund Burke (1729–1797), *On Pitt's First Speech, 1781*

 locks are the main data access point for Forms and there are a number of ways to make the use of blocks more efficient. Chapter 4 explains the aspects of what you can and should base a block on. This chapter discusses the following techniques for working with blocks:

- Naming the block your way
- Dynamic block filtering
- Dynamic block sorting

Naming the Block Your Way

The Data Block Wizard uses the table name as the default for the block name. It creates integrity-checking and block-coordination code (for master-detail relationships) using that name. It also uses this block name in the *Copy Value from Item* property on the foreign key item of a master-detail block arrangement. The form will not run or even compile correctly if you change the block name without changing all of the places that the wizard inserts the name.

Your naming standards may state that the block name should be an abbreviation of the table name—the table alias—with an eight-character limit. There are a few workarounds to the default. One is to allow the wizard to name the block and change the name of the block reference in all of the code (using the **Program→Find and Replace PL/SQL** tool). You also need to change the item property *Copy Value from Item* and the relation property *Join Condition*. This is difficult and you may miss a reference, which will cause the form to fail. You could also create a view that is a SELECT * from the table. Name the view the same as the table alias and base the block on the view. The problem is that once you have created the block, you will need to change the block property *Query Data Source Name* to the name of the table and not the view. A better solution is to create the block before actually using the Data Block Wizard as shown in the following steps:

1. Click on Data Blocks in the Object Navigator and click the Create button. In the dialog, select "Build a new data block manually." This will create a block outside of the wizard using the name BLOCK*n* where *n* is a number.

2. Change the block property *Name* to the table alias (or click on the block name once in the Navigator to replace the name). Also, fill in the name of the block property *Query Data Source Name* as the name of the table.

Now the block is named correctly and has the proper link to the table. You are ready to use the Data Block Wizard from the **Tools→Data Block Wizard** menu item. When you run the wizard, you can select the Table tab and click on the Refresh button to requery the columns. If you do this before creating each block, the resulting blocks can use any name you need and comply with the standard of using the table alias as the block name.

TIP

Be certain of the name you need to give the block before starting the process. If you decide to change the block name after running the Data Block Wizard, you will need to change the existing code and the properties referenced earlier.

Dynamic Block Filtering

The standard Enter Query and Execute Query actions in Forms allow the user to enter query criteria that will modify the result set of a query. While you do not have easy access to the SELECT statement that Forms constructs to query the database, you can programmatically control the WHERE clause that it constructs for that SELECT statement. This gives you control over the rows that the query returns. There are two basic ways to do this:

- Entering query conditions into items in a PRE-QUERY trigger
- Constructing a WHERE clause block property

Query Conditions in a PRE-QUERY Trigger

You query the block using the EXECUTE_QUERY built-in. One of the last steps this built-in takes is to construct a SELECT statement based on the columns represented by items in the block. Forms also uses the query criteria that the user entered into items when the form was in Enter Query mode to build the WHERE clause of this SELECT statement. You can add to or change the values that the user entered in Enter Query mode by assigning values in a PRE-QUERY trigger at the block level.

For example, if you wanted to add a predicate to the WHERE clause for "EMPNO = 10", you would place the following in the PRE-QUERY trigger:

```
:emp.empno := 10;
```

As part of a PRE-QUERY trigger, this code does not assign a value to the item as it usually does, but it creates a part of the WHERE clause, for example:

```
WHERE empno = 10
```

The effect is the same as if the user had typed the values into the items when the form was in Enter Query mode. If the user had typed a different value into the item, the PRE-QUERY trigger code would overwrite it. You can enter more complex values this way too if you prefix them with the # character. For example, if you wanted to return all rows for employee numbers between 7300 and 7500, you would place the following code in the PRE-QUERY trigger:

```
:emp.empno := '#BETWEEN 7300 AND 7500';
```

Normally, Forms creates a WHERE clause by placing an equals sign (=) before the value assigned to the item as in the :EMP.EMPNO := 10; example mentioned before. The pound sign (#) signals Forms that it should not use the equals sign but copy the string after the "#" to the WHERE clause as is.

One restriction to this technique is that the item must have a character datatype. You can change the *Data Type* property to "Char" even if the column is not character data and Forms will convert the value before constructing the SELECT statement. The other restriction is that the item *Query Length* property must be set high enough to accommodate the number of characters you assign to the item in the PRE-QUERY trigger.

WHERE Clause Block Property

Another method that is more flexible is to load the block property *WHERE Clause* with the entire WHERE clause. Forms will use this property when constructing the SELECT statement. It will add this to any criteria entered by the user or generated by the PRE-QUERY trigger. An example follows:

```
v_where := 'EMPNO IN (101, 102, 103)';
SET_BLOCK_PROPERTY('EMP', DEFAULT_WHERE, v_where);
```

Another example follows:

```
set_block_property('EMP', DEFAULT_WHERE, 'JOB=''CLERK''');
```

Although you can include the word "WHERE" to start the clause, it is not required.

Using the *WHERE Clause* block property is a more flexible technique because you can place the call in any trigger (not just in the PRE-QUERY trigger). It also does not require special datatypes or sizes for items as does the PRE-QUERY technique. Therefore, it is better to use this property instead of loading values into items in the PRE-QUERY trigger.

Last Query Conditions

If you need to change the last query performed on the block, you can obtain the full SELECT statement with the :SYSTEM.LAST_QUERY system variable. You can parse this to obtain just the WHERE clause using the following code where V_POS is an index number into the WHERE clause portion of the :SYSTEM.LAST_QUERY value. v_where stores the WHERE clause (without the word "WHERE"):

```
v_pos := instr(name_in('SYSTEM.LAST_QUERY'), ' WHERE ');
IF v_pos > 0
THEN
   v_where := substr(name_in('SYSTEM.LAST_QUERY'), v_pos + 7);
END IF;
```

Since bind variable syntax (using the symbol ":") cannot be used in an attached library, this example uses the NAME_IN function to return the value of the system variable.

NOTE
The WHERE Clause *property persists until you change it or exit the form. If you need to eliminate the* WHERE Clause *property without replacing it, you can set the property to "NULL."*

What About a Block Based on a Procedure?

If you are basing the block on a procedure (as discussed in Chapter 4), you can pass query conditions to the procedure as parameters, as mentioned before. The parameter values are loaded from items on the screen and passed to the procedure using the parameters you set up in the Data Block Wizard. The procedure would need to work these into the WHERE clause of the cursor. For example, if the EMP table procedure used parameters for EMPNO (P_EMPNO) and ENAME (P_ENAME), the WHERE clause of the procedure's cursor would look like this:

```
WHERE    empno = nvl(empno, p_empno)
AND      ename LIKE nvl(ename, p_ename) || '%'
```

The calls to NVL are required because Forms may pass a NULL value in a parameter if no query criteria are specified for the corresponding item.

Dynamic Block Sorting

You can sort the block using a method similar to the one described earlier for filtering a block. Set the block property *ORDER BY Clause* to the list of columns you want to use for sorting (the "ORDER BY" keywords are optional). For example, to sort by LAST_NAME and by FIRST_NAME, set the *ORDER BY Clause* property to "LAST_NAME,FIRST_NAME" (without the quotes). If you want to let the user specify this while the form is running, use a call to SET_BLOCK_PROPERTY such as the following:

```
set_block_property('EMP', ORDER_BY, 'DEPTNO,ENAME');
```

Implementing Dynamic Sorting

There are a few ways you can design this runtime sorting into a form. One way is to offer menu items for each type of sort. This is a bit inflexible because each time you want to add a column to sort on, you have to add a menu item. The procedure you call from this menu item could be written generically to use the name of the menu item. You can then add a menu item without a large amount of work. Another limitation of this method is that the menu items would be potentially different for each block so you would need to modify the menu programmatically whenever the cursor moves to a new block.

List Item Order By

Another method for dynamic sorting is to create a non-base table poplist item containing the sort columns. The List Item Value field in the *Elements in List* property dialog contains the names of the columns; the List Elements fields are set to whatever makes sense to the user. For example, you might use a poplist item called CONTROL.SORT_BY that contains a list of columns represented by items in EMP block. The following shows the List Elements dialog that you will see when editing the *Elements in List* property for a list item.

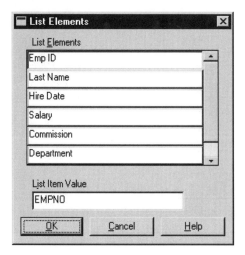

You would write a WHEN-LIST-CHANGED trigger on that item with the following code:

```
set_block_property('EMP', ORDER_BY, :control.sort_by);
go_block('EMP');
execute_query;
```

This programmatically sets the *ORDER BY Clause* property to the name of the column and executes the query whenever the user selects a list value. The list item would appear on the same canvas as the other items in the block as Figure 26-1 shows.

You can extend this concept to offer more than one sorting list so that the user can sort by multiple columns (for example, DEPTNO and ENAME). Each list would have the same columns and same WHEN-LIST-CHANGED trigger, but the trigger code would have to look at all list items to construct the clause for the *ORDER BY Clause* property. You could also offer an ascending-descending list item (or check box) that would work into the code in the same way. If you use more than one value and setting for the sort order, it is best to allow the user to specify when all list items

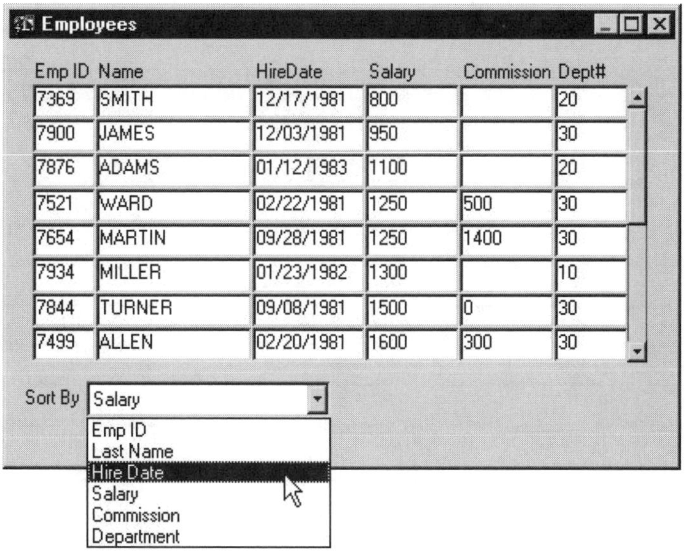

FIGURE 26-1. *List item used for sorting*

are set correctly instead of querying the block each time the user changes a list item. You can add a Sort button and move the WHEN-LIST-CHANGED trigger code to the button's WHEN-BUTTON-PRESSED trigger in this case.

Column Order by Buttons

Another method you can use to allow the user to dynamically sort a multirecord block is a bit more involved from the setup standpoint but is easy to install in a new form once the preparation steps are completed. It presents an interface that is familiar to most users. This method allows the user to select the sort columns by clicking buttons at the top of each column. Figure 26-2 shows a multirecord block with buttons at the top of each column. When the user clicks on a button, the form will requery and sort by the column clicked. The sort is one-dimensional—only one column is used in the sort. If the user clicks on another column button, the block will sort by that column alone. If the user clicks that same column button again, the sort order will switch to descending. Subsequent clicks of the button will toggle between ascending and descending sorts.

This method uses the components listed next.

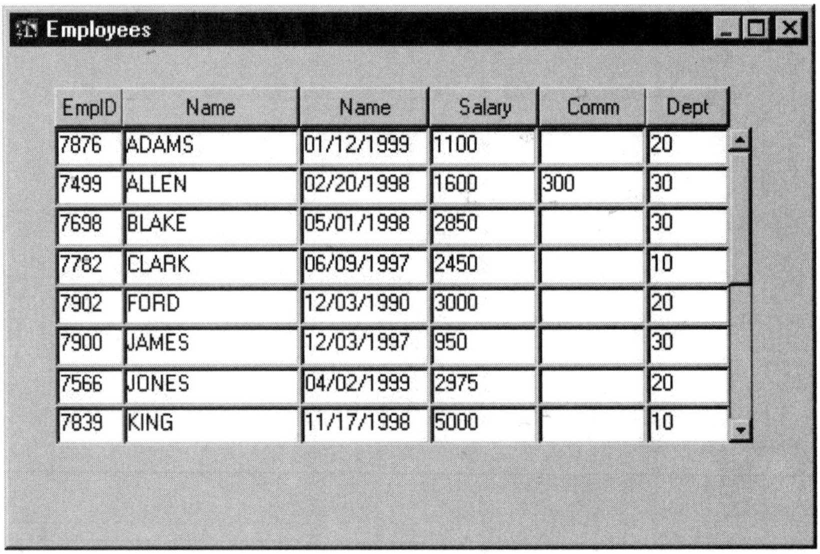

EmpID	Name	Name	Salary	Comm	Dept
7876	ADAMS	01/12/1999	1100		20
7499	ALLEN	02/20/1998	1600	300	30
7698	BLAKE	05/01/1998	2850		30
7782	CLARK	06/09/1997	2450		10
7902	FORD	12/03/1990	3000		20
7900	JAMES	12/03/1997	950		30
7566	JONES	04/02/1999	2975		20
7839	KING	11/17/1998	5000		10

FIGURE 26-2. *Column order by buttons*

Button Block

A separate block contains the buttons. To enable the generic code, the block name is the same as the data block it is sorting with a _HDR suffix to indicate that it is a header. For example, sorting in the EMP block is managed by the EMP_HDR block. The button properties *Keyboard Navigable* and *Mouse Navigate* are set to "No." Since the cursor will not navigate to the block, the hint will never show. The generic code relies on this and uses the *Display Hint Automatically* property as a flag value to indicate whether the sort is ascending or descending. This is not the normal purpose for this property, but it suffices for this purpose because the hint will never show. The block with one button is saved to the object library so that it is easier to include in new forms.

Once this setup is completed, you can create a new button block from the object library by dragging and copying. You then rename the button block, and copy the single button for each column of data. You also subclass all new buttons from a SmartClass button object in the object library. This ensures that the correct property values (as mentioned before) appear on each button. The last step is customizing the button labels, which act as the prompts for the columns. These are the only steps involved to create the button sort objects in a new form.

NOTE

Hint text normally appears if the cursor navigates to the item and Display Hint Automatically *is set to "Yes." If* Display Hint Automatically *is set to "No," the user needs to press the Help key (F1) after moving the cursor to the item.*

Trigger and Generic Procedure

The button block (as stored in the object library) has a WHEN-BUTTON-PRESSED trigger that fires for each button press in the block. This trigger calls a procedure in a PL/SQL library that performs the following steps:

1. Determine the name of the button pressed using the following:

```
v_button_block_item := name_in('SYSTEM.TRIGGER_ITEM');
```

   This call uses the NAME_IN function because it is located in a PL/SQL library where you may not use bind variable formats such as :SYSTEM.TRIGGER_ITEM.

2. Derive the name of the data block by stripping off the _HDR extension of the button block name. The name of the button item is the same as the name of the data block item that will be used for the sort.

3. Determine the last sort direction (ascending or descending) for the item by examining the *Display Hint Automatically* property of the button. If the

property value is "TRUE" ("Yes" in the Property Palette), the last sort direction was ascending. If the property value is "FALSE," the last sort direction for that item was descending. The following built-in call returns the value of this property for the button name in the V_BUTTON_NAME variable:

```
get_item_property(v_button_name, AUTO_HINT);
```

4. Parse the WHERE clause from the last query (if there was a last query) and strip off the ORDER BY clause, if there is one. The code (shown in the "Dynamic Block Filtering" section before) assigns the WHERE clause from the last query to a variable V_WHERE. There is additional code, as follows, to remove the ORDER BY clause.

```
v_pos := instr(name_in('SYSTEM.LAST_QUERY'), ' ORDER BY ');
IF v_pos > 0
THEN
    v_order_by := substr(name_in('SYSTEM.LAST_QUERY'), v_pos + 10);
END IF;
```

5. Set the block's *WHERE Clause* property to the new value. The V_DATA_BLOCK variable is the name of the data block:

```
set_block_property(v_data_block, DEFAULT_WHERE, v_where);
```

6. Set the block's *ORDER BY Clause* property to the name of the column (the button name) and the opposite value from the one determined in step 3. Therefore, if step 3 determined that the last direction was ascending, the new order will be "DESC."

7. Query the data block. The new WHERE and ORDER BY clauses will take effect.

```
go_block(v_data_block);
execute_query;
```

8. Set the button *Display Hint Automatically* property to the value corresponding to the direction (ascending or descending) used for the last query. The variable V_SORT_ORDER stores the direction that was passed to the ORDER BY clause.

```
IF v_sort_order = 'DESC'
THEN
    set_item_property(p_button_name, AUTO_HINT, PROPERTY_FALSE);
ELSE
    set_item_property(p_button_name, AUTO_HINT, PROPERTY_TRUE);
END IF;
```

This code is completely generic and will work for all blocks that are set up in this way.

What About a Block Based on a Procedure?

The method for implementing sort buttons is a bit different if the block is based on a REF CURSOR procedure or on a PL/SQL table procedure that uses a SELECT statement (as discussed in Chapter 4). You have to add a parameter to the call to the SELECT procedure for the direction (ascending or descending) and for the order column. The ORDER BY clause of the procedure's cursor will use these in a decode function. For example, your procedure queries the EMP table and you need to pass the query direction as "ASC" or "DESC" (in a variable such as P_ASC_DESC) and the sort column name (in a variable such as P_ORDER_BY). The ORDER BY clause of the procedure's query would look like the following:

```
ORDER BY
    decode(p_asc_desc, 'ASC',
        decode(p_order_by,
            'ENAME', ename,
            'EMPNO', TO_CHAR(empno, '099999999999999'),
            'HIREDATE', TO_CHAR(hiredate, 'j'),
            job
        )
    ) ASC,
    decode(p_asc_desc, 'DESC',
        decode(p_order_by,
            'ENAME', ename,
            'EMPNO', TO_CHAR(empno, '099999999999999'),
            'HIREDATE', TO_CHAR(hiredate, 'j'),
            job
        )
    ) DESC
```

Why Does this Work?

This technique exploits the power of setting property values programmatically. There are other ways to accomplish the same task. You could use global package variables, Form Builder global variables, parameters created in the Object Navigator, or text items to store the ascending and descending state of each button, but you would have to create a new variable each time you create a sort button. Using a property on the existing item ensures that the storage container for this value is always available. This is a principle that can be used to accomplish other tasks, but you have to be careful of using a property that will not adversely affect the behavior of an object.

TIP
The Display Hint Automatically *property only stores a Boolean (true or false) value. If you need to programmatically store text about a button, you could use the* Prompt *property and locate the prompt under other items or use a font foreground color that is the same as the canvas color.*

CHAPTER
27

Forms Module Tips and
Techniques

It is interesting to contemplate an entangled bank
...and to reflect that these elaborately constructed forms,
so different from each other, and dependent on each other in so complex a manner,
have all been produced by laws acting around us.

—Charles Darwin (1809–1882), *The Origin of Species*

here are a number of techniques that you can use on the form-module level. Many of these techniques will become reusable objects in the Object Library or PL/SQL library. This chapter contains the following techniques:

- Handling errors and messages

- An alert system

- Looping through objects

- Tuning your forms

- Finding code and objects

- Changing the cursor shape

- Calling other forms

- Calling other programs

- Other tips and techniques

Handling Forms Errors and Messages

Oracle Forms returns error messages in the hint line using the form *error_type-error_code*: *error_text*, for example, "FRM-40301: Query caused no records to be retrieved. Re-enter." This may not be the message format that you want to provide to your users. The error type (FRM) and code (40301) might be confusing and look to the users like a more severe error than it really indicates. In addition, if there is a database error, the users need to select **Help→Display Error** to see the error text. For example, if a user tried to update a record for a table on which the UPDATE privilege was not granted, the following message would appear in the hint line:

```
FRM-40509: ORACLE error: unable to UPDATE record.
Record: 1/?
```

You probably would write code to check the user's privileges and set the *Update Allowed* property of the block to "No" if there was no update privilege for that user. However, a situation may arise that would cause this message to appear anyway, and when it occurs, users have to know that the next step is selecting **Help→Display Error**. This will display the following dialog:

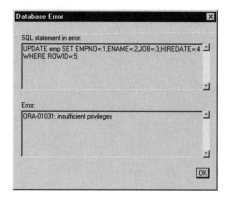

This dialog would probably confuse users. A friendlier message would be the following:

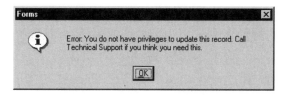

This technique requires triggers in your form that call procedures in the PL/SQL library attached to your form.

The Triggers

There are two categories of codes that Forms issues: *errors* and *messages*. Both use the same error type ("FRM") and numbering system, and the only way to tell the difference between the two categories is by looking up the code number in the help system. You need to create separate triggers to capture the normal Forms messages and errors, and issue your own text to the user.

The *ON-ERROR* trigger replaces the mechanism Forms uses to issue error text. The *ON-MESSAGE* trigger replaces the mechanism Forms uses to issue message text. Both triggers fire in response to Forms events. They do not fire if you use the MESSAGE built-in in your PL/SQL code to display text in the message line. It is easiest to be as generic as possible with the messages and create the triggers at the form level. That way you will not need to place them under each block you create. If a particular block needs special handling, you can use conditional logic in the form-level trigger to provide that special handling. Therefore, you can safely place the ON-ERROR and ON-MESSAGE triggers in the set of triggers that you subclass to the form level from the object library.

The code in these triggers is a one-line call to a local packaged procedure, for example:

```
util.on_error;
```

The Procedures

The UTIL package in the form contains the ON_ERROR (and ON_MESSAGE) procedures as follows:

```
PROCEDURE on_error
IS
BEGIN
    f_util.on_error;
END;
--
PROCEDURE on_message
IS
BEGIN
    f_util.on_message;
END;
```

Since both procedures call PL/SQL library procedures, this may seem like an extra step. However, this strategy allows you to issue text that is specific to a form or block instead of or before calling the library procedure. If you have no special needs for a particular form or block, you can leave the call to the library procedure intact. For example, although the text notifying the user of a problem with update privileges can be worded generically, you may want to issue specific text for a particular block. You can determine the error information using Forms built-ins, as Table 27-1 shows.

The built-ins that use a prefix of "ERROR" and "DBMS_ERROR" are set for the errors, and you read them in the ON-ERROR trigger. The built-ins with a prefix of "MESSAGE" are set for messages and read in the ON-MESSAGE trigger. Using these built-ins, you would change the UTIL procedure in the form to the following:

```
PROCEDURE on_error
IS
    v_text       VARCHAR2(200) := ERROR_TEXT;
    v_code       NUMBER := ERROR_CODE;
    v_dbms_code  NUMBER := DBMS_ERROR_CODE;
BEGIN
    IF v_code = 40509 AND :system.cursor_block = 'EMP'
    THEN
```

Built-in Function	Meaning
ERROR_TYPE	The category of error code (FRM for Forms codes).
ERROR_CODE	The error code number itself (documented in the help system).
ERROR_TEXT	The descriptive text that Forms issues for this error code.
MESSAGE_TYPE	The category of message code (FRM for Forms codes).
MESSAGE_CODE	The message code number itself (documented in the help system).
MESSAGE_TEXT	The descriptive text that Forms issues for this message code.
DBMS_ERROR_CODE	The Oracle error number (usually negative) that displays in the Display Error dialog and states the actual database error.
DBMS_ERROR_TEXT	The error text that Oracle associates with the DBMS_ERROR_CODE. If there are a series of errors, this text shows the entire stack of errors.

TABLE 27-1. *Message and Error Built-ins*

```
    IF v_dbms_code = -1031
    THEN
        f_alert.ok('Error: You do not have privileges to update the SPMTS' ||
            'Employee table. Call Technical Support if you need to do this.',
            f_alert.g_fail);
    ELSE
        f_alert.ok('Error: There is a problem with accessing the SPMTS ' ||
            'Employee table. Call Technical Support and report Oracle ' ||
            'error number ' || to_char(v_dbms_code) || '.', f_alert.g_fail);
    END IF;
  ELSE
    f_util.on_error;
  END IF;
END;
```

The F_ALERT.OK call displays a one-button alert with the message that you pass to it. The F_ALERT.G_FAIL parameter is a constant value stored in a global package variable. It indicates that the procedure should raise a form trigger failure exception to stop the processing. This alert system is described later in this chapter. This

ON_ERROR procedure would present the customized messages for this block if the 40509 error were encountered. Otherwise it would call the library procedure.

You can create message procedures to handle message states in the same way that you handle error states.

The library procedure contains the following code:

```
PROCEDURE on_error
IS
    v_code      NUMBER       := ERROR_CODE;
    v_text      VARCHAR2(200) := ERROR_TEXT;
    v_dbms_code  NUMBER := DBMS_ERROR_CODE;
BEGIN
    -- The cursor call ensures that the waiting cursor is not displayed
    f_cursor.cursor_default;
    IF v_code = 40509
    THEN
        IF v_dbms_code = -1031
        THEN
            f_alert.ok('Error: You do not have privileges to update this ' ||
                'record. Call Technical Support if you think you need this.',
                f_alert.g_fail);
        ELSE
            f_alert.ok('Error: There is a problem with database access. ' ||
                'Call Technical Support and report Oracle error number ' ||
                to_char(v_dbms_code) || '.', f_alert.g_fail);
        END IF;
    ELSE
        f_alert.ok('Error: ' || v_text);
    END IF;
END;
```

The call to the F_CURSOR package changes the mouse cursor to a normal icon in case the alert that appears changes it to a waiting icon. You would add other conditional statements to this procedure to handle messages for specific errors. There are some messages and errors you may want to ignore by using the following type of code (from the ON_MESSAGE procedure):

```
IF v_code IN (40100, 40352)
THEN
    -- 40100 cursor at first record
    -- 40352 last record of query retrieved
    NULL;
ELSE
    f_cursor.cursor_default;
    f_alert.ok('Warning: ' || v_text, f_alert.g_fail);
END IF;
```

Using MESSAGE

You can use the MESSAGE built-in (instead of the F_ALERT.OK procedure mentioned) to display customized text in the hint line. The problem is that if more than one MESSAGE call appears in a trigger, the second MESSAGE will cause the first MESSAGE to issue an alert with the text inside it. The second MESSAGE text will appear in the hint line as usual. You can use the NO_ACKNOWLEDGE parameter for MESSAGE to eliminate this effect with a call such as the following:

```
message('Error: You may not query from this block. Select another ' ||
    'block for the query', NO_ACKNOWLEDGE);
```

However, this means that if there is a series of messages, only the last one will display in the hint line.

You can use the alert effect of MESSAGE to show one-button alerts without using the alert object by coding two messages as in the following example:

```
message('Error: You may not query from this block. Select another ' ||
    'block for the query');
message(' ');
```

The first message will display in a one-button alert because this message must be acknowledged before the second MESSAGE statement. The second message is just a space character (a null string will not work in this situation) so the hint line will appear to be blank when it is shown.

Standards for Error and Message Text

You need to come up with a standard message format to assist users in understanding the text. The content of the message should inform the user that there was a problem or that there is something to pay attention to. It should also give a concise but descriptive explanation of the error, and tell the user what to do next. Error text can begin with "Error:" and message text can begin with "Warning:". The rest of the text depends on the error or message state, but should consist of two sentences for the description and action. Users need to be trained to know that an error is a problem and that a warning is just an informative message.

Variations

Your message and error handling can be made even more generic and flexible if you store the codes and text in a table. The message and error procedures query that table based on the code number and present the code and text in the same kind of alert box. Centralizing the messages gives you easier control over the text because you do not need to open, recode, recompile, and retest a form every time you need to change the text.

Although storing the codes and text externally requires an extra query to the database, the impact should be minimal because the frequency of calling messages should not be high. If you are concerned about this impact, you could embed the codes and text in the PL/SQL library package specification. If the list of messages is not too long, you can load and store them in a PL/SQL table (in the package specification) at the start of the session. The PL/SQL table would either be queried from the database or loaded into the package variables by the package startup code. All forms in the same connection session can then look up messages in that PL/SQL table instead of querying the database. If the likelihood of an error is low or you have too many messages to cache, you may decide to query the database each time there is an error and suffer the (minor) hit that occurs whenever a query is performed.

These methods centralize the messages and allow you to make all changes in only one place. However, after changing the library, you would need to recompile all forms that use that library and this could be tedious.

Storing the text in the file system is another alternative to storing it in a table. The file can be available on a drive that is accessible to all users. This file would contain the code and text. Instead of querying from a table, your code could open the file, loop through it to find the code number, extract the text from the same line or the next line, and close the file. There would be no database access and no form recompilation necessary. The biggest drawback to this method is that you have to use the TEXT_IO package to access the file, and looping through a text file is not very efficient (although it should not be time-consuming).

Another variation is that you can present the text in your own alert window. This window could be written into the template and subclassed from the object library so you would not need to do any extra development work in each form. While this idea does not eliminate the need to store the error text somewhere, it does allow you to provide extra features when displaying the alert. One such feature can be a More button that would jump to additional text about the error or message in the help system or show the DBMS error code and text if appropriate.

An Alert System

Alerts in Forms implement the standard Windows and GUI concept of a message box. You use alerts when you need to inform the user of an action or to ask a simple question. The alert window is *modal* to the application; that is, the alert window must be dismissed before processing can continue. Alerts can contain a title, message, one of three icons, and from one to three buttons. You can define any one of the buttons as a *default button* that will be activated if the user presses ENTER or SPACEBAR. Figure 27-1 shows the components of an alert.

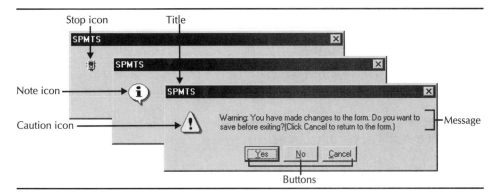

FIGURE 27-1. *Alert components*

The icons allow you to categorize your messages. For example, you can use the Stop icon for messages that present an error or invalid operation message. The Caution icon can be used to present messages that indicate potential problems or actions that require some thought from the user. The Note icon indicates a message that is intended to provide information only. These icons look slightly different when the form runs on the Web, as shown next.

When you run a form on the Web using the new "Oracle look and feel" (as described in Chapter 2), the icons are animated and appear as follows:

The standard method for working with alerts includes the following steps:

1. Create an alert object in the Object Navigator.

2. Assign the *Title, Alert Style* (the icon), *Message, Button 1 Label, Button 2 Label,* and *Button 3 Label* properties.

3. Write code to display the message using the SHOW_ALERT built-in.

4. Process the button pressed in the alert.

This set of steps is required each time you want to use an alert. The steps are not difficult, but there are a number of steps that can be made generic. Therefore, a better method is to create a full alert system containing a set of generic alerts and a generic function to dynamically load them with a message and return information about the button that the user pressed.

Generic Alerts

All the important properties of an alert can be changed programmatically except the *Alert Style* property that designates which icon will show in the alert window. Therefore, you need to create three alerts, one for each icon. Call them NOTE, CAUTION, and STOP, and assign the appropriate icon to each. The only other property to set is the *Visual Attribute Group* property that manages the visual aspect of the alert. Assign a visual attribute that contains standard canvas colors. All alerts are part of an object group that is copied into the object library and subclassed into the template form.

Alert Function

The key to the alert system is a function called MSG in the PL/SQL library F_ALERT package that loads the alert with message text, selects a particular alert based on its icon, displays the alert, and returns the value of the button label that the user clicked. An excerpt from the package specification for this function follows:

```
g_caution_icon   CONSTANT VARCHAR2(10) := 'CAUTION';
g_note_icon      CONSTANT VARCHAR2(10) := 'NOTE';
g_stop_icon      CONSTANT VARCHAR2(10) := 'STOP';
--
FUNCTION msg(
   p_button_names   IN VARCHAR2,
   p_msg            IN VARCHAR2 :=
                    'Message missing. Contact Administrator.',
   p_alert_style    IN VARCHAR2 := g_caution_icon)
   RETURN VARCHAR2;
```

The variable declarations create constants that represent the icons. The parameters to this function include the following:

■ **The button names** This is a comma-delimited string containing the text that will be assigned to the button labels. An example would be "Yes,No,Cancel".

■ **The message text**   This is a character string that will appear as the alert message. There is no fixed limit to the number of characters. The alert will display five lines of text (wrapping it at word breaks), but the alert width will adjust to the number of characters on the largest line. You can also format the text a bit by inserting space characters and line feeds (using the CHR(10) character).

■ **The alert style**   This is an optional parameter that you can use to specify the icon used for an alert. The default is the Caution icon. You can use the global constants that represent the icon names so the developer does not need to know the value that the function will use to evaluate which alert to show. This strategy provides a compile-time check on the function call because, if you spell the name of the variable incorrectly, the code you write to call the function will not compile. If you just used a character value inside quotes (such as 'NOTE') to represent the icon, the misspelling would not be noticed until runtime.

The function goes through the following steps:

1. Checks that the alert style passed into the function represents an existing alert.

2. Parses the string containing the button labels into three variables and assigns the labels to the buttons.

3. Assigns the message text from the parameter passed into the function.

4. Assigns the alert title. Typically, the alert title contains the name of the application. Therefore, one of the steps in the standard startup procedures is to assign a variable value that will be used as the alert title. The F_ALERT package uses this variable when it constructs the alert.

5. Shows the alert and captures the return value in a variable. The return value from an alert is a number represented by the three Forms constants ALERT_BUTTON1, ALERT_BUTTON2, and ALERT_BUTTON3.

6. Returns a value to the calling code with the uppercase label of the button represented by the constant. For example, if the labels of the alert buttons were Yes, No, and Cancel, clicking the Yes button would return "YES" to the calling code.

Sample Call

The following is an example of how you would call the alert function from code in a KEY-EXIT trigger. This is excerpted from the trigger code that checks the :SYSTEM.FORM_STATUS variable to see if there are any uncommitted changes.

```
DECLARE
    v_button    VARCHAR2(20);
BEGIN
    v_button := f_alert.msg('Yes,No,Cancel', 'Warning: You have ' ||
        'made changes to the form. Do you want to save before ' ||
        ' exiting? (Click Cancel to return to the form.)');
    --
    IF v_button = 'YES'
    THEN
        exit_form(DO_COMMIT);
    ELSIF v_button = 'NO'
    THEN
        exit_form(NO_VALIDATE);
    ELSE
        raise form_trigger_failure;
    END IF;
END;
```

NOTE
For a two-button alert, you can embed the call to the function in the IF clause and eliminate the need for a variable to store the return from the function. Here is a brief example:

```
IF f_alert.msg('Yes,No',
    'Warning: You are about to delete the record. Are you sure?',
    g_caution_icon) = 'YES'
THEN
    delete_record;
ELSE
    NULL;
END IF;
```

This example uses hard-coded message text, but, in most applications, you would query the text from a table or PL/SQL procedure, as mentioned earlier in the "Handling Forms Errors and Messages" section of this chapter.

Standard Button Labels

When you call the alert system, you need to pass the button label text. A small number of button label sets are commonly used in GUI programs. If you follow the standards, users will have to spend less time thinking about how to answer a dialog. The most common sets of buttons are the following:

- OK
- OK and Cancel
- Yes and No
- Yes, No, and Cancel

The other important aspect about these button sets is the order that you use to present the buttons. You will most likely frustrate your users, for example, if you order the buttons in a dialog No, Cancel, and Yes.

Standard Alert Message Text

Just as you have a standard for error and message text from Forms events, you also need a standard for text that you place in an alert. The first standard is the format, which can be similar to the format for Forms errors and messages: "*alert_type*: *alert text*" where *alert_type* is "Note" for the Note icon, "Warning" for the Caution icon, and "Error" for the Stop icon.

The alert text should be clear but short. For user-friendliness, be sure you are able to answer the question or statement you place in the alert message with the button labels. It helps to look at the alert as what it is intended for, namely, a dialog. Therefore, to check your messages, pretend that you are having a dialog with yourself. Read the message text and then read a button label and determine if the response makes sense for the message. Repeat this for each button label. The examples in this part of the chapter provide samples of this type of wording.

The OK Alert Procedure

The MSG function makes calling an alert much easier and more generic. Many times you may want to issue a message to the user but do not care about the response. In this case, you would show an alert with an OK button and go on to the next step of the code. There is another procedure called OK in the F_ALERT package that presents the alert without requiring a variable to accept the button name return value. The procedure declaration follows:

```
PROCEDURE ok(
    p_msg           IN VARCHAR2 :=
                        'Message missing. Contact Administrator.',
    p_fail          IN VARCHAR2 := g_no_fail,
    p_style         IN VARCHAR2 := g_note_icon);
```

Here is an example of how to use this procedure:

```
f_alert.ok('Note: The records have been successfully saved.');
```

An optional parameter is the failure flag that you set to F_ALERT.G_FAIL if you want the OK procedure to raise a FORM_TRIGGER_FAILURE exception. The other optional parameter is the icon (alert style) if you want to use something other than the default Note icon.

Looping Through Objects

There are times when you need to set properties on all items in a block and perform a SET_ITEM_PROPERTY action on selected items. For example, you want to disable all buttons in a block. There is a way to determine the names of all items in a block using a loop structure in PL/SQL. The best method for this purpose is a generic routine (as mentioned in Chapter 7 and Chapter 11) that looks at all items and performs some action.

Looping Through Items

The generic routine uses two built-ins to query properties that you can access programmatically. The code "GET_BLOCK_PROPERTY('BLOCK', FIRST_ITEM);" will determine which item appears first in the Object Navigator under the particular block (substitute your block name for 'BLOCK'). The code "GET_ITEM_PROPERTY('BLOCK.ITEM', NEXTITEM);" returns the name of the next item after 'BLOCK.ITEM' in the Object Navigator. The method, therefore, is to find the first item in the block, process it, then go to the next item after that one, and so on, until the next item is "NULL."

An example follows. This example passes in a block name and loops through the block's items. If the item is a button, the following code disables it. When the next item shows as "NULL," the loop stops.

```
PROCEDURE disable_all_buttons(
    p_block_name IN VARCHAR2)
IS
    v_curr_item     VARCHAR2(30);
    v_block_item    VARCHAR2(61);
BEGIN
    -- validate the block name passed in
```

```
IF id_null(find_block(p_block_name))
THEN
   f_alert.ok('Error: The block name passed in (' ||
      p_block_name || ') is not valid. Contact the ' ||
      'administrator.', f_alert.g_fail);
ELSE
   -- loop through all items in this block
   v_curr_item := get_block_property(p_block_name,
      FIRST_ITEM);
   WHILE v_curr_item IS NOT NULL
   LOOP
      v_block_item := p_block_name || '.' ||
        v_curr_item;
      --
      -- turn off the enabled property for the buttons
      IF get_item_property(v_block_item, ITEM_TYPE) =
         'BUTTON'
      THEN
         set_item_property(v_block_item,
            ENABLED, PROPERTY_FALSE);
      END IF;
      v_curr_item := get_item_property(v_block_item,
         NEXTITEM);
   END LOOP;
END IF;
END;
```

Looping Through Blocks

A similar principle applies if you need to loop through all the blocks in a form.
You can get the name of the first block in the Object Navigator list by using the
following:

```
GET_FORM_PROPERTY('FORM_NAME', FIRST_BLOCK);
```

where *FORM_NAME* is the name of your form. The next block name is accessible
using

```
GET_BLOCK_PROPERTY('BLOCK_NAME', NEXTBLOCK);
```

where *BLOCK_NAME* is the name of the block. When this returns a null value, you
are at the last block.

Looping Through Other Objects

Although you can determine the names of all items in a block and all blocks in a form, you cannot do the same for canvases, windows, or any other form object. You can, however, emulate this ability with other objects by storing their names in a delimited string value (PL/SQL table or record group). For example, if you wanted to loop through all canvases and change their color when the form was in Enter Query mode, you could do so if you had a variable that contained their names. The loop would parse a variable that contains the names of the canvases separated by commas. For each canvas name in the variable, the code would change the item's *Background Color* property. You would assign the names to this variable in the startup procedures for the form.

The only drawback to this method is that you have to maintain the list. Whenever you add, delete, or rename a canvas in this example, you have to remember to make the change to the variable value as well. This is a manageable problem, though, and gives you the same ability to write generic code to perform the identical action in a number of forms. If you name your canvases with a number suffix, you will not require this list, but the canvas names will not have meaning as to their use. This makes finding a canvas more difficult if the form contains many canvases. You will have to decide which is more important—significant names or the ease of looping through objects—when coming up with a naming convention for canvases and other Forms objects.

Tuning Your Forms

You want your forms to be as efficient as possible, and you can tune them in a number of ways. The general objectives of tuning forms are the following:

- Reduce the load and run times for the form.
- Optimize database access from the form.
- Reduce memory requirements on the client.
- Minimize network traffic.

Whether you are deploying on the Web or in a client/server environment, many of the same tuning principles apply. There is an additional factor on the Web because of the multi-tier architecture. Chapter 13 provides more tips on how to tune forms in the Web environment. The technique that follows concentrates on Forms-specific tuning tips that will help on a client/server and on the Web. First, there are some tuning concepts worthy of an initial mention that lie outside the form.

TIP
If you want to improve the performance of a frequently used database package, use the DBMS_SHARED_POOL database package's KEEP procedure to load the package into the shared pool memory area of the database. The package will run faster if it is loaded from memory than if it has to be loaded from disk. This will benefit your form.

Tuning from Outside the Form

Often, factors other than the programs are out of bounds to the developer. There is usually someone other than the developer who handles hardware, network, and database installation and maintenance. However, all these factors affect how quickly a form runs and accesses the database, so the developer needs to be sure that these areas are being handled as efficiently as possible by whoever needs to configure them. The main areas outside the form that affect its performance are the following.

Client Tuning

The client machine must have enough resources installed to execute the runtime program whether it uses the browser or the Forms client/server runtime. Although processor speed is important and you want to run on a machine with the fastest processor possible, the main other resource is memory. If a form runs out of memory, the operating system will use virtual memory. This means that there will be disk access to save and swap the contents of the memory space. Disk access takes much more time than memory access and can be avoided with a sufficient amount of memory. Pay attention to the minimum runtime requirements listed in the *Getting Started* manual and, if possible, double them. At this writing, the suggestion is 8MB of RAM for each client/server runtime session (in addition to the operating system requirements). With web deployment, the requirements are similar. In both environments, the more RAM available, the less the runtime engines will need to swap memory to disk, and the faster the application will run.

The minimum requirements for a development machine are much greater because developers often use many tools at the same time. The suggestion in the *Getting Started* manual is 16MB for each builder (for example, Form Builder) that you run. It is important to test the forms on machines that emulate the typical (or even minimum) user's setup. Testing forms using a development machine will not give you a true picture of what users will see if their installed memory and processor is different.

Network Tuning

In the multi-tier web environment, there are network connections between client and middle-tier servers and between middle-tier servers and the database server.

(This architecture is explained more fully in Chapter 13.) All these connections affect the speed at which a form runs. It is therefore important for the network connections to be as fast as possible. This involves both network hardware—interface cards, network lines, hubs, routers, and concentrators—and network software configurations—for user account access validation, domain scope, and network protocol and architecture (LAN or WAN, modem or faster connection). Most of this is clearly beyond the developer's duty, but the data in the form, and even the form itself, is communicated across the network, so the developer must be satisfied that all factors external to the form are working at peak efficiency.

If you work in a client/server environment, you can install Forms Runtime on a network server. The promise of this strategy is that there is less maintenance when the Forms version changes; only one machine needs to be upgraded. However, there are files that must be locally installed in the client's Windows directory, and there are registry settings required on the client side as well, so this benefit is reduced. In addition, running client/server forms from a network drive can cause major drains on the network. When the Forms Runtime is "downloaded" to the client machine's memory during startup, the network is transmitting many tens of megabytes of executable files and .DLLs. This process is much faster if the runtime files are located on the client machine.

With the multi-tier web deployment strategy, this effect is lessened significantly because the runtime files are located on the application server tier. The client only needs the browser and whatever Java support files are required to display the form running on the server. Tuning focus, in this case, shifts from the client and network file server to the application server and database server.

Database Tuning

Other than the application logic that you write (discussed next), Forms' native access to the database requires no special database tuning, but it is important to be sure that data access in general is making the best use of the shared pool area so disk access is minimized. The Oracle8i cost-based optimizer usually chooses the most efficient access path for a SQL statement, but it requires a recent set of statistics that must be collected as a maintenance procedure (using the ANALYZE command) on a regular basis.

There are many other factors, such as INIT.ORA parameters and rollback segment sizes, that affect how efficient the database is across all of its applications. These subjects are really in the realm of the DBA. However, as before, this affects the efficiency of the form and is a factor that the developer must consider.

NOTE
Other Oracle Press books can provide valuable hints and techniques on database and application tuning. Look for the keyword "Tuning" when searching for these references.

Application Tuning

Along with client, network, and database tuning, the design of the data structures for your applications critically affects their efficiency. If you denormalize columns (to store summary information, for example) and the denormalized column data is loaded at runtime, the system could slow down and the form will seem to be running slowly. If you are missing indexes that would speed a query by many times, the form queries will be affected. However, too many indexes can slow down a DML statement, so you have to be judicious in index use. These are only a few of the hundreds of factors that affect how efficiently your application accesses data.

Application tuning is usually performed only when there is an inefficient program component. There are many tools you can use to determine how quickly a SQL statement is running and what path it takes to find the data. If a form appears to be running slowly, you can ALTER SESSION SET SQL_TRACE TRUE, as you would in SQL*Plus, by setting the Statistics preference (in the Reference tab of **Tools→Preferences**) to log the SQL statements in the session to a trace file on the server. There is also a runtime parameter, STATISTICS, that accomplishes the same thing. The trace file will give you clues as to which statement is taking a long time and what the access plan is for the data.

The topic of designing efficient databases is the subject matter for many more chapters of a different book. The main tip here is not what kinds of application tuning to perform, it is that application tuning is key to how efficient the user perceives your forms to be.

Tuning from Inside the Form

Once you have tuned the infrastructure as just mentioned, you can examine your form and see if there is anything that would make it more efficient. Many of these factors are merely tools in the developer's toolbox that should be part of normal form design and coding. The form-oriented tuning tips can be grouped into categories of General Tips and Block Properties as follows.

General Tips

The following tips provide general guidelines that you can follow for tuning your forms.

■ **Partitioning of the code**   The guidelines on where to place the code apply as discussed in Chapter 7. It is important for performance to store database access code in the database. This strategy will save network round-trips and allow you to place a one-line call to the database in your form to represent a block of code.

■ **Modularization**   The smaller your forms are, the faster they will load. There are always logical groups of objects in a form that you could consider making into separate forms that you call or open. However, you have to weigh the benefits of smaller Forms modules (shorter load time and less client memory) against the load time required for the forms that the user will call. For example, if you split FormA into two smaller forms, FormB and FormC, when FormB calls FormC, there is a short lag in time. If this call must be made many times in the course of a session, the accumulated wait time could frustrate the user. The guideline is that if there are parts of a large form that are used only occasionally, they should be considered as candidates for separate forms.

■ **Fewer objects** Using fewer objects in a form logically leads to modularization. There are things you can do, however, within the form to reduce the number of objects. If you are using stacked canvases to hide items, try setting the display property of the items instead. You can eliminate the canvas if you can use the item property. If you are using items on the null canvas to store variable values, use package specification variables instead because items, even though they are not rendered, take more memory because they have property values. The same principle applies to form parameters—avoid parameters unless you are using them to receive values passed into the form. Also avoid global variables because they use extra memory and are difficult to manage. Use package variables instead because there is less overhead.

■ **Eliminate unnecessary boilerplate objects** Boilerplate text and graphics add to the size of the form. In particular, an embedded graphic on a canvas can add significantly to the .FMX file size. For example, a 20K graphic .TIF (Tagged Image File Format) file can increase the size of the .FMX file by 100K because the file is stored in an internal Forms format not as an optimized TIF. The larger the .FMX file is, the longer it takes to open initially. Use the technique discussed in Chapter 25 to load image items from the file system. This requires an image file load, but the size of the file can be smaller if it is stored in a compressed graphics format (such as .TIF). This will eliminate the requirement for boilerplate graphics. Graphics drawn with the Form Builder drawing tools have slightly less impact on the canvas, but still take up enough room that the image file strategy is worth considering.

■ *Interaction Mode* **property** The *Interaction Mode* property of the form module allows you to specify that the user can stop a query before it has completed. If you set this to the value "Non-Blocking", Forms will present a dialog box as follows:

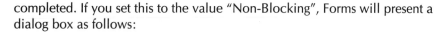

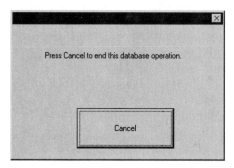

Press Cancel to end this database operation.

Cancel

If the user selects the Cancel button, the query will stop. However, there is overhead with this operation, and the query may take more time because of this. The best advice is to leave this property at its default value, "Blocking".

- **Forms Runtime Diagnostic**   As mentioned in Chapter 2, the Forms Runtime Diagnostic (FRD) is a method for capturing all events that occur in a form session and writing a file with the details of those events. There is overhead in writing this file, so you should only use this for the purposes of development and debugging.

- **Avoid database lookups**   Consider a form built on the EMPLOYEE table that has a manager ID value. When you query this record into a form, you want to show the manager's name instead of the ID. A standard technique for accomplishing this is to write a POST-QUERY trigger that opens a cursor using the ID, fetches a record, closes the cursor, and loads the value into the non–base table item. This technique is inefficient because you have to open and close a cursor for each row retrieved in the query.

A better method is to create a view that contains the manager's name and use the view as a source for the block. You need to worry about DML statements, but this is a manageable concern if you use the techniques described in Chapter 4. The time saved is significant because the database will return all required values without any need for cursors and POST-QUERY processing.

Another technique you can use for querying non–base table values for a lookup is to store the names and ID numbers in a PL/SQL variable (or Forms record group) and use this as the source for the lookups. You can load the record group or table of records when the form starts, and use this source to look up the values in the POST-QUERY trigger. This method allows you to use a table as the basis for the block, but eliminates the cursor processing for each row. If you use a record group, you can load it from a query without having to write cursor loops. You can also find records using the GET_GROUP_RECORD_NUMBER built-in. If you use a PL/SQL table of records, the loading of the values requires a bit more programming.

If the potential number of values you need to look up is small, you can load the values on an as-needed basis. For example, if you just need to look up the manager's name, instead of loading all manager IDs and names into a variable, you can query them when required in the POST-QUERY trigger. After querying an ID and name, you load it into the record group or table of records. When the next row comes in, the POST-QUERY trigger looks in the variable to see if there is a match. If not, it opens, fetches from, and closes a cursor for that row and stores the retrieved value in the variable. This technique is indicated only when the number of rows required in a certain query is small but the number of records in the entire table is large enough that you don't want to load it into a variable.

NOTE
The Performance Event Collection Services (PECS) form that was included with earlier Oracle Developer releases has been discontinued. You can gather much of the information that was available in that tool through the Forms Runtime Diagnostic referred to before.

Block Properties
The block is the main link to the database. There are a number of block properties that can assist in tuning.

- **DML Array Size**   This property can reduce the number of network trips. If you set this to a number greater than the default of "1", the form sends more than one record to the database when you commit a DML statement. This takes more memory on the client or middle-tier side, but can dramatically reduce the number of messages on the network. The best setting for this property is the number of records that require committing in one transaction. Since this will most probably be different for each transaction, you have to make an educated guess. Every row that is sent takes more memory, so there is a drawback in setting the number too high.

- **Update Changed Columns Only**   The default value of this property is "No", which means that, regardless of what column values changed, all columns participate in the update. The UPDATE statement is made up of all columns with their current values. Setting this property to "Yes" might help if there are many items in the block but you usually update only a few of them (and always the same ones). If you only have a subset or a small number of columns in your form and you are not updating the same ones each time, this will not help because the SELECT statement will be different each time. If the statement is the same as one that was issued before, that statement might be found pre-parsed in the database's shared pool area. If so, the statement's execution will be more efficient.

■ **Optimizer Hint**   This property can specify that the optimizer use a certain access plan for a set of data. You can change this programmatically if you need different optimization paths for different situations. For example, you want the optimizer to use a certain index, but you have determined by using SQL_TRACE and examining the plan that it is not using the index. You can enter a hint in this property, and Forms will use this when it accesses the table. While hints for normal statements are enclosed with comment markers ("/* */"), you don't need to use comment markers in this property.

■ **Query Array Size**   The number of records fetched at one time can affect the perceived response time. The default value is "0", which indicates that the array size is the same as the number of records displayed. Setting this property higher can reduce the network trips, but will take more memory on the client or middle-tier side. You set this property higher mainly for multirecord blocks where users will most probably scroll after seeing the initial set of rows. Setting it higher for single-record blocks will make the form appear a bit slower, but this effect may be worthwhile if the user will probably scroll to another record after the first record. Since a low number increases the network traffic, you should try to strike a balance between setting this property value too high and setting it too low. Experimentation may be the only way to tell what the exact setting should be. When in doubt, use the default of "0".

■ **Number of Records Buffered**   The default for this property is "0", which means that the number of records in the block that are held in memory is equal to the number of records displayed plus three. If the user scrolls back and forth through the block (usually more common with multirecord blocks), you want to set this higher. The more records held in memory, the faster the records will reappear in the form when the user scrolls. Records that exceed this setting are buffered to disk. Therefore, the form always stores the records and does not reissue the query to the database. However, even disk access of records swapped to disk can take a noticeable amount of time. Therefore, set this property high enough that the user will be able to scroll without a lot of disk activity, but low enough that the available memory is not taxed by being filled with record data. The size of a record also plays into this consideration because you will use more memory for larger records.

■ **Query All Records**   You usually want to leave this property at its default of "No". This means that the block will initially query only the number of rows set in the *Query Array Size* property, which is faster than returning all records. The benefit for setting this property to "Yes" is that you will be able to calculate summary values of all the rows. You also need to set this to "Yes" if you have calculated items and the *Precompute Summaries* property is set to "No". The *Precompute Summaries* property issues a SELECT statement requesting the values of the calculated items before the query is sent. One of the two properties has to be set to "Yes" if the block contains summary items. If a query could return a large number of rows, you should set this property to "No" so that the user does not have to wait for all rows to be retrieved before working with the form. If there are few rows, then "Yes" is a reasonable value for this property.

TIP
The ORA_PROF built-in package (documented in the Forms help system) allows you to create, destroy, and restart timers in your forms. These functions are all possible with the standard timer built-ins, but ORA_PROF also contains an additional function called ELAPSED_TIME that allows you to query the current time that has elapsed since the timer started. You can use this package for displaying the elapsed time between operations in your form without destroying or restarting the timer.

Finding Code and Objects in a Form

Developers often ask "How do I find all occurrences of a particular item in my form?" Another common question is "How can I be sure that I have located all code that references this item?" These questions usually stem from the need to perform an impact analysis to determine what the effect will be of renaming or deleting an object in the form. If the form is a large one, this can be a daunting task.

Finding the Code

Finding code in the form, or in a number of form files, is as simple as using the Find and Replace in the Program Units utility. You run this utility by selecting **Program→Find and Replace PL/SQL**. The window in Figure 27-2 will be displayed.

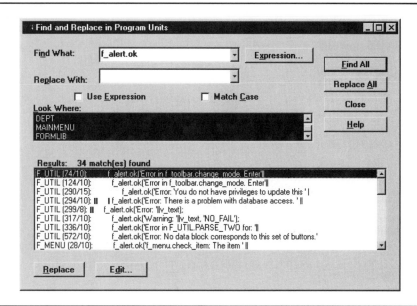

FIGURE 27-2. *Find and Replace in Program Units utility*

You can enter a search string and select files (forms, menus, libraries, and object libraries) that are open in the Form Builder session. Clicking Find All will search for this text in the selected files and present the results in the Results field. You can select one of the locations and navigate to the program unit (using the Edit button) or replace the search string with other text (using the Replace button).

Finding Objects

Finding objects is a bit more involved because there is no search utility that will find all occurrences. The Object Navigator contains a Find box at the top that will locate the names of objects, but you have to match the first letter or two of the object to find it. Also, this utility will not find references that you type into property values, such as an item reference in the LOV's Return Item field in the *Column Mapping Properties* dialog or in the item's *Copy Value from Item* property. If you delete an object that is referenced in one of these places, you will get a compile error but may not be able to easily find the object. There is hope, however, in the techniques that follow.

Generating the Forms Object List Report

A feature called the Object List Report will list all objects from a form (including code objects) in an ASCII text file that is named the same as the form with a .TXT extension. The report is easy to read and consistently formatted. It contains all properties of all objects and, because it is a text file, is completely searchable. The report also lists information about property inheritance with a single character to the left of the property. The symbols used to indicate inheritance follow:

Symbol	Meaning
-	Default property
^	Subclassed property
o	Overridden subclassed property
*	Modified property

You can run this report from Form Builder by opening the file, clicking on an object from that file in the Object Navigator, and selecting **File→Administration→ Object List Report**. This will create the report for the selected form, library, menu, or object library.

Run from the Command Line

You can also generate the Object List Report from the command line using the IFCMP60 executable. For example:

```
ifcmp60 module=helpabt.fmb userid=scott/tiger@db forms_doc=YES
```

The Compiling Forms Files technique discussed in Chapter 29 provides some hints and tips on how to use the command line.

CAUTION
If you have files with the same base name, for example, EMP.FMB and EMP.MMB, you will get the same named Object List Report file for both (EMP.TXT). Therefore, if the files are in the same directory, one Object List Report file will overwrite the other. If you are in this situation, you need to rename or move the first file after you create it.

Using the Forms Open API

You can also use the Forms Open API feature to search for objects and code in a form. The Forms Open API consists of header and library files that you can use in a

C++ program to read the .FMB file directly. This is an extremely powerful feature, and you can accomplish almost anything you want to do to a form. However, you have to understand C++ and the API itself and, unless you have a recurring need, it may not be worth the time and effort. The Forms Open API is documented in the Forms help system. Look in the index for the topic "Open API." The header files are located in the ORACLE_HOME\forms60\api directory if you have installed the Forms API from the installation disk.

Changing the Cursor Shape

The more clues you give users as to what is happening in your form, the more intuitive your form will be. One of the clues available in a GUI interface is the mouse cursor shape. You can use this to indicate to users what action they should take next. For example, during a long-running calculation, you can show a waiting-cursor icon such as the following:

This indicates to users that a process is taking place. When the calculation completes, you cause the cursor to change back to the original shape, usually an arrow like this:

The cursor shape is easy to control in Forms by using the built-in SET_ APPLICATION_PROPERTY. There are a number of different shapes you can change the cursor to. You can also determine what the cursor shape is by using the GET_APPLICATION_PROPERTY built-in. For example, the call to change to the waiting cursor is "SET_APPLICATION_PROPERTY(CURSOR_STYLE, 'BUSY');". The call to change back to the default cursor is "SET_APPLICATION_ PROPERTY(CURSOR_STYLE, 'DEFAULT');".

The number of available shapes has increased as of Developer Release 6. Chapter 2 provides a complete list of the cursors with their default shapes. Remember that users can change the cursor shapes in the Windows Control Panel Mouse applet. Therefore, the shapes may not be exactly what you intended, although they will represent the state that you want. For example, if the user changes the waiting-cursor icon to a spinning globe, when you set the cursor to the waiting-cursor icon (using the 'BUSY' parameter), the user will see the spinning globe.

NOTE
You should also be able to use your own cursor files. The Oracle Support bulletin Mouse Cursors Available in Oracle Developer Forms 6.0 *(68126.1 available on the Oracle web site TechNet or MetaLink) discusses using .CUR (cursor) files instead of the icons listed in Chapter 2.*

Cursor Control Package

To make using the cursor settings easier, you can create a PL/SQL library package with the program units described in the following excerpt from the F_CURSOR package.

```
PROCEDURE cursor_default;
--
PROCEDURE cursor_help;
--
PROCEDURE cursor_busy;
--
PROCEDURE cursor_insertion;
--
PROCEDURE cursor_crosshair;
--
FUNCTION shape
   RETURN VARCHAR2;
```

The procedures call GET_APPLICATION_PROPERTY with the proper text strings. Using procedures with no parameters is easier than having to remember the syntax and spelling of the GET_APPLICATION_PROPERTY parameters. In addition, even if you thought you remembered the spelling, the actual icon name is in quotes, so it would not be checked at compile time. You would not know until you ran the form that you had a misspelling. Using procedures solves this problem. You do have to remember the name of the procedures, but these will appear in a list under the package specification node in the attached library as follows:

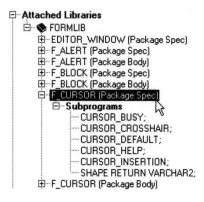

The function SHAPE in this package returns the name of the current cursor icon in case you need to restore the cursor icon and you don't know for sure which icon is showing.

TIP
If you want to know exactly which cursor icon to use at which point in your program, pay attention to other mainstream GUI interfaces that you like and determine how the developers of those products controlled the cursor icon.

The procedures also set a variable (F_CURSOR.V_CURSOR_SHAPE) to the state in which you last set the cursor. As mentioned, there is a function to return the current state of the cursor (F_CURSOR.SHAPE). This may be different from the shape you set as stored in the V_CURSOR_SHAPE variable because Forms may have changed the shape, or you may have used the SET_APPLICATION_PROPERTY variable outside this package to do it.

Calling Other Forms

There are three ways to call forms from other forms using the built-in procedures CALL_FORM, NEW_FORM, and OPEN_FORM. All three allow you to supply a parameter list ID as one of the calling parameters so you can pass values to the second form and share library data as described earlier.

CALL_FORM

Consider you have two forms—FORM_A and FORM_B. You can use CALL_FORM to start FORM_B from FORM_A but leave FORM_A open in memory. When FORM_B exits, control will pass back to FORM_A. Both forms use the same database connection, so it is not possible to commit each one separately. When you call FORM_B, you either have to commit the changes in FORM_A first, or when you want to commit FORM_B, use the POST built-in to post the changes to the database instead. Then you can commit in FORM_A, which will commit the posted changes in FORM_B as well.

One use for this built-in is in modal forms where you want to disable the calling form until the called form exits. However, if you allow FORM_B to do a CALL_FORM back to FORM_A, the user could get confused and not realize that FORM_A is already in the stack of forms loaded.

The GET_APPLICATION_PROPERTY built-in can derive the calling form's name if you use CALL_FORM. Also, CALL_FORM is unrestricted, so you can call it from POST- and PRE- triggers. OPEN_FORM and NEW_FORM are restricted.

NEW_FORM

NEW_FORM will exit FORM_A and remove it from memory before calling FORM_B. This is useful if you know you do not want to come back to a particular form because it exits the first form completely. If you did want to return to the calling form, you would have to store the name of the calling form and pass it to the next form. Then you could issue a NEW_FORM call to return to that first form if needed. Keep in mind that if you use NEW_FORM to return to the calling form, that first form is really being started again, and the state of the form (variables and items) before the original NEW_FORM call is lost.

OPEN_FORM

OPEN_FORM allows more than one form to be open and also lets you open another database session so you can commit FORM_A and FORM_B separately.

Calling Other Programs

There are times when you want to start another operating system process or run another program from within a Forms Runtime session. There are a number of ways to do this in a client/server environment, as follows.

Not on the Web

As Chapter 13 mentions, running programs on the client machine in a web environment is not easy. The form runs on the application server machine that runs the Form Server. Therefore, any HOST or WinExec calls will be passed to that machine, not to the client machine. Depending on your requirement, this may not work. You can code JavaBeans that run in Forms and access the client machine, but this requires some Java programming.

HOST

The HOST built-in allows you to run another operating system command or program synchronously. When the command is running, the form stops processing and you cannot access the form's items. The other process runs in the same Forms Runtime process, so it is a synchronous call. A sample call from a Forms trigger would look like the following:

```
host('NOTEPAD C:\FORMS\DEPT_OUT.TXT');
```

This command will start the Notepad text editor and load the file DEPT_OUT.TXT. When Notepad is running, the form will be frozen. You will not be able to click its buttons or interact with the items. When you exit Notepad, control will be passed back to the form. HOST is not operating-system specific, unlike the solutions that follow.

> **NOTE**
> *Remember that if you have to run another form, a report, or a graphic module, use the RUN_PRODUCT built-in. RUN_PRODUCT allows you to pass parameters to the called program. You can use RUN_PRODUCT synchronously or asynchronously.*

HOST START

The Windows command START runs another process asynchronously. There are command-line parameters you can use to run the command in a minimized or maximized window. There is also a command-line parameter to run the program synchronously. Some Windows operating systems such as Windows NT offer other command-line parameters. You can list the command-line parameters by entering the following in a command-line (MSDOS) window:

```
START /?
```

Using START with HOST is just a matter of including START in the string that you pass to HOST. For example, the following will start Notepad and load the AUTOEXEC.BAT file in an asynchronous way. That is, Forms will be accessible while Notepad is accessible.

```
host('START NOTEPAD C:\FORMS\DEPT_OUT.TXT');
```

WinExec

Another way to run a program asynchronously from Forms Runtime in Windows is by using the WinExec Windows function. The KERNEL32.DLL file in Windows contains a function called WinExec that runs another process. You can register this function into your Form Builder code using the technique described in Chapter 29 for the Foreign Function Interface (FFI). After registering the function, you can call it from Forms and pass it the name of the file you want to execute. The program will run asynchronously with the Forms Runtime.

If you are interested in using this function, you can use the WinExec FFI code that Oracle has written into the WIN_API_SHELL package of the D2KWUTIL.PLL. This file contains all the necessary FFI code and is located in the ORACLE_HOME/devdem60/demos/forms directory if you have installed the Forms demos. The WinExec procedure allows you to run the form in a maximized or minimized window.

Other Tips and Techniques

This section contains some tips and techniques on form modules.

User Notes System

You might want to let users comment on the application while it is in the User Acceptance Test phase. It could also serve as a problem- and bug-tracking system. The idea is that when the user clicks on a button or selects from the menu, a form pops up and allows the user to enter the text of a problem. The form that calls this notes form passes it the identifying information (username, form name, block name, and item names of the cursor location). The form can simply consist of an item where the user enters the problem text and an OK button. If the user has entered text, the form writes a record with the text and the context information to a database table. The development team or support staff can query this table to monitor user feedback. The form has self-contained functionality, and the only requirement for the application form is a call to a library procedure that opens the feedback form in a new database session (so you don't have to worry about the commit state of the calling form) and passes the context information.

This system can be extended by allowing users to query problem notes and to see the progress or history of other notes. You could also write a procedure that is called from the form startup procedure to hide or display the button that calls this form for particular user groups or roles. After you develop the notes form, the entire system can be made available in the template system libraries so it is easy to include in forms. Alternatively, if all forms need to call this notes form, you could build the functionality into the template, and all forms would be able to access the system with no extra development work.

Aligning Objects

An easy way to align objects in the Layout Editor is to drag the *rule guides* out to the canvas by clicking on a rule on the left or top of the editor and dragging onto the canvas. This will help you align objects. You can also group objects together and use the alignment buttons on the top toolbar. If you want to move objects precisely, select them and press the ARROW keys (RIGHT, LEFT, UP, and DOWN).

Viewing Windows and Canvases

To view the size of the window, select **View→Show Canvas** to display the (usually white) canvas border and **View→Show View** to display the (usually black) window border. In the case of a content canvas, the view is the window. In the case of a stacked canvas, the view is the actual view port. You can resize the borders by moving the bottom right corner selection handle. Changing the borders in this way changes the *Height* and *Width* properties accordingly. Figure 27-3 shows lthese two borders.

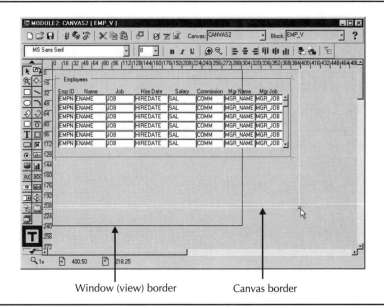

Window (view) border   Canvas border

FIGURE 27-3.   *Canvas and window borders in the Layout Editor*

CHAPTER
28

Forms Menu Tips
and Techniques

I've been sitting here for five minutes and I don't even have a menu!
—Customer at Harry's Diner

 pulldown menu is a simple thing. All it does is provide a hierarchical method for accessing functions (forms, reports, or other modules) in your system. While you can provide this in other ways, such as a form with buttons or image icons that execute the functions, you may decide that a pulldown menu is the best for your users. The following techniques offer information that can help when you design and build menus.

Techniques for Building Menus

Just as with building a form, the easiest way to build a full-featured menu is with a preexisting template (as discussed in Chapter 11).

Creating a Menu

As a review, the basic steps you go through to create a menu from the ground up follow:

1. **Plan the structure** and determine top-level menus and items under each. Be sure to include top-level menus at least for File, Edit, View (optional), Window, and Help because users will expect to see them. Menus you add to this should go between the View and Window menus. Figure 28-1 shows the structure of a sample menu in the Menu Editor.

2. **Create a new menu module** using the Object Navigator. Creating a new menu from a menu template or from an existing menu file is the same as creating a form with a form template: select **File→New→Form Using Template**, and select the menu template file.

3. **Open the Menu Editor** from the right-click menu on the menu module node.

4. **Create top-level menu headings** and fill in their names. CTRL-RIGHT ARROW adds a menu to the right, and CTRL-DOWN ARROW adds a menu item under the menu or item. Use mixed case names and remember that the first uppercase letter will be the underlined access (shortcut) key that will allow the user to select a menu item with a single keypress when the menu is displayed. You can modify the access key assignment by embedding an ampersand "&" in the name. For example, the name "E&xit" will appear with an underlined "x," and the "x" key will serve as the access key.

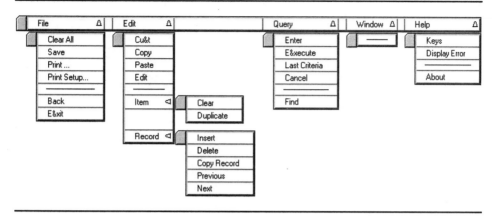

FIGURE 28-1. *Sample menu structure*

5. **Create the items** and fill in the names. If you perform this step in the Menu Editor, the menu items will be named appropriately.

6. **Fill in properties for each item** as described later. Select Property Palette from the right-click menu or press F4 after selecting a menu item to display the Property Palette.

7. **Compile the menu** using the CTRL-T keypress.

TIP
If compiling the menu seems to take a long time, try closing the Menu Editor first.

NOTE
Remember that you cannot run a menu without compiling it into an .MMX file and attaching it to a form. You run the form module that the menu is attached to, not the menu module.

Creating a Popup Menu

The *popup menu,* a new feature as of Developer R.2, is a menu that you create in the form's Popup Menus node, not in a separate menu module. You can attach a popup menu to an item or canvas so that when the user right-clicks an item, a menu will appear, as in the following:

Emp ID	Name	Job	Hire Date
7369	SMITH	CLERK	17-DEC-1995
7499	ALLEN		FEB-1998
7521	WARD		FEB-1999
7566	JONES		APR-1999
7654	MARTIN		SEP-1998

Cut	Ctrl+X
Copy	Ctrl+C
Paste	Ctrl+V
Clear	Delete

Popup menus are handy, user-friendly interface items that users are accustomed to from other GUI applications. They can help users be more productive if you offer commonly used functions (such as Cut, Copy, and Paste for text items) on this menu. Users will then be able to access these functions more quickly than if they had to select them from the main menu at the top of the screen. You can have many popup menus and can attach one menu to more than one item. Also, you can enable and disable items as you can for normal menus, so the menu contents can change based on the item value or other conditions.

You can define a popup menu in the same way as you do a regular menu. You add menus and items in the Object Navigator or in the Menu Editor. The properties and their values work the same way as a normal menu. The main difference is that you have to attach the menu to one or more items or canvases in your form. Create the menu following the guidelines in this section. In the Object Navigator, group the items that you want to apply the menu to, and change the *Popup Menu* property to the name of the menu. You can also attach a popup menu to a canvas so that when the user right-clicks the canvas that has the *Popup Menu* property filled in, the attached menu will appear.

NOTE
Another feature (new as of Developer R.2) is the Switch Orientation button in the Menu Editor toolbar. This button changes the view in the editor from vertical to horizontal orientation and back. This is useful if you have a long or wide menu and need to see part of it in a certain way. This feature only works while you are in the Menu Editor. When you run the form, the menu will display a pulldown menu regardless of what you set as the Layout Editor orientation.

Menu Properties

There are only a handful of properties in the Functional group that you need to set. These properties and their values are described next. Figure 28-2 shows a menu item Property Palette with the Functional group.

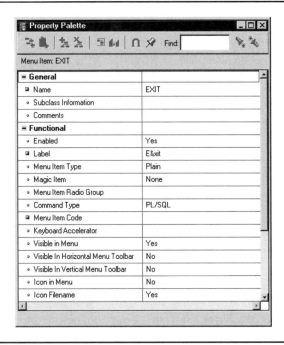

FIGURE 28-2.   *Menu item Property Palette*

Label

Enter the word or phrase you want to appear in the menu at runtime. Normally, Forms will assign the first uppercase letter as the *access key,* which allows the user to activate the item by pressing the access key after the menu is showing. Pressing the ALT key with the top-level menu access-key character activates the top-level pulldown menu. For example, Pressing ALT-F will pull down the File menu; pressing S after that will select the Save menu item.

If you have two items in the same menu pulldown that have the same first uppercase letter (like Cut and Copy in the Edit menu), you can assign a different letter to one by preceding the letter in the label with an "&". For example, if you wanted to use "T" as the access key for Cut, you would use "Cu&t" in the *Label* property. Forms will underline the "t" when you run the menu and will use it as the access key. Figure 28-2 shows this technique applied to the *Label* property of the Exit menu item.

TIP
If you need to change the same property of a number of menu items, you can group them together in the Object Navigator and apply the property to the group, as you can with form objects.

Menu Item Type

The values for this property follow:

- **Plain**   This is the default value used for most purposes.

- **Check**   Use this to show a check mark on an item. These are discussed in the "On Check and Radio Group Items" section.

- **Radio**   Use this to show a radio button as part of a group or as a separate item. This is also discussed in "On Check and Radio Group Items."

- **Separator**   Another design element that you can use in creating menus is separator items, which act to group logical sets of items together within one pulldown menu. Use this menu item type to display a line that separates items. There is no code or action executed for these because separator items cannot be selected. You have to determine what the logical grouping is for your application, and use the separators to help users find particular menu items. This is a common technique and an expected feature of GUI menus.

- **Magic**   Use this value if you want to take advantage of magic item functionality. If you set the type to Magic, you also need to set the *Magic Item* property. Magic items are discussed further in the section "On Magic Items."

Command Type

Set this to one of the following values:

- **Null**   Use this for separators or menu item types.

- **Menu**   Use this if the item is an upper-level menu for another menu item. Fill in the *Submenu Name* property as the name of the menu that this calls.

- **PL/SQL**   This is the default.

- **Plus, Form, and Macro**   Avoid these—they exist only for backward compatibility with older versions of Forms and use languages other than PL/SQL.

Menu Item Code

Double-click the property name in the Property Palette to display the PL/SQL Editor. There is no need to fill this in for Magic types. The code (discussed further in Chapter 11) is just a call to a Forms built-in to call another form, run a report, or perform a Forms function such as Exit. If the item is a PL/SQL command type, the menu will not compile without code in this property. Use "NULL;" for the code if you just want to test the menu and fill in the actual code later.

TIP

Double-click the property name (not the value) to toggle through the values. Using this technique saves the step of activating the poplist and selecting a value. For properties with few values in the poplist, this is very handy. For poplists with many values, it will be faster and easier to pull down the list and make the selection.

On Magic Items

You can use platform-specific features that the environment's presentation manager provides as menu items. For example, in MS Windows, there are Cut, Copy, and Paste functions that manipulate selected text in the clipboard. These allow you to take advantage of some of the Windows default behaviors and incorporate them into the menu by specifying the *Menu Item Type* as Magic and the *Magic Item* as one from the list of items. Assign the magic item type in the menu item property *Magic Item*.

Undo and About

Since they are platform specific, not all Magic items work in MS Windows. Undo and About do nothing by default, so you need to define the *Menu Item Code* property with actual code to perform the action.

Cut, Copy, and Paste

Cut, Copy, and Paste work in MS Windows and are common functions for most Windows applications. Cut, Copy, and Paste do not work on the Web. Therefore, it is better, if you are deploying on the Web, to code these items as PL/SQL command types using the built-ins CUT_REGION, COPY_REGION, and PASTE_REGION. These built-ins will work both in client/server and in web-deployed environments. The sample menu template uses this strategy. The only drawback is that you are not able to take advantage of the standard Windows shortcut keys (CTRL-X, CTRL-C, and CTRL-V for Cut, Copy, and Paste, respectively).

Quit

The magic item Quit will work in both Web and Windows environments. This exits the form by internally executing the DO_KEY('EXIT_FORM') built-in call. You do not need to write any code.

CAUTION
You cannot copy (or even subclass) magic items within a menu, so the toolbar method described later will not work. In fact, this is a major roadblock to using magic items, so you may need to avoid them altogether.

On Check and Radio Group Items

Menu items can also be check or radio types (*Menu Item Type* property). These will display in the menu with a radio button or check mark by them when the form is run, as shown next.

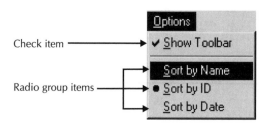

Forms automatically checks or unchecks the check or radio button item when the user selects that menu item. If the menu item is a radio button type, you can group it with other radio menu items by supplying the same name to all items in the same group in the *Menu Item Radio Group* property, as Figure 28-3 shows. This means that only one item of the group may be selected at any one time, and Forms will take care of checking and unchecking the correct items. If the item is a check item, it is treated separately, as a check box item is in a form.

Check and radio group items can be used to let the user select and deselect options or preferences for a default entry value. Windows programs are full of examples of these, but the main purpose is to let the user modify the visual setup of the window. Therefore, one possible use in your forms is to allow the user to show or hide the toolbar buttons or modify the sort order.

The code you place on a check item determines the state of the "check" (a programmatic property that you can query using GET_MENU_ITEM_PROPERTY) and executes conditionally based on this. For example, you can have a check menu item in the Options menu for displaying the toolbar. If the check mark is checked,

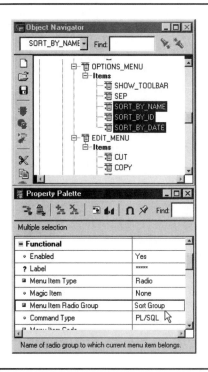

FIGURE 28-3.   *Assigning a radio group name*

the toolbar will be displayed. If it is unchecked, the toolbar is hidden. The code for
this item would be

```
IF get_menu_item_property('OPTIONS_MENU.SHOW_TOOLBAR',
    CHECKED) = 'TRUE'
THEN
    set_menu_item_property('MAIN_MENU.TOOLBAR', DISPLAYED,
        PROPERTY_TRUE);
ELSE
    set_menu_item_property('MAIN_MENU.TOOLBAR', DISPLAYED,
        PROPERTY_FALSE);
END IF;
```

The SET_MENU_ITEM_PROPERTY built-in hides or displays the root menu that
contains all menu buttons. (This is explained further in the "Menu Toolbars"
section.) When you start up the form, you would need to check the menu item

programmatically if the toolbar is to be displayed by default. The code for this would be as follows:

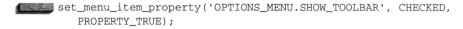

```
set_menu_item_property('OPTIONS_MENU.SHOW_TOOLBAR', CHECKED,
    PROPERTY_TRUE);
```

The code for a radio button menu item is similar. The difference is that, when the item is selected, Forms fills in the radio button indicator and removes the indicator from other items in the group. If you need to investigate a radio group item in the code of another trigger to see if it is selected, you can use the GET_MENU_ ITEM_ PROPERTY built-in as in the following example:

```
IF get_menu_item_property('OPTIONS_MENU.SORT_BY_DATE',
    CHECKED) = 'TRUE'
THEN
    f_block.sort_by('EMP', 'HIREDATE');
ELSIF get_menu_item_property('OPTIONS_MENU.SORT_BY_ID',
    CHECKED) = 'TRUE'
THEN
    f_block.sort_by('EMP', 'EMPNO');
ELSE
    f_block.sort_by('EMP', 'ENAME');
END IF;
```

On Menu Icons

You can assign icons to menu items by setting the *Icon in Menu* property to "Yes" and the *Icon Filename* property to the name of the icon file. Remember that icons in the Windows environment use an .ICO extension and on the Web use a .GIF extension. The *Icon Filename* property shows the name without the extension, however. The following shows a menu with icons. You will have to decide whether the visual clue that the icon provides is worth the extra vertical space that the icons require.

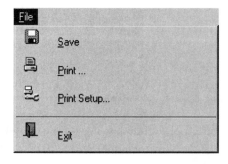

Menu Toolbars

As of Oracle Developer Release 2, menus contain the ability to display items in the menu, in an attached toolbar, or in both menu and toolbar. *Toolbar buttons* are created at runtime based on properties of the menu item. The buttons need no extra canvas and appear in a bar under the menu, as the following shows. You do not need to worry about which window the toolbar will appear on and how it will work in a web environment. This is an easy-to-use feature that allows you to present the most commonly used menu functions in a location that is easy to access.

Including a button for a menu item is as simple as setting the *Visible in Menu Horizontal Toolbar* property to "Yes". If you decide to use vertical menus (that appear on the left side of the window instead of on the top), you can use the *Visible in Menu Vertical Toolbar* property instead. You also need to set the *Icon Filename* property to the name of the icon file (without the extension). If you only want to see the menu toolbar button without the menu item, set the *Visible in Menu* property to "No".

Ordering the Buttons

The normal order of the buttons in the toolbar follows the order in which the items appear in the Object Navigator. You might want to display the buttons in a different order, however, and there is an easy way to do this, as follows:

1. Create the menu with all menus and items.

2. Create another item called TOOLBAR that appears under the top-level menu, as shown next. The *Command Type* property is "Menu", as it is for other items in this menu, but the *Visible in Menu* property is "No".

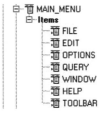

3. Define a menu called TOOLBAR_MENU. Assign the *Submenu Name* property of the TOOLBAR item created in step 2 to "TOOLBAR_MENU".

4. Drag and subclass all the items you want to place in the toolbar into this new menu using right-click, drag, and drop (specify Copy Here and Subclass in the dialogs that follow). You will end up with a menu node that looks like the following:

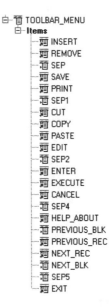

Separator items will show as vertical bars in the toolbar, so place these to group buttons together.

5. Group all items together, and set the *Visible in Menu* property to "No" and *Visible in Horizontal Menu Toolbar* property to "Yes".

6. For each non-separator item, set the *Icon Filename* property to the name of the icon file you would like to display.

7. You can now drag and move the items within the TOOLBAR_MENU menu node to the order that you require.

Although this creates extra items for most functions, the code and other properties are inherited from the menu items. If you change the code on the menu item itself, the code on the button will change, too, because it is subclassed.

CAUTION
Remember that you cannot use this technique for magic menu items because only one copy of each magic item can appear in the same menu file.

Hiding and Showing the Buttons

This system also allows you to manipulate the toolbar as an object, for example, if you want to hide and display it. The code to do this (as it would appear in a menu check item) would look like the following:

```
IF get_menu_item_property('OPTIONS_MENU.SHOW_TOOLBAR', CHECKED)
    = 'TRUE'
THEN
    set_menu_item_property('MAIN_MENU.TOOLBAR', DISPLAYED,
        PROPERTY_TRUE);
ELSE
    set_menu_item_property('MAIN_MENU.TOOLBAR', DISPLAYED,
        PROPERTY_FALSE);
END IF;
```

NOTE
If you define a check menu item to display a toolbar button, when the item is checked, the button will appear as recessed in the toolbar.

Implementing Menu Security

If you need to restrict functions in your menu to certain users, you may be able to use the security feature of menus. This feature allows you to associate specific menu roles with specific database roles. Users who are not granted the associated roles will not see or be able to access the items. There are two main areas of setup involved with this task: the database and the menu.

Database Setup

There are two initial steps to perform so the database contains the proper objects for menu security.

I. Create and Grant to FRM50_ENABLED_ROLES

You or your DBA needs to create the FRM50_ENABLED_ROLES view using scripts that are installed from the Oracle Developer install disk. If you cannot find this view, you need to create it by running the scripts. Be sure you have installed the Oracle Developer Database Tables - Forms Database Tables scripts from the installation disk. If you have installed the scripts, the Installed Products list in the installer will contain a mention of Oracle Developer Database Tables.

Log in to the SYSTEM account and run FRM60BLD.SQL from the ORACLE_HOME/tools/dbtab60/forms60 directory. This creates the Forms tables and roles view (you actually do not need the tables for menu security). Then run FRM60GRT.SQL from the same directory. This grants privileges on the Forms tables and views to the user that you specify. Use PUBLIC as the username, or run the script for each Forms user.

2. Create and Grant Database Roles for Your Application

Determine which groups of users will be allowed access to which menu items. Come up with a plan for which items will be accessible by which user groups. Then create the roles for the user groups and grant users privileges to the role. Normally, only DBAs are able to perform these tasks because they have specific system privileges to create and grant roles. For example:

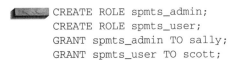

```
CREATE ROLE spmts_admin;
CREATE ROLE spmts_user;
GRANT spmts_admin TO sally;
GRANT spmts_user TO scott;
```

Menu Setup

There are two areas of properties to set up as follows.

Menu Module Properties

- Set *Use Security* to "Yes".

- Set *Module Roles* to the names of the database roles for your application. To delete roles, press CTRL-SHIFT-<. To insert a role, press CTRL-SHIFT-> or move the cursor to the blank line after the last role.

Menu Item Properties

Set the properties for each item:

- Set *Item Roles* to the roles that will have access to the item. Select multiple roles using CTRL-click and SHIFT-click. Deselect roles using CTRL-click. Figure 28-4 shows the role selection window called Menu Item Roles.

- Set *Display without Privilege* to "Yes" if you want the menu item to appear but be disabled if the user does not have a role associated with the item. If this property is set to "No", the menu item will not appear if the user does not have an associated role.

Be sure to assign roles to the top-level menu items as well as to the menu items. Figure 28-5 shows a sample menu. The menu items for FILE, EDIT, OPTIONS, and

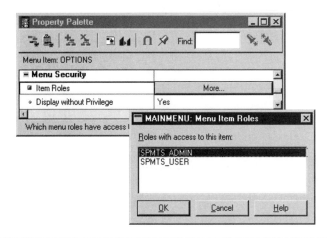

FIGURE 28-4. *Menu Item Roles selection window*

so on represent the top-level pulldown menus. The roles must be set for these items as well as for the items under the menus (such as items under the FILE_MENU node).

Dynamic Toolbars and Menus

Toolbars and menus should be dynamic. That is, as the user moves through the form, only the menu options that apply to the current activity should be available. The technique described here emulates the Forms default menu action. This menu disables menu items in the Query menu when the form is in Normal mode, as shown next:

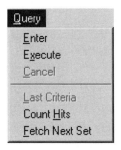

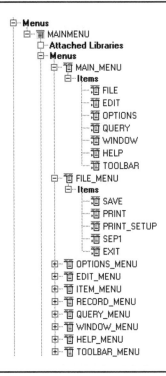

FIGURE 28-5. *Top-level items and menu items*

The Last Criteria and Cancel menu items are disabled because they do not make sense in Normal mode. When the form is placed in Enter Query mode, the menu changes to the following:

In Enter Query mode, the Cancel and Last Criteria items are available because these functions make sense in a query situation, but the Enter (Enter Query) item is disabled because the form is already in Enter Query mode. The toolbar icons associated with these menu items also are disabled in the same way. Another option would be to hide the menu items and toolbar buttons completely, but this would disrupt the layout of the menu and toolbar. You can examine the code that disables and enables these items by looking at the MENUDEFS.MMB file in the Forms' demo directory. The demo form uses SET_MENU_ITEM_PROPERTY to enable and disable the items. It hard-codes the names of the items in these properties.

The template system contains code that accomplishes the same task but is flexibly written to handle any menu items. While you may decide to use code locator forms instead of Enter Query mode, this technique is useful for other purposes because you can use the same type of code to enable and disable sets of menu items and buttons in situations other than query mode.

Preparation

The only preparation step is to create the template system and menu. You also need a sample form that you will attach the menu to.

Ingredients

This solution is purely PL/SQL code. The following program pieces are required.

Package Specification Variable

This variable holds the names of the menu items that will be processed. This is called F_GLOBAL.G_SHOW_MENUITEMS and is assigned in the STARTUP.PRE_FORM procedure that is called by the PRE-FORM trigger. Here is an example of how this variable is assigned:

```
f_global.g_show_menuitems :=
         'MAIN_MENU.FILE:N,' ||
         'QUERY_MENU.LAST_CRITERIA:Q,' ||
         'QUERY_MENU.CANCEL:Q,' ||
         'TOOLBAR.CANCEL:Q,' ||
         'EDIT_MENU.DUP_FIELD:N,' ||
         'EDIT_MENU.RECORD:N,' ||
         'EDIT_MENU.CLEAR_BLOCK:N';
```

This variable just contains a list of buttons delimited by quotes. Normally, all menu items are enabled. If you want to disable items in Normal or Enter Query mode, they will appear in this list. The button name is suffixed with a flag (after the colon) to indicate when it is enabled. The flags indicate Enter Query mode only ("Q") or Normal mode only ("N"). You can also define the item as used in both modes ("B", which is the default) or neither mode ("X", which means it will be enabled programmatically in another way). The flags are used by the CHANGE_MODE procedure.

KEY-ENTQRY and KEY-EXEQRY Triggers

These triggers are written at the form level (subclassed from the object library). These triggers call the KEY_ENTQRY and KEY_EXEQRY procedures in the F_TOOLBAR package in the library. Whenever you need to put the form into Enter Query mode, you use the following call:

```
do_key('ENTER_QUERY');
```

This will fire the KEY-ENTQRY trigger and supply the proper code to manage the menu items. Similarly, when you need to execute a query, you use the following:

```
do_key('EXECUTE_QUERY');
```

CHANGE_MODE Procedure

This procedure appears in the F_UTIL library package that is called by the triggers just mentioned. It is also called by the WHEN-NEW-FORM-INSTANCE trigger to set up the menu items properly when the form starts up. The specification for this procedure is the following:

```
PROCEDURE change_mode(
       p_mode    IN VARCHAR2);
```

The F_TOOLBAR procedures pass in the mode using a package variable that represents a specific mode. These variables are declared in the F_GLOBAL package as follows:

```
g_query_mode      CONSTANT VARCHAR2(10)  :=  'QUERY';
g_normal_mode     CONSTANT VARCHAR2(10)  :=  'NORMAL';
```

For example, the F_TOOLBAR.KEY_EXEQRY procedure would contain the following code:

```
execute_query;
f_util.change_mode(f_global.g_query_mode);
```

The CHANGE_MODE procedure loops through the menu items in the F_GLOBAL variable and enables or disables them based on the flag value associated with each button. The loop is a simple parsing of the variable value, and the enable and disable code looks like the following:

```
IF v_mode = 'H' AND
    get_menu_item_property(v_item, DISPLAYED) = 'TRUE'
THEN
    f_menu.hide(v_item);
ELSIF (v_is_querymode AND v_mode IN ('Q', 'B')) OR
      ((NOT v_is_querymode) AND v_mode IN ('N', 'B'))
THEN
    f_menu.enable(v_item);
ELSE
    f_menu.disable(v_item);
END IF;
```

NOTE
*The code that loops through the list variables and
parses the names of each button is contained in the
sample files available on the authors' and
publisher's web sites. See the front of the book for
the addresses.*

Steps

Once the preparation is finished and the ingredients have been assembled, you are
ready to use the system in a form. The following steps are the only actions necessary
to add this functionality to your form.

  1. Populate the G_SHOW_MENUITEMS variable with a list of the menu items
  (including those that are displayed as menu toolbar buttons). Define the flag
  value for each as described earlier. When you add or remove menu items,
  you need to change the STARTUP.PRE_FORM variable assignment.

  2. The calls to the proper procedures are already written into the template, so
  you just need to be sure to use the DO_KEY calls when you want to place
  the form in Enter Query mode or reset to Normal mode.

Variations

If you need to change the buttons for other purposes, you just need to create
additional package variables to hold the names of those buttons and a section in the
CHANGE_MODE procedure to handle the disabling and enabling.

You can also use a PL/SQL table of records to store the values instead of a
single-valued variable. The table would contain a column for the menu item name
and another for the flag value.

CHAPTER
29

Forms System
Tips and Techniques

Sacrifice is the transmutation of force.
Cosmic archetypes shape this force into spiritual energy,
which can then reappear on the planes of form as an entirely
different type of force to that as which it started.
                    —Kabbalah (BC 1200–700 AD), *Geburah, The Fifth Sephirah*

ome techniques are general ones that you would use to manage the communication between forms files or to handle objects that are not specific to forms, menus, or libraries. This chapter discusses a few techniques that apply to the system level of working with Forms. The following topics are explored:

- Sharing variables

- Compiling forms files

- Setting forms registry values

- Foreign Function Interface (FFI)

- Which files does Oracle installer install?

Sharing Variables

Forms code executes as the result of a triggering event. While the trigger may call other program units in the form, in an attached library, or in the database, the unit of code execution is the trigger. Generally, the variable values you set in the trigger are not available when the code in the trigger is finished. There are a number of ways to make variable values available outside the scope of the trigger. This is particularly useful for values that are not available using standard Forms built-ins.

For example, you want to store the names of all canvases in a variable when the form starts up. This variable allows you to loop through the canvases and change the background color when the form is in Query mode. You may also want to store the names of the menu items you want to disable in Query mode. This is a form-specific list because each form may have slightly different menus. The list of menu items is stored in the list when the form starts and processed each time the form is put in Query mode. You could hard-code this list into the procedure that handles Query mode, but this would make the code specific to the form and defeat the purpose of writing the code in a reusable way.

In addition to being able to share variable values between triggers in the same form, you might also need to share values between forms. One form may base its processing on the values set in the form that called it. You can accomplish variable sharing in the following ways:

- Database package specification variables

- Forms package specification variables

- Parameters

- Items in a block

- Global variables

The following discusses how you can use these for sharing variable values.

Database Package Specification Variables

When you log in to Forms, you are logging in to the database and creating a database session. You can use variables declared in a package specification to store values that are available through the entire session. The same session continues as you use CALL_FORM, NEW_FORM, and OPEN_FORM to start other forms. You can use OPEN_FORM to create a new database connection session, and this will create a new Forms session.

All values that you assign to database package specification variables in one trigger are available in other triggers in that same Forms session, regardless of what form the trigger is in. The benefit of package specification variables is that they can span forms. One form can set values that are used by forms it calls, and the called form can set values that will be known by the caller when the called form exits. The package variables can be any datatype supported by the PL/SQL in Forms and the database.

Forms Package Specification Variables

Forms packages, whether they are in the form itself or in a library attached to the form, act similarly to database packages—and so do Forms package specification variables. The benefit of package variables on the Forms level is that they do not need to access the database. The client runtime engine sets the variable value in its memory and does not need to use the network to reassign or evaluate the value.

Sharing Library Variable Values

Normally package specification variables in Forms are not available between forms. Each new form that starts, whether it is as the result of a CALL_FORM, OPEN_FORM, or NEW_FORM, starts a new set of Forms package variables. If you use an option on these built-ins called SHARE_LIBRARY_DATA, you can make the package variable values global to both the caller and the called form. Values set in either will be available in the other. The syntax varies for each built-in, but an example using CALL_FORM follows:

```
call_form('EMPDEPT', NO_HIDE, DO_REPLACE, QUERY_ONLY,
    SHARE_LIBRARY_DATA);
```

All Forms package specification variable values that are available in the calling form will also be available in the called form. If you set values in the called form and return to the calling form, the calling form will see the same values.

CAUTION
If the shared library data does not work with the NEW_FORM call, try using an OPEN_FORM (with shared library data) to start up the other form. In the WHEN-NEW-FORM-INSTANCE of the other form, issue a CLOSE_FORM to close the form you started from. You have to set a global package variable with the form's ID because CLOSE_FORM requires this. Use the following to derive the form ID:

```
-- v_form_id is declared as a FORMMODULE datatype
v_form_id := find_form(get_application_property(CURRENT_FORM_NAME));
```

Parameters

Parameters are variable values that take two different formats: as parts of a parameter list that you construct programmatically and as objects in the form's Object Navigator.

Programmatic Parameters

You can construct parameters programmatically that you can use to pass values to other forms through CALL_FORM, OPEN_FORM, and NEW_FORM. You can also pass parameters to Reports and Graphics. This is a one-way communication line. The parameter values you set in the calling form are set in the called form (in the case of a CALL_FORM navigation). However, if the values of these parameters are changed in the called form, the new values will not be known in the caller.

The method for setting up a parameter list consists of creating a parameter list (using the CREATE_PARAMETER_LIST built-in) and adding parameters to it (with the ADD_PARAMETER built-in). Single parameter values are considered TEXT_PARAMETER types, and you specify this in the ADD_PARAMETER call. Programmatic parameters may also be a DATA_PARAMETER type that represents a record group. You can use data parameters to pass multiple records to a Reports or Graphics module, but you cannot use data parameters to pass values from one form to another. The following shows a sample CALL_FORM that uses a parameter list ID to pass parameters to another form, DEPT. The DEPT form has all the parameters in its Object Navigator that correspond to the parameters created programmatically in the calling form.

```
DECLARE
    v_paramlist_id     PARAMLIST;
    v_paramlist_name   VARCHAR2(15) := 'emp_params';
BEGIN
    --
    -- Set up the param list
    v_paramlist_id := get_parameter_list(v_paramlist_name);
    IF NOT id_null(v_paramlist_id)
    THEN
        destroy_parameter_list(v_paramlist_id);
    END IF;
    --
    v_paramlist_id := create_parameter_list(v_paramlist_name);
    --
    -- Add the parameters,
    add_parameter(v_paramlist_id, 'IN_QUERY_ONLY_MODE',
        TEXT_PARAMETER, 'N');
    add_parameter(v_paramlist_id, 'AUTO_QUERY_ON_STARTUP',
        TEXT_PARAMETER, 'Y');
    add_parameter(v_paramlist_id, 'QUERY_DEPTNO', TEXT_PARAMETER,
        to_char(:emp.deptno));
    --
    call_form('DEPT', NO_HIDE, NO_REPLACE,
          NO_QUERY_ONLY, SHARE_LIBRARY_DATA, v_paramlist_id);
END;
```

Parameter Objects

Parameter objects (created and displayed in the Object Navigator) can be defined as character, number, or date datatypes. The maximum number of characters is 2,147,483,647 (more than 2Gb). You can use parameters as global variable areas in the form just as you do package-specification variables. If you set a parameter value in one trigger, it will persist through the time during which the form is open. When the control passes to another form, the parameter in the form is no longer available. That is, parameter values stay within the form in which they are defined.

When you call one form from another and pass a parameter list, the parameters that make up the list must exist as Object Navigator parameters in the called form. For example, you have two forms—FORM_A and FORM_B—and you pass a parameter called IN_QUERY_ONLY_MODE as part of a parameter list from FORM_A to FORM_B. FORM_B needs to have an Object Navigator parameter called IN_QUERY_ONLY_MODE. When FORM_B opens, the Object Navigator parameter in FORM_B will be populated with the value passed in using the parameter list parameter. As mentioned earlier, this mechanism is one-way. That is, when FORM_A uses CALL_FORM to navigate to FORM_B, the values you set in the parameter list in the calling form are passed into FORM_B, but the values of the parameters in FORM_B do not pass back to FORM_A.

Items in a Block

Another way to make values available between triggers is to load them into items in a block. The block can be a control block and the items do not need to have a canvas assignment, but the *Data Type* and *Maximum Length* need to be set to accommodate the data that you will load into the variables. The benefit of items is that you can use the COPY and NAME_IN built-ins to read the data. Since both built-ins take a parameter of the name of the item in quotes, your code can construct the item name programmatically and read from different items for different needs. The drawback of using items as shared variable space is that you need to create the items in the Object Navigator. Items take up a bit of form file space, whereas variables do not add significantly to the file size. Another drawback is that if you clear the form, all values in all items will be cleared, including the values in your shared variable value items. This could work to your advantage, but it is an effect to remember. In general, you will not need to use items in this way because you can do most everything you need to with the other shared values techniques.

Global Variables

This is a feature that was available in the early releases of Forms and still used because of the one-way nature of parameters and for backward compatibility. *Global variables* are accessible throughout the same forms session regardless of whether you use CALL_FORM, OPEN_FORM, or NEW_FORM. This means that if FORM_A calls FORM_B, any global variable that is set in FORM_A is accessible in FORM_B. In addition, if FORM_B exits and returns to FORM_A, any global variable set in FORM_B is available in FORM_A. Global variables are sized at 255 characters. To store date and number values, you convert them to character data.

Global variables use bind variable syntax with a prefix of ":GLOBAL". Globals are created when you first assign them, for example:

```
:global.canvas_names := 'MAIN,EMP,DEPT';
```

You can drop a global variable by using the built-in ERASE. You can assign a value to a global that does not exist by using the DEFAULT_VALUE built-in. In fact, it is good practice to call this built-in to assign "NULL" to a global variable before using it for anything other than an assignment. For example:

```
default_value(NULL, 'GLOBAL.CANVAS_NAMES');
f_block.change_canvas_colors(:global.canvas_names);
```

If the global variable had not been assigned (through DEFAULT_VALUE), you would receive an error message from the second line of code.

Global variables are powerful but limited in what they can hold. You cannot pass them between Forms and Reports as you can with parameters. Since they are not declared, it is easy to write code for a global that you think you know the name of, but misspell. Misspelling a global name will not fail at compile time, but the code will not do what you want it to because you have actually created a different global with the misspelled name. Since global variable values remain present for the entire Forms session (unless you reassign or erase them), there is a chance that a global set in one form can unexpectedly affect the way another form works. Using global variables therefore requires great care.

However, there is no reason to use globals now that you can share library variables between forms. Therefore, your standards should strongly state that they are to be avoided.

Table 29-1 summarizes the scope of the different forms of shared variables, assuming you are calling one form from another.

Using "Constant" Variables

You can also hide a literal value from developers so that they do not have to remember the spelling or whether the word is mixed case or not. For example, you could construct a procedure to set the canvas color base if it is in Query mode. The procedure to do this checks the value of a parameter you pass it to determine which color to change the canvases to. You can require the programmer to enter the value as needed by the procedure:

```
change_color('NORMAL');
```

Variable Type	Value Is Available to the Called Form	Value Is Available to the Calling Form	Accesses the Database
Database package specification	Yes	Yes	Yes
Forms package specification	No (default) Yes (optionally)	No (default) Yes (optionally)	No
Parameters	Yes	No	No
Items in a block	No	No	No
Global	Yes	Yes	No

TABLE 29-1. *Shared Variables Scope*

A problem occurs if the developer does not remember or know the valid values for this parameter. The code will compile successfully but fail when the form runs if the value is wrong. Therefore, the better strategy is to put the value in a package variable declared in the package specification for the F_GLOBAL package as follows:

```
g_normal     CONSTANT VARCHAR2(10) := 'NORMAL';
```

Then, when the parameter value is required, you can use the constant value as follows:

```
change_color(f_global.g_normal);
```

This is a useful technique to use even for simple constants such as "Y" and "N" because you do not have to remember if "Y" is spelled as "yes" or "YES" or "Yes" or just "Y". Of course, you do need to remember the name of the global variable, but this is contained in the package specification and, if you spell it incorrectly, you will get a compilation error.

Compiling Forms Files

There are times when you need to recompile a large number of forms or other Forms module files. For example, you may have changed a database package or library package that is referenced by all forms. It is a tedious job to open and recompile a large number of forms manually. The Project Builder component of Oracle Developer allows you to create a project that you can use to group all files related to a project. You can easily recompile a large number of forms using this utility once the project is set up.

Compiling Forms

You can also compile Forms files outside of Project Builder using the Form Builder compiler command line. Although the Forms compiler can only compile one file at a time, you can create command-line files that run the compiler many times. You can compile all Forms files in the current directory with the following command line:

```
for %f in (*.fmb) do start ifcmp60 userid=scott/tiger@db module=%f
```

You run this command from an "MSDOS" command-line window. The ifcmp60 command is the Forms compiler executable, and the userid and module are command-line parameters for the compiler. The rest of the line is batch language syntax for a loop through a directory list. You can place this command in a batch file to make it easier to use. The file can be as follows:

```
@echo off
:: COMPILE_FRM.BAT
cls
ECHO Compiling forms
FOR %%f IN (*.fmb) DO ifcmp60 userid=scott/tiger@db module=%%f
ECHO Finished compiling
```

The double % sign changes to a single % sign when this command is run from a batch file.

Compiling Libraries

You may need to recompile a number of libraries as well. You can also write a compile file for libraries as follows. (The FOR command should appear on one line in the batch file although it is wrapped in this listing.)

```
@echo off
:: COMPILE_LIB.BAT
cls
ECHO Compiling libraries
FOR %%f IN (*.pll) DO ifcmp60 userid=cta/c@d703
   module_type=LIBRARY module=%%f compile_all=yes batch=yes
ECHO Finished compiling
```

This process creates .PLX files from the .PLL files, but retains the source .PLL files. You can run forms using just .PLL files, but the .PLX file offers a version that the users cannot open and examine. The problem with .PLX files is that you have to be careful about which version of the file you are using. Given a library file name in the Attached Libraries node, Forms Runtime will always look for the .PLX file before the .PLL file. If you made a change to the .PLL file before re-creating the .PLX file, the Forms Runtime will use the .PLX file first and you will not see your changes. Of course, this is just a matter of care in handling these files, but a safe standard to operate under is to not use .PLX files or to use them only for test and production directories.

After running batch files such as these, you should check the compiled files to see that they work the way you intended. Also check the messages in any .ERR files that are created.

Command-Line Parameters

The COMPILE_ALL parameter forces a recompile and rewrite of the .PLL file. If you do not include that parameter, the compile process will just create the .PLX file and leave the .PLL file alone. The BATCH parameter indicates that the compiler will not stop for confirmation between each file.

The batch file technique can be used for many types of file conversions. The *Oracle Developer Form Builder Reference, Release 6.0* (available in **Help→Manuals** in Form Builder) contains the command-line parameters you need for the Form Builder executables. Look for the topic "Starting Form Builder Components from the Command Line" in the Options chapter. The executables or components of Form Builder are the Form Builder (design interface), Forms Runtime, Web Previewer, and Form Compiler. All are documented in the manual. You can also enter an invalid command-line option such as nothing=nothing. The screens shown in Figure 29-1 will appear containing the valid command-line syntax.

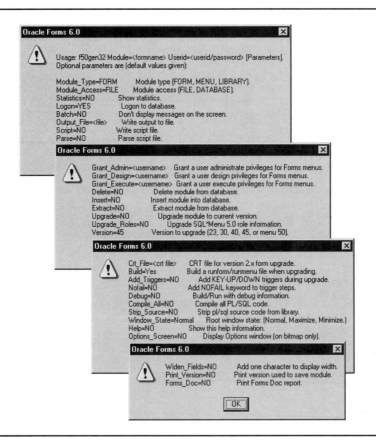

FIGURE 29-1. *Compiler command-line parameters*

NOTE
If you have trouble finding a topic in the Form Builder reference manual, search for a word or a phrase (CTRL-F in Adobe Acrobat). The Adobe Acrobat page numbers do not always agree with the table of contents page numbers, but the search facility is a fast and easy way to find the topic from the table of contents.

The Order of Compilation

The order of compilation matters. You should compile libraries first because the code in forms depends on them. If you have attached libraries to other libraries, you need to compile the attached libraries first and then the libraries that have the attachment. Since the order of compilation matters, you may not be able to rely on the batch file loop method, but you can construct individual command-line commands for each library and place them in the correct order in the batch file. You can then compile menus and forms in any order (and, therefore, use the loop mechanism) because they are not dependent on one another.

CAUTION
Be sure all required object libraries are available in the current directory or in the FORMS60_PATH or ORACLE_PATH when you compile forms and menus.

UNIX Batch Compiles

This batch file technique works equally well in UNIX operating systems, but the loop syntax is a bit different. If you are deploying on the Web, your environment may require you to transfer files from a Windows development environment to a UNIX deployment environment. In this situation, you will need to recompile all files for the other operating system. The following is an example of a file you could create to batch-compile files in UNIX.

```
#
#   compile_all.sh
#
for form_file in `ls *.fmb`
do
    echo Compiling $form_file
    ifcmp60 module=$form_file userid=scott/tiger@db
done
```

Setting Forms Registry Values

One of the key setup tasks for development and rollout of Forms applications is setting up the environment. When you're deploying forms on the Web on a UNIX application server (or when running client/server under UNIX), this involves setting environment variables, which is just a matter of adding variable assignments in a login or shell script. In a Windows environment, this requires setting up values in the Windows registry. While this is not a Forms task, it is worth a mention because setting up the registry is a common requirement.

For example, you need to set a directory into the UI_ICON string value so your forms can find button icons. Open REGEDIT by selecting **Start→Run** from the Windows task menu and entering REGEDIT. If you are using Windows NT, there is also another program that edits the registry called REGEDT32. This has slightly different options; while you can usually use it to accomplish the task, REGEDIT is more standard because it is also available in the Windows 95 and 98 environments.

CAUTION

Working in the registry has its risks. If you delete or change the value of particular system nodes, you can halt the Windows session and even cause an operating system failure. Always back up the registry (by clicking on the top-level node, selecting Registry→Export Registry File, and saving the file to disk). This can help you recover from a registry accident. Alternatively, you can just be very, very careful when working in the registry.

Once you start up REGEDIT, you can navigate to the Oracle node by opening up the hierarchy: HKEY_LOCAL_MACHINE\SOFTWARE\ORACLE. You will see a screen like the one shown in Figure 29-2.

You can find the node you want to change in the list on the left. All Oracle Developer settings (called *string values)* are in the top-level Oracle node. To change a setting, double-click on the name. To add a string value, select **Edit→New→String Value** and type in the name. The list will alphabetize later. Other operations are relatively intuitive, and most everything you need to accomplish is in the right-click menu or top menu. If you are running Form Builder and want to make it aware of a new registry setting, you may have to close and reopen it. If you are just running forms from Form Builder, the next form you run will use the settings because it begins a new Windows session that reads the registry when it starts.

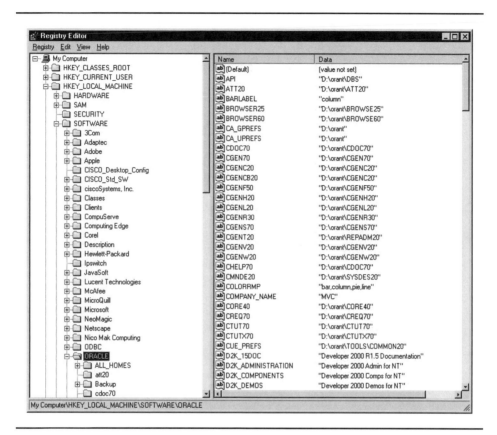

FIGURE 29-2.   *REGEDIT displaying the Oracle node*

Setting Paths

A *path* is a list of directories that Forms uses to find files. There is a Forms path, an icon path, and an Oracle path. All paths are stored in the registry (or environment space in UNIX). Path variables in Windows use semicolons (";") as delimiters. For example, the path Forms uses to find menus, forms, and libraries is the FORMS60_PATH. An example of a value for this path might be "c:\forms;d:\orant\tools\devdem60\demo\forms;c:\forms\lib". This path is not case sensitive in Windows, but is limited to 512 characters. If your path is longer than 512 characters, Forms will ignore it completely regardless of what directories are listed.

TIP
Forms Runtime looks for files first in the current working directory (defined in the Start in field of the Windows shortcut properties) before it looks in the directories in the FORMS60_PATH and ORACLE_PATH. If it seems unable to find the file you have placed in the current working directory, add that directory (".\;" in Windows) to the beginning of the FORMS60_PATH. This hard-codes the current working directory into the FORMS60_PATH regardless of which directory is the current working directory.

Setting the Registry from Within Forms

You can also set and query Windows registry values from Forms code by using procedures in the D2KWUTIL.PLL file. You will find this library file in the ORACLE_HOME/tools/devdem60/demo/forms directory. The READ_REGISTRY function and WRITE_REGISTRY procedure in the WIN_API_ENVIRONMENT package will read from and write to the registry, respectively. The package specification comments contain more information about the parameters that you would use to call these program units.

Foreign Function Interface (FFI)

The Oracle Developer *Foreign Function Interface* (FFI) offers a method you can use to access functions written in an outside non–Form Builder library. For example, in a client/server environment, you might want to call the WinHelp function to display a help file. You need to write extra FFI PL/SQL code to register the Windows function because that function was written and compiled in a "foreign" language—C++.

The following explains how to write the FFI code that you need to call a Windows function in a .DLL—the Windows help engine WinHelp. If your host operating system is not Windows, the same principles apply, but the library and function names will be different.

CAUTION
If you use an FFI call when you are running Forms on the Web, the FFI call will go to the middle-tier application server machine where the Oracle Developer Forms Server is running. Thus, if the FFI call performs an action that requires display to the client, such as this example, that display will not occur on the client, but on the server where the client will not see it. The FFI is still useful in web-deployed forms to access functions in libraries compiled with another language such as C++.

FFIGEN.FMB

The PL/SQL package that you need to create for an external function call requires proficiency with the FFI calling mechanism. In previous releases, Oracle supplied a utility that creates this package code automatically. All you needed was to know the calling interface for the Windows function and the name of the library that it is in. The utility is a normal Oracle Developer form called FFIGEN (Foreign Function Interface Generator) with supporting object library, menu, and PL/SQL library. The form and supporting files used to be available in the EXTRAS directory of the Developer installation CD. However, this is not distributed with the early releases of Oracle Developer Release 6. If you need to use this utility, you can open the Developer R.2 FFIGEN file and run it with R.6 (after creating the necessary tables). Oracle support or the technet.oracle.com web site should also have this file available for downloading in the future. Figure 29-3 shows a sample FFIGEN session from the R.2 FFIGEN form converted to Developer R.6. The authors' web sites (mentioned in the author biographies at the beginning of the book) contain information on how to convert this form from R.5 to R.6.

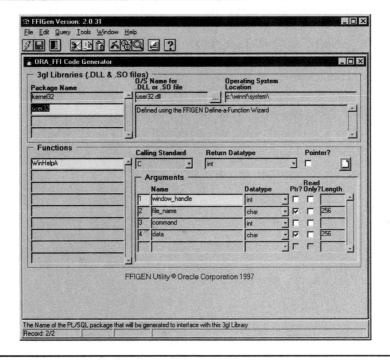

FIGURE 29-3. *Foreign Function Interface generator form*

The first time you run FFIGEN, the form will create tables to store the FFI data. The .HLP help file documents these tables and other internals and steps you through creating an FFI package. Instead of repeating that documentation, the next session will discuss, using an example, the structure of the FFI code that the FFIGEN utility creates.

NOTE
FFI package code can be used by any Oracle Developer component, including Reports, Procedure Builder, and Graphics.

What FFIGEN Creates

The FFI Generator produces a .PLD and .PLL file containing a package specification and header that you compile using Form Builder. The package specification declares the public interface to the foreign function. The package body registers the function so Forms Runtime knows where to find it, declares the calling interface (arguments and return value) for the function, and calls the function through a PL/SQL dispatcher function.

The following example shows code similar to that produced by FFIGEN. It is simplified somewhat to illustrate the steps involved and does not display the exception handlers, but will function on its own. There are other examples of FFI code in the D2KWUTIL.PLL library located in the ORACLE_HOME/tools/devdem60/demo/forms directory. In fact, it is a good idea to look in that library before writing your own FFI code to see if it is included already in the PLL.

FFI Package Specification

A typical FFI package specification appears exactly the same as other PL/SQL specifications. Here's an example of a package specification (without header comments) used to call the WinHelp function:

```
PACKAGE f_winhelp IS
    --
    g_opsys            VARCHAR2(30) :=
                       get_application_property(USER_INTERFACE);
    --
    PROCEDURE call_help(
        p_helpfile IN VARCHAR2);
END;
```

This specification just declares a global variable that is used in the package body and is available to other packages as well. This variable stores the value of the operating system name because you do not want to execute this function in anything other than a Windows runtime environment.

FFI Package Body

The package body contains a few special parts.

Initialization Block

The first part of the package body is the package *initialization block.* This is a block that appears at the bottom of the package body outside all other procedures and functions. The package initialization code is executed the first time a procedure, function, or variable in the package is used. This block uses variables declared in the top of the package body. The following is an excerpt from the package body.

```
PACKAGE BODY f_winhelp
IS
    lh_user           ORA_FFI.LIBHANDLETYPE;
    fh_winhelp        ORA_FFI.FUNCHANDLETYPE;
    v_libname         VARCHAR2(50);
    v_functionname    VARCHAR2(50);
--
-- Private (local) and public procedure and function bodies go here
--
BEGIN
    IF g_opsys IN ('MSWINDOWS32', 'WIN32COMMON')
    THEN
        BEGIN
            lh_user := ora_ffi.find_library('USER32.DLL');
        EXCEPTION
            WHEN ora_ffi.ffi_error
            THEN
                lh_user := ora_ffi.load_library(NULL, 'USER32.DLL');
        END;
        -- Register the function
        fh_winhelp := ora_ffi.register_function(lh_USER, 'WinHelpA',
                ora_ffi.PASCAL_STD);
        -- Register the arguments
        -- HWND argument - the window handle
        ora_ffi.register_parameter(fh_winhelp, ORA_FFI.C_INT);
        -- LPCSTR argument - the file name
        ora_ffi.register_parameter(fh_winhelp, ORA_FFI.C_CHAR_PTR);
        -- LPCSTR argument - the command
        ora_ffi.register_parameter(fh_winhelp, ORA_FFI.C_INT);
        -- DWORD argument - the command data (value)
        ora_ffi.register_parameter(fh_winhelp, ORA_FFI.C_CHAR_PTR);
        -- BOOL argument - the return value
```

```
            ora_ffi.register_return(fh_winhelp, ORA_FFI.C_INT);
    ELSE
        -- Don't call these for other OSes.
        Add an alert if needed.
        NULL;
    END IF;
END;
```

The objective of this code is to find the function in the external library and register the function, the calling arguments, and the return value. The code uses procedures from the built-in ORA_FFI package. Also, each parameter and the return value must map to a specific C language datatype that is declared using the ORA_FFI package datatypes.

Dispatcher Function
The next part of the package body is the *dispatcher function* that calls the foreign function. The following shows an example of this procedure that would be placed in the package body above the package initialization block. It is a private function used only by the package body and is therefore not declared in the package specification.

```
FUNCTION i_winhelp(
    p_funct_handle IN ORA_FFI.FUNCHANDLETYPE,
    p_hwnd         IN PLS_INTEGER,
    p_helpfile     IN OUT VARCHAR2,
    p_command      IN PLS_INTEGER,
    p_data         IN OUT VARCHAR2)
    RETURN PLS_INTEGER;
PRAGMA INTERFACE(C, i_winhelp, 11265);
```

This declaration contains several unusual items. The first is the parameter that passes in a handle or pointer to the function. This parameter is typed with an ORA_FFI datatype. The second unusual item is the datatype of PLS_INTEGER used for the parameters and the return value. The PLS_INTEGER is a PL/SQL NUMBER datatype that maps to a C datatype. In non-FFI PL/SQL, this datatype is equivalent to a NUMBER datatype, but, in the dispatcher function that actually contacts the C function, PLS_INTEGER is required. The last unusual item in this code is the PRAGMA INTERFACE line that identifies to the PL/SQL compiler that this will be a foreign function call.

Caller Procedure
The last part of the FFI code is the public procedure that calls the dispatcher function to display the help file. This code appears after the private dispatcher function and before the initialization block. Here is an example:

```
PROCEDURE call_help(
    p_helpfile IN VARCHAR2)
IS
    v_hwnd_l     NUMBER;
    v_helpfile_l VARCHAR2(512) := p_helpfile;
    -- Shows the contents page, other commands are possible
    v_command_l  NUMBER := 3;
    v_data_l     VARCHAR2(512) := NULL;
    v_rc         NUMBER;
BEGIN
    v_hwnd_l := TO_NUMBER(get_item_property(name_in(
                'SYSTEM.CURSOR_ITEM'), WINDOW_HANDLE));
    -- return value that identifies if the call worked
    v_rc   := i_winhelp(fh_winhelp, v_hwnd_l, v_helpfile_l,
              v_command_l, v_data_l);
END;
```

This procedure translates the somewhat arcane calling interface function (I_WINHELP in this example) to a more developer-friendly PL/SQL procedure. It hides some of the C function's arguments that are not important to the developer and uses standard NUMBER and VARCHAR2 datatypes. The PL/SQL engine performs an implicit conversion between the PLS_INTEGER returned by the I_WINHELP dispatcher function and the V_RC variable.

NOTE
This example shows a call to the WinHelp function to display a help file and show the contents page by hard-coding a "3" as the help command. For a fully featured call interface to WinHelp, you would create a parameter for the command as well, so you could open the help file at a specific topic or at the Index tab. Chapter 14 lists some of the other WinHelp commands.

Error Checking

For production code, you would also write exception handlers (not displayed in these examples). FFI code can be a challenge to debug, and one error is often really an entire stack of errors. The first error in the stack may be the one that tells you exactly what is wrong, but this is hidden unless you pop messages off the error stack. You can use the TOOL_ERR package to determine the entire stack of errors that occurred in an FFI call as follows:

```
PROCEDURE handle_ffi_error
IS
BEGIN
   WHILE tool_err.nerrors > 0
   LOOP
      message(tool_err.message);
      tool_err.pop;
   END LOOP;
END;
```

Place this procedure in a utility package, and call it in a WHEN OTHERS exception on all code in the FFI package body.

Which Files Does Oracle Installer Install?

If you are interested in which files the Oracle Installer installs for a particular option in the Available Products list, open the NT.PRD file (on Windows NT) or the WIN95.PRD file (on Windows 95 or 98) located in the INSTALL directory of the Oracle Developer installation disk. Perform a Windows Explorer search for the file names or just the .PRD extension if you have trouble finding the file. The .PRD is an ASCII text file containing a table that provides the list of products to the Available Products window. Search for the line that contains a description of the product, and note the name of the file in the Filename column.

TIP
Create a directory for your Forms files. Also create a Windows shortcut for the Form Builder executable, IFBLD60.EXE. This will allow you to start the Form Builder without navigating the Windows Start menu. It will also allow you to change the working directory from ORACLE_HOME/forms60 to your Forms files directory (using the shortcut's Start in property). Each time you save or run a file, the Form Builder will use that directory by default. This helps with managing a large number of files.

Search for a file on the installation CD with the name you noted and a .MAP extension. This is usually in the COMPS directory, but the directory structure changes occasionally depending on the version. The MAP file is another text file with a table that indicates the Source (the files that will be installed) and the Destination (the target directories).

If you are interested in the products installed on your machine, open the ASCII text file that has an .RGS extension (the installation registry file) in the ORACLE_HOME/orainst directory. This lists the products you have installed.

CAUTION

Do not edit the .RGS file. You can easily mistype a character and corrupt the installation registry. This will require you to reinstall the products to recover the installation registry. A corollary to this caution is to back up the .RGS file after you have completed an installation.

TIP

Read DEPLOY.WRI in the DEPLOY directory of the installation disk for information on how you can customize the Oracle Installer for your own application. Oracle Developer's Project Builder also provides a method for deployment of customized install sets.

APPENDIX

A

Sample Template
PL/SQL Library Packages

s mentioned in Chapter 10, the template system consists of a number of files that store reusable objects and code. Code is stored mainly in a number of PL/SQL libraries (.PLL files) and attached to the template. Some reusable components (groups of objects used for a specific function) are used only occasionally, and the code for these is stored in separate libraries that are attached when the class is used. There is one main library that supports the template objects and that is attached to the template and all forms created from the template.

When you construct your own template library, it helps to have a starting point. You can use code that Oracle has written in a set of demo libraries. These files are installed into the ORACLE_HOME/tools/devdem60/demo/forms directory if you install the Oracle Developer Demos and Add-ons from the original install disk. The libraries contain a number of generic packages that you can use for your own work. The following libraries are included:

- **D2KCONV**   This file contains procedures to convert an expression (such as 2+2) to a number result and to convert a string to a date.

- **D2KDLSTR**   This file contains a set of procedures to parse and handle delimited strings (such as strings that use commas to separate values).

- **D2KWUTIL**   The most commonly used Windows API functions are available using the procedures in this package. The procedures call the Foreign Function Interface (FFI) to execute Windows calls for the help system, registry, file utilities, mouse cursor, executing Windows programs, emulating keypresses, managing timers, and displaying the print dialog or file dialogs. This is specific to a Windows operating system and does not work on the Web.

- **F60UTIL**   This library provides a package with procedures to write records from a block to an HTML or ASCII text file.

- **WINHELP**   This library contains functions to call the Windows help system.

- *Various names*   There are a number of other .PLL files that support the reusable components for the demonstration help system, Navigator, Wizard, Calendar, Picklist, calls to Excel, Graphics, and drag-and-drop functions.

In addition to the code supplied by Oracle, you can incorporate shareware code that other Oracle users have written. Some online resources for Oracle users are described in Chapter 1. These sources provide tips and techniques that can become part of your library code. The rest of this appendix lists specifications from some of the major packages in a sample template PL/SQL library that is used to support a template system. The package body code is omitted for space reasons, but you can derive the calling syntax from the procedure and function specifications. In addition, the format of the package header has been truncated for brevity reasons from the standard that Chapter 3 suggests. Sample code is available from the publisher's and authors' web sites (see the author information for addresses).

The major packages described are listed here:

F_ALERT	F_BLOCK	F_CURSOR	F_FORM
F_GLOBAL	F_HELP	F_ITEM	F_MENU
F_MESSAGE	F_TOOLBAR	F_UTIL	F_WINDOW

Each package handles a specific object or system as indicated in the name. The F_ prefix denotes that the package is Forms code. References to packages that have an FCA_ prefix point to the application library file (not described here).

F_ALERT

This package gives examples of messages that are hard coded. As mentioned in Chapter 27, for a production system, you would probably place the message text in a database table or PL/SQL table variable in a package.

```
PACKAGE f_alert IS
/*******************************************************************************\
|| Description:
||    Procedures to display alerts. This system requires alerts to be created
||    in the form and named NOTE, STOP, and CAUTION. To do: Add a procedure
||    to set the alert title property from a global package variable set in
||    the startup procedures.
||
|| Usage:
||   MSG
||
||      This function displays a one, two, or three button alert with the
||      message text passed in as a parameter. The names of the buttons are
||      passed in as another parameter. The last, optional, parameter is
||      the name of the alert icon.
||
||      The return value is the name of the button pressed in uppercase.
||      A sample call would be (after declaring v_button as a VARCHAR2(20)):
||
||          v_button := f_alert.multi_button('Yes,No,Cancel',
||                      'Do you want to save before exiting?');
||          -- code here to test the value of v_button (YES, NO, CANCEL)
||
||   OK
||      This displays a single button alert with no return value.
||      The code will raise form trigger failure if the second parameter
||      is f_alert.g_fail. This is a procedure.
||
```

```
\****************************************************************************/
   g_caution_icon  CONSTANT VARCHAR2(10) := 'CAUTION';
   g_note_icon     CONSTANT VARCHAR2(10) := 'NOTE';
   g_stop_icon     CONSTANT VARCHAR2(10) := 'STOP';
   g_no_fail       CONSTANT VARCHAR2(10) := 'NOFAIL';
   g_fail          CONSTANT VARCHAR2(10) := 'FAIL';
   --
   PROCEDURE ok(
      p_msg           IN VARCHAR2 DEFAULT
                      'Message missing. Contact Administrator.',
      p_fail          IN VARCHAR2 DEFAULT g_no_fail,
      p_style         IN VARCHAR2 DEFAULT g_note_icon);
   --
   FUNCTION msg(
      p_button_names  IN VARCHAR2,
      p_msg           IN VARCHAR2 DEFAULT
                       'Message missing. Contact Administrator.',
      p_alert_style   IN VARCHAR2 DEFAULT g_caution_icon)
      RETURN VARCHAR2;
   --
END;
```

F_BLOCK

```
PACKAGE f_block IS
/****************************************************************************\
|| Description:
||    Procedures for block functionality.
||
|| Usage:
||    AUTO_QUERY
||       Does a go_block and execute_query. You are responsible for returning
||       the cursor to the starting point if you want.
||
||    CHECK_REQUIRED_ITEMS
||       Optionally called from WHEN-VALIDATE-ITEM trigger to validate that
||       all items in the list (f_global.g_required_items) have values. Set
||       all items' Required property to False and include the truly required
||       ones in this list.
||
||    DEFAULT_ALL
||       Called from the startup.initialize_form procedure in the form
||       to automatically visit each block in the list passed in through
||       the parameter or, by default, in the variable
||       f_global.g_auto_default_blocks set in the startup.pre_form
||       procedure. The action of moving the cursor to a block will
||       load the value of the property Initial Value into the item.
||
||    MOUSE_BLOCK
||       Return name of current mouse block.
||
||    ON_MESSAGE_QUERY_COUNT
||       This procedure should be called from the ON_MESSAGE trigger in the
||       queried block. If the query was executed with count_record or through
||       the 'query_with_count' procedure, it returns the number of records
```

```
||      retrieved from the query into p_item parameter.
||
||    QUERY_ALL
||      Called from the startup.initialize_form procedure to automatically
||      query blocks in the list stored in the variable
||      f_global.g_auto_query_blocks.
||
||    QUERY_NEXT_BLOCK
||      Executes a query on the next block in the navigation list.
||
||    QUERY_WITH_COUNT
||      This procedure replaces execute_query procedure in case you want to
||      capture the number of records retrieved by the query. This procedure
||      combined with the on_message_query_count procedure that is called from
||      ON_MESSAGE trigger in the relevant block will do the work.
||
||    QUIET_EXECUTE_QUERY
||      Executes a query without displaying the standard message. This, in
||      effect, suppresses the usual message that Forms displays if there
||      are no records retrieved.
||
||    SMART_DOWN
||      Moves the cursor down to a new record or the next record.
\*****************************************************************************/
   --
   PROCEDURE check_required_items
       (p_block_name    IN VARCHAR2 DEFAULT NULL);
   --
   PROCEDURE auto_query(
      p_blockname IN VARCHAR2);
   --
   PROCEDURE default_all(
      p_blocklist IN VARCHAR2 DEAFULT f_global.g_auto_default_blocks);
   --
   FUNCTION mouse_block RETURN varchar2;
   --
   PROCEDURE on_message_query_count(
      p_item IN VARCHAR2 DEFAULT NULL,
      p_concatenate_before IN VARCHAR2 DEFAULT NULL,
      p_concatenate_after IN VARCHAR2 DEFAULT NULL,
      p_show_other_messages IN BOOLEAN DEFAULT TRUE);
   --
   PROCEDURE query_all(
      p_blocklist IN VARCHAR2 DEFAULT f_global.g_auto_query_blocks);
   --
   PROCEDURE query_next_block;
   --
   PROCEDURE quiet_execute_query;
   --
   PROCEDURE query_with_count(
      p_quiet boolean := FALSE);
   --
   PROCEDURE smart_down(
      p_create_rec IN BOOLEAN DEFAULT TRUE,
      p_pop_last_rec_msg IN BOOLEAN DEFAULT TRUE);
    --
END;
```

F_CURSOR

```
PACKAGE f_cursor IS
/**************************************************************************\
|| Description:
||    Procedures that set or query the cursor shape. Developer 6 offers more
||    possibilities of cursor shapes. See the help system for details.
||
|| Usage:
||    CURSOR_DEFAULT
||       Sets cursor to normal arrow.
||
||    CURSOR_HELP
||       Sets cursor to question mark-arrow.
||
||    CURSOR_BUSY
||       Sets cursor to hourglass.
||
||    CURSOR_INSERTION
||       Sets cursor to I-beam.
||
||    CURSOR_CROSSHAIR
||       Sets cursor to cross.
||
||    SHAPE
||       Returns the name of the current cursor shape
||
\**************************************************************************/
    --
    g_cursor_shape      VARCHAR2(30) :=
                        get_application_property
                        (CURSOR_STYLE);
    g_default           CONSTANT VARCHAR2(10) := 'DEFAULT';
    g_help              CONSTANT VARCHAR2(10) := 'HELP';
    g_busy              CONSTANT VARCHAR2(10) := 'BUSY';
    g_insertion         CONSTANT VARCHAR2(10) := 'INSERTION';
    g_crosshair         CONSTANT VARCHAR2(10) := 'CROSSHAIR';
    --
    PROCEDURE cursor_default;
    --
    PROCEDURE cursor_help;
    --
    PROCEDURE cursor_busy;
    --
    PROCEDURE cursor_insertion;
    --
    PROCEDURE cursor_crosshair;
    --
    FUNCTION shape
       RETURN VARCHAR2;
    --
END;
```

F_FORM

```
PACKAGE f_form IS
/*****************************************************************************\
|| Description:
||    Procedures that affect the entire form module. Mainly used to call or
||    open other forms. To do: add a procedure to call OPEN_FORM or NEW_FORM
||    in a new database session. Remember the restrictions of a new session,
||    one of which is that the library data cannot be shared. See the help
||    system OPEN_FORM topic for further restrictions.
||
|| Usage:
||    CALLFORM
||       Calls one form from another. Shares the package variable values.
||
||    CALLFORM_QUERYONLY
||       Calls the form in query-only mode from another form.
||       Shares the package variable values.
||
||    CLOSE_CALLING_FORM
||       Called by startup routine to close calling form if there is a form
||       ID in the variable fca_global. g_calling_form_id. This variable
||       is set in the openform procedure.
||
||    NEWFORM
||       Opens a new form and closes the caller. The called form needs to run
||       the startup routines in FCA_STARTUP that will close the caller.
||       Shares the package variable values.
||
\*****************************************************************************/
   --
   PROCEDURE callform(
      p_form           IN VARCHAR2,
      p_param_string   IN VARCHAR2 DEFAULT NULL);
   --
   PROCEDURE callform_queryonly(
      p_form           IN VARCHAR2,
      p_param_string   IN VARCHAR2 DEFAULT NULL);
   --
   PROCEDURE close_calling_form;
   --
   PROCEDURE newform(
      p_form           IN VARCHAR2,
      p_param_string   IN VARCHAR2 DEFAULT NULL);
   --
END;
```

F_GLOBAL

```
PACKAGE f_global IS
/*****************************************************************************\
|| Description:
||    Variables and Constants used in various procedures. Individual comments
```

```
||    appear above each set of variables.
||
\*******************************************************************************/
    --
    -- Constants
    --
    g_query_mode           CONSTANT VARCHAR2(10) := 'QUERY';
    g_normal_mode          CONSTANT VARCHAR2(10) := 'NORMAL';
    g_no                   CONSTANT VARCHAR2(1) := 'N';
    g_yes                  CONSTANT VARCHAR2(1) := 'Y';
    -- For querying of list items.
    g_query_yes            CONSTANT VARCHAR2(3) := 'YES';
    g_query_no             CONSTANT VARCHAR2(2) := 'NO';
    --
    -- Global variables
    --
    g_visited_logon_form   VARCHAR2(1);
    --
    -- The calling FORM ID structure. Used by
    -- fca_util.openform and fca_util.close_calling_form.
    g_calling_form_id      FORMMODULE;
    --
    -- An indicator of whether we want to exit the application
    -- read in the fca_util.callform procedure.
    g_exit_application     VARCHAR2(1) := 'N';
    --
    -- Whether the form was called in query-only mode.
    g_call_query           BOOLEAN := FALSE;
    --
    g_long_varchar         VARCHAR2(2000);
    --
    -- Files
    --
    g_helpfile             VARCHAR2(500);
    g_help_formname        VARCHAR2(50) := 'HELPABT';
    g_formname             VARCHAR2(15) := get_application_property(
                           CURRENT_FORM_NAME);
    g_opsys                VARCHAR2(15) := get_application_property(
                           USER_INTERFACE);
    g_back_form            VARCHAR2(30);
    g_report_form          VARCHAR2(30);
    g_finder_form          VARCHAR2(30);
    g_sysdir_paramlist     PARAMLIST;
    --
    -- Windows and Canvases
    --
    g_mdi_win_title        VARCHAR2(80);
    g_toolbar_canvas       VARCHAR2(30) := 'TOOLBAR';
    g_query_va             VARCHAR2(30) := 'CANVAS_QUERY';
    g_normal_va            VARCHAR2(30) := 'CANVAS_MAIN';
    --
    -- Assign the alert title in the STARTUP package of each form
    g_alert_title   VARCHAR2(100);
    --
    -- Used for changing the color of canvases in query mode.
    -- Load this in the STARTUP.PRE_FORM for each form.
    g_form_canvases        VARCHAR2(2000);
    --
    -- Menu items
```

```
  --
  g_config_menuitem        VARCHAR2(61);
  g_enterquery_menuitem    VARCHAR2(61) := 'QUERY_MENU.ENTER';
  --
  -- Menu items that show conditionally
  g_show_menuitems         VARCHAR2(2000);
  --
  --  Items and buttons
  --
  -- A list of items to check for values when leaving a record.
  g_required_items         VARCHAR2(2000);
  g_toolbar_tip            VARCHAR2(61) := 'TOOLBAR.HINT';
  --
  -- A list of item:record group names to populate when form starts.
  g_auto_query_lists       VARCHAR2(2000);
  --
  -- These change icons depending on the mode.
  g_enterquery_item        VARCHAR2(61) := 'TOOLBAR.QUERY_FIND';
  --
  -- Buttons that show conditionally.
  g_show_buttons           VARCHAR2(2000);
  --
  --
  -- Item to return to from another window or block.
  g_return_item    VARCHAR2(61);
  --
  -- Blocks
  --
  g_toolbar_block          VARCHAR2(30) := 'TOOLBAR';
  g_auto_query_blocks      VARCHAR2(1000);
  g_auto_default_blocks    VARCHAR2(1000);
  --
  -- Icon files
  --
  -- For the Enter/Execute Query toolbar button.
  g_enter_query_icon       VARCHAR2(20) := 'enterqry';
  g_execute_query_icon     VARCHAR2(20) := 'execqry';
  --
  -- Help-About
  --
  g_form_version           VARCHAR2(10);
  g_form_description       VARCHAR2(60);
  g_form_author            VARCHAR2(60);
  g_form_message           VARCHAR2(60);
  --
  --  Valid do_key built-ins.
  --
  g_dokey_functions          CONSTANT VARCHAR2(2000) :=
        'ABORT_QUERY,BLOCK_MENU,CLEAR_BLOCK,'||
        'CLEAR_FORM,CLEAR_RECORD,COMMIT_FORM,'||
        'COUNT_QUERY,CREATE_RECORD,DELETE_RECORD,DOWN,'||
        'DUPLICATE_ITEM,DUPLICATE_RECORD,EDIT_TEXTITEM,'||
        'ENTER,ENTER_QUERY,EXECUTE_QUERY,EXIT_FORM,HELP,'||
        'LIST_VALUES,LOCK_RECORD,NEXT_BLOCK,NEXT_ITEM,'||
        'NEXT_KEY,NEXT_RECORD,NEXT_SET,PREVIOUS_BLOCK,'||
        'PREVIOUS_ITEM,PREVIOUS_RECORD,PRINT,SCROLL_DOWN,'||
        'SCROLL_UP,UP,';
  --
END;
```

F_HELP

```
PACKAGE f_help IS
/*****************************************************************************\
|| Description:
||    Procedures to apply to the Help system. This help system implements a
||    help window that queries the help table based on the name of the window
||    that the cursor is in.
||
|| Usage:
||    HELP_ABOUT
||       Call help about form and pass it the version number and 2 messages.
||       The final help about box will have the following format:
||          1. Form name, version number
||          2. Description of program
||          3. Author
||          4. User name
||          5. Date
||
||    HIDE_HELP
||       Removes the help window and restores the cursor to its original
||       location. Assumes there is a DUMMY block with NULL_ITEM in it.
||       In case the return item does not exist, the cursor returns to
||       DUMMY.NULL_ITEM.
||
||    SHOW_HELP
||       Displays the help window and saves the cursor location. The help is
||       queried from the database into the HELP block. There is an ability
||       to provide item-level help although this implementation uses
||       window-level help. See comments in the body. The optional parameter
||       signals whether the show keys window should be shown after the
||       help window is hidden (as the result of a button click in the help
||       window). The parameters are the form name and the window name that will
||       be used to find the help row in the help table.
||
\*****************************************************************************/
   --
   g_help_return_item    VARCHAR2(61);
   --
   PROCEDURE help_about(
     p_version         VARCHAR2 DEFAULT '1.0',
     p_description     VARCHAR2 DEFAULT null,
     p_author          VARCHAR2 DEFAULT null,
     p_message         VARCHAR2 DEFAULT 'XXX');
   --
   PROCEDURE hide_help(
     p_show_keys       VARCHAR2 DEFAULT 'NO_SHOW_KEYS');
   --
   PROCEDURE show_help(
     p_form      VARCHAR2 DEFAULT NULL,
     p_block     VARCHAR2 DEFAULT NULL,
     p_item      VARCHAR2 DEFAULT NULL,
     p_window    VARCHAR2 DEFAULT NULL);
   --
END;
```

F_ITEM

```
PACKAGE f_item IS
/***************************************************************************\
|| Description:
||    Procedures that affect individual items (buttons, text items, list
||    items). All issue a message if the item is not found. The parameter is
||    the item name.
||
|| Usage:
||    ACCESS_KEY
||       Moves the cursor to an item of the same name without the _PB
||       suffix. This implements the Access Key property for text items.
||       Create a button in the same block as the text item and subclass
||       the ACCESS_KEY_BUTTON button from the object library. Name the
||       button the same as the item and add a _PB suffix.
||
||    DISABLE
||       Disable the item.
||
||    ENABLE
||       Enable the item. Optionally make the item updateable at the same time.
||
||    HIDE
||       Hide the item.
||
||    LABEL_TEXT
||       Returns the label of the item. Checks to see if it exists and
||       if it is a button or check box.
||
||    SETUP_ALL_LISTS
||       Run setup_list for each item:record group in a list
||       (f_global.g_auto_query_lists).
||
||    SETUP_IMAGE_ITEMS
||       Called from WNFI trigger to load all image items in the specified
||       block with images of the specified type. The default type is GIF.
||       The file names are the names of the items without the trailing
||       "_NN" where "NN" is a number. The default block name is IMAGES.
||       For example, you can have an IMAGES block with LOGO_01 and LOGO_02
||       images items. These will be loaded with a single call to this
||       procedure. The file name loaded will be logo.gif. The parameters are
||       the block name (with a default of IMAGES), graphics file type
||       (default is GIF), and the graphics file extension (default gif).
||
||    RELABEL
||       Change the label for buttons and check boxes.
||
||    SETUP_LIST
||       Populate a list item from a record group. The parameters are the
||       record group name, the item name, and, optionally, whether or not
||       to perform the query again (if this is called more than once in
||       the same form and the data may have changed in between calls). Use
||       the f_global.g_query_yes and f_global.g_query_no package variables
||       to represent "Yes" and "No." The default is to requery.
||
```

```
||    SHOW
||       Show the item (and alternatively enable it). The parameters are the
||       item name and, optionally, if you want to enable it (use the
||       f_global.g_yes and f_global.g_no variables as values. The default is
||       f_global.no.
||
\******************************************************************************/
   --
   PROCEDURE access_key;
   --
   PROCEDURE disable(
      p_item_name IN VARCHAR2);
   --
   PROCEDURE enable(
      p_item_name  IN VARCHAR2,
      p_updateable IN VARCHAR2 DEFAULT 'N');
   --
   PROCEDURE hide(
      p_item_name IN VARCHAR2);
   --
   FUNCTION label_text(
      p_item_name IN VARCHAR2)
      RETURN VARCHAR2;
   --
   PROCEDURE relabel(
      p_item_name IN VARCHAR2,
      p_new_label IN VARCHAR2);
   --
   PROCEDURE setup_image_items(
      p_block     IN VARCHAR2 DEFAULT 'IMAGES',
      p_type      IN VARCHAR2 DEFAULT 'GIF',
      p_extension IN VARCHAR2 DEFAULT 'gif');
   --
   PROCEDURE setup_list(
      p_record_group   IN VARCHAR2,
      p_item_name      IN VARCHAR2,
      p_perform_query  IN VARCHAR2 DEFAULT f_global.g_query_yes);
   --
   PROCEDURE setup_all_lists(
      p_itemlist       IN VARCHAR2 DEFAULT f_global.g_auto_query_lists,
      p_perform_query  IN VARCHAR2 DEFAULT f_global.g_query_yes);
   --
   PROCEDURE show(
      p_item_name IN VARCHAR2,
      p_enabled   IN VARCHAR2 DEFAULT f_global.g_yes);
   --
END;
```

F_MENU

```
PACKAGE f_menu IS
/******************************************************************************\
|| Description:
||    Procedures that affect individual menu items.
||
```

```
|| Usage:
||    CHECK_ITEM
||       Apply a check to a check menu item. First syntax uses ID and second
||       syntax uses name.
||
||    DISABLE
||       Disable the menu item.
||
||    ENABLE
||       Enable the menu item.
||
||    HIDE
||       Hide the menu item.
||
||    IS_CHECKED
||       Return BOOLEAN True if the menu item is checked, False if not checked.
||
||    NORMAL_MODE
||       Turns on and off items in the toolbar for normal mode.
||
||    QUERY_MODE
||       Turns on and off items in the toolbar for query mode.
||
||    RELABEL
||       Change the label on the menu item. Overloaded to take menu item ID
||       or menu item name.
||
||    SHOW
||       Display the menu item (if hidden).
||
||    UNCHECK_ITEM
||       Unapply a check to a check menu item. First syntax uses ID and second
||       syntax uses name.
||
\****************************************************************************/
   -- store the Query menu name
   g_querymenu_name    VARCHAR2(30) := 'QUERY';
   --
   PROCEDURE check_item(
      p_menuid    IN MENUITEM);
   --
   PROCEDURE check_item(
      p_menuitem_name    IN VARCHAR2);
   --
   PROCEDURE disable(
      p_menuitem_name IN VARCHAR2,
      p_fail_msg       IN VARCHAR2 DEFAULT 'MSG');
   --
   PROCEDURE enable(
      p_menuitem_name IN VARCHAR2);
   --
   PROCEDURE hide(
      p_menuitem_name IN VARCHAR2,
      p_fail_msg       IN VARCHAR2 DEFAULT 'MSG');
   --
   FUNCTION is_checked(
      p_menuitem_name IN VARCHAR2)
      RETURN BOOLEAN;
```

```
   --
   PROCEDURE normal_mode;
   --
   PROCEDURE relabel(
      p_menuitem_name IN VARCHAR2,
      p_new_label     IN VARCHAR2);
   --
   PROCEDURE relabel(
      p_menuitem_id IN MENUITEM,
      p_new_label   IN VARCHAR2);
   --
   PROCEDURE query_mode;
   --
   PROCEDURE show(
      p_menuitem_name IN VARCHAR2);
   --
   PROCEDURE uncheck_item(
      p_menuid   IN MENUITEM);
   --
   PROCEDURE uncheck_item(
      p_menuitem_name   IN VARCHAR2);
   --
END;
```

F_MESSAGE

```
PACKAGE f_message IS
/****************************************************************************\
|| Description:
||    Procedures that manage the message item at the bottom of the canvas. This
||    system requires the objects in SUBCLASS_MESSAGE_SYSTEM to be subclassed
||    into the form.
||
|| Usage:
||    CLEAR_MESSAGE
||       Write a null string into the item.
||
||    WRITE_MESSAGE
||       Write the message passed in into the item. Optional parameter allows
||       a trigger failure if 'FAIL' is passed in (default is 'NOFAIL').
||
\****************************************************************************/

   g_message_item   VARCHAR2(61) := 'MESSAGE.MSG_MAIN';
   --
   PROCEDURE clear_message;
   --
   PROCEDURE write_message(
      p_message   IN  VARCHAR2 DEFAULT NULL,
      p_fail      IN  VARCHAR2 DEFAULT 'NOFAIL');
   --
END;
```

F_TOOLBAR

```
PACKAGE f_toolbar IS
/******************************************************************************\
|| Description:
||    Procedures that contain standard code for toolbar (and menu) actions.
||    This code is called from the form-level KEY- triggers that are subclassed
||    from the object library.
||
|| Usage:
||    BUTTON_PRESSED
||       Calls the key trigger associated with the button
||       or executes a user-named trigger based on the toolbar
||       button pressed.
||
||       If the key trigger is called, the control passes from
||       that trigger back to the TOOLBAR package's specific
||       procedure. That TOOLBAR procedure calls a KEY_ procedure
||       listed below.
||    HIDE_HINT
||       Hide the hint shown in the last built-in. Called from
||       WHEN-MOUSE-UP trigger on toolbar block.
||
||    KEY_ procedures
||       Called when the corresponding toolbar button (or menu
||       item) is activated:
||          BACK, CANCEL, COMMIT, CLEAR_FORM, COUNT_QUERY, CREREC, DELREC,
||          DISPLAY_ERROR, DUPREC, EDIT_ITEM, ENTQRY, EXEQRY, PRINT
||          EXIT - has parameters to be used for the standard Forms
||                 constants for the exit_form built-in.
||
||    SHOW_HINT
||       From a right-click mouse button, this displays the hint for the button.
||       Web-deployed forms use this because they can't use the DLL package normally
||       supplied for this.
||
\******************************************************************************/
   PROCEDURE button_pressed;
   --
   PROCEDURE hide_hint;
   --
   PROCEDURE help_about;
   --
   PROCEDURE key_back;
   --
   PROCEDURE key_cancel;
   --
   PROCEDURE key_clear_form;
   --
   PROCEDURE key_commit;
   --
   PROCEDURE key_count_query;
   --
```

```
    PROCEDURE key_crerec;
    --
    PROCEDURE key_delrec;
    --
    PROCEDURE key_display_error;
    --
    PROCEDURE key_duprec;
    --
    PROCEDURE key_edit_item;
    --
    PROCEDURE key_entqry;
    --
    PROCEDURE key_exeqry;
    --
    PROCEDURE key_exit(
       p_commit_mode  IN NUMBER DEFAULT ASK_COMMIT);
    --
    PROCEDURE key_print;
    --
    PROCEDURE last_criteria;
    --
    PROCEDURE show_hint;
    --
END;
```

F_UTIL

```
PACKAGE f_util IS
/*****************************************************************************\
|| Description:
||    Utility procedures and functions that support the general functions of
||    the template form.
||
|| Usage:
||    BLOCK_NAME_ONLY
||       Extracts the block name from a string containing the item and block
||       names.
||
||    CHANGE_MODE
||       Toggles the toolbar, menu, and canvases between ENTER-QUERY mode
||       and NORMAL mode. Relies on list variables being loaded with the
||       names and functions of the buttons and menu items. The values
||       are loaded in the WHEN-NEW-FORM-INSTANCE trigger.
||
||    CHECK_PACKAGE_FAILURE
||       Call this to check for Form Failure after a built in. Raises
||       form trigger failure.
||
||    COMMIT_SUCCEED
||       Returns TRUE if the global.commit_succeed variable is set to 'Y' and
||       returns FALSE otherwise.
||
||    CREATE_SYS_PARAM
||       Create parameter list with system directory name and subdirectory name.
||       Returns the paramlist ID that is assigned in the
```

```
||       STARTUP.PRE_FORM procedure.
||
||    ITEM_NAME_ONLY
||       Extracts the item name from a string containing the item and block
||       names.
||
||    LAST_QUERY_WHERE
||       Function that returns the WHERE clause of the last query (up to 2000
||       characters).
||
||    MOUSE_DOUBLE_CLICK
||       Displays the editor if the item is a text item.
||
||    ON_ERROR
||       Called from ON-ERROR trigger to show error text.
||
||    ON_MESSAGE
||       Called from ON-MESSAGE trigger to show message text.
||
||    PARSE_THREE
||       Divides the string into three. "Gallia est omnis divisa in partes tres."
||
||    PARSE_TWO
||       Divide a string into two parts.
||
||    QUIET_COMMIT
||       Commit the form without a message.
||
||    QUIET_EXECUTE_QUERY
||       Query the form without messages (specifically the one that appears when
||       there is no data returned).
||
||    QUIET_EXIT
||       Exit the form without messages.
||
||    REPEAT_CHAR
||       Create a string of the same character (or characters).
||
||    SETUP_HELP_MENU
||       Disables the help menu items that call files that are not available
||       on the Web.
||
||    SET_CURRENT_RECORD_VA
||       Set the current record attribute for items in all multirecord blocks.
||
||    SET_LOV_BUTTONS
||       Work around a bug in Designer Forms Generator to make all LOV buttons
||       non-navigable.
||
||    SHOW_FORM_KEYS
||       Called from local UTIL procedure to form to display the key list.
||
||    SORT_BUTTON_PRESSED
||       Called from the sort button at top of each item in a
||       multirecord block. This re-sorts the block in ascending
||       or descending order (alternating).
||
||       Assumes the data block is built on a table or view
```

```
||        and that the columns being sorted have the same names as columns in the
||        table or view
||
||        This re-sorts the block and positions the cursor at the top record in
||        the new sort order. If you need to keep the cursor position at the
||        current record, you can supplement this code with the following:
||            1. Storing the primary key value of the record that the cursor is
||               in before sorting. Place this in a package variable.
||            2. Reset a flag variable (Y or N) in a package to indicate that the
||               value has not been matched.
||            3. In the block's POST-QUERY trigger, if the flag variable indicates
||               that there is no match, check the primary key value of the record
||               retrieved with the stored package variable value.
||            4. If it matches, store the record number and reset the flag
||               variable.
||            5. After the query, move the cursor to the record number stored.
||               This means that you have to retrieve all records so you are
||               certain that the record you are matching is available.
||
||        Requirements:
||            1. Heading button block called
||                   CCCC_HDR
||               where CCCC is the data block name.
||            2. Heading buttons called the same name as the item they are sorting.
||            3. Buttons are smartclassed from object library object to inherit
||               the correct property values.
||
||   SUPER_TRIM
||      Strips off leading and trailing tabs, line feeds, and spaces.
||
\*****************************************************************************/
   FUNCTION block_name_only(
      p_block_item_name    VARCHAR2)
      RETURN VARCHAR2;
   --
   PROCEDURE change_mode(
      p_mode   IN VARCHAR2);
   --
   PROCEDURE check_package_failure(
      p_msg  IN VARCHAR2 DEFAULT NULL);
   --
   FUNCTION create_sys_param(
      p_in_sysdir IN VARCHAR2,
      p_in_subdir IN VARCHAR2)
      RETURN PARAMLIST;
   --
   FUNCTION item_name_only(
      p_block_item_name    VARCHAR2)
      RETURN VARCHAR2;
   --
   FUNCTION last_query_where
      RETURN VARCHAR2;
   --
   PROCEDURE mouse_double_click;
   --
   PROCEDURE on_error;
   --
   PROCEDURE on_message;
```

```
--
PROCEDURE parse_two(
   p_full      IN VARCHAR2,
   p_first     IN OUT VARCHAR2,
   p_second    IN OUT VARCHAR2,
   p_delimiter IN VARCHAR2 DEFAULT ',');
--
PROCEDURE parse_three(
   p_full      IN VARCHAR2,
   p_first     IN OUT VARCHAR2,
   p_second    IN OUT VARCHAR2,
   p_third     IN OUT VARCHAR2,
   p_delimiter IN VARCHAR2 DEFAULT ',');
--
PROCEDURE quiet_commit(
   p_fail  IN VARCHAR2 DEFAULT 'FAIL');
--
FUNCTION commit_succeed RETURN BOOLEAN;
--
PROCEDURE set_lov_buttons;
--
PROCEDURE set_current_record_va;
--
PROCEDURE sort_button_pressed(
   p_extra_sort_column   VARCHAR2 DEFAULT NULL);
--
PROCEDURE quiet_exit;
--
FUNCTION repeat_char(
   p_num   IN NUMBER,
   p_char  IN VARCHAR2)
   RETURN VARCHAR2;
--
PROCEDURE setup_help_menu;
--
PROCEDURE show_formkeys;
--
FUNCTION super_trim (
   p_string_in VARCHAR2)
   RETURN VARCHAR2;
--
PROCEDURE quiet_execute_query;
--
END;
```

F_WINDOW

```
PACKAGE f_window IS
/********************************************************************************\
|| Description:
||     Procedures to manage Forms windows.
||
|| Usage:
||     MAX_THE_WINDOW
||         Expands the outer MDI frame or other window to the maximum size
```

```
||      set in the procedure.
||
||    CENTER_IT
||       Centers the window.
||
\*****************************************************************************/
   PROCEDURE max_the_window(
      p_window_name VARCHAR2);
   --
   PROCEDURE center_it(
      p_win      VARCHAR2,
      p_winstyle VARCHAR2 DEFAULT 'DOCUMENT',
      p_console  BOOLEAN DEFAULT TRUE);
   --
END;
```

APPENDIX
B

Interview Questions

he following is a list of the questions from Chapter 23 without the answers, so you can test yourself.

Forms Questions

The following questions test your knowledge of the Forms component of Oracle Developer.

Forms Beginner Questions (5 points each)

1. In building a form, you forgot to add the scroll bar when you created the block using the Block Wizard. How can you add it now?

2. You want to create a multirecord block with overflow items at the bottom, as shown next. All these items are in the same block. How do you make some items appear multiple times and others only once?

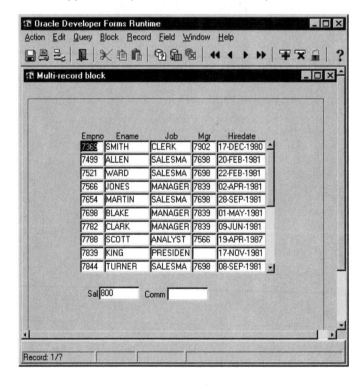

3. When you created a block using the Block Wizard, you forgot to attach it to its parent block. How do you add a parent-child relationship to two blocks that already exist?

4. You want to create a poplist or LOV to show a list of Departments from the database. What are the steps necessary to do this?

5. You want to display the list of employees in a block and show the name of the department each employee belongs to, as shown next. How can this be accomplished if you also want to allow INSERT, UPDATE, and DELETE on the records?

6. You left out one of the five date items in your block. The block has been laid out with triggers included, so you do not want to delete it. List the steps necessary to add an item to the block.

7. When the user clicks on the Save button, you want an "Are you sure?" message to pop up where the user can select "Yes" or "No." What are the steps necessary to accomplish this?

8. You have the following POST-QUERY trigger code in your form:

```
DECLARE
    CURSOR c_avg_sal_nr
    IS
        SELECT  avg(sal)
        FROM    emp
        WHERE   deptno = :dept.deptno;
BEGIN
    OPEN c_avg_sal_nr;
    FETCH c_avg_sal_nr INTO :dept.avg_sal_nr;
    CLOSE c_avg_sal_nr;
END;
```

You want to move the function with the cursor to the database. How would you rewrite the code to do this?

9. You want all the dates in all your forms to use the same format mask, DD-MON-YYYY. What is the best way to do this?

10. When your form opens, you want a block such as EMP to query automatically. How can you do this?

Forms Intermediate Questions (10 points each)

1. You want users to be able to type in an Employee ID. If the Employee ID is valid, it should automatically populate an adjacent item with the name of the employee. If the ID is not valid, the user should get an error message. How do you accomplish this?

2. In the previous question, you were asked about giving the user the capability of typing in an ID and returning the name of an employee. You want to use this same functionality in many places in different forms throughout the application. What is the best way to make this functionality available to other forms?

3. In a multi-tab application with a master block on the first tab and different detail blocks on each of the other tabs, when you query the first block, it takes a long time because you are also querying all of the child blocks. How can you prevent querying of the child blocks and only do so when individual tabs are selected?

4. You have a multirecord Employee block and a poplist to select a Department so that only employees in that department are shown, as seen next. How can you do this?

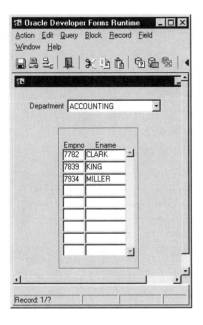

5. A junior programmer created some required items in your form by setting the *Required* property to "Yes" in the Data section of the Property Palettes for each item. Users complain that as soon as they click in the item, they cannot move the cursor without entering something. The junior programmer changes the *Required* property setting to "No." Now when users try to leave or save the form without entering something in the formerly required items, they get the error message "Form 40508 ORACLE error: unable to INSERT record." What is a more user-friendly way to support required items in Oracle Forms?

Forms Advanced Questions (20 points each)

1. Your form has a multirecord block used to select employees as shown next. In the first item, you select a department. Once a department has been selected, you can select employees in the second item. How can you build your form so that once a department is selected in the first item, users will only be able to see employees from the selected department in the second item? (Hint: The objects that look like poplists are really items with buttons next to them that display LOVs.)

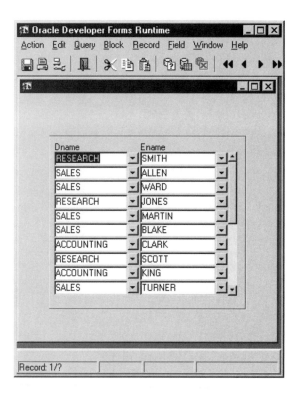

2. You want to create a multitab canvas and also include subtabs. How can this be accomplished?

3. Junior developers approach you with the following problem: They are trying to create a stacked canvas with some items on it. They have used the SHOW_VIEW command to make the stacked canvas appear. When the form is run, the canvas appears and quickly disappears. What is wrong and how can it be fixed?

4. This question assumes you are using a LOCATION table in addition to the EMP and DEPT tables. You want to be able to select a location in a poplist and only see employees at that location, as shown next. Note that there is no Location ID in the EMP table. How can this be accomplished?

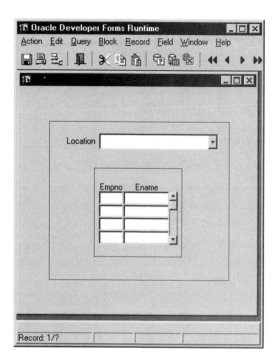

5. You have a form where you want to select a Person from a list activated by a button (as if in an LOV). The database contains a few hundred thousand names so that scrolling through a list of names is not a viable option. You need to use a separate locator window with some selection criteria to help find a specific person. This same functionality will be required in multiple forms.

   a. Should you create this functionality as a form or as a locator object group in an object library?

   b. How would you accomplish this using the selected strategy?

   c. What are the pros and cons of each strategy?

Reports Questions

The following questions test your knowledge of the Reports component of Oracle Developer.

Reports Beginner Questions (5 points each)

All questions in this section refer to the following report: Using Oracle's sample tables in the Scott schema, create a master-detail report showing the names of the departments and the names of employees in each department. Departments should be listed even if they have no employees.

1. Write the SQL query for this report.

   a. On paper, draw the Data Model and groups for the report.

   b. If you were to use the Report Wizard to generate a default layout, how would it look? Draw the frames and place the report objects, labels, and data fields in each frame, where appropriate.

2. For each frame in the Layout Model, what would be the settings for the *Vertical Elasticity* and *Horizontal Elasticity* properties and the repeating direction for the repeating frames?

3. Each department must start on a new page. How can this be accomplished?

4. Rather than have each department listing start on a new page, how can you create a 1-inch separation between each department?

5. You want to display total compensation (salary and commission). How can you modify the existing report to support this?

6. Page numbers must appear in the upper-right corner of each page of the report. How can you make a page number appear in the upper-right corner of the report without using the Report Wizard?

7. You run the report and the page number only appears on the first page of the report. How can this be fixed?

8. A report that has been successfully running has to have a field added. After you add the field, running the report generates an error message that "The xxx field references a column xxx at a frequency below its group." What happened and how can you fix the problem?

9. You want to use a DD-MM-YYYY format for displaying HIREDATE (for example, 17-JAN-1999). How can this be accomplished?

10. You need to create a report-level summary showing the total number of employees in the whole organization with no department-level summaries. How can this be accomplished?

Reports Intermediate Questions (10 points each)

1. In the sample report, if the name of the department appears at the bottom of the page and there is no room for even one employee (an orphaned department header), how can you make the department header move to the beginning of the next page?

2. You want to write a report listing the names of employees from a particular department by passing this information from Oracle Forms. How can this be done?

3. Two independent sets of information need to be displayed on the same page. For example, show all the departments on the top and employees on the bottom, as shown next. What is the process required to accomplish this?

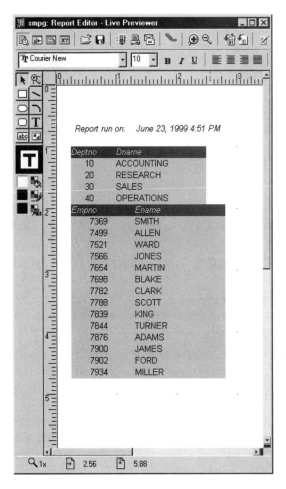

4. You have a report with three independent parts. You want each part to start on a new page. How can you accomplish this?

5. Draw the Data Model and Layout Model to support a basic matrix report where the rows are departments, the columns are locations, and each cell contains a count of employees, as shown next.

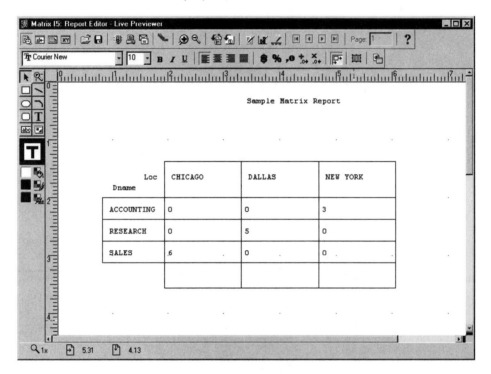

Reports Advanced Questions (20 points each)

1. You need to create a report that is a master with two independent details. For example, a Project may be associated with People and Equipment. What would the Data Model and Layout Model for this report look like?

2. You want to create a report that returns the top *N* Employees (*N* is a parameter passed to the report). How do you do this?

3. You want to start a report on a page other than "1." How can you do this?

4. For the report data model shown in the following illustration and data shown in the database tables below, what is the required SQL query? What does the report Data Model look like? Assume reasonable attributes for the entities.

Question 4–Data Model

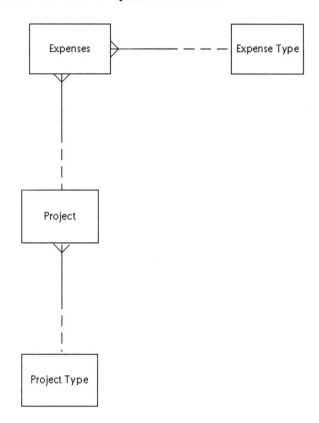

Question 4 Database Tables

Big Projects

Exp Type	Total Amt
People	$10,000
Equipment	$20,000
Misc.	$5,000

Little Projects

Exp Type	Total Amt
People	$5,000
Equipment	$7,000
Misc.	$2,000

5. You want to create a one-page report that folds horizontally in the middle so that the top half of the page is right side up and the bottom half is upside down, as shown next. How can this be done in Reports?

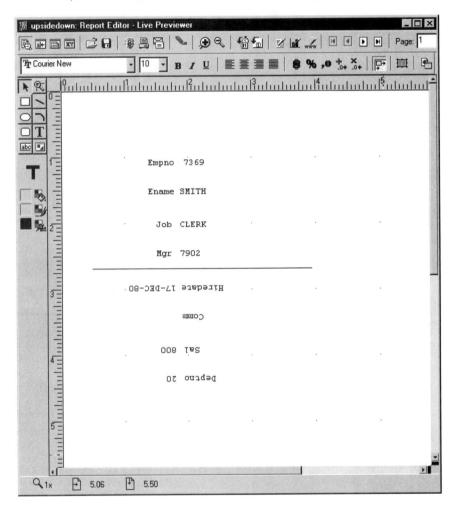

APPENDIX C

WinHelp Concepts

hapter 14 explains how to incorporate help systems into your Forms applications. There are some basic concepts you will need to understand if you decide to use the WinHelp method for help in your forms. In addition to online forums and conferences, WinHelp developers have their own culture that has a particular set of terms. In this case, the terms describe various components of help files: *topic, keyword, context string, hotspot text,* and *hotspot graphic.*

CAUTION
As mentioned in Chapter 14, the WinHelp style of help is not appropriate for web-deployed forms because it uses a Windows API function that displays in the runtime environment. For web-deployed forms, the runtime environment is the Forms Server tier, not the client.

Topic

There is no real concept of a "page" in the help system because help text appears in a window, which allows you to scroll text up and down. Instead of the page, the basic unit in the help system is the *topic,* which can be of any reasonable size. The topic can have a *browse sequence* defined for it so that it can follow and precede other topics. You can browse through topics by pressing the "<<" (previous) and ">>" (next) buttons in the WinHelp toolbar. You can define one topic to be the "Contents Topic" that acts as the launchpad or index so the user can easily navigate to other topics. In this way, the contents topic works like a main menu to the other topics. Alternatively, you can use the Contents tab to display a hierarchical structure of headings (displayed as a book icon) and topics (displayed as a page icon). Figure C-1 shows a Contents tab with headings and topics.

Keyword

When you create the help file, you specify *keywords* that the help system associates with each topic. These keywords display in the Index tab and act as locators for the topics. This means that you can call WinHelp, pass it the help file name and the keyword, and the WinHelp engine will jump to and display the topic for that keyword. This mechanism supplies context sensitivity.

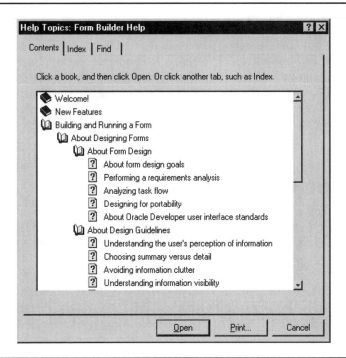

FIGURE C-1.   *Help Contents tab with headings and topics*

Context String

The topic has a *context string* word associated with it that the help file uses internally as a target for a hypertext jump. The topic also has context ID numbers that you can associate with the context strings. Usually there is a file with an .HH extension that contains the mapping of context strings to IDs. The help compiler and programming language compiler normally use this to embed references to a spot in the help file. While Oracle Developer Forms is not a program that can use the .HH file, you can pass the context ID numbers from Forms into WinHelp to create a jump to the topic. You could also write calls to the TEXT_IO Forms package to read the .HH file dynamically and pass the appropriate context string to WinHelp.

Hotspot Text

You can embed in your help topic specially defined text that will appear in a different color (for example, green instead of the normal black). This text is called a *hotspot* and supplies the hypertext feature. The hotspot has a single context string associated with it. When the user clicks on the text, the topic associated with the context string will appear. This makes reading the help file a nonlinear and more intuitive process. It also puts more demands on the help-file author to think of these links while writing the topics.

Hotspot Graphic

Help files are capable of storing bitmapped (.BMP) graphics files internally and displaying them as part of the help file. You need to have an external file initially, but when you compile the help file, the graphic will be stored within the file and is not needed at runtime. The graphics can have hotspots defined for them using the program Shed (Segmented Hypergraphics Editor) supplied by the help-authoring tool or software development kit. This editor lets you define areas on the graphic that reference context strings. You save the graphic as an .SHG file and include it in the compiled help file. The user can click on the area you defined in the graphic, and WinHelp will find the topic associated with the referenced context string. Anyone familiar with web browsers will surely be familiar with this operation.

Other Help Concepts

There are other terms the help system uses to identify its objects:

- **Secondary window**   A window that appears along with the opening help window.

- **Popup**   A topic or part of a topic that appears in another smaller "canvas" on top of the main topic.

- **Glossary**   A topic made up of a list of other topics where each topic listed is a hotspot link to the applicable topic. Clicking on a topic link in the glossary will either display a popup with the topic or show the topic in a window.

- **Macro**   A WinHelp command that performs tasks within the help engine like Next and Previous topic. Macros can be executed from button clicks or hotspot links.

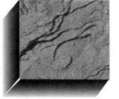

APPENDIX
D

Stepping Through the Report Wizard

he Report Wizard, which first appeared in Reports 3.0, serves two functions. First, it makes it possible for novice developers to create reports that can be modified or extended by an experienced Reports developer. Second, coupled with templates, it can be used to greatly increase the productivity of a Reports developer. Even for complex reports, roughly 50–80 percent of the time spent with the Reports product should be spent using the Report Wizard rather than working directly with the Data Model or Layout Model. The Report Wizard is an extraordinarily powerful feature that can virtually eliminate many of the tedious, manual modifications required to create production reports in earlier versions of the product.

This appendix will provide an overview of the specific features of the Report Wizard. To access the Report Wizard, select **Tools→Report Wizard** or click the Wizard icon.

Style Tab

The Style tab of the Report Wizard is shown here. On the Style tab, you can choose among eight report styles. These report styles govern the overall layout of the report. Depending upon the style chosen, the other Report Wizard tab choices will change to include items relevant to a particular report style. For example, choosing the Matrix with Group style will bring up tabs for Rows, Columns, and Cell that are not available with other style choices.

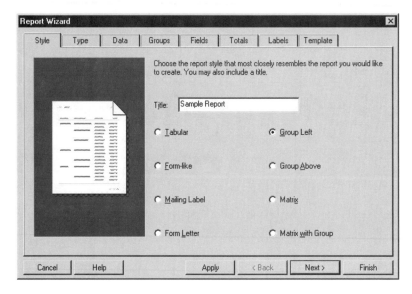

Descriptions of several of these styles follow:

■ **Tabular**   This is a standard columnar report, as shown next, with labels at the tops of columns, which are repeated on every page. If you use summaries, they will appear only at the bottom of the entire report. You cannot specify break groups with a tabular report.

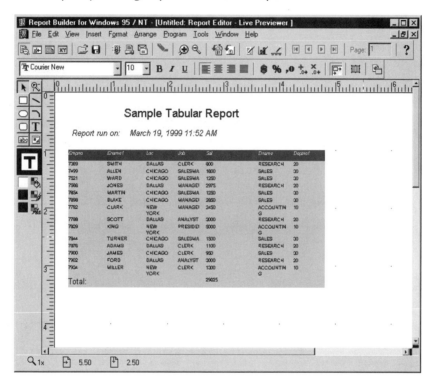

■ **Form-like**   This style option produces a report with a single record per page and data displayed going left to right, top to bottom, as shown next. This style almost never generates a useful report without being modified. If you want to build a report with a form-like style, you will need to modify by hand the report generated by the Report Wizard.

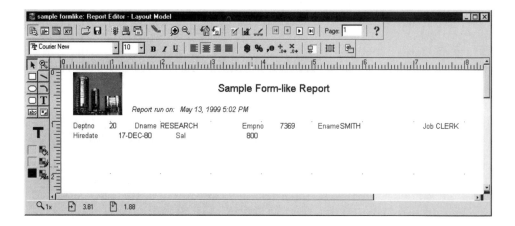

■ **Mailing Label** An example of a mailing label report is shown next. You can specify the font for your mailing labels by creating a special mailing label template. Be aware that the U.S. Postal Service requires mailing label fonts to be at least 8 points (10–12 points recommended), and other countries are likely to have similar restrictions.

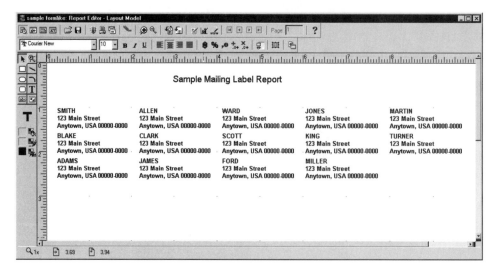

■ **Form Letter** This is used to generate a standard word processing mail-merge file. In this case, the Report Wizard appropriately places one record on each page, which corresponds to the standard that many word processors expect.

■ **Group Left/Group Above**   These types are used for Master-detail reports. In both cases, you can specify multiple break groups. If you specify a summary, the summary will print one time for each group as well as for the whole report. Group Left prints the break groups to the left with the data on the right. Group Above generates a report with the break groups appearing in order above the detail data. These are common kinds of reports. An example is shown here.

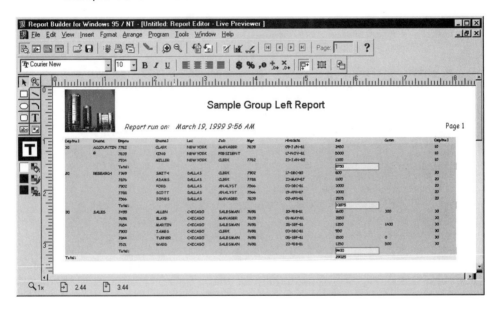

■ **Matrix**   This powerful report type is used for making standard cross-tab reports, as shown next. A *matrix* (cross-tab) report contains a row of labels, a column of labels, and information in a grid format related to the row and column labels. You need at least four groups to create a matrix report: one group must be a cross-product group, two of the groups must be within the cross-product group to furnish the "labels," and a fourth group provides the information for each cell. The groups can belong to a single query or to multiple queries. Matrix reports require special actions in both the Data Model and Layout Model, which will be discussed in the Reports Intermediate Question 5 in Chapter 23.

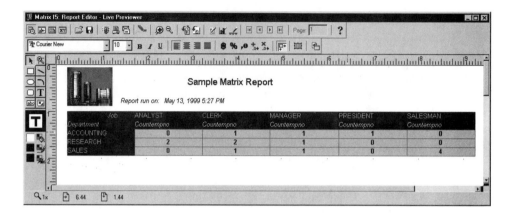

- ■ **Matrix with Group**   This is a special Master-detail report where the detail portion of the report is a matrix.

This by no means exhausts all the types of reports you can build with Reports, but is merely a list of the ones that can be generated automatically.

NOTE
You can use or combine these report types to create complex reports, but you cannot create new report types.

You can customize the report fonts and other properties using templates, but you cannot modify the core functionality of a report type. In this way, the report type specifies the way that the Data Model will be translated to a layout.

Type Tab

This is a new feature in the Report Wizard. It allows you to select either the traditional SQL statement interface or to use an Express query, as shown next. The Type tab is only available if you install the Oracle Express extensions to Developer. It enables you to create reports either against an Oracle database using SQL or against an Express database. This book only covers integration with Oracle databases. Discussion of developing reports using information from an Oracle Express database is beyond the scope of this book.

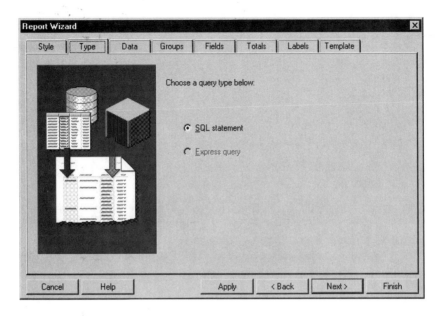

Data Tab

The first step in creating a report is to build a query. The query is a SQL statement that tells the report what information to bring back from the database. On the screen shown here,

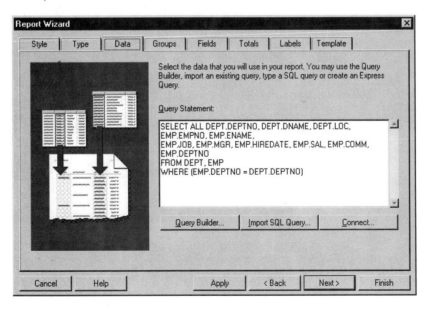

there is also a Connect button, in case you want to connect to the database explicitly. However, Reports is smart enough to automatically give you access to the Connect dialog when necessary. There are three alternatives for creating your query:

- Just as in older versions of Reports, you can type your SQL statement in the SQL Query Statement box. There are two similar query windows available in the Wizard—one for the Wizard and one for whenever you create a new query or attempt to modify an existing query.

- You can use Query Builder to automatically build your query. This use is discussed in more detail in Chapter 19.

- You can import a SQL query stored from a text file. One reason to do this is if you want many reports to share the same query. This method may also be useful for basing a query on a procedure, pulling the text from a SQL file that was used to run a SQL*Plus report, or testing a complex query before basing a report on it as an alternative to cut and paste.

The Check Syntax button will verify that the query is a valid SQL query and will give an error message when it is not valid.

Groups Tab

The Groups tab, shown next, only appears for Group Left, Group Above, and Matrix with Group reports. It allows you to specify the break groups for your report. You can specify any number of break groups and may have any number of fields in each group.

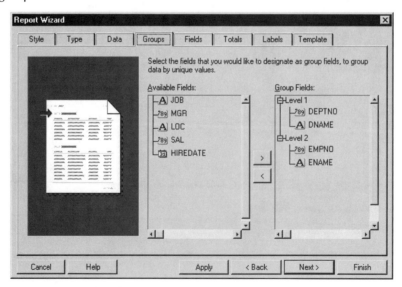

TIP
When selecting fields for groups, once you have selected the first item in the group, you can click that item in the Group Fields column and all subsequent Available Fields you click will be placed at that level after the > button is clicked. Otherwise, separate levels will be created, and you will have to drag the items into the desired group.

You can do this in two steps:

1. Specify all the fields from the Data Model in all the break groups. By default, Reports will place each field in its own level corresponding to its own break group.

2. Drag and drop the fields in the Group Fields area to group the items appropriately. You can delete levels by dragging and dropping out all items from a group, and create a new level by dragging an item to the bottom of the list.

NOTE
If your report has break groups, you must select at least one field from each group.

Fields Tab

The Fields tab, shown next, gives you the ability to specify which fields you actually want to appear in your report.

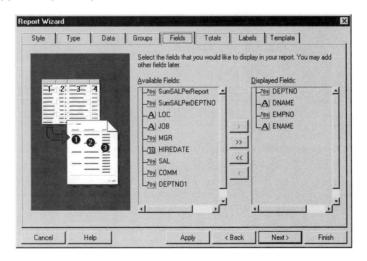

TIP
*These are the fields that will display on the report.
You can drag and drop fields on the Displayed
Fields area to control the order in which they are
displayed when the layout generates.*

NOTE
*You are only able to drag and drop within groups,
even though there is no visual indication of which
fields belong in which groups.*

Totals Tab

When you generate totals in the Totals area of the Report Wizard, as shown next,
you are automatically creating one or more summary columns. Totals are smart.
Not only will Reports calculate the totals, but it will also insert the totals in all the
appropriate places in your report. For example, in a master-detail report, if you
specify the sum of a particular field, you will get a report-level sum as well as a sum
for each break group. However, percent total will only print at the detail level, not
at the report total level (where it is always 100%).

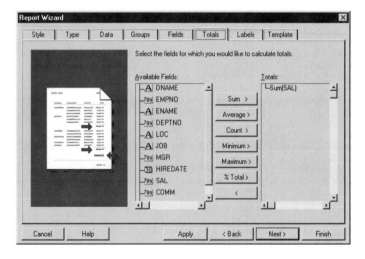

Totals are a special kind of calculated field in Reports that give you the ability to
quickly and easily calculate common functions on your fields. When you perform
one of these functions on a field, the function will be calculated at the report level
and for every break group above the level of the group containing that field. The

only exception is percent total, which calculates the total for every group above the level of the group and including the group containing that field (but not at the report level). If you want multiple totals, you should specify them in the order in which you want them to appear. Functions that are inappropriate for the selected field type are grayed out.

Labels Tab

The Labels tab, shown next, exhibits the fields you have selected for display as well as all total fields, which are automatically displayed. On this tab, you can specify the label for those fields as well as the width in characters of the fields.

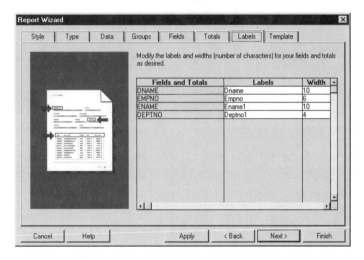

No matter what your unit of measurement is for the report, the Wizard always uses characters. The number of characters will be the same as the number of characters for the database. If you make the text field width too small, the fields will be truncated with no warning message. If you make numeric or date fields too narrow, the field may truncate, appear with stars, or have other unexpected results. Numeric fields with lots of decimal places will truncate the decimal places if the field is too narrow, unless the number of decimal places has been specified in a format mask.

Template Tab

One of the great new features of Reports is templates. By specifying a template, you can easily control much of the look and feel of a report as well as attach libraries and other report objects by default. When creating a report in the Report Wizard, you can specify one of the Oracle-supplied predefined templates, as shown next, or specify a template that you have created. Report template creation and use is discussed in detail in Chapter 21.

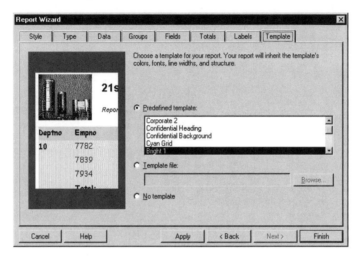

APPENDIX
E

Performing a
Report Audit

A *report audit* is a review and analysis of all the reports generated by the legacy system. The analyst should plan to do a report audit to determine what reports will be retained, discarded, or changed from the original system.

A report audit is a cheap and easy way to determine reporting needs. During the first part of the analysis phase, you should look at the existing reports produced by the system in place. The following information should be gathered as a part of this process:

■ Determine the user requirements associated with the reports—what kind of information do the system users need and use?

■ Determine the reporting requirements for the new system.

■ Determine how the existing reports will need to be modified.

Just because a report has been produced for ten years, analysts should not assume that it is still being read. When users are asked what information they are concerned about, they invariably will leave out important information. The system analyst needs to look carefully at the reports generated by the system and at how they are used by individuals in the organization.

The users should be given copies of all the relevant existing reports and asked to rank them using a scale such as this:

■ **Level 1: Mission Critical**   This report must be converted and in production on day 1.

■ **Level 2: Very Useful**   If possible, this report should be available on day 1; it has high priority for implementation.

■ **Level 3: Useful**   This report is likely to be used in the new system.

■ **Level 4: Marginally Useful**   This report may be used.

■ **Level 5: Not Useful**   These reports are not needed in the new system.

For all reports marked Levels 1 through 3, users should use a highlighter to indicate the information that is specifically useful to them. Frequently, reports have multiple parts. Some users may look only at the summary or for a trend or sample of detail information. It may be possible to decrease the amount of information in reports to make them more concise. Some reports may have been designed for one particular user or class of users and may no longer be relevant—but the system keeps churning out the reports. The cost of doing this in the existing system is small, but the cost of writing a useless report in the new system is prohibitive.

The report audit needs to be completed by a large number of users. Unless the total number of users is very small, the audit should be completed by 10 to 20 users per reporting area (such as payroll, accounting, human resources, and top management). There should be representatives from each reporting area in the audit group. The developer also needs to be aware of the different user groups for which each report is relevant.

The results of the audit can be written in a spreadsheet with the report names listed on the left and the users and user group names across the top. For each report, the priority number (1 to 5) assigned to the report by each user or group should be shown. The users should be asked to look at reports ranked 1 through 3 in more detail. For those reports, users should identify the information that they want in the new system and also identify anything that might be unnecessary.

After all this information is collected, the analyst must decide which reports to incorporate into the new system. Before Oracle Report Builder, the implications of the decision were huge, because putting a report into production used to take two to three person-weeks. With modern reporting tools or report generation using Oracle Designer, this process now takes one to two days. The authors, for example, once developed nine production reports in one day by using Oracle Report Builder.

At the end of this process, the analyst should have three categories of reports that can be collected into separate binders:

1. First-priority reports that must go into the new system

2. Reports that the developer will attempt to implement in phase 1 of the new system

3. Reports without broad enough appeal to be included in the first phase of the new system

Keep in mind that the first two categories may include new reports not yet in production. These binders should also include copies of the actual reports or prototypes.

The cost-benefit trade-off for straightforward reports has also changed over time. Costs have been greatly reduced because of products such as Oracle Report Builder, with its lexical parameter facility. Reports with similar layouts can be combined into a single report. Using the lexical parameters, the system can support the passing of flexible parameters to the report. For example, with this facility, what originally might look like 200 different reports, each requiring a day or two of effort, will become ten or so reports requiring two or three days' effort. An added advantage is that changes to the underlying data structure can be implemented very quickly across the entire reporting environment.

The analyst therefore needs to sort and group the designated reports to support the users' reporting needs. It is not necessary to worry about the total number of reports. As just mentioned, there may be permutations of other existing reports. It is easier to start with more reports and not to be restricted to just the essential ones. Using a combination of Designer and Oracle Report Builder, the analyst should have the ability to support the major reporting requirements of a substantial reports system with about one month's effort.

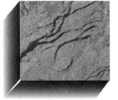

APPENDIX
F

Report Specifications

eport specifications are an essential part of the analysis process. They serve an important function beyond the information gathered about the reports themselves, namely as a validation measure of the analysis data model. Once the reports have been specified at a reasonably detailed level, the analyst needs to make sure that the data model can support all the reporting requirements. There are two levels of report specifications to be created: User Level and System Level. Each will be discussed separately.

User-Level Specifications

All report analysis must begin with copies of the reports to be created. If you are restructuring a legacy system, the reports from that system will be likely candidates for the new system. However, you should not automatically include all the legacy system reports for design in the new system. A report audit should be performed to determine which of the legacy system reports will be brought forward into the new system (see Appendix E) and the number and extent of modifications to be made. The new system may have differently structured information, causing many legacy reports to require significant modifications before development. There will also be some new reports that must be designed from scratch. The complete process of report analysis is beyond the scope of this book. For a more thorough treatment of the Analysis phase, see the *Oracle Designer Handbook* (Peter Koletzke and Dr. Paul Dorsey, Oracle Press, 1999).

There must be a clear description of the business function or functions of the report, including any decisions influenced by the report. The purpose should *not* be vague and general such as "to see information about a project." Rather, it should be something very specific like "to evaluate the cost/benefit performance of a project to help decide whether the project manager is functioning effectively."

A second narrative description should include a statement similar to "This report shows information about..." The sentence should be completed at the report level. This could be about one project, all projects, or several projects, depending upon the given filter criteria. Later, this will be broken down into more detail.

For each type of information on a report, a description should be included for the following: "This group of fields (usually a row) shows information about..." This description should be written for each row in the report. For example, for detailed cost information on a project report: "This group of fields represents information pertaining to a particular expenditure for a particular project." If you are using aggregations, a group of fields might show aggregations of all changes for an entire report.

You need to describe each section of the report. For each group of fields pertaining to a different object (usually a row), specify the object. This is a very important step. Often information concerning different objects is placed in the same row, thus specifying a report that is impossible to build. For example, in a project report looking at a row corresponding to a detailed charge, one of the columns is "Piece of equipment." If a row corresponds to a detailed charge and, in the data model, a detailed charge may include several pieces of equipment, the report will be impossible to build unless you can always allocate the charge to a specific piece of equipment.

Every row in the report should contain information about some precisely defined "object of interest." This object of interest need not necessarily be a table or view in the Data Model.

A report can be logically correct even though each row does not have a one-to-one correspondence with anything in the data model. Each row may correspond to an aggregation of objects.

The concept behind providing users with a flexible reporting system entails including flexible parameters in the reporting applications. These parameters include sorts, breaks, and filters. Within each parameter, selections can be hard coded or user defined. Each will be discussed separately. The implementation of flexible reporting is discussed in Chapter 17.

Sorts

Sorts determine the order in which the report information is displayed. These parameters must be specified independently for every level of subtotaling in the report. In the Project Type example earlier, users would need to specify sorting by project type and location as well as selecting ascending or descending order. Theoretically, it is possible to sort by a column that is not shown on a report. However, this makes little sense and should never be done. Sorting by a column that is not displayed makes the rationale for the sort order invisible to the report reader.

For sorts that are *hard coded* (users cannot change them at runtime), users should specify whether the data should be sorted in ascending or descending order. For example, in a department report, users might always want the data to be sorted by location and department name in ascending order.

You can code in as many levels of sorting as needed given the specific application. In most production reports, you will never need more than four levels. The authors have only seen a few examples where more than four levels of sorting were required.

For sorts that are user specified, the development costs are only slightly higher, but the reports produced are more flexible and robust. Users should be allowed to specify the following as shown in this table:

Sort Parameter	Value	Description
Number of Sort Levels	2	This tells the report designer how many user-definable levels of sorting to support. In the front-end user interface, there are two poplists showing the list of fields available.
Potential Sort Fields	Loc, Dept	These may be available for the user to select from. The user may also have the option of selecting "All" to select from any available columns on the report.

Note that ascending and descending are not specified here. That is because the choice of sorting in ascending or descending order is specified at runtime. In the specifications, only the potential sort fields are specified. Which sort fields are actually used in a particular running of a report and whether those fields are sorted in ascending or descending order is determined when the report is run.

Breaks

Breaks in a report refer to the places in the reports where subtotals are calculated. For example, in an employee report, we could calculate a count of the number of employees and the average salary for each department, or for each location. Of course, there need not be only one level of break in a report. Subtotals could be calculated for each department within a location (or each location within a department). There are two types of breaks:

- **Hard-Coded** These breaks need to be specified by field(s) as well as Ascending or Descending. Aggregation function columns can be a sum, count, average, and so on.

- **User-Specified** The following report characteristics can be user specified:

  - Available fields for breaking

  - Number of potential break levels

  - Aggregations (These can be declared as hard coded as described earlier, or you can allow users to define them on the fly. However, having users specify aggregations at runtime is rarely done.)

This user interface would look the same as the Sorts interface.

The implementation of flexible breaks is discussed in Chapter 24.

Notice that users can only specify a single break column per level. Usually, you won't need to provide more than two levels of breaks dynamically. However, the authors have built systems that required up to four levels of flexible breaks.

Filters

Filters included in a flexible reporting front-end may be a combination of both hard coded and user specified. Using a projects report example, you may want to grant to users the ability to dynamically select what Projects are displayed in a variety of ways but only allow them to aggregate Charges whose status is not "Cancelled."

- **Hard-Coded**   These filters assume the format of a SQL WHERE clause. Using the Project example, the analyst would write in the specifications: "CHARGE_STATUS != 'CANCELLED'" or write out in a sentence "Do not aggregate cancelled charges."

- **User-Specified**   The user can be given the ability to select the fields to filter on. You can filter on a column that would not otherwise be displayed in the report. For example, you could report on Projects and filter the displayed Projects by the Organization Unit to which the Project belongs. You need to disclose what filter criteria were used in the report legend so that the report reader will not be confused.

For each filter attribute, the designer should specify one of the following Filter Types:

- **One-Only**   A single field where the user can either type in something or select from a poplist. For text fields the comparison uses the syntax,

    "value LIKE '<user-entered value>%'"

    so partial values are accepted.

- **Range**   Two fields usually used for dates or numeric values. The user enters two values. The generated syntax is

    "value BETWEEN <user-entered low value> and <user-entered high value>"

    In a range filter, if the user only specifies one value, then the filter is built as an open range. So, if the user only specifies the lower value in the range, then the generated syntax is "value ≥ <user-entered low value>"

If only the high value is specified, then the generated syntax is

"value ≤ <user-entered high value>"

■ **Lists** There are two interfaces for these. Small lists with a limited number of values would have an interface as shown here:

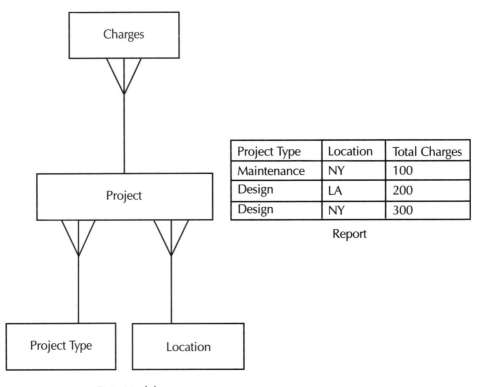

Project Type	Location	Total Charges
Maintenance	NY	100
Design	LA	200
Design	NY	300

Report

Data Model

Large lists require a different format since the interface just shown is not practical for lists with large numbers of selections. For large lists, you need an interface such as the one shown here:

Status	Include	Exclude
Open	○	●
Closed	●	○
Pending	○	●
Complete	●	○

■ **Defined List of Ranges**   This is used primarily for dates, age ranges, or other personnel statistics, as shown here:

People Selected

Joe Hudicka
Kathie Duliba
John Carbone
Popper Dorsey

$<$ $>$

Available People

Edward Van Orden
Charlie Fisher
Yalim Gerger
Dennis Jackson

■ **User-Defined List of Ranges**   This is the same as shown earlier, except that the user can specify the ranges. When using this filter type, take care that users do not enter overlapping ranges.

For all filter types, the user interface must have an Active check box for each field to indicate whether that filter is active.

Fields to Be Displayed

The report specification should contain descriptions of all the fields to be displayed. These should include descriptions of all fields. For user-specified fields, the following information should also be included:

■ Number of flexible columns to be displayed in the report

■ List of all possible fields to be displayed

User-defined fields are useful in systems such as the Project report example. Projects with different milestones can use the same report depending upon the type of project. Users can dynamically select dates when the milestones occur. You can use this method to support many different types of projects with many different milestones. When new project types are added, no changes are required. In a system with many types of cost figures or value types, users can select and display these at runtime.

Other User-Specified Issues

Only rarely is there a need to support user-specified display fields. However, user-specified sorts and filters are used often. User-defined breaks are used occasionally.

All the user-level report specifications just described should be included in the report documentation along with the system-level documentation described in the following section.

System-Level Specifications

System-level specifications in the report should be detailed in such a way that they are consistent with the product being used to build the report. Any logically correct specification format can be translated for use in another product. However, this translation may be a complex step. The way that Oracle Report Builder is designed, the Data Model and Layout Model not only provide a first-rate development environment, but they also provide a way of unambiguously describing how a report should be built.

To be consistent with the way that Reports defines how a report should be built, the process of report specification should include the following parts:

1. A fragment of the data model relevant to the report, including all the columns needed to build the underlying SQL query (or queries) depending upon the level of flexibility being supported. To perform this step, you can use Oracle Designer to extract a small ERD.

2. An Oracle Reports–style data model identifying the relevant groups and key attributes in each group. The data model layout can be hand-drawn and passed to the report developer. If there are any particularly complex formula columns, these should be documented as footnotes.

3. A hand-drawn Oracle Reports–style layout model showing the frames with their appropriate attributes (Repeat Direction and Elasticity).

APPENDIX G

Oracle White Papers on Web-Deployed Forms

here are a number of Oracle white papers that are available on the
Oracle TechNet service (http://technet.oracle.com), Oracle
MetaLink (http://www.oracle.com/support if you have a support
contract), and the Oracle web site (http://www.oracle.com in the
products' collateral sections). These addresses and the selection of
white papers will change over time, but the concept that Oracle provides technical
white papers online is not likely to change. A number of white papers are available
at this writing. Descriptions of some of these follow. Chapter 13 mentions the
documentation supplied with Oracle Developer to support web-deployed forms.

CAUTION
*The names of the white papers change. Look for
contents more than title when you are searching
the web sites.*

- *Oracle Developer Server: How to Tune the Deployment of Internet
  Applications* This is an essential white paper to read if you want to
  understand all possibilities for tuning the Java Archive (JAR) files that
  contain Java classes. The paper also discusses the advanced tuning and
  optimization features introduced with Developer R.6.

- *Client Platform Support Statement of Direction—Release 6.0* This
  white paper provides a description of upcoming features with projected
  delivery dates.

- *Client Platform Support for Microsoft Internet Explorer 5.0 in Developer
  Release 6.0* This document discusses the methods you can use to run
  web-deployed forms in Microsoft Internet Explorer Release 5 without
  JInitiator.

- *Client Platform Support for the Sun Solaris Platform—Release 6.0* This
  white paper describes specifics on how Oracle Developer Release 6.0 runs
  under the Sun Solaris operating system.

- *Developer Forms Server Frequently Asked Questions* This white paper
  contains lots of essential information not found elsewhere, such as how to
  use HTTP instead of sockets so you can cross firewalls.

- *Oracle Developer Server: Deploying Web-Based Applications with Oracle
  JInitiator* This short white paper explains the purpose of JInitiator and
  provides compatibility information. Another paper, *Oracle JInitiator,* also
  explains this material.

■ ***Technical FAQ (Oracle JInitiator)*** This white paper contains essential frequently asked questions and answers that detail how JInitiator works. For example, this white paper discusses the differences between the JavaSoft Java plug-in and JInitiator.

■ ***Deploying Applications on the Web with Oracle Developer Server: Intranet, Extranet, Internet*** This white paper provides an easy-to-understand overview of the various options for using the Developer Server.

■ ***Oracle Developer Server 6.0—A Capacity Planning Guide*** This paper details the scalability features of the Oracle Developer Server.

■ ***Deploying Internet Applications Using HTTP-Enabled Oracle Developer Server*** This white paper discusses how the HTTP protocol can be used for the Developer Servers. It also provides some sample HTML tags and other technical details on how to set this up.

■ ***Oracle Developer Server Tips*** This white paper discusses some common issues that may arise when you are setting up the Developer Server, such as the icons not appearing on iconic buttons.

■ ***Oracle Developer Server—A Benchmark Comparison of Client/Server and Web Deployment by Retek Information Systems*** This paper describes a study done by an outside vendor showing the performance of various activities in client/server, Windows terminal server, and web deployment.

■ ***Oracle Developer Server Scalability Testing*** This is another paper that contains results of benchmark tests to show the effectiveness of the Developer Servers. It is an update to a paper called *Oracle Developer/2000 Forms Server Scalability Testing*.

■ ***Developer Server Troubleshooting Techniques*** This white paper lists some common problems (such as "READ_IMAGE_FILE cannot locate image file") and their solutions (such as checking that the image file is located in a directory in the Forms path).

Index

C

G

J

P

T

Think you're
smart?

**You're an Oracle DBA.
You're implementing a
backup and recovery plan.
Which component stores
the synchronization
information needed for
database recovery?**

a. redo log files
b. control file
c. parameter file
d. trace file

Think you're ready to wear this badge?

The time is right to become an Oracle Certified Professional (OCP) and we're here to help you do it. Oracle's cutting edge Instructor-Led Training, Interactive Courseware, and this exam guide can prepare you for certification faster than ever. OCP status is one of the top honors in your profession. Now is the time to take credit for what you know. *Call 800.441.3541 (Outside the U.S. call +1.310.335.2403)* for an OCP training solution that meets your time, budget, and learning needs. Or visit us at *http://education.oracle.com/certification* for more information.

ORACLE®
Education

Get Your **FREE** Subscription to Oracle Magazine

Stay informed and increase your productivity with every issue of *Oracle Magazine*. Inside each FREE, bimonthly issue you'll get:

- Up-to-date information on Oracle Data Server, Oracle Applications, Network Computing Architecture, and tools
- Third-party news and announcements
- Technical articles on Oracle products and operating environments
- Software tuning tips
- Oracle customer application stories

Three easy ways to subscribe:

1 MAIL Cut out this page, complete the questionnaire on the back, and mail it to: *Oracle Magazine,* P.O. Box 1263, Skokie, IL 60076-8263.

2 FAX Cut out this page, complete the questionnaire on the back, and fax it to **+ 847.647.9735.**

3 WEB Visit our Web site at **www.oramag.com.** You'll find a subscription form there, plus much more!

If there are other Oracle users at your location who would like to receive their own subscription to *Oracle Magazine,* please photocopy the form and pass it along.

☐ **YES! Please send me a FREE subscription to Oracle Magazine.**   ☐ NO, I am not interested at this time.

If you wish to receive your free bimonthly subscription to *Oracle Magazine,* you must fill out the entire form, sign it, and date it (incomplete forms cannot be processed or acknowledged). You can also subscribe at our Web site at **www.oramag.com/html/subform.html** or fax your application to *Oracle Magazine* at **+847.647.9735.**

SIGNATURE (REQUIRED) ✓ _____   DATE _____

NAME _____   TITLE _____

COMPANY _____   E-MAIL ADDRESS _____

STREET/P.O. BOX _____

CITY/STATE/ZIP _____

COUNTRY _____   TELEPHONE _____

You must answer all eight questions below.

1 What is the primary business activity of your firm at this location? (circle only one)
- 01 Agriculture, Mining, Natural Resources
- 02 Architecture, Construction
- 03 Communications
- 04 Consulting, Training
- 05 Consumer Packaged Goods
- 06 Data Processing
- 07 Education
- 08 Engineering
- 09 Financial Services
- 10 Government—Federal, Local, State, Other
- 11 Government—Military
- 12 Health Care
- 13 Manufacturing—Aerospace, Defense
- 14 Manufacturing—Computer Hardware
- 15 Manufacturing—Noncomputer Products
- 16 Real Estate, Insurance
- 17 Research & Development
- 18 Human Resources
- 19 Retailing, Wholesaling, Distribution
- 20 Software Development
- 21 Systems Integration, VAR, VAD, OEM
- 22 Transportation
- 23 Utilities (Electric, Gas, Sanitation)
- 24 Other Business and Services _____

2 Which of the following best describes your job function? (circle only one)
CORPORATE MANAGEMENT/STAFF
- 01 Executive Management (President, Chair, CEO, CFO, Owner, Partner, Principal)
- ~~Finance/Administrative~~

IS/IT Staff
- 07 Systems Development/Programming Management
- 08 Systems Development/Programming Staff
- 09 Consulting
- 10 DBA/Systems Administrator
- 11 Education/Training
- 12 Engineering/R&D/Science Management
- 13 Engineering/R&D/Science Staff
- 14 Technical Support Director/Manager
- 15 Webmaster/Internet Specialist
- 16 Other Technical Management/Staff

3 What is your current primary operating platform? (circle all that apply)
- 01 DEC UNIX
- 02 DEC VAX VMS
- 03 Java
- 04 HP UNIX
- 05 IBM AIX
- 06 IBM UNIX
- 07 Macintosh
- 08 MPE-ix
- 09 MS-DOS
- 10 MVS
- 11 NetWare
- 12 Network Computing
- 13 OpenVMS
- 14 SCO UNIX
- 15 Sun Solaris/SunOS
- 16 SVR4
- 17 Ultrix
- 18 UnixWare
- 19 VM
- 20 Windows
- 21 Windows NT
- 22 Other _____
- 23 Other UNIX _____

4 Do you evaluate, specify, recommend, or authorize the purchase of any of the following? (circle all that apply)
- 01 Hardware
- 02 Software
- 03 Application Development Tools
- 04 Database Products
- 05 Internet or Intranet Products

5 In your job, do you use or plan to purchase any of the following products or services? (check all that apply)

SOFTWARE	Use	Plan to buy
01 Business Graphics	☐	☐
02 CAD/CAE/CAM	☐	☐
03 CASE	☐	☐
04 CIM	☐	☐
05 Communications	☐	☐
06 Database Management	☐	☐
07 File Management	☐	☐
08 Finance	☐	☐
09 Java	☐	☐
10 Materials Resource Planning	☐	☐
11 Multimedia Authoring	☐	☐
12 Networking	☐	☐
13 Office Automation	☐	☐
14 Order Entry/Inventory Control	☐	☐
15 Programming	☐	☐
16 Project Management	☐	☐
17 Scientific and Engineering	☐	☐
18 Spreadsheets	☐	☐
19 Systems Management	☐	☐
20 Workflow	☐	☐
HARDWARE		
21 Macintosh	☐	☐
22 Mainframe	☐	☐
23 Massively Parallel Processing	☐	☐
24 Minicomputer	☐	☐
25 PC	☐	☐
26 Network Computer	☐	☐
27 Supercomputer	☐	☐
28 Symmetric Multiprocessing	☐	☐
29 Workstation	☐	☐
PERIPHERALS		
30 Bridges/Routers/Hubs/Gateways	☐	☐
31 CD-ROM Drives	☐	☐
32 Disk Drives/Subsystems	☐	☐
33 Modems	☐	☐
34 Tape Drives/Subsystems	☐	☐
35 Video Boards/Multimedia	☐	☐
SERVICES		
36 Computer-Based Training	☐	☐
37 Consulting	☐	☐
38 Education/Training	☐	☐
39 Maintenance	☐	☐
40 Online Database Services	☐	☐
41 Support	☐	☐
42 None of the above	☐	☐

6 What Oracle products are in use at your site? (circle all that apply)
SERVER/SOFTWARE
- 01 Oracle8
- 02 Oracle7
- 03 Oracle Application Server
- 04 Oracle Data Mart Suites
- 05 Oracle Internet Commerce Server
- 06 Oracle InterOffice
- 07 Oracle Lite
- 08 Oracle Payment Server
- 09 Oracle Rdb
- 10 Oracle Security Server
- 11 Oracle Video Server
- 12 Oracle Workgroup Server

TOOLS
- 13 Designer/2000
- 14 Developer/2000 (Forms, Reports, Graphics)
- 15 Oracle OLAP Tools
- 16 Oracle Power Object

ORACLE APPLICATIONS
- 17 Oracle Automotive
- 18 Oracle Energy
- 19 Oracle Consumer Packaged Goods
- 20 Oracle Financials
- 21 Oracle Human Resources
- 22 Oracle Manufacturing
- 23 Oracle Projects
- 24 Oracle Sales Force Automation
- 25 Oracle Supply Chain Management
- 26 Other _____
- 27 **None of the above**

7 What other database products are in use at your site? (circle all that apply)
- 01 Access
- 02 BAAN
- 03 dbase
- 04 Gupta
- 05 IBM DB2
- 06 Informix
- 07 Ingres
- 08 Microsoft Access
- 09 Microsoft SQL Server
- 10 Peoplesoft
- 11 Progress
- 12 SAP
- 13 Sybase
- 14 VSAM
- 15 **None of the above**

8 During the next 12 months, how much do you anticipate your organization will spend on computer hardware, software, peripherals, and services for your location? (circle only one)
- 01 Less than $10,000
- 02 $10,000 to $49,999
- 03 $50,000 to $99,999
- 04 $100,000 to $499,999
- 05 $500,000 to $999,999
- 06 $1,000,000 and over

OMG